Fundamental
Reference
Sources

Fundamental Reference Sources

THIRD EDITION

160101

JAMES H. SWEETLAND

AMERICAN LIBRARY ASSOCIATION
Chicago and London
2001

James H. Sweetland is professor in Library and Information Science at the University of Wisconsin–Milwaukee, where he teaches collection management, computer information retrieval, and advanced reference in both social sciences and humanities. Prior to becoming a teacher, he was involved in reference work in special and academic libraries. Before coming to UWM, he served as head librarian at the State Historical Society of Wisconsin. He has been president of the American Library Association's Reference and User Services Association (RUSA) and chair of RUSA's Machine-Assisted Reference Section. He holds the 1991 Special Service Award of the Wisconsin Library Association, Distinguished Alumnus Award from Beta Phi Mu, and the 1997 Literati Club Award for the best article in the journal *Collection Building.*

Project editor, Eloise L. Kinney

Text and cover design by Dianne M. Rooney

Composition by the dotted i in Garamond Book and Novarese using QuarkXPress 4.0 on a Macintosh

Printed on 50-pound white offset, a pH-neutral stock, and bound by Edwards Brothers.

The paper used in this publication meets the minimum requirements of American National Standard for Information Sciences—Permanence of Paper for Printed Library Materials, ANSI Z39.48-1992. ∞

Library of Congress Cataloging-in-Publication Data
Sweetland, James H.
    Fundamental reference sources / James H. Sweetland.—3rd ed.
      p.   cm.
    Rev. ed. of: Fundamental reference sources / Frances Neel Cheney and Wiley J. Williams. 2nd ed. 1980.
    Includes bibliographical references and index.
    ISBN 0-8389-0780-6 (alk. paper)
    1. Reference books—Bibliography.   I. Cheney, Frances Neel, 1906– Fundamental reference sources.   II. Title.
    Z1035.1.C5 2000
    011′.02—dc21   00-024311

Printed in the United States of America.

04   03   02   01   00   5   4   3   2   1

Contents

Preface

This third edition of *Fundamental Reference Sources,* like the first two, is an introduction to selected sources of bibliographical, biographical, linguistic, statistical, and geographical organization. However, the changes in both practical reference work and in the publishing world (now often considered part of the "information industry") have led to some substantial changes in organization. The introductory chapter has been revised and updated to reflect the literature of reference and information services in the past generation, notably the increased emphasis on evaluation. Guides to reference materials include both the current editions of old standbys and a number of new ones. Perhaps symbolic of the changes that took place at the end of the millennium is the elimination of the reference to the *Wilson Library Bulletin (WLB),* no longer published, and its replacement by "Rettig on Reference," which continued the excellent reviews by James Rettig from that journal but on the World Wide Web. This excellent feature appeared on two different websites but has now been dropped—also a sign of the volatility of this new information medium.

The arrangement of this edition follows, in some detail, but it is also fitting to make some points about the basic selection criteria used.

Although the emphasis has remained strongly on materials in English and published in the United States, recognition of the true cultural diversity of the United States had led to more material in other languages, especially Spanish and French, and in more sources that deal with U.S. neighbors to the south and north. Similarly, in addition to the "standard" sources—for example, in biography or language—as appropriate, additional sources dealing with the rich ethnic and linguistic heritage of the United States have been added as supplements.

This edition also reflects the increasing use of electronic formats, particularly CD-ROMs, which were still a laboratory experiment in 1980, not to mention the common use of remote systems, from what are now called "traditional" text-based ones to various parts of the Internet, including the Web. Because the intention remains of providing a list of *fundamental* sources, and because one implication of that term is a degree of stability, generally the primary listing is for a traditional format, nearly always in print, with additional reference to electronic formats. However, many sources are only available in electronic formats.

The terms and definitions for formats used in this book follow:

Print and *microform* need little discussion. They are similar (manual, fairly stable technology and access), but print is almost always more convenient.

CD-ROM format is similar to print and microform in that libraries actually own it (in some cases, at least as long as they pay the rent), but CD-ROMs do give users machine access.

World Wide Web means the information can be found on the Web. The Web is just one of several kinds of online options, but there are resources that are Web based only. In such cases, the URL is given for these, rather than using just the term *online.*

Online, a live, interactive connection, means the information is in several forms, which could include being on the Web. *Online,* however, is intended to be used for such commercial services as Dialog, for tape loads for local systems, and the like. Note that many services are available in multiple formats; the System for Information on Grey Literature in Europe (SIGLE), for example, is not available in print, but it can be accessed through the British Library Automated Information Service (BLAISE), as well as directly at its own website. And, of course, it can also be purchased or leased as a CD-ROM. *Online resources,* regardless of specifics, means libraries have electronic access, but they do not have the database in the library. Note that for online access, libraries need phone or similar lines, which can go down, eliminating access for a time; and if the library stops paying, all access to the information is lost.

Another change in the library environment with implications for this edition is the growth of resource sharing as a way of life. For good or ill, very few libraries are in a position to meet all information needs from their own resources. As a result, both the smaller and larger library find a greater need for sources that do not so much answer a question as point to a source that does. Thus, the second edition of this title devoted a great deal of space to bibliographic tools. The third edition increases this attention to such "pointers," expanding the amount and proportion of traditional bibliographies, indexes and abstracts, and adding a new chapter listing some of the more important directories to people and organizations.

In brief, this edition puts more emphasis on the following types of material than did the first two editions: nonprint and electronic media, government publications, and collective indexes and abstracts. More specific comments, arranged by chapter, follow:

Chapter 1 has been substantially rewritten to reflect the changes in the practice and theory of reference work in the past twenty years.

Chapter 2 has been expanded and divided into two chapters, with *bibliographies* (in essence, lists of whole documents or collections) in chapter 2 and with *indexes* (access to specific parts of documents or collections, or to information) in chapter 3. Chapter 2 discusses *sources of bibliographic information* (broadly defined to include print, audiovisual, and electronic media).

Chapter 3 includes indexes and abstracts, which were formerly part of chapter 2, and adds more titles as well as more types of material.

Chapter 4 is a wholly new chapter, listing *directories* (defined as indexes to people and places that provide information, rather than to documents). In some cases, it was difficult to distinguish between a *directory* and a *biography.* Generally, the latter is expected to do more than merely list a person with his or her address and possibly a sentence on the person; thus, sources that were formerly listed in the biography chapter may now be found in this chapter.

Chapter 5, on sources of biographical information, shows no real conceptual changes, except adding more sources on groups that tend to be underrepresented in more traditional sources and accounting for the creation of new major sources and computerized sources.

Chapter 6 characterizes the principal sources of information on words. In addition to updating the listing of English-language word books (dictionaries, thesauri, usage guides, and the like), this chapter now includes visual dictionaries, English as a second language (ESL) and American Sign Language (ASL) sources, and bilingual dictionaries in more languages than the second edition.

Chapter 7 covers the problems and responsibilities of encyclopedia editors. There are no real changes, except for updating and accommodating the changes in electronic formats. The outlines of the strengths and weaknesses of selected multivolume encyclopedias have been retained as a useful feature.

Chapter 8, on statistical sources, has been substantially changed. First, the section discussing basic statistical methods has been eliminated because most professionals (regardless of degree) should know such basic information; but if they do not, they need more information than could be provided in such a short space. For convenience, all the current texts in library- and information-related statistical research have been listed. The impact of electronic formats is greatest here, as a growing number of data sources are becoming available in electronic form, often replacing all other formats. Finally, this chapter includes more sources of data and expands coverage to include more non-U.S. material than previous editions.

Chapter 9, covering geographical sources, remains essentially the same in outline. The major differences are the recognition of the importance of GIS (Geographic Information Systems) in cartography and the addition of more topical atlases.

All titles were selected on the basis of their importance in general reference collections in U.S. libraries, and although foreign-language sources were not deliberately avoided, they are not emphasized. The debt that any compiler of any list of reference tools owes to Robert Balay and A. J. Walford (hereinafter referred to as *Balay* and *Walford's*) and their colleagues is fully acknowledged, as is the debt owed to the editors, compilers, and authors of the many other sources used and listed in this work.

Other debts must also be acknowledged: first, to Marlene Chamberlain of ALA Editions for her initial suggestion to undertake this project and for her strong support during its production. Second, to Mohammed Aman, dean of the School of Library and Information Science at the University of Wisconsin–Milwaukee and to the university for the sabbatical semester that provided the necessary time; and to Assistant Dean Wilfred Fong for his technical expertise and for providing additional computer space. And, of course, to my wife and son for putting up with me hiding in the study or the library for days on end.

Particular thanks are due to Elizabeth Buchanan for her work on the early stages of the project and to Peggy Potter and Asia Gross for their assistance in the final stages. Another special note of thanks is due Eloise L. Kinney for her editorial work—I thought I was a careful writer; she made me live up to that thought. And, of course, thanks to Frances Neel Cheney for her work on the basic outline of this book and the creation of the first edition and, with Wiley J. Williams, the second edition.

Finally, a note of thanks is certainly in order to a number of colleagues and friends at the Bristol Renaissance Faire for their interest and moral support, especially to Jim and Tobi and Megan, who rather surprisingly were actually interested in the project and its outcome. Although it is unlikely they will ever read this, it is they—as users of libraries and seekers after information—who are the ultimate audience of this and similar works.

1

The Nature of Reference and Information Service

Libraries exist for their users. Many of these users have not yet appeared, and many others may never appear in person, so it is for the potential user and the remote (or off-site) user that librarians select and either acquire what has been recorded in any available form or be aware of what has been recorded so that the library can acquire it if needed. It is at this point that reference and information service begins, for without a body of knowledge and information, it is not possible to provide any assistance.

It is for the user that librarians attempt to organize the materials for easy access through some system or systems that will provide clues to their location. Librarians also acquire or prepare indexes and abstracts of the contents of many types of recorded information, such as periodicals, pamphlets, films, videos, recordings, maps, and databases. The nature and the extent of the information organization in various libraries will vary according to the library's perceptions of the needs of the potential users.

It is also for the user that libraries provide persons who are qualified to assist the user in his or her search for information and who are designated as reference librarians, information specialists, or some similar term.

To fulfill these responsibilities to the user for selecting, acquiring, organizing, and retrieving the body of recorded knowledge, librarians have developed codes for cataloging, systems of classification, and standards of service. In some cases, librarians have also adopted such systems set up by others, often modifying them to better meet the needs of the users. All these systems are constantly in a state of change, subject to continuous inquiry into their effectiveness in meeting current and potential future demands.

Definitions

Efforts to set standards for reference and information service must begin with definitions, and reference librarians through the years have tried to define *reference service*, the exact terminology reflecting the times in which they lived. Thus, William Warner Bishop, in the days before computers, stated with some conviction that "reference work is organized effort on the part of libraries in aid of the most expeditious and fruitful use of their libraries." It is still hard to disagree with this statement, but it is too broad to be of practical use.

In 1930, James I. Wyer, in his *Reference Work: A Textbook for Students of Library Work and Librarians* (Chicago: ALA; 315p.), described reference work as "sympathetic and informed personal aid in interpreting library collections for study and research." This is worth remembering as a reminder that respect for the user is essential to good reference work.

In 1943, the *A.L.A. Glossary of Library Terms* reflected both Bishop and Wyer in defining reference as "that phase of library work which is directly concerned with assistance to readers in securing information and in using the resources of the library in study and research." Changes in the way we look at libraries may be seen in the most recent definition (Chicago: ALA, 1983; 245p.), where "reference service" receives a cross-reference to "information service," which is defined as "personal assistance provided by members of the reference staff to library users in pursuit of information. Synonymous with reference service."

Other definitions are similar, both in tone and in generality. For example, *Harrod's Librarians' Glossary* (8th ed. Brookfield, Vt.: Gower, 1995; 692p.) uses the term *reference work* with three meanings: "That branch of the library's services which includes the assistance given to readers in their search for information on various subjects, . . . Personal assistance given by the librarian to individual readers needing information, . . . The work of the Reference Library" (p. 521). ALA's *World Encyclopedia of Library and Information Services* (3d ed. Chicago: ALA, 1993), using the phrase "reference and information services," says, among other things,

> The purpose of reference service is to help a library's clientele use its collections and external resources effectively to meet their information needs. The distinguishing features of reference services are a staff designated to provide

the service; a collection of reference works accessible to the public in an area set aside for the provision of the service; adequate guides to the library's services (such as a classification scheme, a catalogue, and indexes); and a high degree of interaction between the staff and the clientele (p. 703).

In 1961, Samuel Rothstein and Henry Dubester developed a statement for use by a committee on reference standards and statistics of the Reference Services Division of the American Library Association (now the Reference and User Services Association) that is notable for its outline of the kinds of services reference librarians should be prepared to offer (Louis Shores, "The Measure of Reference," *The Southeastern Librarian* 11 [winter 1961]: 297-302; and reprinted in Arthur Ray Rowland, *Reference Services* [Hamden, Conn.: Shoe String Pr., 1964], p. 135-44). Often reprinted, in brief it describes two types of service to the library's users: direct and indirect.

Direct service is instruction in the use of the library and information services, ranging from answering simple questions to "supplying information based on search in the collections of the library, combining competence in bibliothecal techniques with competence in the subject of inquiry." *Indirect reference service* "involves the preparation and development of catalogs, bibliographies, and all other reference aids which help in providing access to the library's collections. . . . This recognizes the significant role of the technical or processing services of the library as indispensable to the reference function."

A further expansion of Rothstein and Dubester's statement appeared in "A Commitment to Information Services: Developmental Guidelines" (*RQ* 15 [summer 1976]: 327-30; *RQ* 18 [spring 1979]: 375-78, with an added section on "Ethics of Service" adopted January 1979).

This statement was replaced in 1990 by "Information Services for Information Consumers: Guidelines for Providers." These guidelines define information service as

> characterized by a high degree of interaction between staff members and individual users or specifically identified groups of users or potential users. Information services in libraries take a variety of forms including direct personal assistance, directories or signs, exchange of information culled from a reference source, readers' advisory assistance, dissemination of information in anticipation of user needs or interests, and direct end-user access via telecommunications hardware and software (*RQ* 30 [winter 1990]: 262-65).

Unfortunately, although such guidelines provide excellent goals, the reality appears to be rather far from them. Notably, results of studies by Thomas Childers and T. Crowley while pursuing doctoral work at Rutgers, later combined in the book *Information Service in Public Libraries: Two Studies* (Metuchen, N.J.: Scarecrow, 1971; 210p.) suggest just how far the goals and reality are apart. They engaged in "unobtrusive studies" in which a person, posing as a library user, asks specific questions in person or by phone (as needed, the proxy is prepared to engage in a reference interview to provide more background about the question, thus approximating as closely as possible a real reference transaction). Their results, confirmed generally by many subsequent studies, established that only between 50 percent and 60 percent of questions were answered, or referred, correctly. This finding has become enshrined in the library literature as "the 55 percent rule" (a term apparently first popularized by P. J. Burton, "Accuracy of Information Provision: The Need for Client-Centered Service," *Journal of Librarianship* 22 [Oct. 1990]: 201–15). Although criticized as relying almost totally on the ready-reference factual question, which is not the whole of reference work, the studies, and later work as well, are disquieting.

One of the most important ways to determine users' needs is the *reference interview,* a subject that has received considerable attention in library periodicals. For example, there were more than eighty articles on this subject indexed in *Library Literature* in the 1990s. This work, among others, is well synthesized by Elaine Jennerich and Edward Jennerich (*The Reference Interview as a Creative Art,* 2d ed. [Englewood, Colo.: Libraries Unlimited, 1997; 128p.]) and informs the "Guidelines for Behavioral Performance of Reference and Information Services Professionals," adopted in 1996.

Rothstein's "Across the Desk: 100 Years of Reference Encounters" (*Canadian Library Journal* 34 [Oct. 1977]: 391–99) is valuable for its review of the pertinent literature on the subject, from Samuel Green's paper in 1876 to the ALA centennial year of 1976. Rothstein believes that, generally, knowing how to find the truth and harboring a spirit of service are the essential ingredients of the reference encounter over the last 100 years. "I suggest that, with some modernization, but also with some moderation, that same recipe might serve equally well for the foreseeable future." Which nobody can deny.

In 1966, Alan M. Rees, speaking before a conference at Columbia University, posed the question: "What, in fact, is the fundamental nature of the reference process?" In answer, he stated:

> I wish to make a clear differentiation between reference *process,* reference *work,* reference *sources,* and reference *services.* The reference process incorporates the sum total of variables involved in the performance of reference work by an intermediary designated as reference librarian. It includes both the psychology of the questioner and the environmental context within which the need is generated, together with the psychology of the reference librarian and the reference sources employed. Reference service is the formalized provision of information in diverse forms by a reference librarian, who is interposed between the questioner and available information sources. Reference work is the function performed by reference librarians in providing reference service. The perception on the part of the librarian of the need of the questioner is an important part of the

reference process. The formalized representation of this need is the question, which may or may not be an adequate expression of the underlying information requirement.

Rees continued, "The reference process, therefore, comprises a complex interaction among the questioner, reference librarian, and information sources, involving not only the identification and manipulation of available bibliographic apparatus, but also the operation of psychological, sociological, and environmental variables which are imperfectly understood at the present time" ("Broadening the Spectrum," in Winifred B. Linderman, *The Present Status and Future Prospects of Reference/Information Service* [Chicago: ALA, 1967], p. 57-58).

Ironically, until about the same time as this presentation, very little hard data existed on the variables or even on the number and quality of reference transactions. In an analysis of the literature, Mary B. Haley found little solid data in a search covering 1940 to 1970 ("Reference Statistics," *RQ* 10 [winter 1970]: 143-47).

Librarians' concern for whether users do or do not retrieve their information has made them more conscious of the need to know more about these users. Since the Columbia conference, some efforts have been made to examine the process from the point of view of the users. A notable example of this effort is the Wisconsin-Ohio Reference Project (WOREP), developed by Charles Bunge and Marjorie E. Murfin. In brief, over a sample period, each user who asks a question is given a survey checklist with a set of questions about the transaction, while the librarian also fills out a similar checklist for the same transaction. The responses are later compared.

Matthew L. Saxton studied the whole literature on this subject, finding a total of 197 documents (articles, books, theses, dissertations, reports, and the like) issued between 1967 and 1996 on the subject of reference service evaluation, of which 59 were classified as research studies. Although Saxton concluded that there were too few studies at this time on user satisfaction to apply the techniques of meta-analysis to this work, most of the work used the amount or percentage of questions answered correctly as the measure of accuracy. Unfortunately, Saxton concludes (as did Julie Van Dyke before him) that the definitions used in the studies and the measures used were so diverse that it was not possible to make any definite conclusions. However, he concluded that the factors most likely to be related to accuracy of reference transactions are total library expenditures, number of volumes added, size of the population served, hours the library is open, and absolute change in library size ("Reference Service Evaluation and Meta-Analysis: Findings and Methodological Issues," *Library Quarterly* 67 [July 1997]: 267-89).

On the other hand, John C. Stalker and Murfin have provided more detail on the WOREP as applied to a very successful library, concluding that user satisfaction appears related to library size (medium-sized libraries are more successful than either small or large ones). The in-depth analysis of the most successful library also found that it had a "superior" reference collection, relatively high use of online databases and an online catalog, and a higher than typical amount of training. However, the factor that they found most likely related to success overall was the effect of time: Brandeis University librarians (Waltham, Mass.) spent more than five minutes on a transaction about 72 percent of the time (versus about 21 percent for the average medium-sized academic libraries studied in WOREP). Perhaps the most unsettling note in this discussion, however, is that the WOREP, having data on seventy-four general reference departments over twelve years, has found an average success rate of 57 percent, and that the most highly successful library studied had success 72 percent of the time (John C. Stalker and Marjorie E. Murfin, "Quality Reference Service: A Preliminary Case Study," *Journal of Academic Librarianship* 22 [Nov. 1996]: 423–29).

The emphasis on the user and his or her satisfaction has continued in recent years, with reference work per se becoming only part of a larger point of view, in which the "user" has become the "customer," and the issue is neither quantity nor quality, input nor output, but rather "customer satisfaction."

For example, Danuta Nitecki ("Changing the Concept and Measure of Service Quality in Academic Libraries," *Journal of Academic Librarianship* 22 [May 1996]: 181–90) studied the application of "SERVQUAL," an instrument designed for commercial applications, to libraries and found it has promise. The purpose of SERVQUAL is to measure customer expectations compared with what the customer perceived as the reality. Peter Hernon and Ellen Altman summarize and extend the work of Nitecki and others, providing a number of specific measurement instruments and various methods for applying them. In *Service Quality in Academic Libraries* (Norwood, N.J.: Ablex, 1996; 187p.), they present measurements developed over several successive iterations and recommend that all libraries adopt customer satisfaction as a primary goal of their operations.

It is interesting that the current emphasis of customer satisfaction appears as part of the adoption by many libraries of Total Quality Management (TQM) and that, overall, there are comparatively few questions either about reference work or the quality of the library, its collections, or its reference service in the measures suggested. In fact, there is considerable feeling that the traditional library definitions of *quality* have little to do with user satisfaction, to a large degree because the traditional measures are not what the user defines as quality.

The past twenty years have seen some dramatic changes in reference "work," many, but not all, related to the integration of computers into information work. In particular, most of the standard definitions suggest the work is done in a library, with heavy reliance on bibliographic tools, and by people called librarians. In fact, much user assistance is now done using sources not in the library and may be done by people not called librarians (the buzzword of the late 1990s was "knowledge manager," a term that was often applied to people with little or no library training, who generally did not work in places called libraries). In fact, at least some of the thrust toward developing new measures of library service is directly based on the perception that electronic sources, particularly the Internet, have now provided the library with serious competition and have changed user expectations.

An indication of the changes in reference work even within the library environment may be seen by the classification of types of reference services in a popular textbook on the subject (Richard E. Bopp and Linda C. Smith, *Reference and Information Services: An Introduction,* 2d ed. [Englewood, Colo.: Libraries Unlimited, 1995], p. 5–16). These include the following types:

1. Information
   (a) Ready-Reference Questions (giving factual information, such as a telephone number or address);
   (b) Bibliographic Verification (providing a correct and complete citation to a document, which often is not owned in the library where the question is received);
   (c) Interlibrary Loan and Document Delivery (obtaining a document or a copy from some remote library and delivering it to the local user—a very popular service in many libraries);
   (d) Information and Referral Services (identifying community resources, including people and institutions as well as documents);
   (e) Research Questions (detailed assistance in getting fairly complex and often somewhat vaguely defined information);
   (f) Selective Dissemination of Information (customized alerting of new publications or information for the specific needs of a given client);
   (g) Database Searches (in which the librarian assists the user in obtaining information from electronic information sources, usually by doing the search for the user);
   (h) Information Brokering (in effect, where a librarian is doing reference work wholly outside the confines of a library, usually without being employed by a library).

2. Instruction in the use of a given library, libraries in general, or in information sources
   (a) One-to-One Instruction;
   (b) Group Instruction (often conducted as part of a class, in schools at all levels).

3. Guidance

   (a) Readers' Advisory Services (usually found in public libraries, in which a librarian guides a given reader by suggesting other items of interest based on his or her past reading or expressed needs). (This was a very popular function in early libraries but seemed to peak in the 1930s, nearly dying out by the late 1950s. However, in recent years, the concept has seen increasing popularity, possibly related to the development of computerized "advisory services," along the lines of, "If you like A, you will also like B." EBSCO's CD-ROM Nove-List is a good example of this sort of product);

   (b) Bibliotherapy (a specialized form of guidance in which specific readings are suggested to aid an emotional or psychological healing process);

   (c) Term Paper Counseling (usually offered by appointment, away from the reference desk, in response to a student's need for assistance in completing a specific research project, usually in response to a course assignment). Such sessions can be one-on-one but also are seen in the form of "term paper clinics," which are less focused group sessions but again with the emphasis on completing a specific assignment;

   (d) Research Assistance and Consulting (this could be seen as a form of readers' advisory but is usually related to a nonfiction research need and often includes suggestions on the research method, as well as recommendations of and instruction in use of specific sources).

The present emphasis on the need for gathering data and conducting research on the information-searching process will continue, stimulated in part by the increasing computerization of libraries and information systems. In fact, Pierre Papazian attributed this questioning to the advent of mechanization. In "Librarian, Know Thyself" (*RQ* 4 [July 1965]: 7-8), he proposed an analytical study of the human search process, advocating two levels of research on this question: the practice of information searching and the psychology of information.

James Rettig, in "A Theoretical Model and Definition of the Reference Process" (*RQ* 18 [fall 1978]: 19-29), analyzed various statements on reference service found chiefly in journal articles and theoretically defined reference service as "the interpersonal communication process, the purpose of which is to provide a person who needs information with that information, either directly by culling the needed information from an appropriate information source (or sources) or indirectly by (1) providing the person with the appropriate information source(s) or (2) teaching the person how to find the needed information in the appropriate information source(s)." This paper is well documented, as is Kenneth Whittaker's "Toward a Theory for Reference and Information Service" (*Journal of Librarianship* 9 [Jan. 1977]: 49-63). After reviewing the development of this service from its origins to the present, he offers a base plan for systematic and comprehensive research, including terminology, nature and purpose of the service, its scope, and relationships with other subjects.

Another type of continuing investigation is concern with information needs in specific subject fields. Numerous examples of these investigations exist in science and technology, psychology, and the social sciences in general. A recent series summarizing at the least the scholars' needs includes *Information Needs in the Humanities: An Assessment* (Mountain View, Calif.: Research Libraries Group, 1988; 62p.); *Information Needs in the Social Sciences: An Assessment* (Mountain View, Calif.: Research Libraries Group, 1989; 56p.); and *Information Needs in the Sciences: An Assessment* (Mountain View, Calif.: Research Libraries Group, 1991; 79p.). An indication of the interest in the subject is the fact that more than 770 articles on the subject appear in *Library Literature* just in the 1990s.

Search

Meanwhile, as the analysis goes on, individual librarians, attempting to provide direct and indirect service in a given librarian environment, must try to deal intelligently with the individual questioner who seeks assistance. Seasoned reference librarians develop confidence in their ability to help patrons as they develop a knowledge of the sources of information, although they may not express themselves as lyrically as S. R. Ranganathan did in "Reference Service and Humanism" (Rowland, p. 31-34). In his inimitable style, he wrote, "When the reader comes amidst the library . . . he will meet a person, who with radiant geniality whispers into his ears, 'Take my hand; For I have passed this way, And know the truth.'"

Less certain of the trust but with some degree of confidence, the reference librarian should be able to say to the questioner, "Take my hand, for I have passed this way, and know some of the sources of information." Once the questioner has taken this hand, or, more literally, has stated the question, the reference librarian joins in the quest, though not necessarily with "radiant geniality." These first steps are usually referred to as the "reference interview" and more recently as the "librarian-questioner dialogue." By whatever name, it is the heart of the matter, and if it is not done successfully, there will be no resulting restatement of the question, which is so often necessary.

At this point some of the variables noted earlier become important. *Variable* can be defined as "having no fixed quantitative value" or as "anything which varies or which is prone to variation." Recognizing that continuing analysis is expressed in more technical terms, yet daring to use less technical language, we may note a few of these "things" that vary:

1. How much the questioner already knows about the subject field in which the question falls
2. How articulate the questioner is in expressing the information need
3. How interested he or she is in the search itself
4. How defensive the questioner's attitude is toward the librarian
5. How much information is wanted
6. How soon the information is needed
7. How much assistance is wanted: Does the questioner want to do the work alone or would he or she prefer someone else do it? Or does the questioner primarily want instruction along with assistance this time, so that in the future he or she will be able to do it alone?

These same variables may also be expressed from the librarian's point of view, as follows:

1. How much the librarian knows about the subject field in which the question falls
2. How skillful the librarian is at determining what the questioner really wants
3. How interested the librarian is in the search
4. How defensive the librarian is toward the questioner
5. How much information the librarian is prepared to provide
6. How quickly the librarian can provide the information
7. How much assistance or instruction the librarian is prepared to provide
   a. Minimum
   b. Middling
   c. Maximum

These are only a few of the variables, expressed in very general terms and not in the language of a discipline such as psychology, sociology, or another behavioral science. But, let's follow them with a few questions:

1. If the questioner knows more about the subject field of the question than the librarian, is the librarian's attitude more apt to be defensive?
2. If the librarian knows more about the subject field than the questioner, is the questioner's attitude more apt to be defensive?
3. What happens if the questioner is more interested in the search than the librarian?

4. What happens if the librarian is not skilled or sympathetic enough to interpret the question and relate it to the proper source(s) of information?
5. What happens if the library's resources are not adequate to meet the questioner's need?
6. What happens if the questioner wants the answer more quickly than the librarian can supply it?

The continuing concerns of those engaged in reference and information services are reflected in the activities of the Reference and User Services Association (RUSA) of the American Library Association (ALA). Formed in 1972 (as the Reference and Adult Services Division) by a merger of the former Adult Services Division and Reference Services Division, it is "responsible for simulating and supporting in every type of library the delivery of reference/information services to all groups, regardless of age, and of general library services and materials to adults" <http://www.ala.org/rusa/org.html>.

Already noted are its developmental and behavioral guidelines for information services. RUSA has also prepared guidelines on other subjects itself and cooperates with other ALA units in still further guidelines and standards.

It should also be noted that RUSA services to the reference community also include the ongoing development of suggestions, policies, and procedures on such activities as interlibrary loan, computerized information searching, and cooperative reference. Of particular note in the present context are the Wilson Indexes Committee, which advises the H. W. Wilson Company on the coverage of its many indexes; the Notable Books Council, which selects those adult books of each year that are most notable in quality; and the Reference Sources Committee, which, among other things, selects the Outstanding Reference Sources of each year.

RUSA's official journal is *Reference and User Services Quarterly*, formerly titled *RQ*, which expanded from a small leaflet in November 1970 to a substantial refereed journal with valuable articles on all aspects of reference and information work, including reviews of reference and professional sources, printed and electronic. The association also prepares an annual list of outstanding reference sources, published in *American Libraries*, and also gives a number of awards for reference publishing.

A good overview of the kinds of services rendered and current issues being faced is found in the division's newsletter, *RUSA Update*, or on its Web page <http://www.ala.org/rusa/update.html>.

One convenient source of well-selected articles in recent years is *Reference and Information Services: A Reader for the Nineties* (Metuchen, N.J.: Scarecrow, 1991; 415p.), edited by William A. Katz.

The most exhaustive bibliography of sources in English is Marjorie Murfin and Lubomyr Wynar, *Reference Service: An Annotated Bibliographic Guide*

(Littleton, Colo.: Libraries Unlimited, 1977; 249p.) and its supplement, *Reference Service: An Annotated Bibliographic Guide: Supplement, 1976–1982* (Littleton, Colo.: Libraries Unlimited, 1984; 353p.).

And for a background in the history of some of the classic tools, not only enlightening, but interesting, every reference librarian should read *Distinguished Classics of Reference Publishing* (Phoenix, Ariz.: Oryx, 1992; 356p.), edited by James Rettig, which describes the birth and development of thirty-one tried-and-true reference sources, with background about their creators.

What Is a "Reference Source"?

Presumably, the profession would have some agreement upon the tools of the trade, if not precisely what was done with them. Unfortunately, not only is there little help from the standard dictionaries and glossaries, but there is some evidence that in practice, there is not even a rough-and-ready rule of thumb for defining such a source. Turning to the *ALA Glossary* again, the reader is told that a reference book is "1. A book designed by the arrangement and treatment of its subject matter to be consulted for definite items of information rather than to be read consecutively. 2. A book whose use is restricted to the library building" (p. 188); and *Harrod's* says much the same thing.

However, an attempt to study reference collection policies found that librarians rarely had much of an idea of what they were looking for. Or, as they put it, "Although in almost all libraries, materials are sometimes added to the reference collection on the basis of a reference librarian's in-hand inspection, there was also evidence of much automatic selection to reference by category of work. Asked about this, one puzzled librarian notes, 'We put reference books in reference,' apparently believing that the definition of *reference book* is obvious and that the collection parameters it suggests are inviolable" (Mary Biggs and Victor Biggs, "Reference Collection Development in Academic Libraries: Report of a Survey," *RQ* 27 [fall 1987]: 67–79).

Perhaps the most useful definition to date is that proposed by Marcia Bates. Her approach, unlike most of her predecessors, in essence treats of all kinds of reference sources, not only books, but electronic sources as well. She points out that some kinds of books are composed purely of discourse—they lack any ordered records of any kind. On the other hand, some books are composed purely of files of data, with little discourse at all. Comparing the general stacks with the reference stacks, she found that the majority of books in the stacks had little file structure, while the majority of reference books had a very high percentage devoted to files. Thus, her conclusion is that reference books as such are manual databases (Marcia J. Bates, "What Is a Reference Book: A Theoretical and Empirical Analysis," *RQ* 26 [fall 1986]: 43–50).

What Is a "Fundamental" Reference Source?

How does one define *fundamental,* especially in a era when the number and variety of titles continue to increase at the same time that even older standard titles are available in an increasing number of formats?

In a sense, this is a variant of the question of how to teach reference—does one concentrate on the type of sources in general, specific sources (and if so, which ones), or on the process, leaving the student to discover which sources are of most value to a given situation?

One approach to an answer is a survey of what sources are taught in the programs that teach reference librarians. The classic work in this approach remains that of Wallace J. Bonk, who surveyed all accredited library schools in 1960. His results, issued as *Composite List of Titles Taught in Basic Reference by 25 of the Accredited Library Schools* (Ann Arbor, Mich.: Univ. of Michigan Department of Library Science, 1960; various pagings), found "less agreement . . . than was expected" but also that more than half of the schools did teach 115 titles in common, out of a total of 1,202 titles taught by at least one school in the basic course, and 47 percent of the titles were taught in only one course. Bonk found only five titles taught by all twenty-five schools *(Encyclopedia Americana, Encyclopaedia Britannica, World Book Encyclopedia, Funk & Wagnall's New Standard Dictionary, and the Oxford English Dictionary).*

The same basic approach was used by John C. Larsen in 1978 and 1979, surveying the then sixty-three ALA-accredited schools. Larsen found that thirty-one schools had some sort of list of sources taught, while ten consciously did not provide any list as such, and three did not base the course on sources at all. Although a total of 2,014 different titles were taught at the thirty-one schools, only 147 were taught by at least half the schools and 70 by at least 75 percent of them. Of these, only 7 were listed by all thirty-one schools *(New Encyclopaedia Britannica, World Book Encyclopedia, Current Biography, Dictionary of American Biography, New York Times Index, Readers' Guide to Periodical Literature, and the World Almanac).* Overall, Larsen found a larger number of titles and even greater diversity in those titles than did Bonk ("Information Sources Currently Studied in General Reference Courses," *RQ* 18 [summer 1979]: 341–48).

Another approach to the problem of defining the "basic" or "core" list is to find out which sources working librarians use. Again, Bonk provides one of the classic attempts. He sent a list of 352 titles (essentially those titles listed by at least 25 percent of the library schools) to 1,750 reference librarians, asking them to rate each title as "vital," "recommended," or "peripheral" based on degree of use. Librarians were also asked to list other titles of value that were not on the list. Of the 1,090 respondents, no title was rated as vital by all. Ph.D.-granting university librarians agreed on nine titles; librarians at bachelor's- and master's-granting universities, junior colleges, secondary schools, and pubic libraries did not agree on even one vital title. Overall, at least half the respondents agreed on 73 vital titles and on another 69 titles as recommended (Wallace J. Bonk, *Use of Basic Reference Sources in Libraries* [Ann Arbor, Mich.: Campus Publishers, 1966; 236p.]).

Although no study of similar size has been conducted since, it is telling that a survey of the public libraries in Anne Arundel County found that none of them could, at the time of the survey, produce a core list of important titles and that a survey of Latin American bibliographers in 1986 found of twenty-three replies the most agreed-upon title was listed by only ten librarians (Ellen Berkov and Betty Morganstern, "Getting to the Core: Training Librarians in Basic Reference Tools," *The Reference Librarian*, no. 30 [1990]: 191–205).

A third approach is to compare lists of recommended titles in other sources, such as textbooks. Although in one sense begging the question (because it assumes the textbook writers have defined *core* in some fashion), the method does at least provide another way of defining "core"—as "best" rather than "most taught" or "most heavily used." Here, the most useful (if not only) such study is that of Arthur Coren (reported in Richard L. Hopkins, "Ranking the Reference Books: Methodologies for Identifying 'Key' Reference Sources," *The Reference Librarian*, no. 34 [1991]: 141–65). Coren first compared a number of lists of distinguished sources found in *Reference Services Review* and *RQ* over the period from 1980 to 1985, finding only fourteen sources listed by three of more commentators. Hopkins followed this up with a more formal study comparing the titles recommended in four standard reference "textbooks" (including the second edition of *Fundamental Reference Sources*), finding only eighty-one sources listed in all four (about 6 percent of all titles mentioned) and agreement among three of the four books on an additional 132 titles.

The same approach, using seven textbooks and bibliographies, but limited to business-related sources, again found full agreement on only 4 titles and only 29 titles agreed upon by at least four sources (for a total of 9.5 percent of the total of 306 titles) (Debra J. Sears, "The 'Best Books' on Total Quality Management: A First Review," *RQ* 33 [fall 1993]: 85–87).

From the above, one must conclude with William A. Katz that "there is not a single list upon which all reference librarians will agree" (*Introduction to Reference Work*, volume 1, *Basic Information Sources* [New York: McGraw-Hill, 1969], p. 30).

However, before one despairs entirely, note that the lack of a general consensus or core collection is not confined to reference collections. Several studies of library networks in general have found surprisingly little overlap among members of a given network (see William G. Potter, "Studies of Collection Overlap," *Library Research* 4 [spring 1982]: 3–21; and Larry Hardesty and

Colleen Mak, "Searching for the Holy Grail," *Journal of Academic Librarianship* 19 [Jan. 1994]: 362-71). And, on a completely different tack, this author and a colleague, using the entire Online Computer Library Center (OCLC) database, found very little consensus in the collecting of adult fiction by public libraries: out of literally millions of records in about 4,700 public libraries, the most popular title, John Jakes's *North and South,* was held by only 1,090 libraries, or about one-fourth (Judith J. Senkevitch and James H. Sweetland, "Public Libraries and Adult Fiction: Another Look at a Core List of 'Classics,'" *Library Resources and Technical Services* 42 [April 1998]: 102-12).

One should not despair, however. The apparent lack of consensus is not necessarily bad—it may be seen as evidence that librarians have in fact been conscious of local needs and have been successful in developing collections to meet such needs.

The point of this book, as with other guides to reference materials that follow, is, after all, not to provide a required list of materials that *must* be held in every library, but rather to provide suggestions of titles most likely to be useful. It remains the responsibility of the individual librarian to know both the materials and the users and to act accordingly.

Guides to Reference Sources

Although inquiry into the reference process will continue, one thing is agreed upon by all librarians: they must know sources of information. Because of this, guides to reference sources and selection aids have been prepared. There are many notable examples, and only a few are singled out here.

Possibly the best known and most used in the United States is Robert Balay's *Guide to Reference Books* (11th ed. Chicago: ALA, 1992; 2020p.). Carrying on the reputation established by its earlier editors, including Isadore Mudge, Constance Winchell, and Eugene P. Sheehy, its 15,875 entries were selected by fifty librarians, all of whom do reference work and most of whom work in general reference situations. This work is updated between editions by an annotated semiannual list of selected reference materials appearing in *College and Research Libraries.*

Walford's Guide to Reference Material (6th ed. 3v. London: Library Assn. Pub., 1993-95) has about 8,100 more titles listed than *Balay* but is roughly similar in arrangement to it. With a more British slant, better representation of European and Commonwealth titles, and often fuller and more-critical annotations, this source is an often-overlooked but valuable complement to *Balay.*

Although out-of-date, Louise-Nöelle Malclès's *Les Sources du Travail Bibliographique* (3v. in 4, Geneva: Droz; Lille, France: Giard, 1950-58) must be mentioned as a classic, strong in French titles. Although *Balay, Walford's,* and *Malclès* differ to some extent in arrangement and individual titles, they are international in scope and all include the following types of reference materials:

1. Bibliographies and indexes, which direct the user to other sources of information
2. Sources of biographical information
3. Dictionaries of all kinds
4. Encyclopedias
5. Yearbooks
6. Directories of persons and organizations
7. Atlases and gazetteers
8. And, in recent years, *Balay* and *Walford's* have included a growing number of electronic sources

All are annotated; and as reference materials continue to proliferate, they serve as a record of those titles considered worthy of inclusion at the time the guides were published.

A useful current annual source, in some senses updating these sources, is *American Reference Books Annual* (Englewood, Colo.: Libraries Unlimited, 1970-). Roughly 1,800 titles, produced or distributed in the United States, are arranged by subject and provide brief (about 250 words) signed critical reviews primarily by subject specialists, with citations to reviews in several library periodicals, including *Booklist/Reference Books Bulletin, Choice,* and *Library Journal.* In addition to annual indexes to author, title, and subject, these are cumulated every five years. Although its timing does not make it the primary selection source, it is the most complete record of reference source production in the United States, as well as a good source of discriminating reviews and a guide to additional reviews of a title.

As reference sources increase in number and complexity, need increases not only for selective, less exhaustive guides, but for guides to the literature of a special subject field or country or aimed at a particular type of library.

Introductory textbooks, such as Richard E. Bopp and Linda C. Smith, *Reference and Information Services: An Introduction* (2d ed. Englewood, Colo.: Libraries Unlimited, 1995; 626p.), Jean Key Gates, *Guide to the Use of Libraries and Information Sources* (6th ed. New York: McGraw-Hill, 1989; 348p.), and William A. Katz, *Introduction to Reference Work, Volume 1, Basic Information Sources* (6th ed. New York: McGraw-Hill, 1992; 485p.), are examples of useful, less selective guides.

Similarly, the *American Library Association Guide to Information Access* (New York: Random House, 1994; 533p.) is a selective guide aimed at the general reader but with plenty of information helpful to the professional librarian as well.

For a list of guides to the literature in special subject fields, see chapter 2, Sources of Bibliographic Information.

Examples of lists prepared for a particular type of library are Margaret I. Nichols, *Guide to Reference Books for School Media Centers* (4th ed. Englewood, Colo.: Libraries Unlimited, 1992; 463p.) and *Reference Books for Children's Collections* (Dolores Vogliana, ed.; 3d ed. New York: New York Public Library Office of Children's Services, 1996; 97p.), aimed primarily at public libraries, as well as *Reference Sources for Small and Medium-sized Libraries* (Scott E. Kennedy, ed.; 6th ed. Chicago: ALA, 1999; 376p.).

Small libraries with limited budgets will find Andrew L. March, *Recommended Reference Books in Paperback* (2d ed. Englewood, Colo.: Libraries Unlimited, 1992; 263p.) helpful.

Other guides to reference sources include the following:

■ Best reference books, [year]. Englewood, Colo.: Libraries Unlimited, 1981– . Quinquennial.

Selected from reviews in *American Reference Books Annual (ARBA)*, with minor updating. Includes serials as well as books. First edition covered from 1970 to 1980. Arranged by broad subject. Indexes by title, author, and subject.

■ Dority, Kim. A guide to reference books for small and medium-sized libraries, 1984–1994. Englewood, Colo.: Libraries Unlimited, 1995. 372p.

Based on reviews in *ARBA*, selected for those of most value to smaller libraries. Updated by *Recommended Reference Books for Small and Medium-Sized Libraries*, annual, by Libraries Unlimited. Reprints with minor updates reviewed in *ARBA*, with same indexing and arrangement. Has been criticized for unclear selection criteria, which sometimes seem to lead to inappropriate recommendations—the titles are good, but not clearly suitable for smaller libraries.

■ Guide to reference materials for Canadian libraries. 8th ed. Toronto and Buffalo, N.Y.: Univ. of Toronto Pr., 1992. 596p.

A guide specifically for Canadian libraries, listing about 4,600 titles, most with annotations. Classified by subject, with indexes by author, title, and subject. Emphasizes Canadian publication, Canadian editions of international publications.

■ Lewis, Audrey. Madame Audrey's guide to mostly cheap but good reference books for small and rural libraries. Chicago: ALA, 1998. 352p.

Aimed at the smallest library, concentrating on the least expensive acceptable reference books wherever possible, and written in a style that has been likened to "Miss Manners as your local librarian."

■ Reference sources for small and medium-sized libraries. Scott E. Kennedy, ed. 6th ed. Chicago: ALA, 1999. 376p.

> Earlier editions used the term *reference books*. A standard work, covering printed and electronic sources, compiled by a subcommittee of the Reference Sources Committee of the Reference and User Services Association and thus representing, in a sense, the consensus of working reference librarians. Classified by subject, most entries have annotations. Indexed by author or compiler and title.

■ The reference sources handbook. Peter W. Lea and Alan Day, eds. 4th ed. London: Library Assn. Pub., 1996. 446p.

> First three editions as *Printed Reference Material*. From a British perspective, but including much U.S. material (as well as that of other nations). Annotations vary in length, but often provide information as well as perspectives not available in the standard U.S. sources.

Current Reviewing Sources

Library-oriented sources that regularly review reference sources, chiefly those in the English language follow:

> *Booklist/Reference Books Bulletin (RBB)*. *RBB* is, in effect, a separate journal bound within *Booklist*. It includes regular lengthy evaluations of encyclopedias, dictionaries, atlases, and other types of reference materials prepared by the *RBB* Editorial Board, as well as shorter reviews of all types of reference materials, including electronic sources and Internet sites. *RBB* is suitable for all types of libraries, not limited to the smaller school and public library as is *Booklist*. Biweekly, monthly, July and August.

> *Choice*. Brief critical reviews by college and university faculty and libraries, aimed at the college library, and subject-specific essays in each issue, which normally include reference material. *Choice* also has begun an annual supplement covering recommended websites, as well as its regular reviewing of electronic formats. Monthly.

> *Library Journal*. Brief, signed reviews by librarians and others. The April 15 issue publishes an annual "Best Reference Source." Biweekly, except for two months.

> *Reference and Research Book News*. A reasonably complete listing, classified by Library of Congress system. Covers material suitable for all age levels and all types of libraries, providing some information

not in the other sources. However, the annotations are generally only descriptive, rather than evaluative. Eight issues per year.

Reference and User Services Quarterly (formerly *RQ*). Signed reviews, often lengthy, of printed and electronic reference sources by librarians, as well as occasional articles evaluating and comparing sources. Quarterly.

Reference Services Review. Rather than covering a large number of sources in traditional reviews, *Reference Services Review* specializes in state-of-the-art surveys of reference sources in specific fields. Prepared by librarians with experience in the field, the lists of selected titles, well annotated, are usually prefaced with general comments on the field. Quarterly.

Selected lists and current reviewing media are helpful to librarians in developing collections on which effective service is based, as well as awareness of sources of value that are not in one's own collection, but they are no substitute for discriminating judgment in selection of titles best suited to the library's clientele. This requires a thorough knowledge of the library's existing reference collection, not only to use it effectively, but also to avoid needless and expensive duplication of subject matter already available. Such judgment is just as critical in the decisions not to buy and in what formats to buy, with the increasing availability of electronic sources online, on CD-ROM and similar compact disc formats, such as DVD (digital versatile disc), and, for an often hefty fee, on tape, which can be installed on one's own library catalog system.

In short, given a reference source, one may have any or all of the following options:

1. Purchase a printed copy
2. Purchase a CD-ROM from one or more different suppliers
3. Purchase (or usually rent) a magnetic tape
4. "Rent" the source via one or more traditional commercial online sources
5. Access the source, or a significant part of it, for a fee or for free via the Internet or World Wide Web, again often from several sources

Considering that these choices may apply to any given title, and that there is still the likelihood that several different titles may cover approximately the same ground, the need for informed judgment is clear.

Evaluation of Reference Sources

Not only are evaluation skills necessary in collection building, but also in evaluating the adequacy of the reviewing sources themselves, for as a number of studies have shown, the reference-reviewing media have their shortcomings.

These have been examined in several studies, including Margaret Know Goggin and Lillian M. Seaberg, "The Publishing and Reviewing of Reference Books" (*Library Trends* 12 [Jan. 1964]: 437–55); Harry E. Whitmore, "Reference Book Reviewing" (*RQ* 9 [spring 1970]: 221–26; Alma A. Covey, *Reviewing of Reference Books* (Metuchen, N.J.: Scarecrow, 1972; 142p.); James H. Sweetland, "Reference Book Reviewing Tools: How Well Do They Do the Job?" (*Reference Librarian,* no. 15 [fall 1986]: 65–74); and James Rettig, "Reference Book Reviewing Media: A Critical Analysis" (*Library Science Annual* 2 [1986]: 13–29).

Overall, each of these studies finds that the reviews tend to be rather positive, which may or may not be a problem, but also that too often the reviewer does not clearly indicate whether the source under review is particularly good, or for what it is good for, or what sort of library might find it of most use. In other words, the basic failing of reference reviewing is that it is too often not evaluative enough. In addition to the courage of one's convictions, the reviewer may be assisted by detailed and specific guidelines for reviews, whether writing for publication or selecting for one's library.

Although many sources, from general guides to reference materials to individual journals, supply guidance in the evaluation of reference and information sources, few of them are sufficiently detailed to assist the reviewer (a number of such guidelines are reproduced in the appendix). The guidelines for reviewing English-language dictionaries and encyclopedias, bibliographies, atlases, and statistical compilations represent the considered judgment of the editorial board of the ALA's *RBB* and are scrupulously followed by that committee in preparing its reviews. They emphasize the thoroughness required for careful evaluation of these types of reference works and should aid the individual librarian and the library- or information-studies-school student in determining the value of a title, as well as give them a glimpse into the working of the committee.

This brief overview of the nature of reference and information service is intended only as an introduction to the chapters on various types of sources that follow. It is deliberately salted with numerous references to other works, not only to give credit where credit is due (a cardinal rule in reference work), but also to stimulate the reader to use these sources for fuller understanding of this process in a spirit of free inquiry.

2

Sources of
Bibliographic Information

Our efforts to record and to organize for future use our discoveries, meditations, and observations of the universe have never been adequate to the never-ending flow of manuscripts, published works, films, recordings, and machine-based data that constitute our means of communications with one another. This variety of forms of communication is greatly exceeded by the varieties of bibliographic activity, and a serious study of their development would take years of reading. They range from short title lists to data banks, from indexes that use broad Library of Congress subject headings to those with highly specific index entries in very technical fields, to various mechanical and electronic "search engines" based on the full text of selected documents.

Louise-Nöelle Malclès's *Bibliography* (rev. ed. New York: Scarecrow, 1973) remains one of the best sources for a brief history of bibliography as a science and an art, related to the social and intellectual movements that provided the climate for its development and stimulated men and women to compile such lists. Malclès is concerned with systematic bibliography, that form of publication compiled to meet the need so aptly stated by the historian Charles Victor Langlois in 1904: "What can be done so the public will have the means to find out, rapidly and accurately, the resource of all kinds, offered by that great library formed by the work of authors of all times and all countries?"

But, as Malclès points out, the desire to record sources of information pervades the history of scholarship. We find early examples of it in the ancient Babylonian catalogs of cuneiform tablets; in the list compiled by the Greek physician Galen in the second century; and in the list of Bede's own works, appended to his *Ecclesiastical History,* written in the eighth century. But it was the invention of movable-type printing that gave the greatest impetus to bibliographical activity, and lists of published works began to appear as early as 1494. The founders of bibliography in the sixteenth century were men of science whose research into printed books was an extension of their special studies. They did original work, searching out books in libraries, in homes, and in bookstores. They were interested in the authors of the works, producing biobibliographies that more nearly resemble biographical dictionaries, with less attention to the full bibliographic description of the works themselves.

Interest in books for their own sake came later, with the increasing dependence on lists already in existence, but the sixteenth century gave bibliography its direction for the next two centuries (Malclès 1973, 52). The seventeenth century saw the rise of enumerators, concerned with a census of all books and not merely those in which they happened to take a personal interest. By then, there was not only specialized bibliography, but also the beginning of universal and national bibliography. The science flourished in the eighteenth century, with a new generation of researchers to whom the book was as important as its author. The century also saw the development of rules for cataloging and systems for classification. Between 1790 and 1810, booksellers began to publish periodicals that recorded the new books of their countries (sometimes with content annotations), a kind of beginning of current national bibliography.

Nineteenth-century bibliography was affected by the great scientific movement that completely changed the conditions of intellectual activities. Other important factors affecting its development were the exploration of new countries, the progress in public education through curriculum reform and the reorganization of universities, the increase in numbers of major schools and learned societies, the growth of the book trade and periodical press, and the establishment of archives and libraries open to the public. These factors led to an increase in investigation and research, which in turn helped change the emphasis of bibliography from recording the works of the past to dissemination of current advances in learning.

By the beginning of the twentieth century, the goals and methods of bibliography had been defined. If, in the language dictionaries, it kept meaning "the science of the book," the facts contradicted this assertion. It became much more than the science of the book. Unlike those of the sixteenth century, bibliographies concentrated on the author's works, not the author. More than at any other period, bibliography was awareness of the distinct products of the mind. The growth of knowledge and the publication of other bibliographies encouraged this change. Authors had been subordinated to their particular works. Today, bibliography carefully identifies distinct works and editions to record intellectual activity.

From 1914 on, we see the rapid development of current bibliography in almost every subject field. Also, we find specialists working together to produce "collective syntheses," which list the source material considered essential to the subject. But the most dramatic development has been that of documentation centers, which have continued to increase in all subject fields, with those in science and technology taking the lead.

About midcentury, UNESCO became a powerful force for extending and improving bibliography, working with other international organizations. In 1950, UNESCO and the Library of Congress prepared a working paper on the present state and possibilities of improvement of bibliographical services, with an appendix by Katherine Murra entitled, "Notes on the Development of the Concept of Current Complete National Bibliography." The resolutions of the UNESCO Conference on the Improvement of Bibliographical Services emphasized the need for national planning bodies for bibliography and named eleven categories that member states should consider for coverage in current national bibliographies.

In the 1970s, UNESCO's focus changed a bit, with the creation of the General Information Programme by combining several previous programs and the gradually changing emphasis from "bibliography" as such to bibliographic control and a general concern with the entire "information infrastructure." This has tended to more concern on the one hand with the development of coordinated communication formats for computer-based exchange of records, notably a database management system called CD-ISIS, and, at the same time, concentration on education and communication as well as on the preservation of documents and artifacts, as opposed to concern with the science and art of "bibliography."

In many ways, the International Federation of Library Associations and Institutions (IFLA) has taken over the lead role in international bibliographic work. There are two components in modern thinking on the subject—Universal Availability of Publications (UAP) and Universal Bibliographic Control (UBC). The latter became a formal IFLA program in 1974, endorsed by UNESCO and developed by the 1977 International Conference on National Bibliographies. In brief, each nation would have a national bibliographic agency that would catalog all material published in that nation, in a format that would be acceptable to all other nations. Thus, when UBC was achieved, no one would have to catalog any material produced in another country, and all libraries connected to the scheme would have access to all relevant bibliographic records. Obviously, this program assumes not only general availability of computers and of agreed-upon standards for cataloging and for the entry of data, but also for agreement as to the application of standards. However, the attractions of UBC are such that we do seem to be approaching it, while more nations are at least setting up "national bibliographic agencies." For a discussion of the problems and successes, see Edgar A. Jones, "In Search of UBC" (*Cataloging and Classification Quarterly* 23, no. 3/4 [1997]: 85–163; and 24, no. 3/4 [1997]: 59–124). UAP, on the other hand, although also with a fairly lengthy history of its own, involves not only the identification of material, but its delivery to a user when needed (or, at least, approximately when needed), and thus is beyond the scope of this book. However, the reference librarian must always remember that, regardless of one's title or place of work, the user is only partially served with identification of a document, when what is needed is actual possession of the document or, even better, of the needed information.

The advent of the computer in midcentury and especially the development of easy-to-use, inexpensive desktop (and now laptop) computers, followed by the rapid growth of the Internet after about 1990, have dramatically affected our access to stored information. For many years primarily the province of governments and universities, and geared initially to analysis of numeric data, computer databases are now routinely accessed by even small businesses. One might date the change to the entry of Lockheed Information Systems (the parent of the Dialog system) and Systems Development Corporation into the information market with the availability of common command systems for retrieval of information from textual databases in the 1970s, or the start-up of OCLC in the same decade, but in any event, the popular media's awareness of the computer as an information storage and retrieval device really began with the development of the World Wide Web in the 1990s.

Ironically, while bibliography as a science was well developed, as was a field known as information science, few of the current developers of the Web appear to have been aware of even elementary aspects of bibliographic control. At the present time, considerable effort has become devoted to what is tagged *metadata*, or information about information, such as authorship, subject terms, "publishing" responsibility, and the like, for Internet-based information. This is reminiscent of the work of earlier bibliographers and catalogers, and one may wonder if we need to cover the same ground in the twenty-first century because of the change in format from ink on paper to electrons on disks.

With the computer came the rapid development of information systems and services that have dramatically affected our access to stored facts. These systems were first prominent in the sciences and technology and are now common in most areas of endeavor. It is now hard to remember that, although Vannevar Bush's "As We May Think" appeared in 1945 (*Atlantic Monthly* 176, no. 1 [1945]: 101–8), readily accessible systems, using mainframes, did not appear until the 1960s; OCLC became available in the early 1970s; CD-ROMs were considered quite exotic into the early 1980s; and the World Wide Web did not reach any degree of public awareness until about 1995 (with the development of Mosaic, the first easily learned graphics browser). Moreover, storage size and transmission speed have also increased dramatically in about one generation. When this author began searching online in 1976, the 1,200-baud modem was only just available; at this writing, 56K modems are readily available. Similarly, between around 1985 and 1998, CD-ROM access speeds (in terms of the hardware, at least) have gone from the original speed to thirty-two times that original.

For our purposes, the most important point in these changes is in the availability of electronic formats, in the cost of retrieving data, and in the amount of data retrieved. It is now becoming common for library users to expect the full text of requested sources, complete with any graphics, photographs, or other illustrations, and with all the colors of the original, and to expect this within minutes of articulating the request. Ironically, some estimates of the amount of human knowledge (actually data) in machine-readable form at the present are in the order of one-half of 1 percent.

Thus, for at least the immediate future, "bibliographic" activities will continue to be important. In fact, as immediate access to information increases, it is likely that the importance of organized, consistent, and accurate pointers to such information will increase.

It is not the purpose of this chapter to trace the history of bibliographic activities but to describe some of the kinds of systematic bibliography and their general characteristics and uses. For practical purposes, Luther Evans's definition still applies (although many other definitions exist): "A bibliography is a compilation of information regarding recorded sources of information."

Definitions

The two principal elements in bibliographic activity may be understood immediately by anyone who has learned to catalog and classify a book. These elements are traditionally designated descriptive bibliography and systematic bibliography. With the document in hand, the student must first describe its physical state, its format. This description involves recording its author or authors, title, place of publication, publisher, date of publication, size, number of pages, illustrations, and, where applicable, the series to which it belongs. This record is a simple form of *descriptive* bibliography.

The student's next concern is the intellectual content of the book, its subject matter. The student must designate its place in some system of classification—must assign its proper subject headings in terms of some established system. In so doing, the student has engaged in a simple act of *systematic* bibliography.

Descriptive bibliography, then, is concerned with accurate identification and description of a book, or nonbook item, as a physical object. In his *Elements of Bibliography* (Metuchen, N.J.: Scarecrow, 1989; p. 6), Robert Harmon presents a useful table (based on Roy Stokes's classic chart in *Library Trends* 7, no. 4 ([April 1959]: 495), which sets forth the two purposes of bibliography and clarifies the preceding, oversimplified statements:

I. Study of the Book itself, as a Physical Entity, a material object:

PURPOSE: Accurate, precise identification and description	Analytical or Critical Bibliography	*Textual Bibliography* Study and comparison of texts and their transmission through editions and printings
		Historical Bibliography Placing and dating of individual books or other graphic material
		Descriptive Bibliography Identification of the "ideal copy" and all its variants

II. Study of graphic materials as *intellectual entities:*

PURPOSE: Assembling of information about individual books or other graphic materials into a logical and useful arrangement	Enumerative or Systematic Bibliography	*Compilation of lists of books or other graphic materials* Author Bibliographies Bibliographies of Bibliographies Catalogs Guides to the Literature National Bibliography Selective or Elective Bibliography Subject Bibliography Trade Bibliography Universal Bibliography

For a fuller treatment of the subject, see Harmon's *Elements of Bibliography* and also Roy Stokes's *Function of Bibliography* (2d ed. Aldershot, England: Gower, 1982; 201p.). Stokes believes that much of the confusion in use of the term *bibliography* comes from its application to a book both as a physical and as an intellectual entity.

Paul S. Dunkin states simply, "A bibliographer tells us one or more of at least three things about a book he has examined as a physical object: (1) He classifies it as an edition, issue, state, or variant; (2) He transcribes its title; (3) He states its collation" (p. 13). Each of these tasks Dunkin reviews in some detail in his *Bibliography: Tiger or Fat Cat?* (Hamden, Conn.: Archon Books, 1975). His analyses of the writings of Fredson Bowers, Walter Greg, Ronald McKerrow, and other classic writers on the book as a physical object remove some of the controversy and confusion that characterized earlier discussions of the role of descriptive bibliography. Harmon extends the discussion to the equivalent tasks involved in electronic documents, further clarifying the concept of enumerative bibliography.

This chapter and the following are concerned with bibliography as broadly defined by Luther Evans, with full recognition that certain types, such as library catalogs and periodical indexes, are not admitted to the category by all who have written on the subject; and other types, such as electronic lists of electronic documents, or lists of nonprint material, possibly should not even be called by the name *biblio*graphy (since the root word refers to the ink on paper/vellum/papyrus document). These types are all part of systematic bibliography; and for those who seek information on recorded sources of information, it is practical to outline the whole range, without quibbling over differences in definition.

In particular, as we move into an era when the typical library, even the largest, is able to house a smaller and smaller fraction of the world's information resources, the knowledge of the forms and characteristics of those things that are a systematic representation of recorded knowledge in whatever format becomes critical to more than basic functioning of the library. The following attempts to summarize the more common types, giving some clue to their purpose and content.

Library Catalogs

Because libraries and archives remain the principal repositories of recorded knowledge, it follows that the library catalog, which systematically records the holdings of a collection by author, title, and subject, is an important form of systematic bibliography.

Union Catalogs/Union Lists

From catalogs of individual libraries have developed general union catalogs, which record in one sequence the holdings or part of the holdings of two or more libraries, either in book form, microforms, or, increasingly in the last twenty years, electronic form. The classic example of such a catalog is the *National Union Catalog* of the Library of Congress (LC), initially compiled on cards held at the LC, then published in book form, and now also produced in microform. The classic example of an electronic union catalog, of course, is the OCLC Online Union Catalog (OLUC, also called WorldCat), which is based in part on the machine records of the Library of Congress. Containing records for every sort of recorded knowledge known, WorldCat comes closest to the ideal of a universal bibliography.

National Book Bibliographies

Place and date of publication are the principal factors that determine what is included in national bibliographies, such as *Books in Print (BIP)*. Another similar type of such bibliography is based on language, of which the *Cumulative Book Index* (familiarly known as *CBI*) is an important example for American librarians. National and language-based bibliographies may be further restricted by form of publication. Thus, for the most part, *CBI* includes books in the English language, wherever published in the world, published by trade publishers, and is commonly refered to as trade bibliography. Just as a library catalog serves, in effect, as an inventory of a library's collections, a national bibliography serves, within its limits, as an inventory of titles published in a given country.

Subject Bibliographies

As the name implies, subject bibliographies are restricted to one subject but usually not to one form of publication or one language. They may be retrospective or current, comprehensive or selective. Interest in individual writers has been responsible for a large number of author bibliographies, which record works by and about a given author.

Selective Bibliographies

Selective is most often applied to bibliographies that record the best titles for a particular type of user, library, or subject. But note that all the types listed so far are selective in another sense. A library catalog is selective in the sense that it lists only the holdings of a particular library. National or language bibliography is selective in being restricted to the output of one country, type of publication, or language. Subject bibliographies are selective in dealing with only one subject or aspect of a subject and may also be selective in the other sense, by including only the best or most useful material on that subject.

These forms of bibliography are viewed as selective—not to create a confusion of terms but to serve as a reminder of the interdependence of the various forms and of the necessity of using more than one form in many kinds of searches for information. In general, selective bibliographies are compiled with stated criteria for selection of their contents.

Indexes

Indexes differ from catalogs in recording, under appropriate entries, the *contents* of documents of some kind, thus providing access to parts of a whole, rather than the whole item as such. For the most part, they are either prepared by humans using computers or even solely by computers. They range from the general to the ever-increasing number of indexes in special fields, notably science, technology, and business. Typically, printed indexes are arranged alphabetically by subject. Because of their importance, they are treated at length in chapter 3.

Abstracting Services

Abstracting services resemble indexes in providing access to the contents of a document. They differ in providing a summary of the contents. Most printed abstracting services are arranged in a subject classified system, rather than strictly alphabetically. Note that all systematic bibliography contains the element of descriptive bibliography, because any document must be described to be identified. Again, these are treated in chapter 3.

Concordances

Alphabetical lists of the important words in a test as they occur in context are called *concordances*. Older examples include those to the Bible or to the works of important authors, such as Shakespeare. These lists began increasing with the application of computer technology to text and now often include nearly every word in a text (with the exception of very common words such as articles, "a," "an," "the," and the like). In a sense, many modern computer indexes to textual material are concordances, although this term is rarely, if ever, used to describe them.

Internet Directories

Much of the previous discussion is based on the traditional systems developed over several hundred years and primarily assumes that the work will be done by humans, with assistance of some sort of machines (pens, printing presses, typewriters, computers). However, with the wider availability of computers in the 1950s, some attempts have been made to have all the indexing work done by the computer itself, with little human intervention. Early attempts, using keywords from titles or other parts of a record (such as keyword in context, or KWIC), were not completely successful.

However, since the late 1980s, the very rapid development of the Internet, and especially the World Wide Web, has made purely computer indexing nearly essential, even with its flaws, because the amount of material to be indexed and cataloged appears to increase exponentially. One of the major problems with relying on computers to self-index is the complex nature of human language, in which the same word can mean many different things (homographs), in which different words can mean the same or nearly the same thing (synonyms), and in which the same expression can mean different things in different contexts. For example, *bridge* can refer to a structure built over an obstruction (such as a river), a dental appliance, a device for keeping the strings of a musical instrument away from the body of the instrument, or a type of card game, among other things.

At present, particularly for the Web, and to some degree for more purely text-based systems, this problem is dealt with by various schemes for weighting a search request based on the terms. Weights can be determined by how often a word appears in a given document, how many of the words requested appear in the document, the ratio between how often the terms requested appear compared with the average appearance of the terms in the entire database of documents, the proximity of requested terms to each other, and the like. The theory of such indexing, although not completely new, is still in its infancy; and the experience of most people in retrieving information tends to be based on assumptions deriving from use of print-based (even if computer-assisted) indexing. Traditional indexing has depended very heavily on use of controlled vocabularies, in which the terms have clearly defined meanings and in which the problems noted here have several conventional solutions.

Although some predict that the proliferation of Web-based sites must decline, and thus that more traditional indexing and cataloging methods will eventually catch up, for now access to such information remains a problem. One solution, which seems to be at least partly effective, is to have a "spider" or "bot" (robot) select sites of potential interest but a human actually review the selected site and assign some subject terms as assistance to the user.

Computer-based documents that do not appear in some printed form also create another problem—that of descriptive bibliography. Because the site's true existence is in the form of electronics on one or more computers, it is not clear what, other than the site's address, to use as a description. And, because the ease with which a site may be moved from one address to another is not much less than that with which the entire site may be redone, it is not clear yet that even the address is a sufficient identification.

Library Catalogs

When two or more books are acquired by a library, the problem of their relationship to one another arises; thus, some method must be devised to show these relationships and, at the same time, preserve the individual identify of each. Go to a catalog in your nearest library and observe that it contains records accessible at least by author, by title, and by subject. In the case of cards, the distinctions among these records are a bit easier to see; in an online catalog (or OPAC—online public access catalog), the different elements may be indicated by labels or may be most clearly distinguishable by their location on the screen, but the principles remain the same.

Look at the author: observe the author's name is usually given in full, with dates of birth and death, in order to distinguish John Amos Brown from John Andrew Brown or one John Brown from another. For a better understanding of the author concept in codes of cataloging rules in the English language, consult James A. Tait, *Author and Titles* (Hamden, Conn.: Archon Books, 1969; 154p.); for full details, of course, there is also the current edition of the *Anglo-American Cataloguing Rules* (2d ed. Chicago: ALA, 1998; 676p.).

Next, look at a subject entry. Note that the subject was assigned according to a system of subject headings, whose arbitrariness Joseph Becker and R. M. Hayes were not the first to recognize (Joseph Becker and R. M. Hayes, *Information Storage and Retrieval* [New York: Wiley, 1963], p. 25).

The chief problem for the user of a traditional catalog, then, is terminology. Most larger American library catalogs contain subject headings whose authority was established by the Library of Congress and published in *Library of Congress Subject Headings* (22d ed. Washington, D.C.: Library of Congress, 1999; 5v.), available in print and in several electronic forms. According to its preface, this list is the product of evolutionary forces. Familiarity with this list is a prerequisite for any librarian who attempts to give instruction in the use of the catalog. This familiarity involves an awareness of its *scope* notes, which explain the distinction between headings; of its *see* references, which direct the user from a term not used to a term for the subject that is used; and of its *see also* references, which bring together related headings that are often more specific aspects of its subject.

In the 1988 edition of the *LCSH,* the indication of relationships was amplified and the overall display format revised, to follow the conventions of a thesaurus, with the use of the indicators Broader Term, Narrower Term, and Related Term, and the use of the more active Use and Used For to replace the *see* and *see also* tags. Although probably easier for the user, this approach has been criticized as making the authority list of subject headings look like a thesaurus when it is not, thus misleading users (Mary Dykstra, "LC Subject Headings Disguised as a Thesaurus," *Library Journal* 113 [March 1, 1988]: 42–46; 113 [Sept. 15, 1988]: 55–58).

Small libraries often use *Sears List of Subject Headings* (16th ed. New York: Wilson, 1997; 786p.), which follows the Library of Congress form of headings, abridged and simplified to meet the needs of smaller libraries.

But the point to remember is that a thorough knowledge of the system of subject headings used in a particular library catalog or bibliography is essential to the intelligent use of that catalog. Those without this knowledge, or unsure of the best subject heading(s) to use for a given search, can rely on what has been termed "pearl growing." Knowing the author of at least one book on a given subject, the user may then search under that author and then resort to the subject headings usually transcribed with the entry, known in cataloging parlance as the "subject tracings." This approach will work with any information storage system in which the subject terms are included with the entry.

And, lest one argue that machine-readable catalogs, generally permitting keyword searching, obviate the need for the more rigorous subject approach, consider the routine complaint of the catalog user (beginning to pale before the similar complaint of the Internet user): "I got too much stuff." The major attractions of a controlled vocabulary system are the facts that the terminology is consistent and that this terminology is based on an actual human being's careful decision that the terms used actually reflect the document's subject focus.

Other information included with a full machine-readable cataloging (MARC) record is the classification number, which not only indicates the book's location in the library collection, but gives a clue to its subject matter. The classification number is also often a clue to the nationality of an author (e.g., 810 is the Dewey number for American authors, while the Library of Congress uses PR and PS for American and British authors). The catalog record also usually indicates whether a book contains a bibliography, not only by the use of the subheading "—Bibliography," but by a note that a bibliography is included in addition to the text.

From around 1960 to 1980, there was considerable discussion about the use of microform to replace hard-copy cards for library catalogs, and a number of firms developed to meet this need. Ironically, one of the more popular approaches to creation of such a catalog was the computer output microform (COM). With the improvement of computer technology, COM catalogs were rapidly replaced in most libraries by direct computer access to the database. And, in a relatively short time, as microcomputers became readily, and cheaply, available, even smaller libraries began replacing their card catalogs with OPACs.

Another format that had some revival midcentury was the book catalog. Ironically, this revival harkened back to the days *before* the card catalog, which had been developed in part as a response to the increased complexity of the catalog resulting from increased size of libraries. The revival was also, in part, a response to increased complexity as well as an attempt to make the record of a library's holdings available outside the library, and in more than one copy. The widespread use of networked computers seems to have relegated the book catalog to history a second time, but one never knows. . . . And, in the meantime, some important collections published their catalogs in book form. For further information, modern catalogs are well covered in Robert L. Collison, *Published Library Catalogues: An Introduction to Their Contents and Use* (London: Mansell, 1973; 184p.); a more historical approach is Archer Taylor, *Book Catalogues: Their Varieties and Uses* (rev. ed. New York: F. C. Beil, 1986; 284p.). A rather complete list of these sources may be found in Bonnie R. Nelson, *A Guide to Published Library Catalogs* (Metuchen, N.J.: Scarecrow, 1982; 342p.).

An excellent example of a printed book catalog of a major library is

■ New York Public Library. Research Libraries. Dictionary catalog of the research libraries of the New York Public Library, 1911–1971. New York: New York Public Library; distributed by Hall, 1979–83. 800v.

> *Scope*: Holdings of the library as cataloged from 1895 through 1971, when the book catalog went into production. Includes books of all kinds and many book and periodical analytics, plus media of other kinds. Excludes manuscripts, maps, prints, and other primarily graphic materials.

> *Access*: The only major research library catalog in dictionary form, with full records for main entries but usually abbreviated records for analytics.

National Library Catalogs

At first glance, it may seem a great jump from the catalog of a small general collection to the multivolume catalogs of such great libraries as the Library of Congress, the British Library, and the Bibliothèque Nationale, but this jump should be made with the realization that they have certain features in common. They also supply dramatic contrasts between the collections in small libraries and those in the great libraries of the world. No less dramatic is the fact that these great collections are accessible to qualified users all over the world. What, then, are their general characteristics?

National library catalogs traditionally have been restricted to printed books and pamphlets; periodicals, if included, are entered only by title, not analyzed by contents. Each catalog gives fuller representation to material published in its own country than to those of other countries and is usually the most comprehensive record of publications in that country, containing types of publications not listed in trade bibliographies, such as government publications. They are usually arranged by author, with certain notable exceptions. Subjects are usually shown in separately published catalogs or indexes.

Catalogs of the great libraries differ greatly from one another in form of entry and amount of bibliographic detail. Differences in form also occur within a catalog, reflecting changing rules for entry that have developed over the years. At the same time, it must be recognized that the catalogs have been prepared by professional catalogers who have observed a body of rules for cataloging and who have seen the items described. This preparation often distinguishes library catalogs from trade bibliographies (the latter are often compiled from information supplied by the publishers, without examining any actual copy).

United States

First, remember that the Library of Congress, although considered a national library, is not officially such. And, although the *National Union Catalog* is usually considered to be the LC's catalog, actually it is a union catalog of records from many libraries. The public use catalog of the Library of Congress is called SCORPIO and is readily available on the World Wide Web. Thus, the following reflect holdings that are not in SCORPIO.

■ National union catalog: books. Washington, D.C.: Library of Congress, 1983- . Monthly, with indexes cumulating to an annual cumulation. Also cumulations for 1983–87, 1988–91.

   Scope: All books cataloged by the Library of Congress and about 1,100 contributing libraries, including all imprint dates, but with a strong emphasis on post-1955 publications. Created by a merger of the *National Union Catalog, Chinese Cooperative Catalog, Library of Congress Subject Catalog,* and *Library of Congress Monographic Series.*

   Access: A full entry by order of cataloging. Indexes have a short version of the record with each entry and the "register" number of the full record. Indexed by main and added entry, title, series, subject. Gives a full catalog record following *AACR2* for main entry, including all tracings and both Dewey decimal and Library of Congress classifications. Index entries are brief, with register number referring to the main section.

■ National union catalog: a cumulative author list. Washington, D.C.: Library of Congress, 1956-82. Quinquennial cumulations, 1953-57; 1958-62; 1963-67; 1968-72; 1973-77.

> *Scope:* Books, pamphlets, maps, atlases, periodicals, and other serials cataloged by the Library of Congress or reported by cooperating libraries.

> *Access:* Arranged by author/main entry, with no added entries. Entry is Library of Congress catalog card, with full citation, including subject and additional tracings, contents notes, collation, and other entries. Library locations shown by symbol.

■ National union catalog, 1956 through 1967: a cumulative author list, representing Library of Congress printed cards and titles reported by other American libraries. Totowa, N.J.: Rowman & Littlefield, 1970-72. 125v.

> Cumulates the cumulative *NUC*s for the years from 1958 to 1962 and from 1963 to 1967.

■ National union catalog on microfiche. Washington, D.C.: Library of Congress, 1983- .

> Includes *NUC: Books, NUC Audiovisual Materials,* and *NUC Cartographic Materials.* In a register-plus-index format. The indexes for books cumulates monthly; for the others, quarterly.

Much of the material in these catalogs is also available in RLIN (Research Libraries Information Network) and OCLC and other databases, but this remains, in the words of one reviewer, "the most extensive printed catalogue of modern works in existence."

■ National union catalog, pre-1956 imprints: a cumulative author list, representing Library of Congress printed cards and titles reported by other American libraries. London: Mansell, 1968-81. 754v.

> *Scope:* Replaces all earlier LC catalogs except for the film records from 1948 to 1952 and volumes 27-28 of the 1953 to 1957 set. Includes all records in the Library of Congress catalogs plus contributed

records from about 700 research libraries in the United States and Canada. Includes books, pamphlets, maps, atlases, microforms, music, and serials, but *Union List of Serials* and *New Serial Titles* are more complete. Primarily has records for Latin alphabet, plus works in uniform transliteration.

Access: By main entry, with *see* references and some added entries. In addition to the basic set (volumes 1–685), includes a supplement of sixty-nine volumes in one separate alphabet for items found during the project but after the relevant volume was printed and records where the original had very sparse holdings. Entries consist of reproductions of cards; thus, same as the originals with some additions and notably edited to standardize entries.

This set supersedes all earlier Library of Congress catalogs, for the most part, but is restricted to books, pamphlets, atlases, maps, music, and periodicals. But users should remember that

1. different works by the same author are sometimes found under different forms of the author's name, and
2. copies of the same work reported by cooperating libraries may use different forms of the author's name.

Also, some forms of material in the earlier catalogs have been omitted. These include

1. books for the sight impaired, such as those in Braille;
2. phonorecords, motion pictures, and filmstrips; and
3. all works in non-Latin alphabets, unless represented by LC cards.

And, of course, some types of material are more fully represented elsewhere:

1. Periodicals, whose holding libraries are more fully represented in the *Union List of Serials* and *New Serial Titles.*
2. Manuscript collections are much more fully listed in the *National Union Catalog of Manuscript Collections.*

William J. Welsh, in "Last of the Monumental Book Catalogs" (*American Libraries* 12 [Sept. 1981]: 464–68), provides a fascinating history and discussion of the project, which was actually published by a British firm (Mansell).

For subject access, the following are necessary.

■ U.S. Library of Congress. Library of Congress subject catalog. Washington, D.C.: Library of Congress, 1975–83.

■ Library of Congress catalog. Books: subjects. Washington, D.C.: Library of Congress, 1950-74.

> Quinquennial and annual cumulations include titles dated 1945- and cataloged by LC or cooperating libraries during the period covered. Introductions should be read carefully, because exact coverage has varied over time (e.g., motion pictures and music scores are excluded after 1952). Arranged by Library of Congress subject headings. Citations with each entry are essentially the same as the LC author catalogs, with minor variations.

Subject access since 1983 is via the subject index to the *NUC* on fiche.

Great Britain

■ British Library. British Library general catalogue of printed books, 1976- . London and New York: K. G. Saur, 1983- . Cumulations, 1976-82; 1983-85; and several two-year cumulations. Also available in fiche and online as BLAISE (British Library Automated Information Service) file Humanities and Social Sciences and Science Reference and Information Service (from 1974).

> *Scope*: All books and periodicals (not analytics) cataloged since 1975. Complete records of social sciences and humanities, but includes only those science and technology titles that appear in *British National Bibliography* and is selective for music and cartography.

> *Access*: Accessible by authors and editors and all distinctive titles as well (the latter are not available on the cumulation up to 1975). Also provides access to persons, corporate bodies, and publications as subjects (these entries are noted with an asterisk). Entries give main entry, title, place, publisher, year, and collation, but still in a brief form (versus the Library of Congress approach).

■ British Library. General catalogue of printed books to 1975. London: Bingley; New York: K. G. Saur, 1979-87. 360v. Supplement. 1987. 6v. Also online and on CD-ROM.

> Supplements every five years derived from the *British National Bibliography* and other sources and are less complete than the basic set. Generally, these have the same features as the basic, especially the lack of subject headings. First supplement adds in one alphabet about 85,000 books missed or added during the compilation of the set. Later supplements are under a slightly different title, with main entry as British Library after 1975.

Scope: Books, pamphlets, and periodicals in Western languages, and reproductions of these from the period from 1450 to 1975. Replaces several earlier catalogs with one cumulation. Includes many titles not found in the Library of Congress. A random sample of earlier material found that 77 percent of the works listed did not appear in the *Library of Congress Catalog of Books,* and fully 95 percent of those published before 1870 did not appear. Especially strong in British authors, history, and imprints. Sections on the Bible, England, London, and periodicals are especially noteworthy.

Access: Arranged by author, titles, or catchword titles for anonymous works, with cross-references for editors, translators, etc. Generally lacks any subject entries, but note the following:

1. Biographies and biocriticism of authors are listed under the author, providing an excellent bibliography for individual authors;
2. Family histories are listed under family name;
3. Periodicals are listed in volumes 252 to 254 under the heading "Periodicals" and place of publication;
4. Texts and commentaries on scriptures are listed under the name of the scripture;
5. Official publications, some works about a country, and many titles (but not all) in which a country names occurs are listed under the name of the country.

Citations are generally much briefer than *NUC,* omitting author dates, collations, publisher, and subject tracings, although an author's occupation is often noted.

The CD-ROM, from Chadwyck-Healey, depending on exchange rates, can be cheaper than the printed version.

■ British Library general catalogue of printed books to 1995 on CD-ROM. Cambridge, England: Chadwyck-Healey, 1995. CD-ROM only.

Combines the above title with Humanities and Social Sciences and Science Reference and Information Service files through 1995, with additional and updated pre-1975 records.

SUBJECT ACCESS

■ British Library. Subject catalogue of printed books. London: British Library, 1985– . Decennial. Fiche only.

■ British Library general subject catalogue 1975–1985; 1986 to 1990. Munich and New York: K. G. Saur, 1986; 1991–92. 75v.; 42v. Also on fiche as Subject Catalogue of Printed Books.

- British Library. Subject index of modern books acquired, [year]. London: British Library, 1946–50. Published 1968. 4v. 1951–55. Published 1974. 6v. 1961–70. Published 1982. 12v. 1971–75. Published 1986. 14v.
- British Museum. Department of Printed Books. Subject index of the modern works added to the library, 1881–1960. London: British Museum, 1902–74, 13v. in 30v.
- Peddie, Robert A. Subject index of books published before 1880. London: Grafton, 1933–48. Reprint, London: Pordes, 1962. 4v.

  In effect, a subject index to the *BMC (British Museum Catalogue)*, which is now subsumed in the *General Catalogue of Printed Books to 1975*, but with many titles not in the *BMC*. Covers about 50,000 titles in many languages, but emphasizing English, to 1880, when the British Museum began its subject catalog. Arranged A–Z in each volume, with very specific headings (more so than the *BMC*) but excluding personal names.

France

- Bibliographie National Française. Bibliographie établie par la Bibliothèque Nationale de France à partir des documents déposés au titre du dépôt légal. Paris: Bibliothèque Nationale, 1976– . Semimonthly. Also online and on CD-ROM.

  Scope: All items obtained on legal deposit, in five series: Books (semimonthly), Series (monthly), Official Publications (bimonthly), Music (three per year), Atlases, Maps, and Plans (annual).

  Access: Full cataloging, including ISBN and price for all items. Arranged by Universal Decimal Classification, with author, title, and subject indexes. Individual issues cumulate three times a year on fiche, with an annual index.

- Paris. Bibliothèque Nationale. Catalogue général des livres imprimés: auteurs. Paris: Impr. Nationale, 1897–1981. 231v. Auteurs 1897–1959; supplement dur fiches. Paris: Chadwyck-Healey, 1986. Fiche only.

  Scope: Because the *Bibliothèque Nationale* traces its origins to the private library of John II, fourteenth-century king of France, its catalog is rich in early works, particularly strong for French history and literature and French and continental imprints. Works of certain important non-French authors (Cervantes, Shakespeare) are included, in some cases constituting mini-union catalogs of Parisian library holdings. Each volume includes titles acquired up to the date of the volume (e.g., volume 1 represents the collection as of 1897). Beginning with volume 189, however, only additions through 1959 are included, with more recent material listed in a new series. Omitted are anonymous classics, periodicals, society transactions, government publications, and works by corporate authors.

Access: Arranged by personal author. Under authors of voluminous works are title indexes, including alternative and changed titles, citing volumes or editions in which each may be found. Citations are more complete than those in the British Library catalogs, including author's full name, title, place, publisher, date, edition, collation, and occasional contents notes and citations to original publications where the title is a reprinted periodical article.

Union Catalogs

A logical outgrowth of the intent of the national library catalog is the union catalog. Just as the more traditional library catalog provides a list and access to the holdings of one library, the union catalog provides similar access to the holdings of many libraries. Although in theory possible with any form of document reproduction, the union catalog began in earnest in the early part of the twentieth century, especially with the U.S. National Union Catalog (NUC). This massive access engine initially involved adding codes of other major libraries' holdings to the cards representing the Library of Congress's cataloging in a separate card catalog held at the Library of Congress. The resulting records were then published in book form, thus combining the book catalog of the LC with the union catalog.

A massive change in the basic concept of library catalogs occurred in the early 1970s with the development of several computer-based catalogs, notably that of the Ohio College Library Center, later renamed the Online Computer Library Center (OCLC). Following the same general principles of the NUC, OCLC's catalog involved the development of a database of records from the Library of Congress to which other libraries' holdings could be attached. Member libraries agreed to enter original records to the database if any items held were not already there. Thus, while originally serving primarily as a centralized generator of catalog cards, OCLC also became a union catalog of all its members' holdings. The attraction of having such a complete union catalog led many libraries to begin retrospective conversion, entering their holdings symbol for items already cataloged by them and, in the process, entering new records for items not in the database. Today, OCLC has more than 8,300 members, with more than 30,200 different libraries participating in at least part of its programs, and well over thirty-eight million bibliographic records.

- OCLC online union catalog. Dublin, Ohio: Online Computer Library Center, 1971- . Nearly continuous updates. Also called OLUC or WorldCat. Online only.

  Scope: All forms of material, printed and otherwise, including many manuscript collections. Since 1976, the U.S. government has entered *Monthly Catalog* records into OCLC; thus, this is one of the few library catalogs of any kind to include a high percentage of government documents (though many libraries have yet to enter their holdings into OCLC). All LC records are also loaded. As of mid-1998, more than 38 million records were held, with books the largest category (more than 22 million). This is the closest thing yet to a true union catalog, with current cataloging from more than 8,000 libraries of all types, mostly academic and public, but with many school systems and special libraries participating. Many of these libraries have also engaged in retrospective conversion, so OCLC holdings are nearly complete for a growing percentage of U.S. libraries.

  Access: For many years, access to the records was limited, but that is now changed. All words in the entries, as well as all entries, are searchable, with Boolean combinations allowed. LC and Dewey decimal classification numbers (as well as other systems, if entered) are also searchable, as are additional subject headings, such as MeSH (Medical Subject Headings), where entered. For all practical purposes, records are full MARC following *AACR2* rules. In addition to the full cataloging record, including all tracings, the MARC fixed fields are also available and searchable. Attached to the record are library holding symbols, displayable in several arrangements (all, by state, by network, etc.). Records may be displayed in varying formats. OCLC still displays only a primary record, so not all local information is available—notably, local notes, subject headings, and call numbers cannot be retrieved. Periodicals are not analyzed, but there is a current project to provide complete periodical holdings for cooperating libraries.

- Research Libraries Information Network (RLIN). RLG union catalog. Mountain View, Calif.: Research Libraries Group, 1975- . Nearly continues updates. Online only.

  Scope: Material of all types, from the collections of major research, academic, and national libraries (notably the Library of Congress and the National Library of Canada); special libraries in law, medicine, theology, art, and music; museums, archives, and historical societies; area studies collections; and public and corporate libraries.

The main difference between OCLC's OLUC and the RLG union catalog is the latter's primary emphasis is on research libraries and collections. RLG was a pioneer in the development of a machine-readable format for archives and manuscript collections, containing about 500,000 records for such material. RLIN also supports original scripts in non-Roman alphabets (Japanese, Arabic, Chinese, Korean, Persian, Hebrew, Yiddish, and Cyrillic). As of mid-1998, RLIN contained more than ninety-four million records.

Access: All elements of the full MARC record are searchable, as are keywords. Unlike OCLC and most other online union catalogs, the full record for each library is available; so individual variants (notes, alternate subject headings) can be searched and displayed. Non-Roman records may also be searched, either in the original script or in Roman transliteration.

Similar catalogs exist at the regional level (notably the Western Library Network [WLN], which has now merged its database with OCLC) and in other nations. A more recent development is the creation of state and regional union catalogs, often on compact disc as well as online, which may contain records from libraries not members of the larger union catalogs.

Any online union catalog, whether of a given library, a small group of libraries, or a major national union catalog, has one great advantage over published catalogs—timeliness. Generally, as soon as a published item is accessioned by a library with such a catalog, it is searched against the records already in the catalog; if a suitable record is found, the library's own holdings information is added, and the item is ready for the shelf. If the item is not found, most libraries will wait a few days or weeks, and after several searches, if it is still not found, will create an original record and add it. For truly online catalogs, such as OCLC and RLIN, this means that many new records are added to the catalog each day. For subsets of such databases, although records are added each day, the publicly available database may only be updated weekly or monthly.

Another development facilitating rapid dissemination of bibliographic information is Cataloging in Publication (CIP). Started as a pilot project with twenty-seven publishers in 1971, it is now a regular program of the Library of Congress, with nearly all mainstream publishers in the United States participating. The LC catalogs books most likely to be purchased by libraries from proofs submitted by the publisher. The original intent was that the cataloging record could be printed on the copyright page and thus used at once by the library, freeing up cataloger time for material not in the program. In fact, though CIP information still appears on the verso of the title page, the real advantage now is that the cataloging records, in machine-readable form, are available to libraries, booksellers, and scholars, in many formats. Uses include selection of material (from subject headings plus author and publisher reputation), purchase, and cataloging before the item is published, thus making the actual book available even before the user will have heard about it. An interesting brief summary of CIP's history can be found in "Making Cataloging Hum" (*Library of Congress Information Bulletin* [Sept. 16, 1996]: 322–23), along with a discussion of the pilot program to use the Internet to supply the text for CIP ("One More Way to Use the Internet," op. cit., p. 321, 323.) Full details on the program (how to join, what is and isn't included, and the like) may be found in the *CIP Publishers Manual*, 3d ed. (Washington, D.C.: Library of Congress, 1994; 32p.).

In brief, then, although a library catalog contains records for things held in that library, a union catalog contains similar records for things held in many libraries, with each item held in at least one of the group of libraries and most held in many of them.

Meanwhile, a growing number of libraries are providing access to their catalogs over the Internet. Although lacking the convenience of a union catalog, this approach permits users to see what a given library holds and to peruse the notes and different subject classifications (and sometimes subject headings) used. The most complete directory of these to date is the *OPAC Directory*.

■ OPAC directory. Westport, Conn.: Meckler, 1990– . Annual.

> Title and publisher vary. A detailed directory to libraries with remotely accessible (via the Internet) Online Public Access Catalogs (OPACs). Each entry describes subject strengths and gives information on dial-up and Internet access and searching capabilities. As relevant, also gives information on other databases generally available via the OPAC.

National Book Bibliographies

Current

If we adopt LeRoy H. Linder's definition of national bibliography, we must include in this category not only the Library of Congress catalogs already discussed, but also bibliographies of government publications, pamphlets, periodicals, and newspapers, which will be discussed later to set forth more clearly their distinguishing characteristics. Linder, in his study of current national bibliographies, states: "For this study, then, current complete national bibliography is a complete or nearly complete listing, in one or more parts, of the records of a nation, about a nation, copyrighted in a nation, in a single language, issued serially at appropriate intervals as the records appear" (*The*

Rise of Current Complete National Bibliographies [New York: Scarecrow, 1959], p. 18).

William A. Katz defines "national bibliography" as follows: "The system must have two elements: (1) It needs a legal deposit system which ensures that the national library receives a copy of everything to be listed in the bibliography; and (2) the records must be from direct examination of the materials, not from the publisher or author" (William A. Katz, *Introduction to Reference Work*, volume 1: *Basic Information Sources*. 7th ed. [New York: McGraw-Hill, 1997], p. 90). Coverage may include only material published in a particular nation, or it may include materials about the country, even in the language of the country, as may be seen from some of the listings that follow.

For the current purpose here, however, current national bibliography, described in the following section, is restricted to inventories of books published in a single country or language (even though this is an obvious misnomer), with only a few examples cited. These book inventories are usually referred to as trade bibliographies because they emphasize books published by trade publishers and serve the book trade as well as other persons seeking information on recently published book titles.

To relate them to national library catalogs and union catalogs, it is pertinent to note what information they supply that is not generally found in the former types of catalogs. It includes the following:

Price of a book at the time of publication, in nearly all cases

Descriptive annotations, in some cases

Lists of publishers and their addresses

Title entries that are not given in printed national library catalogs

Titles in trade series (i.e., those from a single publisher)

Evidence that a book was in print when the trade bibliography was issued

Some books not recorded in national library catalogs, either because of their recent or forthcoming publication or because they had not been acquired or cataloged by those libraries

In other words, national and union catalogs record holdings of libraries in a given geographic area; national bibliographies record items produced in a given geographic or linguistic area, regardless of whether they are held there.

Remember that some books announced for publication never actually appear, at least under the announced title.

How do trade bibliographies differ from national and union library catalogs in their arrangement? Here, it is more difficult to generalize, because trade bibliographies do not follow one pattern. The following examples illustrate the wide differences in arrangement in only a few of the most frequently used British and American trade bibliographies:

Dictionary arrangement, with authors, titles, and subjects in one alphabet (e.g., *Cumulative Book Index*)

Alphabetical by name of publisher (e.g., *Publishers' Trade List Annual*)

Alphabetical in two indexes: (1) by author and editor, and (2) by title and series (e.g., *Books in Print*)

Alphabetical by subject (e.g., *Subject Guide to Books in Print*)

Classified (e.g., by Dewey decimal classification, as *American Book Publishing Record*)

Because every classified bibliography must have an index, it should be noted that the *British National Bibliography*'s classified arrangement is followed by an alphabetical author, title, and subject index, which includes editors, translators, and series.

As noted earlier, place and date of publication (and occasionally language) are the principal factors that determine the scope of trade bibliographies. To these may be added the form of publication, such as books, and the kind of issuing agency, such as trade publishers. The following titles are those most frequently used:

UNITED STATES

■ American book publishing record. New Providence, N.J.: Bowker/Reed Reference, 1960- . Monthly, with annual and quinquennial cumulations.

Scope: All books published in the United States, with separate sections for adult and juvenile fiction. A useful acquisitions tool, called by *Walford's* the "nearest equivalent to an official United States national bibliography."

Access: Arranged by Dewey decimal classification, with separate sections for adult fiction, juvenile fiction, and mass-market titles. Entry includes citation, Library of Congress card number, subject tracings, Dewey and LC classifications, ISBN, and price. Indexed by author, title, and subject.

■ American book publishing record cumulative, 1876-1949: an American national bibliography. New York: Bowker, 1980. 15v.

■ American book publishing record cumulative, 1950-1977: an American national bibliography. New York: Bowker, 1978. 15v.

Scope: Based on records from Library of Congress catalogs, excluding government publications.

Access: For each set, volumes 1 to 10 by Dewey decimal classification; volume 11, fiction, including juveniles; volume 12, non-Dewey titles. Author and title indexes and a subject guide to the classification in volumes 13 to 15.

■ Books in print. New York: Bowker, 1948– . Annual, with midyear supplements. Fiche, quarterly. Also online and on CD-ROM, as often as weekly.

Scope: More than 1.5 million titles published in the United States or with U.S. distributors. Listing in separate alphabets by author and by title, with complete citation in each case. Sets include full publishers' addresses and contact information; citations include price, ISBN for multiple formats, as needed (e.g., cloth and paper). Prior to 1972, this title was an index to *Publishers' Trade List Annual (PTLA);* since then, it is an independent publication, thus more inclusive. For a few years, *Books Out-of-Print* was also part of this title; now it is separately published. Note this title is the basis for a number of specialized print and electronic products and is also part of *Global Books in Print.*

■ Subject guide to books in print. New Providence, N.J.: Bowker/Reed Reference, 1957– . 5v. Annual. Also online, on CD-ROM, and as part of several Bowker database products.

A subject arrangement of *Books in Print,* excluding fiction, literature, and belles lettres generally. Based on Library of Congress subjects. Same basic citation format as *BIP,* covering about two-thirds of the titles in *BIP.*

■ Books in print with book reviews on disc. New Providence, N.J.: Bowker/Reed Reference, 1979– . CD-ROM only. Monthly updates.

Adds full-text reviews from twelve major library and bookstore selection tools, 1985– . This source is searchable by eighteen elements, including free text, and comes with software to use as an ordering and acquisitions tool. Its companion is, naturally enough, *Books Out-of-Print with Book Reviews on Disc* (quarterly updates), which lists titles from 1979 as they go out of print.

■ Books in series. New York: Bowker, 1980– .

Lists series title, authors, and individual titles in popular, scholarly, and professional series published since 1867.

■ Children's books in print. New Providence, N.J.: Bowker/Reed Reference, 1962- . 2v. Annual.

  Similar to *Books in Print,* with titles drawn from it. Many titles include annotations, and entries include grade level. Volume 1 also includes a section listing awards.

■ Subject guide to children's books in print. New York: Bowker, 1970- . Annual.

  A subject listing, with the same information, based on Library of Congress and *Sears'* headings.

■ Children's books in print on CD-ROM. New Providence, N.J.: Bowker/ Reed Reference, 1992- . CD-ROM only.

  Several titles in one source: records from *Children's Books in Print, Subject Guide to Children's Books in Print, El-Hi Textbooks and Serials in Print,* dozens of monographic bibliographies and lists of recommended children and YA titles, and relevant records from *Bowker's Complete Video Directory* and *Ulrich's.* Includes reviews from *Booklist, Library Journal, School Library Journal, Kirkus,* and *Publishers Weekly.* Up to eighteen searchable fields per record. Uses the same software as the *Books in Print* CD-ROM family, but with the additional sources included is more than just a subset of *BIP.*

■ El-Hi textbooks and serials in print. New Providence, N.J.: Bowker/Reed Reference, 1956- . Annual.

  Based on but much more complete than *Books in Print.* Includes textbooks, teacher manuals, various audiovisual aids, maps, achievements texts, and similar material. Main section arranged by subject. Indexes by author, title, series, series subject, and series titles. Includes publishers' contact information. Entries include grade level, price, and indication as to the availability of a teacher's manual or teacher's edition of the item.

■ Forthcoming books. New York: Bowker, 1966- . Bimonthly, with each issue a cumulation. Also online and on CD-ROM.

  Books eligible for inclusion in *Books in Print,* scheduled for publication in the next several months, plus books published since the most recent *BIP* and not yet in it, with subject, author, and title sections. Each issue overlaps and updates the preceding one. Gives basic bibliographic information and publication date.

■ Small press record of books in print. Paradise, Calif.: Dustbooks, 1966– . Annual.

> Covers output of about 3,000 publishers, mostly titles not listed in *Books in Print.* Indexes by author, title, publisher, and subject; the primary entry, usually author, often includes brief annotations.

■ The complete directory of large print books and serials. New Providence, N.J.: Bowker, 1988– . Annual.

> Successor to *Large Type Books in Print.* Duplicates much of the *title* coverage of the previous title, but provides access to a different *format.* Arranged by subject, listing children's books, textbooks, reference, etc. for all age levels that are in fourteen-point or larger type and are published in the United States. Newspapers and serials are listed separately. Indexes by author and by title.

GREAT BRITAIN

■ Bookbank. London: J. Whitaker: New Providence, N.J.: Reed Reference, 1988– . CD-ROM only. Monthly.

> The electronic version of *Whitaker's Books in Print,* plus out-of-print and forthcoming titles. Issued in several editions (e.g., one covering Australia and New Zealand). There is a separate title, *Bookbank O.P.*

■ British national bibliography, 1950– . Boston Spa, England: British Library, National Bibliographic Service, 1950– . Weekly, with quarterly and annual cumulations. Also British National Bibliography on CD-ROM, online as BNBMARC, 1950– , on the Web as part of BLAISE, and in several fiche cumulations.

> Scope: Based on "Legal Deposit" copyright deposit material from the United Kingdom and the Republic of Ireland. Excludes periodicals except for first issue of new or changed title, music, maps, and most government publications.

> Access: Brief bibliographic citation, including Cataloging in Publication (CIP) for in-press titles, as well as subject tracings and price. Arranged by Dewey decimal classification, with weekly indexes by author and title as well as monthly author/title cumulations and a subject guide. The bibliographic history is a bit complex, but in essence, older material has been cumulated, and indexes have been cumulated from time to time as well.

■ Whitaker's books in print: the reference catalogue of current literature. London: J Whitaker; New Providence, N.J.: Reed Reference, 1874- . 5v. Annual. Formerly *British Books in Print*. Computer produced since 1971, available in print, microform, and CD-ROM as Bookbank.

> *Scope:* Covers all books published in the United Kingdom, in English language in Europe, and in the English language published in the rest of the world if there is a sole U.K. agent; also includes "important" government publications.

> *Access:* Listing by author/title, with keyword subject where subject is part of the title. Children's material coded for age level. Entries include author, title, publication year, size (height) and page count, edition and series, and publisher and ISBN. Updated by *Bookseller* entries and by *New and Forthcoming Books Weekly* (1992-) on fiche, as well as monthly and quarterly fiche.

CANADA

■ Canadian books in print. Toronto and Buffalo: Univ. of Toronto Pr., 1973- . Quarterly, with annual cumulations. Also online and part of Global Books in Print CD-ROM.

> *Scope:* Attempts to fill the gap between *Books in Print* and *Whitaker's,* listing English-language books published in Canada, plus Canadian titles in French if by a publisher who primarily produces English-language titles.

> *Access:* Entry gives citation (but not place of publication), price, and binding. Separately published author/title and subject index quarterly, with annual cumulations.

■ Canadiana: Canada's national bibliography. Ottawa: National Library, 1951- .

> The formal and complete Canadian bibliography, much more complete than *Canadian Books in Print*. Monthly, with annual cumulations. Currently only fiche and online. Includes both French and English titles.

FRANCE

■ Un an de nouveautés. Paris: Éditions Professionelles du Livre, 1980- . Cumulated quarterly and semiannually under Trois mois de nouveautés and Six mois de nouveautés. Annual.

Replaces *Les livres de l'année* (1933-79). Cumulates listings in the weekly *Livres Hebdo* and the monthly *Les livres du Mois.* Arranged by Dewey decimal classification, with author, title, and subject indexes.

■ Bibliographie nationale française. Livres. Paris: Bibliothèque Nationale, 1990- . Twenty-six times per year. Also on CD-ROM, 1970- . Quarterly.

   Scope: Books. One of several sections, others being *Series, Music, Maps, Atlases and Plans,* and *Official Publications.* Replaces *Biblio* (1933-71); *Bibliographie de la France—Biblio* (1972-79); and an earlier title, *Bibliographie de la France: journal général de l'imprimerie et de la librairie* (1811-1971), published as *Bibliographie de la France* (1976-89); publisher varies.

   Access: Full cataloging, including price and ISBN. Indexed by author, title, and subject.

■ Les livres disponibles. 1977- . Paris: F. Electre, 1977- . 3v. in 6. Annual. Also online and on CD-ROM as Electre, updated monthly and quarterly.

   Scope: Replaces *Le catalogue de l'édition française* and *Répertoire des livres disponibles.* Covers books in French language regardless of where published, excluding pamphlets, theses, periodicals, music scores, and association annuals.

   Access: Separate author and title volumes arranged alphabetically; subject volumes by Dewey decimal classification. Entry gives brief citation, collation, and price.

MEXICO AND SOUTH AMERICA

■ Bibliografía Mexicana. México: Universidad Nacional Autónoma de México, Biblioteca Nacional Instituto Bibliográfico Mexicano, 1967- . Annual only since 1986. Monthly updates, only electronic versions available since 1990.

   Absorbed *Anuario Bibliográfico* (1958-69). Arranged by subject classification, with author, title, and subject access.

■ Libros de México. México: Cepromex, 1985- . Quarterly.

   Publishing trade journal with section listing new books, similar in many ways to *Publishers Weekly* (when it included "Weekly Record").

- Libros en venta en America Latina y España. New York: Bowker, 1964- . Annual, formerly biennial. Up to the seventh edition, titled *Libros en venta en Hispanoamérica y España.*

  Updated by *Fichero bibliográfico hispanoamericano,* eleven times per year. Main set now in multiple volumes, with authors, titles, subjects separate. Covers more than 170,000 titles currently in print, primarily from Latin America and, of course, Spain, but includes Spanish-language titles published in the United States. Entries tend to vary, with many lacking publication date, most lacking ISBN, etc.

- Palau y Dulcet, Antonio. Manual del librero hispano-americano; bibliografía general española o hispano-americana desde la invención de la imprenta hasta nuestros tiempos, con el valor comercíal de los impresos descritos. Barcelona, Spain: Librería Palau, 1948-77. 2 ed. corr. y aum. ed. 28v.

  Covers material published in Spain and Spanish America from the beginning of printing to the 1950s, arranged by author, under title of anonymous works, with a title index. Basic volume in the process of updating with meticulous editing as *Manual del librero hispano-americano de Antonio Palau y Dulcet. Addenda y corrigenda o volumen complementario.*

INTERNATIONAL

- Bowker/Whitaker global books in print on disc. New Providence, N.J.: Bowker/Reed Reference, 1993- . CD-ROM only. Monthly.

  Scope: Lists only English-language titles, based on the following, but is clearly currently the most comprehensive listing:

  Books in Print (about 1.5 million titles)

  Bookbank (about 500,000 titles)

  International Books in Print (about 250,000 titles)

  Australian and New Zealand Books in Print (about 70,000 titles)

  Canadian Telebook (including Canadian imprints from *International Books in Print,* about 200,000 titles)

  Access: Gives full citations in integrated records for each title, including all editions and bindings. Generally lacks subject headings, except for *Books in Print* records. Has sixteen access points, plus the ability to use as an online ordering system.

- Cumulative book index: a world list of books in the English language. Bronx, N.Y.: Wilson, 1898- . Monthly, except August, with annual cumulations. Also online and on CD-ROM.

  Scope: Reasonably complete coverage of all books (longer than fifty pages and not government publications), scholarly pamphlets, proceedings in the English language published anywhere in the world.

  Access: Author, title, and subject listings in one alphabet, with full entry usually under author. Full entries include price, LC card numbers, and collation. Includes a detailed publisher listing with full contact information for all publishers. Has been criticized for not listing all English titles from all sources but is the most complete such source available and is apparently complete for English-speaking countries. Fiction is a subject heading and is also a subheading under appropriate subjects.

  The CD-ROM, tape, and online versions permit Boolean and field searching, thus allowing quite sophisticated access, starting with 1987 issues. As a side note, the earlier cumulations are very large, possibly the largest books the library will contain other than unabridged dictionaries and, perhaps, some atlases; as such, popular as show-and-tell with school groups.

- International books in print [year]. Munich and New York: K. G. Saur, 1979- . 4v. Annual. Also on CD-ROM.

  About 200,000 English-language titles not published in the United States or Great Britain. Not as comprehensive as *Cumulative Book Index*, but has useful annotations for most titles. An author-title listing, with separate subject listing. Available as part of *Global Books in Print Plus*.

Summary

The scope, arrangement, and frequency of these current national book bibliographies indicate the ways in which they may be used in searching. Of course, for the online versions, the arrangement may be replaced by the access points.

  As a record of what is currently in print, listed in *Publishers' Trade List Annual, Books in Print* and its *Subject Guide,* and the other national equivalents

  As a record of books to be published, listed bimonthly in *Forthcoming Books* and *Subject Guide to Forthcoming Books*

  As a record of recently published books, as in *American Book Publishing Record* and *Cumulative Book Index*

As a record of books recently cataloged, including those nearly in print, via the CIP program of the Library of Congress, on OCLC, RLIN, and LC's own database; and those in print and most likely recently acquired, on any of the cooperative cataloging systems

American imprints may be listed in trade bibliographies, the National Union Catalog, and the major online union catalogs, although some titles will be found in only one or two sources.

This entire field is in a constant state of flux, with new titles appearing and old standbys disappearing or changing format and frequency. The current prognosis is that either some form of laser disc or online database will become the only form of national and trade bibliographies in the near future (say, within a generation). However, the research and the reference librarian should keep in mind that the great retrospective catalogs in particular, based in many cases on considerably more attention to name authority work than modern practice allows, are likely to remain of value for much longer.

For a fully annotated list of trade and national bibliographies, consult *Walford's Guide to Reference Material,* volume 3 (7th ed. London: Library Assn. Pub., 1998).

An older title, still useful for its level of detail, is

■ Bell, Barbara L. An annotated guide to current national bibliographies. Alexandria, Va.: Chadwyck-Healey, 1986. 407p.

> Alphabetical guide, based on two international surveys of more than 150 nations. Although becoming outdated, the lengthy annotations describing coverage, scope, and classifications will remain useful even in the online environment, and the information on arrangement and indexing will be needed as long as the older material remains in print.

More detailed coverage (with more than one source per country listed, and greater depth of analysis) for the lesser-developed countries may be found in G. E. Gorman and J. J Mills, *Guide to Current National Bibliographies in the Third World,* 2d ed. (New York: Hans Zell, 1987; distributed by K. G. Saur. 372p.).

Retrospective

Remember that the examples of current national bibliography mentioned thus far have been considered current because they provide a continuing record of what was published or in print at a given time, this record appearing soon after the titles were published or, in a few cases, were announced for publication. Although none of the American examples began publication before 1872, it is apparent that the early volumes may also be used as retrospective bibliographies when viewed from the standpoint of the late twentieth century. But what about the earlier periods not covered?

Here are cited a few examples of the American predecessors, and some modern replacements, listed by period covered.

1500-1800 ■ Sabin, Joseph. Dictionary of books relating to America, from its discovery to the present time. New York: Sabin, 1868-92. 29v.

■ Thompson, Lawrence S., ed. The new Sabin: books described by Joseph Sabin and his successors, now described again on the basis of examination of originals and fully indexed by titles, subject, joint authors and institutions and agencies. Troy, N.Y.: Whitson, 1974-86. 10v. plus index.

Adds to Sabin, plus corrects his entries. No new volumes have appeared since Thompson's death. The major advantage of this set is the good subject access.

■ Molnar, John E. Author-title index to Joseph Sabin's Dictionary of books relating to America. Metuchen, N.J.: Scarecrow, 1975. 3v.

1500-1901 ■ Bibliography of American imprints to 1901: compiled from the database of the American Antiquarian Society and the Research Libraries Group. New York: K. G. Saur, 1992. 92v.

More than 400,000 titles printed in the area that became the United States, including pamphlets and leaflets but excluding maps and serials. Essentially complete up to about 1820; after that date, *Checklist of American Imprints* (Scarecrow) is more comprehensive. Full MARC entries. Arranged by title, with indexes by author, subject, place, date.

1639-1800 ■ Evans, Charles. American bibliography: a chronological dictionary of all books, pamphlets, and periodical publications printed in the United States of America from the genesis of printing in 1639 down to and including the year 1800. Chicago: the author, 1903-59. Reprint, New York: Peter Smith, 1941-67. 14v.

Readex Microprint issued a microform set of all items in this bibliography, now available on fiche (replacing the original microcards).

■ Bristol, R. P. Supplement to Charles Evans' American bibliography. Charlottesville: Univ. Pr. of Virginia, 1970. 636p.

Adds about 11,000 items to the basic Evans in date order. A separate index to this also exists, but the Shipton and Mooney title, below, includes these items in its index.

■ Shipton, Clifford K., and James E. Mooney, eds. National index of American imprints through 1800: the short-title Evans. Worcester, Mass.: Barre and American Antiquarian Society, 1969. 2v.

1801-1819 ■ Shaw, Ralph Robert, and Richard H. Shoemaker. American bibliography: a preliminary checklist for 1801-1819. New York: Scarecrow, 1958-66, 1983. 23v.

Nineteen volumes for the bibliography, plus addenda with corrections, library symbols, and indexes by title, author, publisher/bookseller/printer, and, most recently, a geographical index.

1820-1829 ■ Shoemaker, Richard H. Checklist of American imprints for 1820-1829. New York: Scarecrow, 1964-71. 10v. Title index. Metuchen, N.J.: Scarecrow, 1972. 556p. Author index. Metuchen, N.J.: Scarecrow, 1973. 173p.

1820-1875 ■ A checklist of American imprints for [year]- . Metuchen, N.J.: Scarecrow, 1972- .

Has had several compilers. Covers from 1820; intended to replace Roorbach and Kelly (below) when complete to 1875. The arrangement and precise criteria for inclusion have changed a bit over the years; since 1838, no longer lists U.S. government publications; since 1840, the accession numbering includes the last two digits of the year of publication. Arranged by author (by title if anonymous). Entries include author, title, place, publisher, date, and location symbols for holding libraries. As with the originals, there is lack of complete authority control (so that both "St." and "Saint" appear as entries). Cumulative indexes currently cover every ten years, giving only entries and accession numbers, not citations. Given the expense of production and the (expected) small market, it is commendable that Scarecrow, a commercial publisher, continues to issue volumes.

1820-1861 ■ Roorbach, Orville Augustus. Bibliotheca Americana, 1820-1861. New York: Roorbach, 1852-61. Reprint, New York: Peter Smith, 1939.

1861-1870 ■ Kelly, James. American catalogue of books (original and reprints), published in the United States from Jan. 1861 to Jan. 1871. New York: Wiley, 1866-71. Reprint, New York: Peter Smith, 1938. 2v.

1876-1910 ■ American catalogue of books, 1876-1910. New York: Publishers' Weekly, 1876-1910. Reprint, New York: Peter Smith, 1941. 8v. in 13.

1899-1927 ■ United States catalog: books in print. 4th ed. New York: Wilson, 1928.

International

Pre-1500 ■ Incunable short title catalogue. London: British Library, 1996- . Online through BLAISE.

A detailed cataloging record of materials printed with movable type before 1501, including Britain, much of Europe, North and South America, New Zealand, and Japan, with more records added all the time.

1475-1640 ■ Pollard, A. W., and G. R. Redgrave. A short-title catalog of books printed in England, Scotland and Ireland and of English books printed abroad, 1475-1640. Rev and enl. ed. London and New York: Bibliographical Society, 1976-99; distributed by Oxford Univ. Pr. 3v.

Revision of the 1926 classic, including books, pamphlets, broadsides, and similar material published in the named countries, regardless of language, and of English-language titles in the rest of the world. Excludes non-English titles by English authors not published in England. Arranged by author, with entries including fairly full citations plus up to 500 holding libraries and various notes. Because some of the accession numbers changed from the first edition, contains cross-references from the old to the new number. The third volume contains indexes.

1640-1700 ■ Wing, Donald G. Short-title catalog of books printed in England, Scotland, Ireland, Wales and British America and of English books printed in other countries, 1641-1700. Rev. and enl. ed. New York: Index Committee of the Modern Language Assn. of America, 1972-94. 3v. Also on CD-ROM.

A classic, recently revised with many new entries as well as corrections and additions to existing entries. All monographic titles published in England, Ireland, Scotland, Wales, and British America in the time period, plus all English-language monographs printed anywhere in the world in the period. Note that volume 1 had a number of problems and was issued in, in effect, a third revised edition. Entries include brief citations, plus up to five holding libraries in the United Kingdom and the United States.

The material in these two monumental collections (abbreviated *STC,* for *Short-Title Catalog*) has been microfilmed (although not all editions of all works), but this was done over time starting in 1942; thus, the entries in the *STC* cannot directly be used as locations in the microfilm. For that, see *Early English Books, 1475-1640: A Guide to the Microfilm Collection* (Ann Arbor, Mich.: University Microfilms International, 1942-), which provides a shorter author-title index, plus an index from the *STC* numbers to the microfilm locations.

1701-1800 ■ Eighteenth century short title catalogue. London: British Library, 1983- . Available online via RLIN and others, on CD-ROM, and in microform. Monthly updates.

All letterpress material published in the British Isles and the colonies, plus all other material in English or other British languages published from 1701 to 1800. Includes library holding symbols for major libraries and microform reference numbers to Research Publications microform copies. Although not a full MARC record, cataloging is much fuller than the title indicates. Many entries have extensive notes, including subjects, but there is no direct subject access.

All of the above international titles are included in

■ English short title catalogue. Online via Research Libraries Group (RLG) database, RLIN, and CD-ROM.

Also known as *ESTC.* Includes records for all known English-language letterpress materials published between 1473 and 1800, with most of the cataloging done afresh by the Center for Bibliographical Studies and Research, University of California–Riverside. When complete will have all items records in Pollard and Redgrave and Wing, plus many new records not in those (mostly editions of known titles) and indication of "ghosts." Full MARC records include citations to microform sets of the books as well as locations for items not in the sets. The records also include Library of Congress subject headings for titles up to 1700.

1801–1919 ■ Nineteenth century short title catalog: extracted from the catalogues of the Bodleian library, the British library, Harvard university library, the Library of Congress, the library of Trinity College Dublin, the national library of Scotland, and the university libraries of Cambridge and Newcastle. Newcastle-Upon-Tyne and Alexandria, Va.: Avero; distributed by Chadwyck-Healey, 1984–96. Also on CD-ROM.

Same basic coverage as the *ESTC*—all British and colonial books, U.S. books, and other books in English wherever published, plus translations into English. Because entries are based on major library catalogs rather than examination of a copy, there are some multiple entries for the same item. When completed, contrary to the implications of the title, coverage will extend to 1919.

A complete listing of all such sources may be found in Marcelle Beaudiquez, *Retrospective National Bibliographies: An International Directory* (Munich and New York: K. G. Saur, 1986; 189p.).

Bibliographies of Other Publications and of Audiovisual Materials

However convenient it might be to consult one current national bibliography for all forms of publication, it is hardly feasible at this time. At present, although OCLC and RLIN notably do include all formats of material, trade bibliographies for printed books produced by trade and university publishers, religious denominations, societies, and organizations must be supplemented by other bibliographies that record other forms of publications or nonbook materials. These lists are sometimes restricted to the output of a single county, such as the *Monthly Catalog of United States Government Publications;* sometimes by form, regardless of place of publication, such as *Ulrich's.* Singled out for description are examples of useful sources for all types of materials likely to be of interest to the librarian, including print, microform, manuscripts, music, sound recordings, visual recordings, and computer sources.

Computer Databases, Including CD-ROMs

Although beginning only in the early 1960s, a category of machine-readable information called "traditional computer databases" now exists. Many of these are computer-readable versions of printed sources or are based on such sources. Some guides to reference material, including the present one, indicate such availability for sources, as do *Walford's* and *Balay* to some degree, but it is often useful to have a dedicated guide as well.

■ CD-ROMs in print [year]: an international guide. Detroit: Gale, 1987– . Annual. Also on CD-ROM.

> Intended to be the resource of record for this format, listing more than 8,000 commercially available titles in all subject areas, covering CD-ROM, CD-I (Compact Disc, Interactive), and other formats of laser discs. Entries include bibliographic citation, subject terms, a brief content annotation, brief technical specifications, multimedia features, and price. Indexed by company, type of service, geographic area, platform, audience level. The printed version has several indexes; the CD has about eighteen searchable fields. The CD-ROM version has the now-common choices of browsing, using the menu, or direct searching.

■ Gale directory of databases. Detroit: Gale, 1993– . 2v. Semiannual. Also online.

> The most comprehensive guide available. Covers well over 8,000 databases from more than 3,100 producers. International coverage. Entries give a detailed description of each database, including services from which each is available. Indexed by keyword, subject, geography, producer, service. Includes online in one volume; CD-ROM and other types of "portable" databases in the other; each with its own index.

■ The multimedia and CD-ROM directory. London: Waterlow New Media Information, 1981– . 2v. Annual. Also on CD-ROM.

Title and publisher vary. A pioneer in the field (a merger of *CD-ROM Directory* and *Multimedia Yearbook*), listing nearly 20,000 CD-ROMs with one- to two-sentence annotations. Arranged by title, with indexes by subject, format, etc. Although fewer entries than other similar sources, includes information about the producers.

■ World database series. New Providence, N.J.: Bowker/K. G. Saur, 1993- .

A series of print directories to all types of databases, including those on the Internet. Annotations provide some detail and are often evaluative. Generally perceived to be better than those in the *Gale Directory*. Intended to become the de facto authority in the field, but given the rapid changes in the industry, each volume is at least partially out of date by the time it is published. Each consists of a master record, arranged by broad subject, with "bibliographic" citation and a detailed description of the contents, plus citations to reviews of the sites. Each is indexed by vendor, subject, producer, database name. Titles to date include *Agriculture, Biosciences and Pharmacology, Chemistry, Company Information, Geography and Geology, Humanities, Industry, Management, Medicine, Patents, Physics-Mathematics,* and *Social Sciences.*

For a selected list, concentrating on products that are likely to be around for some time, *see*

■ Ensor, Pat. CD-ROM research collections. Westport, Conn.: Meckler, 1991. 302p.

Rather long descriptions of more than 100 regularly updated CD-ROM databases likely to be of use to libraries, excluding directory and numeric sources. Many of these also have online and Internet-based versions, which are similar but not identical to those listed, but this guide remains handy and valid.

Conferences

The following are general bibliographies of conference proceedings, but the most useful reference approach to such materials are the indexes to the individual papers and presentations, treated in chapter 3.

■ Bibliographic guide to conference publications. Boston: Hall, 1974- . Annual.

International coverage with an emphasis on the United States and the English language. Based on Library of Congress cataloging and the holdings of the New York Public Library, covers proceedings, reports, summaries, collections, etc. presented at conferences, most of them of scholarly associations. Arranged by main entry, plus title, series, subject, and added entries in one alphabet, with a full bibliographic record under the main entry only.

■ Proceedings in print. Halifax, Mass.: Proceedings in Print, 1964- . Bimonthly, with cumulated index.

Initially covered only science and technology; humanities and social sciences included since 1967. Access by corporate authors, sponsors, editors, subject. Cumulated annual index is also available separately.

Another useful source, with coverage extending from the 1890s, is *Document Supply Centre Conference Proceedings,* available online via BLAISE and on CD-ROM as *Boston Spa Conferences* (Boston Spa, England: British Library Document Supply Centre, 1991-). The online version is updated monthly, the CD-ROM quarterly.

Film and Video

■ The American film institute catalog of motion pictures produced in the United States. Berkeley, Calif.: Univ. of California Pr., 1988-98. 15v.

The complete and definitive catalog of all motion pictures produced in the United States, arranged by date of production. Provides detailed descriptive information on films, but no evaluative comments. Segments each cover a decade (except for *Film Beginnings, 1893-1910* and *Within Our Gates: Ethnicity in American Feature Films, 1911-1960*) and include indexes by name, date, series, producer, genre, location, source, and subject, as well as producer and songwriters.

■ Bowker's complete video directory. New Providence, N.J.: Bowker/Reed Reference, 1990- . 4v. Annual. Also on CD-ROM; updated quarterly.

Began life as *Variety's Complete Home Video Directory.* Covers about 50,000 entertainment and more than 80,000 educational and information videos in various formats, with more than 6,000 having reviews from *Variety.* Entries include full citation, MPAA and similar ratings, running time, format(s) in which the title is available. Classified by subject and genre. Indexed by nine elements; CD-ROM is searchable by nineteen different criteria.

■ British Film Institute. Film index international. Cambridge, England: Chadwyck-Healey, 1993– . CD-ROM only. Annual.

Base disk covers 1930 to 1991, with annual updates thereafter. Provides key details of more than 100,000 feature films, including references to periodical articles about the film and its actors.

■ Film and video finder. 5th ed. Albuquerque, N.M.: National Information Center for Audiovisual Media, 1996. 3v. Also on the Web, online, and on CD-ROM from several vendors under variant titles.

Replaces and updates the NICEM indexes of various kinds. Covers more than 130,000 items (feature films, educational and training materials, etc.) but has briefer annotations than Bowker's *Educational Film Locator. ARBA (The American Reference Books Annual)* likes *The Video Source Book* better.

■ Goble, Alan, ed. The international film index, 1895–1990. Munich and New Providence, N.J.: K. G. Saur, 1991. 2v.

The most ambitious project to date for films. Truly international coverage, with emphasis on the United States and Europe, but covering about 120 countries for a total of more than 177,000 films. The main index is by film title, giving release date, director, country of production, and type of film (e.g., animation). The second volume is by director, giving film title, date, and type. In addition to an index by country of production, there is also a list of directors of animated films and a fairly lengthy bibliography of film reference books. Although containing much less information per film than the other sources in this section, this source is one of the few to cover the entire world.

■ Magill's survey of cinema. Englewood Cliffs, N.J.: Salem, 1980–85. 21v. Also online.

In separate sets for *English Language Films, Foreign Language Films,* and *Silent Films,* for a total of about 3,000 titles. Covers films from all nations, giving basic citation, including credits and principal cast. The set's major attraction is the fairly lengthy plot summary and synopsis of reviews and criticism for each film. Although other sources are more complete in coverage, this remains a useful compendium of evaluations and (as one would expect from a Magill product) plot summaries. Updated by *Magill's Cinema Annual* (Pasadena, Calif.: Salem, 1982–).

▪ Museum of Broadcast Communications encyclopedia of television. Chicago: Fitzroy Dearborn, 1997. 3v.

> The most detailed source on television programs currently available, covering 1937 to 1984, including more than 7,000 series as well as pilots and specials. Entries include title, plot summary, cast and crew credits, any guest stars, network, and original air date. Arranged by program name, with an index to people.

▪ Nash, Jay Robert, and Stanley R. Ross. The motion picture guide. Evanston. Ill.: CineBooks, 1985–87; distributed by Bowker. 12v.

▪ The motion picture annual. New York: CineBooks, 1986– . Annual.

> The basic set covers 1927 to 1984 in the first nine volumes; silent era is in volume 10; the complete index is in volumes 11 and 12. The *Annual* updates the basic set, for theatrically released films in the English language. Includes a review of each film, plus plot summary and reference to various rating systems. Arrangement is complex, but is basically by film title, with indexes by series, alternate title, awards, and every name listed in every entry.

▪ U.S. Library of Congress. NUC: audiovisual materials. Washington, D.C.: Library of Congress, 1983– . Quarterly.

> Motion pictures, video recordings, filmstrips, and all other visual material cataloged by the LC. As with other current *NUC* versions, consists of a register, with a number of indexes.

Earlier coverage is in U.S. Library of Congress, *Audiovisual Materials* (Washington, D.C.: Library of Congress, 1979–82), *Films and Other Materials for Projection* (Washington, D.C.: Library of Congress, 1972–78), and *Motion Pictures and Film Strips* (Washington, D.C.: Library of Congress, 1958–72).

▪ The video source book. Detroit: Gale, 1979– . Annual. Also on CD-ROM as VideoHound, 1990– . Annual.

> *Scope*: More than 145,000 programs of all kinds in all video formats likely to be available in North America; roughly the equivalent for the format of *Books in Print*. Includes features, how-tos, rock videos, television programs, etc.

> *Access*: Entries include full "bibliographic" information plus full cast (at least all speaking parts), plot summary/description, MPAA and other rating services' ratings, price (purchase and rental, if relevant). Indexes by director and cast, subject category, alternate titles, distributor, and

special formats. The indexing and information provided are extremely detailed, to the level of one-line appearances by actors.

For very brief evaluative annotations, and a brief citation (title, variant title, director, starring roles), both of the following are helpful:

■ Halliwell's film and video guide. John Walker, ed. New York: Harper-Collins, 1977– . Annual.

Generally considered the most complete and best of the brief film guides. Covers more than 20,000 films, giving running times, dates, brief plot summaries, comparative and critical comments, often including excerpts from reviews, and a short list of credits. *Halliwell's Who's Who in the Movies* (formerly *Halliwell's Filmgoer's Companion*) (New York: Harper, 1965– ; irregular) may be used as an index to this.

■ Maltin, Leonard. Leonard Maltin's movie and video guide. New York: Penguin, 1987– . Annual. Also online with additional material as Cinemania.

A classic guide to films, aimed at the home user and filmgoer. Very short evaluative reviews of more than 19,000 films available on video, plus made-for-television movies whether or not available. Arranged by title, with some cross-references from variant titles. Entries give brief information (stars, director, title, running time, date of release).

Government Publications

UNITED STATES

These important sources of scientific, technical, and socioeconomic information, from international, national, state, local, and regional government agencies, are too voluminous to be included in trade bibliographies. Nor are they always listed adequately in library catalogs, although this is changing slightly. They are recorded, with varying degrees of accuracy and completeness, by government agencies, which may include publications of many agencies, as in the *Monthly Catalog,* or the publications of one agency, as in the *Census Catalog and Guide.* For an overview and suggested titles, see the following.

■ Herman, Edward. Locating United States government information. 2d ed. Buffalo, N.Y.: W. S. Hein, 1997. 580p.

With very strong emphasis on current materials, including references to CD-ROM and online sources, and a special "Internet Supplement," plus many sample pages and entries; presently the most up-to-date guide. Each chapter includes sample questions and exercises (and answers).

■ Robinson, Judith Schiek. Tapping the government grapevine: the user friendly guide to U.S. government information. 3d ed. Phoenix, Ariz.: Oryx, 1998. 286p.

> Focuses on U.S. federal government but also includes information on state, county, and local, as well as foreign, governments; international organizations; and the European community. Arranged by type of information, with many interesting side comments on the working of agencies, and a separate "Documents Toolkit" consisting of a basic list of government reference sources. Designed as a textbook, complete with exercises (and answers). Highly recommended by reviewers.

■ Sears, Jean L., and Marilyn K. Moody. Using government information sources, print and electronic. 2d ed. Phoenix, Ariz.: Oryx, 1994. 538p.

> Arranged by topic rather than by issuing agency. Some annotated citations are followed by discussion of their use in relation to the topic at hand. Includes print, microform, and electronic sources integrated under each heading, with some sample pages for heavily used or complex sources. Indexes, of course.

■ Morehead, Joe, and M. Fetzer, eds. Introduction to United States government information sources. 6th ed. Englewood, Colo.: Libraries Unlimited, 1999. 491p.

> First to third editions used the term "Public Documents." Although getting some criticism for less than lively writing, this is the current classic guide to all types of federal information sources in all media over the entire history of the government. Each edition since the fourth has added more coverage of electronic sources.

The primary source for the federal government remains the next entry, often referred to by librarians as "MoCat":

■ U.S. Superintendent of Documents. Monthly catalog of United States government publications. Washington, D.C.: Govt. Print. Off., 1895- . Monthly. Also online and on CD-ROM from several sources.

> Although continuing for more than 100 years, this source underwent a major change in concept and format in 1976. Since July of that year, entries are based on OCLC MARC records, with the main entry consisting

of the full record (except for the fixed fields), and the subject index changed from a more traditional index to Library of Congress subject headings. Primary arrangement is by Superintendent of Documents (SuDocs) classification. Indexes by author, title, LC subject, series/report number, contract number, stock number, title keyword in each issue; cumulated twice a year. Librarians should be aware that this annual actually comes out in thirteen parts, the thirteenth being the *Periodical Supplement,* with one listing for periodicals, rather than having each issue appear in the regular MoCat as it is published.

Cumulated subject indexes are available:

■ Buchanan, William W., and Edna A. Kanely, comps. Cumulative subject index to the Monthly catalog of United States government publications, 1900–1971. Washington, D.C.: Carrollton Pr., 1973–76. 15v.

■ Kanely, Edna A., comp. Cumulative subject index to the Monthly catalog of United States government publications, 1895–1899. Washington, D.C.: Carrollton Pr., 1977. 2v.

■ Kanely, Edna A. Cumulative index to Hickcox's Monthly catalog of United States government publications, 1885–1894. Arlington, Va.: Carrollton Pr., 1981. 3v.

A subject and author index to the predecessor to the current *Monthly Catalog.*

Other sources, of course, are available:

■ Guide to U.S. government publications. McLean, Va.: Documents Index, 1972– . Annual.

Often called just *Andriot* after the compilers (John Andriot and, later, Donna Andriot). A guide to publications by agency, thus arranged by SuDocs number. Most entries have at least brief annotations and cross-references to earlier and later versions of the same title. Because the SuDocs number is based on government organization, numbers change even for continuing titles as the precise placement of an agency changes. *Andriot* includes chronological tables of number changes and even defunct agencies. Indexes by author, title, keyword in title.

■ GPO sales publications reference file. Washington, D.C.: Govt. Print. Off., 1978– . Biweekly. Fiche and electronic formats. Also available on the Web as Sales Product Catalog, soon also to be the title of all the versions.

Title varies. In effect, a books in print for U.S. government publications. Provides keyword access to titles, with each entry giving full bibliographic information, SuDocs number, price, and availability. A separate database provides a listing for things formerly listed but now out of print. Usually just called *PRF.*

■ Hellebust, Lynn. State reference publications. Topeka, Kans.: Government Research Service, 1990– . Annual.

Replaces an earlier title: *State Blue Books, Legislative Manuals, and Reference Publications.* Around twelve to forty entries per state, District of Columbia, and Puerto Rico. Entries give full citations and a detailed description of the contents. Includes a section with full contact address, phone, fax numbers.

■ Hoffman, Frank W. Guide to popular U.S. government publications. 5th ed. Englewood Colo.: Libraries Unlimited, 1998. 285p.

This title began in 1972 as a continuation of LeRoy Schwarzkopf's 1968 work of the same title. Each edition includes older titles still judged of value, serials, annuals, periodicals, etc. plus new titles since the last edition. Arranged by subject category, listing more than 2,000 titles, with a full citation and content annotation for each entry. Indexed by title and subject. Although not everyone's idea of "popular" is the same, this is a reliable guide to the titles probably most likely to be needed in any library.

■ Monthly checklist of state publications. Washington, D.C.: Govt. Print. Off., 1910–94.

Covers official publications of U.S. states, territories, and insular possessions received by the Library of Congress. Arranged by state, then by agency. Periodicals are listed twice a year in June and December. Has a subject index in each issue, which is cumulated annually the following year.

■ Subject bibliographies. Washington, D.C.: Govt. Print. Off., 1975– . Irregular. Also available on the Web as part of GPO Access (*see* below, page 83).

A series of about 250 short bibliographies listing in-print U.S. government publications on given subjects, with full bibliographic information, prices, and ordering information, including SuDocs classification. Many are annotated.

State publications may also be located in lists issued by individual states, although these lists vary greatly in currency and completeness.

A number of online services, normally available through the Web as well as directly by subscription, provide access to very current information, such as tracking bills through the lawmaking process, listing committee hearings, and reporting the debates of both Houses of Congress, as well as the full text of *Congressional Register, Federal Register,* and similar sources. For a comparative review of the four main systems, which is now somewhat out-of-date but still generally valid, see Paura Peritore, "Congress Watching on LEXIS, WESTLAW, LEGISLATE and Congressional Quarterly's CQ: Washington Alert" (*Database* 16 [Oct. 1993]: 104-7).

Even in a time of privatization and outsourcing, the government itself provides similar access, through FedWorld Gateway (Springfield, Va.: NTIS, 1992- . <http://www.fedworld.gov>), which is a gateway, with a fairly good search engine, to U.S. government information, including bibliographic sources and such sites as the Federal Job Announcements Database, U.S. Customs Travel Information, and nearly all U.S. government agency websites.

UNITED NATIONS

■ Directory of United Nations information sources. 5th ed. New York: United Nations, 1994.

> Listing of nearly 1,000 data sets produced by or in association with the United Nations. Arranged in three sections: by organization producing, with a description of the organization; by service; by database. These last two are arranged by subject. Indexes by subject and by name/acronym. ACCIS, the UN agency responsible for the compilation, is now defunct, but the UN website UNBIS appears to replace this title for the time being.

■ Index to United Nations documents and publications on CD-ROM. New Canaan, Conn.: Newsbank/Readex, 1990- . CD-ROM only. Monthly. Archival disk, 1946-91. Also available as AccessUN on the Web.

> Each new disk is cumulative. Indexes UN publications and documents, including periodicals, mimeographed material, etc., as well as printed material. A second database includes full text of documents deemed of particular value.
>
> *Access:* The usual Newsbank search engine allows reasonably sophisticated searching. Entries include author, title, conference name (as relevant), using agency, main UN agency, language, ISSN/ISBN, type of publication, plus an annotation. Searchable by subject, name,

conference, location. Includes a key to the related microfiche set, which covers 1945 to date.

▪ UNBIS United Nations bibliographic information system. New York: Dag Hammarskjöld Library, 1979- . Online. Also available as UNBIS Plus on CD-ROM. Alexandria, Va.: Chadwyck-Healey, 1980- . CD-ROM only. Quarterly updates.

> The official bibliographic access to UN material, including the UN itself and its related agencies, plus speeches made by UN officials and several data sets (e.g., UN voting records). Also lists non-UN books and articles related to its interests.

▪ UNDOC: current index: United Nations documents index. New York and Geneva: United Nations, 1979-97. Annual cumulations on fiche, 1985-97.

> Successor to *UNDEX* (1970-78) and *United Nations Document Index* (1950-73). Comprehensive coverage of UN production, with full citations. Each issue includes indexes, which are cumulated annually. Indexes include access by subject, name, title.

The older material is indexed in

▪ United Nations. UNDEX. United Nations documents index. Series A: subject index, volume 1- , Jan. 1970- ; Series B: country index, volume 1- , Jan. 1970- ; Series C: list of documents issued, volume 1- , Jan. 1974. New York: United Nations, 1970-80.

▪ United Nations. Dag Hammarskjöld Library. United Nations documents index, 1950-1973. New York: United Nations, 1950-75. 24v. Cumulated index, 1950-62. Millwood, N.Y.: Krause, 1974. 4v. replaces those years in one cumulation.

And the librarian should never forget *PAIS International,* which indexes both monographs and articles. It includes a substantial amount of UN as well as U.S. material at all levels. For a fuller description, see chapter 3.

GENERAL GUIDES

▪ Guide to official publications of foreign countries. Chicago: Government Documents Round Table, ALA, 1997; distributed by Congressional Information Service. 494p.

> Covers more than 150 countries, with emphasis on current serials. Arranged by country, then standard list of categories of publication (e.g.,

general guides, health). Gives full citation, publisher, availability, and a brief annotation. No indexing. Still useful, although becoming outdated.

■ New York Public Library. Research Libraries. Catalog of government publications in the Research Libraries. Boston: Hall, 1972. 40v.

Another of the massive Hall catalogs, providing card images for about 1 million government publications. Strongest for the United States, Britain, western Europe, and Scandinavia. Although the collection began in the 1840s, it holds substantial material published before 1800. Arranged by political jurisdiction, with separate listing for serials and monographs under each agency. Unlike most similar Hall products, lacks subject entries.

This source is continued by two publications:

■ Bibliographic guide to government publications, foreign, 1975- . Boston: Hall, 1976- . Annual.

■ Bibliographic guide to government publications, U.S. Boston: Hall, 1975- . Annual.

These two sources provide current access to government publications cataloged by the New York Public Library and the Library of Congress. Arranged in dictionary format with author, title, and subject access and a full record only with the main entry. Both libraries' full catalogs are available on the Web; the records are also available on OCLC and several other online services in varying disguises.

Manuscripts

■ Archives USA. Alexandria, Va.: Chadwyck-Healey, 1998- . CD-ROM and the Web only. Annual on CD-ROM, quarterly on the Web.

Includes all records from the *National Union Catalog of Manuscript Collections* (1959-97), indexing for the *National Inventory of Documentary Sources in the United States,* and a detailed directory of archives and manuscript collections in the United States.

■ National inventory of documentary sources in the United States. Teaneck, N.J.: Chadwyck-Healey, 1983-85. Fiche. Also on CD-ROM.

Copies of finding aids (published and unpublished) produced by state and federal archives, historical societies, academic libraries, and other repositories. Includes two volumes of indexes.

- National union catalog of manuscript collections. Washington, D.C.: Library of Congress, etc., 1959–93. 29v. Continued online only, 1986– . Available on RLIN and on the Web at <http://lcweb.loc.gov/coll/nucmc>.

    Describes collections in libraries and archives, mostly personal papers, and since 1970 oral history transcripts as well. Arrangement varies over time, but indexing is quite complete. Entries include main entry, title, size of collection, scope and content, identification number, as well as accessibility and restrictions, availability of microforms.

    Cumulative indexes to the above are available as *Index to Personal Names in the National Union Catalog of Manuscript Collections, 1959–1984* (Alexandria, Va.: Chadwyck-Healey, 1988. 2v.) and *Index to Subjects and Corporate Names in the National Union Catalog of Manuscript Collections, 1959–1984* (Alexandria, Va.: Chadwyck-Healey, 1994. 3v.).

Microforms

- Guide to microforms in print. New Providence, N.J.: K. G. Saur, 1961– . 2v. Annual.

    International coverage of all types of commercially published microforms of all types, except theses and dissertations (which are covered in *Dissertation Abstracts International*). Arranged by author/title and by subject. Annual, with midyear supplement.

Newspapers

Many newspapers are now available in some version online or in CD-ROM format. Unfortunately, in many cases, the entire text of the paper is not available, and the images, such as photographs, graphs, etc., are rarely available. Thus, it is still useful to know where a full file of the paper can be found. Of course, few of the papers have machine-readable versions going back before the 1990s, so even those papers must be consulted in print form for the earlier years. Fortunately, the National Newspaper Project has been both cataloging and microfilming U.S. papers for some years, so it is often possible to obtain microform copies of older papers (although the images will still be in black and white, rather than color).

- United States newspaper program national union list. 4th ed. Dublin, Ohio: OCLC, 1993. Microform. 70 fiche.

    A title guide to newspapers that are part of the program to catalog fully all U.S. newspapers. Currently has more than 100,000 titles, giving details about the paper plus location of holding libraries. Indexed by subject, place of publication, geographical area covered, beginning and ending dates. The data are online as part of the OCLC database. In effect, this replaces all earlier sources. Note that many of the newspapers are or have been microfilmed in the process of this project.

Older guides, still of some use for the citations follow:

■ Bringham, Clarence S. History and bibliography of American newspapers, 1690–1820. Worcester, Mass.: American Antiquarian Society, 1947. 2v.

■ Gregory, Winifred, ed. American newspapers, 1821–1936: a union list of files available in the United States and Canada. New York: Wilson, 1937. 791p.

■ U.S. Library of Congress. Catalog Publication Division. Newspapers in microform: United States and foreign countries, 1948–1983. Washington, D.C.: Library of Congress, 1984. 3v.

And, for a related format, *see*

■ Newsletters in print. Detroit: Gale, 1966– . Annual. Available as part of Gale Directory of Publications and Broadcast Media database.

Lists serials with national or broad regional interest that treat specialized subjects or interests. Arranged by broad topic, then specific narrower subjects. Includes full citation, intended audience, frequency, circulation size, ISSN, online availability. Indexes by title, subject, publisher, online sources, free sources, those that carry advertising.

Pamphlets and Report Literature

Though some scholarly pamphlets are listed in *Cumulative Book Index,* a much more extensive list is given in *Vertical File Index:*

■ Vertical file index: subject and title index to selected pamphlet material. New York: Wilson, 1935– . Monthly, except August. Also online and on CD-ROM, 1986– .

English-language pamphlets, brochures, and similar material, including maps and charts, published in the United States and Canada. Although all levels of interest are covered, from children to the specialist, the emphasis is on the needs of the general library user. Contrary to the usual Wilson format, this is not a dictionary arrangement but is arranged by subject, with a separate title index in each issue and a subject index in quarterly and semiannual numbers. Entries give full citation, including collation, plus price and a content annotation. A special section, "References on Current Topics," provides a few citations with abstracts to journal articles on currently hot topics.

A type of publication that could be listed as "pamphlet" but is usually considered separately is often called "report literature" but in much of the world goes by the name of "grey literature." Without getting into the details of exactly what constitutes "publications," in short this is material that is generally produced in small quantities for a specific audience and is rarely if ever listed in the other sources noted in this chapter. This category of material can include technical research reports; final reports of government (and privately funded) research; experiments; handouts given during presentations at scholarly and professional conferences; material produced for local use in libraries, schools, and similar institutions; and the like. Often, the original material becomes unavailable within a few weeks or months of its production, but it may be available on request (usually for a fee) in a microform or xerographic copy from the original. Also, such organizations as the ERIC and NTIS services collect such material and make it available in microform.

■ Auger, Charles P. Information sources in grey literature. 4th ed. New Providence, N.J.: Bowker/K. G. Saur/Reed Reference, 1998. 170p.

All aspects of dealing with this format, including cataloging, acquisitions, user concerns, etc. A British point of view but the best complete discussion of the subject.

■ NTIS Database. Washington, D.C.: National Technical Information Service, 1964– . Monthly. Online, on CD-ROM from several vendors; free Web access to much of the 1990– material. Replaces the printed source, *Government Reports Announcements and Index.*

Indexes and abstracts for technical and scientific reports and a surprisingly large amount of audiovisual media (usually training oriented) collected by and/or produced by many U.S. government agencies, often the result of nongovernment research. There is some overlap with ERIC documents, particularly in the social sciences and library/information science. Although the printed full-abstract journal has ceased, the individual reports (by subject) are still available as a monthly bulletin. As with ERIC, nearly all these reports are available on microfiche, and a growing number are also on the Web in PDF (Portable Document Format) format.

■ Resources in education. Washington, D.C.: U.S. Department of Education, Educational Resources Information Center, 1966- . Monthly. Formerly *Research in Education* (1966–75). Online, on CD-ROM, and on the Web.

> Indexes and abstracts documents in educational areas, broadly defined to include formal and informal education, training, and the like, with considerable material produced by libraries, with nearly all subjects covered. Includes many conference papers, proceedings of conferences, and final research reports (e.g., on library automation, curriculum reform). Most of the material indexed is available on microfiche and paper copies from the ERIC Document Reproduction Center and is held by most larger academic libraries. The paper form consists of citation plus abstract and indexes. Electronic access varies with the system but generally includes author, title, subject, keyword, and various classifications. *RIE* is usually packaged with *Current Index to Journals in Education* in the machine-readable formats. Most of the machine-readable formats also include the Eric Digest series, brief state-of-the-art reviews of literature on current educational topics.

■ SIGLE: system for information on grey literature in Europe. The Hague: European Association for Grey Literature Exploitation, 1980- . Monthly. Online, including the Web, and CD-ROM only.

> Covers European research reports, theses, proceedings, translations of these, various official documents, and other similar material made publicly available since 1980. Adds more than 3,000 new items per month. Most items cover science and technology, although social sciences have respectable representation; most are in English. Most material is available from the British Library's Document Supply Centre.

Periodicals

Periodicals are sometimes included in national library catalogs, and government agencies list their periodicals in catalogs of government publications. Periodicals are more fully covered in the following sources, some of which list also some of the larger libraries holding them; however, one should be aware of the CONSER program. Originally standing for **CON**version of **SER**ials, and renamed **C**ooperative **ON**line **SER**ials in 1986, this is a project to convert manual serial records into online records, eventually to have all serials records in an online form. The database is used as the source for New Serial Titles, including U.S. National Newspaper Program information, and officially resides on the OCLC database. CONSER records are full MARC cataloging for serial publications, including variant titles, a list of editors, and indication of what sources index the serial. Eventually, many of the following may be replaced by the records in the national and local online catalogs, but for the present, the following sources are important:

▪ Union list of serials in libraries of the United States and Canada. Edna Brown Titus, ed. 3d ed. New York: Wilson, 1965. 5v.

> Given the changes in information technology, this is very likely the last edition of this title and the last such cumulation to be published. Eventually, CONSER will replace this source. A worldwide list of more than 156,000 titles in existence in December 1949, with holdings (in some detail) for more than 950 libraries in the U.S. and Canada, including periodicals, proceedings, and annual reports of associations. Excludes ephemera and items of highly limited value, some government publications, and newspapers. Arranged by most recent title, with references to earlier titles. Entries give a full history of the title changes, place of publication, publisher, date of first (and last, if ceased) volume, with the holding libraries giving summary holdings and the library symbol.

This is updated by

▪ New serial titles: a union list of serials commencing publication after Dec. 31, 1949. Washington, D.C.: Library of Congress, 1953- . Monthly, with three quarterlies cumulating, and the last issue an annual cumulation. Also cumulated every five years, with 1971-75 as the first cumulation.

> Maintained as part of the CONSER database, lists new serials and new holdings for older serials just reported in about 700 U.S. and Canadian libraries. Record is a copy of the MARC record, including price and publisher address for most records and notes on coverage by indexing and abstracting services.

▪ New serial titles, 1950-1970. Washington, D.C.: Library of Congress, 1973. 4v.

> Cumulates the monthly with additional library locations and revisions to entries, covering about 800 libraries in the U.S. and Canada and about 250,000 entries. Arranged by latest title, with cross-references to earlier titles, and a separate list of publications that have ceased. Gives the same information as the *Union List of Serials,* with the addition of

ISSN numbers. Also arranged by about 250 broad subjects as *New Serial Titles, 1950-1970: Subject Guide* (New York: Bowker, 1975; 2v.).

The following cover currently published serials and provide access by subject, as well as more-detailed information on each publication.

■ Serials directory. Birmingham, Ala., and Peabody, Mass.: EBSCO, 1986- . Online as EBSCONET and on CD-ROM.

Scope: Originally a list of serials available from EBSCO, this is now a major contender with *Standard* and *Ulrich's*. International coverage of more than 180,000 titles of serials, indexing and abstracting services, and newspapers.

Access: With bibliographic citations, price, and frequency, as well as, where available, reference to refereeing process and to the Institute for Scientific Information's "journal impact factor" (a measure of how significant a journal is based on how often it is cited in other journals). Information is based on CONSER, EBSCO's own files, and mail questionnaires, but it has been criticized as not fully up-to-date. As compared with *Ulrich's*, has slightly more entries, and slightly more information per entry, but the indexing has been criticized as not as good. Entry is generally a full CONSER MARC record. Arranged by subject. Indexed by subject, title, publisher, coverage by indexing and abstracting service.

■ Standard periodical directory. New York and Detroit: Oxbridge, 1964- ; distributed by Gale. Also online and on CD-ROM as SPDCD.

Covers only North American titles, and publisher claims it is more comprehensive than its competitors within its scope; it does seem to be better for newsletters and similar publications. Arranged by subjects, entries are longer than EBSCO or *Ulrich's*, giving much the same information in a bit more detail.

■ Ulrich's international periodicals directory: including irregular serials and annuals. New Providence, N.J.: Bowker/Reed Reference, 1932- . Annual. Also on CD-ROM with quarterly updates and online with monthly updates. Updated semiannually by *Ulrich's Update*, which comes automatically with purchase of the printed version.

The scope and exact title of this classic have changed over the years, to become more inclusive. Primary arrangement by subject for serials and newspapers. Entries include full bibliographical information and price,

ISSN, plus indication of major indexing tools, availability of online and CD-ROM versions, e-mail addresses and URLs (Uniform Resource Locators) (but still very incomplete for these) and full-text availability from delivery services, with a total of forty-three potential types of accessible information. Includes lists of refereed serials, controlled circulation titles, electronic serials. The electronic versions also retain all ceased titles.

Additional sources of value follow.

■ Katz, William A., and Linda Sternberg Katz, eds. Magazines for libraries. 9th ed. New Providence, N.J.: Bowker/Reed Reference, 1997. 1350p.

A regular and important reference tool, with nearly all entries revised in each new edition. This is a selective guide to periodicals recommended by the compilers for libraries, arranged by subject. Entries provide basic bibliographic information, plus availability in different formats, ISSN, and price. As relevant, they also note refereeing policy, audience level, and presence of book reviews. The real value of this tool is in the frank evaluations for every entry, including both a content note and true evaluations (not just descriptions). The editors try to provide a reasonable balance among subjects, type of reader, and the like, but they do tend to cite mostly U.S. publications.

■ Fulltext sources online. Medford, N.J.: Information Today, 1989– . Semiannual; each issue replaces previous issue. Also online.

The most complete guide to newspapers, newsletters, and periodicals that have full-text online, including Internet versions. Updated by the website Private Zone <http://www.infotoday.com/fso/private.html>. Formerly published by BiblioData.

■ Hoornstra, Jean, and Trudy Heath. American periodicals, 1741–1900: an index to the microfilm collections; American periodicals, 18th century; American periodicals, 1800–1850; American periodicals, 1850–1900, Civil War and reconstruction. Ann Arbor, Mich.: University Microfilms International, 1979. 341p.

Contrary to the title, this is really a bibliography of the journals, not an index to their content. Main arrangement is by periodical title, giving full bibliographic citation and reel numbers. Indexed by subject, title, editor, and reel number. Because multiple titles are often on the same reel, this is indispensable to use of the microform collection. The subject index is also of value, because few libraries have provided subject access to older periodical titles. Many larger libraries have some or all of this collection on microfilm, often available for interlibrary lending.

■ The international directory of little magazines and small presses. Paradise, Calif.: Dustbooks, 1965- .

About 5,000 entries for magazines and small presses, usually with annotations for the latter, giving editorial policies, types of publications. Geographical and subject indexes. Emphasizes the United States, but Great Britain and Canada are well covered.

Union lists of serials have multiplied greatly in the last few years. However, union catalogs of all kinds now also include serial records, and thus they will probably soon replace separately published lists. To date, one of the frustrations of union catalogs in seeking serials is that they often do not indicate holdings of individual libraries, except in a very general way, while the best of the traditional serials union lists gave very detailed holdings statements. There is a big difference between being told that library *A* holds periodical *Z* from volume 6 to date and knowing that the exact holdings are for volumes 6-18, 22, 66-99, and 112 to date, with specific issues missing. However, the trade-off here is that an online union list is likely to cover vastly more libraries in a given area than the printed list. In any event, because the holdings information in the typical union catalog is increasing in detail, this problem should eventually solve itself.

Sound Recordings

■ U.S. Library of Congress. Music catalog. Washington, D.C.: Library of Congress, 1981- . Fiche, quarterly; CD-ROM, semiannually.

Continues *Library of Congress Catalog—Music, Books on Music, and Sound Recordings* (1973-89) and *Library of Congress Catalog— Music and Phonorecords, 1953-72*. Main entries, with full cataloging record, for the material listed. Scores, sound recordings, books, and serials on music. Indexed by publisher, name, title, subject, series. The CD-ROM includes additional material, such as the Schatz Collection of opera librettos.

■ Words on cassette. New Providence, N.J.: Bowker/Reed Reference, 1992- . Annual.

Formed by the merger of *On Cassette* (Bowker) and *Words on Tape* (Meckler) to provide an "in-print" listing of audiobooks. Includes readings of books, lectures, old radio programs, etc.

Access: Primary entry is under title, with citation, content notes, and running time, plus indication of full or abridged text, availability for rental, and reader's name(s). Indexed by author, reader/performer, subject, producer/distributor. However, many of the main entries provide incomplete information.

Reprints

A number of reprints are issued each year, many of which are not found in *BIP* or similar publications.

■ Guide to reprints, 1967– . Kent, Conn.: Guide to Reprints, 1967– . Annual.

Cumulates with each edition. International coverage of reprints of originals in at least 75 percent of original size and in an edition of at least 200 copies; primarily books but includes serials and government publications as well. Includes the usual bibliographic information and price, reprinter and original publisher, but not the date of the reprint. Arranged by author of books and title of periodicals.

Standards

Although sometimes considered esoteric, and certainly not among anyone's definition of *literature,* the various standards adopted by industries are critical to modern industrial society. And, between the library and computer discussion of the Z39.50 standard, and general discussion of problems related to the turn of the millennium, more people than ever before have become aware of the existence of such standards. Probably the most complete general listing of these is

■ Index and directory of industry standards. 15th ed. Englewood, Colo.: Global Engineering Documents, 1998. 3v.

Primarily international standards, plus major industry standards in Canada, Japan, Germany, the United States, and Great Britain, plus joint European standards, with reference to microforms availability. This is the first comprehensive subject-indexed international directory.

Tests

Although specific copies of educational and psychological tests are rarely held in the average library, it is possible to obtain many of them, if requested by a user. For instance, parents often wish to know more about a given test when asked to give consent for their children to take it, and current and potential employees also may want this information before they take such a test.

■ Test collection catalog. Phoenix, Ariz.: Oryx, 1993–95. 6v. Also available on the Web at the ETS Test File.

> A directory and description of the more than 15,500 tests and measurement devices held by the Educational Testing Service (ETS). Bibliographic citations plus descriptive, but not evaluative, annotations and indexing terms (reminiscent of the ERIC indexes). Arranged by broad type of test. Indexed by title, author, and subject, but no cumulative index. The Web version is searchable; thus, in effect, it is indexed.

■ Mental measurements yearbook. Lincoln, Nebr.: Buros Institute of Mental Measurements, 1938– ; distributed by Univ. of Nebraska. Irregular (most assuredly not a "yearbook"). Index is also available on the Web, in combination with the above title.

> The classic in this field. Lists and evaluates commercially published English-language psychological, educational, vocational tests. Describes the test in some detail, and gives at least one review, as well as review citations. Arranged by test name, with indexes by title, publisher, type of scoring, names of reviewers and test authors. Each edition includes only new or revised tests, so the entire set must be retained and consulted for older, still-used tests. Updated between editions by supplements.

■ Tests in print V. Lincoln, Nebr.: Buros Institute of Mental Measurements, 1999. 2v.

> Covers more than 3,000 tests in English produced by commercial publishers, plus all eleven editions of the *Mental Measurements Yearbook.* Arranged by test with full citation, including price and any restrictions, plus citations to literature (reviews, validations, critiques, etc.) about the test. Indexed by reviewers, acronyms, test titles, and (classified) subject. Also includes an index by type of test (e.g., for abstract reasoning).

Translations

■ Index translationum. International bibliography of translations. Repertoire international des traductions. Paris: UNESCO, 1932- ; distributed by UNIPUB. Annual. CD-ROM only, since 1994.

A bibliography of translations from books as well as serials, unlike the other titles listed here. About 50 percent are "literature," about 25 percent social sciences, and about 15 percent sciences; the rest, all other subjects. Each year adds about 60,000 new entries. International coverage. Arranged by nation, then subject. Entries include full citation for translation and reference to original title and language, author, and translator, as well as price. This is especially useful for translations from non-Latin alphabets. Indexed by author, translator, and publisher. CD-ROM covers all items from 1979 to date, with more than 800,000 titles listed as of 1998.

■ Transdex index. Wooster, Ohio: Bell & Howell, 1984- . Annual cumulations on fiche.

Began as *Catalogue Cards in Book Form for United States Joint Publications Research Service Translations* (1957 to date), with several changes in title and publisher since then. Indexes non-U.S. materials (especially former Soviet-bloc nations) translated by the Joint Publications Research Service, with a strong emphasis on science and technology but other coverage as well, from newspapers, speeches, and broadcasts to periodicals. Indexed by keyword and personal name.

■ World translations index. Delft, Netherlands: International Translations Center, 1987–97. Online 1979–97.

Continues *Translations Register-Index* (1967–86) and *World Trans-index* (1978–86). An index to translations in all fields of science and technology.

These lists and catalogs, which augment national and union library catalogs and trade bibliographies, represent only a small segment of the sources that may be consulted. Others—such as those more limited in scope, for example, guides to manuscripts in individual repositories, translations from one language to another, and national and trade sources for other languages and nations—are described in *Balay* and *Walford's.*

World Wide Web and Internet Access

In addition to printed and CD material, the Internet contains a plethora of access tools of its own. At the present time (and the foreseeable future for that matter), suggesting which "bibliographic" tools are "fundamental" is, to mix metaphors, a crapshoot in the dark while blindfolded. Since 1990, even since 1995, the composition of the Net has changed drastically, particularly with the development of the World Wide Web and the introduction of graphically oriented "Web browsers," starting with Mosaic, which made searching the Web (and much of the rest of the Internet) technologically easy. Thus, one cannot really refer to historical longevity, nor any of the other criteria that would usually be used (and have been used in this book) to define, even in a general way, *fundamental.* The following sites appear to be likely to stay for a while and to provide some level of selectivity in their contents; thus, they are roughly equivalent to bibliographies.

The Web appears to be growing at a substantial rate, with an unknown percentage of essentially worthless sites added alongside those whose value ranges from nearly useless to excellent and whose focus ranges from the very specific to the very general. Given the novelty of this form of information access, it is not clear just how we will eventually deal with this plethora of information.

In practice to date, most Web users tend to select a search engine of some sort, type in some terms, and then be somewhat satisfied with what they get. Oddly, much of the commercial hype has been to emphasize the size of the database indexed and the amount of material retrieved, yet most people really might prefer a smaller but more highly relevant set of material, preferably with some level of quality (or at least minimal accuracy).

Using printed and more traditional online sources as a model (a position that is itself controversial), one could argue that search services like Excite or Hotbot are equivalent to general bibliographies such as *Books in Print* and that more selective sites, often called *directories,* are the equivalent of selective bibliographies. "Gateways" are networks that actually act as entry points to other networks, but behave in many ways like directories, and so are listed with them below. In any event, the following emphasizes the latter, especially those that are particularly selective and that often contain at least abstracts, and often reviews, of the sites contained.

Other excellent and similar sites are available. The following list does not include those mounted by a single person, regardless of quality, as these personal sites have a history of changing addresses, focus, or even disappearing as the person changes institutions or jobs, or as the institution concludes that too much of its own computer resources are being used by the site.

DIRECTORIES OF GATEWAYS AND OTHER DIRECTORIES

■ AlphaSearch. Grand Rapids, Mich.: Heckman Digital Library, Calvin College, 1998– . Monthly updates. <http://www.calvin.edu/library/as>

> This rather new site is a directory of "gateway" sites, which are approximately equivalent to subject bibliographies. Calvin College librarians select and index those gateways that have high quality, contain current material aimed at college-level users, are free, and are maintained by human beings (not computers). The site is searchable by keyword in several fields and browseable.

GUIDES TO SITES

■ Argus clearinghouse. Ann Arbor, Mich.: Angus Associates, 1993– . <http://www.clearinghouse.net>

> A very selective listing of recommended sites, with signed "reviews." Sites are rated by librarians and library school students, and one site each month receives the Digital Librarian's Award. Searchable by a somewhat difficult-to-use engine.

■ Britannica.com. Chicago: Encyclopaedia Britannica, 1999– . <http://www.britannica.com>

> An excellent commercial site, connected to the *Encyclopaedia Britannica,* roughly equivalent to the "research service" provided by that company for years. Sites (more than 75,000) are selected, rated, and reviewed by the *EB* staff on a stated list of criteria, including currency. In addition to the brief review, each site gets from zero to three stars for overall quality. A classified arrangement (sixteen very large subjects, each subdivided), also browseable by subject, and searchable within itself or by use of the AltaVista engine.

■ GPO access. Washington, D.C.: Govt. Print. Off., 1993– . <http://www.access.gpo.gov/su_docs>

> The free U.S. government site, providing access to about 1,000 federal databases and more than 7,500 downloadable files, plus a searchable directory of all federal sites, a directory of depository libraries, and access via e-mail to a "user support team" who can answer questions.

■ Great sites (also known as Parentspage). Chicago: ALA, Children and Technology Committee, 1998– . <http://www.ala.org/parentspage/greatsites>

A classified listing of more than 700 sites, aimed at children (with sections for parents and for teachers and librarians). In part a response to the attempt to require filters in schools and libraries, this site tries to be "child safe" by recommending good sites, as opposed to filtering out possibly objectionable sites. Much more selective in terms of quality than Yahooligans and generally highly respected among children's librarians.

■ Infomine. Irvine, Calif.: University of California at Irvine Library, 1994- . <http://infomine.ucr.edu>

Begun in 1994, a conscious attempt to create a "virtual library," emphasizing scholarly material in ten broad topics. Each site receives detailed indexing using Library of Congress subject headings plus keywords and a description from librarians at the University of California libraries and Stanford. Accessible both by browsing and searching, with easy access from within a given topic to other parts of the listing. Particularly useful features are the inclusion of "what's new" within each topic, rather than as a separate section of the database, and the searchable tags for "document" type (subject guide, virtual library, etc.).

■ Librarians' index to the Internet. Berkeley, Calif.: University of California at Berkeley, 1993- . <http://lii.org/search>

Part of the UC–Berkeley Sunsite, classified into broad topics and subdivided. The annotations at this site are particularly well regarded. A special feature here is the list of related topics (not unlike subject tracings) for each item; these are hot links to other sites in the database. Browseable and searchable.

■ Scout Report signpost. Madison: Internet Scout Project, Univ. of Wisconsin-Madison, 1997- . <http://www.signpost.org/signpost>

A cumulation of the weekly Internet Scout Report site annotations, indexed with a combination of Library of Congress subjects and the "Dublin Core" metadata standard. More recent selections (more than 3,000) are browseable by LC subject headings and by LC classifications. The full file (more than 7,000 sites) is keyword searchable; the fully cataloged sites are also searchable by fields. Selection and annotation are done by a combination of librarians and subject experts at the university. Updated by the Scout Report at <http://scout.cs.wisc.edu/scout/report>, issued weekly on the Web and via e-mail.

- WWW virtual library. East Anglia, United Kingdom: W3 Consortium, 1994- . <http://vlib.org>

  Claims to be the oldest directory to the Web and has developed a reputation for high quality. A catalog of lists maintained by a consortium of subject experts around the world; many are comprehensive within their subject, and most are selective. Many lack clear update dates, so beware. Generally, there are no annotations on this list, but it remains a useful, nonlibrarian-based catalog.

- Yahoo! Santa Clara, Calif.: Yahoo! 1994- . <http:www.yahoo.com>

  The name gives an idea of its approach. One of the oldest, and often said to be the largest, classified selective list of Internet sites, with a very hierarchical classification system. Yahoo! is developing into a full gateway service; among other features, a typical Web search engine (with some Boolean capability) is available to use as an alternative to the classification system. Although Yahoo! claims to be selective, evidence suggests that it accepts a high percentage of the sites suggested to it or found by its bots, so quality is not a high factor in this site. If most of these site guides can be considered equivalent to annotated subject bibliographies, Yahoo! is roughly equivalent to *Books in Print.*

- Yahooligans: the web guide for kids. Santa Clara, Calif.: Yahoo! n.d. <http://www.yahooligans.com>

  Another service from Yahoo! the first classified guide to the Internet. This indexes material deemed suitable for the seven- to twelve-year-old set. Sites are selected by staff from material submitted to them and from sites found by a 'bot that searches the Web automatically. Sites are browseable by classifications and also can be searched by keyword for title, URLs, and comments (which appear supplied by the suggestors). One important feature for many parents is the serious attempt to screen out any sites that are "inappropriate" or make users "uncomfortable," so selections in some areas (e.g., sex education) are minimal.

DIRECTORIES TO OTHER INTERNET RESOURCES

Although the Web has received most of the hype in the last few years, it is only part of the Internet. The following are useful directories to other parts of the Internet.

There are several types of discussion-oriented systems on the Internet, notably a set of e-mail-based "lists," often called "discussion lists," in which one subscribes and then receives material directly via one's electronic mail. In general, such lists are fairly technical, usually academic in nature, and often include known subject experts in the group.

The Usenet is a collection of "news groups," which tend to be more popular but often also include highly skilled, technically competent people. These groups also accept subscriptions but can often be browsed or read without subscription, and they do not automatically send new messages to subscribers. Unlike the e-mail-based discussion lists, the institution or Internet service provider actually subscribes to the group, so not all groups are available to all people (however, see Deja.com Usenet Discussion Service, which follows).

Some systems offer "real-time" discussions, among them the "chat rooms." Anyone can sign up to a chat at any time—logging in means that you are in the chat until you log out. There seems to be a culture in chats where few people give their real names; some regulars adopt personae, age levels, and even genders that are not their own.

Generally speaking (but with many exceptions), one would use an e-mail-based discussion for more academic and scholarly questions and news groups for more popular questions, such as, "What is the best bandsaw for a home hobbyist?" An important caveat for the reference worker: although some e-mail lists do some screening, there is rarely any imputation that the members are particularly knowledgeable in the subject of the list. Usenet groups are even more eclectic, so that, until one knows the regular posters to a given discussion, one should be very wary of the quality or accuracy of the information. It might be useful to think of the e-mail lists as equivalent to an informal presentation at a scholarly conference (with anyone in the audience enabled to join in the panel discussion at will) and the Usenet as the equivalent of the chat at the neighborhood bar or hardware store. And chat rooms in general are the equivalent of a costume party.

The following are useful directories to this Internet material:

■ Deja.com Usenet discussion service. New York: Deja.com, 1995– . <http://www.deja.com/usenet/>

A search engine and archive for Usenet groups, formerly called Deja-News. Browseable and searchable by keyword and complex Boolean, which can be restricted to any specific field. Convenient features are the ability to post to the group once you find something and to subscribe to a group directly from this site. Deja.com also includes information about the groups. Although this site seems to be turning into another gateway, its main value is the archive—a user can search for a term and not only get older postings (going back several years), but identify the Usenet groups that tend to discuss the topic of interest while getting an indication of the flavor and tone of the discussions on the different groups.

■ Directory of scholarly and professional e-conferences. N.p.: Diane Kovacs and the Directory Team, 1998– . <http://www.n2h2.com/KOVACS>

A classified listing of the more serious "conferences" on the Internet, including chat rooms, discussion lists, MOOs (MUD-Object Oriented discussion; MUD means Multi-User Dimension or Multi-User Dungeon), news groups, and the like, as long as they appear to have scholarly or professional interest. Only one predominant subject is assigned per item, but the site is searchable by keyword and includes descriptions of each site.

■ Liszt. San Francisco, Calif.: Topica, 1995– . <http://www.liszt.com>

Browseable and also searchable, this contains a standardized description of mailing lists, Usenet, and IRC (Internet Relay Chat) chat groups of all kinds (including the software on which each is based), plus forms for subscribing to each.

■ Tile.net. <http://tile.net>

This includes both e-mail and Usenet groups, as well as FTP (File Transfer Protocol) sites and directories of vendors and service providers. The listing also includes subscription forms and, commonly, a brief description, including its country of origin and total membership.

Subject Bibliographies

Bibliographies devoted to a single subject or aspect of a subject constitute the largest body of bibliographic publication and are often the first point of departure in a search for information. They may be either retrospective or current, comprehensive or selective, annotated or unannotated, indexed or not. They may exist as separate books or parts of books, in periodicals, on cards or film, online, or otherwise. But, regardless of form, their purpose is "to give information on intellectual activity, international or national, in each branch of knowledge" (Malclès, *Bibliography,* p. 2). The development of subject bibliography since the Middle Ages and its role in the flow of information are analyzed in Barbara M. Hale's *The Subject Bibliography of the Social Sciences and the Humanities* (New York: Pergamon, 1970; 149p.).

Though library catalogs and trade bibliographies provide a series of subject bibliographies through their subject headings, they are less comprehensive than bibliographies of a single subject. As noted earlier, they are only inventories of the collections of a given library or group of libraries or a record of materials published or in print in one country during a specific period of time.

Useful in the evaluation of subject bibliographies is the definitive statement of ALA's Reference Services Division, "Criteria for Evaluating a Bibliography" (*RQ* 11 [summer 1972]: 359-60), and the related "Guidelines for the Preparation of a Bibliography" (*RQ* 32 [winter 1992]: 194-96).

Retrospective—Comprehensive

Ideally, subject bibliographies represent the work of subject authorities and reflect their informed judgment and knowledge of sources, including printed and other formats pertinent to the subject. When they are logically arranged and critically and descriptively annotated, they provide the most useful overview of the literature of a subject for those who are less familiar with it.

The access points to such bibliographies are extremely important and add much to the ease (or lack thereof) of use. In traditional sources, the arrangement plus the indexes to it are critical. In electronic sources, the actual arrangement is less critical, but the design of the database, in both its means of access and its displays, is at least as critical. For the traditional approach to this sort of work, A. M. Lewin Robinson's *Systematic Bibliography* (4th ed. rev. New York: K. G. Saur, 1979; p. 41-78) is still of value. The creator of electronic bibliographies should also at least be familiar with this source, as well as with good principles of database design.

One form of comprehensive bibliography that became very popular in the middle of the twentieth century was the reproduction of catalog cards of special collections in large libraries. In many cases, these appear to have been done about the time the library converted from manual to machine-readable cataloging. Where the older material has been retrospectively converted and where the additional notes, subject tracings, and the like, not to mention the records for book and periodical analytics, were retained in the new version, they are now primarily of historical interest. In many cases, however, these catalogs remain useful for the information they contain not currently in any other version.

In the mid-1990s, a writer and columnist noticed the closing of the card catalog, which had been going on for more than a decade at that point, and was shocked to find that the online versions did not always contain all the notes to be found on the cards (Nicholson Baker, "Discards," *New Yorker* 70 [April 4, 1994]: 64-70, 72-76, 78-86). This led him to look at libraries more closely and thus generate a rather bitter and notorious attack on automation and weeding in general ("The Author vs. the Library," *New Yorker* 72 [Oct. 14, 1996]: 50-53, 56-62), which generated considerable consternation in the library world. Although a bit extreme in statement, many of his points were valid, especially in showing that decisions made in practice do not always match the theoretical ideal and that users of libraries have different points of view from library administrators.

Though card catalogs have been replaced, book forms are still available. Two examples of book forms of specialized catalogs follow:

■ Columbia University. Libraries. Library of the School of Library Service. Dictionary catalog of the Library of the School of Library Service, Columbia University. Boston: Hall, 1962, 7v. Supplement, 1976, 4v.

A classic example of a specialized book catalog, recording titles published since 1876 in all aspects of library resources and librarianship, histories of books and printing, research methods, and other related topics. An author, title, and subject dictionary catalog, with many analytics. The records are direct reproductions of the library's cards, with generally full cataloging in the Library of Congress form as it existed at the time.

■ Dictionary catalog of the Schomburg collection of Negro literature and history in the New York Public Library. Boston: Hall, 9v. and three supplements, 1962-76. Annual supplement as *Bibliographic Guide to Black Studies*. Boston: Hall, 1975- .

Reproduction of catalog cards covering the world's published output in African and African American studies.

Retrospective—Selective

In one sense, all bibliographies are selective, in that they do not list everything potentially relevant to the topic of the bibliography (there are always some books, often privately published, that are missed; others should have been found but aren't until a negative reviewer points them out, long after the bibliography was published). In the sense used here, however, a selective bibliography is one that records the best or most important titles for a particular subject or subjects and a particular type of library or user. Any selective bibliography reflects the biases of the compiler or compilers, their depth of knowledge of the subject, the amount of writing on the subject, and the era and country in which it was compiled. All these factors should be borne in mind in their evaluation and use.

One type of selective bibliography that deserves special consideration is the guide to the literature in a broad subject field. These guides have developed as a result of the increased number and complexity of reference materials in various fields and are intended to guide the beginning researcher in the selection of the most pertinent sources. They augment the general guides, such as *Walford's* and *Balay*, and many of them conform at least in part to the following pattern:

> Overview of the subject
>
> Description of the nature of research in the field
>
> Often, a more exhaustive list of reference tools, sometimes but not always more fully annotated, in terms of their subject, than the general guides
>
> Lists of important texts and syntheses in the field
>
> Separate chapters or sections on types of material that are of particular importance in individual fields (e.g., patents in guides to chemical literature, maps and atlases in geographical literature, statistics in many social sciences and business, industrial standards in engineering, and the like)
>
> Lists of important journals in the field, including indexing, abstracting, and review sources
>
> Lists of libraries, museums, and other collections of material (not limited to published material)
>
> Lists of important associations and societies in the field, often with brief lists of their publications and descriptions of their activities
>
> Lists of authorities in the field, with special interests
>
> Sometimes, typical reference questions in the field

Many examples of such guides may be found in *Balay* and *Walford's;* a few are listed here as examples. For the most part, the following list includes those covering either very large subjects or multiple disciplines. *Balay, Walford's,* and these guides may be consulted for future titles in more limited subjects.

Bibliographies of Specific Groups

AFRICAN AMERICANS

■ Black studies on disc. New York: Simon & Schuster, 1995– . CD-ROM only. Annual updates.

> Includes *Index to Black Periodicals* (1989–), the *Dictionary Catalog of the Schomburg Collection,* and *Bibliographic Guide to Black Studies,* which is based on the Schomburg Collection of the New York Public Library. All types of material relating to the African and African

American experience are included, with access by subject, author, title. Unfortunately, with the combination of the catalogs, there is no attempt to consolidate names under one standard entry.

NATIVE AMERICANS

■ Bibliography of native North Americans on disc. Santa Barbara, Calif.: ABC-Clio, 1992– . CD-ROM only. Semiannual updates.

All entries from the printed *Ethnographic Bibliography of North America*, 4th ed., 1941–90 (now out of print), plus about 10,000 new citations. Covers more than 280 tribes, nations, and groups from the 1600s to 1992, although not very complete after the mid-1980s. Includes books, journal articles, essays, theses, conference papers, and government publications; generally excludes popular material, as well as newspapers, maps, unpublished material, and audiovisuals. A total of twelve searchable fields, using the same engine as the historical abstracting services of the publisher. Conveniently, its thesaurus is on the disc.

WOMEN

■ Henry, Dawn, ed. DWM: a directory of women's media. New York: National Council for Research on Women, 1972–94. Biennial.

International coverage of all sorts of media, including libraries, bookstores, museums, speakers' bureaus, and the like but concentrating on audiovisual and print media (the majority of entries are for periodicals). Entries include full purchase/subscription information and a content annotation. Indexed by publication/organization name, individual name, and location.

Bibliographies of Specific Subjects

BIOLOGY

■ Wyatt, H. V. Information sources in the life sciences. 4th ed. New Providence, N.J.: Butterworths, 1997. 191p.

BUSINESS

■ Daniells, Lorna M. Business information sources. 3d ed. Berkeley: Univ. of California Pr., 1993. 725p.

■ Freed, Melvyn N., and Virgil P. Diodato. Business information desk reference. New York: Macmillan, 1991. 513p.

■ Lavin, Michael R. Business information: how to find it, how to use it. 2d ed. Phoenix, Ariz.: Oryx, 1992. 299p.

CHEMISTRY

■ Antony, Arthur. Guide to basic information sources in chemistry. New York: Halstead, 1979. 219p.

CLASSICS

■ Jenkins, Fred W. Classical studies: a guide to the reference literature. Englewood, Colo.: Libraries Unlimited, 1996. 263p.

DANCE

■ Bopp, Mary S. Research in dance. New York: Hall, 1994. 296p.

EDUCATION

■ Buttlar, Lois J. Education: a guide to reference and information sources. Englewood, Colo.: Libraries Unlimited, 1989. 258p.

HISTORY

■ American Historical Association. The American Historical Association's guide to historical literature. 3d ed. New York: Oxford Univ. Pr., 1995. 2v.
■ Fritze, Ronald H., Brian E. Coutts, and Louis A. Vyhnanek. Reference sources in history: an introductory guide. Santa Barbara, Calif.: ABC-Clio, 1990. 319p.

HUMANITIES IN GENERAL

■ Blazek, Ron, and Elizabeth S. Aversa. The humanities: a selective guide to information sources. 4th ed. Englewood, Colo.: Libraries Unlimited, 1994. 504p.

MUSIC

■ Duckles, Vincent H., Ida Reed, and Michael A. Keller. Music reference and research materials: an annotated bibliography. 5th rev. ed. New York: Schirmer Books/Macmillan, 1997. 812p.
■ Mixter, Keith E. General bibliography for music research. 3d ed. Warren, Mich.: Harmonie Pr., 1996. 200p.

SCIENCE AND ENGINEERING

■ Davis, Elisabeth B., and Diane Schmidt. Using the biological literature: a practical guide. 3d ed. New York: Marcel Dekker, 1998. 421p.
■ Hurt, Charlie D. Information sources in science and technology. 3d ed. Englewood, Colo.: Libraries Unlimited, 1998. 346p.

- Information sources in engineering. 3d ed. New Providence, N.J.: Bowker/ K. G. Saur/Reed Reference, 1996. 772p.

- Malinowski, H. Robert. Reference sources in science, engineering, medicine and agriculture. Phoenix, Ariz.: Oryx, 1994. 355p.

SOCIAL SCIENCES IN GENERAL

- Webb, William H., and others, eds. Sources of information in the social sciences. 3d ed. Chicago: ALA, 1986. 777p.

Other examples include carefully prepared bibliographies of individual authors, which provide accurate and complete bibliographic descriptions of first editions of an author's works; contributions to periodicals, anthologies, and other collections; and sources of biography and criticism. Author bibliographies are being published at a great rate, for living as well as dead writers. In addition, examination of possible bias in the criticism of literature in the past has led to the "rediscovery" by scholars and critics of many authors not traditionally part of the so-called literary canon, especially those from Asia and Africa, the native peoples of all of the world, and women.

Increased publication and the specialization that characterizes much of scholarly research have led to bibliographies restricted to rather narrow subjects. These are best located through bibliographies of bibliographies and through indexes to periodicals and dissertations. Because of the large number, and their specialized nature, no examples of these limited author and subject bibliographies are given here, but they must be kept in mind as important adjuncts to the more general sources listed.

Not to be overlooked are guides to the resources of libraries that differ from library catalogs by describing the collections of one or more libraries. These guides note subject strengths and occasionally list outstanding titles, rather than listing the entire contents. For a list of some of the more important such guides, see chapter 4, "Directories."

Selection Aids

Quite different in scope, arrangement, and method of compilation are selective bibliographies that include all subjects and are aimed primarily at one type of library. They often augment library catalogs and trade bibliographies by including descriptive annotations, and sometimes they include evaluative annotations of some kind. Though more often referred to as selection aids than as subject bibliographies, they may be viewed as starting points for those seeking titles considered suitable for addition to the library. These sources are also commonly used as evaluation tools; by examining such a list, one can compare one's own selection to that of presumed experts in the field.

Selection of the titles is in one of two ways:

1. by vote of experienced librarians and/or subject experts (e.g., the Wilson Standard Catalog series), or
2. by one or more compilers, with the assistance of subject specialists (e.g., *Books for College Libraries*).

The following examples are widely used in libraries in the United States for selection, evaluation, and readers' advisory services:

■ Books for college libraries: a core collection of 50,000 titles. 3d ed. Chicago: ACRL, ALA, 1988. 6v.

> Intended to be a basic, core collection for any college library, following the tradition of C. B. Shaw's *List of Books for College Libraries* (New York: Carnegie, 1930; 2v.). This list is based on the Association of College and Research Libraries (ACRL) standards for college libraries; most titles published since 1980. Generally, science coverage has increased over the last edition, as have biography and psychology. Arranged by Library of Congress classification. Indexed by author and title; includes a subject guide to the classification. Entries give full citations. The *Choice* annual "Outstanding Academic Books" updates this.

■ Children's catalog. Bronx, N.Y.: Wilson, 1909– . Quinquennial, with annual supplements.

> Wilson Standard Catalog for preschool through sixth grade, with about two-thirds nonfiction. Arranged by Dewey decimal classifications, with indexing for analytics, authors, subjects, and titles. Entries provide full citations, plus evaluative annotations and extracts from reviews. Recent editions have dropped the former coding by grades but retain indicators for particularly recommended titles.

■ Elementary school library collection: a guide to books and other media. Williamsport, Pa.: Brodart, 1965– . Biennial. Also on CD-ROM.

> Regularly revised to keep up with curriculum and publishing changes, this provides a larger list than the Wilson equivalent for the same readership. Covers about 10,000 titles in a dozen different formats, including CD-ROM, audiovisuals, computer software. Selection, as with the Wilson Standard Catalog series, is done by a committee set up by the publisher (but not by the American Library Association, as with Wilson's series). As of the twentieth edition, also contains a list of "ESLC classics" for a basic core collection and references to titles in earlier editions still considered classics. All entries contain appropriate biblio-

graphic information plus annotations, with three levels of recommendation. Indexed by author, title, and subject. CD-ROM format has all fields searchable.

■ Herald, D. T. Genreflecting: a guide to reading interests in genre fiction. 4th ed. Englewood, Colo.: Libraries Unlimited, 1995. 367p.

Has developed a solid tradition. A lengthy discussion and analysis of each genre is followed by recommendations, usually a list of citations with annotations, but occasionally discussions of authors, with general recommendations for the corpus of their work. Index of genre authors and themes and by author/title to secondary material.

■ The Horn Book guide to children's and young adult books. Boston: Horn Book, 1989– . Semiannual. Also available as Horn Book Guide Interactive on CD-ROM.

Short reviews of essentially all children's and young adults' trade books published in the United States, arranged by grade level/genre and then by subject. In addition to a full citation and the review itself, each book receives a ranking number (one to six). Indexed by author, illustrator, title, series, and subject, with a list of new editions and reissues.

■ Husband, Janet, and Jonathan F. Husband. Sequels: an annotated guide to novels in series. 3d ed. Chicago: ALA, 1997. 688p.

Useful for its inclusion of genres, especially mystery and science fiction, where series are very common. Excludes most nonfiction and juveniles. Each section begins with a brief description of the series, followed by titles (with brief citations) in the "preferred order for readers" rather than publication date, and with a one-sentence annotation for each title. Arranged by author, with indexes by title and subject.

■ Middle and junior high school library catalog. 7th ed. New York: Wilson, 1995– . Quinquennial, with annual supplements.

Formerly the *Junior High School Library Catalog* (from 1965 to 1990). Unlike some similar titles, this is based more on "literary" criteria for the age level rather than reference to the typical U.S. middle-school curriculum. With the name change, now includes references to CD-ROMs of print equivalents. Part of the Wilson Standard Catalog series. Arranged by classification, with indexes by author, title, subject, and analytics. Entries include citation, price, classification and subject terms, and extracts, quotations, and citations to reviews.

■ Public library catalog: guide to reference books and adult nonfiction. New York: Wilson, 1934– . Quinquennial, with annual supplements.

Another one of the Standard Catalog series, based on librarians' recommendations for a core collection. All titles are published or distributed in the United States. Excludes periodicals, ephemeral works, and fiction. Arranged by Dewey decimal classification, with author/title/subject indexes. Includes annotations, review extracts, and many analytics. Although sometimes criticized for being a bit conservative, still a standard source.

■ The reader's adviser: a layman's guide [title varies]. 14th ed. New York: Bowker/Reed Reference, 1994. 6v. Also on CD-ROM. Annual updates.

This is a major revision and expansion of the series, adding essays for each national literature and chronologies. Provides recommended reading in all subject areas and national literatures, with an emphasis on literature and the humanities, but with improving coverage in the sciences and technology as well. Arranged by subject, with a brief essay and then a list of recommended titles; full citations, including prices; and, often, with references to reviews, along with the annotations. Indexed by author, title, and subject in each volume and in a cumulative index. The CD-ROM version of this edition allows full-text searching, as well as field searching, and provides hypertext links as well.

■ Senior high school library catalog. Bronx, N.Y.: Wilson, 1926– . Quinquennial, with annual supplements.

Earlier editions titled *Standard Catalog for High School Libraries.* Another of the Standard Catalog series, with recommendations for high-school-age readers, covering all subjects, with most items recent imprints, although classics are also retained. Arranged in classified order by Dewey decimal numbers, with an author, title, subject, analytic index. Because of an attempt to remain parallel with curriculum, this catalog contains more adult titles along with young adult and children's books.

■ Sequels, volume 1: adult books. 10th ed. Mandy Hicken, comp. London: Assn. of Assistant Librarians, 1991. 287p.

■ Sequels, volume 2: children's books. 8th ed. D. Fraser, comp. Newcastle-under-Lyme, England: Assn. of Assistant Librarians, 1988. 145p.

A serious attempt to be complete, at least for English-language literature, including fiction and some nonfiction. Arranged by author, then name of series, then title of each book. Very sparse entries, but much more complete than the Husbands' book. Because much out-of-print material has been removed from the *Adult* volume, the eighth edition of it should be consulted for older material.

Current Selection Tools

The need for the most recent publications on a subject has led to an increasing number of current subject bibliographies, issued separately or as part of a subject-oriented journal. Because many of them take the form of indexes to periodicals, they are listed in the next section of the chapter. Useful approaches by subject are provided in *Bibliographic Index,* described later in the section "Bibliographies of Bibliographies," and Marion Sader's *Topical Reference Books* (New Providence, N.J.: Bowker, 1991; 892p.).

Only current selection sources that are aimed primarily at one type of library, and cover all (or most) subjects, are discussed here. The following reviewing and selection sources are the most commonly used in the United States.

■ Booklist. Chicago: ALA, 1905– . Twenty-two per year. Also online.

Reviews of titles recommended for small and medium-sized libraries, with an emphasis on English but with regular sections for other languages. For the most part, reviews are done from proofs, in advance of publication. Arranged by broad subject following Dewey decimal classification, with separate sections for children, young adults, fiction and nonprint formats, Internet and CD-ROM sources, and more. A special, if not unique, feature is the inclusion of *Reference Books Bulletin,* a separately edited review journal with different scope and policies, within this title. Indexed by author in each issue, with semiannual and annual cumulations. Entries include full citation, collation, Dewey decimal classification, Library of Congress subject heading, LC card number, ISBN/ISSN, and price. Officially, a listing in *Booklist* is a recommendation to purchase, yet the reviews can be fairly critical. The online variant permits more search options and includes a cumulative index, among other additional features. "Editors Choice" consists of the titles selected by *Booklist*'s editors and appears in a double issue as the first numbers of the calendar year (as opposed to the volume year).

■ Choice: current reviews for academic libraries. Middletown, Conn.: ACRL. Monthly except July–August. Also online and on CD-ROM.

The premier source for academic libraries, reviewing material of possible value to the four-year liberal arts college library. Reviewers are college faculty. Covers about 6,000 titles a year in all subjects. Reviews are arranged by broad, and then narrow, subjects; then, by author. Citations include full bibliographic data and collation, LC card number, ISBN, and price. By policy, reviewers are supposed to compare the current title with others, but this is not always apparent. Notable are the monthly bibliographical essays on a subject of current interest (including books, periodicals, articles, and other relevant material), providing a small core collection for the subject. *Choice* also covers periodicals and is reviewing more electronic sources as well. The most recent feature is a special annual Internet issue, available separately. "Outstanding Academic Books" features the editors' selections from the best of the titles reviewed in *Choice,* and currently appears in the January issue each year.

■ The Horn Book magazine: about books for children and young adults. Boston: Horn Book, 1924- . Bimonthly.

Takes children's books seriously as a form of literature but still with an eye to the child as reader. Unlike *The Horn Book Guide (see* p. 95, above), reviews only books likely to be recommended (but some of these get fairly negative reviews). In addition to the reviews, includes articles, interviews, review essays, and the like. The reviews are arranged by age level and format. *See also The Horn Book Index, 1924-1989,* Serenna F. Day, ed. (Phoenix, Ariz.: Oryx, 1990; 534p.) for single-alphabet access to reviews in the journal.

■ Library journal. New York: Cahners, 1876- . Twenty-two per year.

A general trade journal for the library profession, with a substantial review section in each issue. Reviews, mostly from advance proofs, adult material in all formats, but the primary section remains a *book* review section. (Children's materials are covered in *School Library Journal.*) Evaluations are aimed at the needs of the general library collection, but recommendations may be for any type of library, not only public libraries. Arranged by broad and then narrow subject. Entries give full citation and collation, price, LC card number, and ISBN. Other sections of *LJ* include columns reviewing periodicals and other special formats.

■ School library journal. New York: Cahners, 1954- . Monthly.

Very similar to *Library Journal* in covering the "trade" of school and children's libraries. Includes reviews of children's and young adult materials, primarily books but also computer and audiovisual sources. Initially was part of *Library Journal* as *Junior Libraries,* then as *School Library Journal.*

Subject bibliographies and reviewing tools may supplement library catalogs and trade bibliographies in supplying the following:

A more exhaustive list of titles or a more selective list of titles

A broader range of materials in addition to books

A more specific or logical approach through their internal arrangement

Critical or descriptive annotations

Bibliographies of Bibliographies

Nearly all forms of bibliography that have been noted thus far may serve as bibliographies of bibliography, for in many of these indexes an element of the citations indicates the presence of a bibliography. Briefly, library catalogs, by their use of the subdivision "bibliography" in subject headings and their indication of the presence of a bibliography in their collations, serve as a record of bibliographies found in one or more libraries' collections. To a certain extent, this is also true of some trade bibliographies, such as *Cumulative Book Index.* Guides to the literature of subject fields always include lists of bibliographies. Periodical indexing and abstracting services also indicate bibliographical articles and often may also indicate those that contain substantial bibliographies in their text. But the proliferation of bibliographies in general has created the need for separate works devoted entirely to this form, which allows the user to find quickly what has been published.

■ Besterman, Theodore. A world bibliography of bibliographies and of bibliographic catalogues, calendars, abstracts, digests, indexes, and the like. 4th rev. and greatly enl. ed. Lausanne, Switzerland: Societas Bibliographica, 1965-66. 5v.

> The classic, still useful. Besterman examined nearly all the titles listed in one of the last monumental one-person efforts, which includes about 117,000 separately published works, carefully cataloged and indicating the number of items in each. It is arranged under about 16,000 subjects and subheads, with adequate cross-references, plus an index to authors, titles of serials and anonymous works, libraries and archives, and subjects covered by abstracts to British patent specifications. Its chief limitation is that it omits bibliographies appearing as parts of articles or books. Besterman is updated by

■ Toomey, Alice F. World bibliography of bibliographies, 1964-1974; a list of works represented by Library of Congress printed catalog cards; a decennial supplement to Theodore Besterman, A world bibliography of bibliographies. Totowa, N.J.: Rowman & Littlefield, 1977. 2v.

Some 18,000 titles listed under about 6,000 subjects, also found in the Library of Congress subject catalogs. Entries are reproduced from catalog cards. Although convenient to use, this title serves as a reminder of the value of the LC subject access. Many of these titles, by the way, do not appear in

■ Bibliographic index: a cumulative bibliography of bibliographies. New York: Wilson, 1938– . Annual.

This subject index gives complete citations to articles devoted wholly or in part to bibliographies appearing in the approximately 2,800 periodicals indexed by Wilson, to books, and to parts of books and pamphlets. Only bibliographies with fifty or more citations are indexed, unless they are by or about a person or a specialized topic. The preface to the first cumulation (1937–42) should be read for an understanding of the principles of compilation. Lack of author and title access does not restrict its use, because bibliographies are usually sought by subject, not author. Personal name entries are for things *about* a person, not *by* him or her.

■ Gray, Richard A., comp. Serial bibliographies in the humanities and social sciences. Ann Arbor, Mich.: Pierian, 1969. 345p.

Although now somewhat dated, this is very useful for historical coverage and for suggestions of sources that are often still published. Gray omits national bibliographies, book-review sections, government publications, monographic bibliographies in series, and the like; but he does include many regular bibliographies appearing in journals. Augments *Besterman* by including parts of journals and *Bibliographic Index* with additional foreign sources. Each title is given ten descriptive codes indicating language, selectivity, and the like. Subject, keywords, and characteristic indexes are included.

■ Wortman, William A. Guide to serial bibliographies for modern literatures. 2d ed. New York: Modern Language Assn., 1995. 333p.

The standard, updating and expanding the first edition (1982). Covers all languages and types of literature, listing all types of serial bibliographies, including separates, journal articles, and special issues, and electronic formats that were in print in 1960 or that have appeared since then. Indexed by title, author, and compiler, but subject access is only through the classified arrangement.

■ Ingles, Ernest B., G. R. Adshead, and Douglas Lochhead. Bibliography of Canadian bibliographies. 3d ed. Toronto: Univ. of Toronto Pr., 1994. 1178p.

> Arranged by subject, with most titles receiving annotations in English or French, a listing of monographs, articles, and chapters about Canadian subjects or of Canadian interest and generally available. Does not include bibliographies attached to articles. Includes a short bibliographic listing by main entry as well as indexes by title and by subject (in French and English).

For guides to collections compiled by and for the library or archive itself, the following are helpful:

■ DeWitt, Donald L. Guides to archives and manuscript collections in the United States: an annotated bibliography. Westport, Conn.: Greenwood, 1994. 478p.

■ Sable, Martin H. Research guides to the humanities, social sciences and technology: an annotated bibliography of guides to library resources and usage arranged by subject or discipline of coverage. Ann Arbor, Mich.: Pierian, 1986. 181p.

The following three titles form a series, with the first title having several chapters on general selection principles. Each has subject chapters that, unlike most similar books, consist of an essay on the bibliography of the subject, rather than an annotated bibliography. Although becoming a bit dated in some areas, these remain good introductions to the fields in question.

■ Selection of library materials in the humanities, social sciences, and sciences. Patricia A. McClung, ed. Chicago: ALA, 1985. 405p.

■ Selection of library materials in applied and interdisciplinary fields. Beth H. Shapiro and John Whaley, eds. Chicago: ALA, 1987. 287p.

■ Selection of library materials for area studies. Chicago: ALA, 1990-94. 2v.

For Latin America, the following cover the field very well:

■ Gropp, Arthur E. A bibliography of Latin American bibliographies. Metuchen, N.J.: Scarecrow, 1968; 515p. Supplement, 1971; 277p.

■ Bibliography of Latin American and Caribbean bibliographies. [location varies]: SALALM Secretariat, 1986- . Annual.

Currently the most complete such work. Earlier volumes are consolidated in

▪ A bibliography of Latin American and Caribbean bibliographies, [year]. Metuchen, N.J.: Scarecrow, 1982- . Irregular.

Covers 1975-79; 1980-84; 1985-89. Earlier material may be found in the next title.

▪ A bibliography of Latin American bibliographies published in periodicals. Metuchen, N.J.: Scarecrow, 1976. 2v.

The fullest such compilation. Updated by *A Bibliography of Latin American Bibliographies: Social Sciences and Humanities* (Metuchen, N.J.: Scarecrow, 1979, 1982), with different compilers, covering both monographs and periodicals. The title and scope changed with the previous two titles.

Summary

This chapter has reviewed the development of bibliographic work and some of the sources, describing the characteristics of the following types of bibliographic access:

1. Library Catalogs (for a single library)
2. National Library Catalogs
3. Union Catalogs
4. National Book Bibliographies
5. Bibliographies of Other Publications and of Audiovisual Materials
6. Subject Bibliographies
7. Selection Aids
8. Current Selection Tools
9. Bibliographies of Bibliographies

These bibliographic forms are among the most used and most important reference sources in libraries, especially those that serve scholars and researchers of any kind. They are helpful in selecting, cataloging, and identifying material that is not held in a given library. As the amount of information continues to expand in size and complexity, such access sources will continue to become more important, especially as more of the general public become aware of the vast amount of information potentially available.

3

Indexing and Abstracting Services

As pointed out earlier, indexes differ from catalogs and bibliographies in recording analytically, under appropriate headings and access points, the contents of books, periodicals, databases, and the like. Already noted are examples of indexes in subject bibliography—author, title, and subject indexes to the classified parts of the Standard Catalog series, for example. Included in this section are indexes to periodicals and newspapers, with brief discussions of many other forms. Indexes to individual books are compiled on somewhat different principles from those to a body of material.

John L. Thornton has said that the characteristics of a "born indexer" are an orderly mind, infinite patience, and an ability to approach a book from the reader's angle ("Indexing," in Robert L. Collison, ed., *Progress in Library Science* [Washington, D.C.: Butterworths, 1965], p. 34). These same characteristics are still needed by indexers today and are just as valuable to users of indexes.

John Rothman has noted four problems of index making that cause problems in index using: (1) selectivity, or scope of coverage in the index; (2) depth, or the extent to which items selected for indexing are analyzed through index entries; (3) structure of the index, or the pattern in which the entries are arranged; and (4) terminology, such as how to handle synonyms, technical versus popular terms, current terms versus their predecessors ("Communicating with Indexes," *Special Libraries* 57 [Oct. 1966]: 569–70). Although item number three does not apply to electronic indexes (it is replaced by the points of access—full term, individual words, possibility of searching by given fields, such as author), the others remain valid for all formats today. Also informative is his "Index, Indexer, Indexing," in *Encyclopedia of Library and Information Science* (New York: Dekker, 1968–91; v.11, p. 286–99).

Some knowledge of the basic principles and methods of indexing is essential to users of indexes, not only because it leads to more intelligent use, but also because it provides a basis for judging the adequacy of an index. Users must determine whether terms employed in the index are specific enough and consistent, whether location is accurately indicated, and whether decisions to omit certain types of material in a collection being indexed have been wisely made (e.g., advertisements in periodicals, short letters in scholarly journals, etc.).

The American Society of Indexers and its British counterpart, the Society of Indexers, are dedicated to the improvement of this important form of information retrieval. This is reflected in the Society of Indexers' official journal, *The Indexer,* and in its directory of courses for those who wish to learn more about this interesting field or who wish to become indexers (*Directory of Indexing and Abstracting Courses and Seminars* [Medford, N.J.: Information Today with American Society of Indexers, 1998; 29p.]).

Different methods are used for indexing different formats. These are described in Donald Cleveland and Ana Cleveland's *Introduction to Indexing and Abstracting* (2d ed., Littleton, Colo.: Libraries Unlimited, 1990; 329p.) and include books, periodicals, music, recordings, films, and other material.

Printed abstracting services, referred to interchangeably as abstracts, abstracting journals, or abstracting services, differ from indexes in their arrangement, which is usually classified by subjects and arranged in terms of appropriate divisions and subdivisions of the subject. Because of this arrangement, they also contain alphabetically arranged subject and author indexes. This difference is obviously less clear in machine-readable versions, except for the presence of an additional field or fields representing the classified subject as well as the descriptor fields. The most important difference from indexes is that abstracting services supply a summary of the contents of the items indexed. These abstracts vary in form from a brief descriptive note to a fairly lengthy summary of the text.

Harrod's Librarian's Glossary (compiled by Ray Prytherch, Aldershot, England: Gower, 1990, p. 2–3) defines an abstract as "a form of current bibliography in which sometimes books, but mainly contributions to periodicals, are summarized; they are accompanied by adequate bibliographical descriptions to enable the publications of articles to be traced, and are frequently arranged in classified order." The abstract types are indicative, informative, evaluative, general, selective, author, locative, and illative—reflecting the different ways they have been described.

Most abstracting services are compiled by an independent publisher or a learned association; some originate in U.S. government agencies. Abstracts are sometimes supplied by the author of the original work, by volunteer abstractors who are specialists in the subject, by a central staff of paid abstractors, or by various combinations of these. One problem that has concerned both users and compilers of abstracts is the time lag between publication of the original and publication of the abstract. Further information will be found in Charles L. Bernier's "Abstracts and Abstracting," in *Encyclopedia of Library and Information Science* (v.1, p. 16–38). Also of use are Jennifer E. Rowley's, *Abstracting and Indexing* (2d ed. London: Bingley, 1988; 181p.) and F. W. Lancaster's *Indexing and Abstracting in Theory and Practice* (2d ed. Champaign: Univ. of Illinois, 1998; 412p.).

These tools were among the earliest to benefit from computerization, both in compilation and production and in access. By the early 1970s, such pioneers as Dialog and the Systems Development Corporation were mounting a growing number of abstracting tools for general access, accelerating a trend already seen in larger institutions that had mounted some databases on their own computers. By the mid-1980s, most indexing and abstracting sources were either online (often on multiple services) or planning to do so. After 1985, more sources also became available on CD-ROM. Since the mid-1990s, even more sources are available directly from the publisher on the World Wide Web, a trend likely to continue. Many project that, within the next decade, the attractions of sophisticated searching, rapid updating, and reduced production costs will lead to the electronic formats being the only choice.

Note, however, that the "Access" part of the descriptions given here applies to the printed source. For most electronic versions, including CD-ROMs, tape-loaded products, traditional online systems, and Web-based systems, all (or nearly all) words in the record are searchable in some fashion. Thus, nearly any element can become an access point. However, the ease of such access and the exact nature of the searching can vary considerably across search engines. For example, it is generally not possible to search authors' first names or specific page numbers on most systems. Words in articles and book titles are nearly always searchable, but words in journal titles are often not individually accessible. Some systems permit a variety of word-proximity searches, others only immediate proximity as phrases. For example, "last-in first-out" can be considered either as a whole four-word phrase, as two two-word elements (which can be phrased as last-in first-out or first-out last-in), or as a string of words consisting of *last* within two words of *out;* there are other variants as well. Rather than try to cover all the variations on all the systems, and the constantly changing Web versions, the following attempts to indicate what elements are present, leaving it up to the reader to contact current vendors as to the exact methods of access.

General Periodical Indexing and Abstracting Services

Probably the most used form of subject bibliography is the periodical index, not only because of the number and variety of periodicals currently published, but also because of the need for the most recent information on topics not covered well by books. These indexes augment bibliographies and library catalogs in many important ways:

> They provide a subject, and often author and title, approach to individual articles in periodicals.

> They are generally more up-to-date, reflecting contemporary opinion on subjects or the current state of knowledge about a subject at a specific time.

> They usually employ quite specific subject headings, reflecting current terminology in the specific subject of interest, rather than the necessarily more general terminology of catalogs and bibliographies.

> They reveal trends in certain subject fields. (For an example of this, *see* Katharine S. Diehl, "Indexes Examined: Reference without Periodicals," *RQ* 4 [Nov. 1964]: 11–14.)

> They provide access to relatively small bits of information, which often appear only in article form, rather than entire books.

Like any other serial publications, individual periodical indexes are subject to change, not only in the titles indexed, but also in the forms of entries. For example, indexes published by Wilson are regularly reviewed for possible additions and deletions of titles, with the assistance of the Wilson Indexes Committee of the ALA Reference and Users Services Association (as mentioned in chapter 1). A very important point, often apparently forgotten (if ever known) by too many users, is that indexes also tend to change their terminology over time in an attempt to reflect the thinking of their time. Thanks to the widespread use of computer databases, it is theoretically possible for the publisher to attempt to avoid the resulting access problems by reindexing items using the old terminology with the news terms on a regular basis. The most well known example of this approach to terminology is probably the National Library of Medicine's MEDLINE, in which the entire database is reloaded every year with that year's current terminology. Unfortunately, this approach also means that (1) the user must have access to the most recent terminology, (2) it becomes nearly impossible to use the machine-readable versions to trace the development of terminology over time, and (3) the printed or microform versions of the older index will not always have the same indexing terms for the same item as does the online or CD-ROM versions of the same index. Note that although many indexes do change terminology over time, not all of them redo their older indexing.

Note, too, that some indexes usually designated as periodical indexes also include books, pamphlets, audiovisual materials, and other formats as well—*PAIS International Index*, for example.

Because there are often two, three, or even more of these periodical indexes for a given subject, published in different countries and covering many of the same titles, the problem of expensive duplication of effort has engaged international agencies and learned societies for many years. These same groups have been further concerned with (1) the great amount of current publication not listed in any current access tool, (2) the time lag in publication, and (3) the need for more specificity in indexing. The need for improvements in these areas has led to many experiments in new forms of information storage and in designing of indexing systems. At the same time, however, in many areas wholly new indexes have appeared, some covering new subject areas, others new audiences and points of view (e.g., women's studies), and some consciously duplicating existing coverage but with improved access such as the addition of more journals, the use of presumably better indexing terminology, the addition of abstracts (and, more recently, full text of some of the items indexed), and the like.

In the mid-1970s, attempts to integrate indexes into online public access catalogs (OPACs), for example, appeared promising (e.g., Information Access Company's Magazine Index), a promise not fulfilled as planned. The major problem in this case was terminology—the Library of Congress subject heading system, reasonably suitable for a general collection of books, is not very good as an indexing approach. The basic idea has been generally adopted, however, but in the form of providing a menu of access tools available from the library's OPAC terminal, with each indexing and abstracting service remaining a separate entity with its own terminology.

For all practical purposes, computers have taken over the indexing field, especially from the user's point of view. Although most indexing and abstracting services are still available in print, the attractions of computer-format indexes are nearly overwhelming:

> They can be updated daily, as new items are indexed (although most are updated monthly).

An entire run of an index can be searched at once, versus the need to look up the same headings in multiple printed volumes.

As noted above, terminology can be changed, added, or subtracted almost at will.

Some multiple indexes can be searched at the same time; multiple years of the same index can nearly always be searched at the same time.

Output can be modified to suit the user (e.g., the user can usually sort the output by author, journal title, date, etc., and the user can often generate either a printout or a download or even e-mail the results to his or her personal computer).

The user can print or download the information on the spot, rather than copying citations manually.

In many cases, the records can be customized by the library by the addition of notes with the library's own holdings or call numbers, for example.

Increasingly, the full text or even the full image of the original articles can be supplied with the indexing. Usually, this text can itself be searched word by word, thus increasing the chance of retrieving information on a more obscure subject or one that the indexer did not feel was important at the time.

From the library's point of view, online indexes can be "rented" as needed, so that a library with no real ongoing need for, say, *Chemical Abstracts* can access it on a pay-as-you-go basis for the occasional need.

Machine-readable indexes take up very little space compared to their print counterparts and are generally easier to use than microform equivalents.

Points to consider in evaluating periodical indexes include the following:

1. Scope of index
2. Length of period covered
3. Frequency and promptness of publication
4. Completeness of indexing of the material
5. Quality of indexing

Computerized databases are, of course, a relatively recent phenomenon. In all but a few cases, coverage rarely extends back much before the 1960s, although there are a few exceptions. Thus, any serious attempt to look for the literature in any subject almost always should require using older printed indexes as well as searching the current version. Keep in mind that various versions of any index may cover very different time periods (a CD-ROM version of the database may cover only the last 10 years, the online version may cover 30 years, and the printed version may approach 100 years of coverage); moreover, various suppliers' versions of the same format may vary both in the extent of the time period covered and the frequency of the updates.

The preceding paragraphs deal largely with machine-readable bibliographic indexes. Nonbibliographic databases are also rapidly increasing and include—among others—statistical and economic data, patents, marking projections, credit records, medical histories, travel information (including airline schedules and prices), and much more.

The following is a very selective list of current periodical indexes, emphasizing those covering more than one field. After some agonizing on the part of the author, the entry is under the most complete form of the index—usually but not always the printed version. For a full, nearly complete guide to databases of all types, *see The Gale Directory of Databases,* described in chapter 2, p. 59.

Readers will find many useful articles, including reviews of specific products, in such periodicals as EMedia/EContent *Professional* (monthly, 1988-); *Online* (bimonthly, 1977-); *Online & CD-ROM Review* (bimonthly, 1977-); and *Searcher* (10/yr., 1993-).

General

General periodical indexes are a good source for subjects of general current interest, usually from a nontechnical perspective. The standard for many years in U.S. libraries follows:

■ Readers' guide to periodical literature (cumulated), 1900- . Bronx, N.Y.: Wilson, 1905- . v.1- . Monthly, with annual cumulations. Online, on CD-ROM, and on tape, with updates as often as daily, covering 1983- .

 Scope: About 240 U.S. periodicals of broad general and popular character, including nontechnical magazines and some more scholarly ones, representing all fields; access to the *New York Times* added in 1993. Titles are selected based on users' needs and are regularly reviewed by the Wilson Indexes Committee; thus, coverage has varied over time.

 Access: Indexed by author, subject, and usually by title (e.g., poetry is entered only under author). Book reviews in the magazines are indexed (in a separate section in the print form since 1976). Entries include full citation (author, title, periodical, volume, date) but not always full pagination (articles continuing on part pages, e.g., with other articles or advertisements, indicated with a plus: 137–39+ means the article occupies the full pages from 137 to 139 and is then continued on one or more later pages in part).

■ Readers' guide abstracts. Bronx, N.Y.: Wilson, 1984– . Online and on CD-ROM only.

Began as microform in 1984. *Readers' Guide to Periodical Literature,* with the addition of 150-word abstracts for about 240 of the journals in *RG* and with the full text of about half available since 1994.

Since the early 1970s, some competitors to this standby have appeared, generally covering more titles. These follow:

■ Academic index; Expanded academic index. Foster City, Calif.: Information Access, 1985– . As often as daily updates. Online and on CD-ROM only.

Scope: One of several variants of the Information Access Company (IAC) indexing database. Covers about 1,600 English-language popular and scholarly journals; 250 "core" titles covered since 1976, with more titles added over time.

Access: Detailed indexing, including all types of reviews (e.g., book, film, but also restaurants, products, etc.). Citations include the usual elements, but give only the initial page number and an indication of total number of pages. Abstracts are included for most articles; *selected* full text for about 750 titles as well. Review citations include a grade (A–F) to represent the overall direction of the review. Exact coverage depends on which product and format used: the CD-ROM has the current four years of all journals plus the last six months of the *New York Times;* the CD-ROM, *Expanded Academic Index,* includes four years of all journals.

As is the case with some electronic products, there is a bewildering variety of choices, with varying numbers of journals indexed or in full text. The previous description covers the most complete version.

■ Academic search. Ipswich, Mass.: EBSCO, 1993– . Monthly. Online and on CD-ROM only.

Scope: Indexing for more than 2,000 journals of likely interest to academic libraries, with a number of non-English titles. Includes indexing to the *Wall Street Journal, Christian Science Monitor,* and *New York Times.*

Access: Full citation, including subject headings, but with only the first page (and total number of pages) indicated, plus abstracts. In the fullest version, provides full text to about 1,000 periodicals and indexing for around 3,000.

As with the IAC products, comes in several variants, including *Academic Abstracts* (about 800 titles of the full set), *Academic Abstracts Full Text Elite* (same as the previous, but adding full text of around 100 titles), plus several subject-specific versions as well.

■ Magazine article summaries. Birmingham, Ala.: EBSCO, 1987– . Also online and on CD-ROM.

A subset of EBSCO's *Academic Search,* aimed more at public libraries. Covers about 400 general-interest magazines, with many business periodicals. Available in several formats, with varying numbers of journals indexed. Several machine-readable versions include a select number of full-text journals.

■ Magazine index; Magazine index plus. Foster City, Calif.: Information Access, 1977– . Online and on CD-ROM only. Updates as often as weekly, depending upon the system, with some daily updating (often in a separate file).

Scope: Another very useful index, but hard to describe because of its multiplicity of incarnations. The basic title, *Magazine Index,* covers more than 400 general-interest popular magazines, including the full text of about 100 of these. Indexing goes back in most cases to 1959, making this the most complete in date coverage of electronic indexes. Except for very short letters and advertisements, it covers everything, including reviews of all types.

Access: Depends on the version, but in essence by all words in record, as well as specified fields, Boolean, browsing. Entries include author, title of article, journal title, volume, date, but only initial page number and indication of length, plus abstract, indexing terms, document type. Review entries include indication of direction of review, using letter coding (A–F). A growing number of full-text articles, 1983 to date, in a forum usually called Magazine Database.

■ Periodical abstracts; Newspaper and periodical abstracts. Louisville, Ky.: University Microfilms International, 1986– . Online and on CD-ROM only, in several variants. Updated as often as daily. Formerly *Courier Plus.*

Scope: In its full form, indexes 1,600 general-interest periodicals, plus about twenty-five newspapers, almost all in English, plus about eighty U.S. radio and television programs, all with a strong emphasis on business topics. Coverage varies, with some periodicals covered since 1986, newspapers since 1989.

Access: Most entries have short abstracts. Includes indexing for reviews of all kinds. As is customary with most electronic sources, has a number of variants: *Resource/One* (in several versions), including full text of about 500 titles; *Magazine Express* (in effect, *Resource/One* with full image rather than merely full text).

Retrospective coverage is available in several forms, notably the following:

■ Cumulated magazine subject index, 1907–1949. Boston: Hall, 1964. 2v.

Scope: The *Annual Magazine Subject Index* in one alphabet. Covers about 360 periodicals, with a strong emphasis on U.S. history, especially local and state periodicals. Includes retrospective coverage of forty-four "core" titles from their initial publication date.

Access: Subject indexing excludes fiction, poetry, and short articles. Given differences in indexing practice, this is a useful source even for those titles covered in other indexes.

■ Nineteenth century readers' guide to periodical literature, 1890–1899, with supplementary indexing, 1900–1922. New York: Wilson, 1944. 2v.

Fifty-one titles indexed by author and subject, including fourteen beyond the first decade to their inclusion in other Wilson indexes. More thorough indexing than *Poole's*.

■ Poole's index to periodical literature, 1802–1906. Boston: Osgood; London: Turner, 1882–1908. 6v.

Scope: Covers 479 titles, mostly English and American. Arranged by keyword subject, with title entries for works of fiction, drama, etc.

Access: No author given; citations are very brief, and titles are often rotated, so that the subject word in title appears first. As a collaborative effort, some periodicals were not indexed in full because of failure of a collaborator. Must be used with the *Cumulative Author Index for Poole's Index to Periodical Literature, 1802–1906* (Ann Arbor, Mich.: Pierian, 1971; 488p.) and, usually, *Poole's Index: Date and Volume Key* (Chicago: Assn. of College and Research Libraries, 1957;

61p.). With all this said, this is still the pioneering periodical index from which all others descend and is very useful.

▪ Subject index to periodicals, 1915-1961. London: Library Assn., 1919-62.

Scope: Title varies. Varies in approach over time, but essentially an index to about 500 U.S. and British periodicals up to 1940, with an emphasis on smaller British periodicals from antiquarian societies and the like. After 1940, drops the non-British titles, and thus covers about 300 titles. Succeeded by *British Humanities Index* and *British Technology Index*. To 1922, was a classified index by subject with authors indexed; after 1926 is subject only.

For material and points of view not generally well covered in the above, the following are useful:

▪ Alternative press index. Baltimore, Md.: Alternative Pr. Ctr., 1970- . Quarterly.

Scope: Subject indexing for more than 200 "alternative" periodicals, newspapers, and other serials, mostly North American and nearly all of leftist political persuasion.

Access: Full citation, arranged by subject. Has a tendency to skimp on cross-references, but is very useful for coverage of periodicals not in other indexes. Includes some letters to the editors and excludes poetry, but otherwise complete indexing. Book reviews in a separate section. Cumulations for 1969-1990 and 1991-1995.

▪ HAPI: Hispanic American periodical index, 1970/74- . Los Angeles: UCLA Latin American Studies Center, 1977- . Annual. Also online and on CD-ROM, updated monthly.

Scope: Index to about 250 journals that cover Latin America and Hispanics in the United States. Full coverage for Mexican and Latin American journals; selective coverage for the others. Excludes science and technology articles.

Access: Subject, author, and book reviews in separate sequences. Full citation, in language of original only.

▪ Index to black periodicals. New York: Hall, 1950- . Annual. Formerly *Index to Periodical Articles by and about Blacks,* originally *Index to Selected Periodicals.* Part of *Black Studies on Disc,* 1995- .

Scope: Coverage varies, but tends to index about thirty-five to forty journals, with an emphasis on African Americans (not Africans or South Americans).

Access: Indexed by author and subject. Reviews for some formats (books, film, theater) grouped together. Full citations, with use of plus sign for run-on articles (similar to the Wilson Standard Catalog series format). Has received some criticism for inconsistency in indexing, but the major problem is that it tends to be about two years behind. A useful and important source.

■ The Kaiser index to black resources, 1948–1986. Brooklyn, N.Y.: Carlson, 1992. 5v.

Scope: An index to about 174,000 articles, reviews, obituaries, and so forth from about 150 black journals and newspapers, as well as relevant material from general publications for the period. Based on the "Reference Aids" file of the Schomburg Center for Research in Black Culture.

Access: By subject, with a citation and usually at least a brief annotation. Entries include a key to the Schomburg Center Clipping File plus title, journal (if relevant), date, and pages but not volume. Lacks consistency in use of terms and cross-references but is the only indexing source for most of the titles listed.

■ The left index: a quarterly index to periodicals of the left. Santa Cruz, Calif.: Reference and Research Services, 1982– . Quarterly, with annual cumulations.

Scope: Index to about 100 small periodicals, mostly U.S. but some from Great Britain and Australia.

Access: Author and subject using Library of Congress subject terms. Includes a separate book review index. Full citations are given only in the author and book review lists.

■ U.S. government periodicals index. Bethesda, Md.: Congressional Information Service, 1994– . Quarterly, with annual cumulations. Also online and on CD-ROM.

Scope: Continues *Index to U.S. Government Periodicals* (Chicago: Infordata, 1974–87). An index to about 200 periodicals published by the U.S. government, most not indexed elsewhere. Coverage starts in 1988 to complete the indexing begun by *Index to U.S. Government Periodicals*.

Access: Subject and author index. Full citation, without abstracts.

■ Women studies abstracts. New Brunswick, N.J.: Rutgers Univ., 1971– . Quarterly. Also online and on CD-ROM as part of Women's Resources International.

> *Scope:* More than 160 journals on the subject, with some popular material.

> *Access:* Indexes by author and subject, cumulating annually. Book reviews are listed separately. Complete citations, but contrary to the title's implication, only about 20 percent have abstracts. Not as comprehensive as the British *Studies on Women Abstracts* but very useful for U.S. publications in particular.

■ Women's studies index. Boston: Hall, 1991– . Annual. Also on CD-ROM as part of Women's Studies on Disc, semiannual.

> *Scope:* Covers about 100 titles, from 1990 to the present. Selective for popular magazines but complete indexing for scholarly journals, including reviews and creative works.

> *Access:* Indexed by author, title, subject; searchable electronically by keyword and journal title as well.

Besides the English-language sources above, the following foreign-language materials are of obvious value:

■ Bibliographie der fremdsprachigen Zeitschriftenliteratur/International index to periodicals. Osnabrück: F. Dietrich, 1911–64. Reprint, New York: Kraus Reprints, 1964. 76v.

> Indexing to about 1,400 periodicals and general works in non-German languages. The first series, 1911 to 1921/1925, provides only subject entries; from 1925/1926 includes author indexes as well. Good coverage for American and British periodicals not in other sources, as well as French, Italian, and other European publications. A few years are missing. Merged with a similar index to German-language periodicals to form *IBZ*.

■ Canadian index. Toronto: Micromedia, 1992– . Monthly, with annual cumulations. Also online as Canadian Business and Current Affairs, and on CD-ROM as KIOSK. Coverage from 1980.

> *Scope:* Formed by the merger of three titles: *Canadian News Index, Canadian Business Index,* and *Canadian Magazine Index.* Covers

about 500 periodicals and ten newspapers in the English language, with most published in Canada but about a dozen published in the United States.

Access: Indexing by name, author, subject, corporation. In print, arranged chronologically. Includes book reviews. Full citation with increasing amounts of full text since 1993.

■ Canadian magazine index. Toronto: Micromedia, 1985–92. 8v.

Subject and name index, in separate sections, to about 300 Canadian popular magazines, including many Canadian editions of U.S. titles and many regional magazines. Coverage includes reviews and even rather short articles.

■ Canadian periodical index. Toronto: Gale Canada, 1949– . Monthly, with annual cumulations.

Scope: A subject and name index to about 400 Canadian periodicals, including some major U.S. magazines often found in Canadian libraries. Good coverage of reviews. Unlike *Canadian Index*, tends to cover more scholarly journals.

Access: Full citations are in English, but subject headings, based on *Canadian Thesaurus* (2d ed. Toronto: Info Globe, 1989; 521p.), are in English with French cross-references.

Earlier coverage may be found in *Canadian Periodical Index, 1920–1937: An Author and Subject Index* (Ottawa: Canadian Library Assn., 1988; 567p.) with indexing for twenty periodicals using the format and subject terms in this index. This is followed by *Canadian Index to Periodicals and Documentary Films: An Author and Subject Index, January, 1948–December, 1959* (Ottawa: Canadian Library Assn., 1962; 1180p.).

■ CLASE: Citas Latinoamericanas en ciencias sociales y humanidades. México: Centro de Información Científica y Humanística, 1975– . Quarterly. Also online and on CD-ROM.

An author and keyword index, with abstracts (in Spanish) to about 1,000 social science and humanities periodicals published in Latin America.

■ French periodical index, 1973/74– . Star City, W.Va.: Ponchie, 1974– .

Publisher varies. Covers general-interest French-language magazines, including several Canadian publications. Arranged by fairly broad subject in French.

■ Index to Latin American periodical literature, 1929–1960. Boston: Hall, 1962– . 8v. 1961–65 supplement, 2v. (1968); 1966–70 supplement, 2v. (1980).

Scope: Indexing to about 3,000 periodicals, with coverage beginning in 1929.

Access: To 1951, provides subject access only (but with entries for authors of "literary value"); after 1951, includes author entries. The first supplement excludes coverage of the titles listed in *Indice General de Publicaciones Periódicas Latinoamericanas*, another Hall publication.

■ International African bibliography. London: Mansell, 1971– . Quarterly.

Scope: Replaces the quarterly bibliographic section in the journal *Africa*, 1929–70. Contrary to the title, includes periodical articles. Since 1992 in two parts: one for books; the other, journal articles. Covers about 1,000 periodicals.

Access: Indexes by subject, name, ethnic group, language.

■ Internationale bibliographie der Zeitschriftenliteratur aus alien gebieten des wissens. Osnabrück: Zeller, 1963– . Semiannual. Also on CD-ROM and on the Web, with semiannual updates. Familiarly known as *IBZ*.

Scope: Subject keyword indexing to about 9,000 periodicals, with an author index to these. Continues *Bibliographie der fremdsprachigen Zeitschriftenliteratur* (1911–64) and *Bibliographie der deutschen Zeitschriftenliteratur* (German periodicals, 1896–1964).

Access: Indexing is in German, with a French and English keyword cross-reference. Remains the largest general international index to periodicals. CD-ROM coverage since 1989.

■ Point de repère: index analytique d'articles de périodiques de langue française. Montreal: Services Documentaires Multimedia, 1980– . Ten per year, with annual cumulations. Also online (daily updates) and on CD-ROM (three times per year) as REPÈRE. Continues *RADAR* and *Periodex*, which were a continuation of *Index Analytique*.

About 500 popular and scholarly periodicals in all subjects, with an emphasis on Canadian publications. Includes full text for forty Quebec periodicals, with some hypertext links for the Web version.

Citation Indexes

A few words must be said about a different kind of index with great potential, especially as an access tool—the index by citation. The concept is quite simple, although the execution is not. Most scholarly and technical publishing, especially in the twentieth century, generates citations to sources in the form of footnotes and bibliographical references. Although there are many different reasons to cite material (as further evidence of claims, for amplification of data, to give appropriate credit, even in some cases merely to appear erudite), the fundamental reason a citation appears is that the item cited is related in some way to the document doing the citing.

Thus, the ability to search by the items cited provides a fairly accurate type of indexing by subject, using the relationship of documents rather than codes, words, or terms. This avoids difficulties involved with language and reliance on the indexer's own perception of the subject(s) of a document and the time usually taken to analyze the document.

Although the basic concept can be traced at least to English common law, with its reliance on precedent (and thus the use of citations to existing cases and laws in later cases) (*see* Fred Shapiro, "Origins of Bibliometrics, Citation Indexing and Citation Analysis: The Neglected Legal Literature," *Journal of the American Society for Information Science* 43 [June 1992]: 337–39), the modern citation index really begins with Eugene Garfield's *Science Citation Index* (Philadelphia: Institute for Scientific Information, 1961–) in 1961. Just as, for many years, verbal subject indexes were heavily associated with the Wilson Company, citation indexes remain associated with the Institute for Scientific Information (ISI), a commercial firm founded by Garfield. The following, therefore, describes the general approach of an ISI citation index.

ISI indexes are created by examination of relevant journals in many languages from many countries. Selection of these journals is basically by an analysis of the literature, so that any journal routinely cited by other journals, and itself containing citations, becomes a candidate for indexing. As each new journal is received, staff at ISI prepare an entry for every citation in every article; thus, a review article with 500 different items cited will obtain 500 different citation access points (one point per document cited). These citations may be any form of communication, including periodical articles, book chapters, books, patents, laws, letters, personal communications, and any other communication format. (Although the documents indexed are, with few exceptions, journal articles, the access points to these are the citations to any type of communication medium.) In addition to the citations, a "Permuterm Subject Index" consisting of keywords from the article titles is created, as is a broad classification code based on the general subject matter of the journal. And, in recent years, the indexes also include keywords assigned by the author (as many journals now require) and other terms based on the titles of the documents cited. The three main citation indexes, *Arts and Humanities Citation Index, Science Citation Index,* and *Social Sciences Citation Index,* are listed later in this chapter in more detail within the appropriate subjects.

For further discussion of citation indexing and the products of ISI, see Eugene Garfield, *Citation Indexing—Its Theory and Application in Science, Technology and Humanities* (New York: Wiley, 1979; 274p.). A brief account is also available in a series of articles within the title "The ISI Essays" <http://www.isinet.com/hot/essays> and on the ISI Web page as "Cited Reference Searching: A Primer" <http://www.isinet.com/training/jobaids/citrefpr/>.

Table of Contents Services

Another newer type of access to periodicals is the table of contents service. When many special libraries began circulating photocopies of the contents pages of journals they received to their staff, it was probably inevitable that sooner or later collective services would begin, much as Poole began replacing the individual periodical article analytics for subject access. The following are general sources; similar tools are listed under the appropriate subject section.

An interesting comparison of four of the major electronic services may be found in Janice M. Jaguszewski and Jody L. Kempf, "Four Current Awareness Databases: Coverage and Currency Compared" (*Database* [Feb./March 1995]: 34-44), which provides a detailed comparison, with examples from mathematics and chemistry.

▪ Contents first. Dublin, Ohio: OCLC, 1990- . Daily updates. Online only.

> *Scope*: Tables of contents for more than 15,000 journals, nearly all in English, with many titles from the British Library's *Inside Information Series* (*see* below, p. 120-21) being added. Titles are those most likely to be held in U.S. libraries and include many from the standard indexes. Covers science, technology, and medicine, with considerable coverage for the social sciences.

Access: The usual access points, but also has Library of Congress subjects for the journals, allowing focused access. Document delivery and an alerting service are available.

■ Current contents. Philadelphia: Institute for Scientific Information, 1959– . Weekly. Also on diskette, CD-ROM, and online.

Scope: In printed form, in several pamphlets, each covering a broad subject, for a total of about 6,000 journals. Covers all journals indexed in the ISI citation indexes. Unlike the other services, includes many multiauthor books, monographic series, and some conference proceedings. Current editions cover *Agriculture, Biology and Environmental Sciences; Arts and Humanities; Clinical Medicine; Engineering, Computing and Technology; Life Sciences; Physical, Chemical and Earth Sciences; Social and Behavioral Sciences.*

Access: Arranged by broad subject, then journal title and issue number within subjects. Author and keyword indexes weekly. Online author, keyword, journal access. Each edition also includes an author and publisher name and address directory. Because entire tables of contents are listed, all book reviews are also accessible. Document delivery for any title published in the last four years available from ISI through a service that can, if desired, nearly always provide the actual pages (rather than a photocopy or electronic copy). An alerting service is available for an additional fee. The electronic versions also include author abstracts.

■ Faxon finder. Westwood, Mass.: Faxon, 1993– . Online and on CD-ROM only. Updates weekly.

Scope: Tables of contents for about 12,000 periodicals in all subjects since 1990, covering many languages. Includes book reviews, letters, etc.

Access: By broad subject only. Keyword, author, etc. searching possible. Gives full citation and abstracts for many articles.

■ Inside science plus. Boston Spa, England: British Library Document Supply Centre, 1997– . CD-ROM only. Updated monthly.

Scope: Contents pages of about 13,000 international science and technology journals, with abstracts for many articles. Covers from 1971 to date. Includes many journals not in the other tables of contents sources.

Access: In addition to the usual access points, this includes hypertext links. Unlike the other sources noted here, users cannot re-create the exact tables of contents by volume and issue. Document delivery is available via Research Libraries Group (RLG) as well as the British Library.

■ Inside social sciences and humanities plus. Boston Spa, England: British Library Document Supply Centre, 1997– . CD-ROM only. Updated monthly.

Scope: Contents pages of about 7,000 journals in business, the arts, and humanities from many countries. Covers from 1971 to date. Includes many journals not in the other tables of contents sources.

Access: In addition to the usual access points, this includes hypertext links. Unlike the other sources noted here, users cannot re-create the exact tables of contents by volume and issue. Document delivery is available via RLG as well as the British Library.

The contents of the two titles above are also available as Inside Information Plus, from RLG, on the Web.

■ Periodicals contents index. Cambridge, England: Chadwyck-Healey, 1993– . CD-ROM only.

Scope: In two series, one covering 1900 to 1960, the other 1961 to 1990/1991. Tables of contents for about 3,500 humanities and social sciences journals held in the Harvard University libraries; international coverage.

Access: This is searchable by title keyword and author, as well as browseable by journal title and issue; each periodical title (but not article titles) is assigned a broad subject classification.

■ UnCover. Denver, Colo.: UnCover, 1988– . Online only. Updated daily. Formerly known as CARL UnCover.

Scope: Tables of contents of about 15,000 English-language periodicals held in major Colorado libraries. Emphasis is on science and technology, but all subjects are covered in some detail.

Access: Journal title, author, and title keyword searching possible. Also provides Reveal, an alerting service, in which new articles of interest (based on a user's profile) will be brought to the user's attention as they are entered into the database.

An important feature is that search access to this database on the Web is free; however, Reveal and document delivery still incur charges.

Additional indexes may be found in sources listed not only in general guides to reference books, such as *Balay*, but also in guides to individual fields and in the general periodicals directories. Also William A. Katz and Linda Sternberg Katz's *Magazines for Libraries*, 9th ed. (New Providence, N.J.: Bowker/Reed Reference, 1997; 1350p.) gives bibliographic data and descriptive and evaluative annotations for many periodical indexing and abstracting services in an introductory section. The most complete coverage at this time is probably

■ Index and abstract directory. Birmingham, Ala.: EBSCO, 1989– . Biennial.

> Lists more than 950 indexing and abstracting services, giving coverage, publisher, and price.

This sort of information is also available in online sources, such as Dialog's Journal Name Finder database (which tells which Dialog databases index a given journal) and in CONSER records on such cataloging utilities as OCLC (and often, the records based on these as found in local and regional union catalogs). Cooperative ONline SERials (CONSER) is a Library of Congress-sponsored program to provide high-quality cataloging for serials and, beginning in the 1980s, to add information as to coverage by indexing and abstracting services for each title to online records. In addition, *Ulrich's*, the *Standard Periodical Directory*, and EBSCO's own *Serials Directory*, all described in chapter 2, also carry such notations with the periodical's title entry.

Subject Indexes to Periodicals

Art

■ Art index. Bronx, N.Y.: Wilson, 1929– . Quarterly, with annual cumulations. Also online and on CD-ROM, 1984– . Updated as often as twice weekly. Electronic cumulation from 1929 to 1984 coming soon.

> *Scope*: About 300 periodicals as well as yearbooks and museum bulletins in many languages covering all types of art, media, and periods.

> *Access*: Indexing by author and subject. Includes indexing to reproductions of individual works of art (under artist's name unless there is considerable text with the illustration). Separate index to book reviews. Also includes film and TV reviews. Full citation with each

entry, following usual Wilson format. *Art Abstracts* adds 50- to 150-word abstracts for items added since 1994.

■ Avery index to architectural periodicals. New York: Columbia Univ. Avery Architecture and Fine Arts Library, 1963- . 15v., with annual supplement. Also online and on CD-ROM as Avery Architecture Index, 1977- .

> *Scope*: About 1,000 periodicals in art history, architecture, decorative arts.
>
> *Access*: Author, title, subject, location, in one sequence. Includes "significant" book reviews and obituaries.

■ BHA: bibliography of the history of art. Santa Monica, Calif.: J. Paul Getty Museum, 1991- . Also online and on CD-ROM.

> *Scope*: Replaces *RAA* and *RILA*—covers Western art in all its aspects, indexing periodical articles, books, dissertations, and other formats. Exact coverage of a given journal title varies so that there is no gap in indexing between this and its predecessors.
>
> *Access*: Classified by subject, with subject, journal, and author indexes. Provides full citation. Available in both English and French editions.
>
> RAA: le répertoire d'archéologie. Paris: Morancé, 1910-89. Annual. Formerly *Répertoire d'art et d'archéologie.*
>
> Indexed periodical articles and, after 1920, books in all fields of art. Classified by subject, with indexes by author and place. After 1973, indexed by artists, author, and specific subject.
>
> RILA: international repertory of the literature of art. New York: College Art Assn. of America, 1975-89.
>
> An index to articles, books, dissertations, exhibition catalogs, and similar material in all art fields. Arranged by broad subject, with author and detailed subject indexes.

Biological Sciences

■ Biological abstracts. Philadelphia: Biological Abstracts, 1926- . Semimonthly, with indexes cumulated twice per year. Five-year cumulations. Online as part of BIOSIS Previews, 1969- , and on CD-ROM, 1980- .

> *Scope*: International coverage of more than 9,500 journals, serials, proceedings, and the like in all languages, with abstracts. Includes not

only biology, but also agriculture, psychology, basic medicine, and veterinary medicine.

Access: Print is arranged by broad subject classification. Subject, author, taxonomic headings (Biosystematic Codes). Entries give exact citation and abstracts for most records and foreign and English translation for article titles.

■ Biological and agricultural index. Bronx, N.Y.: Wilson, 1964– . Monthly except August; annual and quarterly cumulations. Also online and on CD-ROM, 1983– . Updated as often as two times per week.

Subject index to all aspects of both subjects, but about half the 225 or so periodicals are agricultural in nature, and most are U.S. publications. Excludes general journals such as *Nature*. Full citations following Wilson indexing format, with book reviews in a separate section.

Business

■ ABI/INFORM. Ann Arbor, Mich.: Bell & Howell, 1971– . Online and on CD-ROM only. Updated as often as weekly.

Scope: Indexes about 1,000 journals in business, management, and related areas, including information technology, all in English.

Access: Indexing by geographic area, subject, and broad subject and product codes. Full citations include both exact pages and a page count. In many ways is similar to *Wilson Business Abstracts* in covering more general practical and theoretical topics, with less detailed access to individual companies and products. Includes full text for a growing number of titles.

■ Business periodicals index. New York: Wilson, 1958– . Monthly except July, with quarterly and annual cumulations. Also online and on CD-ROM (1982–), with updating as frequently as daily.

Scope: Covers about 400 periodicals in English, including the *Wall Street Journal* and the business section of the *New York Times,* with increasing coverage for Asia in recent years. Covers all aspects of business in general, as well as specific industries and companies, plus taxation, public administration, labor and management, and related topics.

Access: Has geographic and name headings and selected author indexing in one sequence, with book reviews in a separate section, like other Wilson indexes. Full citation, in usual Wilson style.

Wilson Business Abstracts (1982–) includes 50- to 150-word abstracts. *Wilson Business Abstracts Full Text* includes full text of about 150 of the periodicals indexed since 1995. Both are online and on CD-ROM only.

■ Consumers index to product evaluations and information sources. Ann Arbor, Mich.: Pierian, 1972– . Quarterly, with annual cumulations. Also online and on CD-ROM, 1986– .

Scope: Includes service industries, such as restaurants, clubs, hotels, etc., as well as tangible products. Covers about 100 English-language periodicals, including *Consumer Reports* and *Consumer's Digest*, plus company and government bulletins.

Access: Arranged by broad classifications. Indexed by subject, product, company, items recalled. Full citations, plus abstracts (many quite detailed) and evaluation codes. Includes websites for recalls and product alerts, when available.

■ F & S index. Foster City, Calif.: Information Access. Monthly, with quarterly and annual cumulations. In three parts: United States, 1960– ; Europe, 1978– ; International, 1967– . Also online and on CD-ROM, 1972– , in one file.

Scope: Printed coverage as noted; electronic formats usually contain all three sections. Indexes more than 2,000 periodicals.

Access: Indexing by product, company, event (e.g., news event, type of manufacturing), country covered. Full citation, including brief abstract. The major emphasis here is on specific companies and products.

Chemistry

■ Chemical Abstracts Service. Chemical abstracts. Columbus, Ohio: American Chemical Society, 1907– . Weekly. Also online and on CD-ROM, 1967– .

Scope: More than 14,000 journals in all languages, plus patents from about thirty countries. Part of a family of products that includes a subject-related weekly alerting service, CA Select, which is a registry of chemical compounds (roughly equivalent to the ISBN for books), ring indexes, etc.

Access: Weekly indexes by keyword, patent, and author. Six-month cumulated indexes by author, general subject, chemical substance, formula, and patent. The print version is being rapidly replaced by online and CD-ROM versions, which have the advantages of computer searching and a substantial lack of bulk compared to the printed product. Also notable is the version mounted by CAS's own search service, STN, which allows graphical searching by use of chemical structures and symbols. Gives full citation, including abstract.

Education

■ Current index to journals in education. Columbus, Ohio: Macmillan (published by Oryx since 1979), 1969- . Monthly, with semiannual cumulations. Also online and on CD-ROM, 1966- .

> *Scope*: Contrary to the title, *CIJE* is actually an abstracting service, covering about 1,000 journals, nearly all in English. *Education* is broadly defined to include considerable coverage of librarianship and information transfer, vocational training, continuing education, etc.

> *Access*: Arranged by broad classification, also has author and subject indexes, which include the citation. Online and on CD-ROM, as well as several (incomplete) website versions, include thesauri and *ERIC Digests* (state-of-the-art reviews on topics of current interest). Most electronic versions include this and *RIE (Resources in Education)* in the same database. Includes full citation, including (usually) a short abstract and subject indexing fields. Printed version indexes by author and subject and gives full citation as well.

■ Education index. New York: Wilson, 1929- . Ten per year, with annual cumulations. Also online and on CD-ROM, 1984- . Updated as often as twice weekly.

> *Scope*: About 350 English-language periodicals (mostly U.S. periodicals), yearbooks, and monographs.

> *Access*: Subject and author index; separate book review section. Full citation, following Wilson conventions; reviews in a separate section. Has been compared both favorably and unfavorably with *CIJE*, but it seems to be holding its own to date.

> *Education Abstracts* adds abstracts to the indexing from 1994; *Education Abstracts Full Text* adds full text of about 130 periodicals to this. Both are available online and on CD-ROM only.

Film, Television, and Video

■ Film literature index. Albany: State University of New York at Albany, 1973- . Quarterly, with annual cumulations.

Scope: About 340 titles, from more than thirty countries, relating to film, television, and video. Includes obituaries and reviews.

Access: Subject and author index, with separate sections for film and video materials. Book reviews are under both author and subject. Gives full citation with, as relevant, notes as to the presence of filmographies, credits, biographical notes, etc.

■ International index to film periodicals. London: International Federation of Film Archives, 1972– . Annual.

Scope: About eighty-five periodicals, including references to individual films and persons.

Access: Classified by subject, film title, and biographical entries. Indexes by author and director. Gives full citation; many entries have brief annotations.

Genealogy

■ Genealogical periodical annual index. Bowie, Md.: Heritage Books, 1962– . Annual.

■ Successor to D. L. Jacobus, *Index to Genealogical Periodicals* (Baltimore, Md.: Genealogical Pub., 1978; 365p.).

Scope: Covers about 300 English-language genealogical periodicals, mostly local journals and newsletters.

Access: Indexes to names, localities, topic. Also indexes book reviews.

■ Periodical source index. Fort Wayne, Ind.: Allen County Public Library, 1986– . Annual.

Scope: Indexes about 5,000 periodicals, making this the most complete such index available. Retrospective coverage in sixteen volumes (from 1847 to 1985) is continued by the annuals. As a new title is added, the full run is indexed up to that point in the year added, so publication date is not reflective of coverage date.

Access: Full citation, with indexes by family name, place-name, and subject. Tied to a document-delivery service for all items, available for a fee from the library, which has one of the world's largest genealogy collections.

History

■ America: history and life. Santa Barbara, Calif.: ABC-Clio, 1964– . Five per year. Also online and on CD-ROM.

> *Scope*: The history and prehistory of North America. More than 2,000 journals in about forty languages, books reviewed in major journals, and dissertations in history.

> *Access*: Indexing includes a permuted subject display, plus indexing by date(s) covered in each item, in effect treating the historical period covered as a subject. There is also a volume 0, with citations and abstracts on this area from *Historical Abstracts,* published from 1954 to 1963. Gives exact citation plus the abstract.

■ Historical abstracts, 1775–1945: bibliography of the world's periodical literature. Santa Barbara, Calif.: ABC-Clio, 1955– . Also online and on CD-ROM. Three per year, plus annual index.

> *Scope*: Covers the rest of the world not covered by *America: History and Life (AHL)*. In two parts. Part A covers from 1450 to 1914; part B, 1914 to the present. Otherwise, nearly identical to *AHL,* with appropriately variant time and national divisions.

Humanities

■ Arts and humanities citation index. Philadelphia: Institute for Scientific Information, 1976– . Three per year, with annual cumulations. Also online and on CD-ROM, with weekly updates.

> *Scope*: Interdisciplinary in many languages in the humanities, including Asian studies, folklore, archaeology, history, film/radio/television, as well as the usual humanities subjects. Indexes about 1,000 journals in full with selective coverage of related articles in around 6,100 more.

> *Access*: Follows the pattern of all the ISI indexes. Each artwork is treated separately as a "citation" even if there is no formal footnote; similarly, general in-text references are also separately treated (e.g., citations from classical authors, as in Aristotle, *Politics,* II, b, 2). Indexed by author/editor/artist, Permuterm subject, and corporate body. Primary entry is by source journal; gives full citation, usually a brief abstract (since 1993), and a complete list of citations in abbreviated form. Entries include author addresses and affiliations, indication of document type, and the total number of citations made.

- British humanities index. East Grinstead, England: Bowker/K. G. Saur, 1962- . Quarterly. Also on CD-ROM, 1985- , as BHI PLUS.

  Scope: Partial continuation of *Subject Index to Periodicals, which see* (p. 113). About 350 British journals, with some newspaper coverage. Has a very broad definition of *the humanities* to include history, economics, society in general. Includes some indexing of humanities-oriented articles in science and technology journals.

  Access: Classified by subject, with indexes by author, subject, and source journal. Gives full citation, with abstracts included since 1993.

- FRANCIS. Vandoeuvre-lès-Nancy: France Institut de l'Information Scientifique et Technique, 1972. Monthly updates. Online and on CD-ROM only, 1991- .

  Scope: Includes the nineteen humanities and social sciences parts of *Bulletin Signalétique*. Indexing for philosophy, religion, psychology, history of science, sociology, education, the arts, history and archaeology, area studies, business, economics, public health, etc.

  Access: Full citation with abstracts in French. Indexing in French, with keywords also in English.

- Humanities index. Bronx, N.Y.: Wilson, 1974- . Quarterly, with annual cumulations. Also online and on CD-ROM, 1984- .

  Scope: About 350 scholarly English-language journals in archaeology, folklore, history, literature, philosophy, and related subjects.

  Access: Author and subject entries, with book reviews in a separate section. Follows the Wilson pattern of nearly complete citations.

  Humanities Abstracts adds abstracts to the indexing, 1993- .

Law

- Index to legal periodicals and books. Bronx, N.Y.: Wilson, 1908- . Monthly, with quarterly and annual cumulations. Also online and on CD-ROM, 1981- .

  Scope: Covers about 800 U.S., British, Canadian, Australian, and New Zealand (but definite U.S. slant) English-language periodicals, yearbooks, and annuals, with monographs added since 1993 and a few non-English journals starting to appear as well.

Access: Index by author and title, cases, and statutes, with a separate section for book reviews. Standard legal citation format, which is a bit different from the usual Wilson format.

■ Index to periodical articles related to law. Dobbs Ferry, N.Y.: Glanville, 1958- .

Covers legal and law-related articles in general periodicals and other periodicals not in the legal indexes. Cumulations for 1958 to 1988 in four volumes; from 1989 to 1993, one volume; and from 1994 to 1998, one volume.

The LEXIS-NEXIS and WESTLAW databases also include files indexing legal periodicals.

Library and Information Sciences

■ Information science abstracts. Wilmington, N.Y.: Plenum, 1966- . Monthly, except June and July; annual cumulations. Also online and on CD-ROM. Formerly *Documentation Abstracts.*

Scope: Indexes journals plus books, reports, conference proceedings (a particular strength), patents, etc. in all aspects of information science, including many not covered in *Library Literature* and Library and Information Science Abstracts (LISA). International coverage, but most indexed items are in English, with some other languages.

Access: Arranged by classified subject, with subject and author indexes, cumulated annually in last issue. Indexing by keyword to 1983, by controlled vocabulary descriptors from 1984 to date. Full citation plus abstract. Titles in original and English translation.

■ LISA: Library and information science abstracts. East Grinstead, England: Bowker/K. G. Saur, 1969- . Monthly, with annual cumulations. Successor to *Library Science Abstracts,* 1950-68.

Scope: Very strong international coverage of journal articles, books, pamphlets, and reports, with surprisingly little overlap with *Library Literature.* Coverage is selective, so this does not always cover all articles in all journals covered.

Access: Major revision in 1993 in indexing and arrangement. Indexes by author, subject, source journal. The older issues make use of what, to many, was a complex and abstruse classification system. Americans should remember that terminology is British (e.g., "interloan" for "interlibrary loan"). Note, too, that there was an author index before 1979 and since 1993; in between, the index included personal names, not only authors. Full citation, plus an abstract usually prepared by a British librarian.

■ LISA plus. Available online and on CD-ROM.

Includes LISA and *Current Research,* a description of current and recent research in progress, with abstracts written by the principal investigator. LISA attempts to get the investigators to update the entries in the latter with progress reports and citations to final products but is not always successful.

■ Library literature: an index to library and information science. Bronx, N.Y.: Wilson, 1934– . Bimonthly, with annual cumulations. Also online and on CD-ROM, updated up to twice a week.

Scope: Articles from about 230 English- and foreign-language periodicals as well as current books, pamphlets, unpublished theses. Coverage tends to emphasize library science and bibliography more than information science.

Access: Author/subject indexing, with a separate book review section in printed form. Standard Wilson approach, with generally full citations.

Retrospective coverage may be found in

■ Barr, L. J., and others. Libraries in American periodicals before 1876. Jefferson, N.C.: McFarland, 1983. 426p.

Coverage predating Cannon's *Bibliography.* Reprints articles of less than 150 words, with similar-length abstracts for longer articles. Arranged geographically, with indexes by author, title, and subject. Because there were no periodicals formally given to librarianship at the time, coverage extends to many types of literary and technical journals.

■ Cannon, Harry George Turner. Bibliography of library economy: a classified index to the professional periodical literature in the English language relating to library economy, printing, methods of publishing, copyright, bibliography, etc. from 1876 to 1920. Chicago: ALA, 1927. Reprinted by several different publishers.

English-language articles in sixty-five journals with some coverage of general periodicals. Classified with an alphabetical subject index.

■ Jordan, Anne H., and Melbourne Jordan. Cannon's bibliography of library economy, 1876–1920: an author index with citations. Metuchen, N.J.: Scarecrow, 1976. 473p.

> Full citations to all Cannon's items with a known author; because Cannon did not give author, essential for such searches.

Mathematics

■ Mathematical reviews. Providence, R.I.: American Mathematical Society, 1940– . Monthly, with annual cumulations. Also online and on CD-ROM as MathSci.

> *Scope:* Abstracts plus signed critical reviews of math-related books, from around 1,500 U.S. and foreign journals, books, and proceedings.

> *Access:* Classified by subject, with monthly and cumulated author indexes. Full citation, with abstracts; for books, an evaluative review.

Medicine

■ Cumulative index to nursing and allied health literature (CINAHL). Glendale, Calif.: CINAHL Information Systems, 1956– . Bimonthly, with annual cumulations. Also online and on CD-ROM.

> *Scope:* Journals and pamphlets in nursing and the allied health fields, including consumer health, health science librarianship, medical records, dental hygiene, legal issues, and related topics. Covers about 800 English-language journals in nursing plus about twenty in allied health.

> *Access:* Full citation plus abstracts. Author and subject indexes.

■ Excerpta medica. Amsterdam: Elsevier Science, 1947– . Also online and on CD-ROM, with updates as often as weekly.

> *Scope:* Indexes about 3,600 journals in biomedical and biological topics related to medicine. Includes good coverage of history of medicine, anthropology, health economics, forensics, occupational and public health, and medical topics.

> *Access:* On paper in thirty-three bulletins covering separate subjects, plus a drug literature bibliography. Gives full citation, with abstracts for about 75 percent of file. Indexed by a classified system, EMTREE (*Excerpta Medica* Tree Structure), and subject.

■ Index medicus. Washington, D.C.: National Library of Medicine, 1879-99, v.1-21; 2d series, 1903-20, v.1-18; 3d series, 1921-27, v.1-6; 1916-56 as *Quarterly Cumulative Index to Current Medical Literature;* new series, 1960, v.1- . Monthly. Annual cumulations under title *Cumulated Index Medicus.* Online and on CD-ROM in several formats and such vendors as MEDLINE.

> *Scope:* Very comprehensive index to articles from more than 3,000 medical journals in all languages, giving English translations for foreign titles. Detailed and extensive coverage of even short articles, important letters, etc., with a specific emphasis on rapid indexing of a core of important journals.

> *Access:* The monthly and annual print volumes are arranged by subject and use Medical Subject Headings (MeSH), which are updated annually, with an author index, which includes coauthors. The print entry is the bare citation; in the electronic versions, abstracts are included. The print version also contains a separate listing of review articles that includes the number of citations in each article.

Music

■ MUSE. Baltimore, Md.: National Information Services, 1992- . CD-ROM only. Semiannual update.

> *Scope:* Includes all entries from the *Library of Congress Catalog— Music, Books on Music and Sound Recordings,* from 1960 to date, and from *RILM Abstracts of Music Literature* (New York: International Repertoire of Music Literature, 1967- ; annual).

> *Access:* Citation and abstracts, searchable by fields and by keyword.

■ Music index: the key to current music periodical literature. Warren, Mich.: Harmonie Pr., 1949- . Monthly, with biennial cumulations. Also on CD-ROM since 1979; annual updates.

> *Scope:* About 350 European and American music journals, plus some music-related articles from general periodicals and books.

> *Access:* Author, proper name, and subject indexes, with music reviews listed under composer, title, and medium; book reviews under that heading. Gives full bibliographic citation.

Philosophy

■ The philosopher's index. Bowling Green, Ohio: Philosopher's Information Center and Bowling Green State Univ., 1967- . Quarterly, with annual cumulations. Also online and on CD-ROM.

> Scope: Major American and British philosophical journals, with some coverage of other languages and interdisciplinary publications, for a total of about 350 periodicals, plus a varying number of books.

> Access: Author index with full citation; indexes by subject. Separate book review section. Books receive an entry; anthologies also have analytics. Full citations, normally with an abstract.

■ The philosopher's index: a retrospective index to U.S. publications from 1940. Bowling Green, Ohio: Bowling Green State Univ., 1978. 3v. Also online and on CD-ROM.

> Covers journals, 1940 through 1966, as well as books, 1940 through 1976. The online and CD-ROM versions include both this and the current index.

Psychology

■ Psychological abstracts. Lancaster, Pa., and Washington, D.C.: American Psychological Assn., 1927- . Also online and on CD-ROM.

> Scope: U.S. and foreign books, periodicals, dissertations, report literature, in many languages.

> Access: Arranged by broad classification, with indexes by author, brief subject, and book title. Annual cumulated index has greatly expanded subject access. Full citation, plus abstract. The electronic versions include the indexing fields and also a brief telegraphic abstract (used as an entry point in the cumulative subject index) as well as the citation and longer abstract.

> Online as PsychINFO, with greater coverage than the printed version since 1980; same as print, from 1967 to 1979.

> Retrospective access is assisted by the following:

■ Author index to Psychological index 1894 to 1935 and Psychological abstracts 1927 to 1958. Boston: Hall, 1960. 5v.

■ Cumulative author index to Psychological abstracts, 1959–63- . Washington, D.C.: American Psychological Assn., 1965- . Triennial.

■ Cumulated subject index to Psychological abstracts. Boston: Hall, 1968. 5v.

Covers 1927 to 1968.

■ Cumulative subject index to Psychological abstracts. Washington, D.C.: American Psychological Assn., 1971–77.

Covers 1969 to 1977.

Religion

■ Catholic periodical and literature index. Pittsfield, Mass.: Catholic Library Assn., 1930– . Quarterly, with biennial cumulations.

Scope: Combines and continues *Catholic Periodical Index* (from 1930 to 1966) and *The Guide to Catholic Literature*. About 160 Catholic periodicals (mostly American), books by and about Catholics, and major papal documents.

Access: Author, subject, book review, book title indexes. Uses the same subject authority list as *Religion Index One* and *Two,* making searching easier between these indexes.

■ Religion index one: periodicals. Evanston, Ill.: American Theological Library Assn., 1978– . Semiannual, with annual cumulations. Part of ATLA Religion Database online and CD-ROM, covering 1960– .

Scope: Continues *Index to Religious Periodical Literature* (from 1949 to 1976). About 150 American and foreign periodicals, with good coverage of archaeology as well as religion. Mostly Protestant point of view.

Access: Arranged by author, with abstracts. Separate indexes by subject, scriptural reference, book reviews. Shares subject authority list with *Catholic Periodical and Literature Index.* Gives exact citation. The companion volume is *Religion Index Two: Multi-author Works.*

Science and Technology

■ Applied science and technology index. Bronx, N.Y.: Wilson, 1913– . Monthly except July; annual cumulations. Also online and on CD-ROM since 1983; updated as often as semiweekly. Formerly *Industrial Arts Index.*

Scope: Subject index to about 400 journals in English or with English abstracts from all fields of engineering and applied aspects of technology. Emphasis is on applications over theory.

Access: Arranged by subject. Book and product reviews in a separate section. Complete citation, as in other Wilson indexes.

Applied Science and Technology Abstracts adds abstracting to the indexing since 1993; available online and on CD-ROM only.

■ General science index. Bronx, N.Y.: Wilson, 1978– . Ten times per year, with annual cumulations. Also online and on CD-ROM, 1984– . Updated as often as semiweekly.

Scope: The newest of Wilson's subject indexes, covering about 150 general science periodicals, including some also in *Readers' Guide*. A useful collection of journals, but the clear emphasis is the student and layperson.

Access: Indexed by subject, with a separate book review section in printed form. Full citations, as with all the Wilson indexes.

General Science Abstracts, 1993– , includes indexing plus abstracts. *General Science Abstracts Full Text* adds the full text of about forty periodicals, 1995– . Available online and on CD-ROM only.

■ PASCAL. Vandoeuvre-lès-Nancy: France Institut de l'Information Scientifique et Technique, 1973– . Online and on CD-ROM only.

Scope: A replacement to about sixty-five sections of *Bullétin Signalétique* science indexes. Indexes about 5,000 periodicals plus books, theses, reports, and proceedings. International coverage in many languages.

Access: Full citation, plus abstract and subject indexing (classification and specific subjects). Most citations include French, plus English and German subject terms.

■ Science citation index. Philadelphia: Institute for Scientific Information, 1961– . v.1– . Bimonthly, with annual cumulations. The online versions are updated weekly, with many journals indexed the same week received. Also on CD-ROM.

Scope: Covers about 3,600 journals, plus relevant articles in social sciences and humanities and, since 1977, books, symposia, and proceedings. Subject emphasis is biology, chemistry, physics, engineering, mathematics, and some behavioral science journals, although the latter are better covered in *Social Sciences Citation Index.*

Access: Available in a multiple-section printed form, but online, CD-ROM, and Web versions are much easier to use. The important feature of this, as with the other ISI citation indexes, is the indexing by cited reference as well as by author and subject. *See* above (p. 118-19) for comments on citation indexing. Full citations for citing references are given in the *Source Index;* only abbreviated ones for the cited references. Includes abstracts since early 1991 if the journal contains them.

Cumulative backfiles are available for 1945 to 1954 and 1955 to 1964; five-year cumulations, 1965 to date.

Social Sciences

■ ASSIA: applied social sciences index and abstracts. East Grinstead, England: Bowker/K. G. Saur, 1987- . Bimonthly, with annual cumulations. Also online and on CD-ROM as ASSIA PLUS.

Scope: An interdisciplinary index to the applied aspects of all the social and behavioral sciences, covering about 600 journals, about 46 percent U.S., 40 percent British, the rest from Europe and the Commonwealth.

Access: Classified subject arrangement, with indexes by specific subject, author, and source. Available online as ASSIA PLUS. Entries include an abstract.

■ FRANCIS. Vandoeuvre-lès-Nancy: France Institut de l'Information Scientifique et Technique, 1972. Monthly updates. Online and on CD-ROM only, 1991- .

Scope: Includes the nineteen humanities and social sciences parts of *Bulletin Signalétique. See* under "Humanities" for description.

■ PAIS international in print. New York: Public Affairs Information Service, 1915- . Monthly, with quarterly and annual cumulations. Also online and on CD-ROM, 1972- . Formerly titled *Public Affairs Information Service Bulletin;* combined with the PAIS *Foreign Language Index* (which began in 1968).

Scope: Social sciences material of all kinds, including about 3,000 periodicals but also monographs, government publications, statutes, etc. in English, French, Spanish, German, Italian, and Portuguese. Has a broad definition of "public affairs," well beyond political science and diplomacy, and is also useful for its broad coverage yet detailed indexing of government documents, especially non-U.S. items.

Access: Author and subject index. Full citations in all entries, with many short annotations, and such additional information as UN and U.S. SuDocs classifications where relevant.

■ Social sciences citation index. Philadelphia: Institute for Scientific Information, 1969– . Three per year. Cumulations for 1956-65, then five-year cumulations. Also online and on CD-ROM.

Scope: Citation index to about 2,000 journals in all languages in all areas of the social sciences, plus additional entries for relevant articles from the other ISI citation indexes.

Access: See under Citation Indexes for details of coverage and arrangement. Updated weekly. Includes very good coverage for book reviews.

■ Social sciences index. New York: Wilson, 1974– . Quarterly, with annual cumulations. Successor to *Social Sciences and Humanities Index,* 1907-74. Also online and on CD-ROM since 1984. Updated as often as semiweekly in electronic form.

Scope: Subject and author access to about 350 key journals in social sciences, all in English but international in place of publication. Note that, unlike some other indexes, history is considered one of the humanities and thus is not particularly covered in this index.

Access: The usual Wilson arrangement, in one alphabet, with book reviews in a separate section. Full citations, except for run-on articles. *Social Sciences Abstracts,* 1994 to date, adds abstracts to the indexing. *Social Sciences Abstracts Full Text* adds full text to the abstracts for more than 100 periodicals since 1995.

A Proquest version is available via UMI's Proquest system, which includes the full image (including all graphics) for nearly all the journals indexed.

For retrospective coverage, *see*

■ Cumulative subject index to PAIS bulletins, 1915-1974. Arlington, Va.: Carrollton Pr., 1977-78. 15v.

Gives subject terms plus citation to the bulletin, not the original citation.

Newspaper Indexing and Abstracting Services

Tremendous strides have been made in recent years in newspaper indexes, with well over 500 in North America alone. They vary greatly in scope and form, and the best known are produced by commercial firms, although many libraries have maintained at least partial indexes to local papers for many years. In the past, many librarians relied heavily on the *New York Times Index* as a first source, because most metropolitan papers publish news on a given subject at about the same time. Although this is changing with the increase in availability both of indexes and of the full text of more newspapers online or on CD-ROM, the *New York Times* and London *Times* indexes remain very important.

■ Canadian news index. Toronto: Micromedia, 1977–92. Formerly *Canadian Newspaper Index*, absorbed into *Canadian Index* (*see under* "General").

Subject access to the microfilmed editions of seven Canadian newspapers, with a personal name index. Includes various types of reviews. Excludes very local material. Is keyed to a service that provides copies of individual articles.

■ Ethnic newswatch. Stamford, Conn.: Softline Information, 1991– . Monthly updates. Online and on CD-ROM only.

Scope: An example of what newspaper indexes may look like in the future. Nearly 200 newspapers and periodicals covering all ethnic groups (including some for European-American groups). There is no print equivalent.

Access: Indexing both in Spanish and English. Full text of papers, with broad term indexing terms added.

■ New York times index. New York: New York Times Co., 1913– . Semimonthly, with quarterly and annual cumulations. Also online and on CD-ROM as New York Times Abstracts.

Scope: Covers the late city edition (the one available in microform), weekly and Sunday, including all the sections, such as the *Book Review, New York Times Magazine,* etc.

Access: Arranged by subject, organization, location, then chronologically under each heading. Reviews are indexed under the appropriate heading, then alphabetically. Entries give byline and title where available, section, column, page, and date, but, because the year is given on each page in the paper version, not year. (Novices often forget to write down the year, which is frustrating.) Citations give author, title, date, section, page number, with very brief abstracts, arranged in chronological order under each subject.

Given the purpose of this newspaper as the newspaper of record, and the detail of indexing, this index has often been used as a key to other papers' coverage. Having obtained the date(s) of coverage in the *Times,* one can then check other newspapers for dates a few days before and after these, with a good probability of finding relevant articles.

■ New York times index: prior series. New York: Bowker, 1966–76. 15v.

A combination of reproductions of an internal index (handwritten in the early years) with new indexing to cover the years 1851 to 1912.

■ National newspaper index. Foster City, Calif.: Information Access, 1979– . Online and on CD-ROM only. Online versions updated daily; CD-ROM, monthly.

Scope: Covers *Christian Science Monitor, New York Times,* and *Wall Street Journal* since 1970; *Los Angeles Times* and *Washington Post,* 1982 to date. Also covers *PR Newswire* (which gives text of public relations releases of businesses and organizations) and *Businesswire* (a similar service for business-related press releases).

Access: Very full indexing, excluding only such things as weather charts, horoscopes, cartoons, etc. Entries include full citation, including date (unlike the indexes to specific papers, which tend to leave this out) and size in columns. Some titles are enriched with brief "abstracts"; personal names are emphasized. Includes good coverage of reviews of all formats.

■ Newspaper abstracts. Ann Arbor, Mich.: University Microfilms International, 1984– . Also online and on CD-ROM. CD-ROM updated monthly; online versions are part of Periodical Abstracts.

Indexing with abstracts to nine major newspapers; coverage varies over time. *See Periodical Abstracts* (p. 111).

■ The Times index. Reading, England, and Woodbridge, Conn.: Research Pub., 1973– . Monthly and annual cumulations.

Scope: Coverage and format have changed a bit over the years. Covers the final edition of the daily, plus Sunday, plus the *Times Magazine,* and the Literary, Educational, and Higher Educational supplements. During *Times* strikes, indexed the daily and sunday *Telegraph.*

Access: Unlike the *New York Times,* the indexing authority list shifts constantly. Book reviews are conveniently under both the author and under the general subject of "book reviews"; other types of reviews found only under the format type (e.g., "theater reviews"). Citation to author, date, section, page, with a very brief abstract.

Earlier versions of this index, *Official Index to the Times* and *Index to the Times,* cover the period from 1906.

■ Palmer's index to the Times newspapers. London: Palmer; Cambridge, England: Chadwyck-Healey, 1790–1943. Also on the Web and on CD-ROM.

Briefer and less accurate than the *Index to the Times,* but covers from the beginning of the newspaper. Particularly useful for its obituary coverage.

■ The Times index. Reading, England: Newspaper Archive Developments; Woodbridge, Conn.: Research Pub., 1978–83.

Coverage for the years 1785 to 1790, completing indexing before Palmer started. As far as possible, uses the terms in the current index.

For a somewhat dated but still useful guide to local indexes produced by newspapers, historical societies, research libraries, and the like, based on surveys of likely holdings, see Anita Cheek Milner, comp., *Newspaper Indexes: A Location and Subject Guide for Researchers* (Metuchen, N.J.: Scarecrow, 1977–82; 3v.).

Current Events

Allied to newspaper indexes in their subject matter are several other ways of supplying information on current events. Among those found most often in American libraries are the following:

■ EXEGY: The source for current world information. Santa Barbara, Calif.: ABC-Clio, 1994– . Bimonthly. CD-ROM only.

Scope: Statistics and current events information on the United States and Canada (including states and provinces) as well as all nations and international organizations. Includes statistics, political information, biographies of government officials, profiles of political parties and businesses, and summaries of major treaties, constitutions, etc. Also includes pictures and a collection of maps. Also has stories from the last three years.

Access: Full text is searchable by keyword and subject.

■ Facts on File world news digest with index. New York: Facts on File, Oct. 30, 1940– . Weekly, with annual bound volumes.

> *Scope*: Originally and still issued in loose-leaf format, is more convenient in electronic versions. (A machine-readable version, titled *Facts on File News Digest CD-ROM,* is available as an annual and, from EBSCO, as a quarterly, covering 1980 to date. The print annual is called *Facts on File Yearbook.*) A weekly summary of news from about seventy U.S. and foreign newspapers and news magazines. Includes general news, economics and business, science and technology, and social science. Paper indexes cumulated every month, quarterly, and annually. Tends to have less diplomacy and generally more popular coverage than *Keesing's,* and, of course, emphasizes U.S. news and world news of interest in the United States.

> *Access*: Arranged by general geographic location, with top stories of the week placed first. Biweekly cumulated indexes by subject, including proper name, for the paper. Also cumulated indexes for 1946 to 1985. Yearbook has quinquennial cumulated indexes as well.

■ Keesing's record of world events. Cambridge, England: Longman, 1931– . Monthly, with annual cumulations. Also online and on CD-ROM. Formerly titled *Keesing's Contemporary Archives,* 1931–86.

> *Scope*: As with *Facts on File,* summarizes events on a weekly basis from newspapers, newsmagazines, and wire services. Emphasis on British and Commonwealth events, with generally better international coverage than *Facts on File,* but weaker on business and economics in general. Includes background information, texts of speeches, treaties and laws.

> *Access*: Indexes similar to *Facts on File.* Includes access by country, international organizations, and subject; cumulation includes a name index. CD-ROM covers from 1960 to date.

■ NewsBank newsfile. New Canaan, Conn.: NewsBank, 1982– . Also on fiche and on CD-ROM.

> *Scope*: An interesting approach to indexing: in effect, a clipping service to about 500 newspapers including some news wires and international papers, with focus on general news, especially political news, giving a good access to the local slant. Various sections cover arts and popular culture in general and biographical information.

> *Access*: Arranged in a broad classification, then by subject and geographic location. Original has index referring to fiche copy of origi-

nal article. CD-ROM version includes full text of about 100 of the titles covered. Abbreviated citations both to the original and to the microfiche (available separately) lack dates, which makes use a bit inconvenient.

■ NewsBank reference service. New Canaan, Conn.: NewsBank, 1981– . Online and on CD-ROM only.

> *Scope*: A much more convenient, if more expensive, version of *News-Bank*. Includes the basic *NewsBank* (1981 to date), plus *NewsBank Review of the Arts* (1980 to date), *NewsBank Names in the News* (1981 to date), as well as *NewsBank Index to Periodicals*.

> *Access*: By keyword and by all the access points of the printed material.

Other Indexes and Concordances

For retrieving bits of information too specific for inclusion in national catalogs and bibliographies, others types of indexes and concordances are also useful. They also supplement periodical indexes and abstracts by providing additional approaches, or added information for individual items, and by drawing on a wider range of indexed sources. They fall roughly into several categories, each of which has its own heading below: "Indexes to Single Books"; "Indexes to the Works of a Single Author," including concordances; "Indexes to Multiple Books" (similar in conception to indexes to multiple periodicals); "Indexes to Literary Forms"; and "Indexes to Nonliterary Forms." Given the increasing importance of the Internet, indexes to it are considered a fifth type, although they could be included under the fourth category.

Indexes to Single Books

If carefully prepared, indexes to single books supply an alphabetical list of names, facts, places, and other subject content, often in a single alphabet, sometimes in two or more alphabets (basic principles are discussed in the titles by Cleveland and Cleveland and by Rothman, Rowley, and Lancaster, cited earlier on pages 103 to 105). But their present state is far from satisfactory. Librarians need to be aware of their inadequacies and should work with publishers to bring about better book indexes. One way of doing this is to comment on the index when one reviews any book for publication in any format.

Editors of multivolume encyclopedias are particularly aware of the importance of a complete and well-organized index to the persons, places, things, and abstract ideas treated in articles, which more often than not are arranged by broad subject. But no one should expect to find all the information pertinent to any subject in only one article. Not even in an encyclopedia that favors short articles should one expect to find separate articles on every subject. Thus, the need for an index is evident.

One approach to this problem avoids indexing as such entirely and merely provides the full text of the encyclopedia, or other book, in a searchable form. If the search engine permits all the extant varieties of searching—notably, single word, truncation, word proximity (so that one can search phrases), Boolean operators, and possibly some form of relevance ranking—this approach is better than no index at all. It does tend to lead to very large amounts of retrieval, however, much of which (even with supposed relevance ranking) is not relevant.

Indexes to the Works of a Single Author

Indexes to an author's works may resemble indexes to single books or, in the case of important authors, take the form of concordances, which index all significant words in the text, such as a Shakespeare concordance. Thanks to the common use of computers both for indexing and for text production, concordances have become more common but may in fact be becoming obsolete. A machine-readable and searchable full-text database can be used as a concordance, and with the proposed search capability noted above, it could provide much more sophisticated access to the text than the traditional concordance.

Indexes to Multiple Books

Computerization has also made possible a relatively new form of index—the collective index to a collection of books. Although such indexes have been around for some time, they have become much more common. A few, covering general sets of books, are listed below. Others are also listed in the appropriate section.

■ Gale's literary index CD-ROM. Detroit: Gale, 1993– . Semiannual updates. CD-ROM and the Web only.

> A master index on CD-ROM and the Web to all forty-three of Gale's literary series (both biographical and biocritical), covering more than 130,000 authors and 150,000 titles. Includes title, author, and Boolean searching approaches. Includes criticism, biography for all time periods, and languages in all areas of belles lettres.

■ Index to scientific book contents. Philadelphia: Institute for Scientific Information, 1985– . Quarterly, with a four-issue annual cumulation. Also online and on CD-ROM.

Tables of contents for about 2,500 multiauthored books and single-author books that are part of multiauthor series. Indexed by author, editor, corporate author, and Permuterm subject index with broad category index.

■ John Davis Williams Library, Reference Department. University of Mississippi. Plot locator: an index to summaries of fiction and nonfiction. Hamden, Conn.: Garland, 1991. 704p.

A cumulative index to eighty-two sources, from 1902 to 1990, which have at least one-page summaries of books. Includes *Masterplots* (also indexed in *Magill Index to Masterplots,* below). Although emphasis is on belles lettres, includes nonfiction sources as well, so covers more than plots. Arranged by author, then title, with full citations to source. Index by title.

■ Magill index to critical surveys: cumulative indexes, 1981–1994. Rev. ed. Pasadena, Calif.: Salem, 1994. 379p.

Cumulated index to Magill's Critical Survey series by author, title, foreign language title, pseudonyms. New edition now includes drama, long fiction, short fiction, poetry. Indexed by author and title, including cross-references from pseudonyms and foreign titles.

■ Magill index to Masterplots: cumulative indexes, 1963–1993. Pasadena, Calif.: Salem, 1994. 309p.

Title and author indexes to the full set, which remains very popular among students.

■ Pettus, Eloise S., and Daniel D. Pettus. Master index to summaries of children's books. Metuchen, N.J.: Scarecrow, 1985. 2v.

More than 18,000 titles from eighty-six bibliographies, textbooks, and activities books aimed at students from preschool to grade six. Arranged by author, with full citation to original book, including codes and page numbers for each summary. Index by subject and title. Emphasizes American sources and American editions of multiple-country publications. Does not index selection aids.

■ Proper names master index. Detroit: Omnigraphics, 1994. 2v.

> Covers entries in sixty-eight standard reference books that use proper names and adjectives, such as song titles, fictional characters, wars and battles, etc. Does not index biographies or biographical entries (unless the person lived before about 500 B.C. or is legendary). Useful, although it does not always index the most recent edition of each source.

■ Stevenson, Rosemary M. Index to Afro-American reference resources. Westport, Conn.: Greenwood, 1988. 315p.

> Analytical index to 181 sources, including books, chapters, essays. Most are reference books published from 1970 to the mid-1980s, but some are much older. Arranged by subject, with title and author indexes.

■ Weiner, Alan R., and Spencer Means. Literary criticism index. 2d ed. Metuchen, N.J.: Scarecrow, 1994. 580p.

> Author index to about 150 bibliographies or checklists of criticism covering multiple authors, such as the Gale Information Guide Library. Arranged by author, then general criticism, then titles of individual works.

Indexes to Literary Forms

Indexes to literary forms augment the catalogs, bibliographies, and other indexes already mentioned by (1) supplying authors, titles, and often subjects of individual essays, plays, short stories, speeches, dissertations, etc. in collections whose contents are not analyzed in other types of bibliography; (2) supplying citation to the exact location of *words* in a quotation; (3) supplying citation to or quotations from reviews of individual titles; or (4) supplying additional descriptive information and indexing, as for plays.

Remember that many periodical indexes cover such forms as they appear in the periodicals indexed and refer to the appropriate periodical indexes as well.

Examples of titles frequently consulted in American libraries follow, alphabetically by form:

BOOK REVIEWS

■ Book review index. Detroit: Gale, 1965– . v.1– . Quarterly, with annual cumulations. Also online and on CD-ROM.

> *Scope*: All reviews (even omnibus and very short notices) in about 500 periodicals and some newspapers, of books longer than fifty pages, periodicals and reference books, and books on tape. Emphasizes

general-interest materials, but complete coverage of all reviews means that it contains many technical, scientific, and scholarly book reviews as well, as long as they were reviewed in the periodicals in question.

Access: Arranged by author, with entries giving a brief citation (review title and reviewer omitted), and necessary codes for type (e.g., reference, juvenile, periodical). Indexed by title since 1976. Master cumulations cover from 1965 to 1974, then from 1965 to 1984 and other variants, although the electronic versions as an ongoing cumulation are the best bet. All cumulations include title indexes, even for pre-1976 issues.

■ Book review digest. Bronx, N.Y.: Wilson, 1905- . v.1- . Monthly, with semiannual and annual cumulations. Author/title index, 1905-74, Wilson, 1976, 4v.; Author/title index, 1975-84, Wilson, 1986, 1488p.; Author/title index, 1985-94, Wilson, 1996, 1261p. Five-year cumulative indexes beginning with volume 17, as part of appropriate cumulation. CD-ROM and online, from 1983 to date, with updates as often as twice weekly.

Scope: Not actually an index but often treated as one. Covers books published or distributed in the United States and Canada. Includes works of nonfiction for which two or more reviews have appeared in the approximately ninety titles indexed, works of fiction for which there are at least three reviews, and children and young adult works if there are at least three reviews. Exceptions for books in *Reference Books Bulletin,* which are all indexed regardless of other reviews. Emphasizes books of general interest, thus excludes government publications, textbooks, highly technical titles.

Access: Arranged by author, with indexes by title and subject. Indexes are cumulated every five years. Entries include citation, with Dewey decimal classification and *Sears'* subject headings, plus exact citation to reviews, number of words per review, and up to three (for fiction) or four (for nonfiction) excerpts from selected reviews. Covers many fewer titles and vastly fewer periodicals than *Book Review Index* but includes the annotations, review excerpts, and subject access not in *BRI.*

■ National library service cumulative book review index, 1905-1974. Princeton, N.J.: National Library Service, 1975. 6v.

A useful, single alphabet author/title index to *Book Review Digest,* plus all reviews in *Choice, Library Journal,* and *Saturday Review* (in its various titles).

For retrospective coverage, the following are some useful sources.

▪ Combined retrospective index to book reviews in humanities journals, 1802-1974. Woodbridge, Conn.: Research Pub., 1982-84. 10v.

Covers about 500,000 reviews in literature, music, and philosophy journals, with other subjects included for a total of about 150 journals. Author (of item reviewed) arrangement, with citation including reviewer name; tenth volume is a title index.

▪ Combined retrospective index to book reviews in scholarly journals, 1886-1974. Arlington, Va.: Carrollton Pr., 1979-82. 15v.

A companion volume to the previous entry, covering more than 450 mostly history, sociology, and politics journals and about a million reviews. Arranged by author of item reviewed, giving journal, volume and date, and initial page (but not reviewer as does its companion). International coverage includes both full reviews and many shorter notices. Title index in last volume gives citation to author entry.

▪ Index to book reviews in the humanities. Williamston, Mich.: Phillip Thomson, 1960-91. Annual.

Covers about 450 periodicals in the humanities, with history dropped in 1970. Indexes adult books in both English and foreign languages with a very brief citation.

▪ The New York times book review index, 1896-1970. New York: NYT and Arno Pr., 1973. 5v.

A convenient cumulation of the reviews from the *Book Review* section. Indexes to all the reviews by author, title, subject, category/genre, and reviewer byline.

For a general guide to sources of book reviews, the following, while dated, remains useful, especially for foreign and scholarly sources not in *BRD* and *BRI*. However, the electronic versions of periodical bibliographies can also be used to find which titles review books as well.

▪ Gray, Richard A. *A guide to book review citations: a bibliography of sources.* Columbus, Ohio: Ohio State Univ. Pr., 1968. 221p.

REVIEWS OF OTHER FORMATS

▪ Dintrone, Charles V. Television program master index. Jefferson, N.C.: McFarland, 1996. 133p.

Covers comments on about 1,000 television programs in more than 340 books published from 1956 to 1995, including as little as one sentence "if it says something useful." Shows must have appeared on ABC, NBC, CBS, or Fox, but it includes some public television series, such as *Sesame Street*, as well. Index of titles by genre.

■ Film review index. Phoenix, Ariz.: Oryx, 1986-87. 2v.

Indexes more than 3,000 feature film reviews in both popular and technical/scholarly sources from 1882 to the mid-1980s. Primarily covers periodicals but includes a number of books as well. Arranged by film title, with indexes by directory, year of production, country of production.

■ Media review digest, 1970- . Ann Arbor, Mich.: Pierian, 1970- . Annual.

In a sense, the media version of *Book Review Digest,* covering mostly educational and informational nonprint but also listing feature films. Covers about 200 journals. Indexes by general classified subject terms, alphabetical subject, reviewer, producer/distributor, and reviewer (of feature films). Entries typically include a twenty- to twenty-five-word abstract of the review and a similar length summary of the medium. Recent years also have a separate section of mediagraphies, with longer annotations.

■ Salem, James M. A guide to critical reviews. Metuchen, N.J.: Scarecrow, 1971-91. 6v.

Covers American drama (1909-82), musicals (1909-89), drama (other than American) (1909-78), screenplays (1927-80). Arranged by title of work, with citation to journal reviews.

■ Schwann CD review digest—classical. Voorheesville, N.Y.: Peri Pr., 1983- . Irregular.
■ Schwann CD review digest—jazz, popular, etc. Voorheesville, N.Y.: Peri Pr., 1983- . Irregular.

Similar in many ways to *Book Review Digest,* these index and give extracts from reviews for recorded music on laser discs.

DISSERTATIONS

■ Dissertation abstracts international. Ann Arbor, Mich.: University Microfilms International, 1969- . Monthly. Also online and on CD-ROM.

Scope: Succeeds earlier titles, *Dissertation Abstracts* and *Microfilm Abstracts,* 1938-1968. Nearly full coverage of U.S. universities, most

Canadian institutions, and a growing number of British and European institutions. In three parts: *A* for humanities and social sciences, *B* for sciences and engineering, and *C* for all subjects from non-U.S. sources.

Access: Includes full citation, including issuing university and date, plus approximately 350-word abstracts supplied by the authors. Main arrangement by broad subject, with indexes by author and keyword in title. Online in several formats and on CD-ROM as well. Some online versions include the whole file since 1861 and abstracts since 1980, as well as *Master's Abstracts,* a sister publication covering master's theses. Most of the U.S. titles indexed may be obtained in photocopy or microform from UMI.

■ Comprehensive dissertation index, 1861–1972. Ann Arbor, Mich.: Xerox Univ. Microfilms, 1973. 37v. Supplements cover 1973–82, 1983–87, and later.

Scope: Not entirely complete, but the most complete source available for dissertations accepted in U.S. universities, with increasing coverage of Canadian and, more recently, other universities as well. Based on *Dissertation Abstracts International, Doctoral Dissertations Accepted by American Universities, List of American Doctoral Dissertations,* and several lists from specific universities.

Access: Arranged by broad subjects with keyword in title under these; author index. Gives full citations to sources indexed, plus full bibliographic information, including issuing university and date of dissertation.

DRAMA

■ Karp, Rashelle S., June Schlessinger, and Bernard Schlessinger. Plays for children and young adults: an evaluative index and guide. New York: Garland, 1991. 580p. Supplement 1, 1989–94. Garland, 1996.

A selective guide and index to several thousand plays, choral readings, and similar performances for ages five to eighteen, covering *Play Index, Plays* (the magazine), and both editions of *Index to Children's Plays in Collections,* as well as other sources. Includes plot summary and staging information (number of characters, special staging needs, age level, etc.). Indexed by author, subject, grade level, cast size, playing time.

■ Keller, Dean H. Index to plays in periodicals. Metuchen, N.J.: Scarecrow, 1979. 824p.

■ Keller, Dean H. Index to plays in periodicals, 1977-1987. Metuchen, N.J.: Scarecrow, 1990. 391p.

Indexes about 14,000 plays by author and title. Gives full citation to journal, with no other annotation except language if not English.

■ Kreider, B. Index to children's plays in collections, 1965-1974. 2d ed. Metuchen, N.J.: Scarecrow, 1977. 227p.

■ Trefny, Beverly R., and Eileen C. Palmer. Index to children's plays in collections, 1975-1984. 3d ed. Metuchen, N.J.: Scarecrow, 1986. 108p.

An author, title, and subject index (in one sequence) to collected plays—totaling about 2,000 in these two sources. Full entry, including number of actors needed, is only under author. "Subject" includes non-subject headings, such as type of character (e.g., mice, trolls), holiday, historical period, etc.

■ Ottemiller's index to plays in collections: an author and title index to plays appearing in collections published between 1900 and 1985. 7th ed. B. M. Connor and H. G. Mochedlover, eds. Metuchen, N.J.: Scarecrow, 1988. 564p.

Primarily U.S. and British publications, but recent editions have increased coverage of Canadian, South American, and Australian titles. Author and title index to about 6,500 full-length plays in approximately 1,400 collections.

■ Play index, 1949/52- . Bronx, N.Y.: Wilson, 1953- . Quinquennial.

Regularly supplemented every five years, each including both plays published during the time period covered and earlier ones missed in the appropriate volume. Very specific subject indexing, with author/title/subject in one alphabet. Also includes a full citation to the anthologies and separate plays and a list by cast size and gender. A fourth section lists names and addresses of all publishers. Full entries under author include citation, plot, number and type of characters, scene and setting information. Plays suitable for children are indicated with a symbol.

■ Samples, Gordon. The drama scholar's index to plays and filmscripts: a guide to plays and filmscripts in selected anthologies, series and periodicals. Metuchen, N.J.: Scarecrow, 1974-86. 3v.

Covers periodicals, anthologies, series. Arranged by playwright and title of play, with indexes by author/compiler and title of anthology.

Unlike similar titles, includes eighteenth- and nineteenth-century plays that have film scripts.

ESSAYS

■ Chicano anthology index: a comprehensive author, title, and subject index to Chicano anthologies, 1965–1987. Francisco Garcia-Ayvens, comp. Berkeley, Calif.: Chicano Studies Library Publications Unit, Univ. of California at Berkeley, 1990. 704p.

An index to about 5,000 essays in 280 anthologies published since 1965, arranged by subjects. Indexed by author and title.

■ Essay and general literature index. Bronx, N.Y.: Wilson, 1934– . Semiannual, with annual and five-year cumulations. Also online and on CD-ROM; updated as often as semiannually.

Primarily humanities, especially criticism, including reviews and criticism of film, theater, and social sciences (since about 1970). Covers titles published since 1900 (continuing the ALA *Index to General Literature, 1901–1914*). Provides the usual Wilson author/title/subject approach, with full bibliographic information in a separate section. Although it has been criticized for "quaint" subject headings, it remains very useful for subject access and for biographical information.

■ Essay and general literature index: seventy year index, 1900–1969. Bronx, N.Y.: Wilson, 1972.

A cumulated author index, with cross-references from titles, pseudonyms, editors, and the like.

FICTION

■ Fiction catalog. Bronx, N.Y.: Wilson, 1908– . Every five years, with annual supplements.

Novels and some short story collections, based on selections of the "best books" by Wilson with the assistance of U.S. librarians. Covers primarily English, with some foreign titles translated into English. Retains classics from one edition to the next, adding and dropping titles based on the ongoing evaluation of their long-term value and demand in smaller public libraries. Main entries include a brief plot summary, review extract, and list of contents for short story collections. Title and subject index. Although this source has been criticized for its conservatism, recent editions appear to keep up with current points of view and are certainly reflective of the collecting policies of U.S. public libraries.

FOLKLORE AND FAIRY TALES

■ Ashliman, D. L. A guide to folktales in the English language: based on the Aarne-Thompson classification system. Westport, Conn.: Greenwood, 1987. 368p.

> A guide, classified as noted, to both well-known and more obscure English versions of all sorts of folktales, from all nations, cultures, and time periods, with an emphasis on European, English, and Near Eastern work. Includes a brief plot summary and citations to well-known collections. Indexes by title and keywords from the plot summaries. The subject arrangement and plot summaries make this a useful complement to the following title.

■ Index to fairy tales, myths and legends. Mary Huse Eastman, comp. Boston: Faxon, 1926–52 3v.

■ Index to fairy tales [year], including folklore, legends and myths. Norma O. Ireland, comp. Westwood, Mass.: Faxon, 1973, 1989; Metuchen, N.J.: Scarecrow, 1989. 3v.

■ Index to fairy tales, 1987–1992: including 310 collections of fairy tales, folktales, myths, and legends: with significant pre-1987 titles not previously indexed. Joseph W. Sprug, comp. Metuchen, N.J.: Scarecrow, 1994. 587p.

> Consists of a basic volume and supplements, each indexing several hundred more collections. A strong emphasis on European and Native American tales but with some other coverage. Includes full citation, usually citations to reviews, indication of reading level. More recent volumes include a Stith Thompson motif-index code (following). Indexed by a detailed subject index, plus author and title.

■ Thompson, Stith. Motif-index of folk literature. Rev. ed. Bloomington, Ind.: Indiana Univ. Pr., 1955–58. 6v.

> Uses a different classification from Aarne-Thompson, but the same basic idea: related versions of the same story are classified together across cultures. Arranged by motif. Includes detailed index of motifs and subjects, as well as citations to all sources. The classic work of its type.

■ ———. Motif-index of folk literature. New ed. Bloomington, Ind.: Indiana Univ. Pr., 1993. Also on CD-ROM.

A thorough update of the original edition.

GOVERNMENT PUBLICATIONS

The Congressional Information Service (CIS), started in the 1970s, has provided an increasing number of detailed indexes to U.S. government materials. Most follow a similar pattern—primary arrangement by title or issuing agency, with a very detailed contents listing/abstract, followed by a number of analytical indexes. And, with few exceptions, all items indexed are available from CIS in high-quality microform. Citations include both full bibliographic reference and necessary ordering information for the CIS versions. Thus, the indexes can be used as access points to government document collections, freely available in many depository libraries, as well as finding aids or catalogs to products of a commercial firm. Another attraction is that all the products use the same controlled vocabulary, so searching becomes easier, once one learns that vocabulary. CIS mounts nearly all these services on the Web as well.

■ Congressional masterfile 1. Bethesda, Md.: Congressional Information Service, 1988– . CD-ROM only.

Contains, in one database: *U.S. Serial Set Index* (parts 1 to 12), *Congressional Committee Hearings Index,* indexes to both the House and Senate unpublished hearings, committee prints, and U.S. Senate executive documents.

■ Congressional masterfile 2. Bethesda, Md.: Congressional Information Service, 1970– . CD-ROM only.

A CD-ROM version of the *CIS Index,* from 1970 to date, with optional additions of access to *Reports Required by Congress,* executive communications, and materials published by congressional caucuses and member organizations.

Specific titles in the two "Masterfiles" include the following:

■ CIS index to presidential executive orders and proclamations. Washington, D.C.: Congressional Information Service, 1987. 2v. in 22.

Covers Washington through Reagan, with supplements indexing material not found during the compilation.

- CIS index to U.S. executive branch documents, 1789-1909: a guide to documents listed in Checklist of U.S. public documents, 1789-1909, not printed in the U.S. serial set. Bethesda, Md.: Congressional Information Service, 1990. 6v. in 24.

- CIS index to U.S. executive branch documents, 1910-1932: a guide to documents listed in Checklist of U.S. public documents, 1910-1932, not printed. Bethesda, Md.: Congressional Information Service, 1996- . (In progress).

    Coverage as listed, but excludes documents indexed in other CIS indexes, such as the *Serial Set.*

- CIS index to U.S. Senate executive documents and reports. Washington, D.C.: Congressional Information Service, 1987. 2v.

    Covers executive documents and reports from 1817 to 1969 not in the *Serial Set.* The latter did not generally contain this material until 1980. (*CIS Index* includes those published from 1970 to date.) Main section includes citation and abstract. Indexed by subject, names, places, titles, document and report numbers. All indexed items available on fiche.

- CIS index to unpublished U.S. house of representatives committee hearings, 1833-1936; 1937-1946; 1947-1954; 1955-1958; 1959-1964. Bethesda, Md.: Congressional Information Service, 1988- . 2v. in each of three sets.

    The usual CIS approach to indexing, but selection is a bit different. For example, different committees had different policies regarding the recording of hearings, so not all are in this set, and not all are complete records. Similarly, many of the hearings of some committees, such as the House Unamerican Activities Committee, are restricted by law, thus are not included. The main record includes lists of witnesses, date, etc. as with the other CIS indexes. Fiche is available for all items indexed.

- CIS index to unpublished U.S. senate committee hearings, 1823-1964; 1965-1968; 1969-1972. Bethesda, Md.: Congressional Information Service, 1986- . Ongoing, multivolume.

    As with the House set, this is not a complete record, but only as complete as the copies of transcripts the CIS staff could find. However, this is claimed by the publisher to be more than are held in the National Archives or any other government agency. Indexed by subject, organization, personal name, bill numbers, and titles. Main entries include abstract, list of witnesses, bill numbers. All documents indexed are on fiche.

■ CIS U.S. congressional committee hearings index. Washington, D.C.: Congressional Information Service, 1981–85. 42v.

Covers published hearings, from 1833 through 1969. Entries are similar to the later *CIS Index*, with witness names and annotations of content as well as full citations. Indexes by subject, organization, personal names, bill numbers, titles, report, document and SuDocs numbers. All hearings are also available on fiche.

■ CIS U.S. congressional committee prints index: from the earliest publications through 1969. Washington, D.C.: Congressional Information Service, 1980. 5v.

Covers from 1830 through 1969; starting in 1970, committee prints are indexed in the basic *CIS Index*. Although incomplete, because many prints are not known, it is more complete than any other listing of these. Main section includes full bibliographic citation plus short abstract. Indexes by subject, name, publication title (alphabetical and chronological), bill and SuDocs numbers. Indexed document available on fiche.

■ CIS U.S. serial set index. Washington, D.C.: Congressional Information Service, 1975–79. 40v.

Begins with 1789, covering all items in the official *Serial Set* (also known as the "Sheep Set" from its bindings). Citations permit use with the printed set or with the CIS fiche, as with the other titles. Indexing is in two parts—subject and keyword in one section and a separate index to personal names or organizations in a separate set. Also includes indexing by bill numbers, report and document numbers, and serial set volume. Part 14, *Index and Carto-Bibliography of Maps, 1789-1969,* provides access to maps. Indexed by geographic area, subject, map title, personal name, corporate name. Main section provides a detailed description of the maps, including scale, surveyor, publisher, date, etc., as well as citations to the CIS fiche and *Serial Set* volumes.

■ Congressional Information Service/CIS annual. Washington, D.C.: Congressional Information Service, 1970– . Monthly, with annual cumulations. Four-year cumulations after 1970–74.

Congressional publications of both houses, including all active committees. Cumulations revise and correct entries from the annuals. Indexes by subject, name (including all persons who testify at hearings), title, bill number, publication number. Detailed abstracts include brief abstracts of each witness at hearings. The annual includes legislative histories.

■ Congressional Information Service/CIS index to publications of the United States Congress. Washington, D.C.: Congressional Information Service, 1970- .

The serial title, versus the previous title, which is the cumulation title.

■ Index to current urban documents. Westport, Conn.: Greenwood, 1972- . Quarterly, with fourth cumulative for year. Also on the Web and on CD-ROM.

Publications from about 300 large cities, counties, and some school and other special districts and regional planning agencies. Includes budgets, audits, planning reports, and special studies. Though hardly complete, covers the larger metropolitan areas and is by far the easiest and most complete source for these materials. Geographic and subject indexes, providing full citations. Indexed documents are available on fiche. The subject authority list is also available separately.

POETRY

■ Columbia Granger's index to poetry in anthologies. 11th ed. New York: Columbia Univ. Pr., 1997. 2150p.

The standard source for poetry indexing, with the format continuing changes adopted in the eighth edition. Covers about 400 anthologies, with about 150 changed from the last edition, so all editions should be retained. Covers English and American anthologies, including (since the ninth edition) translations of foreign poetry into English. Indexes by title and first line give full citation; author entries give only title; and subject entries give only author and title. Recent editions also include a partial last line index and birth and death dates for authors.

■ Columbia Granger's index to poetry in collected and selected works. New York: Columbia Univ. Pr., 1996. 1913p.

The same approach as the previous title, for individual author collections.

■ Columbia Granger's index to poetry quotations. New York: Columbia Univ. Pr., 1992. 1132p.

Unlike the other *Granger's,* this indexes interior lines of about 4,000 of the most-anthologized poems. Arranged by poet, with a section for the ever-popular "anonymous." Indexes by subject and keyword.

■ Columbia Granger's world of poetry on CD-ROM. New York: Columbia Univ. Pr., 1995. CD-ROM only.

More comprehensive than *Poem Finder,* its major competitor. Contains the full text of 10,000 poems not under copyright and selections from many others. But the primary value is the index to about 135,000 poems in some 700 anthologies, with evaluations of the anthologies. In effect, cumulates the printed editions of *Columbia Granger's Index to Poetry,* beginning with the eighth, and *Columbia Granger's Index to Poetry in Anthologies.*

■ Hoffman, H. H. Hoffman's index to poetry: European and Latin American poetry in anthologies. Metuchen, N.J.: Scarecrow, 1985. 672p.

Complements *Granger's* by covering non-English poetry in major European languages. Indexes about 100 anthologies likely to be in U.S. and British libraries by author, title, first line. Bibliography of anthologies indexed includes a note as to which are also in English translation.

■ Index to poetry for children and young people [year]; a title, subject, author, and first line index to poetry in collections for children and young people. Bronx, N.Y.: Wilson, 1942– . Supplements every five to six years.

A dictionary index to author, title, subject, and first line. Supplements *Granger's.*

■ Poem finder. Great Neck, N.Y.: Roth, 1995– . CD-ROM only. Updated every six months.

Covers about 400,000 poems in more than 2,500 English single-author collections as well as about 3,000 *issues* of periodicals (not 3,000 *different* periodicals), as well as 1,700 anthologies. Includes biographical information on about half of the more than 44,000 writers. Surprisingly little duplication with *Granger's* CD-ROM. Indexed by author, translator, title, first line.

PROCEEDINGS

■ Directory of published proceedings: series SSH—social sciences/ humanities. Harrison, N.Y.: InterDok, 1968– . Quarterly updates, with annual cumulations.

Cumulated index every two years. Also online since 1993.

■ Directory of published proceedings: series SEMT—science, engineering, medicine, technology. Harrison, N.Y.: InterDok, 1964– . Updated ten times per year, with annual cumulations. Index cumulates three times a year, annually, and about every two to five years. Also online since 1993.

Usually just called "InterDok" for its international coverage. Indexed by editor and by subject/sponsor. Entries give citation to whole item. Also has several more subject series (such as *Series PCE—Pollution Control/Ecology,* from 1974 to date, which includes relevant citations from the other two series and appears annually).

■ Index of conference proceedings. Boston Spa, England: British Library Document Supply Centre, 1964- . Also on CD-ROM as Inside Conferences on CD-ROM, 1993- . Quarterly updates.

About 15,000 "worthwhile" proceedings in all subjects and languages covered annually. Subject/keyword index to individual papers in published conference proceedings, with hypertext links in the CD-ROM version.

■ Index to scientific and technical proceedings. Philadelphia: Institute for Scientific Information, 1978- . Monthly, with annual cumulations. Also online, with Index to Scientific Book Contents, 1978- , and on CD-ROM, which covers 1981- .

Access to individual papers in more than 4,000 published conference proceedings each year. Main entries include full citation and contents of each proceeding. Indexes by author/editor, keyword subject (using the Permuterm system), sponsor, meeting location, corporate body, broad subject category.

■ Index to social sciences and humanities proceedings. Philadelphia: Institute for Scientific Information, 1979- . Quarterly, with annual cumulations. Also online and on CD-ROM, 1990- .

International coverage, but with a strong preponderance of English-language material. Indexes more than 21,000 individual papers per year. In addition to the usual humanities and social sciences subjects, includes law. Same arrangement and indexing as its scientific and technical sister.

■ Inside conferences on CD-ROM. Boston Spa, England: British Library Document Supply Centre, 1993- . CD-ROM only. Quarterly updates, cumulating annually.

Adds about 15,000 conferences, with access to about half a million papers each year. All in English, all subjects covered. Includes journals, monographs, series, and fiche publications. Based on conferences collected by the Centre. Author, title of paper, conference citation and details, editor, and volume/series title are all searchable.

QUOTATIONS

Collections of quotations from prose and poetry exist in great numbers, varying considerably in exactness and completeness of citation to the original source. They may be arranged alphabetically by author or subject or chronologically by birth date of author or by date of quotation. For a representative list, see *Balay,* which also contains comments on their reference use. Some librarians feel that, even with considerable overlap, you can never have too many books of quotations; others obviously do not. The following include the general-coverage standbys as well as some newer, more specialized sources:

■ Bartlett, John. Familiar quotations: a collection of passages, phrases, and proverbs traced to their sources in ancient and modern literature. 16th ed. Edited by Justin Kaplan. Boston: Little, Brown, 1992. 1405p.

In many ways, the standard, with well over 20,000 quotes in each edition. Each edition adds and drops some hundreds of speakers; thus, all editions should be retained and used. Includes quotations from scripture and other classical material (mostly Western). Arranged by author/ speaker chronologically, giving full, accurate, and exact citations. Author index includes birth and death dates; a keyword index is also provided. Includes footnotes with additional information.

■ Biggs, Mary. Women's words: the Columbia book of quotations by women. New York: Columbia Univ. Pr., 1996. 500p.

A conscious supplement to other quotation sources, this includes about 3,000 entries, all by women, not in any of the other sources. Similar to the *Columbia Dictionary of Quotations* in general appearance and layout but arranged by date within subject. Gives context of the quotation, as well as the exact citation. Index by person quoted provides a brief identification of the person.

■ Colombo, John R. The dictionary of Canadian quotations. Toronto: Stoddart, 1991. 671p.

Contains about 6,000 quotations by Canadians and by non-Canadians about Canada, with an emphasis on contemporary quotes. Arranged by subject, with index by person quoted. The 1974 edition, called

Columbo's Canadian Quotations, and its 1987 supplement, *Colombo's New Canadian Quotations,* are almost wholly different, with an emphasis on history and culture.

■ The Columbia dictionary of quotations. Robert Andrews, comp. New York: Columbia Univ. Pr., 1993. 1092p.

About 18,000 entries, mostly American and mostly contemporary, about two-thirds of which (states the publisher) have not been in previous compilations. Arranged by topic, with many modern topics (birth control, abortion, political correctness). Gives full citation to sources, including a note as to the context, where needed; makes a distinction between the writer's words and words of a fictional character. Indexed by sources.

■ The Columbia world of quotations. New York: Columbia Univ. Pr., 1996. CD-ROM only.

About 70,000 quotations from some 5,000 people. Includes brief biography and full citation for each quote. Searchable by author, subject, source, keyword, genre, nationality, occupation.

■ Dictionary of contemporary quotations. John Gordon Burke, comp. Evanston, Ill.: J. G. Burke, 1976– . Triennial.

A conscious attempt to augment the standard sources with contemporary quotations of significance (especially political, historical, sociological), and those that are, in the compiler's opinion, particularly "quotable." Mostly one- to two-liners from periodicals and newspapers. Though useful, and generally approaching its goal, this is flawed by many errors in citation and the lack of identification of the person being quoted in many cases. This is also available online and is also updated by a loose-leaf service.

■ Gale's quotations: who said what? Detroit: Gale, 1995. CD-ROM only.

About 117,000 quotations from all time periods and subjects. Access by quoted person, keyword, phrase, quotation. Includes biographic information, including birth and death dates.

■ Langer, Howard J., comp. American Indian quotations. Westport, Conn.: Greenwood, 1996. 260p.

Extends other such sources by including contemporary quotations. Arranged by person in date order. Citation excludes the page number but is otherwise complete; first entry under a name gives brief biographical information.

■ The Macmillan dictionary of quotations. New York: Macmillan, 1989. 736p.

About 20,000 modern and contemporary quotes arranged by subject. This source's main value, however, is the biographical information on about 100 figures quoted in the source, including quotes by and about them. Indexed by author and keyword.

■ Maggio, Rosalie. The new Beacon book of quotations by women. Boston: Beacon, 1996. 844p.

Contains about 16,000 quotes from women on six continents, with about 80 percent unique to this source (says the publisher). Arranged by topic. Indexed by subject, name, key line.

■ Oxford dictionary of quotations. 5th ed. Oxford: Oxford Univ. Pr., 1998. 1152p. Also on CD-ROM.

With an emphasis on English literature, quotes about 17,500 passages arranged by author, with expanded coverage of women and non-English speakers. Includes the full and exact citation, birth and death dates, and other biographical information, with foreign quotes in translation and original. Indexes by keyword include the page number with the item and author, unlike the briefer entries of many other sources. Because each of the four editions is revised considerably, all should be retained. This source, with its companion, *Oxford Dictionary of Modern Quotations* (Oxford: Oxford Univ. Pr., 1991; 371p.) is also available on CD-ROM.

■ Partnow, Elaine. The new quotable women. Rev. ed. New York: Facts on File, 1992. 714p.

More than 15,000 quotations by women, beginning with Eve. Estimates are that less than 1 percent of the quotations in the current edition of *Bartlett's* are from women. Arranged by person in date order, indexed by subject. Cites date and title of source only; gives brief biographical information; and gives lists by career and by ethnic background.

■ Petras, Kathryn, and Ross Petras. The whole world book of quotations. Reading, Mass.: Addison-Wesley, 1994. 476p.

Another attempt to supplement and rectify the coverage of the traditional standards, this includes about 3,000 quotations by non-Westerners and people of color, with a brief biography of each person quoted under his or her name, with references to all of his or her quotes in the book. Arranged by general category, with index by name, giving biographical information.

■ Platt, Suzy. Respectfully quoted: a dictionary of quotations requested from the Congressional Research Service. Washington, D.C.: Congressional Research Service, Library of Congress, 1989. 520p.

Although this has only about 2,100 quotations, all based on requests from members of Congress over seventy-five years, about half are not in any other source. Mostly from and about politics, each item has a brief contextual annotation along with exact citations. Indexes by subject, author, and keyword.

■ Riley, Dorothy Winbush. My soul looks back, 'less I forget: a collection of quotations by people of color. New York: HarperCollins, 1993. 498p.

Although most modern quotation books include a few items from people of color, they are hard to find, a problem remedied in this source. Covers about 7,000 quotes, mostly from African Americans but also from other ethnic groups, under about 450 subjects, including many controversial topics. Many cited items are from contemporary newspapers and broadcast media, but some range back to classical times.

■ Stevenson, Burton Egbert. The home book of quotations, classical and modern. 10th rev. ed. New York: Dodd, Mead, 1967. 2816p.

More than 50,000 quotations, arranged by subject, unlike *Bartlett's* and *Oxford*. Usually gives full and exact citation. Index by keyword omits words used as subject entries. This title is still valuable for its access system and for older quotations.

■ What they said, 1969– . Alan F. Pater and Jason R. Pater, eds. Beverly Hills, Calif.: Monitor, 1969– . Annual.

Current quotations arranged by topic, with speakers identified. Sources are news conferences, speeches, lectures, broadcasts, congressional hearings, and the like, rather than the usual literary sources. Indexed by speaker and subject.

SHORT STORIES

■ Short story index. Bronx, N.Y.: Wilson, 1953– . Annual, with cumulated supplements about every five years.

Indexes about 5,000 English-language (original or translated) adult stories per year in collections and about 100 periodicals by author, title, and subject, with many cross-references. Full set provides coverage since 1900. In one alphabet, with citation to source and pages under author only, to author name under title, and to author and title under subject; full bibliographic information.

■ Weiss, Alan. A comprehensive bibliography of English-Canadian short stories, 1950–1983. Toronto and Cheektowaga, N.Y.: ECW Pr., 1988; distributed by Univ. of Toronto Pr. 973p.

A nearly complete record of short stories by Canadians or residents of Canada, written from 1950 to 1983, indexing about 14,000 stories in anthologies and periodicals.

■ Yancy, Preston M. The Afro-American short story. Westport, Conn.: Greenwood, 1985. 171p.

Lists 850 stories by about 300 writers, written from 1950 to 1982, with commentaries on about 100 of the stories. Includes contents of the anthologies with full tables of contents and an author index that is really an annotated bibliography.

SPEECHES

■ Sutton, Roberta Briggs. Speech index: an index to 259 collections of world famous orations and speeches for various occasions. 4th ed. New York: Scarecrow, 1966. Speech index: an index to collections of world famous orations and speeches for various occasions: supplement, 1966–1980. Metuchen, N.J.: Scarecrow, 1982. 466p.

Scope is clear. Access by author/speaker, subject (based on *Sears'*), and type of speech in one alphabet. Gives full citation in all entries.

Indexes to Nonliterary Forms

As with other indexes, those to nonliterary forms such as works of art, laws and court cases, music, illustrations, patents, formulas, etc. are based on providing access to important characteristics of the form, almost always by subject. A few examples are given here; for further details and many more such titles, guides to the literature of the pertinent fields should be consulted. As with other forms of indexes, more and more of these are most readily and easily consulted via computer systems. In all cases, the basic principle of the index is the same: a systematically arranged list that gives enough information about the item in question so that it can be identified and traced and that provides a useful access point to that information.

FILM AND TELEVISION PROGRAMS

- Enser's filmed books and plays. Ellen Baskin and Mandy Hicken, comps. 5th ed. Brookfield, Vt.: Ashgate, 1993. 986p.

  More than 6,000 entries for sound film versions (since 1928) of novels, plays, short stories, and other literary forms. Covers both English and other languages, and includes television movies, miniseries, and similar programs. Main entry by film title, with citation to original form, availability on videotape, and other information. Indexed by author of literary form, giving film title and title of original work.

- Gifford, Denis. Books and plays in films, 1896–1915. Jefferson, N.C.: McFarland, 1991. 206p.

  Complements coverage of *Enser's.*

- Rouse, Sarah, and Katharine Loughney. Three decades of television. Washington, D.C.: Motion Picture, Broadcasting and Recorded Sound Division, Library of Congress, 1989. 688p.

  A listing of more than 100,000 programs held by the Library of Congress since 1949. Some are complete series, others only individual programs; all are available for viewing at LC. Arranged by title, giving cast and credits, format, content, and summary of program and classified by forty-one descriptors.

- Television news index and abstracts. Nashville, Tenn.: Vanderbilt Univ. Television News Archive, 1968- . Monthly.

Major network news programs, with some coverage of specials, such as the nightly news coverage of the Iran hostage crisis. Detailed abstracts of each program, with indexing by subject, personal name, and place. Copies of all programs are available. The Archive will also, for a fee, create compilations of parts of programs by subject, person covered, and the like.

ILLUSTRATIONS AND MAPS

■ Havlice, Patricia P. World painting index. Metuchen, N.J.: Scarecrow, 1977. 4v. Supplements, 1982, 1995; each in 2v.

An index to reproductions of paintings in American and European books and catalogs. The main edition covers 1,167 books and catalogs; the supplements cover about 1,300 more. Citations, arranged by painting, include a brief description of work, including whether it is black and white or color, and citation. A title index lists painters.

■ Illustration index. Metuchen, N.J.: Scarecrow, 1957-98.

■ Illustration index. New York: Scarecrow, 1957. 527p.

■ Illustration index. First supplement. New York: Scarecrow, 1961. 230p.

■ Illustration index. 2d ed. New York: Scarecrow, 1966. 527p.

■ Illustration index. 3d ed. New York: Scarecrow, 1973. 164p.

■ Illustration index. 4th ed. Metuchen, N.J.: Scarecrow, 1980. 458p.

■ Illustration index V, 1977-1981. Metuchen, N.J.: Scarecrow, 1984. 411p.

■ Illustration index VI, 1982-1986. Metuchen, N.J.: Scarecrow, 1988. 531p.

■ Illustration index VII, 1987-1991. Metuchen, N.J.: Scarecrow, 1993. 492p.

■ Illustration index VIII, 1992-1996. Lanham, Md.: Scarecrow, 1998. 464p.

Coverage varies with edition but usually covers about ten heavily illustrated U.S. periodicals, including *American Heritage, National Geographic, Smithsonian, Sports Illustrated,* and others since 1950. Indexes each illustration (of any type, including maps) in an article, including names of people important enough to get a separate entry in the *World Book Encyclopedia.* Excludes advertising.

■ National geographic index, 1888-1988. Washington, D.C.: National Geographic Society, 1988. 1215p.

A detailed index to the contents of this journal, including articles and maps.

■ Teague, Edward H. World architecture index: a guide to illustrations. Westport, Conn.: Greenwood, 1991. 447p.

Covers buildings (description, plans, photographs, etc.) in about 100 books on architecture published from 1945 to 1989 that the compiler feels are likely to be held in larger libraries. Includes coverage of the *Encyclopedia of World Art* and the *Macmillan Encyclopedia of Architects*. Index by site, architect, type of building, and common name of building.

MUSIC

■ Ferguson, Gar L. Song finder: a title index to 32,000 popular songs in collections, 1854-1992. Westport, Conn.: Greenwood, 1995. 344p.

Just what it says, covering 621 books of songs by title, with about 30 percent not indexed in similar sources. Includes references to fifteen similar indexes. Indexed by song title, with citation to book, but no other information, except to distinguish songs of the same title.

■ Goodfellow, William D. SongCite: an index to popular songs. Hamden, Conn.: Garland, 1995. 433p.

A more modern index to songs, covering more than 7,000 titles in about 250 music books that contain both words and music, published since 1988. Access by composer, lyricist, themes (from plays, television, or films), titles of songs. Includes first lines in indexes.

■ Havlice, Patricia P. Popular song index. Metuchen, N.J.: Scarecrow, 1975-89. 4v.

Indexes songs in anthologies, both adult and children's. Indexes by title, first line, and chorus. By far the most complete such index available.

■ Pallay, Steven G. Cross index title guide to classical music. New York: Greenwood, 1987. 206p.

■ Pallay, Steven G. Cross index title guide to opera and operetta. Westport, Conn.: Greenwood, 1989. 214p.

Emphasis on European works. Index by title and composer, including popular title (but not first line, as with arias), to about 1,400 works.

■ Popular music: an annotated index of American popular songs. Detroit: Gale, 1985- . Annual.

Continues the work begun by Nat Shapiro in covering recorded sound. Does not cover music in anthologies, which is done by Havlice's *Popular Song Index*. Includes a review of the year. Indexes of performances, composers, awards, songs; arranged by title. Citations give brief title, type of recording, firm producing recording.

Cumulations of this and previous versions may be found as

■ Popular music, 1900–1919: an annotated guide to American popular songs including introductory essay, lyricists and composers index, important performances index, chronological index, and list of publishers. Barbara Cohen-Stratyner, ed. Detroit: Gale, 1988. 656p.

■ Popular music, 1920–1979: a revised cumulation. Nat Shapiro and Bruce Pollock, eds. Detroit: Gale, 1985. 3v.

■ Popular music, 1980–1989: an annotated guide to American popular songs, including introductory essay, lyricists and composers index, important performances index, chronological index, awards index, and list of publishers. Bruce Pollock, ed. Detroit: Gale, 1995. 911p.

■ Snow, Barbara. Index of songs on children's recordings. 2d ed. Eugene, Oreg.: Staccato Pr., 1993. 210p.

Covers about 7,300 songs on approximately 680 recordings, including all items listed in the first edition. All songs must have words and music; does not cover song fragments, words only, etc. even if on an indexed record. Arranged by recording title, with a separate section by song title, performer.

MICROFORM COLLECTIONS

■ Niles, Ann. Index to microform collections. Westport, Conn.: Meckler, 1983–85. 2v.

An author and title index to seventy large microform sets, with contents listed for each set indexed. This source emphasizes smaller sets that were not likely to be included in the Association of Research Libraries Microform Project. Because many libraries that purchased these sets have not made analytics, this provides a very useful source, sometimes the only title-by-title access available to the user.

Summary

This chapter has reviewed and listed some types of indexes and abstracts, giving examples of the following:

1. General Periodical Indexing and Abstracting Services
2. Citation Indexes
3. Table of Contents Services
4. Subject Indexes to Periodicals
5. Newspaper Indexing and Abstracting Services
6. Other Indexes and Concordances

As the amount of information continues to expand in size and complexity, such access sources will continue to become more important, especially as more of the general public become aware of the vast amount of information potentially available.

4

Directories

With the growth of resource sharing of all kinds, including the Internet culture, boundaries between geographic areas are becoming less and less relevant. In addition, the rapid (and apparently growing) proliferation of information sources in both numbers and variety, combined with a failure of even the best-supported library's budget to keep pace with inflation, means that any library's collection represents a dwindling fraction of the information available. At the same time, improvements in even the most basic levels of information access via cable television and the Internet mean that a growing fraction of the public is, at least in theory, more aware of the resources available to it. Ironically, then, as any given library is less likely to have "everything you need," the definition both of *need* and of *everything* by clients is broadening.

One way of dealing with these related phenomena is to place increased emphasis on the library not as a stand-alone collection, but rather as an information nexus, as a connection to the "virtual library" of all information. This point has already been made in the discussion of bibliographic access tools in chapter 2. However, in addition to the need for reliable, well-constructed access to information-as-package, we see a growing need for access to people with information. Thus, the modern library, regardless of size, must have at least a basic collection of directories to such people, institutions, and organizations.

The ideal directory would probably be a combination of a major biographical tool, such as the *Dictionary of National Biography (DNB)* or *Contemporary Authors,* with a complete list of publications (traditional and electronic) for each person listed, plus detailed indexing by areas of interest and expertise; reliable comments on the quality of the advice, publications, and information held by each person; plus a constantly updated record of the person's address, phone, e-mail, fax, and other ways of communicating with them. Unfortunately, such a project, if even feasible, is nowhere in sight.

In the meantime, however, some excellent standard sources give much of the needed information, available in print, online and on CD-ROM, and via the Web. A few examples of these follow.

Personal Directories

The most obvious and probably most common directories are those listing people with some common characteristic, such as membership in an organization or residence in a given place. At least at the beginning of the twenty-first century, probably the most common such directory is the telephone directory. At one time, and not that long ago, American libraries were able to obtain as many of these (for the United States at least) as they desired, at no charge. The combination of the breakup of AT&T and the phone companies' decision to charge for the formerly free directory information (and possibly a general realization that even phone numbers and addresses are information for which one can charge) led to the decision to charge for most or all of these. At about the same time, however, some commercial firms appeared with microform and, later, machine-readable cumulations of such directories. Under the circumstances, many libraries have bought these.

The most recent stage (as of this writing) is both an evolution and devolution—some firms have mounted nationwide directories on the World Wide Web (the evolution) and made them available for free (the devolution).

Directories of Institutions and Organizations

In some ways, directories of organizations are more useful to the library than to individuals, because the library is more often in need of information from a group of experts such as a trade association than of locating a specific individual. The ideal guide to an organization would include its location; contact information, such as address, phone, e-mail, and similar data; some indication of the purposes and functions of the group; and, as relevant, an indication of the services provided to members and nonmembers. Many such guides also include lists of officers, publications, and the like. A growing number of organizations are mounting their own sites on the Web, giving even more information of this type; but, to date, many do not have such sites (which are, in any case, sometimes difficult to find). The following directories have proven value for the librarian in search of information:

Handbooks

■ Gunderson, Ted, with Roger McGovern. How to locate anyone anywhere without leaving home. Rev. ed. New York: Plume, 1996. 250p.

Although similar books are available, especially on the subject of finding individuals, this has the attraction of being accurate and of listing only methods that are legal. On the one hand, a useful source; on the other, a frightening one, as the reader soon realizes how much personal information is readily and legally obtainable. The only problem with this book is its age—the number and variety of Internet sources with personal information are not listed.

■ Johnson, Richard S. How to locate anyone who is or has been in the military: armed forces locator directory. 8th ed. Burlington, N.C.: MIE, 1999. 299p.

Covers all bases in the United States, contacts for Navy ships, overseas locations, and the various related agencies, libraries, and the like. Useful for the curious but especially for the genealogist and for potential heirs of former military personnel.

Bibliographies and Directories of Directories

■ Directories in print. Detroit: Gale, 1989– . Annual. Also online.

Replaces *Directory of Directories* (1983–88). A subject listing with descriptions of about 16,000 directories, with indexes by subject, title, keyword. Includes references to electronic formats as well as printed ones.

■ Directory of technical and scientific directories: a world bibliographic guide to medical, agricultural, industrial, and natural science directories. 6th ed. Phoenix, Ariz.: Oryx, 1989. 302p.

About 1,500 directories of all types, including handbooks and encyclopedias. Indexed by author/editor, title, publisher.

■ Guide to American directories. New York: B. Klein, 1954- . Irregular.

> Title varies. Covers all trades and professions for the United States plus major directories for many foreign countries. Indexes by subject and title.

■ Guide to American educational directories. 8th ed. Rye, N.Y.: Todd, 1998. 300p.

> Includes directories as such, plus yearbooks, handbooks, bibliographies, who's who-type publications, etc. Arranged by broad subject; indexed by subject and title.

General Directories

City Directories

City directories are a useful source of both current and historical information. Going back to the early nineteenth century, the city directory generally lists all businesses and people by their addresses (rather than by names). The listing usually includes the person or persons living at the address, their occupation, and, later, their telephone number. Over time, the amount of information available has increased, and with the development of machine-readable databases, the newer directories provide access by essentially every data element in every record.

The most prolific publisher of such directories is the Polk Company, founded in 1870 in Detroit and current publisher of about 1,300 directories to more than 6,000 communities. The basic title is now *Polk Directory [city name]*. Other sources, such as PhoneDisc, are based on the data in telephone directories, but the Polk Company employs surveyors, who collect much more data per person and address—relying always on either personal surveys or publicly available information.

For historical work, the series American Directories through 1860; City Directories of the United States, 1860-1901; and City Directories of the United States, 1902-1935 (Woodbridge, Conn.: Research Pub.) provide every identified city directory on microform. Catalogs are available for the series, and many libraries holding pieces of the collection have added their records to the big national union catalogs, such as OCLC's WorldCat.

The first source listed is a collection of other sources, most of which are also listed here as separates.

■ Gale's ready reference shelf. Detroit: Gale, 1996- . Web and on CD-ROM only.

Includes *Encyclopedia of Associations: National Associations, International Associations, Regional, State, and Local Associations; Gale Directory of Databases; Publishers Directory; Directories in Print; Newsletters in Print; Gale Directory of Publications and Broadcast Media; Directory of Special Libraries and Information Centers* (excluding the appendixes); *Research Centers Directory; Encyclopedia of American Religions* (excluding religious essays); *Gale Guide to Internet Databases;* and others, for a total of fourteen of Gale's directories.

The following directories include persons, businesses, and other types of organizations.

■ Associations Canada. Toronto: IHS Micromedia, 1991– . Annual.

More than 20,000 Canadian (and some foreign organizations of Canadian interest) organizations—private and public, charities, professional groups, etc. Entries include directory information, basic description, founding date, membership dues, and other information similar to that in *Encyclopedia of Associations.* Indexed by subject, location, publication, acronym, personal name of executive.

■ Business phone book USA. Detroit: Omnigraphics, 1977– . Annual. Also on CD-ROM.

Formerly *National Directory of Addresses and Telephone Numbers.* About 25 percent of the listings change each year. Covers companies and organizations, with a separate section for U.S. government agencies; classified listing by subject.

■ Canadian almanac and directory for the year [year]. Toronto: Micromedia, 1847– . Annual.

Almost the entire text is devoted to directory- rather than almanac-type information. In ten major sections, provides basic directory information and occasionally a brief annotation. A definitive, reliable, and essential work for Canadian interests.

■ Cross-border links: a directory of organizations in Canada, Mexico, and the United States. Albuquerque, N. Mex.: Inter-Hemispheric Educational Resource Center, 1992. 257p.

One-, two-, and three-nation organizations related to the North American Free Trade Agreement (NAFTA) in some fashion. Arranged in eight broad categories giving basic directory information including e-mail address and contact person, a short description and history, publications, and activities. Indexed by organization.

■ Encyclopedia of associations. Detroit: Gale, 1956– . Annual. Also online and on CD-ROM.

A set, with multiple volumes for each part.

National Organizations of the U.S.: consists of several text volumes, index volumes, and a interedition supplement. The original covers national-level nonprofit organizations, including national organizations, international organizations that are generally North American in scope and that have a U.S. office; local and regional associations with a national office; nonmembership organizations if they provide information to the general public; for-profit organizations with a name that suggests they are not for profit. Includes brief entries for informal organizations that lack a national headquarters. Also lists, in the index, organizations in the last edition that are or appear to be defunct. Arranged by broad subject, then keyword in names. Provides full directory information, including phone, fax, e-mail, and Web address; a brief description, including founding date, membership numbers, and requirements; indication of information services, such as publications or libraries; and indication of major meetings or conferences, with approximate dates. Indexed by a number of elements, including name of organizations, location, and key executives, plus a keyword index. The electronic versions are fully searchable.

Regional, State, and Local Organizations: covers nonprofit organizations and associations at the state, county, city, neighborhood, and other local levels, including those with multistate memberships. Also includes multistate organizations. Selection criteria, entries, and indexing as for the previous section. In five volumes, each for one U.S. region. Arranged by state, city, town, based on organization mailing address. Coverage varies—based on mail survey. Indexed by name and keyword in each volume.

International Organizations: originally volume 4 of the encyclopedia, but became a separate volume in 1989. Again, similar overall to the basic national volumes. Covers national and international nonprofit organizations, with a growing attention to social-welfare and human-service organizations. Arranged by fifteen broad categories.

■ Fenton, Thomas P., and Mary J. Heffron. Third world resource directory. Maryknoll, N.Y.: Orbis Books, 1994. 785p.

Related to *Third World Resources,* a quarterly (1985–). Covers about 2,500 documents, including slide shows, films, etc. and more than 2,000 organizations. Indexes by organization, personal name, title, subject. Especially good coverage of nongovernmental and social activist organizations.

■ National e-mail and fax directory, [year]. Detroit: Gale, 1989– . Annual.

Approaching about 100,000 U.S. organizations, libraries, etc., giving name, address, e-mail address, fax, and phone number.

■ PhoneDisc. Foster City, Calif.: InfoUSA, 1997. Web and on CD-ROM only.

The product name seems to be in a state of flux, with the major advertising billing it as "The American Business Disc." A total of six discs, providing access to the telephone directories in the United States. Can be searched by name, number, address, county, metropolitan area, business type, SIC code, and even alternate spellings (Kathy, Catherine, and Cathy treated as the same word). Includes phone and fax numbers, plus a growing number of Uniform Resource Locators (URLs), at least for businesses. Available in several configurations, such as residential only, business only, the entire nation, and others. The business versions include additional information on business type, number of employees, and similar data.

■ Scotty's Canadian sourcebook. Don Mills, Ontario, Canada: Southam, 1974– . Annual.

Formerly *Canadian Sourcebook,* previously the *Corpus Almanac and Canadian Sourcebook,* this includes basic directory information (including e-mail and fax numbers) for all types of organizations in Canada; government agencies get longer descriptions than entries in the other sections. Arranged by type of organization, then by subject or geographical area, with indexes by subject and proper name. In some ways, it retains some of the statistical features of an almanac, but this really has turned into a directory.

■ U.S. Postal Service. National five digit zip code and post office directory. Washington, D.C.: Govt. Print. Off., 1979– . 2v. Annual.

Arranged by state, then city, then by street, giving the zip code. Includes separate sections for post offices by name and by zip code. A much more detailed directory, available in microform and on the Web <http://www.usps.gov/ncsc> is the *ZIP + 4 State Directory.* Many commercial services also provide the same data for a fee or a larger price than the government.

■ Washington information directory. Washington, D.C.: Congressional Quarterly, 1975– . Annual.

Basic directory information for all sorts of government and private organizations, including congressional committees, lobbyists, etc., with basic directory information plus a very brief description. Also includes governors and secretaries of state, mayors of larger cities, and some other state officials. Indexed by name and subject.

■ WhoWhere people finder. Waltham, Mass.: Lycos Network, 1988– . <http://www.whowhere.lycos.com>

One of many similar directories found in most search systems and gateways on the Web. This one has the attraction of permitting full searching of phone directories, e-mail lists, and Web pages either by full or by partial name. Results include the phone number, street address, e-mail and/or URLs, a detailed map (at least for most people living in a town) of their address, and directions from any given location in the United States to that place. Text and search capabilities are available in English, French, and Spanish.

■ World Pages. St. Louis, Mo.: WorldPages.com, 1996– . <http://www.worldpages.com>

An example of a growing phenomenon on the World Wide Web. As with PhoneDisc, contains the white and yellow pages for the United States and Canada. The search options are somewhat limited—a proper name must also have a state or province and a country location (i.e., you can't search for all people with the same name nationwide in one command). However, when the results are displayed, in addition to basic name, address, and telephone number, a detailed map is available, showing approximately where in a given city block the address is located. One can zoom out to see the entire neighborhood, city, or even greater area.

■ Yearbook of international organizations. Munich: K. G. Saur, 1948– . Annual. Also on CD-ROM.

More of a directory than a yearbook, with generally better coverage than any other source listed here for international organizations from NGOs (nongovernmental organizations) to fraternities and churches. Fairly lengthy descriptions, with separate volumes indexed by location and by subject.

Specialized Directories

The following is a selection of directories for specific subjects, interests, or groups. Remember that another source of information about both specific groups and their members is the membership directories, often included with handbooks, published by the organizations. The *Encyclopedia of Associations* and similar directories, listed here, indicate the title, frequency, and availability of such directories and should be consulted for that information.

A growing number of organizations have much of their general membership information on a website. This often includes considerably more information about the organization than is found in the printed handbook, but it rarely includes individuals other than the current major officers and staff of the organization. However, in many cases, a query from the Web page will elicit a response, say, to confirm the membership of a given person.

Alternative Directories

The "alternative" category is difficult to define, because some forms of organization, schools of thought, and the like eventually become "mainstream." Generally, the following cover organizations working for some type of social change or engaging in some behavior that is not generally found in the United States (e.g., vegetarianism).

■ American Library Association. Social Responsibilities Round Table. Alternative publications: a guide to directories, indexes, bibliographies, and other sources. Jefferson, N.C.: McFarland, 1990. 90p.

> Mostly subject and trade bibliographies but also indexes and abstracts, review sources, mail-order outlets. Index by author, title, publisher, subjects. The basis for subject access is the Hennepin County (Minnesota) Library authority list.

■ Communities directory. 2d ed. Rutledge, Mo.: Fellowship for Intentional Community, 1999. 440p.

> A combination handbook and directory to "alternative communities," including a wide variety of groups but with best coverage for the United States. About one to three paragraphs per group plus basic directory information and keyword index.

■ Gardner, Richard. Alternative America. Cambridge, Mass.: Copies from Resources, 1995. Unpaged.

Alternative lifestyles, radical causes, food co-ops, religious sects, etc. Arranged by zip code, followed by name, address, phone, descriptor. Indexed by name and subject.

Architects

■ American Institute of Architects. Pro file: the official directory of the American Institute of Architects. Topeka, Kans.: Archimedia, 1978- . Annual. Also partially on the Web.

> Arranged by state, this lists U.S. architectural firms, with full directory information (including fax, e-mail, and URL), a list of staff, recent projects, and the firm's focus. The many indexes include firm, persons, and specializations.

Art

■ American art directory. New York: Jacques Cattell Pr., 1898- . Annual.

> Editor and publisher vary. Originally known as *American Art Annual.* Covers organizations, schools, museums, libraries in all areas of art, emphasizing the United States but with a foreign section. Arranged by type and indexed by organization/institution name, persons, subjects.

Awards

Although most almanacs and encyclopedia yearbooks list the winners of a given year's awards, there is a demand both for a more complete list of such winners and for the awards and their criteria themselves. The following are helpful for such questions.

■ Awards, honors, and prizes. Detroit: Gale, 1969- . 2v. Annual.

> Covers the entire world, with the United States and Canada in the first volume and the rest of the world in the second. For each organization giving an award, lists basic directory information (including e-mail and URLs) and each award, with a brief description; but it does not list recipients. Arranged by organization, with indexes by subject (to each volume), by organization, and by award (comprehensive in each volume). Does not list scholarships and grants.

■ Smith, Laura. Children's book awards international. Jefferson, N.C.: McFarland, 1992. 649p.

Lists more than 400 awards given by about 40 countries, for a total of about 11,000 awards given up to 1990. Arranged by country, then name of award. Entries give award name, sponsor (and contact information), criteria for award, and a list of winners through 1990. Indexed by author, award, illustrator, title, sponsor.

■ World of winners. 3d ed. Detroit: Gale, 1998. 1315p.

Covers winners of about 2,900 awards in all areas, including sports, literature, science, and other fields. Arranged by award name, listing organization that gives the award and then all winners, most recent first. Some entries include brief information about the award and the winner. Indexed by exact name of award, subject, organization, and winner.

Broadcast Media

■ Bacon's directories on disc. Chicago: Bacon's Information, 1952– . Annual. Web (as MediaSource International) and on CD-ROM only.

Covers all of the Bacon directories—newspapers, magazines, TV (broadcast and cable), radio, news services, syndicators. These are also available separately in print, but the electronic formats are much more convenient. Bacon is a well-respected publisher of media-oriented directories.

■ Broadcasting and cable yearbook. New Providence, N.J.: Bowker, 1982– . Annual.

Title varies. Covers all aspects of U.S. and Canadian broadcasting— radio and television, plus cable and similar systems, advertising, services, trade associations, etc. Indexes by people and organizations.

■ Burrelle's media directory. Livingston, N.J.: Burrelle's Media Services, 1997. 5v. Annual. Also on CD-ROM.

One of the standard media directories in the United States, covering newspapers, news services, magazines and newsletters, radio and television stations, and cable systems. Aimed at the business, rather than the listener, provides detailed directory information, including phone, fax, e-mail, URL if available, information on advertising and acceptance of press releases, frequency, and the like. Also indicates special sections (for print media) or special local shows (e.g., talk shows, for broadcast media). Includes a very brief annotation as to format, audience, and topical emphasis.

Business

As an area with a large number of directory-type sources, the business field has naturally generated a general "bibliography" of such sources:

■ Directory of business and financial information services. 9th ed. Washington, D.C.: Special Libraries Assn., 1994. 471p.

> First published in 1924. Lists about 1,300 services by about 370 vendors. Emphasis on the United States, but it includes more than 150 foreign sources. Covers books, CD-ROMs, loose-leafs, etc. Publisher, title, and subject indexes.

■ D & B million dollar directory. New York: Dun & Bradstreet, 1959- . Annual. Also on CD-ROM as Million Dollar Disc.

> No other set comes close to this one. *Standard & Poor's* (S & P's) *Directory* has only about 25 percent as many companies but more data per company, with this an honorable second. Alphabetical by company, with indexes by location and by industry.

■ Directory of corporate affiliations. New Providence, N.J.: National Register, 1973- . Annual. Also online and on CD-ROM.

> Concentrates on companies traded in major U.S. stock exchanges and over the counter but lists some private companies as well. Provides access by company name, parent company, brand name, SIC code, and personal names (corporate executives).

■ Standard & Poor's register of corporations, directors and executives. New York: Standard & Poor's, 1928- . Annual, with three supplements per year. Also online as Standard & Poor's Corporation Descriptions and on CD-ROM as Standard & Poor's Corporations.

> Covers more than 55,000 U.S. corporations and more than 70,000 of their executives. Gives brief corporate description and data (number of employees, annual sales volume) plus profiles of executives and corporate directors. Indexed by SIC code, location, corporate family. Includes obituaries of those included in last edition, list of the S & P 500, and other lists.

Much directory use can be made out of the standard business data sources, notably those published by Standard & Poor's and Moody's. These sources, because they are much more than directories, are treated in chapter 8.

■ American manufacturers directory. Omaha, Nebr.: American Business Directories, 1992– . Annual. Also online as American Business Directory (quarterly updates) and on CD-ROM as Business America (semiannual updates).

Manufacturing businesses with at least twenty employees, giving basic directory information plus names of CEO, president, and owner; ranges of employees and sales; and a credit rating. The main entries are arranged by firm name; other sections give brief information arranged by city and SIC code. The same publisher provides a *State Business Directory* for all states and a CD-ROM called Business America (or Business Disc) combining a number of its directories.

■ American wholesalers and distributors directory. 7th ed. Detroit: Gale, 1999. 1700p.

Covers more than 27,000 firms in the United States, giving basic directory information including e-mail addresses and URLs, chief officers, and business emphasis with some data. Classified by subject. Indexed by SIC code, location, company name.

■ Brands and their companies. Detroit: Gale, 1976– . Annual. Also online as Trade Names Database.

Formerly *Trade Names Dictionary.* Lists more than a quarter of a million consumer brand names, giving a brief description, name of company who makes or owns it, and a citation to the source of this information. Company names listed with basic directory information. A companion volume, *Companies and Their Brands,* provides the reverse information.

■ Consultants and consulting organizations directory. Detroit: Gale, 1973– . Annual. Also online.

Covers the United States and Canada. Gives basic directory information, including e-mail addresses and URLs and a brief description. Arranged by broad topic. Indexed by location, firm and personal name, activity. Updated by *New Consultants.*

■ Thomas register of American manufacturers. New York: Thomas, 1905/06– . Annual. Also on the Web and on CD-ROM.

The premier directory of manufacturers and of the goods they manufacture. Arranged in three sections: "Products and Services," listing products under nearly 63,000 headings, using an alphabetic-classified arrangement, then listing suppliers by state and then by city. This section also includes an alphabetical index to the classification systems. The second part, "Company Profiles," is arranged by company, giving basic directory information, ratings of assets, and locations of major offices, factories, and the like; most also include a listing of the full product lines. The "catalog file" includes catalogs for more than 2,200 firms, arranged by company name. And, in some ways a very turn-of-the-last-century feature, the entire directory is peppered with advertisements from the companies. Indexes include those by product heading and by trademark and brand name.

Disabled People

■ ABLEDATA. U.S. Department of Education. National Institute on Disability and Rehabilitation Research. Online database available at no charge on the Web.

A directory of "assistive technology" products of all kinds and of all levels of technology, from white canes to wheelchairs to computer-assisted voice-recognition systems. Provides a detailed description of the product, including full company directory information and price ranges. The directory includes references to items no longer made and to experimental, customized, and do-it-yourself designs. Searchable by keyword, subject headings, phrase, brand name, company.

■ AFB directory of services for blind and visually impaired persons in the United States and Canada. New York: American Federation for the Blind, 1932– . Biennial. Also on CD-ROM.

Schools, government and private agencies, organizations, etc. for blind and visually impaired people, their families, and people who work with them. Includes publications, services, products, and media. Geographically arranged; indexed by subject and by organizations.

■ The complete directory for people with disabilities. Lakeville, Conn.: Grey House; Detroit: Gale, 1991– . Annual.

Basic directory information plus brief description of service or product, emphasizing the United States but with many other countries having at least a few entries. Covers camps, schools, products, services, publications, travel, etc. Indexed by entry name, locations, disability.

Education

There seem to be almost as many education directories as there are business directories. Nearly every professional association and interest group seems to have its own list of recommended educational programs, while several popular magazines provide annual rankings of one kind or another. The following is just a sampling of pure directories useful in the typical library, with a conscious attempt to recognize the educational interests of those not planning for college as well as those who are.

■ Accredited institutions of postsecondary education [year]: programs, candidates. Washington, D.C.: American Council on Education, 1976/77- . Annual.

   A directory of both degree and nondegree (e.g., auto repair) programs in the United States, with basic directory information, program, and by whom accredited. Does not list any program where there is no accrediting body; thus, is not a complete list of programs or degrees. Arranged by state, with an institution index. Unfortunately, no subject index.

■ American trade schools directory. Queens Village, N.Y.: Croner, 1953- . Monthly.

   A loose-leaf source listing private and public trade schools of all types, giving brief directory information and course of study code. Indexed by state and course of study.

■ American universities and colleges. Washington, D.C.: American Council on Education, 1928- . Quadrennial.

   The definitive standard directory, with more information than in most others. Covers about 1,900 institutions in detail. General and institutional index. Unfortunately, given the publishing schedule, much of the information becomes out-of-date. A companion volume covering the two-year colleges is *American Community Colleges: A Guide* (10th ed. Phoenix, Ariz.: Oryx, 1995; 909p.).

■ Baird's manual of American college fraternities. 20th ed. Indianapolis, Ind.: Baird's Manual Foundation, 1991. Multiple pagination.

   The standard guide to both fraternities and sororities. Includes a general history of fraternities, then a listing in some detail (two to three pages each) followed by the colleges that have chapters. The listings are in several sections for members of the different umbrella associations. Includes a list of defunct groups and other similar recognition societies and groups.

■ Barnhart, Phillip A. Guide to national professional certification programs. 2d ed. Amherst, Mass.: Human Resource Development Pr., 1997. 325p.

All types of programs certifying any occupational group (engineers, hairdressers, secretaries, etc.). Describes programs, including how one obtains the certificate, with basic directory information and size of program. An important source for those who do not choose the college route but wish some other sort of formal training.

■ College blue book. New York: Macmillan, 1923– . 5v.

A classic, covering about 3,000 institutions with general descriptions, basic data (e.g., number of students), and lists of degrees offered by subject. Includes e-mail addresses and URLs for a growing number of institutions. Arrangement is narrative descriptions; tabular information; index of degrees by college and by subject, occupation, and education; and a section on grants, loans, and other financial aid.

■ Commonwealth Universities yearbook. London and New York: Assn. of Commonwealth Universities, 1914– ; distributed by Stockton Pr. Annual.

Detailed profiles of about 500 universities in thirty-two nations and to about 200,000 staff members in them. Includes fairly long descriptions of the educational system for many of the nations. Indexes by topics, institution/organization, subjects of study, personal names.

■ Handbook of private schools. Boston: Porter Sargent, 1915– . Annual.

The standard in the field, usually called Porter-Sargent. Covers about 1,700 private boarding and day schools, with full directory information, details of curriculum, special programs (e.g., military schools), enrollment, faculty size, and colleges attended by graduates and a description of the surrounding community. Indexed by school name.

■ HEP higher education directory. Falls Church, Va.: Higher Education, 1979– . Annual.

Covers the more than 3,600 agencies accredited by all bodies recognized by the U.S. Department of Education. Gives basic directory information plus enrollment size, typical fees, and programs at the college. By state, then institution. Indexed by institution, by accrediting agency, and by names (with phone numbers) of major administrators. Includes both four-year and two-year institutions.

■ National faculty directory. Detroit: Gale, 1970– . Annual.

About 606,000 faculty members at about 3,700 institutions in North America. Arranged by name, giving very brief directory information (institution phone number, basic address) and academic department. Excludes those who are not classroom teachers and unlikely to adopt textbooks for class use. Data are from catalogs and faculty directories; thus, the listings are not always accurate or current.

■ Patterson's American education. Mount Prospect, Ill.: Educational Directories, 1904– . 2v. Annual.

Now combines this title with *Patterson's Schools Classified,* formerly a separate publication. Covers public and private junior high and high schools and school districts. Volume 1 is arranged by state, community, district, then school, giving directory information and principals. Volume 2 lists the schools by specialty. Includes several specialized lists as well, such as U.S. territories, Catholic schools, Lutheran schools, etc.

■ Patterson's elementary education. Mount Prospect, Ill.: Educational Directories, 1989– . Annual.

Covers public elementary schools in the United States, excepting specialty and kindergarten-only schools and private schools with more than 100 students. Similar to *Patterson's American Education.*

■ Peterson's annual guide to graduate study. Princeton, N.J.: Peterson's, 1983– . Annual. 6v. Also online and on CD-ROM as Gradline.

Includes a general overview, with considerable tabular and narrative comparative information. The other five volumes, arranged by subject, provide in-depth discussions of specific programs at specific schools, usually focusing on all faculty and research, as well as details of the department or program.

■ Peterson's guide to four-year colleges. Princeton, N.J.: Peterson's, 1970– . Annual.

■ Peterson's guide to two-year colleges. Princeton, N.J.: Peterson's, 1960– . Annual. Both also online and on CD-ROM as Peterson's College Database.

Both are standards, with about half-page standardized descriptions of each institution, giving details of enrollment, fees, programs, student aid. These are followed by much longer, detailed descriptions of a smaller number of institutions, written by their own staff, discussing lifestyle, the general environment, and the like.

■ World higher education database. New York: Grove's Dictionaries, 1996– . Web and on CD-ROM only.

Formerly World Academic Database. Based on data in *International Handbook of Universities* and *World List of Universities,* plus further information from UNESCO data, this source covers more than 12,000 institutions in 175 nations.

■ World list of universities and other institutions of higher education. New York: Stockton Pr., 1962– . Biennial.

Very brief entries for more than 11,000 universities, as defined by each nation, in 178 nations, plus other three- and four-year schools and national educational agencies concerned with the university level. Excludes military academies and independent theological schools. Arranged by nation, then category, then name. No index by institution name. The index is really only a table of contents.
The *International Handbook of Universities,* by the same publisher, contains more information on about roughly half of the institutions.

■ The world of learning. London and Detroit: Europa, 1947– ; distributed by Gale. Annual.

Has been called a perennial standard. Lists 26,000 institutions, including learned societies, research institutions, libraries, museums, etc., with directory information, staff size, major administrators. Some universities list all faculty. Arranged geographically, with an index by institution name.

Ethnic Groups

■ Asian Americans information directory. 2d ed. Detroit: Gale, 1993. 577p.

Arranged by nineteen ethnic groups, listing national and state organizations, government agencies, libraries, media, etc. related to each of the groups. Most entries give directory information and a brief descriptive annotation.

■ African Americans information directory. Detroit: Gale, 1990– . Biennial.

Has become a standard work, in part because of the frequency of updates. More than 5,000 entries arranged in eighteen chapters, more or less by format (awards, periodicals, etc.). Includes a video section. Most entries are from other Gale publications, but it also includes information from the *U.S. Government Manual, Catalog of Federal Domestic*

Assistance, and *Black Enterprise* magazine. *American Reference Books Annual (ARBA)* has called this an "essential reference source for most libraries."

■ Hispanic resource directory. Juneau, Alaska: Denali Pr., 1988– . Triennial.

More than 6,000 entries for associations, research and resource centers, schools at all levels, libraries, migrant and bilingual associations, media, diplomatic offices, etc. Gives basic directory information and contact person, including fax numbers and in some cases (libraries and publications) a brief annotation.

■ Native Americans information directory. 2d ed. Detroit: Gale, 1998. 372p.

Much overlap with the *Reference Encyclopedia of the American Indian,* but this includes Hawaii and a very good index. Many entries are annoated. Indexed by name and keyword.

■ Reference encyclopedia of the American Indian. 8th ed. West Nyack, N.Y.: Todd, 1997. 735p.

Much more of a directory with statistics than an "encyclopedia," this covers the United States and Canada. Considerable overlap with Gale's *Native Americans Information Directory,* but each has material the other lacks.

Events

■ Eventline. New York: Elsevier, 1989– . Monthly. Also online.

A multidisciplinary directory to conventions, trade shows, professional meetings, sports events, and the like, including dates and locations, contact information, organizers.

■ World meetings: United States and Canada. New York: Macmillan, 1963– . Quarterly.

■ World meetings outside the United States and Canada. New York: Macmillan, 1968– . Quarterly.

Each issue covers current information plus two years in the future. Main section is by date with full descriptions of location, date, times, sponsor, theme, exhibits, anticipated number of attendees, etc. Indexed by date of meeting, keyword in meeting name, location, deadline, sponsor.

Government and Politics—National

GENERAL

■ The capital source. Washington, D.C.: National Journal, 1986– . Semiannual.

A basic directory, including e-mail addresses and URLs of all types of organizations in the District of Columbia area, including government offices, embassies, corporations, consultants, news contacts, and the like. No index.

■ Washington information directory. Washington, D.C.: Congressional Quarterly, 1975– . Annual.

Basic directory information for all sorts of government and private organizations, including congressional committees, lobbyists, etc., with basic directory information plus a very brief description. Also includes governors and secretaries of state, mayors of larger cities, and some other state officials. Indexed by name and subject.

■ Wilcox, Laird. Guide to the American left: directory and bibliography. 21st ed. Olathe, Kans.: Editorial Research Service, 1999. 108p.

■ Wilcox, Laird. Guide to the American right: directory and bibliography. 24th ed. Olathe, Kans.: Editorial Research Service, 1999. 102p.

Gives basic directory information plus a one-sentence annotation (description or biography) for organizations, serials, and some people. Each also contains an annotated bibliography. Includes other information such as pithy quotations and some articles (original and reprints) on relevant topics.

PERSONS

■ Carroll's federal directory. Washington, D.C.: Carroll, 1995– . Annual. Also online and on CD-ROM.

The "library edition" includes the *Regional Directory* as well, which covers federal officials who work outside the Washington area. Probably the most complete such directory currently in print, with full directory information for each agency, congresspersons, etc., with lists of aides or other heads of departments, including fax and e-mail and beginning to include URLs. Indexed by keyword and location, with a separate phone directory of "key executives." Includes maps of congressional districts, plus (unlike most similar sources) maps of other such districts as defined by regulatory agencies.

■ Clements, John. Taylor's encyclopedia of government officials, federal and state. Dallas, Tex.: Political Research, 1968– . Biennial, with quarterly updates.

> Top officials of federal and state governments, plus ambassadors. Gives basic directory information and considerable data on each state, recent elections, etc. Indexed by personal name, arranged by state. This source also includes a political research service for subscribers, which will answer questions and provide documents.

■ Congressional staff directory. Mount Vernon, Va.: Staff Directories, 1959– . Three times per year. Also on CD-ROM.

> Nearly all staff of all members of Congress in color-coded sections. Gives basic biographies, pictures of the congressperson, zip codes for the districts, and other features. Has an index by person and a subject index.

■ Congressional yellow book. Washington, D.C.: Leadership Directories, 1976– . Loose-leaf, with four updates per year. Also online and on CD-ROM.

> Very useful source providing basic directory information, plus some statistics and a little biographical information.

■ Federal regional yellow book. Washington, D.C.: Leadership Directories, 1993– . Semiannual.

> Most permanent staff in regional offices of all branches of the federal government outside of Washington. Basic directory information indexed by location, name, and subject.

■ Federal staff directory. Mount Vernon, Va.: Staff Directories, 1982– . Three times per year. Also on CD-ROM.

> Covers executive branch, giving information about each agency (including quasi-government bodies such as the Smithsonian) plus a high percentage of its staff. Basic directory information, plus brief biographies for upper-level staff. Indexed by name and keyword.

■ Federal yellow book. Washington, D.C.: Leadership Directories, 1976– . Quarterly. Also on CD-ROM.

> Executive departments, giving name and basic directory information. Presidential appointees also noted in table of contents. General phone numbers for agencies and offices, as well as for specific people. Indexed by agency and personal name.

■ Judicial staff directory. Mount Vernon, Va.: Staff Directories, 1986– . Annual. Also on CD-ROM.

Lists all judges and clerks for all federal courts, giving basic directory information. Includes maps of each state and territory federal jurisdiction; also includes the Department of Justice and all state courts. Has the most detailed indexes of all of these.

■ Official congressional directory, [year]. Washington, D.C.: Govt. Print. Off., 1888– . Biennial.

Title varies. Official directory of members of Congress, with short biographies, committee assignments, etc. Includes lists of other major federal officials, foreign diplomats, governors, and members of the press, radio, and television galleries. Really more of a directory *for* members of Congress than merely a directory of them.

■ Staff directories on CD-ROM. Mount Vernon, Va.: Staff Directories, 1993– . Semiannual. CD-ROM only.

Congressional, Federal, and Judicial Staff Directories on one disc. Good search capability, but one can only search one directory at a time.

And, for historical research, the following is indispensible:

■ Official register of the United States. Washington, D.C.: Department of Commerce, Bureau of the Census, 1861-1959. Biennial, 1861-1923; annual, 1925-59.

Title and issuing agency vary, as does coverage, with postal service dropped in 1912 and most "minor staff" excluded after 1925. Arranged by agency with a name index. Basic directory information plus salary and title.

ORGANIZATIONS

■ Federal regulatory directory. 9th ed. Washington, D.C.: Congressional Quarterly, 1999. 760p.

Directory information plus detailed history of each agency. Includes pictures and short biographies of commissioners plus directory information for middle- and upper-level staff. Amount of information varies with section, roughly with importance of agency. Also provides information on how to use *Federal Register* (Washington, D.C.: Office of the Federal Register, 1936– ; daily, except Saturdays, Sundays, and federal holidays) and *Code of Federal Regulations* (Washington, D.C.: Office of the Federal Register, 1938– ; regular updates). A detailed name index and an agency/subject index.

Government and Politics—State and Local

■ Carroll's municipal/county directory. Washington, D.C.: Carroll, 1995– . Annual. Also online and on CD-ROM.

The library edition includes both county and municipal government, with the level of detail the same as for *Carroll's Federal Directory,* including the same approach to indexing.

■ Carroll's state directory. Washington, D.C.: Carroll, 1995– . Annual. Also online and on CD-ROM.

Covers state government agencies with the level of detail the same as for the federal government, including the same approach to indexing, except no geographic index because the basic arrangement is geographical.

■ Hellebust, Lynn. State legislative sourcebook, [year]: a resource guide to legislative information in the fifty states. Topeka, Kans.: Government Research Service, 1985– . Annual.

Now in hardcover versus earlier loose-leaf. Covers fifty states, the District of Columbia, Puerto Rico. Detailed background and full bibliographic citations plus URLs.

■ Municipal yellow book. Washington, D.C.: Leadership Directories, 1991– . Semiannual.

Basic directory, including fax numbers for larger cities and counties, plus some "authorities" such as bus, tunnel, and harbor authorities. Lists more people per city but fewer cities than the Carroll directory.

Grants, Fellowships, and Scholarships

■ Annual register of grant support. New Providence, N.J.: Bowker/Reed Reference, 1969– . Annual.

Lists more than 3,300 organizations, both government and private, corporations, trusts, and similar groups that give funding. Basic directory information for each organization is followed by a listing of each grant program, with recent deadlines, eligibility, sizes of awards, number of awards, and the like. Includes a contact person. Classified by type of support (e.g., engineering, arts), with indexes by subject, organization, personal name, location.

■ Catalog of federal domestic assistance. Washington, D.C.: Office of Management and the Budget, 1971– . Annual. Punched for three-ring binder. Also on the Web and on CD-ROM.

A list of all federal assistance programs, including both financial and nonfinancial programs. Unquestionably the most complete listing by program but generally felt to be rather difficult to use. This has led to the following, which essentially reformats the information into a more user-friendly arrangement: J. Robert Dumouchel. *Government Assistance Almanac, [year]* (Detroit: Omnigraphics, 1985– ; annual).

■ Complete grants sourcebook for higher education. 3d ed. Phoenix, Ariz.: Oryx, 1995. 340p.

Unlike most of its competitors, this actually provides brief *evaluations* of the funding source and process for each agency listed. Includes directory information plus basic data (high, low, and average awards), a brief description of the process, and a listing of recent grants. Indexed by subject, foundations, name, and state. Also has an annotated bibliography.

■ Directory of research grants. Phoeniz, Ariz.: Oryx, 1975– . Annual. Also online and on CD-ROM as GRANTS. Updated every two months.

Although this overlaps with the *Annual Register of Grant Support,* its emphasis on research funding and its extensive and detailed index make it worth considering. The regular electronic updating increases its value.

The Foundation Center, a nonprofit organization based in New York, provides a number of services for the seeker after private funding. These services include the titles listed below, among others, and also the maintenance of research centers in many cities. These centers include all the directories listed here, many other sources, and detailed information on the local and regional funding agencies, as well as staff trained to assist users who may seek funding. The center's website, at <http://fdncenter.org>, should be familar to everyone who has tried or might try to obtain funding for a worthy project. A number of the sources listed below are also available on FC Search, a CD-ROM (New York: Foundation Center, 1996–).

■ Foundation directory. New York: Foundation Center, 1960- . Annual, with supplement. Also online.

Part 1 lists independent, corporate, community, and private foundations with assets of $2 million or more or annual giving of at least $200,000. Gives directory information, officers, basic data on size and size of grant, and application information. Indexes by location, type of support, subject, foundation name, with a list of new foundations. Part 2 (1990-) provides similar coverage from smaller foundations.

■ Foundation grants index. New York: Foundation Center, 1970- . Annual cumulations of *Foundation Grants Index Quarterly.*

Lists awards of $10,000 and more, with a brief description of the reason for the award and information about the awarding organization. Arranged by broad subject, with indexes by several points. Includes an alphabetical list of foundations with addresses. The *Foundation Directory* lists the awarding body, but this lists the awardees.

■ Foundation grants to individuals. New York: Foundation Center, 1977- . Biennial.

Lists grants for as little as $64 and as high as $20,000 plus, with detailed information on the grant. Covers all types of aid (grants, scholarships, internships, etc.) to individuals from private foundations.

■ Guide to U.S. foundations, their trustees, officers and donors. New York: Foundation Center, 1993- . Annual. Formerly *The National Data Book of Foundations.*

A complete listing of funding agencies, covering more than 25,000 private organizations and about 250 community organizations giving grants of at least $1. Also provides information on 700 other groups that only give funding internally. More complete in listing, but with less information per entry, than the *Foundation Directory;* and it can be used as an index to all the center's other publications.

■ Margolin, Judith B., ed. The Foundation Center's user-friendly guide: grantseeker's guide to resources. 4th ed. New York: Foundation Center, 1996. 40p.

A brief pamphlet organized under ten headings, with bibliographies. Many longer books, not to mention a number of television infomercials, purport to tell the seeker how to do it; this title actually does so, and it should be in every reference library.

Gale A. Schlachter, with the assistance of R. David Weber, produces some detailed directories to financial aid for specific groups of people. Although some duplication exists among the volumes, the amount of information per grant or award (including the size and number of awards along with the usual descriptions) and the indexing by program, sponsor, location, subject, and deadlines make these very useful. Current titles, all published biennially by Reference Services Press, include the following:

College Student's Guide to Merit and Other No-Need Funding

Financial Aid for African Americans

Financial Aid for Asian Americans

Financial Aid for Hispanic Americans

Financial Aid for Native Americans

Financial Aid for Research and Creative Activities Abroad

Financial Aid for Study and Teaching Abroad

Financial Aid for the Disabled and Their Families

Funding for Persons with Visual Impairments

High School Senior's Guide to Merit and Other No-Need Funding

Money for Graduate Research and Study in the Humanities

Money for Graduate Research and Study in the Sciences

Money for Graduate Research and Study in the Social Sciences

RSP Funding for Nursing Students and Nurses

Historical Agencies and Museums

■ America preserved: a checklist of historic buildings, structures and sites. Washington, D.C.: Library of Congress, 1995. 1179p.

A brief checklist of sites based on the Historic American Buildings Survey and the Historic American Engineering Record, with data on documentation available (e.g., written material, photographs, measured drawings, etc.), including informal documents such as field notes. The entry includes the street address. This includes many buildings now gone and many not on the National Register.

■ Directory of historical organizations in the United States and Canada. 14th ed. Nashville, Tenn.: American Assn. for State and Local History, 1990. 1108p.

All sorts of professional and amateur organizations arranged by location. Gives a brief description of activities, publications, collections or programs, and a contact person, as well as basic directory information and a list of key staff.

■ Folklife sourcebook. Washington, D.C.: Library of Congress, 1994. 165p.

Directory of folklife sources, complete for the United States and including Canada and Mexico in the appendixes. Includes archives, programming (such as demonstrations and living history displays), societies, serials, publishers, mail-order dealers in reproduction clothing and artifacts, books and music, and related material for those interested in American folk culture.

■ Hudson, Kenneth, and Ann Nicholls. Directory of museums and living displays. 3d ed. New York: Stockton Pr./Grove's Dictionaries of Music, 1985. 1047p.

Includes more than 35,000 living-history farms, botanical gardens, zoos, aquariums, and similar places, giving name and address and a two- to three-line general statement. The United States gets most coverage, but 170 countries are listed. No index, but there is no real need for one.

■ Museums of the world. 5th ed. New Providence, N.J.: K. G. Saur/Reed Reference, 1995. 672p.

The first revision since 1981, with basic directory information, museum director's name, and brief annotations about the collections. Indexed by subject.

■ National register of historic places, 1966–1994: cumulative list through January 1, 1994. Washington, D.C.: National Park Service, 1994. 923p.

Each new edition replaces previous cumulation. Lists about 58,000 sites by state, county, and then name. Gives address, date of designation, coding by type of property, and a reference number. No description to speak of; this is almost a classic directory. Chadwyck-Healey has published much of the documentation for each property on fiche.

■ Official museum directory. Wilmette, Ill.: National Register, 1961– . Annual.

Title varies. More than 7,000 for the United States by state, then city. Directory information, plus a profile of the collection, description of the physical facilities, and other information about each museum. Affiliated professional organizations, regional associations, and other similar bodies are also listed. Indexed by museum name, personnel, museum category, collection subject. Canada was included through 1983 but is now in a companion, *The Official Directory of Canadian Museums* (Ottawa: Canadian Museums Assn., 1984/85– ; irregular).

■ Smith, Allen. Directory of oral history collections. Phoenix, Ariz.: Oryx, 1988. 141p.

Lists 476 U.S. repositories, arranged by state, then city. Though somewhat out-of-date, the basic descriptions are still valid, and many newer collections are not readily accessible. The best approach is probably to use Ash and Miller's *Subject Collections* (*see* below, p. 199) to identify the topic of interest, and then confirm the presence of oral history with the specific collection.

Genealogy

■ Bentley, Elizabeth P. County courthouse book. 2d ed. Baltimore, Md.: Genealogical Pub., 1996. 405p.

Guide to courthouses from a genealogical perspective, giving general background on each state's court system, basic directory information for each courthouse, and a description of its holdings.

■ Bentley, Elizabeth P. Directory of family associations. 3d ed. Baltimore, Md.: Genealogical Pub., 1996. 355p.

Basic directory information, contact persons, and publications of about 6,500 family associations engaged in some form of genealogical research.

■ Filby, P. William. Directory of American libraries with genealogy or local history collections. Wilmington, Del.: Scholarly Resources, 1988. 319p.

Covers the United States and Canada, describing nearly all libraries with such collections, arranged by state or province. Although much of this information is in theory available in the general library directories, not all is; and this is much easier to use.

■ The genealogist's address book. 4th ed. Baltimore, Md.: Genealogical Pub., 1998. 832p.

Updates about 80 percent of the last edition and adds many new addresses. Although the index is hard to use because of a lack of keywords, this is essential for any serious genealogical researcher. Includes national, state, ethnic, and special resources, including governments and libraries, as well as periodicals and serials.

The following four sources provide information about the various legal records of use in genealogical research.

■ The sourcebook of county court records. 4th ed. Tempe, Ariz.: BRB, 1998. 656p.

Gives a description of each state's court structure, followed by a county-by-county listing of the court records sources, including address and phone number and any restrictions on access.

■ The sourcebook of federal courts: U.S. district and bankruptcy. Tempe, Ariz.: BRB, 1993. Various paging.

The same arrangement and entry as the above but for the federal courts.

■ The sourcebook of local court and county record retrievers. Tempe, Ariz.: BRB, 1993. 431p.

By state, then county, giving full contact information and descriptions of people and firms who do this work. Excludes genealogists in general.

■ The sourcebook of state public records. 4th ed. Tempe, Ariz.: BRB, 1998. 448p.

Well over 5,000 state-level locations for more than twenty types of information. Each entry includes directory information, time period coverage of available records, hours, turnaround time, restrictions. An added feature is a how-to chapter on the use and retrieval of these records.

Law

■ Martindale-Hubbell law directory. Summit, N.J.: Martindale-Hubbell, 1868– . Annual.

This directory has been essential since the 1860s. Includes U.S. and Canadian attorneys, plus some other nations. Colleges, law schools, etc., as well as firms. Appendixes include full text of a number of important documents. The same publisher also issues the *Martindale-Hubbell International Law Directory* to cover the rest of the world.

■ Martindale-Hubbell law directory on CD-ROM. New Providence, N.J.: Martindale-Hubbell, 1995– . CD-ROM only.

Combines the eight volumes into one. Keyword searching makes this much easier to use than the print version. Records include both full and short entries (i.e., a full entry for a firm includes all lawyers' names and biographies; a short entry, just the names). CD-ROM users don't need to know where lawyers practice to look them up.

Libraries and Archives

■ American library directory. New Providence, N.J.: Bowker/Reed Reference, 1908– . Annual. Also online and on CD-ROM. Updated by American Library Directory Updating Service.

Another standard, now including e-mail addresses, URLs, and OPAC dial-in numbers. Arranged by state, then city, this lists basic directory and statistical information for all types of libraries, except those in elementary and secondary schools. The entries typically include size measures (such as the number of volumes held and budget figures), department heads, and other staff of interest to outsiders, such as interlibrary loan librarians, curators of special collections, and the like. Special collections are usually described in brief. Includes a growing number of libraries in Canada and Mexico. A useful feature is the recent addition of an index by people listed. As with other Bowker directories of this type, data are based on annual surveys and thus limited to the responses received, but this generally has reasonably up-to-date statistics on budget, services, staff size, and the like.

■ Ash, Lee, and William G. Miller. Subject collections: a guide to special book collections and subject emphases as reported by university, college, public, and special libraries and museums in the United States and Canada. 7th rev. and enl. ed. New Providence, N.J.: Bowker, 1993. 2v.

The standard and the most complete such directory for libraries and museums, but it excludes college and university archives and small local history and genealogy collections. Each entry, arranged by subject then state, includes directory information, a description of the collection, and holdings information.

■ Burwell directory of information brokers. Houston, Tex.: Burwell, 1978- . Annual. Also on the Web and on CD-ROM.

Basic directory information to independent information workers, listing more than 1,500 people and organizations worldwide, but with a strong U.S. slant. Standard information includes a paragraph about each group, including fees. Indexed by city, company, contacts, foreign country experience, etc., including subject covered.

■ DeWitt, Donald L. Guides to archives and manuscript collections in the United States: an annotated bibliography. Westport, Conn.: Greenwood, 1994. 478p.

A bibliography of finding aids, directories, and similar material.

■ Directory of government documents collections and librarians. 7th ed. Bethesda, Md.: Congressional Information Service, 1997. 624p.

Directory of libraries and librarians, especially useful for state, local, international, and highly specialized collections.

■ Directory of special libraries and information centers. Detroit: Gale, 1963- . 2v.

Libraries with specialized collections or services in all subjects, arranged by library name, with well over 8,000 cross-references within the text. Provides full directory information, details on the library (much like those in the *American Library Directory*), and descriptions of the specialized areas. Indexed by subject, with a number of type-of-library listings as well. A second volume provides indexes by persons and by geographic locations. Updated between editions by *New Special Libraries*. For a subject rather than library name arrangement, *see* Subject Directory of Special Libraries. This is in several volumes, each of which may be purchased separately.

■ Downs, Robert B. American library resources: a bibliographical guide. Chicago: ALA, 1951. 428p. Updated by supplements for 1950-61, 1961-70, 1971-80.

Lists only libraries with catalogs, bibliographies, articles about the collection; does not list similar collections that have no such publications. There is also a cumulative index by author and subject.

■ Information industry directory. Detroit: Gale, 1971– . Annual.

Formerly *Encyclopedia of Information Systems and Services.* An alphabetical listing of agencies, businesses, and organizations in the industry, including database producers and services, hardware and software firms related to information handling, and the like. Is definitely the most complete source in the field, with the usual collection of detailed indexes common to Gale products.

■ National inventory of documentary sources in the United States. Teaneck, N.J.: Chadwyck-Healey, 1983– . In progress fiche/CD-ROM.

Also known as *NIDS.* Includes state and federal agencies, historical societies, academic libraries, etc. Lists guides to manuscripts and archives, both published and unpublished finding aids. As with several other products from this publisher, the full text of the sources listed is available in microform.

■ Special collections in children's literature: an international directory. 3d ed. Chicago: ALA, 1995. 235p.

The definitive directory in its field, with about one-fourth of the listings outside the United States. Very specific descriptions plus directory information.

■ World guide to special libraries. 4th ed. New Providence, N.J.: K. G. Saur/Reed Reference, 1998. 2v.

About 50,000 libraries arranged by subject strength. Index of libraries but not of subjects. Includes freestanding libraries, plus departmental and similar university library collections.

Medicine and Health

■ ALA fingertip guide to national health-information resources. Chicago: ALA, 1995. 97p.

An address and phone directory, including toll-free numbers and very brief annotations. Has a good subject index; also a hot-line section.

■ American dental directory. Chicago: American Dental Assn., 1947- . Annual.

By state and city, giving directory information, specialization, and place and year of dental degree. Includes lists of military dentists and a list by specialty.

■ A.H.A. [American Hospital Association] guide to the health care field. Chicago: Healthcare Infosource, 1972- . Annual.

Four sections: hospitals, health-care systems, health organizations and agencies, networks. Generally provides more information per entry than the ALA guide.

■ Directory of health care professionals. Chicago: American Health Care Assn., 1990- . 2v. Annual.

Basic directory information of professionals in hospitals in the United States covering about 7,000 hospitals. Volume 1 lists more than 7,000 hospitals; volume 2 lists about 183,000 individuals.

■ Directory of nursing homes. Baltimore, Md.: HCIA, 1982- . Annual.

Directory information plus admission requirements, size, facilities, and an index by affiliation and a list of names.

■ Directory of physicians in the United States. Chicago: American Medical Assn., 1906- . Irregular.

Formerly *American Medical Directory.* Arranged by name, with a geographical listing.

■ DIRLINE. Bethesda, Md.: U.S. National Library of Medicine, Quarterly updates. Online database only.

Directory plus description of information resources.

■ Encyclopedia of health information sources. 2d ed. Detroit: Gale, 1993. 521p.

Citations to more than 6,700 sources including CD-ROMs and online databases. Gives phone and fax numbers. No evaluations for sources, but selected from reputable selective bibliographies such as Brandon's core lists, reviews. An excellent starting point, although not exhaustive.

■ Medical and health information directory. 10th ed. Detroit: Gale, 1998. 3v.

Similar to other Gale directories, covering organizations, libraries, publications, etc. in the broad area of health care. Gives basic directory plus membership, purpose, meetings, and publications. Each volume is self-contained and available separately or together. Volume 1 covers organizations and institutions; volume 2 covers libraries, publications, audiovisual (AV) material, and databases. Volume 3 covers health services, with briefer entries than volume 1.

■ Rees, Alan M., ed. Consumer health information source book. 5th ed. Phoenix, Ariz.: Oryx, 1998. 226p.

An annotated directory of sources, including newsletters, organizations, books, and Internet sites, with an emphasis on the consumer/patient. Indexes by author, title, and subject.

Military

■ American military cemeteries: a comprehensive illustrated guide to the hallowed grounds of the United States, including cemeteries overseas. Jefferson, N.C.: McFarland, 1992. 512p.

Covers most military cemeteries (national and state, including Confederate), giving basic description, names of important persons buried there, types of monuments and markers used, and address, often with a map.

■ Cragg, Dan. Guide to military installations. 5th ed. Harrisburg, Pa.: Stackpole Books, 1997. 416p.

U.S. and overseas bases and facilities but omits National Guard and Reserve and Coast Guard. Arranged by location, giving general history, description, housing, services, etc. Includes addresses and contact information and many maps. Indexed by base.

■ Evinger, William R. Directory of military bases in the U.S. Phoenix, Ariz.: Oryx, 1991. 197p.

All bases and installations in the United States including Coast Guard and National Guard and Reserves, plus Department of Defense offices, recruiting offices, training camps, etc. Arranged by location, with basic directory information, a brief description, and numeric data.

■ Neagles, James C. U.S. military records: a guide to federal and state sources, colonial America to the present. Salt Lake City, Utah: Ancestry, 1994. 441p.

An excellent guide, covering all engagements from 1622 to 1975.

Publishing and Media Production

PRINT MEDIA

■ AB Bookman's yearbook. Clifton, N.J.: Bookman's Weekly, 1954- . Annual.

The standard for specifically antiquarian information, as well as news of the trade. Its primary function is the identification of subject-specialist booksellers. Related to *AB Bookman's Weekly,* the bible of the trade.

■ American book trade directory. New Providence, N.J.: Bowker/Reed Reference, 1925- . Annual. Also on CD-ROM.

Originally *American Book Trade Manual.* The standard source for information on all aspects of the U.S. book trade, including booksellers, wholesalers, and suppliers. Includes miscellaneous book trade information, statistics and graphs, and results of some surveys. Not every store listed, especially chain stores. Indexed by type of store and by names for retailers and wholesalers. The same publisher produces *International Book Trade Directory* for the rest of the world.

■ Antiquarian, specialty, and used book sellers: a subject guide and directory. 2d ed. Detroit: Omnigraphics, 1997. 861p.

Nearly 3,000 stores with up to sixteen items of information per entry. A detailed subject index under about 2,000 subjects, plus indexes by store name, store manager. Does not list book fairs or used-book dealers who work out of their own homes, but is the most comprehensive and current directory of its type.

■ Editor and Publisher international year book. New York: Editor and Publisher, 1921- . Annual. Also on CD-ROM.

Newspapers, syndicates, equipment, organizations, services (e.g., clip art), and personnel. Arranged geographically, with some topical arrangements. Brief indexes. Entries include basic directory information plus data varying with type of entry (e.g., news circulation statistics, newsprint consumption). Lack of title index makes this hard to use, although the CD-ROM's search capability obviates the problem. Lots of statistics and directory information. Complete listing of U.S. daily papers, weekly papers, schools of journalism, etc., as well as listing of Canadian and international daily papers.

■ Literary market place. New Providence, N.J.: Bowker/Reed Reference, 1940- . Annual. Also on CD-ROM.

Publishers, printers, suppliers of binding services and graphics, bookstores, etc. Arranged by type of service with full directory information and usually very brief annotations. Well indexed. A complementary source, covering the world outside North America, is *ILMP: International Literary Market Place* (New Providence, N.J.: Bowker, 1971- ; annual).

■ Publishers directory, [year]. Detroit: Gale, 1984- . 2v. Annual.

More than 18,000 publishers and 600 distributors. Includes commercial publishers, interest groups, museums, divisions, imprints, etc. under main entry. Although *Literary Market Place (LMP)* has information on services, suppliers, and book manufacturing not found here, this is complete for publishers. Index by publisher, imprint, distributor; by subject; by location.

■ Publishers, distributors and wholesalers of the United States. New Providence, N.J.: Bowker/Reed Reference, 1979- . Annual. Also online and on CD-ROM.

More comprehensive than *LMP,* covering about 100,000 active publishers, distributors, wholesalers, museums, software manufacturers, cassette manufacturers, etc.

AUDIOVISUAL AND ELECTRONIC MEDIA

■ AV market place. New Providence, N.J.: Bowker, 1984- . Annual.

Covers North America. Basic type of coverage and arrangement are very similar to *LMP.* In addition to producers, manufacturers, distibutors, etc., also lists awards, festivals, reference books, upcoming conferences, etc.

■ Children's media market place. 4th ed. New York: Neal-Schuman, 1995. 284p.

Names, addresses, etc. of publishers, computer software and AV producers/distributors, children's booksellers, grant sources, reviewing sources, etc. Now includes discussion groups, user groups, etc. Index has brief directory information as well as pointer to main entry.

■ Educational media and technology yearbook. Englewood, Colo.: Libraries Unlimited, 1973– . Annual.

Includes annotated bibliography plus general review-type articles, directory information, and the like. Indexes by author, name, title, subject.

■ Information industry directory. Detroit: Gale, 1971– . Annual.

Formerly *Encyclopedia of Information Systems and Services.* As one reviewer put it, the "most comprehensive source in the field, enhanced by the thorough indexing." Covers database producers, services, and brokers, as well as software related to information retrieval.

Religion

■ Melton, J. Gordon. Directory of religious organizations in the United States. 3d ed. Detroit: Gale, 1993. 728p.

About 2,500 for-profit and nonprofit organizations with headquarters in the United States and involved with religion. Excludes the offices of Christian denominational bodies in the *Encyclopedia of American Religions* (Wilmington, N.C.: McGrath, 1978; 2v.) (except archives and historical offices); Roman Catholic religious orders in *The Official Catholic Directory* (New York: Kenedy, 1886– ; annual); social service organizations serving primarily one community. An increasingly important work.

■ Melton, J. Gordon. National directory of churches, synagogues and other houses of worship. Detroit: Gale, 1994. 4v.

The most comprehensive directory of its type, but with less information than some of the specific denominational directories.

■ Melton, J. Gordon. Religious bodies in the United States: a directory. Hamden, Conn.: Garland, 1992. 340p.

In many ways a complement and supplement to Melton's *Directory,* listing many groups not in standard directories. Entries include the usual directory information, plus a brief description of the group.

■ Melton, J. Gordon, and Michael A. Koszegi. Religious information sources: a worldwide guide. Hamden, Conn.: Garland, 1992. 569p.

All types of religion, all over the world, and all types of sources: print and nonprint, databases, oral histories, CD-ROMs, professional associations, etc. Indexes by author, title, subject, organization.

■ Yearbook of American and Canadian churches. Nashville, Tenn.: Abingdon, 1916– . Annual.

Title and publisher vary. Covers all faiths—churches, seminaries, periodicals, archives, etc. Primarily a detailed directory, with narrative information on various denominations and some statistics.

Research Centers and Laboratories

■ Directory of American research and technology. New York: Bowker, 1986– . Annual. Online as INFOLINE and on the Web.

Formerly *Industrial Research Laboratories of the United States,* with format and purpose remaining the same. More than 6,000 parent companies and about 5,000 subsidiaries. A directory of nongovernment facilities involved in commercial research.

■ European research centres. 9th ed. Harlow, England, and Detroit: Longman, 1993; distributed by Gale. 2000p.

Complements *Research Centers Directory.* Based on survey data; thus, entries vary in level of detail. Follows the usual Gale format, with about 12,000 entries. Indexed by title and subject.

■ International research centers directory. Detroit: Gale, 1982– . Annual. Also online and on CD-ROM.

More than 8,000 entries. Excludes the United States and Canada. Indexed by subject, nation, master (name, acronym, keyword).

■ Research centers directory. Detroit: Gale, 1960– . Annual.

About 13,000 organizations by subject, with full directory information and a description of the organization and its functions and services. Indexed by subject, place, name of institution, and a master index. Updated between editions by *New Research Centers* (Detroit: Gale, 1975– ; loose-leaf service). Special emphasis is given to university-based research centers and other nonprofits, unlike the other directories.

■ Research services directory. 7th ed. Lakeville, Conn.: Grey House, 1999. 1089p.

More than 4,400 contract and proprietary research firms in the United States and Canada. Basic directory information plus description, although the latter varies a lot. Generally lists principal clients, publications, services provided. Index by subject, operating name (e.g., Eastman Kodak, not Kodak), location, personal name. Geographic and personal indexes list basic directory information with each entry.

■ Selective inventory of social science information and documentation services. 5th ed. Paris: UNESCO, 1998. 453p.

Based on the DARE information bank (an online and Web directory produced by UNESCO since 1974), plus a questionnaire. A worldwide guide to centers that compile, produce, and distribute social science information and that have permanent staff and service those outside the institution. The typical entry includes a list of publications, type of software and systems used, subject focus.

■ World guide to scientific associations and learned societies. 7th ed. Munich and New York: K. G. Saur, 1998. 529p.

Title varies. Lists currently active national and international organizations, giving directory information, publications, brief description, size of membership. Fifth and later editions include a listing of periodicals published by such societies.

Women

■ Henry, Dawn, ed. DWM: a directory of women's media. New York: National Council for Research on Women, 1972-94. Biennial.

International, with considerable nonmainstream materials. Includes bookstores, writers' groups, speaker's bureaus, libraries, archives, museums, music organizations, and various types of media. Based on mail surveys. Index by publication/organization, individual name, location. Most entries have annotations and subscription or membership information.

■ Stafford, Beth. Directory of women's studies programs and library sources. Phoenix, Ariz.: Oryx, 1990. 154p.

Though outdated, this consolidates a considerable amount of information otherwise difficult to find in the more general directories. Provides access by type of degree or individual courses and detailed information about library strengths. Note that this includes courses and nondegree programs.

■ Women's information directory. Detroit: Gale, 1992. 763p.

More than 11,000 listings relevant to U.S. women and women's issues, including organizations, museums, galleries, etc. Covers national- to state-level services, libraries and museums, awards and other financial aid, publications, electronic sources, etc. related to women. Indexed by name and by subject.

Summary

This chapter lists a few examples of directories for people, institutions, and organizations. Some feel that, given the amount of personal information available on the Internet, these sorts of tools are obsolete. However, when looking at reference works, remember to consider accuracy. One example of the dangers of overreliance on the Internet will suffice: In spring 1999, the author searched for himself by full name on several directories, both on the Web and in more traditional commercial services, nearly all of which are based on public records collected by other agencies. In some cases, there was no entry at all; in others, the only entry was under first intitials rather than names. I was listed as still living in New Orleans, which I left in 1982; as living in a duplex, which is no longer true; and as not having a car (true—I have a van). A slightly broader search found my father still living (he died several years ago), in two different cities, and with an active telephone number.

It has been noted that several of the print and CD-ROM directories listed are not always completely up-to-date, and that no directory can ever be fully accurate, yet none of the standard sources are so out-of-date or inaccurate as all that. So, as one tends to prefer a free source on the Internet, with its user-friendly features, one should always remember that it's the content that is critical—or, as with many other things, let the buyer beware.

5

Sources of Biographical Information

It is not rare to encounter persons who confuse the word *biography* with *bibliography*. Instead of being supercilious about this mistake, librarians should be reminded that biographic searching is very dependent upon bibliographical sources and that early bibliographies resembled biographical dictionaries, their compilers being more concerned with the writers of the works than with scrupulous recordings of their writings. The bibliographies often included details on birth, death, and career and should not be overlooked in biographical searching. Also, national library catalogs, such as those of the Library of Congress, often include some biographical information.

Familiarity with sources of biographical information requires, first of all, some knowledge of their nature and some understanding of the generalizations that apply to their use.

The Nature of Biographical Sources

Look in any good encyclopedia and you will find a brief history of biographical writing, its changing viewpoints and approaches throughout the centuries, and the names of the great biographers who produced this body of knowledge about men's and women's lives. Dryden, who first used the word

210

biography as "the history of particular men's lives" (*Oxford English Dictionary.* 2d ed. [Oxford: Oxford Univ. Pr., 1989; v.2, p. 208]), little dreamed of the proliferation of published biographical reference sources since his time, which must be seen in terms of their usefulness if biographical data are to be retrieved accurately, quickly, and with discriminating judgment.

The value of biographies to reference work (as opposed, say, to historical research) lies in the biographic data they make available. But these data may be presented unclearly, incorrectly, or not at all. In her excellent classic chapter on biographical reference questions, Margaret Hutchins discusses identification problems—those involving obscure persons, disputed facts, and hidden facts about famous people. Attempting to verify disputed facts, she warns that "the correct information is not determined by a mere accumulation of testimonies but by an evaluation of them and by careful checking of a variety of sources against one another" (*Introduction to Reference Work* [Chicago: ALA, 1944], p. 61). Thus, checking a subject in a number of secondary sources, such as biographical dictionaries or encyclopedias, will not necessarily verify a disputed fact, because erroneous "facts" may have been drawn from a single source. Rather, one must attempt to find information whose accuracy can be trusted. Often, this means its origin is as close as possible to the subject in place and in time.

In the discussion that follows, only sources—not types of questions—are considered. No effort has been made to be exhaustive, only to point out the patterns of publications of the sources—bibliographies and indexes, encyclopedias and biographical dictionaries, collective biographies—together with some of the generalizations that apply to them.

Generalizations

A number of general statements apply to all biographical sources:

1. Biographical sources are apt to reflect the prevailing critical opinion of the age in which they are published. The *Dictionary of National Biography,* for example, reflects a late Victorian/Edwardian view, both in who is selected (there are notoriously few women or native colonials listed) and the length of the entries on each person.
2. International biographical dictionaries usually give more emphasis to nationals of the country in which they are published. *Merriam-Webster's Biographical Dictionary,* for example, has British and American emphasis in its number of biographees and length of sketches.
3. Encyclopedias are a good source of information about persons no longer living, but they are generally less useful than current biographical directories for contemporaries, such as *International Who's Who.*

4. Responsibly edited encyclopedias and national biographical dictionaries are apt to include evaluation as well as narration of a biographee's accomplishments, for responsible editing involves a discriminating selection of contributors, verification of facts, and an effort to reflect established judgment of a biographee's contribution to society. Photographs often accompany the sketches.

5. National biographical dictionaries record more nationals and usually give more information about them than international dictionaries. Thus, the *Dictionary of American Biography* gives more information about John Quincy Adams than does *Merriam-Webster's Biographical Dictionary*.

6. State and county histories, with long biographical sections, are a good source of information about less prominent persons and often give fuller treatment to more prominent persons than do national biographical dictionaries. On the other hand, many late-nineteenth- and early-twentieth-century state and county histories are notorious for having sold space in their biographical sections. Thus, they may overemphasize the (positive) contributions of those able to pay, regardless of their objective importance, and underestimate or even ignore those who either could not or would not pay or who weren't even approached as likely customers (especially members of the working class and minorities of any kind).

7. Newspaper and periodical indexes give good references, in some cases, for obituaries, outstanding accomplishments, contemporary opinion, and eyewitness accounts, such as *New York Times* references to a controversial figure. These indexes also serve to bring earlier sources up-to-date. Notably, however, many newspaper indexes and even full-text electronic sources do not include obituaries as a matter of course, unless the person in question was quite prominent or notorious.

8. Special biographical dictionaries of writers and artists usually give more biocritical information and more citations to their work than do general sources.

9. Special biographical dictionaries of scientists, like *American Men and Women of Science,* usually give more information on a scientist's special field than a general source, as well as listing more scientists in the field than the general source.

10. Contributor's columns in general periodicals and literary quarterlies are seldom indexed, but they often serve to identify a young (or new) writer in the issue that published his or her work. The same sort of information is also found, and not indexed, in many scholarly journals as well. Thus, if an item is found by the person of interest, it may also pay to obtain the full issue of the journal as well, and check for the list of contributors (often at the very beginning or end of the textual section of the issue).

11. It is usually less difficult to find information on a writer than a non-writer of equal prominence, because a writer's works appear in bibliographies, indexes, and catalogs.

12. Literary histories and handbooks, such as the *Cambridge History of English Literature* and *Benét's Reader's Encyclopedia,* are a good source of biographies of poets, dramatists, and novelists, often containing more discriminating biocriticism than general sources.

13. In general, the "big fish, small pond" phenomenon will apply: a person of given accomplishments will more likely be listed in a biographical dictionary of narrower scope, whether by subject field or geographic area; similarly, the amount of space devoted to a person usually varies inversely by the range of scope of the source. For example, a person not even in an international biographical directory might receive a line or two in a national source, one or two paragraphs in a listing of film actors, and a page or more in a listing of science-fiction film actors.

From the previous generalizations, the following may be observed:

When the nationality of a person is not known, consult an encyclopedia or international biography first.

When the nationality of a person is known, begin with a national biographical dictionary.

If it is known that a person is no longer living, consult a retrospective source.

If it is known that a person is living, consult a current source first.

If a person's profession is known, consult sources for that profession first.

If a person's place of residence or major contribution is known, consult a source for that area, if possible.

Always keep in mind the increasing availability of collective indexes to biographical sources, which help obviate some of the above.

Evaluation

The following questions should be answered satisfactorily in evaluating the relative worth of a biographical dictionary.

1. How were the biographees selected? Is the selection based on sound criteria, clearly stated in the preface and consistently applied? Are persons of interest included? Are notables within the particular field for which the dictionary claims coverage fully represented? Does it duplicate information readily available in more general reference sources?

2. What sources of information are used? Have they been compiled by an authority who used clearly cited published and unpublished sources? Have they been supplied by the biographee? Were questionnaires or interviews used?
3. Are the sketches factual or evaluative or both? Are they interestingly written? Are the criteria used for evaluation clear?
4. Are references to further information provided? Are the citations full enough to be easily used?
5. Are photographs or other images used? What is their quality?
6. If it is a current biographical dictionary, issued at intervals, is it kept scrupulously up-to-date?
7. Is there an appended index to vocations, geographical locations? Are there any other similar indexes?

Some or all of these points will apply to the individual titles discussed in this chapter, though they are less applicable to the indexes to biography, which often serve as a starting point in searching for biographical information.

Bibliographies

The demand for biographical information, as well as its proliferation, has led to the publication of bibliographies and indexes that make biographical reference work much easier. The most comprehensive current work follows:

■ Bibliography of biography on CD-ROM. Boston Spa, England: British Library, 1992– . Annual updates. CD-ROM only.

A compact disc version of the *Bibliography of Biography,* which is on fiche. Includes entries from the *British National Bibliography, Library of Congress Catalog, University of London Catalogue,* and the British Library's *Humanities and Social Sciences Catalogue.* Lists biographies, autobiographies, collective biographies, and memoirs, mostly in English, and is searchable by fourteen fields (names as subject, keywords, author, title, subjects, year, etc.) and browsable on nine. Given the varied sources used, there is some difference in name authorities and some duplicate records, but this is by far the most complete and easiest to use current tool.

The older literature, especially for the United States, may be found in

■ Biographical books, 1876–1949. New York: Bowker, 1983. 1768p.
■ Biographical books, 1950–1980. New York: Bowker, 1980. 1557p.

Based on the *American Book Publishing Record* cumulations, these provide nearly complete historical coverage for U.S. publishing. Indexes by name, subject, and vocation, as well as author and title. Provides full LC cataloging for all titles.

Other sources of use include the following:

▪ Slocum, Robert B. Biographical dictionaries and related works. 2d ed. Detroit: Gale, 1986. 2v.

Lists about 16,000 sources of collective biography (some annotated) of all kinds, including some biobibliographies, collection of epitaphs, genealogies, government manuals with biographical material, and so forth. Arranged in three sections: universal; United States and foreign by area; United States and foreign by vocation. Indexes by author, title, subject.

Libraries Unlimited has also published a selection from *American Reference Books Annual* as the *ARBA Guide to Biographical Dictionaries* (Littleton, Colo.: Libraries Unlimited, 1986; 444p.). Its main value is the excellent critical annotations, mostly reprinted verbatim from the parent source.

Indexes to Biography

Many general sources can be used as indexes to biographies, the following among them:

Library catalogs, with subject entries for individual biographies

Trade bibliographies, with subject entries for individual biographies

Periodical indexes, with entries for persons who are subjects of articles

Newspaper indexes, which include references to obituaries and names in the news

These should not be overlooked in libraries that lack more specialized titles, for they often give at least birth and death dates and clues to a person's nationality and occupation.

Special indexes to biography fall into two broad categories:

1. those that index a wide range of biographical information appearing in current or recently published books and periodicals, *Biography Index,* for example; and

2. those that index collective biography found in books and/or periodicals published during a specified period in a specified country or countries.

As the number of published biographies continues to increase, both types of indexes are becoming more common. A number of these are listed here; others may be found listed with sources covering specific occupations or groups.

Both types often supply birth and death dates and nationality and occupation of biographees, which will be useful even if the indexed references are unavailable in the libraries where they are consulted. Careful attention to scope of any biographical index or source will save considerable time; for instance, if a name is not found in Hyamson's *Dictionary of Universal Biography*, it is not necessary to consult volumes of the *Dictionary of National Biography* published before 1934, which are completely indexed in Hyamson's *Dictionary.*

General Indexes

The following current biographical indexes cite sources of information both for living persons and for those no longer living.

■ Biography and genealogy master index. Detroit: Gale, 1975– . Annual and five-year cumulations. Also on fiche, online, and on CD-ROM.

Indexes about 4 million names in about 700 works of collective biographies, including most of the who's who volumes, with about 450,000 new entries added per year. Emphasis remains on currently living Americans, although many deceased and non-U.S. people do appear. Given the capabilities of electronic sources (e.g., the CD-ROM version allows libraries to add local call numbers to the works cited), these are far preferable to the printed version.

Contrary to the title, because passenger lists and similar sources are not indexed and the emphasis is on living Americans, this does not cover genealogical sources very well at all. And, because many different sources are indexed, the same person sometimes appears under multiple forms.

■ Biography index: a quarterly index to biographical material in books and magazines. Bronx, N.Y.: Wilson, 1947– . Quarterly, annual, and biennial cumulations. Also online and on CD-ROM, 1984– .

This source covers the approximately 2,700 periodicals indexed by Wilson, plus some obituaries in the *New York Times* as well as current books of individual and collective biography, including juveniles. Arranged alphabetically by name, with valuable index to occupations and professions. The CD-ROM and online versions cover July 1984 to date.

Although Wilson indexes are heavily oriented to English-language publications, many of the publications are international in scope; thus, foreign persons are reasonably well covered. The books are completely analyzed. Because portraits and illustrations are indicated (and searchable as a format type in the electronic versions), this source is also a useful index to portraits.

The following titles cover older material:

■ Hyamson, A. M. A dictionary of universal biography of all ages and of all peoples. 2d ed. London: Routledge; New York: Dutton, 1951. 680p.

Useful when the nationality of a biographee isn't known and you lack access to the sources noted here. Covers persons no longer living who appear in twenty-three biographical dictionaries. Includes full indexing for the *Dictionary of National Biography* and the *Dictionary of American Biography.* Other titles are indexed only for those whose work or memory "has survived until today." Name entries include nationality, country of adoption, profession, dates (if known), and citations to sources of fuller biography.

■ Lobies, Jean-Pierre. Index bio-bibliographicus notorum hominum. Osnabrück, Germany: Biblio Verlag, 1972– (in progress).

Intended to cover 3 to 5 million names, based on a bibliography of more than 6,200 works of collective biographies from all periods and countries. When completed, will be close to the ultimate collective biographical index.

■ Riches, Phyllis M. Analytical bibliography of universal collected biography: comprising books published in the English tongue in Great Britain and Ireland, America and the British dominions. London: Library Assn., 1934. 709p.

These 50,000 entries from about 3,000 volumes include many lesser-known names. Entries often include birth and death dates, nationality, and profession. Includes chronological and occupational indexes and an author and subject bibliography of biographical dictionaries.

Several recent sources combine the text of sources with a cumulated index. The most ambitious of these follows:

■ World biographical information system. Munchen and London: K. G. Saur, 1980– . Print and fiche. Indexes also online and on CD-ROM as World Biographical Index.

> Consists of separate sets (thirty-seven as of mid-2000), all following the same basic pattern: the full text of several hundred collection biographies, published from the seventeenth to the mid-twentieth century, and cumulated in one alphabet by name, subarranged by date of publications, and produced on fiche. An index, in print, in one alphabetical sequence, not only gives name, dates of birth and death, and occupation, but also gives both the citation to the original source and a reference to the fiche set. Reflecting the nature of the sources collected, the sets are unbalanced toward certain occupations and have relatively few people of color; where there is a second series, it tends to add more nonwhites and women than the first series.

> Because the indexes are sold separately, they can be used without the fiche. Entries include profession or occupation, office, country, place of origin, source code, and fiche/frame reference. The CD-ROM and online versions cumulate sixteen of the indexes and are searchable by the usual approaches; the electronic versions also include a multiple-language list of occupations. With the additional date provided, the indexes can be used, in effect, as a type of historical who's who.

The following sets are currently available.

■ *African biographical archive.* 1994–97.

> Contains 231 sources, published from 1807 to 1990, covering about 75,000 names, from the pharaohs to the 1980s. *African Biographical Index* (1998, 3v.) includes closer to 90,000 names, from more sources.

■ *American biographical archive I and II.* 1986–96.

> The first segment consists of 367 works from the earliest period of North American history to the early part of the twentieth century. The second adds 127 more titles, mostly published in the twentieth century. *American Biographical Index Series II* (1997, 10v.) covers the whole archive.

■ *Arab-Islamic biographical archive.* 1995–98.

> Covers 100 titles published from 1858 to 1993 in major European languages, for about 80,000 names from pre-Islamic times to the present.

- *Australasian biographical archive.* 1990-95.

  Nearly 200 sources published from 1866 to 1983, covering Australia, New Zealand, Papua New Guinea, and the South Pacific islands, from European discovery to the present. Unlike most of the other series, the lack of collective biographies means this set includes more material from periodicals and newspapers. *Australasian Biographical Index* (1996, 3v.) covers the full set.

- *Baltic biographical archive.* 1995-98.

  Biographical information on more than 80,000 people from 218 sources published from 1650 to 1993, indexed by *Baltic Biographical Index* (1999, 3v.).

- *Biographical archive of the Benelux countries I and II.* 1992- .

  Series one covers 123 sources published from 1581 to 1938, listing about 65,000 names. In addition to Europeans, this set also covers residents of the former Dutch colonies. Coverage expands with series two to cover 68 sources published from 1920 to the present, adding about 55,000 more names. *Biographical Index of the Benelux Countries* (1994, 4v.) currently covers only the first series.

- *Biographical archive of the classical world.* 1996- .

  Covers about 100 works published from classical times to the 1980s, for about 150,000 names beginning with the eighth century B.C.E.

- *Biographical archive of the Soviet Union (1917-1991).* 2000- .

  The most recent series was announced in early 2000.

- *British biographical archive I and II.* 1984-94.

  The first series is based on 324 titles published from 1601 to 1926; the second adds 268 more titles published in the nineteenth and twentieth centuries. Together, the sets cover about 234,000 names, which are indexed in *British Biographical Index Series II* (1998, 7v.).

- *Chinese biographical archive.* 1996- .

  To date, this set covers about 100 works published in both Western languages and Chinese, with the latter translated into English, covering more than 50,000 names from the earliest history of China to the present. *Chinese Biographical Index* (2000, 3v.) indexes the set.

▪ *Czech and Slovakian biographical archive.* 1993–97.

Some 206 sources published from 1559 to 1992, covering about 110,000 names. Indexed in *Czech and Slovakian Biographical Index* (2000, 4v.).

▪ *French biographical archive I and II.* 1989–96.

The two series cover more than 175,000 names from about 300 sources published from the seventeenth century to 1980. Both are indexed in *French Biographical Index Series II* (1997, 7v.).

▪ *German biographical archive I and II.* 1982–93.

Together, these cover about 400,000 people from 538 sources published from 1700 to the 1950s. The series are indexed in *German Biographical Index Series II* (1997, 8v.).

▪ *Greek biographical archive.* 1998– .

Still in progress, the set covers from about 300 C.E. to the present, based on sources published from 1680 to the present. About 70,000 names will be included when this set is completed.

▪ *Hungarian biographical archive.* 1994–99.

More than 90,000 people from 127 sources published from 1559 to 1990 and indexed by *Hungarian Biographical Index* (2000, 3v.).

▪ *Indian biographical archive.* 1997– .

About 180 sources published from about 1700 to 1947 and covering more than 100,000 names from India, Pakistan, Bangladesh, and Sri Lanka.

▪ *Italian biographical archive I and II.* 1987–94.
▪ *Italian biographical archive to 1996.* 1998– .

These three sets include more than 300,000 names from about 600 sources published between 1646 and the mid-1990s. *Italian Biographical Index Series II* (1996, 7v.) covers the first two series.

▪ *Japanese biographical archive.* 2000– .

Covers about 20,000 names from about 87 Japanese (translated) and Western-language sources.

■ *Jewish biographical archive. 1994–96.*

Based on 123 sources published from the end of the eighteenth century to 1948 and covering about 150,000 people; indexed by *Jewish Biographical Index* (1998, 4v.).

■ *Polish biographical archive I and II. 1992–99.*

More than 350 reference sources covering more than 88,000 names. *Polish Biographical Index* (1998, 4v.) indexes the first set.

■ *Russian biographical archive. 1997– .*

Deals with more than 75,000 people listed in 150 sources published from 1827 to 1995, with most of the entries in Russian.

■ *Scandinavian biographical archive. 1989–91.*

Covers 150,000 names from 360 sources published before the mid-twentieth century and indexed by *Scandinavian Biographical Index* (1994, 4v.).

■ *South-East Asian biographical archive. 1997– .*

Includes more than 300 sources covering about 55,000 people. More than 10,000 entries in Asian languages are translated or abstracted into English.

■ *South-East-European biographical archive. 1997– .*

Covers the Balkan area through 200 works from 1711 to 1995, for a total of about 100,000 names.

■ *Spanish, Portugese and Latin-American biographical archive I and II. 1986–93.*

■ *Spanish, Portugese and Latin-American biographical archive 1960–1995. 1961– .*

The first two series cover 604 works listing more than 300,000 names from sources published between 1602 and the 1950s. The new series covers 1950 to date in 200 works, listing about 150,000 more names. The *Spanish, Portugese and Latin-American Biographical Index III* (1999, 10v.) indexes all three of these sets.

■ *Turkish biographical acrhive.* 1999– .

Covers 155 sources published from 1836 to 1999, with about 100,000 names.

Similar in conception and execution to the series are the following:

■ Public figures in the Soviet Union: a current biographical index. Cambridge, England, and Alexandria, Va.: Chadwyck-Healey, 1988–93. Fiche only.

A cumulated index based on newspapers, magazines, abstracts from biographical works, Radio Free Europe news agencies. In Russian. Covers from 1984 to 1993, with some retrospective material. Related to *The Soviet Biograpbic Archive.* Title changed in 1992 to *Public Figures of the C. I. S. and Baltic States* and then ceased.

■ The Soviet biographic archive, 1954–1985. Cambridge, England, and Alexandria, Va.: Chadwyck-Healey, 1986. Fiche only.

Based on newspapers, magazines, abstracts from biographical works, Radio Free Europe news agencies. In Russian. Covers from 1954 to date, updated daily; annual supplement expected. About thirty-five sources scanned regularly. Was called "undoubtedly the largest and most easily accessible" biographical source for the Soviet Union by one reviewer. Related to *Public Figures in the Soviet Union.*

Specialized Indexes

This section covers general indexes to specific types of material or to specific general groups. Indexes to specific professions are listed under the appropriate profession.

CHILDREN'S AND YOUNG ADULT BIOGRAPHIES

■ Breen, Karen. Index to collective biographies for young readers. 4th ed. New Providence, N.J.: Bowker, 1988. 494p. Also on CD-ROM.

Greatly expanded over earlier editions, this source indexes about 10,000 names in 1,129 collective biographies. Arranged by name, with a subject index and a list by book title of names included.

NEWSPAPERS

■ Names in the news. New Canaan, Conn.: NewsBank, 1980– . CD-ROM database, with fiche. Monthly updates.

Part of the NewsBank system, which is an index and clipping file of newspapers. An index to biographical articles (including interviews, obituaries, etc.) in about 450 local and regional newspapers in the United States, with citation to the original as well as a key to the News-Bank fiche.

■ New York times obituaries index, 1858-1968. New York: New York Times Co., 1970. 1136p.

■ New York times obituaries index, 1969-1978. New York: New York Times Co., 1980. 131p.

As it says, indexes obituaries in the *Times.* The update adds those under "Murders and Suicides" and provides many corrections and additions to the original. A current variant of this index that includes the text of the articles is The New York Times Biographical File (online only), with obituaries, interviews, and the like since 1980.

■ Obituaries from the Times, 1951-1960; 1961-1970; 1971-1975. Westport, Conn.: Greenwood, 1977-79.

That is, the London *Times.* About 60 percent of entries do not appear in the *DNB.* Reprints most of the *Times* obituaries in full, and indexes all of them. Those that are not reprinted are for people whose reputation is no longer that held when the original appeared. Includes a subject index.

PERIODICALS

Biography Index, of course, covers periodical articles as well as collections and individual titles. Many useful biographies, especially of the less famous or the more recently famous (or notorious), can be found in periodicals and newspapers.

■ Periodical source index, 1847-1985. Fort Wayne, Ind.: Allen County Public Library Foundation, 1988- . 16v. Annual updates. Also on CD-ROM.

Referred to as PERSI, this is becoming the source of first resort for genealogists. The basic set indexes the library's more than 2,000 genealogical periodicals (one of the largest such collections in the world), covering biographical articles, cemetery and census records, church and court records, deeds, directories, histories, institutions, land and military records, maps. Entries give periodical, volume, issue, month, year, but not article title or page number. Annual (covering 1986-) indexes all periodicals *received* in a given year, regardless of publication date. Arrangement by "U.S. Places," "Canadian Places," "Other Foreign Places," "Research Methodology," "Families." Annual does include article title but still not the page number.

WOMEN

■ Ireland, Norma O. Index to women of the world from ancient to modern times: biographies and portraits. Westwood, Mass.: Faxon, 1970. 573p.

■ ———. Index to women of the world from ancient to modern times: a supplement. Metuchen, N.J.: Scarecrow, 1988. 744p.

The original covers about 15,000 entries from 350 collective biographies; the supplement covers about 380 more titles published from 1971 to 1985. Most entries list birth, death, nationality, occupation, citations to collections. Unfortunately, the emphasis is heavily weighted to more popular sources.

■ Herman, Kaii. Women in particular: an index to American women. Phoenix, Ariz.: Oryx, 1984. 740p.

Covers about 15,000 women in fifty-four works of collective biography, including the *DNB* and *DAB,* but not the *Who's Who* series. Indexes by field and career, religious affiliation, ethnic/racial identity; geographical location, with full information at each entry. A name index gives citations to the first four indexes. Some overlap with Ireland's indexes, but it generally covers the more scholarly sources and, of course, is limited to Americans.

Other indexes to biography that are restricted to one field (e.g., art or literature) are described under those subjects in the following pages.

Many World Wide Web search engines and indexes provide a special category for searching for people. Although many of these websites are of the directory sort (*see also* chapter 4 for some examples), many are more detailed. Possibly the most common type of biographical website, however, is the unauthorized "tribute" page to a given celebrity. Often full of pictures and textual information, these have a tendency to come and go, and they often contain questionable material. However, they may be of some use when used very judiciously. In addition to the classification "People" or similar, most Web search engines have a special way of searching for proper names (for example, searching words with initial capitals) that usually retrieves large numbers of sites on the more famous and notorious people, many of whom are not listed in the more selective and formal indexes.

One last word on biographical information on the Web, with suggestive analogies for other types of websites as well. The combination of graphical interfaces, easy-to-use software, and digital images permits very easy manipulation of graphics. It has become a joke in some circles to "cut and paste" one person's head onto someone else's body or even to add images of people to pictures of celebrities (as in the movie *Forrest Gump*). Thus, it is not impossible to get a wholly erroneous idea of a person from a combination of inaccurate text and bogus pictures. This sort of fakery seems especially common for celebrity biographies. Users should stick to sites of known reliability to avoid being misled.

International Biographical Sources

Consult international biographical dictionaries first if nationality is not known. Some of the so-called university dictionaries are products of the nineteenth century, and they reflect a certain bias of the period, in both the selection and treatment of biographees. In using them, one should also check more recent sources, which may correct errors or include findings based on more recent research. Other, more current one-volume international biographical dictionaries often give very brief sketches, with little or no bibliographical citation. In verifying biographical facts, varied types of sources should be consulted, for errors may be repeated from one biographical source to the next. Thus, the number of times a given fact is found is not necessarily an assurance of its accuracy.

Only a few of the better-known biographical dictionaries, international in scope, are given below:

Classics

■ Biographie universelle, ancienne et moderne. Nouv. éd. J. F. Michaud, ed. Paris: Mme. C. Desplaces, 1843–65. Reprint, Graz, Austria: Akademische Druck-u. Verlagsanstalt, 1966–70. 45v.

> Usually cited as *Michaud*. Long, signed articles with bibliographies (all titles translated into French) and some shorter sketches. Still a very useful work, because of its high standard of scholarship. The strong royalist and Catholic bias of the first edition was corrected in the "new" edition. Although it has many errors of fact and some "inadequacy of treatment," the errors are relatively few. Covers much the same ground as *Hoefer* (see next entry), but it is more carefully edited; articles are signed (initials), longer, and generally better written. *Hoefer* generally has better bibliographies and more names (especially for minor figures) and gives titles in bibliographies in original language.

■ Nouvelle biographie générale depuis les temps plus reculés jusqu'à nos jours, avec les enseignements bibliographiques et l'indication des sources à consulter. Paris: Firmin Didot, 1853–66. Reprint, Copenhagen: Rosenkilde et Bagger, 1963–69. 46v.

Usually cited as *Hoefer,* after the editor. Intended to be more concise and cover more names than *Michaud.* Long articles cover about 545,000 eminent living and deceased. For the most part, this is based on condensations of other work, with no original scholarship. Inclusion of more than 400 pirated articles from *Michaud* in the first two volumes of the first edition led to a famous lawsuit, described by R. C. Christie in the *Quarterly Review* (157: 204–26), reprinted in his *Selected Essays and Papers* (London: Longman, 1902).

▪ New century cyclopedia of names. C. L. Barnhart, ed. New York: Appleton, 1954. 3v.

A revision of the *Century Cyclopedia of Names,* volume 11 of the 1911 *Century Dictionary and Cyclopedia,* but twice as large. Emphasizes the English-speaking world (but gives English and native spelling and pronunciation for non-English names). Covers more than 100,000 names, including biblical, literary, and other fictional characters, with pronunciation noted. Includes many appendixes (e.g., lists of rulers, chronological table of history). The instructions for use should be read carefully, but this remains a useful classic.

Modern Sources

▪ Cambridge biographical dictionary. David Crystal, ed. Cambridge and New York: Cambridge Univ. Pr., 1996. 495p.

The revised American edition of *Chambers Biographical Dictionary,* and a condensed version of the next title. Some names have been dropped from the previous edition, many more names have been added, and more prominence has been given to twentieth-century figures in general; to women; and to business, art, films, media, and other nonmilitary and political figures. This has been cited by reviewers as the best single-volume biographical source and as a "necessary, basic" tool.

▪ Cambridge biographical encyclopedia. 2d ed. Cambridge and New York: Cambridge Univ. Pr., 1998. 1264p.

Some 15,000 short biographies, with an emphasis on the twentieth century. A "Ready Reference" section adds shorter information on about 10,000 other people. Includes a chronological listing, many cross-references, and a subject classification as well. Improves earlier editions by adding more women, people of color, and non-Westerners.

- Encyclopedia of world biography. New York: McGraw-Hill, 1973. 12v. Twentieth century update. Palatine, Ill.: Jack Heraty, 1987–95. 6v. 2d ed. Gale, 1998. 19v. Also on CD-ROM.

  Originally titled *McGraw-Hill Encyclopedia of World Biography.* Long essays with bibliographical notes, further reading, cross-references. At least one illustration per essay, and many locator maps. The Gale edition completely revises all existing entries and adds about 40 percent more, as well as provides one cumulative index. Although there are few names not found in other sources likely to be held in the average medium-sized library, the information is generally in more depth and breadth than other similar sources.

- The International who's who of women. 2d ed. London: Europa, 1997. 628p.

  More than 4,000 concise profiles of the world's most eminent women. Indexes by occupation, name, nationality. Standard brief biographical information based on questionnaires. A direct complement to the *International Who's Who,* with which there is very little overlap.

- Merriam-Webster's biographical dictionary. Springfield, Mass.: Merriam-Webster, 1995. 1170p.

  A complete revision of the former *Webster's New Biographical Dictionary* (1988). Covers only deceased people, with much coverage of non-Western and the Third World in general. A major attraction to this title is the pronunciation guide to the names.

- Wilson biographies. Bronx, N.Y.: Wilson, 1997– . Online and on CD-ROM only. Annual updates.

  Full text of about 100 Wilson publications, including *Current Biography,* the World Authors series, the books of Junior Authors and Illustrators, and other sources. Searchable by name, profession, dates, works, and keywords.

Fiction and Myth

For older characters (real and fictional) the following are the standards:

- Jobes, Gertrude. Dictionary of mythology, folklore and symbols. Metuchen, N.J.: Scarecrow, 1962. 3v.

In spite of its title, a biographical source with many entries for animals, gems, and the like. The third volume is an index, including tables of deities, heroes, personalities, plus mythological affiliations.

■ Thomas, Joseph. Universal pronouncing dictionary of biography and mythology. 5th ed. Philadelphia: Lippincott, 1930. Reprint, Detroit: Gale, 1970. 2550p.

Usually called *Lippincott's Biographical Dictionary.* Brief articles covering all nations and time periods, including Greek, Roman, Norse, Sanskrit, Teutonic, and other mythologies. Bibliographies included in some entries. Particularly useful for the emphasis given to pronunciation. Includes first names with equivalents in various languages and disputed or doubtful pronunciations.

Characters in more recent fiction are a bit more difficult to identify, but the following collectively will probably trace the character:

■ Amos, William, comp. The originals: an A–Z of fiction's real-life characters. Boston: Little, Brown, 1985. 614p.

Covers about 3,000 characters and their real-life models from novels, plays, poetry, and essays, as far back as the 1500s, with a strong emphasis on English but with other languages as well. A name index of both fictional and real persons and numerous cross-references is included.

■ Bold, Alan, and Robert Giddings. Who was really who in fiction. Chicago: Longman, 1986. 383p.

An expanded version of *True Characters* (1984). Gives real-life counterparts of about 600 fictional characters in novels, films, poems, opera, etc. Not as comprehensive as Amos's *The Originals,* but this title has longer entries and doesn't completely overlap the other.

■ Magill, Frank N., comp. Cyclopedia of literary characters. Salem, 1963. 2v.
■ ———. Cyclopedia of literary characters II. Pasadena, Calif.: Salem, 1990. 4v.

Also published as *Masterplots Cyclopedia of Literary Characters.* Indexes more than 28,000 fictional characters in about 3,000 novels, novellas, plays, epics, etc. from around the world, with an emphasis on Anglo-American literature. Includes reference to source and a brief "biography" of the character.

- Rintoul, M. C. Dictionary of real people and places in fiction. New York: Routledge, 1993. 1184p.

  Entries for about 4,000 people and places in some 1,000 English-language novels and short stories, giving a brief biography or description plus evidence for the claim the fictional reference has to reality; this latter differentiates this from all other similar sources. Indexed by fictional and real names. Title index gives only author; author index gives full citation.

- Seymour-Smith, M. Dictionary of fictional characters. 4th rev. ed. Boston: The Writer, 1992. 598p.

  Earlier editions were called *Everyman's Dictionary of Fictional Characters* and *Dent Dictionary of Fictional Characters.* Lists some 50,000 characters by about 3,000 authors, with a very brief description plus citation to work(s). This current edition restores many characters dropped from earlier editions, while adding many more U.S. and Commonwealth women writers.

Nicknames and Pseudonyms

- Pseudonyms and nicknames dictionary. 3d ed. Detroit: Gale, 1987. 2v.

  Covers about 80,000 names, mostly entertainers, athletes, and authors in some 275 sources. The main entry, under the real name, includes dates, nationality, occupation, and pseudonyms; the assumed names cross-reference the main entries. Many entries for obscure and difficult-to-trace people.

Current Sources

Current sources of biographical information require careful reading of their prefaces to determine the source and date of sketches. They should be further examined to determine whether sketches are simply an abbreviated recording of facts or whether they attempt to interpret the biographee in a readable style. They are usually compiled from questionnaires containing biographical data supplied directly by the biographees. However, when questionnaires are subjected to judicious editing and further checked against published sources of information, the result is apt to be more accurate and better balanced. Also, some persons are inclined to report more fully their appointments to local committees, resulting in lengthy biographical sketches that do not necessarily indicate their relative importance.

The following are some of the more generally used current sources:

■ Current biography. Bronx, N.Y.: Wilson, 1940– . Monthly, except December, with annual cumulations as *Current Biography Yearbook.* Also online and on CD-ROM.

> From sixteen to eighteen new profiles each month. Distinguished by careful editing, readable style, clear photographs, and bibliographies. Sketches written by research staff who use information from biographee plus many other sources. Tends to emphasize American artists, film stars, athletes, and other popular figures, but major international figures also covered. Obituaries are included for those listed in past issues. The *Yearbook* updates sketches from the monthlies and indexes by professions the most recent ten years of the set. *Current Biography Cumulated Index* produced every five years.

■ International year book and statesmen's who's who. East Grinstead, England: Bowker/K. G. Saur, 1953– . Annual.

> More than half the content gives facts of birth, education, profession, organizations, publications, address, and the like for about 7,000 persons in government, education, and business. Overlaps a little with the *International Who's Who* and hardly at all with *Who's Who in the World.* Reviewers have criticized this for many errors and lack of stated selection criteria, but it does include names not listed in other standard sources.

■ International who's who. London: Europa, 1935– ; distributed by Gale. Annual.

> Has been called by reviewers "probably the best single source for obtaining brief information about the famous and influential humans of the world." Covers about 20,000 names, with royalty in a separate section; lists those who have died since last edition. Most nations of the world covered, including many that have no such volume or don't update every year. Marquis's *Who's Who in the World* has about 50 percent more names but with less detail and smaller print. There is much less overlap in these two sources than one would expect.

■ Who's who in the world. New Providence, N.J.: Marquis Who's Who, 1970– . Annual.

> Based on surveys, identifies about 40,000 eminent world figures in current affairs, with an emphasis on government, legal and diplomatic figures, scholars, journalists, and heads of major organizations. Has received recent criticism for lack of sufficiently detailed selection crite-

ria and the very brief entries, but it includes many people otherwise hard to find.

National Biographical Sources

Consult national biographical dictionaries first if the nationality of the biographee is known. If carefully edited, they contain well-written accounts of a person's life, outstanding accomplishments, references to further sources of information, and (sometimes) portraits or photographs. When the exact date of death is known, it serves as an aid in locating obituaries in newspapers. Current sources of the who's who type are usually compiled from data supplied by the biographees and resemble the international who's whos described above. The following are well known and often used for information on persons, living or dead.

United States

- American national biography. John A. Garraty and Mark C. Carnes, eds. New York: Oxford Univ. Pr., 1999. 24v.

   A conscious replacement and updating to the *Dictionary of American Biography,* updating many entries from that source based on current research and points of view. All persons selected must have been deceased prior to 1996, but otherwise the criteria are considerably more inclusive than the *DAB,* notably including more women, people of color, people of lower socioeconomic status, and the like. The 17,500 entries are rather long, tracing the person's life from birth to death but emphasizing the events and traits that led to their inclusion. All entries include current bibliographies. Arranged by name, with indexes by subject, contributor (there were more than 6,000 contributors), birthplace, occupations, and areas of renown.

- Cambridge dictionary of American biography. John S. Bowman, ed. New York: Cambridge Univ. Pr., 1995. 903p.

   Some 9,000 notable U.S. residents, including many women and ethnics, but remains skimpy on Canadians and Latin Americans. Many not native United States but had significant impact on United States. From 75 to 200 words, with a few longer. Occupational index. *ARBA96* says this is the "best one volume biographical source on the market."

- Dictionary of American biography. New York: Scribner, 1974– . 11v., plus supplements in varying configurations.

The original set (1928–36) and supplements cover about 19,000 names. Evaluations are long, signed articles about those "who have made some significant contribution to American life" and who lived in the territory now known as the United States of America. Excludes British officers and loyalists by design; the original also excluded most women and people of color as well. This has been rectified in later supplements, as well as in other sources, such as *Notable American Women*. Appended bibliographies often contain references to the manuscript collections relating to the biographee and to the definitive edition of his (rarely her) works. Distinguished for its judicious selection of biographees, the authority of its contributors, and its scholarly approach, it should be consulted first for American males who died before 1980, though less inclusive than *Appleton's Cyclopedia of American Biography* (New York: D. Appleton, 1887–1900; 6v.), which has some Canadian and Latin American names. Names of lesser national importance may often be found in the *National Cyclopedia of American Biography*. The index is a good source for a state's outstanding men and important college graduates, as well as lists of persons prominent at the time in various occupations. Supplements include people who died since preparation of the original set and, to an increasing degree, people omitted from the original volumes for reasons of gender, race, and ethnicity who are now felt worthy of inclusion. A comprehensive index covers the full set and the supplements.

■ Concise dictionary of American biography. 5th ed. New York: Scribner, 1997. 2v.

More than 18,000 entries from the full *DAB* and its eight supplements, covering those who died before 1971. Unlike earlier editions, all entries are in one alphabet. An index to occupations is provided. If you cannot afford the full set, this can be useful.

■ Notable American women, 1607–1950: a biographical dictionary. Cambridge, Mass.: Belknap Pr. of Harvard Univ., 1971–80. 4v.

Essentially, a continuation of the *Dictionary of American Biography,* adding women who should have been listed in that title (in volumes 1 to 3) and generally excluding women who were listed. Resembles the *DAB* in its long, signed articles. Covers about 1,800 notable women deceased as of 1975 who had "significant impact on American life." Includes lengthy bibliographies.

■ Encyclopedia of American biography. John A. Garraty, ed. 2d ed. New York: Harper & Row, 1996. 1263p.

These signed, two-part articles on more than 1,000 people are unique in giving a factual summary (done by Columbia University graduate students) followed by an interpretative essay by an expert on the biographee. Includes short bibliographies.

■ National cyclopedia of American biography. New York: White, 1892–1984. 75v.

Early years spell it as "cyclopaedia." Differs from the *DAB* in having more names of local importance, especially in business and industry; sketches that are more evaluative than descriptive, based on descriptions provided by the family of the biographee; photographs of nearly all biographees; and no bibliographies. Not arranged alphabetically; thus, must be used with the index. Probably the most comprehensive work of its kind for America, certainly with more detail than any similar source. The index, *Notable Names in American History* (Clifton, N.J.: White, 1984; 576p.), covers not only the biographees' entries, but also other names, places, institutions, and events mentioned in the entries.

■ Who was who in America with world notables. New Providence, N.J.: Marquis Who's Who/Reed Reference, 1942– . v.1– (in progress). Historical volume, 1607–1896 (1967).

A good source for exact date of death and often place of burial of persons whose names formerly appeared in *Who's Who in America* (except for the *Historical Volume,* which included Lief Ericsson, John Cabot, etc. who died before the start date). Sketches based on those, with requested revisions appearing in the editors' files, although there is little revision. A useful cumulative index, *Who Was Who in America with World Notables: Index,* appears every few years, the most recent in 1993.

ETHNIC GROUPS

■ Bataille, Gretchen M. Native American women: a biographical dictionary. Hamden, Conn.: Garland, 1993. 333p.

The first solid source for this area. Covers 231 women born from 1595 to 1960, with good representation of Canadian and Arctic women. Includes contributors' backgrounds and a number of separate indexes giving such things as tribal affiliations, state or province of birth, occupation, and the like.

■ Black biographical dictionaries, 1790–1950. Alexandria, Va.: Chadwyck-Healey, 1989. Fiche only.

■ Black biography, 1790–1950. Alexandria, Va.: Chadwyck-Healey, 1991. 3v.

Covers more than 30,000 African American people from 300 collective biographical books and pamphlets with substantial biographical information, from 1790 to 1950. The index includes any name in the sources covered, even if not clearly a person of African ancestry. Arranged by name, with indexes by place of birth, occupation, and religion, and one of women.

■ Mundo Lo, Sara de. Index to Spanish American collective biography. Boston: Hall, 1981– . 6v.

A bibliography of biographical works, this includes encyclopedias, anthologies, general and specialized histories, and collective biographies. Gives annotations and detailed contents notes for each title. Indexes by author and title, biographee, and geographical location. Longer works get more detailed treatment. Also gives U.S. and Canadian library locations for the works cited. Each volume covers a specific geographical area (volume 2 is Mexico; the rest are multiple nations). Separate volumes for Brazil and on general Latin American sources are planned.

CONTEMPORARY

■ Who's who in America. New Providence, N.J.: Marquis Who's Who/Reed Reference, 1899– . v.1– . Annual. Also online and on CD-ROM.

Data, supplied via mail surveys from biographees, are concisely and factually presented for "the best-known men and women in all lines of useful and reputable achievement" selected because of outstanding effort or official position. Primarily American coverage, but includes a few persons of other nationalities of likely interest to Americans. Differs from *Current Biography* in (1) being more inclusive, (2) giving no evaluation, (3) employing many abbreviations to save space, and (4) lacking bibliographies, except brief lists of authors' works. Similar to *International Who's Who* in form and content. Augmented by separate regional and subject volumes.

■ Who's who of American women: a biographical dictionary of notable living American women. New Providence, N.J.: Marquis Who's Who/Reed Reference, 1958/59– . v.1– . Biennial.

About 30,000 entries, following standard Marquis format, with many names not found in the base volume. A good source for professional and club women.

■ Marquis who's who on CD-ROM. Marquis who's who plus [CD-ROM]. Marquis who's who [online]. New Providence, N.J.: Marquis Who's Who, 1993– . Semiannual updates.

Full text of *Who's Who in America* plus fourteen regional and professional volumes (*Who's Who in the World, Who's Who of American Women,* etc.) from 1985 to date. Other packages include just the regional volumes and the professional volumes.

■ Contemporary black biography. Detroit: Gale, 1992– . Semiannual.

International coverage of both famous and ordinary people likely to have been ignored by other sources (although heavy emphasis on living Americans). Includes both contemporary and historical figures. Entries are signed, but no information is given about the authors. Index by nationality, subject, occupation, name.

■ Who's who among African Americans. Detroit: Gale, 1976– . Biennial.

Coverage of about 20,000 people from all states, Canada, Europe, Zimbabwe, Caribbean. Index by occupation, geography; obituary index of entries from earlier editions, but still lists some as living who are now dead. Particularly useful as few African Americans are included in *Who's Who in America.*

■ Who's who among Asian Americans. Detroit: Gale, 1995– . Biennial.

Covers about 6,000 names, either residents or citizens of the United States, of Asian ancestry, but not necessarily born in Asia, with only about 10 percent overlap with *Who's Who in America.* The usual short biographies, with indexes by geography, occupation, and nationality/ethnicity. The same general pattern as Gale's titles for African and Hispanic Americans is used.

■ Who's who among Hispanic Americans. Detroit: Gale, 1990– . Biennial. Also online.

More than 11,000 entries, with few duplicates with the other *Who's Who* editions. Indexes by geographic locations, occupations, ethnic/cultural heritage.

Africa

■ Africa who's who. 2d ed. London: Africa Books, 1991. 1863p.

A companion to *Africa Today* (London: Africa Journal, 1981– ; serial) and *Makers of Modern Africa* (London: Africa Journal, 1981– ; serial). Biographies of more than 12,000 personalities.

■ Rake, A. Who's who in Africa: leaders for the 1990s. Metuchen, N.J.: Scarecrow, 1992. 448p.

Career profiles of 300 political figures in forty-seven south of Sahara nations, A–Z by country. Includes basic political facts about each country.

Australia

■ Australian dictionary of biography. Melbourne: Melbourne Univ. Pr., 1966– . v.1– (in progress).

Unlike the *DNB,* covers a genuine cross section of society. Is arranged by broad chronological period (starting 1788), but otherwise is very similar to the *DNB* in type of article, appended bibliographies, etc. Covers surprisingly few women, except as spouses. A separate cumulative index is published for the first twelve volumes.

■ Who's who in Australia: an Australian biographical dictionary and register of prominent people with which is incorporated John's notable Australians. Melbourne: Information Australia, 1906– . Annual.

About 8,200 biographies with some general information on Australia.

Canada

■ Dictionary of Canadian biography. Toronto and Buffalo, N.Y.: Univ. of Toronto Pr., 1966–91. 1994– (in progress).

Published in both French and English editions. Intended to be twenty volumes, but funding problems led to a hiatus. The first fourteen volumes, arranged by date, cover from 1000 to 1920. A cumulative index lists both main entries and all persons named within entries in separate alphabets.

■ Roberts, Charles G. D., and Arthur L. Tunnell, eds. Standard dictionary of Canadian biography: the Canadian who was who, 1875–1937. Toronto: Trans-Canada Pr., 1934–38. 2v.

Remains the standard historical biography, with signed scholarly articles, including bibliographies, for eminent Canadians who died between 1875 and 1937 and a few others who were born outside of Canada but had a major effect on Canadian life.

■ Wallace, W. Stewart. The Macmillan dictionary of Canadian biography. 4th ed., rev. and enl. London and Toronto: Macmillan, 1978. 914p.

> Brief entries for Canadians who died before 1976. Sketches include bibliographies.

CONTEMPORARY

■ Canadian who's who [year]. Toronto and Buffalo, N.Y.: Univ. of Toronto Pr., 1980- . Annual. Also online and on fiche.

> Series began in 1910 under a different publisher. The standard source for Canadian biography, with entries ranging from three lines to half a page. Entries are similar to the Marquis series and are based on questionnaires. Fiche sets cover 1898 to 1975, combining this title with *Canadian Men and Women of the Time* (1898, 1912). *Canadian Who's Who Index, 1898-1984* (Toronto and Buffalo, N.Y.: Univ. of Toronto Pr., 1986; 528p.) is a cumulative index of more than 33,000 names.

China

■ Biographical dictionary of Republican China. Howard L. Boorman and Richard C. Howard, eds. New York: Columbia Univ. Pr., 1967-79. 5v.

> About 600 scholarly evaluative biographies on persons both living and dead, emphasizing those prominent in all fields during the Republican period, from 1911 to 1949. Most of volume 4 is a useful bibliography. Volume 5 is a personal name index. Titles and names are given in romanized form and Chinese characters.

■ Library of Congress Orientalia Division. Eminent Chinese of the Ch'ing period (1644-1912). Washington, D.C.: Govt. Print. Off., 1943-44. 2v.

> The standard historical dictionary, covering about 300 leaders, with signed, detailed articles that include bibliographies. Updated by the previous title.

CONTEMPORARY

■ Bartke, Wolfgang. Who's who in the People's Republic of China. 3d ed. Munchen and New York: K. G. Saur, 1991. 2v.

First edition, 1981. Based primarily on the Chinese press and BBC broadcasts, covering about 4,100 biographies. Many entries are very abbreviated because of lack of information. Volume 2 includes a list of more than 1,300 people in the last edition, with dates of death or "last appearance." Appendix includes lists of party, government, and organization officials and other background information.

France

▪ Dictionnaire de biographie française. Paris: Letouzey et Ané, 1933– . 16v. plus fascicles (in progress).

Lengthy, authoritative, signed articles with good bibliographies, modeled in part on the *DNB*. Covers men and women from France and dependent territories, plus foreigners important in France, from ancient history. Excludes living people.

▪ Who's who in France: Qui est qui en France: dictionnaire biographique de personnalités françaises vivant en France dans les territoires à Outre-Mer ou à l'étranger et de personnalités étrangères résidant en France. Paris and Detroit: Editions Jacques Lafitte, 1953– ; distributed by Gale. Biennial.

Most up-to-date of the French sources. More than 20,000 biographies of French nationals in France, territories, or other nations, plus notables living in France. Includes several essays on French culture, lists of heads of state, etc.

Germany

▪ Allgemeine deutsche Biographie; hrsg. durch die Historische Commission bei der K. Akademie der Wissenschaften. Leipzig: Duncker, 1875–1912. 56v. (2., unveränderte Aufl.) Neudruck der 1 Aufl. von 1875. Berlin: Duncker & Humblot, 1967–71.

More than 20,000 lengthy, evaluative, signed biographies with bibliographies make this the standard source for those no longer living at the end of the nineteenth century. The arrangement requires that the general index be used first. The *Neue deutsche Biographie* is largely based on this.

▪ Neue deutsche Biographie, hrsg. von der Historischen Kommission bei der Bayerischen Akademie der Wissenschaften. Berlin: Duncker & Humblot, 1953– . v.1– (in progress).

Long, signed articles with appended bibliographies, including many from the previous title as well as from later and a few from earlier periods. Indexes in each volume cite entries to the previous title as well. As of late 1997, the series had reached volume 18, "Nau."

CONTEMPORARY

- Wer ist wer? Das deutsche who's who [title varies]. Lubeck: Schmidt-Romhildt, 1905- . Also online and on CD-ROM.

  Covers about 45,000 names of living people, plus obituaries of listed people who died since the last edition. Emphasizes politics, sports, industry, religion, and the arts and includes names not in *Who's Who in Germany.*

- Who's who in Germany. Essen, Germany: Who's Who International Red Series Verlag, 1992. 2v.

  Updates the title first published in 1955. The 1992 edition includes for the first time biographies and institutional information on the reunited Germany. The appendix gives up-to-date statistics and an outline of various aspects of German life. Like others in the series, the entries are not listed in *Biographical and Genealogical Master Index.*

Great Britain

- Dictionary of national biography. Leslie Stephen and Sidney Lee, eds. London: Smith, Elder, 1908-9 (reissue); London: Oxford Univ. Pr., 1938 (reprint). 21v. and supp. Oxford: Oxford Univ. Pr., 1912-96 (several reprints).

  Largest of the national biographical dictionaries, its full, evaluative sketches, prepared and signed by authorities, treat more than 35,000 no longer living "men and women of British or Irish race who have achieved any reasonable distinction in any walk of life, . . . early settlers in America . . . natives of these islands who have gained distinction in foreign countries and persons of foreign birth who have gained eminence in this county," from ancient times to the present. Supplements, formerly added every ten years, now are added every five years to keep this up-to-date, although original articles are not revised. Recent supplements include a cumulative index to all supplements.

  In addition to the main set, see *Corrections and Additions to the Dictionary of National Biography Cumulated from the Bulletin of the Institute of Historical Research Covering the Years 1923-1963*

(Boston: Hall, 1966; 212p.), a cumulation of corrections published in the *Bulletin of Historical Research.* See also *Dictionary of National Biography: Missing Persons* (Oxford: Oxford Univ. Pr., 1993; 768p.), which contains articles on 1,086 persons editors believe were overlooked by the original and supplements to 1985, selected from about 100,000 candidates. The *Concise Dictionary* (London and New York: Oxford Univ. Pr., 1992; 3v.) also includes corrections and additions to the main set.

There are plans for a full revision into *The New Dictionary of National Biography,* sometime early in the twenty-first century.

■ Concise dictionary of national biography: from earliest times to 1985. London and New York: Oxford Univ. Pr., 1992. 3v.

This is the third edition although not labeled as such. Lists every name in the whole *DNB* set though the 1990 supplement but with condensed material. Uneven; those in the supplement get longer entries, as do very famous people.

■ Who was who. London: Black; New York: St. Martin's, 1920– . Quinquennial.

Generally the *Who's Who* entry with a death-date tag line added. Useful primarily in that one can discard older *Who's Whos.*

CONTEMPORARY

■ Who's who. New York: St. Martin's, 1849– . v.1– . Annual.

The American edition of a British title, covers about 30,000 names. Aims to furnish, in a very compact form, biographical sketches of eminent living persons of both sexes in all parts of the world, but with a distinct bias toward British males. Based on returns from mail surveys submitted annually to listees for updating. Sketches are removed when the person dies or when he or she is no longer of public interest; thus, names may appear in a given earlier volume or volumes but not in later ones. Includes obituaries for those in the last edition who died since it was produced.

Italy

■ Chi è? Dizionario degli italiani d'oggi. Rome: Scarano, 1928–61. Ed.1–7. 7v.

An earlier work with the same title was issued in 1908 by Guido Biagi. Unlike the following title, this is compiled from sources other than the biographees. Unfortunately, it is rarely up-to-date, although good for older personalities.

■ Dizionario biografico degli italiani. Rome: Istituto della Enciclopedia Italiana. 1960– . v.1– (in progress).

The Italian equivalent to the *DNB,* with signed, evaluative articles including bibliographies; also has living people. Unlike most similar sources, even minor figures receive long articles. As of the late 1990s, the set was into the middle of the *F*s. When completed, this will contain about 40,000 names of persons no longer living who lived in the fifth through twentieth centuries.

CONTEMPORARY

■ Who's who in Italy. Essen, Germany: Who's Who International Red Series Verlag, 1992. 2v.

Similar to the volume by the same publisher for Germany, with about 11,000 entries for prominent Italians and appendixes with general current information.

Japan

■ Who's who in Japan. 3d ed. Boca Raton, Fla.: CRC Pr., 1992. 800p.

Short biographies of about 51,000 people, with a directory of institutions.

Latin America

■ Encyclopedia of Latin America. Helen Delpar, ed. New York: McGraw-Hill, 1975. 651p.

About two-thirds of the entries are biographical, with an emphasis on political figures. Good for coverage of recent history.

■ Who's who in Latin America: government, politics, banking and industry. 4th ed. New York: Norman Ross, 1997. 2v.

More than 2,000 biographies of major figures, although many are very short. Name index gives relevant country. Volume 1 covers South America; volume 2 covers Central America and the Caribbean.

CONTEMPORARY

■ Who's who in Latin America. 3d ed., rev. and enl. Stanford, Calif.: Stanford Univ. Pr.; Chicago: Marquis Who's Who, 1946–51. Reprint, Detroit: Ethridge, 1971. 7v. in 2.

Brief factual sketches of about 8,000 people, based on residence, not nationality (which makes for some confusion, but also inclusiveness). Each country is treated separately.

Mexico

■ Camp, Roderick A. Who's who in Mexico today. 2d ed. Boulder, Colo.: Westview Pr., 1993. 206p.

Brief entries for about 400 prominent Mexicans, complementing the author's *Mexican Political Biographies, 1884-1935* (Austin: Univ. of Texas Pr., 1991; 458p.) and *Mexican Political Biographies, 1935-1993* (3d ed. Austin: Univ. of Texas Pr., 1995; 985p.). Includes groups often left out of similar works, such as women, clergy, opposition politicians. Gives references to sources.

■ Diccionario biografíco de Mexico. Monterey: Editorial Revesa, 1968-70. 2v.

Short sketches from colonial and early independence up to 1970.

■ Garcia Granados, Rafael. Diccionario biográfico de historia antigua de Méjico. Mexico City: Instituto de Historia, 1952-55. 3v.

Covers Aztec (volumes 1 and 2) and Christianized Native Americans, from the Spanish conquest through the seventeenth century. Includes bibliography and detailed name and geographical indexes in volume 3.

Russia and the Former Soviet Union

■ Russkii biograficheskii slovar'. St. Petersburg: Kadima, 1896-1918. 25v.

Although incomplete, this remains the best equivalent to the *DNB* and *DAB* for prerevolutionary Russia.

■ The Soviet Union: a biographical dictionary. Archie Brown, ed. 1st American ed. New York: Macmillan, 1991. 489p.

About 1,400 people from the Russian Revolution to 1990, covering nearly everyone who should be covered in such a source. Although not the most comprehensive, probably the first choice for the average library.

CONTEMPORARY

■ Who's who in Russia and the CIS republics. Vladimir Morozov, ed. New York: Henry Holt, 1995. 328p.

Among a number of recent sources, the only one to be based on Russian sources, primarily the magazine *V.I.P.* Somewhat erratic and a bit thin for the CIS states, but good coverage of those people listed.

■ Who's who in Russia and the new states. Leonard Geron and Alex Pravda, eds. London and New York: I. B. Taurus, 1993. 600p.

Brief biographies of about 7,000 people, with a strong emphasis on political figures. Generally considered more accurate and up-to-date than *Who's Who in Russia and the CIS Republics,* but it lacks a subject index.

Professions

Many sources of biographies of persons who have been active in professions or vocations are available in a good library collection. Among them are literary histories for men and women of letters, military and diplomatic histories for soldiers and statespersons, histories of art and music for artists and musicians, and histories of science and technology for scientists, engineers, inventors, and the like. Directories of associations and professions also often provide brief identifying data for their members and sometimes include foreign affiliates as well. Also, special periodical indexes in these fields are useful for supplemental information. But when a living person's profession or vocation is known, it is well to consult first a biographical dictionary in that field, for it often contains more names than the more general who's whos. The titles listed here are only a sampling of this rapidly growing type of publication.

Current biographical dictionaries in special fields have increased in number and variety in recent years, because of the increase in the number of professional men and women, the growth of professional associations, and the prestige attached to being among those considered outstanding in their vocations. Like the national who's whos, professional directories are usually compiled from information provided by the biographee.

These special biographical dictionaries may be supplemented by association membership directories, which vary a great deal in the amount of biographical data contained, from mere name and address listing to a compilation of biographical sketches. Another source of biographical information in special fields is the official journal or journals in the field, which often contain news notes on persons active in the field, such as *American Libraries* for librarians.

In the following list, indexes are listed first, followed by collective biographies.

Artists

■ Havlice, Patricia P. Index to artistic biography. Metuchen, N.J.: Scarecrow, 1973. 2v. Supplement, 1981. 953p.

Indexes 124,000 names in 134 sources published from 1902 to 1980 in ten languages.

■ Mallett, Daniel T. Mallett's index of artists, including painters, sculptors, illustrators, engravers of the past and present. New York: Bowker, 1935. 493p. Supplement, 1940. 319p. Often reprinted.

A standard source, with 25,000 very brief biographies and references to 22 general and more than 1,000 specialized sources.

■ Poorman, Susan, comp. The Neal-Schuman index to performing and creative artists in collective biographies. New York: Neal-Schuman, 1991. 155p.

Indexes about 1,300 names in 127 collective biographies published from 1970 to 1989. Also includes an index to women artists by nation and by profession. Includes name, occupations, nation of origin, birth date, plus amount of information available in the source, whether it is illustrated, and references to standard bibliographies (e.g., *Children's Catalog*).

■ Williamson, G. C. Bryan's dictionary of painters and engravers. 4th rev. ed. London: Bell, 1903–5. Reprint, Port Washington, N.Y.: Kennicat Pr., 1964. 5v.

A respected historical source for turn-of-the-century points of view, giving longer articles by specialists about some 20,000 people. Includes titles and location of major works for each artist.

■ Encyclopedia of world art. New York: McGraw-Hill, 1959–87. 15v. Supplements as v.16–17.

Contains a large number of biocritical entries for artists in all fields, including architects, often with locations of major works. Excellent color plates of many works.

■ Who's who in art: biographies of leading men and women in the world of art today. London: Art Trade Pr., 1927– ; distributed by Gale. Biennial.

The standard British biographical source, listing about 3,000 names in all types of media. As of 1994, it no longer adds any non-British names. Appendix of signatures and monograms.

■ Canaday, John. Lives of the painters. New York: Norton, 1969. 4v.

A useful biocritical work for those who lived before 1900, with the fourth volume containing plates and an index.

■ Who's who in American art. New Providence, N.J.: Marquis Who's Who, 1935- . v.1- .

More than 11,000 people in the United States, Canada, Mexico. Includes active artists, curators, administrators, collectors, librarians, etc. All genres and related crafts. Each edition also has a cumulative obituary section for former entries who have died since 1953 and geographical and professional classified indexes.

■ Who was who in American art: compiled from the original thirty-four volumes of American art annual, Who's who in American art: biographies of American artists active from 1898–1947. Peter Hastings Falk, ed. Madison, Conn.: Sound View Pr., 1985. 707p.

Cumulates the titles noted from 1898 through 1947, with updated information and additional names. (The *Who's Who* title is not to be confused with the modern series, published by Bowker and Marquis since 1953.)

■ Contemporary artists. 4th ed. Joann Cerrito and others, eds. Detroit: St. James, 1996. 1340p.

Since the third edition, in 1989, the publisher has made a special effort to include video and computer art. Offers about 800 biographies, excluding anyone who died before 1960, unless he or she was a major influence. In addition to biographical data, gives a list of exhibitions, bibliographies by and about the artist, and a signed critical essay. Black-and-white photos for many entries. Given the selectivity of the work, earlier editions should be retained.

■ Cummings, Paul. A dictionary of contemporary American artists. 6th ed. New York: St. Martin's, 1994. 786p.

Not truly "contemporary" in that it generally excludes younger artists. Index and name pronunciation guide, as well as lengthy bibliographies.

■ Lester, Patrick. The biographical directory of Native American painters. Norman: Univ. of Oklahoma Pr., 1995. 701p.

> The most complete directory in the field. Gives name, dates, area of residence, media used, a list of published works, illustrations, commissions, and exhibitions. Accepts the artists' definition of "Indianness." Generally supercedes Jeanne S. King's *American Indian Painters* (New York: Museum of the American Indian, 1968; 269p.).

Authors

■ Gale's literary index. Detroit: Gale, 1992– . Online and on CD-ROM only. Seminannual updates. Internet: <www.galenet.com/Servlet/LitIndex>

> An index to all forty-three printed series published by Gale, including the titles listed here and others, covering all languages and time periods. In general, the series provide both biographical information and critical comment. Entries for proper name, pseudonyms, and variants, with cross-references for both names and titles; but citations only to the works by title (and sometimes volume), not the specific page.

For older material, the following remain helpful:

■ Havlice, Patricia. Index to literary biography. Metuchen, N.J.: Scarecrow, 1975. 2v. First supplement, 1983. 2v.

> Index to about 70,000 authors in sixty-four reference sources published from 1902 to 1970, with dates, nationality, occupation, preferred media, pseudonyms, and preferred name spellings. The supplement adds fifty-seven more titles, published from 1969 to 1981.

■ Index to the Wilson author series. Rev ed. New York: Wilson, 1996. 104p. Regular updates.

> Indexes about 11,000 names in the eleven volumes in this series. Author name, dates, key to work(s) are indexed, with cross-references to variant name forms.

■ Contemporary world writers. Tracy Chevalier, ed. 2d ed. Detroit: St. James, 1993. 686p.

> Lists 340 living writers from more than sixty nations whose works have been translated into English. Includes a biographical sketch, current

address, bibliography (mostly of books, but other formats often included), which cites original edition plus first Great Britain and U.S. editions in English. Also lists secondary sources about the author. Includes signed critical essays. Index by nationality, title.

- Contemporary poets. Tracy Chevalier, ed. 5th ed. New York: St. Martin's, 1991. 1179p.

  More than 800 current English-language poets, As with other St. Martin's works, gives a biography, a bibliography of sources by and about the writer, and a lengthy critical essay. A notable feature is the inclusion of many poets' comments on their own work.

- Page, James A., and Jae Min Roh. Selected black American, African, and Caribbean authors: a bio-bibliography. Littleton, Colo.: Libraries Unlimited, 1985. 388p.

  Biographies of 632 authors, including some nonliterary authors, especially in religion and social affairs. Biographical sketch, list of book-length works, references to biographical sources.

- Gay and lesbian literature. Detroit: St. James, 1994- . Irregular.

  In the usual St. James format, more than 200 twentieth-century English-language writers, based on the writing's gay and lesbian content and not the sexual identity of the authors. Includes useful appendixes of authors not included in this title, literary awards, anthologies, general critical studies. Indexes by name, nationality (seventeen nations), gender, subject/genre.

- The writers directory. Detroit and London: St. James, 1971/73- . Biennial.

  About 15,000 living writers from English-speaking nations, including South Africa and Ireland, who have written at least one full-length book in English. Includes a list by genre and subject emphasis. About one-third are nonfiction writers. Entries include brief biographies, list of books written, genres, and most recent address. Those formerly listed and now deceased are included in the next edition after their death.

- The Schomberg Center guide to black literature from the eighteenth century to the present. Detroit: Gale, 1996. 545p.

Mostly U.S. but includes international black writers whose work is available in English. In addition to biographical information for about 500 authors, has 460 plot summaries, photos of about 100 authors, about fifty dust jackets. Includes references to other Gale works.

▪ Contemporary authors, a bio-bibliographical guide to current writers in fiction, general nonfiction, poetry, journalism, drama, motion pictures, television, and other fields. Detroit: Gale, 1962– . Series. Also online and on CD-ROM. Updated semiannually. Internet: <http://galenet.gale.com/>.

A somewhat complex series, with 149 volumes numbered as 160 because of consolidation and replacements. Original volumes and "first revision" and "permanent" series are gradually being superseded by the "New Revision" series, but the originals and first revisions should be retained, as many of these entries will not appear again. Bibliographies are intended to be as complete as possible. Some reviewers have questioned whether the revisions in the latest series are changed enough to be worth doing.

Contemporary Authors Cumulative Index (Detroit, Gale, 1980–) covers the previous series as well as the other Gale authors and criticism series. Cumulates with every other volume.

▪ DiscLit: world authors. New York: Macmillan and Hall, 1994. Online and on CD-ROM only.

Full text of all 146 volumes from Twayne's World Authors series, plus about 200,000 bibliographic records from OCLC about those authors. Includes biographies and critical comments on literary figures, philosophers, historians.

▪ DISCovering authors. Detroit: Gale, 1993. Online and on CD-ROM only. Triennial updates.

In several modules on the same disc, access depending on your subscription. Modules are "Most-Studied Authors," based on U.S. school curriculum, "Poets," "Dramatists," "Novelists," "Multicultural Authors," "Popular Fiction," and "Genre Authors."

Selections from the Gale series, generally four to seven essays (about sixty pages total per name) from the print version, with about one-third of the material updated or new. Very user-friendly, can search on any field in the record. Includes authority list of terms and cross-references. Access by author, subject/genre, work title, literary character, personal data, full text.

There is also a *DISCovering Authors, British Edition* of the 300 most-studied authors, aimed at British curriculum; *DISCovering Authors, Canadian Edition* of about 400 authors, including sixty Canadians studied in that country; and a *Junior DISCovering Authors* containing 300 names, based heavily on *Something about the Author.*

■ DiscLit: British authors. New York: Macmillan and Hall, 1992. Online and on CD-ROM only.

Full text of 145 volumes in Twayne's English Authors series with more than 100,000 citations to authors covered in the series from the OCLC database.

■ DiscLit: American authors. New York: Macmillan and Hall, 1991. Online and on CD-ROM only.

The full text of 143 volumes in Twayne's United States Authors series, with more than 127,000 citations to authors covered in the series from the OCLC database.

■ International authors and writers who's who. Cambridge, England: International Biographical Centre; Bristol, Pa.: Taylor & Francis, 1976- . Biennial.

More than 8,000 entries, mostly from North America and Europe. Has been criticized for lack of clear criteria for inclusion (e.g., the on-again, off-again inclusion of poets). Does include translators (a rare occurrence).

Other frequently used volumes include some in the Wilson Authors series:

■ Kunitz, Stanley J., and Howard Haycraft, comps. American authors, 1600–1900. 8th ed. New York: Wilson, 1977. 846p.

■ Kunitz, Stanley J., and Howard Haycraft, comps. British authors before 1800. New York: Wilson, 1952. 584p.

■ Kunitz, Stanley J., and Howard Haycraft, comps. British authors of the nineteenth century. New York: Wilson, 1936. 677p.

Includes Canada, South Africa, Australia, and New Zealand.

■ Kunitz, Stanley J., and Vineta Colby. European authors, 1000–1900. New York: Wilson, 1967. 1016p.

■ World authors, 1900–1950. Martin Seymour-Smith and Andrew C. Kimmens, eds. Bronx, N.Y.: Wilson, 1996. 4v.

   A reworking of Kunitz's *Twentieth Century Authors* (1942) and *TCA First Supplement* (1955), including nearly all the 2,500 authors of the first work plus others who came into prominence since 1955.

■ Wakeman, John, ed. World authors, 1950–1970. New York: Wilson, 1975. 1594p.

   Some 959 authors, available in English, who gained attention from 1950 to 1970. This is updated by *World Authors, 1970–1975* (1980), with 348 new entries; *World Authors, 1975–1980* (1985), with 379; *World Authors, 1980–1985,* adding 320 new name5s; *World Authors, 1985–1990* (1995), with 345; and *World Authors, 1990–1995* (1999), adding 345 names. Similar to *Twentieth Century Authors* but more truly international. Entries not signed. Many of the authors covered have written autobiographical articles.

The previous titles, as well as the rest of the series, are accessible via the *Index to the Wilson Authors Series* (Bronx, N.Y.: Wilson, 1996; 120p.).

■ Contemporary novelists. 6th ed. Susan W. Brown, ed. New York: St. Martin's, 1995. 1173p.

   Regularly updates essays from previous editions and drops authors. Brief biography, primary bibliography, and a critical essay about living English-language writers. Often a short secondary bibliography as well. Also lists information about published bibliographies and manuscript collections. Index by title to all novels mentioned.

■ Benét's reader's encyclopedia of American literature. George Perkins, Barbara Perkins, and Phillip Leininger, eds. New York: HarperCollins, 1991. 1176p.

   American writers and genres, with good coverage of women, as well as African American, Jewish American, and other ethnic groups. Includes genealogies of famous literary families.

■ Benét's reader's encyclopedia. 4th ed. Bruce Murphy, ed. New York: HarperCollins, 1995. 1144p.

A classic, with more than 9,000 entries. Gives mostly biographical information. Includes legends, allusions, genres, etc., as well as author entries.

■ White, Barbara. American women's fiction, 1790–1870. New York: Garland, 1990. 294p.

Lists and annotates 385 sources discussing 328 women; includes ninteenth-century sources. Index by name of person covered. Covers many more than *American Women Writers,* which does only 143 of the 328 names.

■ Dictionary of literary biography. Detroit: Gale, 1978– . Serial. Also on the Web.

A major reference series, now broadened in scope to include Canadian, French, and German, as well as American and British literature. Each volume has lengthy signed articles on major authors of a given time period or genre, many photos, and primary and secondary bibliographies. Volumes have been ranked as among the best sources in their field.

Subsets of this series are also available, such as the *Concise Dictionary of American Literary Biography.*

■ Latin American writers. Carlos A. Solé, ed. New York: Scribner, 1989. 3v.

A literary history of Mexico, Central and South America, and the Spanish-speaking Caribbean. Arranged by date of birth starting with de las Casas (1474), for a total of 176 authors (149 Spanish, 27 Brazilian). Indexes by country and name, as well as a general index.

Also useful are the various handbooks to literature as well as the standard histories of national literature, such as the *Cambridge History of English Literature,* and the various Oxford *Companions,* such as the *Oxford Companion to American Literature* (6th ed. New York: Oxford Univ. Pr., 1995; 779p.).

Children and Young Adult Authors

■ Children's authors and illustrators: an index to biographical dictionaries. 5th ed. Detroit: Gale, 1995. 811p.

An index to 200,000 entries for about 30,000 authors and illustrators in 650 sources; with good coverage of women and members of ethnic groups. Has been criticized for some weakness on YA authors, but does include "adult" authors who have been adopted by children.

■ Writers for young adults: biographies master index. 3d ed. Detroit: Gale, 1989. 183p.

Covers about 145,000 entries for some 16,000 people in 600 sources. As with the previous title, it includes adult writers whose work is suitable for YAs.

■ Kunitz, Stanley J., and Howard Haycraft, comps. Junior book of authors. 2d rev. ed. New York: Wilson, 1951. 309p.

Continued by *More Junior Authors, Third Book of Junior Authors,* and the fourth, fifth, and sixth *Book of Junior Authors and Illustrators,* the most recent published in 1989. The current volume in the series is

■ Seventh book of junior authors and illustrators. Bronx, N.Y.: Wilson, 1996. 371p.

These 235 entries are based on initial lists of about 1,000 authors and illustrators. The most frequently cited titles are *Something about the Author* and *Contemporary Authors.* Includes authors not listed in most other sources and a cumulative index to the whole set—by both name and pen name. As with many Wilson products, inclusion is based on a panel vote.

■ Something about the author: facts and pictures about contemporary authors and illustrators of books for young people. Detroit: Gale, 1972- . 4v. per year.

An ALA Outstanding Reference Source. One to six pages per biography, usually with a portrait and often examples of illustrations. Cumulative illustrator and author indexes in every odd-numbered volume, plus references to *Yesterday's Authors of Books for Children,* the Children's Literature Review series, and the Something about the Author series.

Businessmen and Businesswomen

■ Standard & Poor's register—biographical. New York: Standard & Poor's, 1987- . Online only.

Who's who–type entries for about 70,000 corporate executives, based on self-completed questionnaires plus press releases and other data compiled for the various Standard & Poor's directories and found in the printed *Standard & Poor's Register of Corporations, Directors and Executives,* volume 2 (*see* chapter 4).

- Who's who in finance and industry. Chicago: Marquis Who's Who, 1936– . Biennial. Also online and on CD-ROM.

  Some changes beginning with the twenty-eighth edition (1993) have led to fewer biographies but more foreign coverage and a new "Professional Area Index." Generally lists top executives of major and medium-sized corporations.

Educators

- Directory of American scholars. 9th ed. Detroit: Gale, 1999. 5v.

  The first eight editions, published by Bowker, covered the most prominent scholars in all disciplines in the United States and Canada, but the last was published in 1982. This is planned to revive the series, and it will include both geographic and master indexes.

See also chapter 4 for the *National Faculty Directory.*

Film and Television

- McNeil, Barbara, and Miranda C. Herbert. Performing arts biography master index: a consolidated index to over 270,000 biographical sketches of persons living and dead, as they appear in over 100 of the principal biographical dictionaries devoted to the performing arts. 2d ed. Detroit: Gale, 1982. 701p.

  Replaces Dennis La Beau, *Theatre, Film and Television Biographies Master Index* (Detroit: Gale, 1979; 477p.).

- Baseline. New York: Baseline, 1970– . Online only.

  An entire system of entertainment information, much of which is available from LEXIS/NEXIS as well as the producer. The system contains current biographies and credits for about 700,000 people, primarily in the film and television industries, including celebrities, but listing anyone who generates a screen credit.

- Halliwell's filmgoer's companion. 13th ed. John Walker, ed. New York: HarperCollins, 1999. 864p.

  A "reference classic" of international scope, comprised mostly of biographies of filmmakers, directors, stars, and writers, plus some articles on movements, trends, techniques, subjects, etc.

■ International dictionary of films and filmmakers. Nicholas Thomas and James Vinson, eds. 2d ed. Detroit: St. James, 1990–93. 5v.

Has been called "the most substantial English-language film encyclopedia available," although it is mostly biographical. Volume 1 lists films; volume 5 is an index. The other three contain "Directors," "Actors and Actresses," and "Writers and Production Artists." Especially valuable for extensive filmographies and bibliographies. Includes cross-references to foreign titles.

■ International motion picture almanac. New York: Quigley, 1929– . Annual.

Mostly a who's who of industry including TV and radio as well as film. Includes awards, obituaries, etc., and an analytical index.

■ International television and video almanac. New York: Quigley, 1945– . Annual.

As above, with the same who's who section but different information for products, corporations, etc.

The previous two sources are now available on one CD-ROM as Quigley's Entertainment Industry Reference on CD-ROM (New York: Quigley, 1997– ; annual).

Labor Leaders

■ Fink, Gary M. Biographical dictionary of American labor. Westport, Conn.: Greenwood, 1984. 767p.

An update of a 1974 title by the same author, now listing more than 700 people, with a conscious attempt to include women and leaders of the end of the nineteenth century. In addition to medium-length biographies, all with bibliographies, this includes a detailed analysis of American labor in the twentieth century.

■ Lane, A. Thomas, ed. Biographical dictionary of European labor leaders. Westport, Conn.: Greenwood, 1995. 2v.

Covers about 1,400 people from all European nations, from the early nineteenth century to the present, including not only union leaders but politicians, the cooperative movement, and various "radical" movements as well. As with the previous title, this title also contains useful appendixes, along with a good index and cross-reference system.

Law

- Martindale-Hubbell law directory. Summit, N.J.: Martindale-Hubbell, 1868- . Annual. 17v. plus indexes. Also on CD-ROM, 1995- .

  U.S. and Canadian attorneys, plus some from other nations. Colleges, law schools, etc., as well as firms; also includes firms catering to the legal profession. Long entries for some firms include all lawyers and short biographies for each; shorter records for other firms just list names. Keyword searching makes the CD-ROM much easier to use.

Library and Information Professionals

- Dictionary of American library biography. Littleton, Colo.: Libraries Unlimited, 1978. 596p. Supplement, 1990. 184p.

  Evaluative signed sketches of about 300 deceased librarians and a few others significant in librarianship (e.g., Carnegie, Franklin). The supplement adds fifty-one new names of those who died before June 30, 1987.

- Directory of library and information professionals. Woodbridge, Conn.: Research Pub., 1988. 2v. Also on CD-ROM.

  Although outdated, the most recent general biographical source in the field, based on surveys sent to all members of the major library and information science professional organizations in the United States. Abbreviated, who's who–type entries. All fields are searchable on the CD-ROM version.

Military Leaders

- Brassey's encyclopedia of military history and biography. McLean, Va.: Brassey's, 1994. 1197p.

  A derivative of the same publisher's *International Military and Defense Encyclopedia* (6v., 1993) but very useful if the parent volume is lacking. Covers all nations and time periods, with an excellent, detailed index.

- Dictionary of American military biography. Roger Spiller and Joseph G. Dawson, eds. Westport, Conn.: Greenwood, 1984. 3v.

  About 400 essays by 200 experts, covering the French and Indian War through Vietnam. Includes numerous cross-references, appendixes giving background, and an index. Each entry has a brief bibliography. Unlike many such compilations, this work is dispassionate, gives credit (and blame) to others, and includes some nonmilitary leaders who had significant influence.

■ Harper encyclopedia of military biography. Trevor N. Dupuy, Curt Johnson, and David L. Bongard. New York: HarperCollins, 1992. 834p.

A companion to the *Harper Encyclopedia of Military History* (4th ed, 1993), this work covers about 3,000 leaders from all nations and time periods. Most are short, just-the-facts entries, but longer biographies include (possibly controversial) one-sentence appraisals; and nearly all entries have short bibliographies. A useful feature is the inclusion of alternative spellings (e.g., for Asian and Middle Eastern figures); the lack of a subject index is less useful. This has been called the standard work on the subject, although the previous title has more detail on the Americas.

Musicians

■ Baker's biographical dictionary of musicians. Nicholas Slonimsky, ed. 8th ed. New York: Schirmer Books, 1992. 2115p.

About 15,000 entries for living as well as deceased persons. The work is highly respected but idiosyncratic. *Reference Books Bulletin* says this is one of the few reference works that can be read for pleasure. Covers all periods and countries; includes bibliographies.

■ International who's who in music. 14th ed. Cambridge, England: Melrose Pr., 1994. 1296p.

Competently done and fairly comprehensive sketches for about 8,000 names. Includes references to agents, with good coverage of popular music.

■ Contemporary musicians: profiles of the people in music. Detroit: Gale, 1989– . Also online, 1994– .

Each volume covers about eighty people and groups, with a strong emphasis on popular music. Entries include a picture, selective bibliographies (mostly journal articles) and discographies, and are all signed. Each volume has cumulative name and subject indexes to the full set. As of volume 11, it is online and earlier entries are being revised.

Political Leaders

■ Biographical directory of the American Congress, 1774–1996. Alexandria, Va.: CQ Staff Directories, 1997. 2108p.

> Brief factual accounts, giving birth and death dates, education, career, and terms of office, based on the official *Congressional Directory.*

■ Biographical dictionary of the American left. Westport, Conn.: Greenwood, 1986. 493p.

> An objective, scholarly work covering about 275 leaders, including utopians, Marxists, etc. All information can be found in other sources, but this is handy.

■ Who's who in American politics: a biographical directory of United States political leaders. New Providence, N.J.: Marquis Who's Who, 1967– . 2v. Also online.

> About 29,000 sketches, including national and state governments, diplomats, and the like, based on survey questionnaires in standard who's who style.

■ Congressional directory. [number] Congress. Washington, D.C.: Govt. Print. Off., 1888– . Biennial. Also online.

> Official, if short, biographies of all members of the Senate and House, including committee assignments, maps of their districts, and current directory information. Also includes directory information for other government officials, including governors, as well as diplomats and accredited members of the print and electronic press.
>
> Nonofficial, and thus often more informative, information can also be found in the *CQ Member Profiles* (Washington, D.C.: Congressional Quarterly, 1990– ; online only), which includes all members since the 100th Congress with comments on home life, personality, and politics, as well as ratings of voting records.

Religious Leaders

■ Who's who in religion. 4th ed. Chicago: Marquis Who's Who, 1992. 580p.

> The usual who's who format covering living clergy, church officials, and lay leaders around the world, based on biographees' responses to a

survey, with additional information. Because this title comes out infrequently, many names change from edition to edition; thus, retain all editions.

■ Who's who of world religions. John R. Hinnells, ed. New York: Simon & Schuster, 1992. 656p.

Not to be confused with the previous title, provides about 1,500 entries for major figures of all times and faiths, with an emphasis on non-Christian (and non-Western Christian) figures. Coverage is very wide, with such figures as Charles Manson and David Berg (Moses of the Children of God) as well as Gilgamesh, Tecumseh, Martin Luther, and the Buddha. Entries include brief biographical material but also discussion of the person's beliefs and influence. Entries are keyed to a bibliography at the end; a topical and general index as well as cross-references provide easy access.

■ Bowden, Henry Warner. Dictionary of American religious biography. 2d ed. Westport, Conn.: Greenwood, 1993. 686p.

About 550 mostly one-page biographies of deceased Americans, with appended bibliographies. General index plus indexes by birthplace and denomination. Overall, well-balanced coverage.

Scientists

■ Ireland, Norma O. Index to scientists of the world, from ancient to modern times: biographies and portraits. Boston: Faxon, 1962. 662p.

Indexes biographies, portraits, and chief contributions of more than 7,400 scientists in 338 biographical dictionaries. Gives name, date, description, source, and page; up to sixty citations for prominent figures (e.g., Galileo). Juvenile sources are indicated with an asterisk.

■ Pelletier, Paul A. Prominent scientists: an index to collective biographies. 3d ed. New York: Neal-Schuman, 1994. 353p.

More than 300 collections published since 1960, indexing more than 15,000 names. Arranged alphabetically by name, with an index to field of activity. Includes not only current and recent scientists, but classical and medieval ones, such as Thales. This is a follow-up to Norma O. Ireland's *Index to Scientists of the World* (*see* above).

- The biographical dictionary of scientists. Roy Porter, ed. 2d ed. New York: Oxford Univ. Pr., 1994. 891p.

  Relatively longer biographies of the "great men and women" of science over all of history. Includes brief histories of each field of the "hard" sciences and a glossary of terms that can be used as a brief scientific dictionary. The index includes names and subjects.

- American men and women of science. New Providence, N.J.: Bowker/ Reed Reference, 1906- . Triennial. 8v. Also online and on CD-ROM as part of the Bowker Biographical Directory.

  Sketches of about 123,000 living people working in computer, biological, and physical sciences in the United States and Canada who have made "significant" contributions to the field. Starting with the nineteenth edition, includes names of spouses and children and phone, fax, and e-mail addresses. Includes several statistical tables.

There is also a *Cumulative Index* to the first fourteen editions, compiled by J. C Press (847p.).

- Dictionary of scientific biography. Charles C. Gillispie, ed. New York: Scribner, 1970-80. 16v. plus 2v. supplement, 1990.

  Prominent scientists who were deceased at time of publication. Very similar in layout to the *DAB,* but with few female scientists included, even in the supplements. The board has been aware of weakness in social sciences, natural sciences, and medicine and hopes to rectify. Volume 16 indexes the basic set and first supplement (i.e., volume 15); volume 18 indexes the second supplement and also has a subject index.

- Herzenberg, Caroline I. Women scientists from antiquity to the present. West Cornwall, Conn.: Locust Hill Pr., 1986. 200p.

  An index to about 130 sources. Includes living scientists as well as those in all time periods.

- Who's who in science and engineering. 3d ed. Chicago: Marquis Who's Who, 1996. 1386p.

  Brief biographies of about 26,000 living medical doctors, scientists, and engineers around the world, although emphasizing the United States. Unlike earlier editions, includes social sciences as well as hard sciences and engineering. Indexes by professional area and by geography. Includes a list of awards, with their recipients.

■ Who's who in technology. 7th ed. Detroit: Gale, 1995. Also online.

Brief biographies of about 25,000 applied scientists and engineers all over the world, with indexes by geography, employer, and field of expertise. Includes obituaries of those from previous editions who are now deceased.

■ Who's who in science in Europe: a biographical guide to technology, agriculture, and medicine. 9th ed. London and New York: Stockton Pr., 1995. 2v. Also on CD-ROM.

A standard, covering about 60,000 people in Europe, including Turkey, and excluding the former Soviet Union. Biographical information is a bit more extensive than the Marquis works, but only major publications are listed. Includes a discipline index.

Theater

■ Wearing, J. P. American and British theatrical biography: a directory. Metuchen, N.J.: Scarecrow, 1979. 1007p.

Indexes about 50,000 names in some 200 sources, with cross-references to stage names, dates, nationality, occupation(s), source code.

■ Who's who in the theatre: a biographical record of the contemporary stage. Detroit: Gale, 1912–81. 18v.

Publisher varies. *Contemporary Theatre, Film and Television* is a successor to *Who's Who in the Theatre* and includes indexing to this set in its volume 4.

■ Who was who in the theatre, 1912–1976: a biographical directory of actors, actresses, directors, playwrights, and producers from the English-speaking theatre, compiled from Who's who in the theatre, v.1–15. Detroit: Gale, 1978. 4v.

Persons dead or inactive by 1976. Covers 41,000 entries from volumes 1 to 15, excluding those carried over to the sixteenth volume.

■ Contemporary theatre, film and television: a biographical guide. Detroit: Gale, 1984– . Annual.

A continuation of *Who's Who in the Theatre,* adding film and TV information from biographies or agents; many include a black-and-white photo. Focus on contemporary in English-speaking nations but some others included; updates previous entries as needed. Includes list of former entries.

Many more national biographies and biographical directories in special fields will be found in *Balay,* which devotes section AH to biography and AJ to genealogy. *Walford's Guide to Reference Material* (volume 2) devotes section 92 to biography and from 929.5 to 929.9 to genealogy and heraldry. Both *Balay* and *Walford's* provide broad coverage of sources, as well as useful descriptive and (especially *Walford's*) evaluative annotations.

A readable account of the most frequently used biographical sources will be found in William A. Katz's *Introduction to Reference Work* (volume 1, chapter 9), as well as Richard E. Bopp and Linda C. Smith's *Reference and Information Services* (2d ed., chapter 15).

An example of an annotated list suitable for the small library, *Reference Sources for Small and Medium-sized Libraries,* includes about 150 biographical sources judged to be the most useful in this type of library by a committee of the ALA's Reference and User Services Association. A similar, if somewhat older, list, aimed at libraries of all types and sizes, was published as "Biographical Reference Sources: A Selective Checklist" in *Reference Books Bulletin* (80 [May 15, 1984]: 1314-27; [June 15, 1984]: 1447-61; and 81 [May 15, 1985]: 1309-11]). This list, in addition to some reviews, is primarily in a matrix format, giving such things as type of biographee covered, frequency, and audience.

Summary

Sources of biographical information are among the most used and most numerous titles. They are widely varied, and their variety is exceeded only in their degree of reliability. This chapter has described the nature of biographical information, the most important indexes, international and national sources, and those restricted to one or more professions. Points to be observed in their evaluation have been noted.

6

Sources on Words

In a world where the need to communicate is keenly felt, no source is more important than one on words and their meanings. Individuals must communicate with individuals, and nations with nations. This need increases with the complexity of society, with the advances in science and technology, and with our concern with our image. We are a far cry from the days when we could be satisfied with glossaries of individual words. Today we are less concerned with rare and obsolete words than with the rapidly increasing living language.

For this reason, this chapter will be concerned with sources of the living language—chiefly, but not exclusively, the English language—fundamental to our understanding of the symbols we use to communicate. Most important and most widely used are general language dictionaries, and some knowledge of why and how they are made is essential if they are to be used intelligently—not as a kind of mystical authority, but as a product of our efforts to record the meanings of words and their pronunciations, not to mention their spelling. Guidelines for reviewing English-language dictionaries may be found in the appendix.

Fortunately, the potential user or purchaser of a dictionary has some recent guidance in the following sources:

Kenneth Kister's *Kister's Best Dictionaries for Adults and Young People: A Comparative Guide* (Phoenix, Ariz.: Oryx, 1992; 438p.) covers about 300 dictionaries published in the United States, Canada, and Great Britain, including electronic formats. Kister, the premier critic of dictionaries and encyclopedias, provides evaluative reviews varying in length but often several pages long, with citations to other reviews.

Although the previous title is the work of one person, the *ARBA Guide to Subject Encyclopedias and Dictionaries* (Susan C. Awe, ed.; 2d ed. Englewood, Colo.: Libraries Unlimited, 1997; 482p.) cumulates and updates reviews from *American Reference Books Annual,* covering an area different from that of Kister. For a slightly different take, a collaborative effort of several prominent reference librarians and teachers, *Encyclopedias, Atlases and Dictionaries* (Marion Sader and Amy Lewis, eds.; New Providence, N.J.: Bowker, 1995; 575p.) also provides lengthy critical evaluations of general works.

Why a Dictionary Is Made

General language dictionaries have been compiled in modern times by individuals, learned societies, or commercial firms with one of two basic purposes, purposes that are inevitably related: (1) to set authoritative standards for spelling, meaning, and usage, or (2) to record the words of the language, with all their uses and meanings. Dictionaries compiled for the first purpose are known as *prescriptive,* an often-cited example being Samuel Johnson's *Dictionary of the English Language* (1755; reprint, North Stratford, N.H.: Ayer, 1980; 2320p.; also available on CD-ROM, New York: Cambridge Univ. Pr., 1996). Dictionaries compiled for the second purpose are known as *descriptive,* the best-known example in English being the *Oxford English Dictionary* (1884–). *OED,* as it is known and usually cited, owes its origins largely to Dean Richard C. Trench's attack on Samuel Johnson's view, which had influenced English lexicography for more than a hundred years. Dean Trench believed that a dictionary should be an inventory of the language and that the lexicographer should be a historian, not a critic, of the language.

That the latter view is more generally accepted in twentieth-century lexicography is evident in *Webster's Third New International Dictionary,* which aims to represent the language as it is now used. That there are objections to this purpose is evident in the storm of controversy that arose soon after publication of *Webster's Third;* for a sample, see James H. Sleed and Wilma R. Ebbitts, eds., *Dictionaries and That Dictionary* (Chicago: Scott, Foresman, 1962; 273p.). Later material on the continuing controversy is covered in Herbert C. Morton, *The Story of Webster's Third: Philip Gove's Controversial Dictionary and Its Critics* (Cambridge and New York: Cambridge Univ. Pr., 1994;

332p.). Noah Webster was a man of many interests—teacher, author, journalist, lawyer, judge, scientist, gardener, traveler—but was best known as a lexicographer. An ardent believer that the American nation needed a language and literature of its own, he wrote a three-volume *Grammatical Institute of the English Language* (part 1), known as the *Blue-backed Speller* (1783; reprint, Bedford, Mass.: Applewood Books, 1998; 198p.), which became a best-seller (about 60 million copies were sold in the course of a century). It helped to bring about reform in American orthography. The year he died (1843), G. & C. Merriam acquired the right to produce further editions of his great work, *An American Dictionary of the English Language,* and this firm continues to revise and publish this standard, unabridged dictionary (as well as many abridgments). In 1970, Johnson Reprint Corporation published a facsimile of the original 1828 edition of the dictionary in two volumes, with an introduction by Mario Pei.

Even Dr. Johnson, though unable to abandon his prescriptive approach, finally admitted, in the preface to the dictionary, that his desire to "fix" the language was one that "neither reason nor experience can justify."

An example of how modern lexicographers defend their objectivity in recording a language is given by Jess Stein, editor in chief of the first edition of the *Random House Dictionary of the English Language,* who states in its introduction (reprinted in the second edition):

> And finally, that lexicographer's Scylla and Charybdis: Should the dictionary be an authoritarian guide to "correct" English or should it be so antiseptically free of comment that it may defeat the user by providing him with no guidance at all? There is, we believe, a linguistically sound middle course. Language, most people agree, is never static—except when dead. It has a capacity for constant change and growth that enables it to serve effectively the requirements of the society in which it exists. It is, therefore, the function of a dictionary to provide the user with an exact record of the language he sees and hears. That record must be fully descriptive. Since language is a social institution, the lexicographer must give the user an adequate indication of the attitudes of society toward particular words or expressions, whether he regards those attitudes as linguistically sound or not. The lexicographer who does not recognize the existence of long-established strictures in usage has not discharged his full responsibility. He has not been objective and factual; he has reported selectively, omitting references to a social attitude relevant to many words and expressions. He does not need to express approval or disapproval of a disputed usage, but he does need to report the milieu of words as well as their meanings [p. x].

Nevertheless, present-day compilers of dictionaries must inevitably, it seems, be concerned with what is considered the "standard" language and must give emphasis to standard words and meanings in their vocabulary. As

Isaac Funk said, in the original preface to his first *Standard Dictionary of the English Language* (1893):

> The chief function of a dictionary is to record usage; not, except in a limited degree, to seek to create it. Yet, when custom or usage varies, it is important that a dictionary should be most careful, in its preferences, to give its sanction to the best forms and tendencies. It has manifold opportunities to render good service to the language by characterizing certain words and variant forms of words, and certain meanings or usages, as archaic or obsolete, as foreign, dialectic, or provincial, as colloquial, vulgar, slang or law, as inelegant or erroneously formed [from "Introductory," *New Standard Dictionary of the English Language* (New York: Funk & Wagnalls, 1963), p. xi.].

On the other hand, again from the second edition of the *Random House Dictionary:*

> Vocabulary once confined to a specialized area becomes generalized in usage, and must be so recognized; some terms once associated only with racing cards and sports cars now apply to the design of the family car; items of clothing once worn mainly by cowboys, athletes or explorers are in widespread everyday use; the jargon of specific groups and activities becomes the slang of a wider social milieu and is then used by much of the general public ["Preface," 2d ed., p. vii].

Increasingly, what was once considered slang is now included in general dictionaries. For example, the supplement to the *Oxford English Dictionary* incorporated Eric Partridge's *Dictionary of Slang,* which was once described by Partridge as containing words not fit to print in the *OED;* and the second edition of that monumental work contains even more of such words. And certainly slang appears more often in newspapers, magazines, and books.

Along with this tendency to include more "substandard" terms from the point of view of grammar and style, there is a growing concern with "offensive" terms from the point of view of ethnic and racial concerns. These include not only the presence of words found objectionable by a given group, but also definitions of otherwise neutral terms and have recently extended to political issues, such as the meaning of *Palestine.* That even historical dictionaries are coming under such fire can be seen in the travails surrounding the second edition of the *Oxford English Dictionary,* well described by its editor, Robert Burchfield, in *Unlocking the English Language* (New York: Hill & Wang, 1991; 202p.). In short, regardless of the opinions of linguists and philologists, to the average person, a dictionary is *not* merely a record of the language, but a recommendation of proper, or at least accepted, usage.

That dictionaries inevitably serve as language standardizers is pointed out by Kenneth Whittaker:

It was commonly accepted in the eighteenth century that dictionaries should try to standardize the spelling, pronunciation, meaning and general usage of words. In fact, it was sometimes held that dictionaries should fix the words of good English for all time. Nowadays, on the contrary, it is generally felt that dictionaries should limit themselves to recording exactly a language's development. However, although the twentieth century point of view is different from that of the eighteenth century, the fact remains that dictionaries do inevitably act as language standardizers. In Elizabethan times, when English dictionaries were still rudimentary, the spelling of words was far more varied than it is today. . . . One of the main reasons for the disappearance of varied spellings since Shakespeare's day is undoubtedly the growth of dictionaries.

Even when dictionaries record different usages and spellings, they can only record a limited number, and so fix usage. Whittaker further points out that in newly developing countries of the world, variations in usage (such as different spellings) are eliminated from the start, because dictionaries are produced alongside the first newspapers, books, and other writings in a language hitherto unwritten (*Dictionaries* [New York: Philosophical Library, 1966], p. 25–26).

When, then, do we discriminate between the two types of dictionaries? The answer lies in the methods of compilation, the former being based on the opinions and judgments of compilers on what they consider to be approved, standard usage; the latter, on the basis of evidence gathered from a careful inventory of recorded sources of the language.

It is a difficult and time-consuming task to produce a good, general English-language (or any other language) dictionary:

A commercial dictionary is a very heavy expense, expensive to set and expensive to write and edit (even if the writing and editing are poorly done). If a dictionary is to sell, these costs cannot be passed on to consumers immediately as they can with many other products. Usually publishers plan to recover costs within a period of five years, but it often takes longer. A reference book does very well to yield 8 to 10 percent in the market, a very small return compared to that of a book club, which might make 25 percent, or of many products that yield 50 percent [cited in *Kister's Best Dictionaries*, p. 26, from Clarence L. Barnhart, "General Dictionaries," *American Speech* 44 (fall 1969): 173–74].

Unabridged Dictionaries

Briefly discussed here are only well-known unabridged English-language dictionaries—their scope and word treatment. Fuller discussion will be found in Kenneth Kister's *Kister's Best Dictionaries for Adults and Young People: A Comparative Guide* (Phoenix, Ariz.: Oryz, 1992; 438p.), an excellent source of thorough, discriminating evaluations of English-language dictionaries and wordbooks. For brief descriptive notes on a wide range of titles, see *Balay* and *Walford's*.

Though the number of entries for each dictionary (listed here) is given as stated by the publishers, these statistics should be used with some knowledge of what is being counted. Sidney Landau, editor in chief of Funk & Wagnalls dictionaries, discussed the point some years ago in an article that concludes: "To regard a dictionary's total entry count as significant in itself, is not very sensible, especially if one has only vague notions of what a dictionary entry is. Properly understood, however, and provided one also is familiar with other aspects of the dictionary in question, entry count can be a useful guide in estimating a dictionary's comparative size and comprehensiveness" ("The Numbers Game: Dictionary Entry Count," *RQ* 4 [Sept. 1964]: 13–15).

Landau explains the various types of entries, defining a main entry as "a word, phrase, abbreviation, or word element (including prefixes, suffixes, and combining forms) that appears in its regular alphabetical place and is there defined." Other types of entries that may be included in the total vocabulary count have been designated by a federal specification, which provides for counting inflected forms, variant spellings, and defined parts of speech other than the main entry (Federal Supply Service. General Services Administration. *Federal Specifications: Dictionaries, English* [Washington, D.C.: Govt. Print. Off., 1974; 8p.]; [SuDocs number GS 2.8: G-D-331D]). Also included in entry counts may be idioms, run-on derivatives, and words or phrases in self-explanatory lists—one beginning with the prefix *un*, for example. Remember that what may appear in main entry form in one dictionary may appear in another form in another dictionary. Thus, we see the validity of including in the total count not only the main entry, but the inflected forms, variant spellings, defined parts of speech, idioms, run-on derivatives, and words or phrases in self-explanatory lists.

Felicia Lampert quotes one lexicographer as saying, "Most publishers either lie or equivocate in their entry claims; no one is likely to sit down and count." She cites no source for this statement, and continues, somewhat frivolously, "Exaggerations of up to 20 percent are considered sporting in the trade" ("Dictionaries: Our Language Right or Wrong," in Jack C. Gray, comp., *Words, Words, and Words about Dictionaries* [San Francisco: Chandler, 1963], p. 70). But it is reasonable to believe that good editors know how many entries are included in the dictionaries for which they are responsible.

One other point should be remembered in comparing the vocabulary counts of one dictionary with another: some dictionaries include nonlexical terms, such as biographical and geographical names, while others do not. This difference should be taken into consideration if sizes of vocabulary are compared.

Historical

■ Oxford English dictionary. 2d ed. Oxford: Clarendon Pr., 1989. 20v. Also on CD-ROM. (Often called *OED II* to distinguish it from the first edition.)

> *Scope*: Includes material from the original and its supplement plus the modern four-volume supplement, with the addition of more than 5,000 words that have appeared in the language since the latter was published. Thus, it contains well over one-half million words known to have been used since 1150. Especially complete for commonly used words, with a tendency to extend "common" more into science and technology than slang and argot. Generally does not include highly technical scientific words and dialects in use after about 1500, unless the word continued in general use.

> *Treatment*: Gives current or most usual spelling, pronunciation (now using the International Phonetic Alphabet [IPA]), part of speech, field or currency label if needed, earlier spellings, earliest appearance of the word in written sources (precise date if known), etymology, meanings, groups of idiomatic phrases or attributive uses, and combinations. Meanings are numbered or lettered, with specifications as to status and date of first appearance; if obsolete, indications of authorship. Definitions are rather brief—this is not a dictionary of definitions per se. Pronunciation is that generally used by both American and British broadcasters and thus more neutral. An excellent source for dating words and for finding quotations, because several generations of scholars searched many sources for the earliest appearance of a word.

> Heavily British in emphasis, so less useful for American terms. The user should also keep in mind that words often appear in the spoken language some time before they appear in written form, and that, inevitably, some written appearances of a word may have been missed.

> The CD-ROM version of this tool is much more versatile than the print, because it allows searching by fields, including author, date, and quotations, parts of speech, etc., as well as the full text, and has printing capability.

For evaluations of the CD-ROM, *see American Reference Books Annual* 28 (1997): 388; and *Booklist* 93 (June 1, 1997): 1736. The *Booklist* review includes comments on the printed version.

■ Oxford English dictionary additions series. John Simpson and Edmund Weiner, eds. New York: Clarendon Pr./Oxford Univ. Pr., 1993– . 3v. as of 1999 (in progress).

Follows the style and format of the parent volume, listing new words and meanings that have entered the language since the beginning of the second edition. Intended to be issued in continuing volumes; until the third edition of the *OED,* each new volume will have a cumulative index. Includes not only British English, but also American, Caribbean, and Australian terms. A very useful feature is the inclusion of cross-references to terms in the *OED II.*

See reviews in *Choice* 32 (Sept. 1994): 74; *Reference Books Bulletin* 90 (April 1, 1994): 1476-77; *Wilson Library Bulletin* 69 (Sept. 1994): 85-86; and *American Reference Books Annual* 26 (1995): 460.

■ New shorter Oxford English dictionary on historical principles. Lesley Brown, ed. New York: Oxford Univ. Pr., 1993. 2v. Also on CD-ROM, 1997.

Covers words in use from 1700 to the present (plus older terms that appear commonly in literature), with about 97,000 entries with 83,000 illustrative quotations. Includes a number of newer words not in the full *OED II,* and quotations from more modern sources, also not in the original. Generally, one would prefer the full *OED II,* but this is a cheaper (and less complete) alternative.

The earlier versions of this monumental work are common in libraries and appear in reprints from time to time:

■ Murray, Sir James Augustus Henry. New English dictionary on historical principles. Oxford: Clarendon Pr., 1888-1933. 12v. and a supplement.

■ ———. Oxford English dictionary, being a corrected reissue, with an introduction, supplement, and bibliography, of a new English dictionary on historical principles. Oxford: Clarendon Pr., 1933. 13v.

■ ———. A supplement to the Oxford English dictionary. R. W. Burchfield, ed. Oxford: Clarendon Pr., 1972-86. 4v.

Gives greater coverage to scientific and technical words, improves upon the poor coverage in the original of vulgar and taboo words, and adds new words and meanings that appeared in British English during the publication dates (1884-1928) of the original plus new words since then. Includes much better coverage of American English than the original.

For a moving account of Murray's editorship for thirty-five years until his death at seventy-eight, see the account by his granddaughter, K. M. Elizabeth

Murray, *Caught in the Web of Words* (New Haven, Conn.: Yale Univ. Pr., 1977; 386p.). See also John Willinsky, *Empire of Words: The Reign of the OED* (Princeton, N.J.: Princeton Univ. Pr., 1994; 258p.), for an interesting yet scholarly account of the dictionary from its earliest planning through the second edition. And, just to prove that neither reference librarianship nor lexicography is always dull, try Simon Winchester's *The Professor and the Madman* (New York: HarperCollins, 1998; 242p.) on the role of Simon Minor, one of the major contributors to the *OED,* who worked from his cell in Broadmoor, an English "lunatic asylum."

Several other dictionaries compiled on historical principles may be used to supplement the *Oxford English Dictionary.* Although they cannot be classified as unabridged dictionaries, their method of compilation and emphasis on illustrative quotations justify their being considered here, rather than with dialect dictionaries.

An interesting and often useful update to all dictionaries of all types is *The Barnhart Dictionary Companion: A Quarterly to Update "the" Dictionary* (Cold Spring, N.Y.: Barnhart, 1982- ; v.1- ; quarterly), which provides detailed definitions and longer than usual quotations to back them up for words that, in the opinion of the editors, are important additions to the English language. Of particular interest is the use of symbols to classify each new term (e.g., *drugs, youth culture*).

For years, the classic equivalent to the *OED* for American English was

- Craigie, Sir Walter Alexander, and James R. Hulbert. Dictionary of American English on historical principles. Chicago: Univ. of Chicago Pr., 1936–44. 4v.

  Scope: For the period before 1900, includes "not only words and phrases which are clearly or apparently of American origin, or have greater currency here than elsewhere, but also every word denoting something which has a real connection with the development of the country and the history of its people" (preface). Excludes technical terms and meanings not in general use, as well as slang words or uses originating after 1875.

  Treatment: Gives definitions and explanations, with chronologically arranged illustrative quotations (with exact citation to sources) before 1925 and symbols to indicate those words in English before 1600, those originating in the United States, and those known only from the passages cited. Unlike the *Oxford English Dictionary,* gives little attention to pronunciation and etymology.

Other dictionaries of the same type include the following:

■ Mathews, Milford McLeod. A dictionary of Americanisms on historical principles. Chicago: Univ. of Chicago Pr., 1951. 2v.

> *Scope*: Some 50,000 entries, differing from Craigie's *Dictionary of American English* in covering only words and phrases originating in the United States up to about 1950. Gives earlier uses of some words than Craigie and corrects some errors.

> *Treatment*: Definitions; illustrative quotations (including many from Craigie) in date order, with exact citation to sources; pronunciation (more often than Craigie). Includes some drawings from catalogs, periodicals, etc., as needed to illustrate words.

■ Thorton, Richard A. An American glossary, being an attempt to illustrate certain Americanisms upon historical principles. London: Francis; Philadelphia: Lippincott, 1912; New Haven, Conn.: American Dialect Society, 1931–39. Reprint, with an introduction by Margaret M. Bryant, New York: Ungar, 1962. 3v.

> *Scope*: Based on books, periodicals, newspapers, and especially the *Congressional Globe* and *Congressional Record*. Includes words of American origin, as well as English words that have acquired an American meaning or that are still in use in the United States but obsolete or provincial in England. Persons and places are included.

> *Treatment*: Definitions and explanations, with illustrative quotations arranged chronologically and giving exact citations to sources.

And, the current complete dictionary, in some ways going beyond the *OED*, follows:

■ Dictionary of American regional English. Cambridge, Mass., and London: Belknap Pr. of Harvard Univ., 1985– . 3v. as of 1998 (in progress).

> *Scope*: A record of American English as used in about 1,000 communities, based on a survey deliberately weighted to older people. Excludes scientific, technical, and learned phrases and anything else that could be considered "standard English" across the country; however, also tends to avoid sexual references or to be a bit coy about them. About 45 percent of the words appear in no other dictionary.

> *Treatment*: Arranged by term, with computer-generated maps showing the distribution of each term, most of which are single words but including some phrases (for example, "Adam's off ox" and "Adam's old fox" as variants). Entries consist of a headword; indication of part of speech and variant forms; etymology, with an emphasis on how the

word entered American English; regional and social labels; the definitions; quotes with brief citations, each also with a regional note where possible (e.g., what part of the country a character lived in); the *DARE* interview question used; data on the responses to the question; and a schematic map showing the approximate area(s) of the country where variant terms are used. Incudes a very detailed pronunciation guide. When completed, this will probably surpass its predecessors. Useful as a dictionary and also enjoyable reading for those interested in words or in the declining regional differences in the United States. The questionnaire and the list of informants are included.

Reviews include those in *American Reference Books Annual* 28 (1997): 383–84; *Booklist* 88 (Oct. 15, 1991): 1992; and *Choice* 23 (Jan. 1986): 724.

To date, the first two volumes have also been complemented by *An Index by Region, Usage, and Etymology to the Dictionary of American Regional English* (Tuscaloosa: Univ. of Alabama Pr., 1993; 178p.), which provides access by nearly all the regional, social, and usage labels used in the work.

Remember that Canada is also, in part, an English-speaking nation:

■ Dictionary of Canadianisms on historical principles. Walter S. Avis, ed. in chief. Toronto: W. J. Gage, 1967. 926p.

Scope: Reprinted in paperback in 1991. Historical record of words used in Canada in English language since the earliest days, including both purely Canadian words and meanings and other words not peculiar to that nation (the latter are marked with a dagger). Includes many compound terms incorporating proper nouns but lacks geographical and biographical entries.

Treatment: Definitions and many illustrative quotations, with complete citation to sources; pronunciation (using IPA) and etymology only when relevant. Many drawings and an extensive bibliography are included.

Modern Unabridged Dictionaries

The classic unabridged dictionary of modern English is that of Merriam-Webster, who is in a direct linear descent from Noah Webster.

■ Webster's new international dictionary of the English language. 2d unabridged ed. William Allan Neilson, ed. in chief. Springfield, Mass.: Merriam, 1934. 3195p.

> *Scope*: Starts with all words in English around 1500, plus all words in Chaucer, and adds to the present day (i.e., around 1930). Main words in upper part of page; the lower part includes the very rare terms, bibliographical quotations, foreign-language quotations, etc. Separate list of abbreviations, signs, and symbols, plus a pronouncing gazetteer and pronouncing biographical dictionary. Original edition has had supplements added to it; the 1986 edition has a full supplement, which is also available separately as *12,000 Words: A Supplement to Webster's Third New International Dictionary* (Springfield, Mass.: Merriam-Webster, 1986; 212p.).

> *Treatment*: Gives spelling, syllabification, pronunciation (diacritics and respelling), parts of speech, very detailed etymologies, definitions in historical order, labels (field, use, geographic), extensive illustrative quotations (incompletely cited), synonyms and antonyms, and many pictures, including color plates.

A classic at the time of publication, and, because of its prescriptive definitions and use notes, still popular, even though long out of print. Replaced, as far as the publisher is concerned, but not always in the hearts of the critics, by

■ Webster's third new international dictionary of the English language, unabridged. Rev. ed. Philip Babcok Gove, ed. in chief. Springfield, Mass.: Merriam-Webster, 1986. 2783p.

> *Scope*: Reprinted in 1993. Some 472,000 entries for words in use since 1755 (the date of Dr. Johnson's *Dictionary*). Adds to the second edition about 50,000 new words and as many new meanings, very full etymologies, and abbreviations in the main alphabet. Deletes many obsolete and rare words, the pronouncing gazetteer and biographical dictionaries, foreign words and phrases (unless part of the English language), and literary and art allusions. Also differs from the second in having new but fewer pictorial illustrations, no divided pages, and less use of labels. Includes the full addendum also published separately (*12,000 Words: A Supplement to Webster's Third New International Dictionary* [Springfield, Mass.: Merriam-Webster, 1986; 212p.]), with new words and meanings since that title was published. Words added since then appear in an addendum updated every couple of years, but easy to overlook.

Treatment: Gives spelling, syllabification, pronunciation, part of speech, etymology, definitions in historical order (*not* most common first), illustrative quotations (still not completely cited), synonyms (with careful distinctions and illustrative quotations), and some pictorial illustrations. Also has about fifty tables and charts in the body of the work.

The major difference between the 1934 edition and the third edition, according to many reviewers at the time of first publication, was the change from *prescriptive* to *descriptive* outlook—the decline in use of labels for slang, "improper" and the like, and the acceptance of synonyms like *isn't* and *ain't*. Regardless of one's opinion on this issue, however, it is currently the only true "unabridged" dictionary of the English language on the market. For a current review, *see Booklist* 93 (June 1, 1997): 1738.

■ Flexner, Stuart Berg, ed. in chief. Random House unabridged dictionary. 2d ed. New York: Random House, 1994. 2478p. Also available on CD-ROM as Random House Webster's Unabridged Dictionary.

Scope: Originally published in 1987, contains about 315,000 entries, completely revising the first edition, with about 55,000 new words. Emphasizes words in current use, including American and foreign terms, biographical and geographical terms, abbreviations, titles of major literary works, and the like (about 10 percent of the entries are for people, places, and events).

Treatment: Gives pronunciation, including respelling and diacritics, syllabification, part of speech, definitions (arranged most common first), staff-written illustrative phrases, synonyms and antonyms, etymologies. Includes more than 2,400 illustrations and more than 200 detailed usage notes, as well as a large number of synonym lists. Although nonprescriptive, entries include labels for vulgarisms and slang. A useful feature is the inclusion of notes for regional variations and dates of first use for many entries.

The CD-ROM includes all illustrations and about 120,000 spoken pronunciations, as well as the addendum of new words from the compact edition. Additional features include four separate bilingual dictionaries for French, Spanish, German, and Italian and several essays on language in general. Curiously, this work has generally been well received by academics and scholars and disliked by writers in the popular press. A smaller version, *The Random House Compact Unabridged Dictio-*

nary (2d ed., 1996; 2230p.), contains all the text of the full-sized version plus an addendum of new words.

This was the first general dictionary to use electronic data processing in its production; for a description, *see Booklist* 63 (April 1, 1967): 803-7. For reviews of the second edition, *see American Reference Books Annual* 19 (1988): 436; and *Library Journal* 113 (April 15, 1988): 34, and 112 (Nov. 15, 1987): 72.

For further reading on the subject of dictionaries, Jack C. Gray's *Words, Words, and Words about Dictionaries* (San Francisco: Chandler, 1963; 207p.), which contains general discussions of words and essays on the history and use of dictionaries by a number of authorities, reviews and comments on *Webster's Third New International,* and prefaces and samples from Dr. Johnson's dictionary, *Webster's Second,* and *Webster's Third.* A useful and interesting shorter discussion is Marie C. Ellis, "The Legacy of Noah Webster: The Merriam-Webster Family of Dictionaries," in *Distinguished Classics of Reference Publishing,* edited by James Rettig (Phoenix, Ariz.: Oryx, 1992; p. 286-305).

Abridged Dictionaries

Although all libraries need a well-edited, up-to-date unabridged dictionary, many people find it too cumbersome and too expensive. Convenience, therefore, explains the popularity of abridged dictionaries, which usually are published because of the demand for a handy, inexpensive dictionary for quick reference. They may be abridgments of larger dictionaries, as in the case of *Webster's New Collegiate Dictionary,* or independent compilations, such as the *American Heritage Dictionary.*

Described here are a few of the better-known and heavily used college or desk dictionaries, with their six general characteristics:

1. A vocabulary ranging from about 100,000 to 200,000 entries, usually giving preference to words in current use, with generous representation of scientific and technical terms and varying emphasis on slang and dialect
2. Less emphasis on etymology than is found in unabridged dictionaries
3. Fewer illustrations of use than are found in some unabridged dictionaries
4. Adequate attention to synonyms and antonyms
5. Supplementary lists of signs and symbols, forms of address, meaning of given names, colleges and universities, and biographical and geographical names, which are sometimes found in the main alphabet
6. Often additional appendixes, such as abridged gazetteers, collections of maps, usage guides, and the like

American

■ The American heritage dictionary of the English language. William Morris, ed. 3d ed. Boston: Houghton, 1992. 2184p. Also online and on CD-ROM.

> *Scope:* First published in 1969. About 200,000 words, placing this between true unabridged dictionaries and collegiate dictionaries. This edition restores the larger size of the first edition, allowing for about 4,000 illustrations (including photographs), all conveniently placed in the margin.

> *Treatment:* Syllabification, pronunciation (diacritics and respelling), part of speech, field and usage labels, concise definitions, with the "central meaning" the first one. Illustrations in margins. Contains biographical and geographical entries. Perhaps the most distinguishing characteristic of *American Heritage* is the reliance on the 173 members of the Usage Panel, who have been asked to comment on questionable uses. The votes of the panel—noted writers, critics, and scholars—are then given with the word. Although it has been criticized by many, knowing, for example, whether *verbal* and *oral* are considered synonyms by the literary establishment can be useful, especially for students. Other useful features are the spelling out of terms in the etymologies (e.g., *Middle English* instead of *ME*) and lengthy synonym notes going far beyond the mere listing in many competitors' volumes. Entries also include many (staff-written) examples.

> This title is also available in a number of electronic versions, for example, as a part of Microsoft Bookshelf and a stand-alone as American Heritage Talking Dictionary. These offer sound, thus giving exact pronunciation, as well as permitting sophisticated searching (the latter more so than the Microsoft version). The electronic versions permit searches by words in definitions, cross-references via hypertext to a thesaurus, and anagram searching. Additional features include an electronic thesaurus, a dictionary of cultural literacy, and maps and photographs.

> Reviews include those in *American Reference Books Annual* 29 (1998): 431; 27 (1996): 441; and 24 (1993): 447–48; *Booklist* 93 (June 1, 1997): 1740; and 89 (Oct. 1, 1992): 350; and *Library Journal* 117 (Aug. 1992): 86.

Although the previous title is, in some senses, an abridged dictionary, there is also the *American Heritage College Dictionary,* 3d ed. (Boston: Houghton, 1993; 1630p.), with fewer words, shorter entries (reduced etymologies, illustrations, etc.), and smaller size.

■ Merriam-Webster's collegiate dictionary. 10th ed. Springfield, Mass.: Merriam-Webster, 1993. 1559p. Also online and on CD-ROM. As of this writing, the Web version, <http://www.m-w.com/netdict.htm>, is free.

> *Scope*: Formerly *Webster's Collegiate Dictionary* (through the ninth edition). About 160,000 entries, founded on the same database as *Webster's Third,* with slight revisions each year and a major revision, leading to a new edition, every ten years or so. Includes trademarks and service marks, many obsolete and archaic terms, and regionalisms, all of which are labeled. Adds usage notes and a somewhat clearer (if less complete) pronunciation system than its parent, so that this is not merely a cut-down version, but a different work. Several appendixes include biographical and geographical entries as well as other useful material.

> *Treatment*: Gives headword, etymology, date of first recorded use in English, definitions in chronological order, with most recent last, and usage notes (not in the unabridged edition). Illustrative quotes are common, but no dates are given; the earliest appearance of a word is dated, however. Unlike many competitors, abbreviations are conveniently placed in the main alphabet. Notes on synonyms discriminate among slight differences.

> The CD-ROM version includes voice technology for 100,000 pronunciations, about 1,000 color illustrations, and *Merriam-Webster's Collegiate Thesaurus.* As with most of its competitors, the text is searchable by Boolean techniques. Every significant word in every definition is also hypertext linked to its definition. The Web version is similar, without the audio technology, but with some modifications to deal with the limitations of hypertext markup language (HTML).

> Reviews include those in *American Reference Books Annual* 29 (1998): 431–32; 27 (1996): 443–44; and 25 (1994): 438; *Booklist* 93 (June 1, 1997): 1740–41; and *Choice* 34 (July 1997): 1789; 34 (Jan. 1997): 780–81; 33 (Dec. 1995): 577–78.

> This work is also the basis for the hot-linked definitions in the electronic versions of the *Encyclopaedia Britannica* and *Encyclopedia Americana.* The Web version has, unfortunately, abbreviated entries, omissions, and less sophisticated search capability than the CD-ROM versions.

■ Random House Webster's college dictionary. Robert Costello, ed. in chief. Newly rev. and updated. New York: Random House, 1999. 1568p.

Scope: Earlier editions were called *Random House Dictionary of the English Language, College Ed.; Random House College Dictionary;* and *Random House American College Dictionary.* Based on the full *Random House Dictionary*, but with additions, especially new terms, relying on the Random House Living Dictionary Project database (a database created from the text of the 1987 edition of the *Random House Unabridged Dictionary* [*see* p. 274, above] and updated daily with words from current popular media). Contains about 180,000 terms, including more than 400 biographical entries and about 7,000 geographical entries. Gives particular emphasis to regionalisms (labeled as such by location) and neologisms. Has about 800 pictorial illustrations. Annual printings add some new words and drop older ones (often neologisms that are no longer current). Definitely the source for recent terms and meanings.

Treatment: Same as the unabridged version, but does label usage, including racial, ethnic, and religious language, as well as sexism, the latter having generated considerable unfavorable comment (especially *Time* [June 24, 1991]: 51).

On a side note, this title also generated the famous lawsuit over the use of the color red plus the words *Webster's* and *College*, which Merriam-Webster argued (successfully at first, but the case was lost on appeal and no changes were made) were intentional infringement of its traditional dust jacket.

Reviews may be found in *Booklist* 93 (June 1, 1997): 1744; *Choice* 34 (March 1997): 1142; and *Library Journal* 122 (Nov. 15, 1997): 53.

■ Webster's new world dictionary of American English. Victoria Neufeldt, ed. in chief. 3d college ed. New York: Prentice-Hall, 1994. 1574p. Also on CD-ROM.

Scope: With a particular emphasis on Americanisms, this edition includes about 150,000 entries, with 20,000 new since 1988 and statistics reflecting the 1990 census. Neufeldt, who replaced David B. Guralnik for this edition, has added racial slurs, vulgarisms, and some obscenities, but she also retains archaic words found in literary works often assigned in U.S. colleges. The main section includes many brief geographical and biographical entries.

Treatment: The roughly 11,000 Americanisms are marked by asterisks. Definitions are arranged historically. Both syllabification and end-of-line divisions are given; pronunciation is based on the publisher's own system. Etymology is very good; even includes place-names. Some entries have usage notes and synonyms lists; about 650 line drawings. Abbreviations, foreign terms; proper names in main sequence. More readable because of change in typeface.

Kister has stated this is among the three or four best college desk dictionaries currently published in North America. Interestingly, the 1988 edition was actually a nonfiction best-seller for twenty weeks on the *New York Times* list. This is said to be the desk dictionary of choice for most major news organizations in the United States.

Reviews include those in *American Reference Books Annual* 25 (1995): 451; *Booklist* 90 (March 1, 1994): 1292; *Choice* 31 (May 1994): 1423; and *Booklist* (June 1 & 15, 1997): 1746.

■ World book dictionary. Robert K. Barnhart, ed. Chicago: World Book, 1996. 2v. Also on CD-ROM as part of World Book Information Finder.

Scope: A companion to the *World Book Encyclopedia* but can stand well on its own. Defines all words in the encyclopedia, except for proper names and historical events; thus, its 225,000 entries in effect understate its size compared to its competitors. Emphasizes active vocabulary, but includes a few archaic words likely to be encountered; updated annually with new words and definitions as needed. Includes much slang, but excludes all vulgarisms. Includes considerable foreign terms and many Briticisms. Has a useful, lengthy introduction on dictionaries and language in general.

Treatment: Most common meaning first. Spelling, syllabification, pronunciation (modified IPA), etymologies (spelling out all terms, rather than using abbreviations like *OE* for *Old English*), excellent definitions. Includes a few descriptive usage notes, many synonym entries, and more-illustrative quotations than its competitors (but with incomplete citations). As part of the Thorndike-Barnhart family, this uses the approach that the definition must be in simpler words than the word defined. Includes more than 3,000 pictorial illustrations, all in black and white but particularly clear and often showing slight differences in meaning.

Often mistakenly considered a children's dictionary, and unfortunately much more expensive as well as more cumbersome than its competitors, this is an excellent stand-alone work for libraries. Reviews may be found in *American Reference Books Annual* 29 (1998): 430–31; and *Booklist* 93 (June 1, 1997): 1748.

Even though many dictionaries add new words with every new edition (and the *Random House Webster's* with every biennial revision), they are unable to keep up with changes in the language. One attempt to keep up on new words is the following:

■ The third Barnhart dictionary of new English. Robert K. Barnhart and others, eds. Rev. ed. Bronx, N.Y.: Wilson, 1990. 565p.

> The most recent version of *The Barnhart Dictionary of New English since 1963* (1973) and *The Second Barnhart Dictionary of New English* (1980), incorporating most of its two predecessors but with an emphasis on words of the past decade, with etymologies added for many entries. Thus, one should not discard the first two editions. Entry includes word or phrase, part of speech, meaning, and at least one usage example. In addition to having longer and more detailed entries than similar sources, this also gives date and citation of the first appearance of a word or meaning and, if it started as a type of argot or jargon, also the date when the term appeared in common use.

Possibly the best ongoing source for new words and terms is the column "Among the New Words," published quarterly since 1941 in the journal *American Speech*. Unlike some other sources (but similar to the Barnhart title), the treatments are scholarly and detailed, with a number of examples. The columns have been cumulated in *Fifty Years among the New Words: A Dictionary of Neologisms, 1941-1991*, edited by John Algeo and Adele S. Algeo (Cambridge and New York: Cambridge Univ. Pr., 1991; 257p.).

One last dictionary, with a specialized audience, follows:

■ Oxford large print dictionary. 2d ed. New York: Oxford Univ. Pr., 1995. 960p.

> Scope: More than 60,000 entries; many geographical and biographical entries. Includes "correct English" notes. Basically British, but gives American spellings, too.

> Treatment: Words in boldface, label for part of speech, definition. No syllabification or etymologies.

> Reviewed in *American Reference Books Annual* 28 (1997): 377; and *Booklist* 92 (Feb. 15, 1996): 1040.

Great Britain

■ Chambers dictionary. Edinburgh and New York: Chambers, 1993; distributed by Cambridge Univ. Pr. 2062p. Also on CD-ROM.

Scope: Formerly *Chambers English Dictionary* (1988) and *Chambers Twentieth Century Dictionary*, with a history going back to 1901. Popular in the United Kingdom because of its authority (it's the official Scrabble dictionary) and the size of vocabulary—about 215,000 entry words. Includes coverage of dialect and regional (especially Scottish), archaic, and literary words (including all words in Shakespeare, Milton, Sir Walter Scott, and other classical writers), with many newer scientific and technical terms.

Treatment: All words from the same root are grouped together under one headword, which may be a bit difficult at first for users accustomed to the American approach. Entries include pronunciation (by respelling), part of speech, labels, definitions (in chronological order), some illustrative phrases, and brief citations to authors. The brief etymologies are at the end of the entries. Useful for coverage of Briticisms and archaic words, as well as clear, succinct, and (sometimes) amusing definitions. American English, while included, is not covered as well as its British sister.

Also available as The Chambers Dictionary on CD-ROM, permitting use of truncation/wild cards and searching by idiomatic phrase, foreign loanwords, and distinction between initial caps and lowercase letters, as well as keyword and Boolean searching.

Reviews may be found in *ARBA* 27 (1996): 442–43; *Booklist* 91 (Nov. 1, 1994): 534, 536; and *Choice* 32 (Jan. 1995): 744.

■ The concise Oxford dictionary of current English. Della Thompson, ed. 9th ed. New York: Oxford Univ. Pr., 1995. 1694p.

Scope: About 150,000 entries based on the same citation file as used for its larger cousin, and the British National Corpus database. Good coverage of current British terms, especially colloquialisms, slang, and technical terms. Truly international, giving British pronunciation and spelling, but also indicating American, Australian, Canadian, and other spellings and definitions.

Treatment: Definitions are organized in order of current usage (in Great Britain). Pronunciation (using English rather than American sounds) uses IPA, and some etymologies go into detail on usage. "Offensive" words are labeled as such, based on current sensibilities.

Not a first choice for the smaller American library, but extremely valuable for current coverage of other varieties of English. Reviewed in *American Reference Books Annual* 27 (1996): 443; and *Booklist* 93 (June 1 & 15, 1997): 1744.

Canada

▪ Gage Canadian dictionary. Rev. ed. Toronto: Gage Educational, 1997. 1718p.

First published in 1967 as *Dictionary of Canadian English*. Has more than 100,000 entries for Canadian English. Provides concise definitions, with staff-written examples, IPA pronunciation, and generally accepted Canadian spelling and usage. Naturally, there are also dictionaries of Canadian French—*see* page 323.

▪ The Penguin Canadian dictionary. Thomas Paikeday, ed. Markham, Ontario: Penguin; Missassauga, Ontario: Copp Clark Pittman, 1990. 870p.

A one-man labor of love, with about 75,000 words, a conscious emphasis on Canadianisms, and with French-Canadian terms included. Has no place-names or biographies. Gives simple definitions (but no etymologies), relying on illustrative sentences and phrases; includes many phrases, like "ahead of time" as entries. Pronunciation is given by respelling.

English as a Second Language

With the growing realization that many English-speaking societies are comprised of many different cultures and language groups, and the increasing globalization of society, the supply of English as a second language (ESL) dictionaries is increasing. The following are the best, and most useful to libraries, of the lot. Unlike bilingual dictionaries, these assume basic English literacy; also unlike bilinguals, they usually do more than merely give equivalent words—they also try to explain idioms and the more subtle differences in usage. As a result, ESL dictionaries can also be useful for native English speakers.

▪ Collins COBUILD English language dictionary. New, expanded [i.e., 2d] ed. John Sinclair, ed. in chief. London: HarperCollins, 1996. 1951p.

Scope: Explicitly for English as a second language, based on an electronic database (the Bank of English) of more than 200 million words from British and American newspapers, novels, etc. (but originally based on the Collins-Birmingham University International Language Database, thus the title). About 75,000 entries, with most attention to the few thousand words most used. Lacks entries for places, people, and highly technical terms.

Treatment: Pronunciation (using IPA) giving both British and American versions, definitions; nearly 100,000 examples emphasize idioms, homographs, etc. Includes a clear indication of slight variations in use and meaning. Cross-references are given, and the word in question usually appears in both entries. A separate "extra column" provides notes on grammar and semantic relationships within the main entries. Other interesting features are the use of one to five diamonds to indicate how often the word defined appears in the Bank of English and the use of complete sentences in all definitions (unlike other ESL dictionaries). Vulgarisms are included, with a note warning about use (including words and phrases deemed taboo). No pictorial illustrations. This work has received very positive reviews.

Reviews may be found in *Booklist* 93 (June 1, 1997): 1748-49; and *Choice* 34 (Dec. 1996): 587.

■ Longman dictionary of contemporary English. Della Summers, ed. 3d ed. White Plains, N.Y.: Longman, 1996. 1668p.

Scope: About 56,000 entries aimed at the intermediate or advanced student of English as a second language. The pioneer in using controlled vocabulary in its definitions (about 2,000 words in this edition), with about 80,000 words based on Longman's Lancaster Corpus and the British National Corpus of about 25 million words, with additions. Emphasizes contemporary spoken English. Includes slang, colloquial, idiomatic, and technical words and some phrases (e.g., "make up," which has several meanings).

Treatment: Provides word, syllabification, pronunciation (IPA), part of speech, definition (most common first), illustrative examples. Idioms at the ends of entries include many phrases. Lengthy introductory usage guide and detailed usage notes with entries. Includes much distinguishing information (e.g., Renaissance vs. renaissance; variant spellings; usage including "formal," "informal," "not formal," and "taboo"). Both British and American use, with British first. Pictorial illustrations are clearly captioned and often include labels for parts. Special and rare features are the use of bar graphs and codes to indicate the most common usages and distinctions between written and spoken English, features found only here and in Collins COBUILD.

■ Oxford advanced learner's dictionary of current English. Jonathan Crowther, ed. 5th ed. Oxford and New York: Oxford Univ. Pr., 1995. 1440p.

Scope: The current version of the standard dictionary of this type, pioneered by A. S. Hornby in 1942 and still considered the standard. Contains about 63,000 entries, aimed at the advanced student of English as a second language and concentrating on those parts of

English most difficult for foreigners to learn, with an emphasis on written English. Uses the resources of the Oxford American English Corpus and the British National Corpus.

Treatment: Uses British spelling but provides American spelling and definitions as well. Provides word divisions (where to divide when writing, as opposed to true syllables), pronunciations (IPA), brief definitions, labeling (including slang, vulgar), many cross-references, derivatives (especially phrases using the word defined), many illustrative examples, and many pictorial illustrations. In particular, there are many usage notes with definitions as well as appendixes with irregular verbs, some large illustrations (reminiscent of a standard visual dictionary), and detailed user-help sections. Definitely aimed at the advanced learner, using a nearly 3,500-word vocabulary for definitions, compared with the more usual 2,000 or so words.

■ Random House Webster's dictionary of American English. Gerard M. Dalgish, ed. New York: Random House, 1997. 800p.

Scope: Based on Random House's Living Dictionary Database, this is the first American-oriented ESL dictionary, giving Americanisms and emphasizing U.S. usage. About 50,000 entries.

Treatment: Pronunciation given both in IPA and the use of diacritics; thus, it is familiar both to users of American dictionaries (which tend to the latter) and users of most ESL titles. Definitions are brief, and illustrations are sparse compared to many similar titles, but the emphasis on Americanisms makes this a very useful supplement to others.

Reviews include those in *Booklist* 93 (May 1, 1997): 1479; *Choice* 34 (April 1997): 1314; and *School Library Journal* 43 (May 1997): 156.

School Dictionaries

School dictionaries are a type of abridged dictionary that are often independently compiled, rather than based on a larger work. Careful attention is given to the selection of the vocabulary and to features that add to ease of use. Their general characteristics follow:

1. A vocabulary ranging from about 2,500 to 80,000 entries, selected on the basis of their frequency in school textbooks and supplementary readings, with an emphasis given to words in current use, though obsolete words from English classics (notably Shakespeare) may also be included.
2. Etymology is either omitted or briefly treated.
3. Pronunciation is shown in an easily understood form.

4. Definitions are simply expressed in terms of a vocabulary suitable for the intended age level, emphasizing standard usage.
5. Verbal illustrations of use are selected in terms of the interests of the intended age level and generally fewer than those in college/desk dictionaries.
6. Pictorial illustrations are more freely used at lower levels, selected in term of the interests of the intended age level and with text captions in large type.
7. Supplementary material, giving instructions on using the dictionary, is tied in with school curriculum.
8. Separately published workbooks often accompany the dictionary.

Selection aids for school dictionaries that supply information on grade level and vocabulary include *Kister's Best Dictionaries for Adults and Young People* (Kenneth F. Kister. Phoenix, Ariz.: Oryx, 1992; 438p.); *Encyclopedias, Atlases and Dictionaries* (Marion Sader and Amy Lewis, eds. New Providence, N.J.: Bowker, 1995; 495p.); and the Wilson Standard Catalog series. The latter includes *Children's Catalog* (New York: Wilson, 1909- ; quinquennial, with annual supplements); *Middle and Junior High School Library Catalog* (New York: Wilson, 1995- ; quinquennial, with annual supplements); and *Senior High School Library Catalog* (New York: Wilson, 1967- ; quinquennial, with annual supplements). Look under both "Dictionaries" (and relevant subheadings) and specific languages, such as "English Language—Dictionaries," and also check the separate section for electronic sources, which are not listed otherwise.

Comments on several standard young people's dictionaries follow:

■ American heritage student dictionary. New York: Houghton, 1998. 1120p.

> *Scope*: Aimed at grades six to nine. Contains about 65,000 entries based on word-frequency counts from textbooks, magazines, encyclopedias, and other sources, primarily the *American Heritage College Dictionary*.

> *Treatment*: Following its parent, gives the Usage Panel's votes and is generally prescriptive. Gives pronunciation, part of speech, simple etymologies, and definitions in language aimed at the readership, as well as use notes, homographs, and fine distinctions illustrated by examples. Biographical and geographical entries are interfiled. Includes more than 2,000 black-and-white illustrations and synonym/antonym lists. The illustrations, use notes, and similar material are located in the wide margins.

Reviews may be found in *American Reference Books Annual* 26 (1995): 457; *Reference Books Bulletin* 91 (Sept. 1, 1994): 74; and *School Library Journal* 40 (Nov. 1994): 134.

■ Macmillan dictionary for children. Rev. ed. New York: Simon & Schuster, 1997. 896p. Abbreviated version also on CD-ROM.

> Also available over time as *Macmillan Dictionary for Students, Scribner Dictionary,* and *McGraw-Hill School Dictionary.* Aimed at ages eight to twelve, with about 35,000 entries (the CD-ROM has about 12,000 entries, but all the words are pronounced). Has clear, up-to-date definitions; many synonym studies; and some usage notes. Illustrative sentences are mostly created by the editors. The text edition includes a short section of activities teaching use of the dictionary.

Scott, Foresman also issues a series of youth dictionaries, based on and continuing the pioneering work of Clarence Barnhart.

■ Thorndike-Barnhart beginning dictionary. Columbus, Ohio: Scott, Foresman, 1997. 832p.

> *Scope*: Formerly published as *Scott, Foresman Beginning Dictionary* and *Thorndike-Barnhart Children's Dictionary.* About 28,000 entries, selected on the basis of word frequency. Intended for the elementary grades as the simplest of the Scott, Foresman series of school dictionaries. Includes geographic names, but omits personal names.

> *Treatment*: Simple definitions, with more than 22,000 illustrative examples, pronunciation using the Thorndike-Barnhart system, and some etymologies. Illustrations, mostly in color, include depictions of abstract concepts—an idea pioneered in this dictionary in 1976. Kister continues to consider it "among the best dictionaries in its class." Includes several exercises in dictionary use.

■ Thorndike-Barnhart intermediate dictionary. Columbus, Ohio: Scott-Foresman, 1997. 1024p.

> *Scope*: Formerly the *Scott, Foresman Intermediate Dictionary* and the *Thorndike-Barnhart Junior Dictionary.* Some 68,500 entries, including geographical and biographical entries.

> *Treatment*: Gives 44,000 examples, 1,800 etymologies, 1,700 illustrations, with about 50 percent color. Good sample sentences. Excellent definitions, in appropriate vocabulary for the audience. Gives syllabification, part of speech, pronunication, often plurals of nouns and participles, and past tenses of verbs.

■ Thorndike-Barnhart advanced dictionary. Columbus, Ohio: Scott, Foresman, 1997. 1280p.

Scope: Formerly the *Scott, Foresman Advanced Dictionary* and the *Thorndike-Barnhart Student Dictionary*. About 100,000 entries.

Treatment: Gives 120,000 definitions, 900 usage notes and synonym studies, 18,000 etymologies, 35,000 illustrative sentences, and 900 usage notes and synonym studies. Includes 1,500 two-color drawings and black-and-white photos. Includes "Word Families," English words with common roots, and "Word Sources," words with related roots—both are a different type of etymology from the usual. Kister calls this, with the possible exception of the *Macmillan Dictionary*, the "best dictionary for classroom use in North American high schools."

Also very useful in school libraries and media centers is the *World Book Dictionary*, discussed above. It is intended as a companion to the *World Book Encyclopedia*.

Etymological Dictionaries

General dictionaries, notably the *OED*, give some attention to word origins, but curiosity about word origins among persons who agree with Ernest Klein's belief that "to know the origin of words is to know the cultural history of mankind" often lead them to dictionaries devoted exclusively to etymology. Names that come to mind, then, are Skeat, Partridge, Onions, and (more recently) Klein. Skeat's *An Etymological Dictionary of the English Language* has long been considered the standard scholarly work, whose histories of 14,000 words have been greatly revised and expanded to about 38,000 in Onions's *Oxford Dictionary of English Etymology*, which has fewer literary allusions than Skeat. Less comprehensive is Partridge's *Origins*, though it may be of more general interest because he groups words that are etymologically related to each other. Also engaging is his enthusiasm, reflected in *Name into Word*, which gives discussions of proper names that have passed into common use in the English language. His foreword concludes:

> He who despises the history of words despises the history of mankind; and he who ignores the history of words ignores that one part of himself which can lastingly affect the world outside himself, the sole part that merits a posterity. By the words of others shall we, using intelligence, know them; by our own words do we, if we strive, know ourselves [p. xiv].

Klein's *A Comprehensive Etymological Dictionary of the English Language* has more entries than the *Oxford Dictionary of English Etymology*. Its subtitle, *Dealing with the Origin of Words and Their Sense Development, Thus Illustrating the History of Civilization and Culture*, reflects

Klein's center purpose. Like Onions, he embodies the findings of modern philological scholarship and gives, for the first time, full reference to Tocharian, the extinct language rediscovered at the end of the nineteenth century.

The development of etymological dictionaries is briefly treated in general encyclopedias and, in a more lively fashion, by James R. Hulbert, *Dictionaries, British and American* (rev. ed. London: Deutsch, 1968; 109p.). The following are a number of the more important dictionaries of this type:

■ The American heritage dictionary of Indo-European roots. Boston: Houghton, 1985. 113p.

> A companion to the *American Heritage Dictionary: Second College Edition.* Aimed at the general public. Arranged by Indo-European root, with examples of English words. Includes an index by English words to the roots.

■ Barnhart dictionary of etymology. Bronx, N.Y.: Wilson, 1988. 1284p.

> The first general vocabulary etymological dictionary in some years, also notable in its emphasis on Americanisms. Contain more than 30,000 entries, many revised from older dictionaries based on new research. Pays particular attention to word elements, such as prefixes and suffixes; uses words rather than abbreviations in its etymologies, for the most part. Also includes two articles on history of English, proto-German, and Indo-European roots. Updated and supplemented but not replaced by the *Barnhart Concise Dictionary of Etymology* (New York: HarperCollins, 1995; 916p.). Compared to Klein, Onions, and Partridge (*Origins,* 4th ed.), this has more of an emphasis on current American vocabulary, more recent scholarship, and is by far the most easy-to-use and readable text.

■ Klein, Ernest. A comprehensive etymological dictionary of the English language: dealing with the origin of words and their sense development, thus illustrating the history of civilization and culture. Amsterdam: Elsevier, 1971. Reprint, Elsevier, 1986. 844p.

> First published in 1966/67 in two volumes; reprinted in one volume. The preface contains much useful information on such dictionaries and discussions of Hebrew, Aramaic, and Arabic loanwords, with a pronunciation and transliteration guide to those words not common in English dictionaries. Contains more terms than the *Oxford Dictionary of English Etymology,* especially names, mythological and real, and technical and scientific vocabulary.

■ Onions, C. T., with the assistance of G. W. S. Friedrichsen and R. W. Burchfield, eds. Oxford dictionary of English etymology. Oxford: Clarendon Pr., 1966. 1025p.

> The first really comprehensive such dictionary since Skeat's *Etymological Dictionary.* Not quite as detailed as Partridge's *Origins,* but much broader in scope. Includes both American and British spelling, many entries for prefixes and suffixes, pronunciation and current meaning, century when it first appeared, and any changes since then. Avoids most slang, personal names, and scientific and technical vocabulary, for which Klein is more useful.

■ Partridge, Eric. Name into word: proper names that have become common property. A discursive dictionary. 2d ed., rev. and enl. New York: Macmillan, 1950. Reprint, New York: Ayer, 1977. 644p.

> Includes common words based on names of persons, places, etc. (e.g., *boycott*), with discursive explanations.

■ ———. Origins: a short etymological dictionary of modern English. 4th ed. London: Routledge & Paul, 1966. Reprint, London: Routledge & Paul, 1990. 972p.

> Covers the 20,000 or so most common words in English, avoiding medical and technical terms, dialect, and slang.

■ Skeat, Walter William. An etymological dictionary of the English language. New, rev., and enl. [4th] ed. Oxford: Clarendon Pr., 1910. 780p.

> The standard older scholarly work, with references to sources; still regularly reprinted.

Usage

Because good dictionaries record the usage of words, why is it necessary to consult other sources on the subject? This question is well answered in the introductory chapter of Wilson Follett's *Modern American Usage* (discussed below in this chapter):

> The first and obvious reply is that a dictionary does not give reasons even when it gives examples of varying usage in one or two brief quotations. Often, what makes a word preferable is its relation to others in a passage. The narrow context of a dictionary sentence gives too few clues to the force and versatility of a particular word. Definitions must be supplemented with discussion. This

discussion draws its authority from the principle that good usage is what the people who think and care about words believe good usage to be. . . . The fact that those who attend to language disagree on many points does not alter the nature and force of good usage, any more than the diverse judgments of critics about fine art or of courts about the law alter the nature and force of art and of law [p. 6].

The same guide also sets forth the two related purposes of a book on usage:

By analyzing structural errors and ambiguities it reminds writers and speakers of grammatical norms that are frequently flouted; and by discussing words and idioms it provides a list of distinctions and suggestions in the realm of tact. In neither department can it be complete; it does not pretend to be a grammar book, nor does it profess to discuss every failure of judgment or subtlety in the use of words. It concentrates on the prevailing faults of current speech and prose. And the most useful service it can render is to make its readers think for themselves on these matters. To become sensibly self-conscious about words is more important than to memorize and act on this or that suggestion without thought [p. 5].

Books on usage vary widely in contents and reflect the view of the individual compilers to a greater extent than unabridged dictionaries. Thus, it is desirable to have a number of them in a well-stocked reference collection, selected with great attention to the authority of the compilers. One of the best known is H. W. Fowler, author of *A Dictionary of Modern English Usage,* published in 1926 and revised in 1965 by Ernest Gowers (Oxford: Clarendon Pr., 1965; 725p.). Margaret Nicholson, author of *A Dictionary of American-English Usage,* based on Fowler's book, considers his dictionary indispensable: "Fowler not only teaches you how to write; he is a demon on your shoulder, teaching you how not to write, pointing out and exhibiting, with terrifying clarity, your most cherished foibles: Love of the Long Word, Elegant Variation, Genteelisms, Pedantry, Battered Ornaments." Her dictionary is intended as an adaptation of Fowler's, not a replacement, with American variations. Longer articles were shortened, and more academic articles and those less pertinent to usage today were omitted, to make room for new entries and illustrations (Margaret Nicholson, *A Dictionary of American-English Usage, Based on Fowler's "Modern English Usage"* [New York: Oxford Univ. Pr., 1957; 671p.]).

In recent years, however, discussions of language usually found only in the halls of the linguists and philologists have become more common among general society, such as the distinction between *which* and *that* or *I* and *me,* the use of *it's* as possessive, or race- and gender-specific terms. In the process, there has been much more attention paid to the fact that languages naturally change over time and thus more and more criticism voiced on the standard works on usage. Thus, a number of the following will also be needed to answer such questions.

- Copperud, Roy H. American usage and style: the consensus. New York: Van Nostrand Reinhold, 1980. 433p.

  Consolidates his *Dictionary of Usage and Style* (1964) and *American Usage: The Consensus* (1970). Gives consensus from nine authoritative works on use and style (but many of these have been updated since 1980), plus his own views. Also uses standard dictionaries, etc. Gives both dissent and agreement for most words. When there is only one opinion, it is not clear whether this means it is one author's or really a consensus. John Bermner's *Words on Words* (New York: Columbia Univ. Pr., 1980; 405p.) also gives citations to other authorities, but this title is unique in its focus on agreements/disagreements.

- Evans, Bergen, and Cornelia Evans. A dictionary of contemporary American usage. New York: Random House, 1957. 567p.

  An informal but scholarly classic, covering rhetoric, literary concepts, clichés, etc.

- Follett, Wilson. Modern American usage: a guide. Edited and completed by Jacques Barzun and others. New York: Hill & Wang, 1966. Reprint, New York: Hill & Wang, 1998. 362p.

  Another classic, still useful as a complement to Nicholson, *A Dictionary of American-English Usage,* and Fowler, *Dictionary of Modern English Usage.*

- Fowler, Henry Watson. Dictionary of modern English usage. 2d rev. ed. by Sir Ernest Gowers, ed. Oxford: Oxford Univ. Pr., 1965. 725p. Republished with corrections, 1983.

  Has been called "indispensable," but keep the first edition because of the many changes. Has definitions interspersed with essays. The revised edition includes a classified guide to help in Fowler's sometime enigmatic titles. Perhaps one of the more enjoyable features is Fowler's use of bad examples to clarify the rule—many are quite amusing as well as realistic.

- Macdonald, Ron. A broadcast news manual of style. 2d ed. New York: Longman, 1994. 224p.

  Primarily a usage guide (e.g., *student* versus *pupil*) in dictionary form, but unlike most, includes recommended pronunciations. Appendixes include discussions of electronic production of news copy. Includes sample scripts, etc., related to the delivery of news in audiovisual formats, but the most likely use for this title in the typical library is for pronunciation of foreign places and persons.

■ Maggio, Rosalie. Talking about people: a guide to fair and accurate language. Phoenix, Ariz.: Oryx, 1997. 436p.

First appeared in 1987 as *The Nonsexist Word Finder,* later as *The Bias-Free Word Finder* and *The Dictionary of Bias-Free Usage.* Covers about 5,000 terms either biased or thought to be so, giving alternatives or explaining why they aren't biased. Section of guidelines for non-biased use. This title has been attacked for calling terms like *Achilles heel* or *Scrooge* sexist, but it does accept many apparently offensive terms when there is a good reason for them.

■ Miller, C., and K. Swift. The handbook of nonsexist writing for writers, editors and speakers. 2d ed. New York: Harper & Row, 1988. 178p.

A well-established, concise manual, also available in a British-English edition. Generally, it is more accepting of apparently offensive terms than the previous title.

■ Morris, William, and Mary Morris. Harper dictionary of contemporary usage. 2d ed. New York: Harper & Row, 1992. 641p.

Usage comments based on a 165-person panel, 29 more than the first edition. For each entry, gives votes and quotes several panelists. With some controversial usages, also gives votes from first edition. Not as complete on grammar and pronunciation as older books, such as Follett's *Modern American Usage,* or *Fowler* or *Evans,* and generally more conservative than the latter, *Burchfield (The New Fowler's)* or *Gilman (Merriam-Webster's Dictionary of English Usage* [Springfield, Mass.: Merriam-Webster, 1994; 388p.]).

■ The new Fowler's modern English usage. Robert W. Burchfield, rev. 3d ed. New York: Clarendon Pr./Oxford Univ. Pr., 1996. 640p.

A totally different book from the first and second editions. Burchfield (editor of the *OED Supplement* and a linguist) largely rewrote the whole book and added comments on American English. Burchfield is a much less witty and drier writer than Fowler, but he is also much less prescriptive; and he uses the IPA instead of respelling to indicate pronunciation. Thus, Fowler will still be preferred by the more traditionalist writer.

■ Nicholson, Margaret. A dictionary of American-English usage, based on Fowler's Modern English usage. New York: Oxford Univ. Pr., 1957. 671p.

A conservative, traditionalist, but American version of Fowler.

■ Partridge, Eric. Usage and abusage: a guide to good English. 3d ed. Edited by Janet Whitcut. London: Hamilton, 1999. 448p.

Similar in format to *Fowler* but intended to be less Olympian and austere. Whitcut has retained the original in concept but also makes many changes: some formerly condemned uses are now accepted; new topics (e.g., sexism) are addressed. Notably, she is aware the audience is unlikely to have had a classical education.

■ Wall, C. Edward, and Edward Przebienda. Words and phrases index. Ann Arbor, Mich.: Pierian, 1969-70. 4v.

A computer-produced index to notes and articles in *American Notes and Queries* (1962-67), *American Speech* (1925-66), *Britannica Book of the Year* (1945-67), and *Notes and Queries* (1925-66); thus, a handy access point to both meaning and use comments.

■ Webster's dictionary of English usage. Springfield, Mass.: Merriam-Webster, 1989. 989p.

Also reprinted as *Merriam-Webster's Dictionary of English Usage.* A major new dictionary of usage, but nonjudgmental. The 2,200 articles, from a few lines to four pages, discuss controversies but then say do as you like. It has an excellent bibliography. The real point is the detailed historical discussions, with more than 20,000 quotes; the entries read like articles. Includes many examples from the Merriam-Webster citation file, with lengthy conversational discussions of usage, including reference to standard usage books like *Fowler, Evans,* etc. *WDEU* is frankly American, but does include references to British usage as needed (which is much of the time).

■ Weiner, E. S. C., and A. Delahunty. The Oxford guide to English usage. 2d ed. Oxford: Oxford Univ. Pr., 1993. 306p.

Not prescriptive, but describes as standard, formal, informal, etc. Both American and British pronunciation and usage are given. Good supplement to *Fowler* for spelling, pronunciation, vocabulary, grammar, idiomatic use, inflexion, pronunciation, etc. *Fowler* tends to concentrate on correct vocabulary; this title devotes less than 25 percent of the text to vocabulary.

■ Wilson, Kenneth G. The Columbia guide to standard American English. New York: Columbia Univ. Pr., 1993. 482p.

More than 6,500 entries, covering both grammar and linguistics and words, phrases, and constructions that are often confused. Lacks the historical information of Webster's similar guide. Includes modern concerns such as race and gender. Entries give "level" of use (degree of formality), with five levels of speech, three of writing. Includes many cross-references and an extensive bibliography.

Most standard personal computer word-processing software include usage and style manuals as part of the package. Although presumably someone chose the individual manual used, and many software users probably at least occasionally rely on the guidance of their guidance, no research to date has indicated if users are aware that opinions on usage may vary or even know which usage guide they are relying upon. There is a good chance that the style manuals selected by the more popular word-processing programs will have a substantial effect on the rhetoric and usage of the American-English language in the next generation, much more so than they or any other source have had in the past, yet without the majority of people even becoming aware of the source.

Because it's a heavily "word-oriented" product, Microsoft Bookshelf should be noted here. Available on CD-ROM, it contains the full texts of various dictionaries, a thesaurus, quotation book, atlas, usage guide, short encyclopedia, and the like. Strangely, the specific sources tend to change from one year to the next.

Idioms and Related Terms

■ Brewer, Ebenezer C., and Ivan H. Evans, eds. Brewer's dictionary of phrase and fable. 16th ed. New York: HarperResource, 1999. 1298p.

The classic, with the first edition published in 1870. The 1970 centenary edition was wholly revised, and the fourteenth and later editions continue adding new terms, up-to-date illustrative quotations, and the like. An index supplements the cross-references. An invaluable source for coverage of phrases and adages, lists, colloquialisms, proverbial phrases, mythological references, fictional characters, and all kinds of miscellaneous information. Because each edition adds and drops terms, the full set should be retained.

■ Brewer's dictionary of twentieth-century phrase and fable. 3d ed. London: Cassell, 1996. 662p.

A supplement to the previous title, listing "the most evocative words and phrases" introduced in the twentieth century and documenting "in a popular fashion many phrases that evade explanation in standard dictionaries." Not quite either a dictionary of slang or comprehensive guide to English idioms (with a strong emphasis on British), but with comprehensive coverage of many types of nonstandard terms. Source details are unfortunately sparse.

■ A dictionary of American proverbs. Wolfgang Mieder, ed. in chief. Edited by Stewart A. Kingsbury and Kelsie B. Harder. New York: Oxford Univ. Pr., 1996. 710p.

Covers about 15,000 proverbs and variants from about 150,000 citations collected by the American Dialect Society in the United States and parts of Canada, emphasizing the mid-1940s to the end of the 1970s. Differs from other such books in emphasizing the oral tradition based on field research, rather than written sources. A typical entry includes date, author, and title of earliest printed appearance; cites other proverb collections; notes distribution of proverbs and variants. Includes information on geographical distribution. Arranged by most significant keyword, with many cross-references. Extensive multisection bibliography.

A recent review in *American Speech* says this title "surpasses, supersedes and includes all previous works on the topic." But as this only cites them, it does not replace them for all older terms. Includes good bibliography of books, collections of proverbs, and articles.

■ Grote, David. British English for American readers: a dictionary of the language, customs, and places of British life and literature. Westport, Conn.: Greenwood, 1992. 728p.

Claims to be "far more than a dictionary of British vocabulary"—terms of all kinds, including events, legal terms, slang, titles, plants, foods, etc. commonly appearing in British literature that Americans may not be familiar with. More of an emphasis on literary language than Schur's similar volume.

■ Idioms and phrases index. Laurence Urdang, ed. in chief. Detroit: Gale, 1983. 3v.

An index to about thirty sources that define or discuss phrases of two or more words that are idioms, slang, and the like. Includes *Brewer's Dictionary of Phrase and Fable*, dictionaries of slang, and *Words and Phrases Index*.

■ Oxford dictionary of current idiomatic English. London: Oxford Univ. Pr., 1975-83. 2v.

Covers about 15,000 idioms, with British emphasis but good at Americanisms as well. Volume 1 lists "Verbs with Prepositions and Particles"; volume 2 covers "Phrase, Clause and Sentence Idioms." A comprehensive authoritative guide, which often gives warnings about incorrect use and constructions. Of particular value for non-English speakers, especially with its use of contemporary speech for examples.

▪ Schur, Norman W. British English A to Zed. 3d rev. ed. New York: Facts on File, 1987. 477p.

First appeared as *British Self-Taught,* 1973, a work by an American scholar. The 5,000-plus entries include words with different meanings in Great Britain and the United States, words rarely used in the United States, and words with no direct U.S. equivalent. Includes slang and outdated words likely to be found in period films and older works, as well as current material. Two appendixes provide fascinating reading on the general differences between the two languages; glossaries and tables of currency.

Synonyms and Antonyms

General dictionaries, both abridged and unabridged, usually treat synonyms and antonyms in their word entries, but many other dictionaries are devoted entirely to these forms. Like books on usage, they attempt to give more discussion and examples than a general dictionary. But they must be used with proper caution, as Eric Partridge warns in his *Usage and Abusage* (6th ed. London: Hamilton, 1965; 392p.).

> The educated person does not need to be told that, in the desire for variety, to consult a dictionary of synonyms (so called) and take haphazard an apparent synonym is to expose himself to the risk—almost to the certainty—of making himself ridiculous. . . . If you wish to use two or more synonyms as a stylistic device, make sure that the choice fulfills your purpose [p. 332–33].

Margaret Nicholson, in *A Dictionary of American-English Usage,* also notes that "misapprehensions of the degree in which words are synonymous is responsible for much bad writing of the less educated kind" [p. 566].

Following Partridge's advice, experienced writers may turn to the following:

▪ Roget's international thesaurus. 5th ed. New York: HarperCollins, 1992. 1141p.

The "definitive unabridged English-language thesaurus," still following the original classified principles, but with some additions and modifications: in effect, the current version of the original. Lists more than

325,000 words in fifteen classes, and more than 1,000 categories. Lacks antonyms, but includes useful word lists (e.g., for types of phobias). Index gives an exact citation to the correct paragraph.

Other thesauri of current value follow:

- The Cambridge thesaurus of American English. William D. Lutz. New York: Cambridge Univ. Pr., 1994. 515p.

  An alphabetical arrangement of about 200,000 words, intended to be both comprehensive and easier to use than *Roget's*. The first synonyms under each entry are those that distinguish it from other similar words, then a list of most common followed by less common. Some antonyms also appear at the end. All words have part-of-speech labels. Much more selective than *Roget's*, with many fewer synonyms and alphabetically arranged. A useful alternative to *Roget's International* and *Webster's New World Thesaurus* (3d ed. New York: Macmillan, 1997; 882p.).

- Choose the right word: a contemporary guide to selecting the precise word for every situation. S. I. Hayakawa and Eugene Ehrlich, eds. 2d ed. New York: HarperCollins, 1994. 532p.

  The current version of *Funk & Wagnalls Modern Guide to Synonyms and Related Words* (1968), with many revisions but no new synonym groups. Explanations are longer, more detailed, and make clearer distinctions than *Webster's New Dictionary of Synonyms*, but illustrative quotes are not from real sentences as they are in Webster's. Index to both headwords and all synonyms.

- Knapp, Sara. The contemporary thesaurus of social science terms and synonyms: a guide for natural language computer searching. Phoenix, Ariz.: Oryx, 1993. 400p.

  Lists 6,000 concepts, based on newspapers, thesauri, actual search requests, subject dictionaries. Entries include term, synonyms, related terms, alternative endings, and cross-references. British and American spellings are both supplied. Supplementary matter, aimed at those new to computer searching, includes information on Boolean logic and strategies. This sort of usage guide may well become more common as the world moves more toward electronic sources that are based on the technical vocabularies of many disciplines and many nations.

- Merriam-Webster's collegiate thesaurus. Springfield, Mass.: Merriam, 1995. 868p. Also on CD-ROM as part of Merriam-Webster's Collegiate Dictionary Deluxe.

Provides uncommon features to deal with perceived defects of standard thesauri. Brief core meaning for each main entry, alphabetical organization, synonyms, antonyms, idiomatic equivalents, vulgarisms, and regionalisms. Excludes archaic, obsolete, rare, technical jargon. Good introduction on development and history of thesauri. Similar to *Roget's II,* but includes more than synonyms and idioms and has a less confusing arrangement.

■ Roget's II: the new thesaurus. 3d ed. Boston: Houghton, 1994. 1200p. Also on CD-ROM.

Contrary to the implications of the title (which, like *Webster,* is now a generic name available to any publisher), this entirely new work is based on the third edition of the *American Heritage Dictionary,* with an unusual two-column format, giving terms, illustrative quotes, and very brief definitions in one column, synonyms and idioms in the other. The 17,000-plus entries exclude related words, antonyms, and contrasting words, but they do include slang and informal language, with appropriate labels. A useful supplement to the full *Roget's,* which does not include definitions.

■ Roget's twenty-first century thesaurus in dictionary form. Barbara Ann Kipfer, ed. New York: Dell, 1992. 978p.

A serious attempt to combine the best features of both the Roget classification and an alphabetical arrangement. The 17,000 headwords, in alphabetical order, are keyed to a "concept index" of 837 broad terms, each of which is keyed to all related headwords. The synonym lists are only provided in the alphabetical portion.

■ Urdang, Laurence. The Oxford thesaurus: an A–Z dictionary of synonyms. Oxford: Clarendon Pr.; New York: Oxford Univ. Pr., 1992. 1005p. Also on CD-ROM.

A major new thesaurus, with about 275,000 synonyms (but no antonyms) under more than 8,500 headwords. Each group includes an illustrative sentence. Terms include notes as to geographic or stylistic variations. A detailed and comprehensive index to each occurrence of each term is also included. Most American libraries will prefer the 1992 U.S. edition to the 1991 British version.

■ Webster's new dictionary of synonyms. 2d ed. Springfield, Mass.: Merriam-Webster, 1984. 909p.

Based on *Webster's Dictionary of Synonyms,* with the first edition published in 1942. Has more than 8,700 entries. Includes examples of usage, antonyms, clear and concise definitions, and multiple illustrative phrases. Strongly current in standard American English. *Balay* calls this "for many purposes the best dictionary of synonyms." Provides useful discriminations of different meanings between related words, illustrated with examples and quotations from classical and modern writers.

Pronunciation

A good general dictionary always gives pronunciation and is adequate in most cases. But pronouncing dictionaries, those giving only pronunciation, are often convenient to use when only pronunciation is sought, saving wear and tear on larger dictionaries. Their characteristics follow:

1. Emphasis on difficult words in selection of vocabulary
2. Indication of variant pronunciations in different regions
3. Inclusion of proper names not always found in general dictionaries
4. No definitions

With good-quality sound reproduction (both in terms of the pronunciation and accent of the speaker and in the hardware and software of the equipment used), the growing availability of pronunciations in machine-readable dictionaries may eventually eliminate this type of dictionary as a category. The researcher must remember, however, that there is often more than one acceptable pronunciation and that regional accents can also modify even that. In other words, just as more than one dictionary is necessary for print-oriented research, more than one aural/oral dictionary will be necessary. Some standard titles are listed here:

■ Kenyon, John S., and Thomas A. Knott. A pronouncing dictionary of American English. 2d ed. Springfield, Mass.: Merriam, 1953. 484p.

Uses IPA to give pronunciation of the colloquial speech of "cultivated Americans," noting regional differences. Includes proper names, with an emphasis on Americans (with some British and a few others), and many names in literature and history. For recent names, the *NBC Handbook* is necessary.

■ NBC handbook of pronunciation. 4th ed. Revised and updated by Eugene Ehrlich and Raymond Hand Jr. New York: Harper, 1984. 539p.

About 21,000 commonly used words, with a strong emphasis on proper names (people, countries, cities, etc.). Uses respelling (not diacritics or IPA), giving primary and secondary stresses as well.

■ Pronouncing dictionary of proper names. 2d ed. Detroit: Omnigraphics, 1997. 1097p.

Gives 28,000 current names (and some older ones) and brief definitions as well. Uses both IPA and respelling. Includes people, places, products, and many other items that have proper names. A recipient of both the RASD Outstanding Reference Book and *LJ* Best Reference Books accolades.

For pronunciation of names not found in the sources listed, one should always try biographical and geographical dictionaries, which often include pronunciation, as well as general unabridged dictionaries, which often include some names. Also, newsmagazines (accessed via indexes and abstracts) and encyclopedias, especially the *Encyclopedia Americana,* often give pronunciations of difficult proper names (e.g., the given name of Pope John Paul II).

Slang

Although slang is increasingly included in general dictionaries, in books on usage, and in dictionaries of synonyms, recourse to dictionaries devoted entirely to slang often produces the following:

1. Definitions of more recent slang
2. Derogatory or taboo words not always found in standard dictionaries
3. More detailed information on the historical origins of slang expressions
4. More illustrative quotations

For an illustrative history of slang and dialect, H. L. Mencken's work is still helpful and nearly definitive (*The American Language,* 4th ed., corr., enl., and rewritten [New York: Knopf, 1936; 796p.]; *Supplements* 1 and 2 [New York: Knopf, 1945, 1948]). The abridged edition, by Raven I. McDonald (New York: Knopf, 1963; 777p.), contains modifications to reflect changes in language and civilization.

When it is completed, the following will be definitive for some time:

■ Random House historical dictionary of American slang. J. E. Lighter, J. Ball, and J. O'Connor, eds. New York: Random House, 1994– . 3v.

Its more than 80,000 entries are intended to be a definitive dictionary—similar to *DARE* or the *OED,* but for slang. Each entry gives the word, part of speech, etymology, field label (group or subculture using the word), definitions, and illustrative examples in historical order. The introductory material is particularly useful as a discussion of the types of slang, its effects, history, and the like. Some reviewers are already proclaiming this to be the definitive dictionary in its field; it is certainly the first to be based entirely on accurately quoted and dated examples, based on 8,000 sources.

For reviews, *see Choice* (Nov. 1994): 436; *Library Journal* (Aug. 1994): 78; *Reference Books Bulletin* (Oct. 1, 1994): 352; and *American Reference Books Annual* 26 (1995): 462–63; 29 (1998): 439.

Other dictionaries, mostly in specialized areas, follow:

■ Berry, Lester V., and Melvin Van den Bark. American thesaurus of slang. 2d ed. New York: Crowell, 1953. 1272p.

Good coverage of older slang, but the second edition does not completely replace the first. Has access by standard English to slang terms, rare for such dictionaries.

■ Chapman, Robert L. New dictionary of American slang. New York: Harper, 1986. 485p.

A revised edition of the classic by Harold Wentworth and Stuart Berg Flexner, *Dictionary of American Slang* (2d supplemented ed. New York: Crowell, 1975; 766p.), which was generally perceived as the best of the American slang dictionaries for its time. The 17,000 entries include strong and offensive language (with labels), with dates of origin for terms before about 1970 but not after. Gives usage examples but not always pronunciations. The preface includes a history of slang dictionaries. Adds new definitions to many terms. Although it adds new terms, it drops others, so it does not completely replace Wentworth and Flexner's volume.

■ Dalzell, Tom. Flappers 2 rappers: American youth slang. Springfield, Mass.: Merriam-Webster, 1996. 256p.

Although it emphasizes the period since the 1920s, coverage begins with the 1850s. Arranged by decades, this is a combination study of etymologies and usage as well as a list and definition of slang terms, based on about 1,000 books and more than 2,000 articles. All the academic apparatus are present, including careful documentation, references to slang sources, and a good, cross-referenced index.

▪ Major, Clarence. Juba to jive: a dictionary of African-American slang. New ed. New York: Viking Penguin, 1994. 432p.

Gives definition, illustrative example, association with a given subculture or occupation (e.g., drug users, jazz musician, etc.), and indicates areas of use in the United States. Cross-references. Citations to about 150 printed sources. More scholarly than Geneva Smitherman's *Black Talk: Words and Phrases from the Hood to the Amen Corner* (Boston: Houghton, 1994; 243p.).

▪ Partridge, Eric. A dictionary of slang and unconventional English. 8th ed. Edited by P. Beale. London: Routledge & Paul, 1984. 1400p.

This edition incorporates all the supplements to the original 1937 edition, with many corrections, additions, etc. Partridge's own notes were used for most of this; post-1978 additions (after Partridge died) carry Beale's initials. *See also A Concise Dictionary of Slang and Unconventional English,* edited by Beale (New York: Macmillan, 1990; 534p.), which supplements the above by including only terms appearing in the twentieth century, adding terms that came into use in the 1980s, and by removing Cockney because it is no longer considered slang but a dialect.

▪ Richter, Alan. Dictionary of sexual slang: words, phrases, and idioms from AC/DC to zig-zag. New York: Wiley, 1993. 250p.

Complements the author's *Language of Sexuality* (Jefferson, N.C.: McFarland, 1987; 151p.). About 4,000 words in English over the last 500 years. Gives etymology (if available), nature, time of use, metaphor, etc. but not pronunciation. Includes ordinary words with sexual meanings. Because many other dictionaries (including those of slang) tend to avoid these sorts of words and definitions, it is a useful supplement to them.

Having listed the above, an important note is in order: much slang is in part intended to differentiate the users from the rest of society. As a result, it not only tends to change rapidly, but the change is accelerated by a term's appearance in the mainstream media, not to mention dictionaries. In other words, much of the slang in current use is unlikely to be found in reference sources. On the other hand, some terms still considered slang have been in the language for some time: "Far out" appears in the mouth of a Californian in Frank Norris's 1899 novel *McTeague,* and "Sock it to 'em" appears at the turn of the eighteenth century (as the Latin "soc et tuum").

Dialect

No attempt is made here to review the controversies in matters of definition, limits, and acceptability of dialect that exist at the present (or any given past) time. Some consider the concept of dialect as a form of language spoken in a particular area as only relative, but general dictionaries continue to label words as dialects. Perhaps Fowler's definition in his *Dictionary of Modern English Usage* will serve: "Dialect is essentially local; a dialect is the variety of a language that prevails in a district, with local peculiarities of vocabulary, pronunciation and phrase." This agrees substantially with the definition in Webster's dictionaries. We have had dialect dictionaries for a long time, with promise of more to come, using the latest compilation methods.

Little has been said to this point about new processes in the preparation of dictionaries, except that the *Random House Dictionary of the English Language* was the first general dictionary to use electronic data processing in its production and that the *American Heritage Dictionary* was produced from data on magnetic tapes. For all practical purposes, however, all dictionaries are now produced in this fashion. One of the earliest to use this approach is the *Dictionary of American Regional English,* described in detail by R. L. Venezky, in "Storage, Retrieval, and Editing of Information for a Dictionary" (*American Documentation* 19 [Jan. 1968]: 71-79), with the accompanying abstract:

> A computer system has been designed for storing, retrieving, and editing data for the *Dictionary of American Regional English* (D. A. R. E.). This dictionary, in contrast to most commercial dictionaries, will consist of words which have regional rather than national currency and will derive its entries from data collected by its own fieldworkers, readers, and researchers. Entries, consisting of a headword or phrase, plus descriptors for such items as the user, meaning, pronunciation, and collection technique for this word or phrase are stored in a central file. Interrogations on this file can be made on the value of any headword or description, or any logical combination of such values.
>
> Any portion of an entry which satisfies an interrogation may be designated for retrieval. An experimental editing system employing an on-line CRT (cathode ray tube) terminal has been developed for the editing process, although a more flexible system will be needed for the actual editing which is scheduled to begin in approximately three years.

It is somewhat astounding that this description, after only about thirty years, now sounds a bit archaic and that the basic technique is now fairly common in the production of most dictionaries. Such methods were unknown to Joseph Wright, editor of the following still-classic dialect dictionary:

■ Wright, Joseph, ed. English dialect dictionary; being the complete vocabulary of all dialect words still in use, or known to have been in use during the last 200 years; founded on the publications of the English Dialect Society. London: Frowde, 1898–1905. Reprint, New York: Oxford Univ. Pr., 1981. 6v.

> *Scope*: Complete vocabulary of all words used in English since 1700 in England, Ireland, Wales, and Scotland, both literary and spoken. Provides much information about popular games, superstitions, customs, etc., with bibliographic references for additional reading.

> *Treatment*: Gives definitions and explanations, geographical area, pronunciation, etymology, and illustrative quotations.

This work has been hailed by Logan Pearsall Smith in his essay on popular speech:

> Of all the various forms of non-literary English, the local dialects have been most carefully documented and studied; glossaries of all, and grammars of some of them have been published, and the material in these has been put together, with that collected by the Dialect Society, in six volumes of Dr. Wright's immense *Dialect Dictionary,* which is not only one of the greatest lexicographical achievements ever performed by one scholar, but a work for the lover of words of inexhaustible fascination, enabling him, as it does, to explore at ease the wide regions which lie around the streets and suburbs of our polite vernacular.

This is quoted in Eric Partridge's *Slang, Today and Yesterday* (3d ed., rev. New York: Macmillan, 1950; p. 133–34), which contains an entertaining chapter on the affiliations of slang with dialect, cant, and vulgarisms.

Abbreviations

Thus far we have considered special dictionaries that are primarily concerned with usage, because not only dictionaries of usage, but also those of synonyms and slang, help a user select the right word for the right time. Also, etymological dictionaries add to the understanding of the true meanings of words. Other special dictionaries are less related to usage but nevertheless supply information that may not be found in a general dictionary. One well-known type is the dictionary of abbreviations.

If slang is increasing, as society becomes fragmented into more and more cultural subgroups, each adding to the general slang vocabulary, certainly the use of abbreviations and acronyms is increasing; and dictionaries of abbreviations and acronyms are hard-pressed to keep up with them. Furthermore, because one set of initials may stand for so many different things, it is necessary to discover the abbreviation's setting to discover the correct equivalent. Thus, "ALA" may bring to mind the American Library Association to librarians, but it brings to mind the American Landrace Association to a hog farmer. And, because abbreviations and acronyms are added daily, dictionaries of these forms must be updated by consulting the periodicals literature in individual fields.

When selecting dictionaries of this kind, comprehensiveness and currency are of prime importance, especially because good unabridged and desk dictionaries include some abbreviations. Dictionaries in special fields also give attention to abbreviations and acronyms pertinent to their fields. Only a few recent tiles are listed here:

■ Acronyms, initialisms, and abbreviations dictionary: a guide to alphabetic designations, contractions, acronyms, initialisms, abbreviations, and similar condensed appellations. Detroit: Gale, 1960– . 3v.

> A comprehensive list, with emphasis on the United States, England, and Canada and the English-speaking world in general, as opposed to *International Acronyms,* for complete coverage of non-English terms. Gives definition, English translation if needed, language of original, source code (referring to the full citation), place of origin, subject, sponsoring entity. If a term has several meanings, these are listed alphabetically. Obsolete and superseded terms are included. The third volume, *Reverse Acronyms, Initialisms and Abbreviations Dictionary,* includes the terms but is arranged by the meaning.

■ International acronyms, initialisms, and abbreviations dictionary. Detroit: Gale, 1985– . 3v. Biennial.

> This title excludes the United States, Canada, and Great Britain. Updated between editions with *New International Acronyms, Abbreviations and Initialisms.* Full three-volume set also includes *Reverse Acronyms, Initialisms and Abbreviations Dictionary.*

■ DeSola, Ralph, and others. Abbreviations dictionary. 9th ed. Boca Raton, Fla.: CRC Pr., 1995. 1347p.

> First edition was in 1958; this adds 15,000 entries to the eighth edition. Various short forms are interfiled with each other. Many special lists (e.g., airlines of the world, constellations, numbered abbreviations, etc.) in fifty-seven supplementary sections (e.g., signs of the Zodiac).

One type of abbreviation that must be singled out for special attention is that of periodical titles. These abbreviations often present real problems of identification. Because many older books and, especially, journals make extensive use of abbreviations in their citations, such a reference source remains necessary.

■ Periodical title abbreviations. 11th ed. Detroit: Gale, 1998. 3v.

> Descriptive rather than prescriptive. Volume 1 lists about 175,000 abbreviations; volume 2 gives the full names, based on about 120 sources; and volume 3 is the interedition update. Very similar to the other Gale titles listed here.

■ Brown, Peter, and George Burder Stratton, eds. World list of scientific periodicals published in the years 1900–1960. 4th ed. London: Butterworths, 1963–65. 3v.

> This edition is the "last to appear in this format," according to the preface. Later work has been incorporated into the *British Union-Catalogue: New Periodical Titles* and its two supplements. Anyone using older materials should keep this title in mind, as the knowledge even of *ibid.* and *idem.*, let alone *Phil. Trans.*, is leaving the common academic vocabulary.

Visual Dictionaries

The number of visual dictionaries has increased substantially in the last few years, possibly in response to the increase in multicultural sensitivity or perhaps merely to the increasing cross-cultural (and cross-language) business traffic. The general pattern is the same—unlike traditional dictionaries, which are verbal and illustrated by some pictures, in these the pictures, usually within broad classifications (drawings or photographs), are the main entry, with parts then labeled. Not only is this useful to the nonexpert, but the better such dictionaries are also useful for learning the "way things work," for instance, the fascinating book by David Macaulay, *The Way Things Work* (Boston: Houghton, 1988; 384p.; CD-ROM, New York: Dorling Kindersley Multimedia, 1994).

First, however, a dictionary for a truly visual language:

■ Sternberg, Martin L. A. American sign language dictionary. 3d ed. New York: HarperCollins, 1998. 614p. Also available as American Sign Language Dictionary on CD-ROM (New York: HarperCollins Interactive, 1994).

The CD-ROM contains about 2,200 words, each with a video clip show-ing how to sign it as well as a definition and both verbal and line-drawing instructions on making the sign. Videos can be viewed at normal speed or slow motion or stopped at any point. This edition includes some ex-ercises for the beginning signer, plus finger-spelling translation of any English-language word entered. A useful feature is the index by English, German, French, Italian, and Spanish. The printed dictionary is much more complete, and its 1981 edition includes many terms dropped from the 1994 version; thus, both print editions should be retained, with the CD-ROM preferred for newer terms and more useful sign-making in-structions, which can also help in interpreting the printed version.

The classic of the more general type is the *Oxford-Duden:*

■ The Oxford-Duden pictorial German-English dictionary. 2d ed. Oxford and New York: Oxford Univ. Pr., 1994. 880p.

A cooperative effort of two publishers, based on *Bildwörterbuch,* which is volume 3 of a ten-volume series by Duden; English text is a di-rect translation of German. The 384 plates, mostly black-and-white line drawings, are fairly small but usually clear, with labels in both lan-guages and indexed by German and by English.

Some examples of related titles follow:

■ The Oxford-Duden pictorial English dictionary. 2d ed. Oxford and New York: Oxford Univ. Pr., 1995. 824p.

More than 28,000 black-and-white illustrations and six color plates, based on the first edition of *The Oxford-Duden Pictorial German-English Dictionary,* with some updating. British vocabulary, with American stems or spelling in parentheses, and both forms indexed. Especially good for recent technical terminology and ESL use. Entries are arranged by class of object; each page has a list of numbered terms that refer to numbers in the pictures. A detailed alphabetical index includes all terms, with reference both to the page and to the numbered item within the picture. Some illustrations are rather small, and not all Briticisms are given their American equivalent. A more serious difficulty for the series as a whole is that the same pictures are used for most of the titles and are becoming out-of-date. For example, the kitchen scene has no mi-crowave, and the library does not show an online catalog. For the most part, technical and scientific scenes are much better portrayed than do-mestic ones.

■ The Oxford-Duden pictorial Spanish-English dictionary. 2d ed. Oxford: Clarendon Pr.; New York: Oxford Univ. Pr., 1995. 884p.

Similar to the others by the publishers. Emphasizes British English, but does include South American Spanish, with variations from different countries given.

The previous titles have been treated at some length to give the flavor of what has become a rather extensive series, all based heavily on the German version but with modifications to represent cultural variations. Other titles include French-English, Italian-English, Hungarian-English, Thai-English, Portuguese-English, Serbo/Croat-English, Chinese-English, and Japanese-English, among others.

Most other similar dictionaries tend to a single language:

■ Bragonier, R., and D. Fisher. What's what: a visual glossary of the physical world. Rev. ed. Maplewood, N.J.: Hammond, 1990. 581p.

Thousands of clear illustrations of objects, labeled. Uses black-and-white photographs rather than the more common drawings. Even when covering the same topics, often the point of view and the parts labeled vary with the dictionary; thus, this title is a helpful complement to the others listed earlier. The first edition of this title sold more than a million copies, by the way.

■ Dorling Kindersley ultimate visual dictionary. New York: Dorling Kindersley, 1994. 640p.

More like a pictorial encyclopedia than a dictionary, emphasizing science and technology. More than 6,000 diagrammatic photos and drawings illustrate about 30,000 fairly technical terms under 270 major entries. Arranged by category with an accurate and extensive index. Not as extensive as the *Facts on File Visual Dictionary* or the *Oxford-Duden* titles, but the essays are clearer in putting unfamiliar items in context, and the pictures are very detailed. Much of this material appeared in a series of single-topic children's dictionaries.

■ Facts on File visual dictionary. Jean-Claude Corbeil, ed. in chief. New York: Facts on File, 1986. 797p.

Claims to be the "first basic dictionary of terminological orientation, comprising within a single volume" about 25,000 terms and 3,000 technical drawings, in twenty-eight thematic chapters. No abstract words. Clear, technical drawings; up-to-date as of 1986. First published in Canada, but American English has been used throughout. Access is by a very detailed table of contents and three indexes: "General" (all terms in alphabetical order); "Thematic" (all terms alphabetically by sections); and "Specialized" (all terms by page by subcategories). However, there are no cross-references and, of course, no definitions. The main arrangement consists of subject sections ("Sports," "Do-It-Yourself," etc.) with detailed drawings; each drawing is then richly labeled. Some users might prefer the colored illustrations of the *Macmillan Visual Dictionary*, but others will appreciate the clarity of the black-and-white drawings in this title.

A number of bilingual dictionaries were issued by the publisher, all based on this edition, and thus some received criticism for missing important cultural aspects of language (e.g., typically French foods are pictured but not typically Chinese foods in the Chinese-English version). In any event, the sales of what seems to have been a very good idea do not appear to have been very good at all.

■ Longman photo dictionary. White Plains, N.Y.: Longman, 1987. 91p.

About 2,000 color photos. Although much shorter than its competitors, it includes emotions, family, and other subtle concepts that they do not. Each photo is labeled and includes lists of vocabulary related to the picture. Although some pictures are rather small, the volume is easier and simpler to use than the *Oxford-Duden* and *Facts on File* works. Bilingual English-Spanish and English-Japanese editions are also available.

■ Macmillan visual dictionary. Jean-Claude Corbeil and Ariane Archambault, eds. New York: Macmillan, 1997. 928p. Also available with CD-ROM with animation, all captions in English, Spanish, and French, with pronunciations.

■ Macmillan visual dictionary: multilingual edition: English, French, Spanish, German. New York: Macmillan, 1994. 959p.

About 3,500 full-color, computer-generated illustrations based on input from more than 175 technical organizations, specialized books, and the like. Includes a section for signs and symbols. Aimed at the general public, but clearly useful for ESL as well. The illustrations are often color versions of the same pictures in the *Facts on File Visual Dictionary.* The multilingual edition is exactly the same, but with English, French, German, and Spanish terms indicated. Arranged under broad categories, each illustration may have several elements, ranging from one animal (e.g., the oyster) to a complex scene (e.g., an airport). Labels for parts are around each object. In addition to the subject arrangement, there is a detailed table of contents. An alphabetical index with cross-references provides access to individual terms. Unlike the *Facts on File* version, uses only American English.

Special Fields

The increasing specialization of our age has naturally led to increasingly specialized vocabularies, which in turn require an increasing number of dictionaries in special fields. They take various forms, including the following:

1. Encyclopedic dictionaries, giving not only definitions of terms, but other descriptive information; brief biographies of persons prominent in the field; and agencies active in the field
2. Monolingual dictionaries, restricted largely to definitions of terms
3. Bilingual dictionaries, restricted largely to pertinent words in one language with their equivalents in another language
4. Polyglot dictionaries, giving equivalents in two or more languages

Only the monolingual dictionary is emphasized here, and a good one should meet the following criteria:

1. It should be sponsored by an active association in the field, concerned with standardizing the vocabulary of the field or, at least, with recording the existing vocabulary used by specialists.
2. It should have an informed editorial board, concerned with setting sound criteria for selection and treatment of terms.
3. Its vocabulary should be selected from a wide range of books and current journals and other publications in the field.

A carefully compiled dictionary in a subject field should supplement a general dictionary by providing the following:

1. More new words and trade names in the field
2. More highly specialized terms in the field
3. Accurate definitions in terms of the subject, more fully treated, and with added descriptive material when pertinent, including diagrams and other illustrations (graphic and textual) as needed
4. Illustrative quotations from cited authorities in the field, where pertinent
5. Balanced and unbiased treatment of abstract terms on which there is a difference of opinion or, failing any consensus, a clear discussion of the differing meanings and some idea of the nature of the controversy
6. Revised editions when necessary to keep up with the current and expanding vocabulary

This last point is of particular importance, because there are amazing differences in vocabulary across fields. Barratt Wilkins compared twelve subject dictionaries (six from the sciences and six from the social sciences) with *Webster's Third New International Dictionary.* Based on a check of 180 terms, he justified the usefulness of subject dictionaries because of the number of terms not found in the unabridged dictionary and because of the quality of their definitions ("Subject Dictionaries," *RQ* 9 [spring 1970]: 234-36). For an interesting global comparison, look into John Christ's *Concepts and Subject Headings: Their Relation in Information Retrieval and Library Science* (Metuchen, N.J.: Scarecrow, 1972; 174p.). Christ compared a sample of terms from the *International Encyclopedia of the Social Sciences* with Library of Congress subject terms and found less than half the index terms had obvious equivalents in Library of Congress subject headings (LCSH).

The demand for specialized dictionaries has led some publishers to issue hastily prepared volumes, which add little to what may be found in a good up-to-date unabridged dictionary, though Hulbert states:

> It is, however, only fair to the general lexicographer, whether commercial or historical, to point out that his main function is to explain the whole vocabulary of the language, and that if one wants sure definition of technical words and uses one should consult a more specialized lexicon, e.g. of philosophy, social sciences, medicine, etc. Heaven help the maker of a specialized dictionary if his definitions are not accurate! It is his job to make them so [p. 76].

Note that special dictionaries often are not concerned with etymology, syllabification, or pronunciation. Thus, special dictionaries must be selected with care, after determining whether they augment the general dictionary sufficiently to warrant purchase, especially in a general library.

Because only a few special dictionaries are discussed here, some of the more useful sources for subject dictionaries should be reviewed. Many can be located in the index to *Balay,* where they are cited under subject, as "Biological Science—Dictionaries." Additional titles will be found in guides to the literature of subject fields (such as those cited in chapter 2, pages 91-93). Also useful for detailed commentary are encyclopedias in special subject fields, an excellent example being the article on dictionaries in the *Encyclopedia of Philosophy* (Paul Edwards, ed. in chief; New York: Macmillan, 1967; 8v.).

An exhaustive list of subject dictionaries in the Library of Congress may be found in *Dictionaries, Encyclopedias, and Other Word-Related Books* (4th ed. Detroit: Gale, 1988; 2v.), which includes titles cataloged since 1966. A similar list is available in Emanuel Molho's *Dictionary Catalogue* (2d ed. New York: French & European Pubs., 1989; 178p.).

Library and Information Sciences

Because all librarians should be familiar at least with their own field, the following is a reasonably complete list. Generally, other fields have a similar set of relevant dictionaries, but only a few examples are listed for them.

■ ALA glossary of library and information science. Heartsill Young, ed. Chicago: ALA, 1983. 245p.

An attempt to be definitive, at least for the United States, although becoming out-of-date. Covers librarianship, printing, publishing, telecommunication, archives, graphic arts, computer science, and related fields.

■ Ayala, Marta Stiefel, Reynaldo Ayala, and Jesus Lau. Technical dictionary of library and information science: English/Spanish, Spanish/English. Hamden, Conn.: Garland, 1993. 647p.

The first bilingual, comprehensive English-Spanish dictionary in the field; even the introductory material is in both languages. Gives a short (ten to thirty words) definition, with emphasis on current use, not historical.

■ Bookman's glossary. Jean Peters, ed. 6th ed., rev. and enl. New York: Bowker, 1983. 223p.

About 1,800 definitions in librarianship, publishing, etc. Includes brief biographies of major figures. As with the *ALA Glossary,* now unfortunately out-of-date for modern printing and inadequate for electronic publishing of all kinds. Still a classic.

■ Glaister, Geoffrey Ashall. Encyclopedia of the book. 2d ed. London: British Library; New Castle, Del.: Oak Knoll Pr., 1996. 576p.

Said by some reviewers to be better than *Harrod's Librarians Glossary.*

■ Harrod's librarians glossary: 9,200 terms used in information management, library science, publishing, the book trades, and archive management. Ray Prytherch, comp. 8th ed. Aldershot, England; Brookfield, Vt.: Gower, 1995. 692p.

Based on the classic *Librarians Glossary,* by Leonard Harrod, this continues to expand. From the eighth edition on, includes addresses of major libraries, co-ops, associations, etc. Is considered the "preeminent source," with many current references. Even though both American and British terms and spelling appear, the British origins are still evident.

■ Isaacs, Alan, and others. Multilingual dictionary of publishing, printing and bookselling. New York: Mansell/Cassell, 1992. 448p.

About 2,000 terms in seven languages, translated into both American and British English where those two differ.

■ Keenan, Stella. Concise dictionary of library and information science. New Providence, N.J.: Bowker/K. G. Saur, 1996. 214p.

Avoids duplication with other standard sources such as the *ALA Glossary* by covering nonconventional terms. Emphasizes current terminology, with a strong emphasis on electronic aspects of information (i.e., the publishing terms concentrate on electronic publishing). Classified arrangement.

■ Soper, Mary Ellen, and others. The librarian's thesaurus. Chicago: ALA, 1990. 225p.

Actually, more of a dictionary than a thesaurus. Essentially, long definitions of terms. Part A, general; part B, procedures and processes; part C, technology. This has very little overlap with *Harrod's* and the *ALA Glossary.*

■ Watters, Carolyn. Dictionary of information science and technology. Boston: Academic Pr., 1992. 300p.

Intended to make highly technical language more understandable. Arranged alphabetically, but with a key to a subject outline, which appears at the end of the volume.

A few examples of general dictionaries in other fields follow:

Business and Economics

■ Banki, Ivan S. Dictionary of administration and management: authoritative, comprehensive. Los Angeles: Systems Research, 1986. 1369p.

Revised and expanded over the previous edition. Brief definitions for about 20,000 terms, concepts, and techniques, plus an extensive list of acronyms and abbreviations and a bibliography.

■ Friedman, Jack P., and others. Dictionary of business terms. 2d ed. Woodbury, N.Y.: Barron, 1994. 700p.

Subject specialists define about 6,000 terms. Ample cross-references, up-to-date with technical terms and jargon. Definitions are especially lucid. Strongly recommended.

■ The McGraw-Hill dictionary of modern economics: a handbook of terms and organizations. 3d ed. Douglas Greenwald and others, eds. New York: McGraw-Hill, 1983. 632p.

More than 1,400 definitions for the nonspecialist, sometimes including charts, graphs, tables. Part 2 lists and briefly describes about 235 organizations involved with the topic. Some reviews say use with *The MIT Dictionary.*

■ Kohler's dictionary for accountants. 6th ed. Eric L. Kohler and W. W. Cooper, eds. Englewood Cliffs, N.J.: Prentice-Hall, 1983. 593p.

The standard in the field. About 2,600 terms are defined and explained.

■ The MIT dictionary of modern economics. David W. Pearce, ed. 4th ed. Cambridge, Mass.: MIT Pr., 1992. 474p.

Aimed at the needs of students in economics, but useful for all users. Includes biographies with summaries of major works (e.g., Galbraith).

■ The new Palgrave: a dictionary of economics. John Eatwell and others, eds. London: Macmillan; New York: Stockton Pr., 1987. 4v.

Updates Sir Robert Palgrave, *Palgrave's Dictionary of Political Economy* (1894–96), revised edition, edited by Henry Higgs (London and New York: Macmillan, 1923–26; 3v.). Generally considered a classic, but may be heavy going for the layperson.

■ New Palgrave dictionary of money and finance. Peter Newman and others, eds. New York: Stockton Pr., 1992. 3v.

A companion to *New Palgrave,* with about 20 percent overlap with it, although some of those entries were revised for this volume.

■ Rosenberg, Jerry M. Dictionary of business and management. 3d ed. New York: Wiley, 1993. 374p.

About 7,500 terms included, 2,500 fewer than in the last edition, but more than the competition. Brief and concise definitions. Only about 30 percent overlap with Friedman et al.'s *Dictionary of Business Terms* —so both should be obtained for complete coverage.

Law

- Black, Henry Campbell. Black's law dictionary. 7th ed. St. Paul, Minn.: West, 1999. 1738p. Also online.

    The standard U.S. law dictionary.

Medicine

- International dictionary of medicine and biology. New York: Wiley, 1986. 3v.

    Still considered *the* unabridged dictionary in the field of medicine. More than 151,000 entries, including terms from the *DSM-III* and other standard nomenclatures, people for whom terms have been named, etc. The user should be aware, however, that both a revised edition of *DSM-III* and a *DSM-IV* have appeared since this title was published.

- Stedman's medical dictionary. 26th ed. Baltimore, Md.: Williams & Wilkins, 1995. 1784p.

    Covers about 100,000 words, with twenty-four color plates, many illustrations, and biographical entries. Generally is more technical than *Dorland's Illustrated Medical Dictionary* (28th ed. Philadelphia: Saunders, 1994; 1940p.).

- The American Heritage Stedman's medical dictionary. New York: Houghton, 1995. 960p.

    Good for both general readers and health-care professionals, with about 45,000 definitions, based on the full *Stedman's,* some with illustrations. Many cross-references from common terms to the correct medical term.

- Taber's cyclopedic medical dictionary. Clayton L. Thomas, ed. 17th ed. Philadelphia: F. A. Davis, 1993. 2590p.

    Another standard, first published in 1940, mostly for the North American market. Less technical than either *Dorland's* or *Stedman's.*

Sciences

- Academic Press dictionary of science and technology. Christopher Morris, ed. San Diego, Calif.: Academic Pr., 1992. 2432p. Also on CD-ROM.

    About 133,000 definitions for nearly 130,000 terms. Includes 122 essays, one for each area of science, and gives general overview. About

2,000 illustrations and a pronunciation guide. Definitions include field of specialty, related terms, cross-references, sometimes pronunciation. Biographical entries for living and dead. Uses International System of Units (SI). No index.

■ Allaby, Michael, ed. The Oxford dictionary of natural history. Oxford and New York: Oxford Univ. Pr., 1986. 760p.

Definitions of about 14,000 terms in entries of around 100 words or less, aimed at students and amateur naturalists. Includes lots of plants and animals. Unfortunately, lacks illustration.

■ Bennett, H. Concise chemical and technical dictionary. 4th ed. New York: Chemical, 1986. 1271p.

More than 85,000 brief definitions mostly accessible to the layperson.

■ Cambridge dictionary of science and technology. New ed. Peter M. B. Walker, gen. ed. Cambridge, England, and New York: Cambridge Univ. Pr., 1990. 1008p.

Also published as the *Chambers Science and Technology Dictionary.* A well-known standard since 1940, for the layperson and professional. Includes about 45,000 entries. Definitions include reference to the specific specialty and alternative forms and trade names, with many boldface cross-references. Appendixes for chemical formulas, elements, periodic table for animal and plant kingdoms, and more.

■ Larousse dictionary of science and technology. New York: Larousse, 1995. 1236p.

A good one-volume dictionary with more than 4,900 entries. Easier to use than the larger *McGraw-Hill* title and thus more likely to be popular with the general public.

■ Lincoln, Roger J. The Cambridge illustrated dictionary of natural history. Cambridge, England, and New York: Cambridge Univ. Pr., 1987. 413p.

Less than 50 percent of the terms overlap with *The Oxford Dictionary.* Includes about 700 small but clear drawings and some maps and charts.

■ McGraw-Hill dictionary of scientific and technical terms. Sybil P. Parker, ed. 5th ed. New York: McGraw-Hill, 1993. 2088p. Includes a diskette to add terms to spell checkers.

More than 105,000 terms defined, adding more than 5,000 since the fourth edition. Includes field of specialty, acronyms, synonyms, abbreviations, and pronunciations; uses U.S. measurement system with equivalent SI metrics. Includes a biographical appendix and copious illustrations. *Wilson Library Bulletin* likes this as the choice, only replaced for a while by *Academic Press Dictionary* because it was newer and a bit bigger. This has more copious illustrations and gives pronunciations.

For two specialties within science, named effects and units of measurement, that often lead to confusion, the following are useful:

■ Ballentyne, Denis W. G., and D. R. Lovett. A dictionary of named effects and laws in chemistry, physics and mathematics. 4th ed. London and New York: Chapman & Hall, 1980. 346p.

Several thousand entries, emphasizing things known by personal name, but provides little biographical information. This edition puts nearly all units into SI units.

■ Jerrard, Harold G., and D. B. McNeill. A dictionary of scientific units: including dimensionless numbers and scales. 6th ed. London and New York: Chapman & Hall/Methuen, 1992. 255p.

About 950 units defined, with historical information added and supported by about 650 references. Appendixes include British and American weights and measures and SI units and conversions.

Social and Behavioral Sciences

■ Campbell, Robert J. Psychiatric dictionary. 7th ed. New York: Oxford Univ. Pr., 1996. 799p.

Gives encyclopedic treatment to many terms as well as shorter definitions. Based on the *DSM-III* but includes older terms if still widely used or generally more familiar.

■ Chaplin, James Patrick. Dictionary of psychology. 2d rev. (shown as 3d on cover) ed. New York: Laurel, 1985. 499p.

A standard dictionary, including related areas such as psychiatry and biology. Concise and accurate definitions.

■ Encyclopedic dictionary of psychology. Rom Harré and Roger Lamb, eds. Cambridge, Mass.: MIT Pr., 1983. 718p.

A major tool for the field. A later edition, published in four volumes, adds a minor amount of updating.

■ Gould, Julius, and William L. Kolb, eds. A dictionary of the social sciences. New York: Free Pr., 1964. 761p.

Despite the date, this remains a standard for the entire area.

■ Longman dictionary of psychology and psychiatry. Robert M. Goldenson, ed. in chief. New York: Longman, 1984. 815p.

Some 21,164 entries based on *DSM-III;* includes biographical entries. Appendixes with *DSM-III* classification scheme and other general information.

■ Miller, P. McC., and M. J. Wilson. A dictionary of social science methods. Chichester, N.Y.: Wiley, 1983. 124p.

Terms and methods in all social sciences, including many statistical terms. Full cross-references.

■ Mitchell, Geoffrey D. A new dictionary of the social sciences. Hawthorne, N.Y.: Aldine, 1979. 244p.

Another standard for general terminology.

■ Routledge dictionary of language and linguistics. New York: Routledge, 1996. 560p.

Translated and updated from the German 1990 edition. Again, a classic, but possibly too scholarly for popular collections.

■ Wolman, Benjamin B., ed. Dictionary of behavioral science. 2d ed. San Diego, Calif.: Academic Pr., 1989. 720p.

More than 20,000 terms in psychology and psychiatry, including biographical entries, but no bibliographies.

Foreign-Language Dictionaries

Monolingual dictionaries of languages other than English follow the same patterns and have the same general purposes as English-language dictionaries.

The same criteria may be applied in evaluating their adequacy. They require that the user have some familiarity with the language represented and are thus not as often consulted by beginning students as the bilingual dictionary, whose characteristics must be considered separately. Compared to general monolingual dictionaries, bilingual dictionaries

1. Have a more limited vocabulary
2. Give little or no historical information
3. Give less (or no) attention to etymologies
4. Give pronunciation and stress
5. Give parts of speech and genders
6. Give equivalents in another language
7. Indicate levels and fields of usage (e.g., slang)
8. Often give illustrative phrases
9. Often include proper names
10. Often include sections on grammar
11. Often consider the nationality of the intended user

The librarian should always remember that there are many people whose native language is not English and who may prefer consulting either the monolingual dictionary in their native language or a bilingual dictionary from that language to English.

Polyglot Dictionaries

Polyglot dictionaries, those that give equivalents in three or more languages, are most often found in scientific and technical fields and are not generally considered here, with one or two exceptions. Two examples of the general type follow:

■ NTC's multilingual dictionary of American sign language. Claude O. Proctor, ed. Lincolnwood, Ill.: National Textbook Co., 1995. 767p.

About 2,500 entries, arranged by English word, giving a small line drawing for ASL and equivalents in twelve other languages, with access by a glossary in each language.

■ Oxford three-in-one bilingual dictionary. New York: Oxford Univ. Pr., 1997. CD-ROM only.

Contains full text and images from the *Oxford-Hachette French Dictionary, Oxford-Duden German Dictionary,* and the *Oxford Spanish Dictionary.* Searchable by keyword and standard dictionary elements (e.g., idioms, usage examples).

Foreign-language dictionaries are generously represented in *Balay,* both in the section on general dictionaries and under special subjects, like chemistry and physics. Further comments or additional titles may be found in the guides by *Balay* and *Walford's,* as well as specialized guides to dictionaries listed in this source.

Guides to individual subject fields (see chapter 2, on bibliographies) are also good sources for bilingual and polyglot dictionaries in a given field.

All of these sources help determine what is available or which are more suitable for various types of libraries or users. But because new editions of established titles, as well as newly compiled dictionaries, are published with increasing frequency, current trade bibliographies should be consulted for more recent publications. For older dictionaries, the following two titles are essential.

■ Collison, Robert Lewis. Dictionaries of English and foreign languages, a bibliographical guide to both general and technical dictionaries, with historical and explanatory notes and references. 2d ed. New York: Hafner, 1971. 303p.

Although aging, still useful for the historical discussions.

■ Dictionaries, encyclopedias and other word-related books. Annie M. Brewer, ed. 4th ed. Detroit: Gale, 1988. 2v.

The most recent edition of a classic work first published in 1975. Lists about 35,000 dictionaries, glossaries, lexicons, encyclopedias, topical indexes, and other word-related books by LC classification, with a detailed subject-title index. The full Library of Congress cataloging record includes the subject tracings, thus providing a useful guide to more recent online records.

The student with a more deep and abiding interest in the subject will want to know about Margaret Cop's *Babel Unravelled: An Annotated World Bibliography of Dictionary Bibliographies, 1658–1988* (Tübingen, Germany: M. Neimeyer, 1990; 195p.).

Listed below are a few examples of general monolingual and bilingual dictionaries for languages most frequently studied and/or used in the United States. Their scope and treatment are noted briefly.

First, however, are two general sources of foreign words and phrases often found in written or spoken English.

■ The Harper dictionary of foreign terms. 3d ed., rev. Eugene Ehrlich, ed. New York: Harper & Row, 1987. 423p.

About 15,000 foreign terms in American and English literature, conversation, print, and broadcast news. Includes both current and archaic words and, unlike others of its kind, an index from English to the foreign term. Its only real deficiency is a lack of pronunciation keys.

■ Pei, Mario, and Salvatore Ramondino. Dictionary of foreign terms. New York: Delacorte, 1974. 366p.

Classical and modern terms and phrases, their pronunciation, and English equivalents, many not found in the general dictionaries.

Arabic

■ Al-Mawrid modern English-Arabic dictionary. Munir Ba'Albakki, ed. Beirut: International Book Centre, 1997. 1254p. Also on CD-ROM.

Copiously illustrated, including many color illustrations. Includes separate sections for biographies, English proverbs, and abbreviations.

■ Arabic-English dictionary of modern written Arabic. 4th ed. Hans Wehr, ed. Ithaca, N.Y.: Spoken Language Services, 1994. 1301p.

Coverage is only one way, but entries are both in transliterated and Arabic form, making it somewhat easier for an English speaker to use.

■ Awde, Nicholas, and Putros Semano. The Arabic alphabet: how to read and write it. Secaucus, N.J.: Lyle Stuart, 1986. 95p.

Because Arabic is a cursive script, letter forms vary considerably depending on position in a word; and vowels tend to be indicated by diacritics, or ignored entirely, while the root words often seem to disappear within derivations. This short book, aimed at English speakers, helps deal with these issues.

■ Modern Arabic English dictionary. 13th ed. Elias A. Elias, ed. Beirut: International Book Centre, 1991. 868p.

■ Modern English Arabic dictionary. 25th ed. Elias A. Elias, ed. Beirut: International Book Centre, 1992. 862p.

Standard complementary coverage, based primarily on Egyptian usage but includes references to all Arabic-speaking countries, with illustrations.

Chinese

■ Far East English-Chinese Chinese-English dictionary. Liang Shih-ch'iu, ed. Taipei: Far East Books, 1991. 676p.

Unlike most current Chinese-English dictionaries, this publication lists the traditional rather than the more recent, simplified characters. Includes radical, Mandarin phonetics, and Wade-Giles romanization system indexes, plus several appendixes giving useful cultural information and a verb-tense table aimed at Chinese speakers.

■ Pinyin Chinese-English dictionary. Hong Kong: Commercial Pr., 1993; distributed by Wiley. 976p.

Useful for the English speaker, the modern, simplified Chinese characters are arranged alphabetically by their phonetic transcription: the character is followed by its combinations with other characters, pinyin pronunciation, English translations, and, often, a usage example. Several useful appendixes include a table comparing Wade-Giles with pinyin, a radical index, and the original complex forms of characters.

French

■ Collins-Robert French-English, English-French dictionary, unabridged. 5th ed. Beryl T. Atkins, ed. New York: HarperCollins, 1998. 1893p. Also on CD-ROM.

Focuses on about 280,000 commonly used terms with common definitions. In addition to the definitions' emphasis, includes many usage examples and a special section on "language in use" as well as the expected French conjugation tables. The *Modern Language Review* called this "the established authority on current French and English."

■ Girard, Denis, and others. New Cassell's French dictionary: French-English, English-French. Old Tappan, N.Y.: Macmillan, 1977. 655p.

A familiar and useful desk dictionary including pronunciations.

■ Harrap's standard French and English dictionary. Margaret Ledésert and R. P. L. Ledésert. Rev. ed. London: Harrap, 1977–80. 4v.

A complete revision of the standard work. Claimed to be the largest bilingual dictionary in existence. Includes Belgian, Canadian, and other idioms. Pronunciation is given but not etymology. The English word list includes both U.S. and Commonwealth terms.

■ Larousse French-English, English-French dictionary. Fay Carney and Claude Nimmo, eds. New York: Larousse-Kingfisher-Chambers, 1994. 2064p.

A frequently reprinted standard. More than 300,000 entries for advanced students and professionals, with an emphasis on the context of terms. Most terms include usage notes and often several sample sentences. Includes both American and British English, as well as Canadian, Belgian, and Swiss, and, of course, the language as spoken in France. A particularly useful feature is the keying of all verbs to standard conjugation tables (plus a list of English irregular verbs) and labeling of colloquial and vulgar terms. Includes the usual map section but also has small maps of major cities. Also available as the *Larousse Concise French-English, English-French Dictionary*, rev. ed. (New York: Larousse-Kingfisher-Chambers, 1997; 1v.), with about 90,000 entries and with the conjugation section intact.

■ Littré, Paul-Émile. Dictionnaire de la langue français. Paris: Jean-Jacques Pauvert, 1956–58. 7v. Reprint, 1983.

Reprint of the famous four-volume 1873 to 1878 dictionary, incorporating the supplement into the main alphabet. Still important for history, grammar, and quotations with exact citations, although many of the etymologies have been corrected by more recent works.

■ NTC's dictionary of Canadian French. Sinclair Robinson and Donald Smith, eds. Lincolnwood, Ill.: NTC Contemporary, 1995. 292p.

More than 5,000 terms, classified by subject, with a master index. Includes English, Quebeçois, and French in parallel columns, with labels for slang. A helpful section on Acadian and Quebec French grammar and pronunciation concludes the work. Colloquialisms include an indication if no North American English equivalent exists.

■ The Oxford-Hachette French dictionary. 2d ed. Marie-Hélène Corréard and Valerie Grundy, eds. Oxford and New York: Oxford Univ. Pr., 1997. 1943p. Also on CD-ROM.

Another standard desk dictionary, based on collaboration between Oxford and Hachette, giving definitions for about 300,000 words based on a 10-million-word corpus. Includes samples of page images of correspondence, irregular verbs, and the like. Particularly useful for the discussion of more difficult translation question between English and French, including much attention to "false friends" (apparent cognates, like "editor/editeur," that are not equivalent—the term means *publisher* in French).

■ Robert, Paul. Dictionnaire alphabétique et analogique de la langue française. 2d ed., rev. and enl. Paris: Le Robert, 1985. 9v.

The full version on which the following is based. A historical dictionary of French, including definitions with extensive quotations.

■ Robert, Paul. Le petit Robert. Le petit Robert 1: dictionnaire alphabétique et analogique de la langue française. New ed., rev. and corr. Paris: Société du Nouveau Littré; Kinderhook, N.Y.: ibd Ltd., 1996. 2171p.

Not to be confused with the *Petit Robert 2,* which is a dictionary of names. Definitions are in historical order. This classic remains important in giving synonyms, antonyms, and variant uses. Includes type of use (e.g., "abstract noun").

German

■ Betteridge, Harold T. Cassell's German dictionary: German-English, English-German. Completely rev. ed. London: Cassell; Old Tappan, N.Y.: Macmillan, 1978. 1600p.

Many new words and terms over last edition. Includes phonetic transcriptions of headwords. Has been called "one of the most useful bilingual dictionaries."

■ Collins German-English/English-German dictionary. 3d rev. ed. Peter Terrell, Eva Vennebusch, and Robin Sawers, eds. New York: HarperCollins, 1997. 613p.

A modern offering (first edition 1980) emphasizing current ordinary spoken language, with more than 280,000 headwords and 460,000 translations. Good coverage of U.S. English and of Swiss, Austrian, and East German German. Notable for extensive and consistent use of stylistic labels (including colloquial, vulgar, offensive) for context and types of use. Useful supplement on grammar of both English and German. Plural verbs use a simple, easy-to-understand system, but only British English pronunciations are given.

■ Grimm, Jakob Ludwig Karl, and Wilhelm Grimm. Deutsches Wörterbuch. Im Auftrage des Deutschen Reiches und Preussens mit Unterstützung des

Reichministeriums des Innern, des Preussischen Ministeriums für Wissenschaft, Kunst und Volksbildung, und der Preussischen Akademie der Wissenschaften. Leipzig: Hirzel, 1854–1971. 16v. Reprint, Evanston, Ill.: Adler's Foreign Books, 1984. 33v.

> Done on historical principles by the brothers Grimm of the fairy tales. Similar to the *OED* but lacks pronunciation and obsolete words and in general is less systematic. The later volumes are better than the earlier. A new edition has been in progress since 1965.

■ Langenscheidt New Muret-Sanders encyclopedic dictionary of the English and German languages. London, New York, and Maspeth, N.Y.: Langenscheidt, 1962–75. 2 pts. in 4v.

> Also known as *Encyclopedic Dictionary of English and German.* *Muret-Sanders* was considered the standard, but this version is a wholly new dictionary. Some reviewers felt American rather than British English is emphasized versus the publisher's claim they are treated equally. Different styles and registers are labeled; pronunication is indicated by IPA. A shorter (and more affordable) version of this is the *Langenscheidt New College German Dictionary: German-English, English-German* (1991; 1421p). The full version is also available in a condensed two-volume edition.

■ Oxford-Duden German dictionary: English-German/German-English. Rev. ed. W. Scholze-Stubenrecht and J. B. Sykes, eds. Oxford and New York: Oxford Univ. Pr., 1997. 1712p. Also on CD-ROM.

> Notable as the first bilingual dictionary ever to be done by a two-language team. Based on databases maintained by Oxford University and by the Dudenredaktion of the Bibliographsiches Institut. The 260,000-plus entries emphasize regional use of English in Britain and the United States and of German in East versus West Germany, Switzerland, and Austria, with good coverage of idioms and scientific terms. This title is particularly useful for making subtle distinctions and commenting on near-synonyms where one language cannot be directly translated into the other. This is generally considered the standard single-volume German-English dictionary.

Greek

■ A Greek-English lexicon. Henry George Liddell and Robert Scott, eds. New ed., rev. and aug. throughout by Henry Stuart Jones. 9th ed. New York: Oxford Univ. Pr., 1996. 2446p.

Basically the same as the 1940 edition, with the addition of a revised supplement. The first edition appeared in 1843. Etymologies are reduced to a minimum; place-names and proper names are usually omitted as well. This dictionary stops about A.D. 600; thus, it misses Byzantine and patristic literature but remains the standard for its period.

■ Oxford dictionary of modern Greek (English-Greek). J. T. Pring, comp. Oxford: Clarendon Pr., 1995. 640p.

A standard for modern (but not classical) Greek that has gone through many editions.

Hebrew

■ Alcalay, Reuben. The complete English-Hebrew dictionary. Tel-Aviv: Masadah, 1990. 2v.

■ Alcalay, Reuben. The complete Hebrew-English dictionary. Tel-Aviv: Masadah, 1990. 2v.

Covers both classical and current terminology.

■ Ben-Yehudah, Eliezer. Complete dictionary of ancient and modern Hebrew. Berlin-Schöneberg: Langenscheidt; Jerusalem: Ben-Yehudah Hozaala'Or, 1908-59. 16v.

This remains the standard for older material.

■ Webster's new world Hebrew dictionary. New York: Prentice-Hall, 1992. 827p.

Definitely aimed at the English speaker, with Hebrew arranged in Roman alphabet order and the Hebrew word preceded by the English transliteration.

Italian

■ Grande dizionario della lingua italiana. Salvatore Battaglia, ed. in chief. Turin: Unione Tipografico–Editrice Torinese, 1961-96. 18v. (in progress).

A scholarly dictionary on historical principles. Gives full definitions and examples of meaning and use in chronological order, with numerous quotations and full etymologies. Numerous citations to sources in a separate volume. Volume 1 through 16 are *A* through *Roba*. Will replace

Nicolò Tommaseo and Bernardo Bellini, *Dizionario della lingua italiana* (Turin: Unione Tipografico–Editrice Torinese, 1861–79; 4v. in 8).

■ Il nuovo dizionario Hazon Garzanti. Milan: Garzanti, 1990. 2429p.

A new edition of the *Garzanti Comprehensive Italian-English, English-Italian Dictionary* (1963). Includes proper names and technical and colloquial terms, but it is aimed at Italian users; thus, phonetic pronunciation is given only for English words. Many reviewers feel this is *the* current dictionary to use.

■ Reynolds, Barbara. The Cambridge Italian dictionary. Cambridge, England: Cambridge Univ. Pr., 1962–81. 2v.

Very inclusive, including many obsolete and archaic words. Although it is both Italian-English and English-Italian, the emphasis is on the speaker of British English.

Japanese

Written Japanese consists of Chinese characters *(kanji)* and a simplified phonetic script consisting of *hiragana* (cursive) and *katagana,* used for non-Chinese loanwords and some special cases.

■ Kodansha's romanized Japanese-English dictionary. Timothy J. Vance, ed. New York: Kodansha America, 1993. 666p. '

A completely rewritten version of the *New World Japanese-English Dictionary* (Kodansha America, 1990). Has about 16,000 entries with sample sentences in Japanese, romanized Japanese, and English translation. Appendixes on particles and other grammar issues. Includes labels for colloquial, honorific, and the like; thus, is generally one of the more prescriptive dictionaries.

■ Merriam-Webster's Japanese-English learner's dictionary. Springfield, Mass.: Merriam-Webster, 1995. 1121p.

Aimed at students at all levels. Each Japanese entry includes roman transliteration (modified Hepburn system of romanization, which is the currently preferred system), then hiragana or katagana, then kanji, followed by the English equivalent. Modern sentences or phrases are given in nearly all cases in romanized Japanese, then normal Japanese, then in English. Many entries have special-usage boxes, which give details on variations in use of idiomatic and similar terms. The introduction to Japanese pronunciation and the outline of grammar are also particularly helpful for the beginner.

■ NTC's new Japanese-English character dictionary. Jack Halpern, ed. Lincolnwood, Ill.: National Textbook Co., 1993. 1992p.

A dictionary of more than 4,400 kanji, for a total of 42,000 words. Two distinctive features of this title are the giving of a central/core meaning for the dominant meaning of each kanji and the use of SKIP (system of kanji indexing by pattern). Each entry has a core meaning, number, and order of strokes, including compounds, homophones, etc., where needed. The 200-page introduction is a good basic introduction to the Japanese language. SKIP is very useful for those who lack previous knowledge of kanji elements.

■ Random House Japanese-English English-Japanese dictionary. New York: Random House, 1995. 600p.

A two-part, handy reference for those with a limited vocabulary in either language. The Japanese-English section is in romanized form, giving part of speech, hiragana, katagana, and/or kanji, plus English. English-Japanese gives part of speech, romanization, and Japanese in hiragana, katagana, and kanji.

Latin

■ Andrews, Ethan Allen. Harper's Latin dictionary: a new Latin dictionary founded on the translation of Freund's Latin-German lexicon. Rev., enl., and in great part rewritten by Charlton T. Lewis and Charles Short. New York: American Book Co., 1907. 2019p.

Frequently reprinted as *A Latin Dictionary* (Oxford: Oxford Univ. Pr., 1956; pagination varies). Often called "Lewis and Short." *Balay* calls it "the most generally useful of the older Latin-English dictionaries."

■ Cassell's Latin dictionary: Latin-English, English-Latin. 6th ed. London: Cassell; New York: Macmillan, 1977. 912p.

Also known as *Cassell's New Latin Dictionary.* A reliable desk dictionary for school and general use, often considered one of the standards. This work is also the source of a more popular title, *Latin for the Illiterati,* edited by Jon R. Stone (New York: Routledge, 1996; 201p.), which provides access to words and terms most often found in modern life.

- Oxford Latin dictionary. P. G. W. Glare, ed. New York: Oxford Univ. Pr., 1983. 2130p.

   The standard reference for classical Latin, up to end of the second century C.E. Includes both literary and nonliterary words, with illustrative quotations in chronological order.

Russian

- English-Russian, Russian-English dictionary. Kenneth Katzner, ed. 2d ed. New York: Wiley, 1994. 1184p.

   The first full-sized bilingual Russian and English dictionary to be compiled in the United States, but includes both American and British English. Includes labels for English words with more than one meaning, showing which is being translated into Russian. Has been called (by *ARBA*) the "only reasonably comprehensive dictionary specifically designed for U.S. students of Russian." Has about 40,000 Russian entries and about 26,000 in English. Excludes slang, obscenities, and acronyms (latter common in Russian text). Appendix listing of family and geographical names.

- Galperina, I. R., and E. M. Mednikova. New English-Russian dictionary. Bol'shoi anglo-russkii slovar'. 4th ed. New York: State Mutual Book and Periodical Service, 1988. 4v.

   Currently the largest English-Russian dictionary available. Has about 150,000 entry words. Emphasizes current vocabulary, with many scientific and technical terms and idioms. Aimed at Russian speakers, with preface and introduction in Russian and English. The stress is marked for Russian words.

- Howlett, Colin, ed. The Oxford Russian dictionary: English-Russian edited by Paul Falla; Russian-English edited by Marcus Wheeler and Boris Unbegaun. Rev. and updated. New York: Oxford Univ. Pr., 1998. 1340p.

   Amalgamates the *Oxford Russian-English Dictionary* by Wheeler and the *Oxford English-Russian Dictionary* by Falla into one title. One of the most current and comprehensive available, with about 180,000 words. The focus is on British English, but American usage and Russian dialects are included. The *Concise Oxford Russian Dictionary* (Oxford and New York: Oxford Univ. Pr., 1996; 1007p.) is based on this title.

■ Müller, Vladimir Karlovich, comp. English-Russian dictionary. 20th ed. French & European Pubs., 1992. 864p.

Probably the most commonly used desk dictionary for beginning users of Russian, with about 70,000 entries.

Spanish

■ Academia Real Española. Diccionario de la lengua español. 21st ed. New York: French & European Pubs., 1995. 2v.

Useful, authoritative, and basic; the unabridged version is *the* monolingual dictionary for the Spanish language.

■ Collins Spanish-English, English-Spanish dictionary: unabridged. Colin Smith and others, eds. 4th ed. New York: HarperCollins, 1996. 1688p.

About 230,000 entries, and about twice as many definitions. Includes adequate definitions, including notes for slang and regional usages. Covers both British (including variants such as Scottish) and American English, Spanish and Latin American Spanish—all clearly marked. Both *ll* and *ch* are interfiled, but *ñ* is still considered a separate letter. In addition to the inclusion of many idioms within entries, an entire section, "Language in Use," provides a classified listing of commonly used terms, such as those for agreeing and disagreeing, making suggestions, using the telephone, and the like—in separate Spanish and English sections. All verbs include a reference to the conjugation tables in the appendix.

■ Harrap's concise Spanish and English dictionary. London: Harrap; New York: Prentice-Hall, 1992. 526, 557p.

Uses the new alphabetizing, where *ll* and *ch* aren't considered separate letters. Contains 115,000 entries. No American English. South American and Central American Spanish are well treated, including idioms.

■ Larousse Spanish-English/English-Spanish dictionary. Gran diccionario Español-Inglese/Inglese-Español. New York: Larousse-Kingfisher-Chambers, 1993. 804p.

Unabridged edition with more than 220,000 entries covering both American and British English, and American and European Spanish, with a good selection of current technical, scientific, and medical terms. Includes a map section. Arranged in the traditional alphabetization (*ch*, *ll*, and *ñ* are treated as separate letters). Noted for its treatment of grammar and usage, as well as references to conjugation charts for verbs. Colloquial and vulgar terms are included and labeled.

■ New revised Velázquez Spanish and English dictionary. New rev. ed. Mariano Velasquez de la Cadena, Edward Gray, and Juan L. Iribas. Rev. by Ida Navarro Hinojosa, Manuel Blanco-González, and R. J. Nelson. Piscataway, N.J.: New Century, 1985. 788p.

A new version of *A New Pronouncing Dictionary of the Spanish and English Languages,* 1973, with a history going back to 1852. This edition includes a 1985 supplement to the Spanish part with new words from both Latin America and Spain and particular emphasis on business, science, and technology.

■ Oliveres, Raphael A. NTC's dictionary of Latin American Spanish. Lincolnwod, Ill.: National Textbook Co., 1997. 375p.

Specialized to only about 6,000 words specific to one or more Latin American countries, with definitions given in both Spanish and English. Access by the usual Spanish and English terms but also by country of origin and an index of words borrowed from English. Obviously, this must be used with a more inclusive dictionary, but it is particularly useful for understanding idioms and avoiding verbal faux pas.

■ Oxford Spanish dictionary. New international ed. 2d ed. New York: Oxford Univ. Pr., 1999. 1829p. Also on CD-ROM.

Good overall coverage, with about 225,000 words, and notably better on Latin American terms than most of its competitors. Includes both British and American English and Castilian and Latin American Spanish, with clearer explanations of words and more emphasis on current technical, scientific, and political vocabulary than most.

■ Steiner, Roger, ed. in chief. Simon and Schuster's international dictionary: English/Spanish, Spanish/English. 2d ed. New York: Macmillan, 1997. 1597p.

One of the larger general bilingual dictionaries. Distinguishes between uses in different South American nations; U.S. versus British pronunciation (using IPA) and usage. Includes many proper and place-names.

■ University of Chicago Spanish dictionary. 4th ed. Chicago: Univ. of Chicago Pr., 1987. 484p.

Particularly useful for words used in the Americas and for regionalisms across the world. Especially noted for its coverage of business and related terminology. In addition to usage notes, provides synonyms and clarifying notes in parentheses plus a list of common idioms and proverbs in different dialects. Also available in a large-print edition from the American Printing House for the Blind.

Summary

Libraries have a responsibility to provide a well-selected range of dictionaries for their users, and librarians must provide information instruction, based on thorough knowledge of a dictionary's purpose, for (as Confucius said long ago) "When words lose their meaning, people lose their liberty."

This chapter has tried to explain how and why dictionaries are made; the differences between unabridged and abridged dictionaries; school dictionaries; dictionaries concerned with etymologies, usage, synonyms and antonyms, pronunciation, slang and dialect, or abbreviations; visual dictionaries; dictionaries restricted to special fields; and monolingual and bilingual foreign dictionaries—with brief descriptions of some in current use.

7

Encyclopedias

How does one begin to discuss those monumental syntheses of knowledge, encyclopedias, so often maligned? Perhaps these attempts of humanity through the ages to bring order to the circle of knowledge should be approached first as reflections of the eras in which they were compiled—an important fact to remember in viewing their assets and limitations.

The era in which they were produced reflects not only the state of knowledge at the time, but also their underlying purposes. As Warren E. Preece, editor of the most recent edition of the *Encyclopaedia Britannica,* has observed, "Encyclopedias may be undertaken, as in classical Greece, to 'make a man whole,' as in Medieval Europe, to 'make a man Christian,' as in 18th-century France, to 'make a man free'" ("The Organization of Knowledge and the Planning of Encyclopedias," *Journal of World History* 9, no. 3 [1966]: 798–818). Challenging Raymond Queneau's statement that encyclopedias are products of culminating civilizations, he suggests that "encyclopedias have enjoyed their greatest successes, have seemed to attain their greatest vitality, in those periods of history of which it might be said—at least in retrospect—that the world was held in an uneasy balance between the death of one age and the birth of another. It is possible to conjecture that it is in the midst of the tensions created by the imminent decline of one intellectual tradition and the imminent evolution of another that the function of the encyclopaedist and the support accorded him have assumed their greatest proportions." And Preece cites examples to prove his point.

Others, in reviewing the history of encyclopedias, have noted the spirit of the age, as in the eighteenth century, the classic age of encyclopedias, when Diderot's great French *Encyclopédie* was said to incorporate the basic philosophy of French rationalism, as has been documented in Robert Darnton's *The Business of Enlightenment: A Published History of the Encyclopédie, 1775-1800* (Cambridge, Mass.: Belknap Pr. of Harvard Univ., 1979; 624p.). In the twentieth century, nationalism, sectarianism, political trends, and new educational theory have been important factors in the production of hundreds of encyclopedias.

Certainly, the growth of public education has affected the making of encyclopedias, and the earlier compilations of information intended for the intellectual elite were gradually replaced by those addressed to the general reader, as in the nineteenth century, when Brockhaus chose *Conversations-Lexikon: oder encyclopädisches handwörterbuch für gebildete Stände* (Altenburg, Germany: F. A. Brockhaus, 1814-19; 10v.) as the title for his simply written, popular encyclopedia to intimate to his readers, largely members of the middle class, that his work contained the polite learning that could provide the means of acceptance into good society.

More recently, the expansion of public education has stimulated the publication of encyclopedias for children and young people whose contents and style of writing are directed to this particular audience.

Most important has been the growth of knowledge, as well as its accessibility. Preece has emphasized the necessity that the encyclopedist have access to this body of extant knowledge:

> It must be pointed out that in practical terms this today is equivalent to saying that he must have access to the scholar, the author, the specialist whose particular work it is, and has been, to husband knowledge. . . . When the encyclopaedist talks today of access to the body of knowledge, he means, therefore, the world of those whose business knowledge is [p. 803].

The encyclopedist must view this body of knowledge with a clear sense of purpose. Much has been written on the purpose of encyclopedias, some of it repetitious and some representing conflicting points of view. Many will agree with Preece, who has attributed the existence of encyclopedias to a desire to bring order to existing knowledge (p. 799), and, later, to "the task of helping all who turn to it to better understand the world in which they live" ("Notes toward a New Encyclopaedia," in *Reference and Information Services: A New Reader,* edited by William A. Katz and Ann Clifford [Metuchen, N.J.: Scarecrow, 1982], p. 380). Among other writers of this century we find Charles Van Doren endorsing the opinion of Lucien Febvre, editor of the *Encyclopédie Française,* that the primary aim should be to teach, and only secondarily to inform ("The Idea of an Encyclopedia," *The American Behavioral Scientist* 6 [Sept. 1962]: 23). On the other hand, Jacques Barzun, in the same journal, views an encyclopedia as first and foremost a work of reference, used only indirectly for understanding ("Notes on Making a World Encyclopedia," p. 7-14). Harry Ashmore, writing as editor in chief of the *Encyclopaedia Britannica* in the same issue, describes the encyclopedia

> as a continuing link between the academic and lay worlds, a work of faculty reference, certainly, but also a major instrument of popular education. . . . It will not, of course, repeat all the expert knows, or needs to know. An encyclopedia is not, and should not be, a textbook—a fact which seems to elude the single-minded who fault the work for its failure to include esoteric matter of their specialized interest ["Editing the Universal Encyclopedia," p. 15-18].

These are all men of the twentieth century, who must inevitably view the encyclopedia in terms of that century. Whether they face a more difficult task than their predecessors cannot be stated with certainty, but the increasing proliferation, complexity, and (many would say) fragmentation of knowledge, together with the responsibility of bringing it into some order and awareness of the changing audience for whom it is intended, present problems. Will it be possible for them to produce a set of volumes (in whatever format) that will meet the needs of the scholar as well as the ever more vaguely defined general reader? Certainly, scholars have become ever more specialized in their scholarly interests, but are they not also people with intellectual curiosity about subjects outside their specialties? And, if this be true, do they not share this in common with the general reader? Alas, this does not seem to be the case, for their realization of the complexity of knowledge makes scholars suspicious of syntheses, contemptuous of generalizations, and often narrowly snobbish about the encyclopedia as a form. Yet editors of encyclopedias are increasingly dependent on scholars as contributors, though often hard put to translate their articles into a language that is comprehensible to the general reader.

Warren Preece believed that the fifteenth edition of the *Encyclopaedia Britannica* answered, at least in part, the needs of the times. In "The New Britannica" (*Scholarly Publishing* 5 [Jan. 1974]: 99-110), he described the planning and the efforts that went into the edition:

> It is reasonable and probably not too flippant to submit that by the twentieth century general encyclopedias had become almost neurotic in their ambivalence. Although their limited size and scale and necessarily broad scope made them unsuitable sources of knowledge for the specialist in his own field, they were written by specialists on the basis of advice provided by specialists, and edited by persons who had begun to acquire editorial skills only after they had first become specialists [p. 101].

Revision of contents is a very sensitive point with editors, for encyclopedias may be revised in a number of different ways:

> *In arrangement.* For example, the *Book of Knowledge* changed in 1966 from topical to alphabetical arrangement.

> *By continuous revision.* This approach is generally favored by American publishers, who develop various kinds of programs (e.g., *Americana*), with revision of areas requiring "urgent" attention and revision volume by volume, with all articles in the volume being reviewed, with some dropped, others added, and others updated or rewritten. *Compton's Encyclopedia* has a program that involves updating population statistics, noting deaths, and revising certain areas, rather than single volumes. Both approaches involve adding new illustrations and dropping old ones when necessary (or when seen as desirable to maintain an up-to-date appearance).

> *By new editions.* This includes the fifteenth *Britannica* and most of the one-volume encyclopedias, such as the *New Columbia Encyclopedia.*

These revisions require editorial decisions. Also, in their efforts to keep the size within bounds, editors must determine the amount of space devoted to various subject fields and to illustrations, bibliographies, and indexes. They must deal with how the contents should be arranged and how to avoid bias. With the increasing use of electronic formats, they must determine the type and variety of access points and either purchase an existing search engine or arrange for the development of a new one. And these are not all the problems to be faced.

Who would undertake this task alone? No one, of course. Thus, the modern encyclopedia has become the product of many people. What are their qualifications? What specific problems do they face? It seems appropriate to outline these points in the making of a good encyclopedia. (For guidelines in reviewing general English-language encyclopedias, see the appendix.)

The Making of Encyclopedias

I. Staff

    A. The editor, his qualities and capacities. According to Otto Whitelock ("On the Making and Survival of Encyclopedias," *Choice* 4 [June 1967]: 381–89), the requirements are

        1. A universal mind, in the sense that the editor is not wedded to a single discipline to the exclusion of all others, able to grasp the

significance of new developments and integrate them into existing material

2. Thorough familiarity with the encyclopedia for whose balance and progress he is responsible

3. Faith in his or her capacities and willingness to enlist the assistance of men and women of equal caliber, without fear of being overshadowed by those more expert in a given field

4. Ability to serve as a competent catalyst.

More practical considerations are mentioned by Robert Collison in *Encyclopaedias: Their History throughout the Ages* (2d ed. New York: Hafner, 1966; p. 13-14). The editor

1. has a strict publication schedule to observe;

2. must keep an eye on his rivals' efforts;

3. must watch the encyclopedia's own staff and outside contributors to ensure that wittingly or unwittingly they do not plagiarize material already published elsewhere;

4. must cooperate with editors' offices in other countries, and with the demands of the sales force who know that scholarship must be tempered with popularity and a due regard for current interests however ephemeral, if the sets of the encyclopedia are not to lie unused on warehouse shelves [Ashmore would not agree with the latter, having "never heard of any of my editorial contemporaries on major encyclopedias complain of pressures toward corruption of editorial content in the name of sales promotion," p. 16);

5. must keep up-to-date with modern scholarship, with political trends and controversies, and with the new topics and names that spring into fame overnight;

6. must be unprejudiced him- or herself and must be cognizant of prejudices in others, and temper the contributors' opinions to safeguard the readers' susceptibilities; and

7. must do all this without lowering standards.

B. Board of editors

1. Selected for their breadth of interests and concern for the organization of knowledge

2. Responsible for suggesting long-range improvements

3. Responsible for advising editors on broad problems, just as the editorial board of a good dictionary functions

Wallace S. Murray also describes some concerns of conscientious editors in "Editorial Policies and Procedures of Grolier Incorporated" (*Booklist* 73 [Sept. 15, 1976]: 207-8).

C. Consultants and contributors

1. Selected for their thorough knowledge of the subject fields for which they are responsible—not necessarily "big names" to be used in advertising the encyclopedia.

2. "The scholar as writer demands the right to be precise and he is aware that technical precision may involve the necessity of using the vocabulary of his own field of authority. He is likely to want the justifiable right to express his own position on matters in which his professional competence entitles his position to serious consideration. He is likely to be suspicious of persons who handle his contribution but who do not share his own eminence in his field, he may regard as 'dangerous oversimplification' any effort to express ideas in languages more likely to be understood by those who are not his peers, and, as his correspondence frequently indicates, he has quite often a proprietary feeling toward the encyclopedia which for nearly 200 years has enjoyed a reputation as being the repository of statements by world-famous scholars of their times" (Preece, p. 815).

3. "Scholarly advisers are still, apparently, glad to be associated with the project and invitations to contributors are still accepted far more often than they are rejected. . . . Editorial suggestions are for the most part accepted when reasons for them are made clear" (Preece, p. 816).

However, Preece gives several amusing examples of the tension between the scholarly writer and the needs of the general encyclopedist in "Notes toward a New Encyclopaedia," in *Reference and Information Services* (p. 370–406).

D. Central editorial staff

1. Researchers and reference librarians who check facts and figures
2. Those who check on the readability of articles
3. Indexers
4. Copy editors and proofreaders
5. Layout artists and photograph editors
6. Systems analysts and programmers, for electronic versions

The making of an encyclopedia is presented in the *Random House Encyclopedia* (3d ed. New York: Random House, 1990; 2911p.), where color photographs illustrate the steps, from an author in the publisher's office to the final proof.

II. Scope

General characteristics, which also reveal the use that may be made of the encyclopedia's contents, are best approached by broad subject field, as noted below:

A. *Science and technology.* Reputable publishers go to great lengths in selecting qualified scientists as consultants and contributors, recognizing the ever expanding body of scientific knowledge as well as the high esteem in which it is held. But rapid advances in this broad area make it impossible for general encyclopedias to monitor and report all the changes; they must often be augmented and updated by special encyclopedias, such as the *McGraw-Hill Encyclopedia of Science and Technology* and its yearbooks and by articles located through specialized abstracting and indexing services. However, they are useful for broad overviews. General encyclopedias are also useful for biographies of important scientists, especially those no longer living, although these are often more fully covered in the *Dictionary of Scientific Biography* and similar sources. Encyclopedias designed for family use generally contain how-to information and career opportunities in science and technology. The family-oriented encyclopedias are also likely to have considerable "popular science" and technological information on such things as repair of appliances, home maintenance, and the like.

Young people's encyclopedias with good coverage of scientific subjects are *World Book* and *The New Book of Knowledge.* Written in a simple, readable style and copiously illustrated, they are often preferred by adults as well, especially those with a limited knowledge of science and its vocabulary.

Science and technology are more fully treated in adult encyclopedias, especially *Encyclopedia Americana, New Encyclopaedia Britannica,* and *New Columbia Encyclopedia.* Some articles, especially in the first two cited, may not be fully comprehensible to those with little background in the field. *Random House Encyclopedia* is distinguished for the well-captioned illustrations that accompany its scientific articles.

All major encyclopedia publishers, conscious of this highly sensitive area, attempt to update topics through continuous revision and special articles on timely subjects in their yearbooks.

B. *History.* In the broadest sense of the term, encyclopedias are all history, especially in the sense of a record of events, including histories of countries, subjects, and biographies of historically important persons. They may be consulted with a fair degree of confidence by those seeking condensed accounts of kingdoms and battles long ago. But can they be expected to include the latest interpretations of historical periods? Because of the historical research constantly being carried out, changing interests and point of view, and occasionally new discoveries, it is often necessary to consult fuller and more recent sources. For example, Kenneth Kister (*Kister's Best Encyclopedias: A Comparative Guide to General and Specialized Encyclopedias,* 2d ed. (Phoenix, Ariz.: Oryx, 1994; 506p.) found few general encyclopedias had updated their articles on Galileo to reflect the fact that his condemnation by the Catholic Church had been lifted.

To check an encyclopedia's coverage of recent history, look at articles on various countries to determine whether current political and economic conditions have been adequately reported. Or, as did Kister, one may take an item of recent general interest and see if it has been integrated into the historical articles.

C. *Geography.* Geographical information has been included since the beginning of encyclopedias, and early ones are interesting reflections of what was known of the world at that time. The increased amount of information on geographic areas is strikingly illustrated by comparing the article on Florida in the first edition of *Britannica* with the one in the most recent edition.

Certain generalizations applicable to encyclopedias at the beginning of the twenty-first century follow:

1. Treatment of individual countries, states, and cities varies greatly according to the nationality of an encyclopedia. Compared with others, American encyclopedias, for example, generally have more entries for American cities and towns and longer articles on individual states (the *Americana* is an outstanding example). Articles on states and provinces vary in emphasis. For example, articles written by American historians are apt to give fuller attention to the history of states. Increasingly, a "state article" is written by more than one contributor, as in *World Book,* in which historians, journalists, and professors of geography or geology are jointly responsible. *Compton's* also contains long, well-illustrated articles on countries and states.

2. In spite of the emphasis on an encyclopedia's country of origin, American and British editors are sensitive to the current interest in newer nations and tend to treat them more fully than in the

past. They give more attention to recent developments in older countries, although, in both cases, yearbooks, current-events sources (like *Facts on File*), and periodical indexes must be used for the most recent events and current statistics. The rise of new nations makes it difficult for general encyclopedias to incorporate current information in sufficient depth. In such cases, other reference sources, such as George T. Kiran's *Encyclopedia of the Third World* (4th ed. New York: Facts on File, 1992; 3v.) should be consulted, as well as regional and national encyclopedias.

3. Maps are an important feature, and most encyclopedia publishers employ cartographers and map publishers who supply maps that accompany the articles, as in *Random House* and *Colliers,* with maps by Rand McNally. Among foreign encyclopedias, *Enciclopedia Universal Ilustrada Europeo-Americana* (usually cited just as *Espasa,* after its publisher) is noted for its many geological, geographical, and historical maps, including some for cities and towns; maps in the *Grand Larousse Universel* are distinguished for their quality. But encyclopedias should be augmented by world atlases, which have more maps on a larger scale and give more detail (these are discussed in chapter 8).

4. The extent of other illustrative material varies widely and is greatest in encyclopedias for young people, although color illustrations are generally increasing in all printed matter. Complaints that illustrations of a foreign country do not always give an accurate picture of life in that country have made editors more sensitive in selection of photographs for other than their "colorful" and "quaint" qualities. Also, the increasing use of illustrations, especially in color, has resulted in many more photographs of countries and the people who live in them, as in *Random House* and the *New Britannica.*

D. *Political science and economics.* Again, the "national origin" of an encyclopedia affects the treatment of politics and economics. Americans are usually more sensitive to national biases in foreign encyclopedias than to those published in the United States, thus missing the fact that they also have biases. For example, Patricia Kennedy Grimstead, in her thorough analysis of the *Great Soviet Encyclopedia* (in English), refers to the omission of disgraced personalities and the "frequent substitution of propagandistic overtones for precise statistics and comprehensive factual background" ("Détente on the Reference Shelves," *Wilson Library Bulletin* 49 [June 1975]: 728–40).

However, most encyclopedias strive for more objectivity in reporting on political and economics topics, and they usually succeed. *Encyclopedia Americana* has been noted for its objectivity and up-to-date coverage of important political changes and election data. *Colliers* and *Compton's* give more emphasis to American political figures and events, and less to the international scene, bearing in mind their American audience. *New Columbia Encyclopedia* has a good representation of American political figures and, to a lesser extent, others throughout the world, both living and dead.

Compton's has been accused of a subtle political bias, mostly corrected in recent years; and the *New Encyclopaedia Britannica,* in spite of its stated aim to avoid expressions of bias or prejudice, has been accused of missing this aim, from a claimed pro-Soviet bias to a demonstrated animal-rights bias. The latter, by the way, was "corrected" by apparent removal of any comments on the moral issue of animal experimentation in the article on "Dogs" ("Dogma," *Washington Post* [Feb. 1, 1992]: A22, quoted in Richard E. Bopp and Linda C. Smith, *Reference and Information Services: An Introduction,* 2d ed. [Englewood, Colo.: Libraries Unlimited, 1995], p. 442).

William A. Katz, in *Introduction to Reference Work* (7th ed; vol. 1, New York: McGraw-Hill, 1997; p. 204-5), recognizes the problem of presenting issues and ideas in his discussion of viewpoint and objectivity, especially in the context of the profit motive, which tends to try to attract the widest audience. He gives examples of solving the problem by adopting a chronological historical approach, attempting to ignore the issue in whole or part, or making an effort to balance an article by presenting all sides.

Bearing this in mind, we may consult encyclopedias for

1. Political and economic theories, although these are more fully covered in more specialized encyclopedias
2. Political and economic history, often treated in articles on individual countries
3. Political and economic conditions in individual countries, usually treated in articles about those countries. This information may be updated by yearbooks but even more so by current-events sources, such as *Facts on File World News Digest* (New York: Facts on File, 1940– ; weekly); *Keesing's Record of World Events* (London: Longman, 1931– ; monthly); and *EXEGY: The Source for Current World Information* (Santa Barbara, Calif.: ABC-Clio, 1994– ; bimonthly), and by current statistical sources and such specialized sources as *CIA World Factbook* (Washington, D.C.: Central Intelligence Agency, 1981– ; annual)

4. Biographies of important political figures, living and dead. These are usually well covered, at least for those who were prominent in the thinking of the nation of the encyclopedia's origin

E. *Education.* Much that has been noted in political science and economics also applies to coverage of education. The same kinds of education information will be found, though more fully treated, in more specialized sources, such as the *Encyclopedia of Education* (New York: Macmillan/Free Pr., 1971; 10v.).

1. Educational theories and methods
2. History of education
3. Educational conditions in individual countries (usually treated in articles on those countries)
4. Biographies of famous educators
5. Accounts of the larger or more famous universities and colleges, sometimes with photographs of the campus or notable buildings

F. *Biography.* The use of encyclopedias in biographical reference has been noted in chapter 5, pages 210 to 211; however, it is well to remember that if the nationality of a biographee is known, an encyclopedia published in that country is most likely to contain an evaluative account of his or her life. (For example, Spaniards and Hispanic Americans are well covered in *Espasa.*) Also, it is often surprising to note the varying selection of biographees, even comparing encyclopedias that are similar in scope and purpose. Because this is often the case, consult several encyclopedias when searching for biographical information.

Reflecting the times, encyclopedias tend to include more persons from the sports and entertainment fields than formerly, as well as more living persons, although this can give them qualms. As W. D. Halsey said, some time ago, "Surely if one can see fame in a person who has died, one should be able to recognize it in one who is still alive. The passage of years has taught me that it isn't this easy. Reference books do not confer immortality, and the price we pay for entering what no one wants or needs is very predictably the elimination of information that is both wanted and needed. And the line between simple notoriety and lasting fame may not be as clear about a particular individual at any given moment as one might wish" ("Remarks on the Maintenance and Continuing Revision of General-Purpose Encyclopedias and Dictionaries," *Booklist* 73 [Sept. 15, 1976]: 209–10).

Other generalizations follow:

1. Appended bibliographies often include the best full-length biographies of persons and, in the case of writers, the definitive editions of their works.

2. Encyclopedias usually give fuller treatment to biographies of important persons than do one-volume universal biographical dictionaries, such as *Webster's Biographical Dictionary.*

3. Well-indexed encyclopedias include references to persons in other articles that often augment information supplied in the biographical account. Some also index persons under vocation and name of country.

4. Family (or "home") encyclopedias often append lists of important persons in the articles on individual states.

5. Young people's encyclopedias often contain interesting illustrations for a biographee, in addition to more conventional portraits, which often accompany the biographical sketches in adult encyclopedias.

6. Yearbooks often contain obituaries and sketches on persons recently prominent.

G. *Philosophy.* It is to the Greek philosophers that we owe the foundations of the classifications of knowledge used in encyclopedias. Now, in an age where there is usually a great gulf between the concerns of academic philosophers (who tend to consider the average person philosophically illiterate) and the layperson's "philosophy of life," the importance of the general encyclopedia as a source of philosophic thought must be considered. This is particularly true for the users of school and public libraries, especially because these libraries usually have otherwise weak collections in the subject.

Though no adequate substitute for the *Encyclopedia of Philosophy* (New York: Macmillan/Free Pr., 1967; 8v.; *Supplement,* New York: Simon & Schuster, 1996; 775p.), a general encyclopedia has certain advantages. For example, encyclopedias for young people contain simple explanations of philosophical concepts that may be easily understood by persons without formal philosophical training. More difficult to comprehend, adult encyclopedias attempt to cover the field in an orderly fashion, though not always reflecting the currently most active schools of thought.

A good analysis of the treatment of philosophy in older general encyclopedias, together with names of outstanding philosophers, is included in the *Encyclopedia of Philosophy* (1967, v.6, p. 170–74). This article (by William Gerber) covers both English-language philosophers and those from other languages and, although somewhat dated, provides a kind of synthesis that is extremely useful to reference librarians.

Philosophy, as a discipline, may not receive the same emphasis or continuous or frequent revision as that given to science in contemporary encyclopedias. Even so, we may consult them profitably for

1. General articles on philosophy, covering history and methodology, with attention to contributions of major philosophers and schools of thought
2. Articles on various disciplines of philosophy (e.g., metaphysics)
3. Biographies of philosophers
4. Analyses of philosophical treatises in summary form
5. Important conferences and recent important books, sometimes found in yearbooks

More extensive articles, with long (if now somewhat outdated) bibliographies, on ideas that have shaped philosophic thought, may be found in *Dictionary of the History of Ideas,* edited by Philip P. Wiener (New York: Scribner, 1973–74; 5v.).

H. *Religion.* Again, we may reflect that religion has been important in the history of encyclopedias, as in medieval Europe when, as noted above, on page 333, they were intended to "make man Christian."

Louis Shores, discussing objectivity in an encyclopedia in a 1960 address to Drexel Institute (now Drexel University, in Philadelphia), said that "at least two American encyclopedias have no biography of Jesus because they have despaired of reconciling the faiths involved. . . . What the encyclopedist knows he must do is submit every article in religion to his 'faiths' advisers" (*Reference as the Promotion of Free Inquiry* [Littleton, Colo.: Libraries Unlimited, 1976], p. 182–83). Of course, editors of encyclopedias seek the counsel of qualified advisers in their efforts to provide impartial treatment of religious subjects.

Today, in the "age of ecumenism," we may expect a more balanced coverage of the world's great religions, especially of the non-Western ones. Thus, a general encyclopedia may be consulted for

1. Articles on the nature and history of religions
2. Biographies of saints, prophets, characters in scriptures (especially the Bible), and religious thinkers, past and present
3. Predominant religions in various countries, usually in the articles on those countries
4. Synopses of the sacred writings of various religions
5. Current concerns, in yearbooks

As might be expected, some of these topics are more fully treated in special reference works in the field, such as Bible dictionaries or denominational encyclopedias. For example, the *New Catholic Encyclopedia* (New York: McGraw-Hill, 1967–89; 15v., 3v. supplement) devotes a great deal of space to biographies of Catholic saints, to accounts of the state of Catholicism in all parts of the world, and to reinterpretations of controversial figures, such as Martin Luther. In addition, its articles on labor, education, agriculture, and marriage (to name only a few) reflect more or less contemporary establishment Roman Catholic theology as of the late 1960s (although the three supplements—volumes 16 to 18—do reflect the most important changes). Also noteworthy, in spite of its shortcomings, is the *Encyclopaedia Judaica.* Its biographies of those who have contributed to nearly 6,000 years of Jewish history augment those in general encyclopedias. The *New Catholic Encyclopedia* issues supplements from time to time; the *Encyclopaedia Judaica Yearbook* (biennial, by the way) contains new and updated articles on subjects covered in the basic set, feature articles on current topics, and a regular feature on Christian-Jewish relations.

These two works are also excellent sources for information on medieval through early modern European history in general and for biographies of important thinkers in the same period. (It is probably an exaggeration to say that every major thinker of the time was either Jewish, Catholic, or condemned by the Roman Catholic Church, but that statement is not far from the mark—and the two encyclopedias cited here do have at least brief articles on nearly everyone of importance in European thought.)

I. *Literature.* It is obvious that editors, in their efforts to achieve balance, must give fuller attention to literature of the past than to that of the present, but encyclopedias may be used as starting points for the following types of information.

1. Biographies of authors, with emphasis on older writers, who have stood the test of time, and less emphasis on current writers unless they have achieved wide popularity or received literary awards. Encyclopedias for young people are strong in accounts of writers for children, especially winners of such prizes as the Newbery and Caldecott. Foreign encyclopedias give emphasis to biographies of their national authors, such as *Espasa* for Spanish and Hispanic American writers or *Larousse* to French and French-speaking authors. They are also a good source for translations of authors of the English-speaking world and for foreign criticism of those authors, both tending to be found in the

appended bibliographies. In recent years, the general American encyclopedias in particular have been improving their coverage of women, people of color, and writers of less-popular schools of thought, in an attempt to expand what has sometimes been called the "literary canon"

2. Histories of literature in various countries, with emphasis on the Western world and on the national literature of the encyclopedia's country of origin, with improving attention to some of the newer nations and writers in recent revisions of American encyclopedias

3. Characteristics of adult literary forms (e.g., poetry, drama, fiction, essays, biography) and children's literature as well, although the latter is more fully treated in young people's encyclopedias

4. Brief synopses of literary works, such as those found in *Americana* and in foreign encyclopedias, such as the famous and still useful nineteenth-century *Larousse Grand Dictionnaire Universel,* which has many such articles

5. Recent best-sellers, awards, etc., often found in the yearbooks

Encyclopedias are not intended as substitutes for multivolume histories of national literature, such as the *Literary History of the United States* (4th ed. New York: Macmillan, 1974; 2v.) or the *Cambridge History of English Literature* (New York and London: Putnam, 1907–17; 15v.). Nor will their bibliographies even approach those of the *Cambridge Bibliography of English Literature* (Cambridge, England: Cambridge Univ. Pr., 1966; 5v.). Moreover, these national compilations are updated by many serial bibliographies, such as the *Annual Bibliography of English Language and Literature* (London: Modern Humanities Research Association, 1920–) and the *MLA International Bibliography* (New York: Modern Language Assn., 1921–), and others cited in William A. Wortman, *Guide to Serial Bibliographies for Modern Literature* (2d ed. New York: Modern Language Assn., 1995; 333p.).

Nor should we expect as many critical reevaluations of authors whose work has been reassessed by newer critics; these must be sought in the literary quarterlies and academic journals. Nor are literary quotations as easily identified as they are in quotation books.

But general encyclopedias may not be safely ignored in the field of literature, especially as many of their contributors are recognized literary critics.

J. *Art and music.* Although encyclopedias have been criticized for not reflecting recent movements in art and music, they are justified in giving more attention to the past—again, to maintain proper balance, for current enthusiasms may fade into ephemera in a few decades. In recent years, many American works have been making more of an effort to at least mention current trends and significant figures in these areas. Encyclopedias' useful features include

1. Biographies of artists and composers
2. Histories of art and music, sometimes with separate articles on individual countries. However, one-volume encyclopedias are really only useful for identification of movements and people, because their treatment is so sketchy
3. Descriptions of musical instruments, orchestras and bands, musical forms and notation, often illustrated, although these are of course more fully treated in specialized sources such as *The New Grove Dictionary of Music and Musicians* (Stanley Sadie, ed. Washington, D.C.: Grove's Dictionaries of Music, 1980; 20v.)
4. Characteristics of various schools and movements in art
5. Reproductions of works of art. *Enciclopedia Italiana* is often cited for its excellent reproductions, although they cannot substitute for those in the *Encyclopedia of World Art*. The *New Catholic Encyclopedia* is a good source of religious art. In general, to date the printed works have much higher quality of reproductions of art than do the CD-ROM and online versions, although the latter are improving. And, overall, because the expense of World Wide Web "publishing" of graphics is much lower than that of print, as access to the Web, and to color printers, becomes more common, the machine-readable versions of both general and specialized encyclopedias will undoubtedly improve as a source of (at least) acceptable quality reproductions of artworks
6. Words and music of songs, as in the nineteenth-century *Larousse* (cited under literature), which gives words and music (melody only) of about 600 songs. Several of the major encyclopedias' online versions now include the words, music, and sound recordings of at least some songs.

K. *Libraries and related subjects.* General encyclopedias are sources of information on libraries, professional library and information science associations, biographies of famous librarians, and histories of famous libraries, as well as on the history and character of such reference sources as dictionaries, encyclopedias, and atlases, as well as the more modern electronic systems and sources, such as online databases and laser discs.

Fuller information on all these topics will be found in the *Encyclopedia of Library and Information Science* (New York: Marcel

Dekker, 1968–), which deserves special mention because of its importance to librarians. Begun in 1968, with sixty-two volumes published by 1998 (the original set of thirty-five volumes plus supplementary volumes), it contains a substantial array of signed articles, ranging in length from a few paragraphs to long monographs. Although subject to criticism for its apparent lack of an ending date, uneven quality, and, as time goes on, lack of currency, its international scope and treatment of both traditional librarianship and information science provide a basis for a better understanding of all the types and kinds of libraries and their services.

This admittedly superficial analysis of the coverage of various subject fields suffers from many generalizations, most of them widely known. However, because too many teachers and librarians seem to denigrate encyclopedias (elementary- and high-school students are often forbidden to use encyclopedias for assignments), it seems important to give at least a brief, if imperfect, account of some of their more important uses.

Kister's Best Encyclopedias: A Comparative Guide to General and Specialized Encyclopedias, 2d ed. (Phoenix, Ariz.: Oryx, 1994; 506p.) is the most valuable source of detailed, recent information on general and specialized encyclopedias currently available. Now in its second edition, it is the latest of a number of encyclopedia-buying guides done by the author, Kenneth Kister, currently the dean of "independent" reference-tool reviewers. Its intention, admirably executed, is to provide advice to any U.S. or Canadian consumer in the purchase of an encyclopedia.

The bulk of the work is devoted to lengthy comparative reviews of seventy-seven general encyclopedias arranged by size—large, medium-sized, and small encyclopedias for adults and older students; large and medium-sized sets, and small sets, for children and younger students; and electronic encyclopedias. Each work gets the same treatment: a full citation, description of coverage, evaluation of coverage based on comparison of treatment of fifty-one topics for the adult and twenty-five for the children's works, plus a summary. Comparison charts are provided to summarize these reviews. The electronic reviews are similar but include information on the access engine and other dynamic features.

The remainder of the book provides shorter reviews for out-of-print, subject, and foreign-language encyclopedias, for a total of about 1,000 titles reviewed. Kister also provides a lengthy, recent bibliography on encyclopedias plus a very good, detailed index. The bibliography includes books, articles, and sources that regularly review encyclopedias, such as *Booklist* and *American Reference Books Annual.* The latter reviewed *Kister's Best* in 1995, recommending it as a "must purchase."

Within *Booklist* is *Reference Books Bulletin (RBB),* which is a separate publication, with its own editor, editorial board, and editorial policies, although it is contained physically within *Booklist. RBB* includes lengthy, detailed analyses of new major encyclopedias, as well as comparative reviews of the extent of revisions of later issues or editions of older encyclopedias (among other types of reference sources). These reviews currently appearing in an early fall issue of *RBB* are prepared by the *Reference Books Bulletin* Editorial Board. In recent years, it has also had an annual omnibus review of online and CD-ROM versions of encyclopedias in different issues (currently November and January). The *Booklist* website includes current reviews, as well as a handy article, "Evaluating Encyclopedias: How We Do It," by the former editor of *RBB,* Sandy Whiteley, at <http://www.ala.org/booklist/v92/rbb-encyc.html>.

Brief, signed reviews of encyclopedias available in the United States appear rather promptly in *American Reference Books Annual* (Englewood, Colo.: Libraries Unlimited, 1970-). The five-year cumulative indexes of subjects, titles, and authors and editors add to the ease of location of particular titles as does the *ARBA Guide to Subject Encyclopedias and Dictionaries* (Susan C. Awe, ed.; 2d ed. Englewood, Colo.: Libraries Unlimited, 1997; 482p.). Reviews, although shorter than those in *RBB,* are usually discerning.

Textbooks on reference sources always include encyclopedias, a notable example being Katz's *Introduction to Reference Work,* volume 1, *Basic Information Sources.* It gives little attention to history but contains both analyses of the major sets and a useful discussion of evaluation points. Also discussed are major foreign encyclopedias and outstanding examples of special encyclopedias in art, history, and science. It can be recommended for its readable style, recency, and good list of suggested readings. Although less detailed on specific titles, Bopp and Smith's *Reference and Information Services* also has helpful information.

Much has been written on the history of encyclopedias, but perhaps best known is Robert L. Collison's *Encyclopaedias: Their History throughout the Ages* (2d ed. New York: Hafner, 1966; 334p.), with extensive historical notes and bibliographies. A more philosophical approach may be found in Richard Krzys "Encyclopedics: The Origin and Development of Encyclopedia Design," in *Encyclopedia of Library and Information Science,* volume 50, edited by Allen Kent (New York: Marcel Dekker, 1992; p. 159-84).

Collison and Warren Preece's article in *The New Encyclopaedia Brittanica-Macropaedia* (Chicago: Encyclopaedia Britannica, 1985; v.6, p. 258-77), briefly summarized in the *Micropaedia* (p. 487-89), is probably the best article on the subject in any general encyclopedia.

Padraig Walsh, in his *Anglo-American General Encyclopedias: A Historical Bibliography, 1703-1967* (New York: Bowker, 1967; 270p.), thanks Collison in his introduction "for his invaluable advice, and also for blazing the trail for me . . ." (p. xix). He includes publishing histories and brief biographical notes on outstanding editors of 419 alphabetically listed works; an index to publishers and distributors; a chronology covering 1703-1967; and a general bibliography. Appended is a forum on encyclopedias, with remarks by Louis Shores, Lowell Martin, William D. Halsey, William H. Nault, and Walsh at a symposium on July 6, 1965, reprinted from *RQ* (5 [winter 1965]: 3 ff.).

Particularly good articles on the *Encyclopaedia Britannica* (generally known as *Britannica 3* or just *EB3*) and *World Book* may be found in *Distinguished Classics of Reference Publishing*, edited by James Rettig (Phoenix, Ariz.: Oryx, 1992; 356p.); an "authorized biography" of the *Britannica* is *Let Knowledge Grow: The Story of Encyclopaedia Britannica* (Chicago: Encyclopaedia Britannica, 1992; 24p.).

Additional books and articles on individual encyclopedias may be located through such sources as *Library Literature* and the *National Union Catalog (NUC)*.

Because the encyclopedia articles and other material listed above only spottily list examples of encyclopedias in special fields, those who seek fuller information must look elsewhere. As noted in chapter 2, the "bibliography" chapter, guides to the literature of individual fields are useful, as are *Walford's*, *Balay*, and *Kister's*. Conveniently, the index to *Balay* lists encyclopedias under subject fields. Also to consider are articles in special encyclopedias, such as the one noted earlier in the *Encyclopedia of Philosophy*.

Because knowledge of the indexes to encyclopedias is fundamental to using them efficiently, articles on the indexing of individual encyclopedias are valuable sources of information. A number are included in *Indexers on Indexing*, edited by L. M. Harrod (New York: Bowker, 1978; 430p.). For a description of the indexing of *EB3*, C. D. Needham's "Britannica Revisited," in *Library Association Record* (77 [July 1975]: 153-68), remains helpful; for more recent discussions of encyclopedia indexing, *see* David Crystal, "Some Indexing Decisions in the Cambridge Encyclopedia Family," *The Indexer* (19 [April 1995]: 177-83), and Ron Gardner and Eve Gardner, "Indexing the *Canadian Encyclopedia*, Second Edition," *The Indexer* (16 [Oct. 1988]: 87-91).

It is apparent that there is no dearth of information on encyclopedias for those who are willing to read it. And librarians *must* read it, because not only are they expected to be knowledgeable about these circles of knowledge, they are also sometimes associated with individual works as researchers, writers, or even editors.

Reference librarians and others concerned with teaching the use of the encyclopedia to beginning users will find a number of audiovisual aids listed in guides to these materials. Such things can be used profitably, especially with large groups.

Multivolume Adult Encyclopedias

It is hardly possible to store in the memory the special features, strengths, and weaknesses of individual encyclopedias, though some of them may be learned by continuous use, especially by those who have near-total recall. Even then, knowledge of particulars must be revised from time to time because good encyclopedias are in a state of continuous revision, and the flexibility of electronic reference sources means that even the basic arrangement and access points of electronic versions can be changed with daunting frequency.

Although modern multivolume encyclopedias, having the same general purpose, are subject to certain generalizations, as discussed earlier, differences in treatment and kinds of information in individual articles almost always occur.

Familiarity with individual encyclopedias, developed only through extensive use, is often conditioned by the critical reception they have received as reflected in the review media. The rest of this section on English-language encyclopedias is devoted to an outline of the strengths and weaknesses of six multivolume adult sets, five one- to three-volume sets, and seven sets intended for children and young adults. All are currently available in the United States and are, with few exceptions, likely to be found in U.S. libraries. Arrangement is by general type and, within type, approximately, by importance to libraries. Further detailed information may be found in *Kister's Best Encyclopedias,* among other sources.

■ The new encyclopaedia Britannica. Chicago: Encyclopaedia Britannica, 1974– . Also available online and on the Web as Britannica Online, and on CD-ROM as Britannica CD.

In 1974, the *New Encyclopaedia Britannica (EB3)* was issued in its fifteenth edition, the first entirely new edition in forty-five years. It differs in arrangement from the fourteenth edition, and from any other encyclopedia, by being in three parts: *Propaedia, Micropaedia,* and *Macropaedia* (coined words that put many people off). When a new edition of an encyclopedia is published in the United States, it is duly noted in the major library and publishing sources but rarely anywhere else; this title received much more publicity. A major reason for this was its new approach to the circle of knowledge; another was its practical elimination of an index, and its replacement with the *Micropaedia.* This latter feature was so objectionable that the publishers eventually relented and in 1985 issued a major restructuring (but *not* a new edition), whose most visible feature was the addition of a two-volume analytical index.

Because the arrangement remains of some interest, the contents should be described in some detail, as follows: *Propaedia,* subtitled *Outline of Knowledge and Guide to the Britannica,* is a topical guide to the *Macropaedia,* arranged in ten parts (which are further subdivided). This outline, with a total of forty-two divisions and 189 sections, was then used as a planning tool for the entire new work. The scheme is in essence a modern version of the encyclopedists' goal to classify all world knowledge. Although of interest as such, the *Propaedia* does not seem to be heavily used by librarians or information seekers, who clearly prefer the more traditional use of the encyclopedia as a source of facts and opinions, rather than a form of education—thus the demands for a conventional index.

The *Micropaedia* was originally intended as this index, with ten volumes of fairly short (about 750 words) articles on many topics not in the *Macropaedia,* as well as cross-references within those articles, and from many other terms, to the larger encyclopedia. The cross-referencing remains, but the *Micropaedia* has been expanded to twelve volumes, with no limit to the articles' length, although they are still fairly short. The *Macropaedia* remains the collection of longer, more philosophical and theoretical articles, but it was consolidated heavily (and reduced from nineteen to seventeen volumes in the restructuring). Although an oversimplification, it may be useful to consider the two latter parts of the *EB3* as one, with the shorter articles separated from the longer. Fortunately, the new index is quite detailed.

Aside from the structural considerations, Britannica retains its basic stature and reputation as an excellent, highly authoritative encyclopedia, with many articles written by noted experts. As most librarians know, of course, other than a tendency to a very slight British bias, mostly seen in the use of British spellings and in the number of British contributors, *EB3* has been published in the United States for most of the twentieth century. Even so, it has a consciously international focus; it has much better coverage of non-Western subjects and geographical areas than the competition.

Emphasis remains on the arts and humanities, with many highly theoretical and technical articles at a quite advanced reading level. Although science and technology certainly are covered, these received relatively less attention in *EB3* than in most of its competitors, although coverage is improving in recent years. Geographic coverage is quite international, with the United States and the United Kingdom receiving proportionately less coverage than in the competition. As one might expect, the bibliographies attached to the articles are particularly authoritative.

The *EB3* has been criticized by some reviewers for its continuing lack of popular appeal: many of its illustrations are small and remain in black and white; many of its articles, notably the scientific and mathematical ones, are nearly beyond the reading comprehension of laypeople. Similarly, *EB3* was a bit later than its rivals in producing an electronic edition (although early experiments were made), and the first versions of this tended to rather heavy text, in a not completely attractive format. The World Wide Web version, however, though still in a state of flux, consciously attempts to take advantage of hypertext and multimedia features, with a reasonable degree of success. Quite simply, Britannica remains a highly authoritative encyclopedia for adults, with particularly good coverage of most subjects within the purview of the educated person.

In addition to the text of the encyclopedia itself, the electronic version includes *Merriam-Webster's Collegiate Dictionary.* The CD-ROM is more of a text dump rather than truly multimedia. Searching is releatively primitive; many articles merely refer to the *Book of the Year* but give no citation, even to which year, and don't give the text.

On the other hand, the Web version not only includes the full text of the printed encyclopedia, enhanced with multimedia features, but it provides hot links to the dictionary from words in the text. Though not strictly part of the encyclopedia itself, the Web version also includes a growing list of selected links to other recommended sites.

Strengths

1. Broad, deep, and well-balanced coverage of topics
2. Very authoritative and reliable
3. Reasonably current, although avoiding fads until they are clearly part of the culture
4. Since 1985, good access via index and cross-references

Weaknesses

1. Three-part arrangement remains confusing
2. Reading level is quite difficult
3. Illustrations tend to be a bit stodgy and lack color even where color is needed (although this is changing)

Reviews

American Reference Books Annual 26 (1995): 35–36 (print and electronic)

Choice 34 (Nov. 1996): 440–41 (CD-ROM)

Reference Books Bulletin 93 (Feb. 1, 1997): 960–61

Reference Books Bulletin 93 (Nov. 1, 1996): 523–24 (CD-ROM)

Reference Books Bulletin 92 (Sept. 15, 1995): 196–98 (print and CD-ROM)

■ The encyclopedia Americana. Bernard S. Cayne, ed. in chief. Danbury, Conn.: Grolier, 1979– . 30v. Also available as the Encyclopedia Americana on CD-ROM and on the World Wide Web.

Unlike its major competitor, *EB3, Americana* is arranged in one alphabet under about 52,000 entries. The first major U.S. encyclopedia, first published in 1829, it retains its frank American point of view, while at the same time increasingly becoming a truly international work. Substantial revision since the early 1990s has increased representation of women and the many cultures that make up the United States, both in articles, treatment within articles, and the illustrations. Also, and apparently in response to negative reviews, illustrations are increasingly in color.

Traditionally, *Americana* has excellent science and technology coverage, a point still true, although some of its competition is improving. Unquestionably, *Americana* retains its lead on North American history and geography, with many little-known facts not covered in its rivals. Its social science coverage also remains strong; another attraction are the many individual articles on specific works of art and literature. Longer articles (and many of the shorter ones) have appended bibliographies, although references tend to be a bit dated.

The index is useful, with about the same depth of coverage as *EB3*, but *Americana* articles tend to have relatively fewer cross-references than many reviewers feel are necessary.

The electronic versions retain the text and illustrations of the original, with the addition of sound, motion, and other multimedia effects.

Strengths

1. Clear style
2. Excellent accuracy and impartial coverage of controversial issues, which it does not avoid
3. Strong coverage of U.S. and Canadian topics
4. Large analytical index

Weaknesses

1. A tendency not to update older articles very rapidly, especially those in the humanities and arts
2. Less than exciting illustrations

3. In recent years, has had a fairly slow pace of revision, although this appears to be improving

4. Some technical articles are difficult to read

Reviews

American Reference Books Annual 28 (1997): 22–23 (print)

American Reference Books Annual 27 (1996): 20 (electronic)

American Reference Books Annual 26 (1995): 27–28 (print)

Choice 34 (Jan. 1997): 778 (electronic)

Choice 33 (June 1996): 1625–26 (electronic)

Reference Books Bulletin 93 (Nov. 1, 1996): 530 (electronic)

Reference Books Bulletin 93 (Sept. 25, 1996): 270–71

Reference Books Bulletin 92 (Sept. 15, 1995): 188–91 (print and electronic)

■ Academic American encyclopedia. Danbury, Conn.: Grolier, 1998. 21v. Online and on CD-ROM as the Grolier Multimedia Encyclopedia, updated monthly.

The first wholly new encyclopedia since *Colliers,* in the 1950s, this was the first to use computer technology in planning, editing, and revising and thus also the first to be available in machine-readable format. As a result, the publisher has claimed as much as 26 percent of the articles and pictures undergo revision in a given year. Initially published by Arete, a French firm, and first available in the United States in 1980, this encyclopedia is particularly known for its illustrations—about one-third of the space is devoted to about 18,000 of them, with a majority in color. Entries are quite short, averaging about 350 words, and tend to reflect interests of U.S. school curriculum; although the work is aimed at adults, reviewers have tended to feel it is somewhere between a high-school–young-adult encyclopedia and a purely adult one.

Although a short-entry encyclopedia, nearly 40 percent of the articles have bibliographies attached, and many of the articles tend to use rather technical terminology. As might be expected, *Academic American* includes a large number of popular and current topics, often covering subjects and people not in most other encyclopedias. Coverage of current science and technology is especially good, and biographical entries occupy nearly one-third of the text. The index, located in the last volume, is quite detailed, more so than any other general encyclopedia; combined with liberal cross-references, this provides very easy access to all the material. Updating varies, but approaches true "continuous revision," with the printed version undergoing the usual annual revision; but the electronic versions vary, often being updated quarterly.

Consciously aimed at giving objective, incontrovertible facts, *Academic American* is quite good at presenting all sides of controversial issues, and generally does not avoid them, although the length of the articles does not always permit sufficient discussion of the full nature of the controversy.

One criticism that might be made of this work is its appearance in many guises and titles, not to mention its multiple formats. Among current and recent titles are *Barnes & Noble New American Encyclopedia, Grolier Academic Encyclopedia, Grolier International Encyclopedia, Grolier Encyclopedia of Knowledge, Global International Encyclopedia, Macmillan Family Encyclopedia,* and the *Lexicon Universal Encyclopedia.*

The CD-ROM version, originally released as Academic American Encyclopedia in 1985, was the first such encyclopedia. Over the years, the publisher has added many additional features, as well as more articles, so that this is nearly a different product than the printed version, rather than just the print plus multimedia. Over time, the CD-ROM has added more illustrations, for a total of about 10,000, including, of course, motion and sound, plus multimedia maps (maps accompanied by images, graphs, and texts, plus a voice-over). It is possible to search by keyword, title, subject, or chronology, with most of the sophisticated Boolean operators also available. Searches can be saved in several formats, and parts of text can be bookmarked for later referral. Because it is fairly easy to save these searches, libraries may find that their drives become full. On the positive side, although material can be saved, there is no word processor attached to the encyclopedia, which might discourage the grosser forms of plagiarism. The online version includes hyperlinks to selected websites and *Brain Jam,* a magazine.

As the new kid on the block, this work has had mixed reviews, although Kister feels it is "one of the best midsized encyclopedias available today."

Strengths

1. Broad and balanced coverage, especially of topics of current interest
2. Good authority
3. Very up-to-date
4. Outstanding illustrations and generally appealing format
5. Very good access via a detailed index and many cross-references
6. Good, if brief, current bibliographies

Weaknesses

1. Too brief, sometimes simplistic articles
2. A generally dry "names/dates/places" style
3. "Busy" layout, which some may find confusing
4. Variety of formats and titles, which can be confusing

Reviews

American Reference Books Annual 26 (1995): 18–19

Choice 34 (Oct. 1996): 260 (electronic version)

Choice 33 (Nov. 1995): 446–47 (electronic version)

Library Journal 122 (Nov. 15, 1997): 122 (electronic version)

Reference Books Bulletin 94 (Jan. 1, 1998): 844 (electronic version)

Reference Books Bulletin 93 (Nov. 1, 1996): 530–31 (electronic version)

Reference Books Bulletin 93 (Sept. 15, 1996): 265–66

Reference Books Bulletin 92 (Sept. 15, 1995): 185–86

School Library Journal 44 (Jan. 1998): 56 (electronic version)

■ Collier's encyclopedia with bibliography and index. New York: Collier, 1997. 24v. Also online and on CD-ROM as part of Middle Search PLUS, an EBSCO product.

First published from 1949 to 1951, and the most recent "big set" before *Academic American, Colliers* reflects the advice and assistance of many notable librarians, among them Louis Shores, who was active in its planning from 1946. Its nearly 25,000 articles remain reliable, although intentionally not always in as much depth as *Britannica* and *Americana.* For all practical purposes, it was nearly completely revised in the 1990s, making it the most current of the larger sets. Unlike most of its rivals, its yearbook consciously attempts to update articles in the main set and is thus worth buying as part of the set (a fact not generally true of encyclopedia yearbooks).

The articles are quite long and thus require a good index; such an analytical index is a reality—with more entries per word than any other major encyclopedia. In addition to facts and general concept articles, *Colliers* is also good for more practical topics and the more practical applications of the more theoretical subjects as well. Although not following the "pyramid style" of works for younger readers (that is, proceeding from the simple to the more complex), many of the articles do begin with definitions and basic facts, then gradually increase in complexity. Although some articles also have glossaries appended, there has still been criticism that some science articles are too technical.

A few articles have appended bibliographies, but most readings are listed in the last volume, along with the index. Although many of the references are a bit dated, most are briefly annotated, something not generally found in the competition.

Colliers has been criticized over time for its handling of controversies or, more accurately, for ignoring or downplaying them. It has also received some criticism for implicit bias, for example, by the use of prominent clergy as authors for religion articles. However, the same critics do not claim that there is deliberate bias to the point of inaccuracy. The most prominent and respected modern critic of encyclopedias today, Kenneth Kister, has said this is "the best of the big sets."

Strengths

1. Usually accurate and authoritative
2. Impartial (with some caveats)
3. Clearly written
4. Up-to-date, especially in topics of current interest
5. Superior, detailed analytical index
6. Annotated 11,500-item bibliography emphasizing books in English likely to be found in U.S. libraries
7. Good, relevant illustrations, increasingly in color

Weaknesses

1. Some bibliographic references are dated
2. Some readers dislike the separate bibliography
3. A tendency to avoid or downplay controversy
4. Though good, illustrations have been said to be too few

Reviews

American Reference Books Annual 26 (1995): 16–17 (print)

Library Journal 122 (Jan. 1997): 160 (CD-ROM)

Reference Books Bulletin 94 (Nov. 1, 1997): 496–97 (electronic)

Reference Books Bulletin 94 (Sept. 15, 1997): 252–53 (print)

Reference Books Bulletin 93 (Nov. 1, 1996): 524–25 (CD-ROM); (Sept. 15, 1996): 266–67 (print)

School Library Journal 43 (Feb. 1997): 128

■ Funk & Wagnalls new encyclopedia. New York: Funk & Wagnalls, 1993. 29v. Also online and on CD-ROM as part of Primary Search, produced by

EBSCO, as the basis for Infopedia, Microsoft's Encarta, and as Funk & Wagnalls Multipedia Encyclopedia.

The low cost of this encyclopedia, and the fact that its primary marketing is via one-volume-at-a-time sales in supermarkets, has tended to affect opinion negatively. However, though not in the same class as *Americana, Britannica,* or *Colliers, Funk & Wagnalls* is actually quite good as a medium-sized encyclopedia.

With about 25,000 entries, about 40 percent of those biographical, this is aimed at the home market and thus has a somewhat less difficult style, including the use of the pyramid approach for the more technical articles. Generally, entries are brief, although there are much longer survey-type articles; only the latter have any bibliographies. Handling of controversy is generally objective, but the editors have not completely replaced the tendency merely to ignore controversy entirely.

Articles, although accurate, have less depth, and often breadth, than many critics feel necessary. Again, though actually updated twice a year, *Funk & Wagnalls* has been criticized for lack of currency, especially in the arts and humanities. Related to its costs, illustrations are much sparser than in its competitors, with somewhat less than ideal clarity and color.

Note, however, that the widely used and heavily advertised Microsoft Encarta electronic encyclopedia is based on the *Funk & Wagnalls* text, and Kister has called *Funk & Wagnalls* the "best buy on the market."

Strengths

1. Authoritative, reasonably well balanced
2. Generally up-to-date
3. Index and cross-references good
4. Bibliographies, though scarce, generally good
5. Good coverage of U.S. and Canadian history, geography, and biography; science; and technology
6. Indexes to place-names in maps

Weaknesses

1. Generally poor coverage of arts and humanities subjects
2. Generally unappealing layout and illustrations

Reviews

American Reference Books Annual 26 (1995): 28–29

Reference Books Bulletin 93 (Sept. 15, 1996): 272–73

■ New standard encyclopedia. Chicago: Ferguson, 1997. 20v.

Although a solid midsized encyclopedia, around since 1930, this has been mostly marketed though supermarkets and directly to home users. The addition of an index volume in 1989 seems to have brought it to the attention of the library and school market. Unlike most other multivolume encyclopedias, all articles are staff written, and then reviewed by outside experts; both the style and the accuracy appear quite good. Generally, this is up-to-date and reasonably good in its treatment of controversies. Clearly aimed at the home market, this encyclopedia is useful for the library for two reasons: first, its regular reading level makes it suitable for about seventh- and eighth-graders, a group that falls between the usual children's and young adult reading levels. Second, the *New Standard* contains a significant amount of practical information on such things as home repair, nutrition, consumer protection, and the like; and it often includes the addresses and contact information for national organizations in these articles.

Strengths

1. Good for junior-high reading level but not obviously a children's work, making it suitable for adults with reading difficulties
2. Trustworthy, especially in factual articles
3. Includes in-text definitions of difficult words as well as pronunciations for nearly all entry words
4. A good, detailed analytical index and many cross-references
5. Bibliographies appended to about 1,000 articles include a mix of adult and children's and young adults' books
6. Updated quarterly with loose-leaf supplements, which include an annual index (versus the annual supplements of most other encyclopedias)

Weaknesses

1. Poor illustrations
2. Lacks depth
3. Even with the quarterly updates, often not as timely as it could be

Reviews

American Reference Books Annual 26 (1995): 36–37

American Reference Books Annual 24 (1993): 28–29

Reference Books Bulletin 93 (Sept. 15, 1996): 276–77

Reference Books Bulletin 92 (Sept. 15, 1995): 198–99

Encyclopedia Supplements

It is generally agreed that encyclopedia supplements (annuals or yearbooks) are more successful in recording the previous year's events than in updating the parent set, although there are some exceptions. Although publishers emphasize in their advertising that their supplements or yearbooks serve to keep the basic set current, they do not systematically update the articles in the encyclopedias. They are less closely related to the parent sets than is usually claimed. There is considerable variation in their arrangement, quantity and quality of illustrations, extent of indexing, and special features. About the only attraction they have over less expensive independent annuals, such as *World Almanac* and *Information Please Almanac,* which contain similar information, is that the encyclopedia annuals have a more pleasing format. With this in mind, one can argue that the individual family should avoid purchasing such yearbooks and opt for an almanac; libraries, on the other hand, could make a good case, because of the additional information, for considering the annuals—in fact, most still do. With the gradual replacement (at least as predicted by some) of printed encyclopedias with online and CD products, complete with considerably easier updating, it is possible in the future that yearbooks will cease to exist, and the typical encyclopedia will be revised and updated "continuously" (or at least, say, monthly).

Remember that much of the material in the annuals is not incorporated into later revisions of the encyclopedia. Also, in searching for an event, remember that annuals usually cover the last three months of one year and the first nine of the next. They also often contain feature articles and special reports, often by well-known authorities, that will not be found elsewhere.

Although the yearbooks' contents vary, certain generalizations hold, and the following indicates the reference use that can be made of them.

1. Brief biographies of persons who have died or become prominent during the year. The obituaries, giving date of death, serve as a guide to the location of longer newspaper accounts
2. Chronologies of recent events
3. Recent socioeconomic statistical data, usually for large areas and not always with citation to source
4. Brief reports of activities in various fields, often noting important conferences and publications
5. Recent developments (especially political) in countries over the world
6. Special sections containing long, signed articles on topics of current interest, usually by well-known authorities
7. Photographs and other illustrations, such as cartoons

Although a bit old, the *Reference Books Bulletin* Editorial Board's "Encyclopedia Annuals, Supplements and Yearbooks: A 1985 Overview" (*Refer-*

ence Books Bulletin 82 [Sept. 1, 1985]: 36–43) remains an excellent comparison. The comments in *Kister's Best Encyclopedias* are also very useful, although it should be remembered that Kister is highly dubious of the value of most of these publications.

One- to Three-Volume Encyclopedias

Libraries with a number of reputable multivolume encyclopedias still find many reference uses for one- to three-volume encyclopedias and often keep them close at hand for quick reference. They are especially useful for identification of persons and places and for brief overviews of a subject. When responsibly edited and well arranged, they provide an admirable starting point in a search. They are also desirable for home use, where cost and space are factors.

Until recently, these condensations saved space by leaving out almost all pictorial illustrations, but with the publication of the *Random House Encyclopedia* in 1977, things changed. More than 11,000 of its nearly 14,000 pictures were in color and geared in with the 896 long articles in its *Colorpedia* section. About four black-and-white photographs on every other page accompanied the 25,000 short articles in the *Alphapedia* section. Since then, all the shorter encyclopedias have been adding more pictures, often in color. Thus, these encyclopedias can no longer be overlooked as pictorial sources.

The strengths and weaknesses of the following five titles, as reflected in the reviewing media, are further detailed below. These encyclopedias were selected because of their recognized excellence and because of their reference value for the library. In several cases, there are even shorter versions of the same title, or paperback editions, more suitable for the home. A reasonably complete listing, with evaluations, may be found in *Kister's Best Encyclopedias;* many are also reviewed in *Reference Books Bulletin* when a new edition appears.

■ The Columbia encyclopedia. 5th ed. New York: Columbia Univ. Pr., 1993; distributed by Houghton. 3048p. Also on CD-ROM and in the CD-ROM version of the *Canadian Encyclopedia.*

The largest and most formidable one-volume encyclopedia in English. Unlike its competitors, it is actually produced and published in the United States. Generally, this work is completely revised with a new edition about every fifteen years. Currently, it has about 51,000 short entries, with rich cross-referencing.

About 45 percent of the entries are biographical, and another 30 percent are geographical, making coverage in these areas better than many multivolume encyclopedias. Although consciously aimed at American readers, there is somewhat of an international focus.

The CD-ROM version includes new and updated articles every year, plus many hypertext links. Searching includes Boolean, hypertext, and keyword approaches, as well as classified category searches (in effect, a form of browsing). Longer articles include subheadings for even more refined searching.

Strengths

1. Excellent authority, with heavy reliance on Columbia University faculty
2. Excellent biographical and geographical coverage, including newer nations
3. Lucid, clear style, even in the more technical articles
4. Currently, well-selected bibliographies, with a tendency to list books that have good bibliographies
5. Clear, well-placed illustrations
6. Often gives pronunciation of unfamiliar and foreign words

Weaknesses

1. Lacks an index, and cross-references are not completely adequate
2. Most illustrations, while clear, are dull and nearly all in black and white

Reviews

American Reference Books Annual 25 (1995): 25

Reference Books Bulletin 93 (June 1, 1997): 1750–51 (electronic version)

■ Concise Columbia encyclopedia. 3d ed. New York: Columbia Univ. Pr., 1994. 920p. Also online and in a handheld version as itself; also on CD-ROM as part of Microsoft Bookshelf and the basis for the free website Encyclopedia.com <http:www.encyclopedia.com>.

As the title says, an abridged version of the *Columbia Encyclopedia,* with about 15,000 articles, no bibliographies. Generally, all the historical material has been cut from the full *Columbia,* and much information is included in tables, rather than articles. The only color illustrations are the sixteen pages of maps.

More for the home market than schools or libraries, this title is noted for several reasons: first, the first edition is also available in large-print format in eight volumes. Second, the text provides the basis for the encyclopedia portion of Microsoft Bookshelf and other general reference CD-ROMs, including a version that also includes the *Canadian Encyclopedia* and the *Gage Canadian Dictionary.*

The various forms of the electronic version include a number of useful features: these include the ability to search either by keyword or menu; a *phonetic* spell checker; the ability to set bookmarks; and the capability to limit searches by subject field, date, or geographic region.

Reviews

    American Reference Books Annual 27 (1996): 19

    Choice 32 (March 1995): 1078

■ The Cambridge encyclopedia. 3d ed. New York: Cambridge Univ. Pr., 1997. 1303p.

A strong British emphasis is seen in this, which has been called the best of the British one-volume encyclopedias. Generally, the hardcover version is preferred to the paperback, as being more complete. Although not really a competitor to the *Columbia,* this has been recommended as useful for the British point of view, such as in its biographies, and as a very good value for the money. The scientific articles include many not in the other one- to three-volume encyclopedias.

Reviews

    American Reference Books Annual 27 (1996): 18–19

    Choice 35 (Feb. 1998): 963

    Library Journal 123 (Jan. 1998): 86

■ Random House encyclopedia. 3d ed. New York: Random House, 1990. 2781p.

Quite different from the *Columbia* is the profusely illustrated *Random House,* whose appearance in 1977 was widely noted in both reviewing and publishing circles. Compare the treatment of several subjects in both encyclopedias, and it is obvious that they complement each other. Much material in *Random House* will be intelligible to young readers, not only because of the extensive use of captioned illustrations, but because the text is less scholarly in tone than the *Columbia.*

Random House also differs from the *Columbia* in arrangement: its *Colorpedia* section is classified under seven categories, each introduced by a brief essay by a well-known scholar. The content is further arranged under about 800 topics, each with a two-page spread, of which more than half is given to color illustrations (for a total of about 11,000 color illustrations). The *Alphapedia* section consists of about 25,000 very short entries (about 100 words each) for concepts, people, and places not in the *Colorpedia,* as well as cross-references to the *Colorpedia.* In addition to the profuse illustrations, the *Random House* includes eighty Rand McNally maps, complete with a 22,000-item index to the map section.

Note that approximately twenty different national editions of this work are available in the appropriate languages. An attempt at a hand-held version of this encyclopedia, however, was not generally perceived as successful and was dropped.

Strengths

1. Extremely good color illustrations
2. Combination A–Z and classified approach
3. Easy reading style
4. Generally authoritative (but see below)
5. Good, objective coverage of controversial topics
6. The fifty-two-page Time Chart can be of use and interest

Weaknesses

1. Arrangement is confusing
2. The *Alphapedia,* intended as an index to the *Colorpedia,* is not an adequate substitute for a detailed analytical index
3. Some critics have noted the omission of people they felt should be included and what they claim is inadequate treatment of other persons
4. Coverage is uneven, with an emphasis on topics that lend themselves to illustrations
5. The bibliographies are sparse and not well selected
6. Attempting to put all large topics into exactly two pages is conceptually flawed
7. Some critics have pointed out coverage of specific topics within a given subject is often misleading and arbitrary
8. The complex cross-reference system can be confusing
9. Has not been updated in some time, and its future is uncertain

Reviews

American Reference Books Annual 22 (1991): 16

Choice 28 (March 1991): 1091

Library Journal 115 (Sept. 1, 1990): 150

Reference Books Bulletin 87 (Jan. 1, 1991): 946

▪ Webster's new world encyclopedia. Stephen P. Elliott and others, eds. New York: Prentice-Hall, 1992. 1230p.

An American version of the best-known one-volume British encyclopedia, *Hutchinson's Twentieth Century Encyclopedia* (7th ed., 5th rev. London: Hutchinson, 1987; 1350p.), this appears in three printed variations—hardcover, "college edition" hardcover, and paperback "pocket edition." The first is most relevant to libraries, of course. It contains about 25,000 short articles, none with bibliographies. The American edition is wholly updated from the British version, with about 1,200 new articles added to reflect Canadian and U.S. topics and interests. This work is especially strong in science, geography, biography, and history. The nearly 2,500 illustrations are mostly in color but are not well indexed.

Strengths

1. Broad, well-balanced coverage
2. Up-to-date
3. Plain, explicit prose
4. Good objective coverage of most controversial topics

Weaknesses

1. No depth to the articles
2. No index and few cross-references
3. Many minor inaccuracies

Reviews

American Reference Books Annual 24 (1993): 29

Choice 30 (Feb. 1993): 947

Library Journal 117 (Aug. 1992): 92

Reference Books Bulletin 89 (Oct. 15, 1992): 449–50

Children's and Young Adults' Encyclopedias

Encyclopedias for children and young people have come a long way since the old *Book of Knowledge,* begun in 1912 and so dear to children of several generations. Now, good sets (including the *New Book of Knowledge*) are compiled with rather scrupulous attention to the school curriculum and the needs and interests of children. Ironically, often these very same encyclopedias are also useful for adults, particularly in scientific and technical areas (including social sciences as well as physical sciences) in which they have had little training or experience.

An important feature is the style of writing, which must be readable, interesting, and geared to the age group for which it is intended. Editors may organize articles in pyramid style, proceeding from the simple to the more complex, as in *Compton's* and *World Book*. Also employed are graded vocabulary lists, such as the Dale-Chall list used by *The New Book of Knowledge* and *World Book*. Some encyclopedias try to match the vocabulary of certain articles to the reading skills of children most apt to consult those articles. Most of the encyclopedias aimed at the younger age groups also define difficult or technical words within the text, as they are used.

Good illustrations, including photographs, diagrams, maps, and charts, are essential, not for decorations, but as a complement to the text. Fortunately, competition generally has forced all publishers to improve the quality and number of their illustrations. Bibliographies are sometimes provided, at least for major articles.

These sets must be well arranged for ease of use and well indexed. Indexing, however, is a bit problematic for encyclopedias aimed at this age group, because studies have shown that relatively few children use them, preferring to look up the relevant headword and then either be satisfied with the resulting article or assume that the given encyclopedia has nothing on the subject. When added to the increasing availability of full-text searching by keyword, even the best index may be ignored—although its use might save considerable time, trouble, and frustration.

Like adult encyclopedias, some of those for the younger ages also have yearbooks, which are more important as a record of what has happened than as updates of the basic set. Often profusely illustrated, they have special articles on subjects of current interest. World Book's *Year Book* is probably the model of such a yearbook (for adults or children), reprinting some articles from the basic set in the yearbook and adding a cumulative index to the last couple years of the yearbook.

The encyclopedias mentioned here may be approached in terms of their strengths and weaknesses, as with the adult works, as reflected in critical comment on recent editions.

■ Children's Britannica. Chicago: Encyclopaedia Britannica, 1993- . 20v.

Formerly known as *Britannica Junior,* this contains about 4,000 main articles, plus about 6,000 shorter ones in the "Reference Index." Attempts to be international, but clearly retains a British flavor; and unlike most other U.S.-published children's encyclopedias, has no direct connection with the school curriculum. Unlike *The New Book of Knowledge,* it lacks bibliographies and does not use a controlled vocabulary, although style is generally suitable to the age level.

Strengths

1. Experienced editorial committee and good authority
2. Good coverage of biography and geography

3. Objective and accurate treatment, with much better treatment of controversy than its predecessor
4. Good index, along with adequate cross-references
5. International flavor

Weaknesses

1. Although it has many illustrations (about 30 percent of the text), the overall appearance remains drab compared with its competition
2. Split of articles into a main section and "Reference Index" can be confusing (evidence suggests children rarely use indexes)
3. Style may be too difficult in some articles
4. Tends to be a bit weak on U.S. coverage
5. No bibliographies

Reviews

American Reference Books Annual 26 (1995): 22–23

American Reference Books Annual 23 (1992): 15–16

Reference Books Bulletin 91 (Sept. 15, 1994): 159

Reference Books Bulletin 90 (Sept. 15, 1993): 174

■ Compton's encyclopedia. Chicago: Compton's Learning Co., 1994. 26v. Also online and on CD-ROM as Compton's Interactive Encyclopedia. Annual updates.

As popular and highly esteemed by some users as *World Book, Compton's* differs from it in using broad articles complemented by a short-article "Fact Index," which is also an index to the longer articles. Although also aimed at the North American curriculum, it is not as directly influenced by it as is *World Book;* notably, in addition to the usual science and technology and geography, *Compton's* includes articles on subjects of general interest to children that have nothing to do with school curriculum.

In fact, given the lack of use of controlled vocabulary and the broadness of coverage, *Compton's* can also be considered a general, adult-level encyclopedia as well. After some decline in the 1980s, this work has been revived, with new illustrations, most in color, and a willingness to deal objectively with controversy that was not present before. Also, the confusing presence of "Fact Index" entries in each volume is being replaced with one alphabetic sequence (possibly an influence of the *Britannica* innovation).

The first major encyclopedia set to become truly multimedia, this work has won a number of awards. Based on the printed set, and containing all of its text with additional illustrations and multimedia material (sound, motion, etc.), at the beginning of the twenty-first century this encyclopedia has remained ahead of its competitors, particularly in terms of its ease of searching and the different ways of searching. These include browsing though article titles, maps, or multimedia listings; keyword searching of the encyclopedia, the atlas, or the dictionary; selecting by topic; and using the "InfoPilot," which produces groups of articles related to the search topic. Although most feel this is easy to use, the combination of all these options, plus an "expert" mode, might confuse some users.

In addition to the encyclopedia, the CD-ROM includes *Merriam-Webster's Intermediate Dictionary* and a thesaurus. Unlike Encarta, there is no word processor attached, but a "notebook" allows taking of notes and cut-and-pasting of articles. A fascinating innovation is the monthly updating of articles on the Internet, with the ability to download these to one's local computer, giving a new meaning to "continuous revision."

Strengths

1. Authoritative contributors
2. Wide coverage, with topics treated in greater depth than in most other sets for the same audience, in part a result of the use of broad over narrow subjects
3. High degree of accuracy and timeliness
4. Use of pyramid style, and definitions of difficult terms, plus use of glossaries in many articles
5. Fact summaries
6. A tradition of excellent illustrations and maps

Weaknesses

1. Has become dated in the past; the publisher's dedication to remaining current in all subjects may be unclear, especially because there have been changes in publisher
2. Not all difficult words are defined
3. Some articles, even with the assistance noted above, are really too difficult for those below high school
4. Many biographies are treated too briefly in the "Fact Index"
5. Because evidence suggests children tend not to use indexes, separation of articles into two parts may mean they do not find the information needed
6. Bibliographies are rare

Reviews

> *American Reference Books Annual* 26 (1995): 25–26 (electronic version)
>
> *American Reference Books Annual* 25 (1994): 15–16
>
> *Choice* 32 (April 1995): 1282 (electronic version)
>
> *Reference Books Bulletin* 94 (Sept. 15, 1997): 254–55; (Nov. 1, 1997): 501–2 (electronic version)
>
> *Reference Books Bulletin* 93 (Sept. 15, 1996): 268–69; (Nov. 1, 1996): 526 (electronic version)
>
> *Reference Books Bulletin* 92 (Sept. 15, 1995): 186–87

■ The Kingfisher children's encyclopedia. New York: Larousse-Kingfisher-Chambers, 1998. 468p.

An outstanding one-volume encyclopedia that has received very positive reaction from the critics. Strong on science and technology, unbiased, and profusely illustrated, this work is especially sensitive to issues of race, gender, ethnicity, religion, and the like. *Kingfisher* is heavily illustrated and also includes many fact boxes, tables, and other useful graphics. Also published as the *Grolier Children's Encyclopedia* in ten volumes, this edition is handier and less expensive. Although there are other shorter children's encyclopedias, this is listed because, unlike other adult and children's shorter encyclopedias, there are two separate indexes (even though the basic arrangement is alphabetical): an analytical index and a 1,500-item classified index.

Strengths

1. Good authority
2. Appealing use of graphics and color
3. Good, clear style
4. Unlike most shorter encyclopedias, has separate index
5. Good cross-references

Weaknesses

1. By its nature, coverage lacks depth
2. Tends to ignore some controversial topics entirely
3. Indexing is incomplete

Reviews

American Reference Books Annual 27 (1996): 22

American Reference Books Annual 25 (1994): 17

Reference Books Bulletin 91 (June 1, 1995): 1826

■ The new book of knowledge. Danbury, Conn.: Grolier, 1999. 21v. plus study guide. Also online.

Encyclopedias for elementary-school children, with their uncomplicated articles and simple vocabulary, are often suitable for older students with reading difficulties or slow learners. Outstanding among these is *The New Book of Knowledge,* which includes more than 9,000 main articles and 5,000 shorter entries in an alphabetical arrangement. Major changes beginning in 1992 include a change from a topical to an alphabetical arrangement, more realistic and generally better treatment of controversy, and the gradual phasing out of the "Dictionary Index." Based on North American curriculum, with the addition of topics of likely interest to children, this is unlike most other children's encyclopedias in being written expressly for them, not a cut-down version of an adult encyclopedia. Articles use controlled vocabulary (the Dale-Chall readability formula), with style varying, so that a lighter style appears in articles of personal interest as opposed to school-related topics.

The electronic version adds the usual multimedia features, with an emphasis on the sort of things younger children like, and Internet links. Note that these links emphasize the American Library Association's "Great Sites" in a conscious attempt to provide a guide to "family friendly" children's sites.

Strengths

1. Experienced advisory board
2. Well-qualified contributors
3. Accurate
4. Objective and realistic treatment of controversial topics
5. Excellent illustrations, nearly all in color
6. Good coverage of science and technology
7. Coverage of arts and humanities good, with the notable inclusion of coverage of children's literature and authors
8. Energetic specific article revision as well as recent overall revision
9. Difficult terms defined in articles, with pronunciation given
10. Practical learning activities included with many articles
11. Home and school reading-and-study guide includes suitable (and graded) bibliographies
12. Use of readability formula plus pyramid style makes for easy reading

13. Individual indexes in each volume as well as a cumulated index in separate volume

Weaknesses

1. Illustrations not completely indexed
2. Some critics feel the readability formula leads to oversimplistic articles

Reviews

American Reference Books Annual 26 (1995): 34–35

Reference Books Bulletin 93 (Sept. 15, 1996): 274–75

Reference Books Bulletin 92 (Sept. 15, 1995): 194–95

■ New Grolier children's encyclopedia. Danbury, Conn.: Grolier, 1998. 10v.

The current version of the *New Grolier Student Encyclopedia,* formerly the *Young Students Encyclopedia,* aimed at the younger elementary student. Each volume is only sixty-four pages long, with a "Factfinder" time line and fact index to the volume. Contains many color illustrations and maps and plenty of sidebars and boxed information. Although arranged A–Z, the set also includes an index, which will probably be used only rarely by the age level in question.

Some might question whether students this young would be better served with one of the larger sets aimed at the older students, because they will rapidly outgrow this title. On the other hand, a number of other sets are aimed at this age level, suggesting there is an ongoing need. All things considered, if such a set is needed, this is probably the most suitable for the library (if not the home as well).

■ The World Book encyclopedia. Chicago: World Book, 1993. 22v. Also available in electronic form as World Book Information Finder and The World Book Multimedia Encyclopedia. Annual updates.

Although considered a children's and young people's encyclopedia, this is consistently the best-selling encyclopedia in the world, and it is certainly of value to adults as well as children. Given the market (children in grades three to twelve), topics and coverage are based on those typical of American schools. An interesting feature is the vocabulary—articles are written in a style and with vocabulary appropriate to the subject, so that, say, the article on "mouse" is simpler than that on "cell." The care in writing is evidenced in consistent use of nonsexist, nonethnocentric language and the use of the metric system for all measurements.

Longer articles tend to have "topical units," tables of contents, and the like. The last volume also includes annually revised study guides. Unlike those of most encyclopedias, the *World Book Year Book* is directly keyed to the main set and so functions as an update.

Editions for other nations are available, with extra volumes to provide appropriate national articles.

A fairly new multimedia contender, *World Book's* database and electronic form are both good, reliable products. The *Information Finder* contains only the matter of the encyclopedia and its associated *World Book Dictionary.* The *Multimedia Encyclopedia* includes the *Information Finder* material, plus illustrations, maps, "virtual realities" (three-dimensional dynamic illustrations), and animations. Articles tend to be longer than in other CD-ROM encyclopedias; the 16,000-plus diagrams, maps, and similar graphics are very well done. The publisher is touting the "virtual realities," multimedia simulations, and other animations. Interesting features include the hot linking of about 250,000 words directly to the *World Book Dictionary,* ability to search by time frame, and a classified list of articles. After a slow start in the multimedia competition, this is certainly worth consideration.

Strengths

1. Excellent authority
2. Annual updates, with relevant yearbook articles as well as continuous revision (up to 50 percent in a year)
3. Outstanding coverage of all subjects in the U.S. school curriculum
4. Routinely tested in about 400 actual classrooms
5. Clear, direct style using appropriate vocabulary, so that more-advanced articles are not too simplistic and simple articles not too advanced for likely readers
6. Technical and uncommon terms defined in articles
7. Excellent maps and other graphics
8. Balanced treatment of controversial subjects
9. Useful reading and study guides
10. Comprehensive analytical index

Weaknesses

1. Biographies not all sufficiently deep
2. Critics have felt there is too strong a conservative Western bias to some articles
3. Not all illustrations are clear and meaningful

Reviews

> *American Reference Books Annual* 28 (1997): 25-26
>
> *American Reference Books Annual* 26 (1995): 38 (electronic version)
>
> *Reference Books Bulletin* 93 (Sept. 15, 1996): 278-79
>
> *Reference Books Bulletin* 92 (Sept. 15, 1995): 201

And, for the younger children—

■ Childcraft: the how and why library. Chicago: World Book, 1996. 15v. plus dictionary.

Not strictly an encyclopedia, but more of a general reference set for younger children. *Childcraft* has about 3,000 articles arranged topically, and it is rather loosely keyed to the U.S. school curriculum. In recent years, it is getting away from its former "white suburban" flavor but retains a cheerful, noncontroversial point of view. Articles, many written by *World Book* contributors, include selections from famous writers and are well illustrated. The set sold to homes includes a high-quality children's dictionary, but this does not come with the set sold to libraries and schools. Kister states that this is "unquestionably the best general reference set for children ages 4-10."

Strengths

1. Good authority
2. Excellent illustrations, most in color
3. Good coverage of social and environmental issues
4. Style and vocabulary appropriate to younger children
5. Includes some bibliographies

Weaknesses

1. Lack of depth in many articles
2. Children outgrow this rather quickly
3. Tends to avoid controversy
4. Some reviewers dislike the general point of view as too protective

Reviews

> *American Reference Books Annual* 24 (1993): 22-23
>
> *American Reference Books Annual* 21 (1990): 19
>
> *Reference Books Bulletin* 86 (June 1, 1990): 1917
>
> *Reference Books Bulletin* 86 (Jan. 15, 1990): 1032

Electronic Encyclopedias

Since the early 1980s, a growing number of encyclopedias, among other reference books, has become available in machine-readable formats. At first, these were only the text of printed versions, generally available online via remote computers. These were followed by CD-ROM encyclopedias, which rather quickly began to include not only the graphics of the printed versions, but also new graphics, plus sound and motion—thus, the "multimedia" encyclopedia. As the World Wide Web gains in popularity, multimedia is being seen on the remote online sources as well. An instructive description of the challenges posed by the changing formats may be found in Robert J. Janus, "From Paper and Ink to CD-ROM: Digitizing the *World Book* Image" (*Library Trends* 45 [spring 1997]: 602–22).

Although it is unclear now precisely how electronics will change the concept of "encyclopedia" overall, one could argue that the improved updating capacity of machine-readable versions means there is no need for the annual supplements. Current trends (as of the beginning of the third millennium) suggest that the encyclopedia will be available in both a local form (such as CD-ROM or its successors) and on the World Wide Web. It will contain text, all types of pictures (still and moving), and sound. Indexes will be searchable and also browseable and will also include hypertext links among articles. Also, most electronic encyclopedias add some sort of indexing to other sites on the Web, only, one hopes, those of a very high quality. Thus far, attempts to produce handheld encyclopedias have failed to catch on, but who knows what may come in the next decade or so?

The following titles are sold only in electronic form; usually these products come from some company other than the original publisher. The versions marketed by the original publisher are considered with the print editions.

■ Microsoft Encarta multimedia encyclopedia. Redmond, Wash.: Microsoft Pr., 1992– . On the Web and on CD-ROM only. Monthly updates.

Some reviewers feel this is the model for what the encyclopedia of the future will look like. The actual text is based on the 1993 edition of the midrange *Funk & Wagnalls New Encyclopedia,* with some rewriting and a growing number of articles from *Collier's Encyclopedia,* plus more than 5,000 new articles and multimedia features. These include more than nine hours of sound (e.g., for given musical instruments), about 8,000 still and motion pictures, interactive charts, and games. Encarta also includes colorful maps of states, countries, continents, and the world. Additional features include a game and a simple word processor that allows the user to take notes, download parts of the text, and write a paper. (Note that, given the reaction of many teachers to *any* use of an encyclopedia for research papers, the encouragement to use nothing but Encarta for such papers may not be considered a positive feature.)

As one would expect from Microsoft, there is full use of the Windows interface, which can lead to rather busy screens. There are a large number of hypertext links, as well as links from text to sound to graphics and back. Searching options include categories, keywords, and Boolean, as well as use of the timeline, table of contents, and the image gallery. Though fun to use, the combination of information, busy screens, and less-than-helpful help screens may confuse users. Even so, this is possibly the shape of the reference book of the future.

■ Infopedia. Spring Valley, N.Y.: Future Vision Multimedia, 1994.

Includes the full text of the *Funk & Wagnalls New Encyclopedia* with multimedia enhancements (notably considerable audio), plus *Merriam-Webster's Dictionary, Webster's New Biographical Dictionary, Merriam-Webster's Dictionary of Quotations, Merriam-Webster's Dictionary of English Usage,* the *Hammond World Atlas,* and *Roget's Twenty-first Century Thesaurus.*

■ Microsoft bookshelf: multimedia reference library. Redmond, Wash.: Microsoft Pr., 1994.

This collection of reference books, aimed at the end user, includes the second edition of the *Concise Columbia Encyclopedia.* Although it contains only the shorter, abridged version of the full *Columbia Encyclopedia,* it is worth noting that this exists, because many computer owners will have Bookshelf.

A pattern seems to be developing in which journals review the new versions of electronic encyclopedias (and other forms of reference tools, for that matter) in omnibus reviews. Some recent articles of value in evaluating electronic encyclopedias follow: Peter Jasco, "The 1999 Editions of General-Interest Encyclopedias," *Computers in Libraries* 19 (June 1999): 30-34; Peter Jasco, "Multimedia Strategies in Online Encyclopedias, Part I," *Information Today* 15 (April 1998): 40- ; Peter Jasco, "Part II," *Information Today* 15 (May 1998): 40; Barbara A. Burg and Amy M. Katzman, "Virtual Knowledge: The Best Buys in 1998 CD-ROM Encyclopedias," *Searcher* 6 (April 1998): 57-62; Stephen Del Vecchio, "Out for a Spin: A School Librarian Test Drives 14 CD-ROM Encyclopedias," *School Library Journal* 43 (Sept. 1997): 118-24; Linda A. Singer, "1997 Encyclopedias: Declining Titles,

Consolidations, from CD-ROM Titles to Online Programs," *Information Searcher* 9, no. 3 (1997): 15–18; and Walt Crawford, "Introductions and Interpedias," *Database* 20 (Feb./March 1997): 76–78.

In addition to the *Reference Books Bulletin* omnibus reviews in November and January of each year noted above, *Computers in Libraries* also published a series by the highly respected Peter Jacso, to date in the April issue of that journal, which should also be consulted.

Foreign Encyclopedias

English-language encyclopedias will naturally be used most often in American libraries, but no good reference librarian can afford to overlook the great general encyclopedias of other countries, some already mentioned earlier in this chapter. Not only should they be part of college and university reference collections, and in public libraries serving non-English-speaking constituents, but also part of good school libraries, where children's encyclopedias can be useful in foreign-language teaching.

Balay's *Guide to Reference Books* (pages 110 to 118) gives a good, brief introduction to foreign-language encyclopedias, pointing out strong features such as quality and number of illustrations, the history and literature of a given country, and other information not found in English-language encyclopedias. *Kister's Best Encyclopedias* also provides relatively short annotations for these, which, though much less detailed than his full entries, can be quite helpful.

In the following notes on outstanding contemporary encyclopedias in several foreign languages likely to be encountered in the United States, their use in American libraries will be emphasized. Appreciation of their history may be gained from Robert Collison's work, cited above.

Canadian

■ Canadian encyclopedia. 2d ed. James H. Harsh, ed. in chief. Edmonton, Alberta: Hurtig, 1988. 4v. Also available on CD-ROM as the Canadian Encyclopedia Plus.

Although in English, this work needs to be mentioned, both as an excellent example of a national encyclopedia and because American librarians should have at least a basic knowledge of their immediate neighboring countries. Given the competition, this encyclopedia has a definite bias—Canadiana and things Canadian, as well as a Canadian point of view. With about 9,500 articles, roughly 90 percent revised since the first edition, about 3,700 are biographical. The illustrations, mostly in full color, are very high quality, clearly rivaling (if not exceeding) the *Britannica* and *Americana*. A good analytical index provides easy access to the material.

The CD-ROM version has multimedia additions (sound, motion, and the like), some updating and additional entries, the full text of the *Gage Canadian Dictionary* (Toronto: Gage, 1983; 1313p.), *The Columbia Encyclopedia* (5th ed., 1993), *Roget's II: The New Thesaurus* (Boston: Houghton, 1988; unpaged), and the *Larousse English/French and French/English Dictionary* (London: Hamlyn, 1983; 352p.). Searching is available by title, by subject term, by use of Boolean operators, and via a term-weighting relevance ranking system.

Reviews

> *American Reference Books Annual* 28 (1997): 22 (electronic)
>
> *American Reference Books Annual* 20 (1989): 51 (print)
>
> *Reference Books Bulletin* 85 (April 15, 1989): 1444 (print)

French

■ Encyclopaedia universalis. 3d ed. Paris: Encyclopaedia Universalis, 1990. Distributed in the United States by Encyclopaedia Britannica. 30v. plus supplements.

Highly respected, and with this edition arranged similarly to the *Britannica*. The first twenty-three volumes (the *Corpus*) contain about 10,000 long articles on broad subjects by eminent French scholars. This is followed by the *Symposium,* in three volumes, consisting of 177 topical essays, primarily on current global problems, with many statistical tables. The third part is the *Thesaurus-Index,* in volumes 27 to 30, consisting of about 25,000 short articles plus an index to the set. France, French Canada, and the francophone world in general receive special emphasis, although the encyclopedia consciously attempts to cover the whole range of human knowledge. Generally, there are few colored illustrations, other than art reproductions. The annual supplement, which also functions much like a yearbook, is titled *Universalia.*

■ Grand Larousse universel en 15 volumes. Paris: Larousse, 1995. 15v.

About 190,000 short entries, following founder Pierre Larousse's approach in combining the functions of a dictionary (about half the entries relate to the French language) and encyclopedia. Includes many illustrations as well. A shorter version, *Actualia,* is also available, notable mainly for the inclusion of an updating service.

■ La grande encyclopédie. Paris: Librairie Larousse, 1971–90. 21v., atlas, and supplements.

Contains about 8,000 entries in alphabetical order, including many quite long articles, especially those for individual nations. Excellent cross-references add to the ease of use. In effect and intent, this replaces the great nineteenth-century work of the same title (thirty-one volumes, 1886 to 1902), although its emphasis on twentieth-century developments may lead the library to retain the earlier edition. The many illustrations, and maps nearly all in color, have been praised highly by reviewers.

German

■ Brockhaus enzyklopädie: in virundzwanzig bänden. 20th ed. Wiesbaden: Brockhaus, 1996. 25v.

Another classic German short-entry encyclopedia, with more than 260,000 entries in this edition. Unlike most encyclopedias listed above, this is wholly revised every few years, in addition to having a yearbook. Another interesting feature is the special section in each sixth volume updating the previous articles. International in scope, with a strong German emphasis, it retains its clear and simple style in unsigned articles addressed to the general reader. Combining the features of dictionary and encyclopedia, this is a useful source for abbreviations, giving the original, its German equivalent, and a brief description. The editors consciously attempt to keep the many bibliographies up-to-date, making them a useful source not only for German works, but also German translations of non-German works and, depending on the article (such as English Literature), citations to works in other languages. More than 33,000 illustrations, still tending to small black and white but with increasing color, are nearly all very clear, and include facsimile autographs, photographs of persons, and excellent small maps. The color reproductions of artworks are particularly good.

The extent of revisions in this edition is not surprising to those familiar with the history of the house of Brockhaus. Its founder, Friedrich Arnold Brockhaus, was a dedicated believer in frequent revisions, and "in 1817 and 1818, volumes of the second, third, and fourth editions were appearing concurrently—a curiosity in bibliography, in the history of the encyclopedia, and in publishing history in general" (Collison, *Encyclopaedias,* p. 159). That it retains the features for which it has long been noted assures its usefulness in American libraries.

■ Meyers enzyklopädisches Lexikon in 25 bänden. 9th ed. Mannheim: Bibliographisches Institut Lexikonverlag, 1971-81. 25v. plus supplements.

A good example of how titles change over time. The eighth edition (*Meyers Neues Lexikon,* published 1936 to 1942) is notable for its heavy Nazi bias; this is an almost wholly new work, returning the quality of the first seven editions. Generally the 250,000 entries are brief, although each volume includes a few longer essays on broader topics. Bibliographies, included with many articles, are brief but up-to-date. The 26,000 small illustrations, only a few in color, are germane and generally quite good. Biographies include living people, rare in general encyclopedias. The annual *Jarhbuch* (1974-) includes a cumulative index to the yearbooks.

Italian

■ Enciclopedia del novecento. Roma: Istituto della Enciclopedia Italiana, 1978-89. 8v.

Deliberately presented as a modern complement to the *Enciclopedia Italiana.* Contains long survey articles on twentieth-century developments in both theory and in objective reality. As with the *Enciclopedia Italiana,* there are many illustrations of high quality.

■ Enciclopedia europea. Milan: Garzanti, 1976-84. 12v.

Another current encyclopedia from a different publisher, but with authoritative articles on modern European events and points of view. Includes many non-Italian contributors (even some from North America). For the most part, articles are short, although geographic entries (nations, cities, provinces) and some general articles (e.g., on schools of philsophical thought) are much longer. A considerable percentage of entries are biographical. This title contains excellent maps and illustrations, mostly photographs, but all are in black and white. The twelfth volume is an index and classified bibliography, which helps make up in part for the lack of such with the articles. In many senses, as well as standing on its own, this is a useful complement to the previous title.

■ Enciclopedia Italiana de Scienze, Lettre ed Arti. Roma: Istituto della Enciclopdia Italiana, fondata da Giovanni Treccani, 1929- . 49v. (in progress).

The basic set consists of thirty-six volumes, with supplements about every ten years; these are true supplements, revising and updating existing articles as well as adding new material. Each volume gives the editorial staff and identifies contributors and their contributions, which are signed with initials. Contributors are chiefly European scholars and professors, with Italians in the majority. Strong in the humanities and biography, but representing the "circle of knowledge" of the 1930s (but, fortunately, without too much Fascist bias), it retains its value for American libraries chiefly for the large number of well-produced illustrations, especially those in sepia. This is an excellent source for artworks, localities, landmarks, and similar material. The colored illustrations are not quite up to the standard of the *Encyclopedia of World Art,* although they range much more widely in subjects; the small black-and-white ones aren't quite up to the standard of the *Brockhaus.* The maps, many of them foldouts, produced by the Touring Club of Italy, are clear but not indexed on the verso (as in *Brockhaus*). The bibliographies appended to the longer articles are very good, emphasizing European and English-language titles, but have rarely been updated in the appendixes.

This work has been hailed by Collison as "one of the most important encyclopedias of the 20th century . . . one of the finest examples of the national encyclopedia ever produced . . . and the standard of reproduction of illustrations has never been surpassed in a work of similar nature" (*Encyclopaedias,* p. 207).

According to Livio C. Stecchini ("On Encyclopedias in Time and Space," *American Behavioral Scientist* 6 [Sept. 1962]: 5), this "outstanding achievement of learning, was made possible by the unique circumstance that in that generation almost all Italian intellectuals, from the Communists to the Fascists, including the radical democrats and the liberals, were under the influence of Hegelian philosophy. The *Enciclopedia Italiana* realized Hegel's program for a universal knowledge. Because of the Hegelian notion that the truth of an idea is in its history, it has approached better than any other encyclopedia the idea of providing complete and objective information; topics are treated historically with a full review of the several opinions on the subject. Therefore, even though the work was written under Fascist auspices, all points of view succeeded in finding some expression in it. Because of the historical method and because of the political circumstances, the *Enciclopedia Italiana* falls short in the treatment of truly contemporary issues."

Russian

■ Bol'shaia Sovetskaia Entsiklopediia. 3d ed. Moskva: Sovetskaia Entsiklopediia, 1970–79. 30v.

■ Great Soviet encyclopedia: a translation of the third edition. A. M. Prok-
horov, ed. in chief. New York: Macmillan, 1973–83. 32v.

The English translation of the Russian text differs from the original in
omitting brief articles—mostly dictionary and gazetteer entries, according to the editors, totaling less than 1 percent of the text (these are
indicated in the list of contents for each volume). Also omitted are
many illustrations from the original—maps, photographs, etc. The editors have updated some of the statistics, dates, and name changes but
not consistently; such updated articles are marked as such.

Reactions of reviewers to the translation have been mixed, with
some feeling that it isn't very good and others finding it smooth and
easy to read. For those who wish to compare the text, each article of
the English includes an exact citation to the original Russian.

This work is of value primarily for the coverage of lesser-known people and places in the former Soviet Union, as well as for what has
turned out to be the ultimate expression of the Soviet point of view
and the current state of Soviet thought just prior to glasnost and the
breakup of the USSR. Surprisingly to some, other than a fairly clear
Marxist-Leninist bias, especially in socioeconomic topics, the articles
are reasonably objective.

Many of the 100,000-plus articles have appended bibliographies, including all found in the original set. Works in languages not using the
Latin alphabet are given in the Library of Congress (LC) transliteration
system for that language or, if there is no LC system, in the transliteration
system used through the English text. Names of authors whose works
are translated into Russian appear in the original language, not in Russian
transliteration. The bibliographies in articles about people are divided
into works by and works about, with the latter first listing those in Russian, then foreign works in Russian translation, then in other languages.
Other bibliographies usually follow the arrangement of the article.

The English translation, arranged by the Latin (not the Cyrillic) alphabet, must be used with the index. Prepared by computer, the index
is detailed and accurate and is estimated to include about 500,000 entries. Clear instructions for use are given.

Spanish

■ Enciclopedia universal ilustrada europeo-americana. Barcelona: Espasa;
Madrid: Espasa-Calpe, 1905–33. 80v. in 81. Suplemento anual, 1934– .
1935– . Irregular.

One of the world's most extensive encyclopedias, it is generally known as *Espasa*. Volumes 1 to 70 and the *Apéndice* volumes 1 to 10 (as well as the new *Apéndice,* which updates a number of articles in the original eighty volumes) are arranged alphabetically by short topic, with many cross-references. Supplements are arranged by broad topics (e.g., Geografia y Historia), further subdivided by countries. It has both dictionary and encyclopedic features. Dictionary entries give etymology and French, Italian, English, German, Portuguese, Catalan, and Esperanto equivalents but no illustrative quotations. Encyclopedic features include its broad international coverage, though it is especially strong for Spain and Latin America and in biographical and geographical entries. Bibliographies for longer articles have been well selected, although most are, of course, dated and do not appear to include Spanish translations from original works of non-Spanish writers. *Espasa* is noted for its large number of geographical, geological, historical, and statistical maps, including those for a number of small cities, and for its many full-color reproductions of paintings (though these are excelled by those in *The Encyclopedia of World Art*). It is an excellent source of Spanish and Spanish-American biography.

The biennial supplements tend to be about two years behind. In spite of the time lag, they are valuable for their large number of brief biographies, often with accompanying photographs, found in the "Biografia y Necrologia" section, and for the more than 400 pages covering socioeconomic conditions by country, with emphasis on Spain. Sports are also well covered, with a separate section on bullfighting. The supplements are also useful for statistics on tourism and for world coverage of the arts, especially dance, theater, and film—profusely illustrated with stills and with lists of award-winning films and a good bibliography. Unlike the basic set, articles in the supplements are signed—nearly all the contributors are Spanish and most are writers or members of the academic professions.

In using the basic set, it may be well to remember the comment of Stecchini that it is "remarkable for its lack of concern with the reliability of the information and for the casualness of the editing, by which two entries may be dedicated to the same person under different names" ("On Encyclopedias in Time and Space," p. 3).

In summary, foreign encyclopedias are useful in American libraries for

1. Viewpoints other than American
2. Biographies of nationals of the countries of publication
3. Excellent illustrations (in some cases)

4. Plots of literary works, dramas, and films
5. Facsimiles of autographs of famous people
6. Abbreviations
7. Subjects of interest to the nation of the encyclopedia
8. Maps of cites and towns (useful, among other things, for travelers)
9. Bibliographies that emphasize the language of the country of publication

General Reference Features of Encyclopedias

One great strength of the modern general encyclopedia is that it incorporates the features of many other types of reference sources:

1. Like an unabridged monolingual dictionary, it defines words and sometimes gives their pronunciation.
2. Like a bibliography, it cites sources of further information (although not as comprehensively as required by some users).
3. Like a universal biographical dictionary, it devotes generous amounts of space to biographies of individuals, both living and dead.
4. Like a gazetteer, it supplies pertinent information on large and small geographic areas, more often than not with accompanying maps.

That it will continue to retain these features, even in electronic formats, seems more than likely; and, as noted, its inadequacies must be filled by additional forms of reference sources, such as

1. Special encyclopedias, for fuller or more highly technical information
2. Bibliographies, indexes, and abstracting services designed to meet the need for fuller and more current information
3. Unabridged dictionaries for further information on words and their usage
4. Statistical sources that provide more detailed and current data, especially on socioeconomic conditions
5. Atlases, which provide maps on a larger scale and in more detail, especially for smaller areas

8

Sources of Statistics

This chapter acknowledges the widespread production and uses of statistics in today's world—with no reason to doubt they will continue to multiply—and suggests that reference librarians can and must improve their understanding of statistics. There are two different common meanings to the word *statistics:* (1) the science of the collection, analysis, and interpretation of numeric data; and (2) collections of numeric data. For the most part, this chapter is concerned with the latter, listing and annotating many different types of compilations of data from among the even vaster number of such compilations available. In addition, the chapter makes a few comments on the types of data available and suggests some sources useful in understanding the processes and methods by which statistics are collected and analyzed.

A conscious effort has been made to indicate the availability of electronic sources for the data, especially those sources available via the Internet; the growth of that source, and the popularity of electronic formats for data in general, means that the odds increase daily that any given source will be in machine-readable format. Thus, the reader who wishes the data in a convenient downloadable format should always double-check online sources to see if the desired information is now available on them.

It is a truism to speak of the pervasiveness of statistics in modern society. So obsessed are we with numbers (though the written or spoken word may be highly suspect, numerical information suggests precision and great accuracy) that we use them to "prove" practically anything. From all sides, including government agencies, research organizations, colleges and universities, corporations, and nearly every other type of organization invented by human beings, we are bombarded with numerical data on every conceivable topic. Important decisions in our national and personal lives are made on the basis of statistics. Alas, the collection and interpretation of statistics is not an exact science, but rather partly an art and partly a science. Librarians therefore should appreciate this wisdom from the authors of a classic introductory statistics text: "Those who accept statistics indiscriminately will be duped unnecessarily; those who distrust statistics indiscriminately will often be ignorant unnecessarily; recognize, therefore, that there is an alternative between gullibility and blind distrust" (W. Allen Wallis and Harry V. Roberts, *Statistics: A New Approach* [Glencoe, Ill.: Free Pr., 1956], p. 17).

The development of and ongoing improvements in the computer appear to have merely increased and accelerated a trend already begun with the development of measuring instruments in the early modern period—both the ability to collect and manipulate data, and to quickly disseminate the results, continue to increase, apparently exponentially. Thus, it is easily possible to become wholly inundated with numerical data, some of very questionable validity and others of great accuracy and importance.

Statistical Reference Service and Evaluation of Statistical Sources

It is a fair question to ask why reference librarians should be concerned with statistics. In answer, at least three reasons present themselves: first, as facilitators or intermediaries between users and information, they are increasingly called upon to assist users not only in locating data, but in interpreting it. Second, the literature of every discipline, even the humanities and arts, reflects increasing use and sophistication of quantitative methods of research. And third, it appears that reference librarians will increasingly be expected to undertake research of their own, which will require at least a basic knowledge of statistics.

Texts, Mostly in Library and Information Work

In recent years, librarians have become more aware of the need to understand at least basic statistical techniques, both to provide intelligent reference service and to study their own discipline. A number of books about statistics and general texts on research methods are available to enhance this awareness.

Strangely, in this author's experience at least, many librarians seem to think that *research* is a synonym for *statistics.* Although much research does require numerical analysis, many methods do not. And, surprisingly, often the data analysis that is required is invalidated by a lack of rigor in research design or data collection in the first place. The following should be useful but, of course, will only be useful if read . . .

■ Baker, Sharon, and F. W. Lancaster. The measurement and evaluation of library services. 2d ed. Arlington, Va.: Information Resources Pr., 1991. 411p.

Arranged by function to be evaluated, rather than method, as are most similar books. An excellent discussion of the topics, although with less detail on the how-to than some.

■ Freed, Melvyn N., and others. The educator's desk reference: a source-book of educational information and research. New York: American Council on Education, 1989. 536p.

A general handbook. In the current context, particularly useful for its statistical section, which lists various standard tests by what the user wishes to accomplish and by the type of data available for analysis. Does not explain how to calculate the statistic but what it does and what it doesn't do, with warnings about dangers of interpretation.

■ Hafner, Arthur W. Descriptive statistical techniques for librarians. 2d ed. Chicago: ALA, 1998. 323p.

A basic text, as it says, discussing descriptive statistics only, with many examples and exercises (with answers). Has added material on continuous improvement, benchmarking, and other currently popular topics. A useful feature for the innumerate is the use of words as well as mathematical formulas to explain calculations. Should be supplemented with a source on inferential statistics.

■ Hernon, Peter. Statistics: a component of the research process. Rev. ed. Norwood, N.J.: Ablex, 1994. 248p.

Complements other texts, with more emphasis on the research background and data collection.

■ Lancaster, F. Wilfrid. If you want to evaluate your library. 2d ed. Champaign, Ill.: Univ. of Illinois Graduate School of Library and Information Science, 1993. 352p.

A simplified "textbook" version of the Baker and Lancaster title.

■ Mellon, Constance A. Naturalistic inquiry for library science: methods and applications for research, evaluation and teaching. New York: Greenwood, 1990. 201p.

General information on qualitative research, but rather jargonish. Lots of library examples (versus the usual social science examples).

■ Powell, Ronald R. Basic research methods for librarians. 3d ed. Norwood, N.J.: Ablex, 1997. 281p.

Offers research design, sampling, data collection, etc., complete with a number of examples. Includes historical and qualitative as well as quantitative research methods. In effect, a basic social science text with emphasis on librarianship.

■ Simpson, Ian S. Basic statistics for librarians. 3d ed. London: Library Assn.; Chicago: ALA, 1988. 242p.

Each edition expands as well as updates the previous. Aimed at managers with relatively little statistical training and background, provides explanations, examples, and helpful information on selecting the appropriate test for a given application.

■ Simpson, Ian S. How to interpret statistical data: a guide for librarians and information scientists. London: Library Assn., 1990. 78p.

Companion to the above, with a clearly defined purpose. Not a textbook for the researcher but a guide for the user of the research, assuming no background at all in statistics.

■ Slater, Margaret. Research methods in library and information studies. London: Library Assn., 1990. 182p.

A basic guide, including information on collecting data and communicating research, as well as statistical analysis, but with an emphasis on survey research. Unlike some of the other sources listed here, includes a substantial discussion of qualitative techniques.

■ Swisher, Robert, and Charles R. McClure. Research for decision making: methods for librarians. Chicago: ALA, 1984. 209p.

Another textbook, but this one is aimed at managers, showing how to use good research to directly inform decision making. Includes many examples along the way.

- Zweizig, Douglas, and others. The tell it! manual: the complete program for evaluating library performance. Chicago: ALA, 1996. 270p.

  Based on the American Library Association (ALA) series of manuals for evaluating and planning public library services. Though somewhat elementary, this is based on solid methodology and tested in actual training workshops. Includes suggestions for communicating the data as well as collecting and analyzing it. An even more simplified textbook approach, again covering all aspects of library operations. The emphasis here is on "action research" for the general librarian; thus, the methods and approaches may be less rigorous than in some of the other sources listed here, but they are still likely to provide information, as in the old phrase, close enough for all but the most rigorous research project.

Visual Data Presentation

The following titles by Edward R. Tufte are generally regarded as the definitive works on the subject, complete with examples, case studies, and dos and don'ts as well as theory:

> *The Visual Display of Quantitative Information* (Chesire, Conn.: Graphics Pr., 1992; 197p.);
>
> *Envisioning Information* (Chesire, Conn.: Graphics Pr., 1990; 128p.); and
>
> *Visual Explanations: Images and Quantities, Evidence and Narrative* (Chesire, Conn.: Graphics Pr., 1997; 156p.).

Titles with less detail and, thus, in some ways more accessible follow:

- Henry, Gary T. Graphing data: techniques for display and analysis. Thousand Oaks, Calif.: Sage, 1995. 161p.
- Schmid, Calvin F. Statistical graphics: design principles and practices. New York: Wiley, 1983. 212p.

Because most of the work in which librarians will be involved concerns social statistics, the following classic should be ready at hand:

- Blalock, Hubert M. Social statistics. 2d rev. ed. New York: McGraw-Hill, 1979. 625p.

Problems with Using Statistics

Reference librarians may next address themselves to considering some reasons for the difficulty of statistical questions and suggestions for evaluating statistical sources. Statistical questions may be difficult because the answers are in a form that is hard to obtain, understand, identify, and evaluate. Often the material needed to answer a single question is scattered, so that one part will be found in one publication and others in other publications; and the parts do not fit together because of differences in bases of coverage or units of measurement, even in the same series. Although the increase in availability and use of electronic sources, and the access afforded by the Internet, have improved the ability to obtain numbers of some kind, the questions still remain as to whether they have been collected at all, and for what purpose, under what assumptions, and with what degree of accuracy. Darrell Huff's *How to Lie with Statistics* (New York: Norton, 1954; 142p.) remains a classic in its description of the difficulties in using statistics.

Experienced librarians well know that some users want more up-to-date statistics than have been published or they want them arranged differently from the way the compilers have published them—by, say, age and county when they have been published by sex and state; or they want consumption statistics when only production statistics have been compiled. Such requests may require librarians to think of extramural sources—for example, the agency that collected the data may have the needed figures on file and will make them available. Or, increasingly, the raw data are directly available, and the user may (with the appropriate combination of knowledge and software) rearrange them to suit the need.

Still, sometimes certain statistics have not been collected or made available, even though the requestor's position may be that, surely, somewhere, there are the data on the desired topic. It is hard to convince this person that the statistics may not have been collected, perhaps because of protests from certain groups, as in the case of the 1970 Census of Population, when the Bureau of the Census was not permitted to include a question on church membership. Or the data may have been lost—the author, for example, had to confront a person who could not believe that the 1890 raw census data (other than a few volumes) had been lost in a fire.

Another aspect of nonavailability may be the confidentiality of records—not whether they have been collected. Other data are not available because of the nature of the subject (e.g., rape or homelessness), for which only widely ranging estimates have been made by different groups. Also, persons often ask for comparable statistics on such subjects as marriage and divorce, or juvenile delinquency, for periods earlier than are available.

It is important in the preliminary reference interview with the inquirer to determine the following:

1. How accurate the data must be (will a rough estimate or rounded figures be sufficient?)
2. Exactly what is wanted (e.g., if statistics of the "largest libraries" are wanted, is size defined by number of titles or volumes in the collection,

by amount of budget, by population served, by cubic capacity of building, etc.?)

3. How the statistics are to be classified (e.g., by year, month, day; by gender, race, or nationality; by weight or count)

4. If any comparisons are wanted, and on what factors the comparisons are to be made

5. What time span is to be covered (how recent, how far back, what intervals are desired [e.g., daily, monthly, annually])

6. In what format the results are desired (tables, graphs, charts, or maps; printed or machine-readable; if graphics, color or black and white)

Evaluation of statistical sources accents the importance of primary (i.e., original) sources in statistical reference work. They are usually more accurate, because in any reproduction other than photoreproduction, errors may creep in. They may and often are more detailed and more complete than in a secondary source. Primary sources may be far superior to secondary ones in providing notes explaining how (and even why) the data were collected and any limitations—recognition of bias in data collection, change in agency responsible for collection of data, change in classification (such as that reflected in a redefinition of "rural" or "metropolitan area"), degree of accuracy of calculation—to be remembered in using the data.

One type of note that is not included in the previous paragraph is singled out for special comment, because it is often a source of confusion. The measure here is the "index number," or "base number," used to measure relative changes over time. Suppose that the average cost of a group of commodities in 1982 is considered as "100" (the base). If the cost in, say, 1990 was 95 percent greater, this would be expressed as "195." But if statisticians converted to a different base year, the index number would change. Thus, merely obtaining an updated index to a previous piece of data is not enough to compare the two numbers unless one also knows the base year (or month or other time period). As the conditions of life change, the older base figure becomes more and more meaningless, so that the base is changed to reflect the new conditions.

Remember that, at any given time, one may encounter several different indexes—a reminder that although a base of 100 for a given time period (e.g., 1992 = 100) may be the one most frequently seen, it is by no means the only one used. For example, the November 1998 *Consumer Price Index* uses the following: 1982–1984 = 100; December 1997 = 100; December 1982 = 100; 1988 = 100, among others, as well as the 1992 figure.

Because the quality of the notes in all statistical sources (secondary as well as primary) is so critical in judging the value of the sources, let us sample their variety from a superior secondary source, the *Statistical Abstract of the United States, 1997* (Washington, D.C.: Govt. Print. Off., 1997; 1023p.). Following each example is an indication of the type of note being illustrated.

p. 8, table 2, headnote: "Total population includes Armed Forces abroad; civilian population excludes Armed Forces." (Statement of universe note)

p. 12, table 9, note 3: "[Chinese immigrants] includes Taiwan." (Clarification of definition of national origin based on two nations' claiming sovereignty)

p. 14, table 12, note 3: "The revised 1970 resident population count . . . incorporates changes due to errors found after tabulations were completed." (Explanation of variation in this table with earlier editions)

p. 27, figure 1.3, headnote: "The mean center of population is that point at which an imaginary, flat, weightless, and rigid map of the United States would balance if weights of identical value were placed on it so that each weight represented the location of one person on the date of the census." (Definition of special term)

p. 29, table 27, note 1: "Persons per square mile were calculated on the basis of land area data from the 1990 census." (Clarification of term that applies in this table to data from 1980, 1990, and 1996)

p. 32, table 32, headnote: "Based on Current Population Survey, see text section 1 and Appendix III." (Source and cross-references within this text)

p. 33, table 33, headnote: "In thousands, except percent. As of July 1." (Unit indicator, time restrictor)

p. 34, table 34, headnote: "These estimates are consistent with data released in PE-47, PE-48, PPL-49, and PPL-50 released August 20, 1996. Consequently the estimates shown in this table are not consistent with subsequently released national and state estimates." (Comparability, and later lack of same)

p. 36, table 36, headnote: "Series A is the preferred series model and uses state-to-state migration observed from 1975–76 through 1993–94." (Definition, time restrictor)

p. 44, table 44, headnote. "As of April 1. Resident population." (Time restrictor, universe)

p. 55, table 58, headnote: "Excludes members of the Armed Forces except those living off post or with their families on post." (Universe defined. Note difference between this and the "civilian population" in table 2)

p. 61, table 72, note 1: "Persons of Hispanic origin may be of any race." (In a table with entries for total; White; Black; American Indian, Eskimo, Aleut; Asian, Pacific Islander; and Hispanic, to clarify why total does not add all categories)

p. 120, table 172, headnote: "Based on the Current Population Survey, and subject to sampling error; see text, section 1 and Appendix III." (Citation, warning about errors, and internal cross-reference)

p. 130, table 191, note 1: "Comparisons beginning 1990 with data for earlier years should be made with caution as estimates of change may reflect improvements in the design rather than changes in hospital use." (Time restrictor, comparability)

p. 131, table 193, note 3: "Figure does not meet standards of reliability or precision." (Explanation of lack of data in some cells of table)

p. 138, table 206, headnote: "Beginning 1985, the levels of estimates may not be comparable to estimates for 1980 because the later data are based on a revised questionnaire and field procedures; for further information see source." (Time restrictor, comparability, data collection method change)

p. 138, table 206, note 4: "Child's loss of more than half a school day because of illness or injury, computed for children 6-16 years of age. Beginning 1985, children 5-17 years old." (Unit indicator for heading "School-loss days," change in universe)

p. 174, table 268, headnote: "Covers children 3-21 served under IDEA, Part B and Chapter 1 of ESEA (SOP)." (Universe defined—note difference in definition of "children" from previous table)

p. 177, table 277, headnote: "Through 1985, data based on 10 percent sample; thereafter based on all ACT tested seniors." (Unit definition, comparability—note substantial change in sample versus universe)

p. 681, table 1117, headnote: "In millions of pounds, except per capita in pounds." (Variation in unit within same table)

p. 681, table 1117, note 2: "Fiscal year for fruits; calendar year for vegetables and potatoes." (Variation in time limit)

p. 725, table 1200, citation note: "Source Bureau of the Census, Internet site <http://www.census.gov/ftp/pub/hhes/www/hvs.html> (accessed 29 July 1997)." (Citation to a dynamic data source on the Web)

Awareness of these notes is critical for careful statistical reference work, especially because many users are apt to overlook them. It should also be noted that prefaces to statistical compilations and articles that discuss problems of data analysis (such as those in the *Monthly Labor Review*) will be valuable in evaluating sources. However, although one would expect the librarian to always read the prefaces and introductory matter of any reference source, such material may not be available. Notably, to date at least, many machine-readable forms of statistical compilations leave out much of the notes and prefatory material found in the printed versions or may effectively bury them within the "help" feature. Or, especially in the case of the original raw data, the explanations may be in a separate publication or file, such as the "code book" used in entering and analyzing the data.

Although most of the remainder of this chapter is devoted to annotating a representative list of statistical reference sources, it may be useful at this point to suggest a short list of the most frequently consulted titles, along with page references to their annotations:

(page 445)   Almanacs
(page 405)   *American Statistics Index*
(page 396)   *Encyclopedia of Statistical Sciences*
(page 407)   *Statistical Abstract* (and supplements)
(page 406)   *Statistical Reference Index*
(page 402)   *Statistics Sources*
(page 421)   *Survey of Current Business*
(page 447)   *UN Statistical Yearbook*
(page 404)   U.S. Bureau of the Census, *Census Catalog and Guide*

Work with statistical sources brings to light a most valuable skill of good reference librarians: the ability to classify or categorize sources rapidly—a bit of mental gymnastics, so to speak—in order to try to connect types of sources and types of questions. A review of the more general types of sources thus seems in order.

1. Bibliographies and indexes
   a. National library catalogs are a source of books on statistical methods and for location of compilations of statistics on broad subjects.
   b. Guides to the literature of subject fields supply pertinent sources of statistics.
   c. Indexes and abstracting services are often a source of current data.
2. Biographical sources. These are useful only for such specific vital statistics as birth and death dates, sex, age, place of residence, and the like.
3. Dictionaries. These are useful only for population statistics of larger geographical areas, for statistics on colleges and universities, and, to varying degrees, definitions of statistical terms.
4. Encyclopedias
   a. General encyclopedias contain (usually for larger geographical areas) socioeconomic statistics such as area, population, education,

production, and the like that must be updated by yearbooks, almanacs, and similar sources.

b. They also contain general articles on statistical theories and methods.

c. Specialized encyclopedias in appropriate subject fields are even better sources on theories and methods, for example, the *International Encyclopedia of the Social Sciences* (David L. Sills, ed. New York: Macmillan, 1968-91; 19v.) and *Encyclopedia of Statistical Sciences* (this latter title is described later in this chapter).

This chapter's emphasis is clearly on collections and sources of statistics, rather than methods and theories, but we may indicate a few such sources, with an emphasis on those of particular use to librarians dealing with statistics.

Terminology

Statistical reference service cannot fail to recognize the problem of terminology. Not unique to the collection and interpretation of statistics, it is faced by all disciplines, especially in the social and behavioral sciences, with a rapidly changing vocabulary, and has resulted in a continuing effort on the part of those responsible for statistical activities to attempt some uniformity in definitions of terms—some standardization that will result in relative stability in the data collected, as well as its interpretation. Evidence of this concern is found in the following special dictionaries and encyclopedias.

■ Colby, Robert W., and Thomas A. Meyers. The encyclopedia of technical market indicators. Homewood, Ill.: Dow-Jones Irwin, 1988. 581p.

More than 100 standard stock-market indicators explained by experts in the respective fields. Gives definitions, examples, graphics. Notably, all indicators have been tested for validity and reliability. Though not for the novice, is the most complete work of its kind.

■ Dictionary of U.S. government statistical terms. Alfred N. Garwood and Louise L. Hornor, eds. Palo Alto, Calif.: Information Pub., 1991. 247p.

Covers about 1,000 terms. Gives term, definition, agency that developed it, and a brief discussion of the data collection and calculation. Although very specialized terms are not included, this should meet the needs of most library users.

■ Encyclopedia of statistical sciences. Samuel Kotz and Norman L. Johnson, eds. in chief. New York: Wiley, 1987-88. 9v.

Intended for both experts and nonexperts but assumes some basic statistics and mathematics. The level of writing on a topic varies with complexity, including what is assumed in the article, with many formulae and a few citations with almost every article. Provides a middle ground between elementary texts and the very detailed Chemical Rubber Company (CRC) handbooks, with broader coverage as well. Cumulative index to the set.

■ Jerrard, H. G., and D. B. McNeill. A dictionary of scientific units: including dimensionless numbers and scales. 6th ed. London and New York: Chapman & Hall, 1992. 255p.

The standard work, with more than 900 entries arranged by name of unit. Gives definition, relevant historical facts, usually some indication of size of unit, and citation to sources. Five appendixes, including British and American weights and measures, International System of Units (SI) units, and conversions. Has a detailed analytical index.

■ Library statistics [Z39.7-1995]. National Information Standards Organization. Bethesda, Md.: National Information Standards Organization, 1997. 18p.

The "official" standard definitions for U.S. library statistics, with definitions. This is probably more technical than most libraries will ever need, but all librarians should be aware that the standard exists.

■ Marriott, F. H. C. A dictionary of statistical terms. 5th rev. ed. Harlow, England: Longman; New York: Wiley, 1990. 223p.

Considerably changed from the previous editions, notably in dropping many foreign, ephemeral, and obsolete terms and adding about 400 new words, especially related to medical statistics and statistical computing.

■ Petersen, William, and Renee Petersen. Dictionary of demography: terms, concepts and institutions. New York: Greenwood, 1986. 2v. Biographies. Westport, Conn.: Greenwood, 1984. 2v. Multilingual glossary. 1 vol.

The first two volumes contain 1,500 entries on demographics and related topics, with listings of national demographic-statistics bureaus. Most articles include bibliographies. Index by name/subject. Another volume provides two-way glossaries of the terms in English and French, Spanish, Italian, and German. English/Russian and English/Japanese and Chinese listings. Biographies are indexed in the glossary's index.

■ Vogt, W. Paul. Dictionary of statistics and methodology: a nontechnical guide for the social sciences. 2d ed. Newbury Park, Calif.: Sage, 1998. 253p.

> More than 1,000 statistics and methodological terms used in social and behavioral sciences. Brief definitions emphasize concepts more than formulas. Less complete than Marriott's volume, but easier for laypersons to understand.

Occupations and Industries

Related to the above, the dictionaries of occupations and industries are often used to define the categories of data collection as well as provide search terms for information retrieval.

■ Dictionary of occupational titles. 4th ed. Washington, D.C.: Govt. Print. Off., 1991. 1404p. Also available in a commercial reprint in hardcover.

> Describes the vast majority of occupations in the United States. *DOT* is widely used by employers (in classifying similar jobs and establishing wages and salaries), by the government, and by many other sources that discuss the job market. *See* below, pages 435 to 438, for several sources that use these codes.

■ Canadian classification and dictionary of occupations. 7th ed. Ottawa: Canadian Govt. Pub. Centre, 1987. 385p.

> Similar to *DOT,* but includes ratings for level of education, time needed to learn the job, physical effort, etc. Must be used with six other booklets that actually describe the jobs.

■ International standard classification of occupations. Washington, D.C.: International Labor Office, 1990. 457p.

> An international approach to the occupational classifications done by the *DOT* for the United States. Based on degree of skill and kind of work. Indexes by both numbers and titles.

The classification systems for business and industry were revised as a result of the North American Free Trade Agreement (NAFTA), but the older classifications are still used in many sources.

■ U.S. Office of Management and the Budget. North American industry classification system. Lanham, Md.: Bernan, 1997– . Also online.

The new standard classification for all sorts of "industry" including nearly every type of occupation, manufacturer, or profession (e.g., information industry, professional services, arts). Combines the *Canadian Standard Industrial Classification for Companies and Enterprises 1980* (Ottawa: Statistics Canada, 1986; 381p.), *Clasificación Mexicana de Actividades y Productos 1999 (CMAP)* (Aguascalientes, Mexico: Instituto Nacional de Estadística, Geografía e Informática, 1998; 481p.), and the *Standard Industrial Classification Manual* (Washington, D.C.: Govt. Print. Off., 1987; 705p.) into one system. However, at the beginning of the new millennium, some printed and electronic statistical sources continue to use the older system, so the older system should be retained. The website includes a cross-reference list between the SIC and NAICS.

An outstanding example of a federal agency concerned with definitions of terms is the U.S. Bureau of the Census, and no user of its statistical array should ignore the prefatory definitions that accompany many of its collections of data, such as the decennial *Census of Population.* These definitions are particularly significant in constructing comparative tables of data, as terminology has been changed and refined since the early censuses and continues to change with every new one.

■ Evaluating censuses of population and housing. Washington, D.C.: Bureau of the Census, 1985. 255p.

   Detailed information on the collection, arrangement, and interpretation of census data.

Professional associations, as well as government agencies, are concerned with this problem of terminology, and those who have struggled with inadequate and inaccurate statistics for libraries were hopeful that they would be improved as a result of the ALA Statistical Coordinating Project. These efforts have borne fruit in part in Mary Jo Lynch's, *Cooperative System for Public Library Data Collection: Final Report of a Pilot Project* (Chicago: ALA, Office for Research, 1987 [123 leaves]). For a brief description of current programs, *see Library Statistics Cooperative Program* (Washington, D.C.: National Commission on Libraries and Information Science, National Center for Education Statistics, 1999; 6p.).

Another aspect of the question of what is being measured is geographic areas. It is important, for example, to be aware that some counties in the United States have changed size and borders since their establishment, sometimes through the creation of several counties from an earlier one, less often by merging of two counties. It is often a problem to locate statistics for a small area, because broad areas such as countries, states, and provinces are usually the units for which statistics are reported. Often, in fact, the local data are only available from commercial sources, such as market research firms. A number of sources for such data are discussed in chapter 9, "Sources of Geographical Information."

General Sources

Bibliographic Sources

The access route to the desired statistics is frequently though the guides, bibliographies, indexes, and abstracts to the statistical literature, as well as to those in individual subject fields. Listed below are some examples of these works that alert the user to the existence of specific statistical data. First, however, some guides to the theoretical field.

BIBLIOGRAPHIES AND INDEXES OF STATISTICAL METHODS

- Current index to statistics: applications, methods, and theory. Washington, D.C.: American Statistical Assn., 1975- . Annual.

  Indexes all the major journals cover to cover, plus selective indexing of other journals, books, book chapters, conference proceedings, etc. Covers mostly fairly technical mathematical material but also application-oriented material (e.g., response rates, interrater reliability). Index by author and by keyword, with some augmented context.

- Kendall, Maurice George, and Alison G. Doig. Bibliography of statistical literature. New York: Hafner, 1962-68. 3v.

  Covers papers, but not books, mostly in Western languages from the sixteenth century to 1958. Books are covered by Oscar Buros's *Statistical Methodology Reviews,* 1933/38-1941/50 (New York: Wiley, 1938-51; 3v.).

- Statistical theory and method abstracts. Edinburgh: Longman, etc., for International Statistical Institute, 1959- . Quarterly.

  Updates *Bibliography of Statistical Literature.* Covers periodical articles, conference proceedings, some monographs. Classified, with author index each issue, and cumulated annually. Annual index to book reviews.

BIBLIOGRAPHIES OF DATA SOURCES

- Andriot, Donna, Jay Andriot, and Laurie Andriot. Guide to U.S. government statistics. McLean, Va.: Documents Index, 1961- .

More than 13,000 annotated references, arranged by Superintendent of Documents (SuDocs) classification. Annotations give date of creation and authority and often the purpose for which the data were collected; OCLC Online Computer Library Center numbers included. Indexed by agency, title, area (world), area (U.S.), subject. This title is recommended for libraries that can't afford *American Statistics Index (ASI)* or as a supplement. Walford prefers this to Wasserman's *Statistics Sources (see* below, page 402) and says the only real competition is *ASI.*

■ Balachandran, M., and S. Balachandran. State and local statistics sources: a subject guide to statistical data on states, cities and locales. Detroit: Gale, 1990-93. 2v.

Similar in arrangement to Gale's *Statistics Sources,* with more than 60,000 citations for the United States, including the District of Columbia, Guam, and Puerto Rico. Arranged by city, other location, then broad subject. Includes an annotated list of nonprint sources of statistics as well as a list of sources used to compile the source.

■ Directory of business and financial information services. 9th ed. Washington, D.C.: Special Libraries Assn., 1994. 471p.

First published in 1924. Lists by title 1,249 services by about 370 vendors. Emphasis is on the United States, but it includes more than 150 foreign sources. The ninth edition adds about 150 new titles, including books, CD-ROMs, loose-leafs, etc. Indexes by publisher, title, subject; references are to entry number rather than page.

■ Goyer, Doreen S. The international population census bibliography, revision and update, 1945-1977. New York: Academic Pr., 1980. 576p.

A straight, unannotated bibliography by nation, then date, with non-English titles translated. Relates to a microform collection of the originals.

■ Handbook of national population censuses. New York: Greenwood.

Emphasizes post-1945 material, with a general description of each nation's censuses, followed by some detail on each iteration, with tables of basic types of data covered.

■ Domschke, Eliane. The handbook of national population censuses. Africa and Asia. New York: Greenwood, 1986. 1032p.

■ Goyer, Doreen. The handbook of national population censuses. Europe. New York: Greenwood, 1992. 544p.

■ Goyer, Doreen S., and Eliane Domschke. The handbook of national population censuses. Latin America and the Caribbean, North America, and Oceania. Westport, Conn.: Greenwood, 1983. 711p.

Earlier material is covered in *General Censuses and Vital Statistics of the Americas* (Washington, D.C.: Govt. Print. Off., 1948; reprint 1974; 174p.) and *National Censuses and Vital Statistics in Europe, 1918-1939: An Annotated Bibliography,* with a supplement covering 1940 to 1948). (Washington, D.C.: Govt. Print. Off., 1948; reprint 1969; 215p.), produced by the Library of Congress Census Library Project.

■ Kurian, George T. Global data locator. Lanham, Md.: Bernan, 1997. 375p.

This replaces Kurian's *Sourcebook of Global Statistics* (1985). Annotated entries for 240 international statistical sources, including the entire table of contents for the printed sources (the only source to do this). Includes print and electronic sources, including CD-ROM, online, diskette, and tape products. The discussion of the International Statistical System is also of value.

Russell H. Powell's *Handbooks and Tables in Science and Technology* (3d ed. Phoenix, Ariz.: Oryx, 1994; 359p.) provides a recent bibliography of the surprisingly large number of such sources.

■ Statistics Canada catalogue. Ottawa: Statistics Canada, 1972- . Also online.

An annotated catalog of the publications (print and electronic) of the Canadian agency that combines the functions of several of the U.S. departments that collect data. Index by subject and title. Essentially the same information, with links to much of the actual data, is available on the website.

■ Statistics sources: a subject guide to data on industrial, business, social, educational, financial and other topics for the United States and internationally. Detroit: Gale, 1962- . 2v. Annual. Also on the Web, by subscription.

Still known as *Wasserman,* after its first editor-compiler, Paul Wasserman (it is now by Jacqueline Wasserman O'Brien and Steven R. Wasserman). Nearly 50,000 citations to all sorts of data sources, including print and online, under about 20,000 subjects, with a full publisher directory and a directory of government subject specialists. Each subject entry gives an annotation and general citation to the source; however, because most are regularly updated, there are no specific citations.

Although this source has received some criticism over the years, it remains the standard. Many of the specific sources cited in this chapter cover about the same ground but in much more detail.

■ Walden, Graham R., comp. Polling and survey research methods, 1935–1979: an annotated bibliography. Westport, Conn.: Greenwood, 1996. 581p.

■ ———. Public opinion polls and survey research: a selective annotated bibliography of U.S. guides and studies from the 1980s. New York: Garland, 1990. 306p.

Annotated citations to items published from when Gallup and Roper began through 1989, with an emphasis on understanding how survey research is conducted. The introduction provides a particularly clear discussion of this form of research.

■ Westfall, Gloria. Bibliography of official statistical yearbooks and bulletins. Alexandria, Va.: Chadwyck-Healey, 1986. 247p.

Replaces earlier Library of Congress publications *Statistical Yearbooks* (1953) and *Statistical Bulletins* (1954). Annotates 374 titles for more than 180 countries, including notes on title changes.

■ World directory of non-official statistical sources. 2d ed. London: Euromonitor; Detroit: Gale, 1998. 2v.

A combination and replacement of the *European Directory of Non-official Sources* and the *International Directory of Non-official Sources,* lists more than 2,000 nongovernmental sources such as trade association publications, opinion surveys, forecasts, etc. A bit expensive, but handy for the international business data.

The Superintendent of Documents Subject Bibliography series has a number of pamphlets related to statistics, updated as needed. These include the following:

Census of Population and Housing, Block Statistics (SB-311)

*Census of Population and Housing, Census Tract*s (SB-312)

Census of Transportation (SB-149)

Educational Statistics (SB-083)

Statistical Publications (SB-273)

Vital and Health Statistics (SB-121)

The entire series is also available on the Internet at <http://www.access.gpo.gov/su_docs>.

■ U.S. Bureau of the census. Census catalog and guide. Washington, D.C.: Govt. Print. Off., 1985- . Annual. Also on the Web.

Replaces *Bureau of the Census Catalog,* from 1964 to 1984. The 1985 issue cumulates volumes from 1980 to 1984. Broad subject areas, with all formats, including microform, tape, and online. Index by subject appendixes. For earlier citations, *Bureau of the Census Catalog of Publications, 1790-1972* (1974), cumulates editions from 1946 to 1972, plus a reprint of the *Catalog of United States Census Publications, 1790-1945* (1950). Each of these has separate indexes.

GENERAL INDEXES

Periodicals, often published by governments or trade and professional associations, are an excellent source of current socioeconomic statistics; and their statistical information may be located in part through such indexes as *PAIS International.* Examples are numerous, as may be seen by consulting *Ulrich's* or *Statistics Sources.* A few examples are listed under the appropriate heading, but one should be aware of the existence of indexes such as the following.

■ Business periodicals index. New York: Wilson, 1958- . *Wilson Business Abstracts,* 1990- , with full text, 1995- . Also monthly, with quarterly and annual cumulations. Also online and on CD-ROM since 1987.

A general subject index to periodicals, almost all American, but with global coverage. Covers all fields of business, with considerable statistical coverage in all such areas. Indexing in recent years has improved geographic headings. The CD-ROM permits keyword and subject access, plus access by author and journal, which print can't do.

■ Public Affairs Information Service. PAIS international. New York: Public Affairs Information Service, 1915- . Also online and on CD-ROM from 1976 (1972 for the *Foreign Language Index*).

Formerly the *Bulletin of the Public Affairs Information Service* and *PAIS Foreign Language Index.* As a combination periodical and monograph and series index, provides good subject access to articles, books, pamphlets, etc., from both commercial and government material, with a good coverage of the United Nations and other national governments. *Statistics* can be a subheading under any subject.

INDEXES TO DATA SOURCES

■ American statistics index. Bethesda, Md.: Congressional Information Service, 1973– . Monthly, with annual cumulations and five-year cumulations. Also on the Web as part of Statistical Universe and on CD-ROM as part of Statistical Masterfile. There is also a retrospective edition for 1960–74.

Indexes and annotates statistical serials, series, monographs, and other types of publications produced by all three branches of the federal government; regulatory, administrative, and similar agencies; and special bodies. Covers both purely statistical publications and those with a substantial amount of statistics. As with other Congressional Information Service (CIS) products, consists of an abstract section (by issuing agency) and separate indexes by subject, name, categories (e.g., by race, by gender), titles, and agency report numbers. Covers social, economic, demographic, and other types of statistics. Includes a key to the CIS fiche editions of all items listed as well as full citations (including SuDocs numbers) to the original.

■ Barbuto, Domenica M. The international financial statistics locator: a research and information guide. Hamden, Conn.: Garland, 1994. 338p.

Indexes twenty-two sources, such as the *Wall Street Journal, Barrons,* etc., including some CD-ROM sources, all of which receive fairly detailed annotations. Arranged by broad topic, then nation and specialized topic. Includes an indication if a given statistic is not available for a given nation.

■ Composite index for CRC handbooks. Boca Raton, Fla.: CRC Pr., 1991. 3d ed. 3v. Supplement, 1992. 413p. Also on CD-ROM.

Indexes all CRC handbooks published to date. These provide statistical data in various scientific areas, as well as basic social science and general statistical methodology data.

■ IIS: index to international statistics. Bethesda, Md.: Congressional Information Service, 1983– . Monthly, with annual cumulations. Also on the Web as part of Statistical Universe and on CD-ROM as part of Statistical Masterfile. A 1983–87 cumulation is also available.

English-language statistics of about 100 major intergovernmental organizations, including European Community, the United Nations (UN), Organization of American States (OAS), and the like. Economic, demographic, industrial, and social statistics. Arrangement is very similar to *American Statistics Index.* Each entry includes full citation, citation to the CIS fiche, and an abstract, with a separate and detailed index. About 90 percent of the indexed material is available on fiche from CIS.

■ Monthly bulletin of statistics. New York: Department of Economic and Social Development, Statistical Division, United Nations, 1947- . Monthly. Also online and on the Web <http://www.un.org/depts/unsd>.

Current economic statistics for most of the world, including both standard monthly data and special topics. Primarily, the data update tables in the *UN Statistical Yearbook* (*see* below, p. 447).

■ Forecast. Ithaca, N.Y.: American Demographics, 1991- . Also online. Monthly.

Formerly *The Numbers News.* A newsletter analyzing demographic, population, and consumer statistics. Includes news of new products of the U.S. Bureau of the Census, government and private marketing, and demographic data.

■ Skapura, Robert. Charts, graphs and stats index. Fort Atkinson, Wis.: Highsmith, 1992-96. 3v.

Covers from 1988 to 1995. Indexes nine popular, widely available magazines, with more than 5,300 entries in each volume.

■ Statistical masterfile. Bethesda, Md.: Congressional Information Service. CD-ROM. Quarterly updates. Also on the Web as Statistical Universe.

Combines all three CIS indexes, complete with an index, thesaurus, the data, and "category breakdowns."

■ Statistical reference index. Bethesda, Md.: Congressional Information Service, 1980- . Also part of Statistical Masterfile on CD-ROM and on the Web. Monthly, with quarterly and annual cumulations.

Indexes more than 2,000 titles, including about 1,400 serial publications, produced by private organizations, state governments, independent research services, and universities. A companion to *American*

Statistics Index, with nearly identical arrangement. Gives citations both to original and to CIS fiche collection. Nearly all items may be purchased from CIS on fiche.

General Collections of Data

■ A matter of fact: statements containing statistics on current social, economic and political issues. Ann Arbor, Mich.: Pierian, 1985– . Online as A Matter of Fact (AMOF) and as Statistical Abstracts from the A Matter of Fact Database. Quarterly updates.

Citations, with excerpts and statistical tables, from about 1,000 general-interest periodicals and newspapers, plus the *Congressional Record* and congressional hearings. Obviously, some overlap with Statistical Masterfile.

■ Profiles of America: an informational, statistical and relocation encyclopedia of all U.S. cities, towns and counties. Milpitas, Calif.: Toucan Valley, 1995. 16v. Also on CD-ROM.

Each volume covers several states. Data for states, counties, and minor civil divisions in the United States are based on the 1990 census, plus other federal and state data and some original research. Generally provides more detail on the smaller community than most other sources. Individual volumes are available.

■ Statistical abstract of the United States, 1878– . Washington, D.C.: U.S. Bureau of the Census. Govt. Print. Off., 1879– . Also online, on the Web, and on CD-ROM, 1993– . Annual.

The most commonly used tool in most libraries and the agreed-upon standard for U.S. statistics, with political, social, and economic summary data. Most tables have time series, some back to 1789 or 1800. Access is by a table of contents by broad subject and a detailed alphabetical index. Offers a number of useful appendixes, including fairly nontechnical descriptions of data collection and censuses. "Supplements" to this source appear irregularly, listed here (and in most library catalogs) in their own right. Interestingly, several versions of this are available from commercial sources, often for less money than the government publication; and most tables are also available on the Web.

This is supplemented by the two following sources:

- Kurian, George T. Datapedia of the United States, 1790–2000. Lanham, Md.: Bernan, 1994. 600p.

  Updates *Historical Statistics of the United States* and is based entirely on that title to 1970. Post-1970 is based on *Statistical Abstract* and many other sources as well. Retains divisions and table numbers of *Historical Statistics,* adding many graphs and highlights sections. Although this title does not include all the material in *Historical Statistics,* the presentation is generally clearer and easier to read than the original.

- U.S. Bureau of the Census. Historical statistics of the United States, colonial times to 1970. 3d ed. Washington, D.C.: Govt. Print. Off., 1975. 2v. Also on CD-ROM, from Cambridge University Press.

  Covers 1610 to 1970 in more than 12,500 time series. Each chapter has introductory text and tables. Includes definitions of terms, descriptive text, and detailed source notes. Most data are national level, but some state and regional information is included. Detailed subject index, as well as an index by starting date for time series. Formally updated by *Statistical Abstract of the United States. Datapedia,* a commercial venture, is a later cumulation.

Although the individual titles could also be listed with their specific subjects, the following series titles are listed here because they are, in a sense, multivolume compendia:

- Statistical handbooks. Phoenix, Ariz.: Oryx.

  A series of compendia on specific groups, heavily based on government data. More user-friendly than the originals but generally a direct reprint of the tables (with varying typefaces, sizes, and the like). In addition to citations to the originals, each volume includes a glossary of terms specific to the statistics of the group in question. Generally, statistics cover several decades.

- Statistical handbook on adolescents in America. Bruce A. Chadwick and Tim B. Heaton, eds. Phoenix, Ariz.: Oryx, 1996. 344p.
- Statistical handbook on aging Americans. Frank L. Schick and Renee Schick, eds. 2d ed. Phoenix, Ariz.: Oryx, 1994. 360p.
- Statistical handbook on the American family. Bruce A. Chadwick and Tim B. Heaton, eds. Phoenix, Ariz.: Oryx, 1992. 312p.

- Statistical handbook on U.S. Hispanics. Frank L. Schick and Renee Schick, eds. Phoenix, Ariz.: Oryx, 1991. 255p.
- Statistical handbook on violence in America. Adam Dobrin and others, eds. Phoenix, Ariz.: Oryx, 1996. 424p.
- Statistical handbook on women in America. Cynthia M. Taeuber, ed. 2d ed. Phoenix, Ariz.: Oryx, 1996. 354p.

- Statistical record series. Detroit: Gale.

    A growing number of titles in a standardized format (with minor variations). Arranged in chapters by topic, each begins with introductory or explanatory text, followed by tables and graphs (mostly pie and bar). A table of contents for each chart and a keyword index provide access. Generally based on government data, but with other sources included. Coverage tends to be inclusive, so that the *Children* volume also has much on adolescents, and the *Hispanic Americans* volume includes considerable data on Asian Americans and the like. Reviewer comments have varied (as one would expect), but overall, each volume has been highly recommended. The major complaint is that not all the necessary notes and explanations on data collection are always included, so that reference to the original is often necessary.

    One caveat: new editions may not supersede older ones, so all editions should be retained.

- Statistical record of Asian Americans. Susan Gall and Timothy L. Gall, eds. Detroit: Gale, 1993. 796p.
- Statistical record of black America. Jessie C. Smith and Carrell Horton, eds. 4th ed. Detroit: Gale, 1997. 1064p.
- Statistical record of children. Linda Schmittroth, ed. Detroit: Gale, 1994. 983p.
- Statistical record of health and medicine. 2d ed. Arsen Darnay, ed. Detroit: Gale, 1998. 1029p.
- Statistical record of Hispanic Americans. 2d ed. Marlita A. Reddy, ed. Detroit: Gale, 1995. 1141p.
- Statistical record of Native North Americans. 2d ed. Marlita A. Reddy, ed. Detroit: Gale, 1995. 1272p.
- Statistical record of older Americans. Charity Anne Dorgan, ed. 3d ed. Detroit: Gale, 1996. 783p.
- Statistical record of the environment. Charity Anne Dorgan, comp. 3d ed. Detroit: Gale, 1995. 1118p.

■ Statistical record of women worldwide. Linda Schmittroth, ed. 2d ed. Detroit: Gale, 1996. 1047p.

Online Sources

As already noted above, a number of traditional sources are also available in machine-readable forms. In addition, a growing number of data collections are available in the "raw" form directly, either online or via CD-ROM. In some cases, only the raw data are available and must be downloaded and then manipulated locally; in others, the service will itself create new tables or other presentations on request. A few examples of such sources are listed below:

Theoretically, the best sources of statistics for most uses, including many casual lookups, are in electronic form. Again, theoretically, online access is the best, as the following reasons clearly show:

1. Electronic sources, such as laser discs and online services, can store a vast amount of data in a small space (the entire *Census of Population and Housing,* for example, can be stored on one compact disc).
2. With readily available software, users can create their own display of the data, in forms of tables, graphs, or, in many cases, maps. (For more on this, see chapter 9.)
3. Again, with readily available software, the user can compare sets of data based on the user's specific need, even if the creator of the data never thought of this need (and thus would have no cross-tabulations, for example, of the chosen elements).
4. The user can readily use the data in calculations, applying all the standard and most of the more exotic statistical tests to the data. With printed or microform sources, of course, the user must first rekey the numbers into a manipulatable database before such calculations can take place.
5. In theory, online databases can be updated as needed; this could be as often as hourly, but it is more likely to be daily, weekly, or less often.

On the other side of the coin, electronic data sources have their faults:

1. The user must have the appropriate software and hardware to use the data, while printed sources merely require opening them.
2. The user must have some understanding of how to use the system and equipment, or must have some training (which, in some cases, requires several hours), merely to obtain a few numbers.
3. Readily available data can be readily misused and misunderstood.
4. Printed sources are sometimes updated more often than are the online sources.

5. Online sources of data may not indicate the original source, making their accuracy suspect.

6. All online sources are at least susceptible to manipulation and revision (*see* George Orwell's *1984,* for example).

7. Too many online sources omit explanatory text and notes or make these difficult to find.

8. Users may rely on inappropriate electronic sources rather than better or more relevant print or microform sources, which may require manual entry of the data for manipulation.

Electronic sources, however, particularly those available on the World Wide Web, are here to stay, and more and more data producers are making at least part of their data available on the Web. The following sites combine the function of bibliography and compendia in providing access to other sites with data and allowing at least some manipulation of the data. As with much of the Web, many of the sites listed as resources on these metasites are the same—the degree of interconnection and overlap among sites will continue to grow, at least in this author's opinion.

■ The American factfinder. Washington, D.C.: U.S. Census Bureau. <http://factfinder.census.gov/>

A free search engine for access to current census data, including the 1997 Economic Census and the 1990 *Census of Population and Housing,* as well as information on the 2000 census. Apparently will add more data sources over time.

■ Data on the net. San Diego: University of California. <http://odwin.ucsd.edu/idata>

Probably the most complete directory currently available. Provides access to more than 430 sites with downloadable data, about 100 data archives and libraries, about 100 data catalogs (libraries, archives, private-vendor catalogs), and about fifty fee-for-service data sources. Also includes an annotated guide to *ICPSR Data Archive (see* below) and links to about 150 social science–related sites that provide other links. Each entry in each of these categories receives a short but very informative annotation. The site itself is searchable, and many of the specific sites linked here are also searchable from this site.

■ Eurostat. Luxembourg, Belgium: Statistical Office of the European Communities. <http://europa. eu.int/en/comm/eurostat/serven/home.htm>

Direct access to all the statistics for the European Union, plus various other material of relevance to the union, especially members of the

European Economic Area. Mostly, however, this is a catalog of sources, rather than a link to the actual data.

■ FedStats. Washington, D.C.: Federal Interagency Council on Statistical Policy. <http://www.fedstats.gov>

A free directory and link to more than seventy U.S. government agencies' general websites and statistics. The selection criteria require the agency to spend at least $500,000 per year in some type of statistical activity, so this site includes access to many smaller programs in agencies that are not necessarily considered "statistical agencies" of the government. This site is searchable by subject, by agency, and by keyword. Although most of the data is at the national level, there are many links to state, county, and local data. This site provides a single source for much of the government-produced data listed here and is growing on a regular basis.

■ Government information sharing project. Corvallis: Oregon State University. <http://govinfo.kerr.orst.edu>

Operated by Oregon State University in cooperation with the Oregon State Library, with significant funding from the Department of Education, this site provides Web-based access to government data on CD-ROM, as well as links to other government websites. In addition to a forms-based query system, this site provides access by title of the source and a useful description of the source in question (many websites leave out information from the foreword and preface of the printed sources).

■ ICPSR data archive. Ann Arbor: University of Michigan, Interuniversity Consortium for Political and Social Research. <http://www.icpsr.umich.edu>

Most of the data sets are available for further use. Emphasizes political, social, and demographic data (including U.S. census materials) and opinion surveys. The primary source of data is material collected by scholars in the course of specific studies, rather than business or government. The website can be browsed by subject or searched by keyword. Much of the data is available directly for a fee (or to dues-paying members).

■ ICPSR guide online. Ann Arbor: University of Michigan, Interuniversity Consortium for Political and Social Research. Quarterly updates. <http://www.icpsr.umich.edu/index.html>

Replaces *ICPSR Guide to Resources and Services* (Ann Arbor: University of Michigan, Inter-university Consortium for Political and Social Research, 1976-97). A detailed record of data sets held by this organization, covering from the seventeenth century to the present. Each record gives a summary and description of the set; universe and sampling methods; dates of data collection; citation to the study and to related publications; and Inter-university Consortium for Political and Social Research (ICPSR) number.

■ Integrated public use microdata series (IPUMS). Minneapolis/St. Paul: Minn.: Department of History, University of Minnesota. <http://www.hist.umn.edu/~ipums98/home.html>

Contains samples of data for individuals selected from each of the U.S. censuses from 1850 to 1990, although the data from 1940 to 1990 have less detail in order to protect confidentiality. Although the data vary from sample to sample, this is a very useful resource for many purposes. The data may be downloaded at no charge, and the documentation is very complete and clear.

■ State statistical information resources. Milwaukee: University of Wisconsin-Milwaukee. <http://www.uwm.edu/Library/Docs/statestt.html>

Arranged by state, a set of links to each of the state's official statistics sites.

■ Statistical agencies (international). Washington, D.C.: U.S. Census Bureau. <http://www.census.gov/main/www/stat_int.html>

A very brief but very convenient list, by country, with links to the official statistical agencies of all countries that have one.

■ Statistical resources on the Web. Ann Arbor: University of Michigan Documents Center. <http://www.lib.umich.edu/libhome/documents.center/stats.html>

A subject- and keyword-searchable directory of Web-based sites, including both government and private sources. Includes a number of very focused sources (e.g., mortgage payment calculators) as well as compendia and links to major data archives.

■ Statistics Canada web site. Ottawa: Statistics Canada. <http://www.statcan.ca/start.html>

The nation's statistical agency, combining the statistical functions of what in the United States are divided among the Bureau of the Census, Department of Commerce, and about seventy other agencies. Includes some online data, catalogs of all publications and other data sources, and links to other statistical sources. The entire site is available in both English and French versions.

■ Stat-USA Internet. Washington, D.C.: U.S. Department of Commerce. <http://www.stat-usa.gov>

A subscription site, but at a reasonable price, mounted by the U.S. Department of Commerce, providing access to economic, business, and trade information, including considerable foreign data. Much of the latter is based on daily updates from U.S. embassies.

■ U.S. Bureau of Labor Statistics. Website. <http://stats.bls.gov>

The main page for the Bureau of Labor Statistics (BLS), a major collector and producer of statistical data relating to employment, labor, the cost of living, and related topics. Although some printed sources, such as the *Consumer Price Index, Monthly Labor Review,* and *Employment and Earnings,* are still available, the BLS is moving quickly to eliminate or drastically reduce its print output in favor of the Web, CD-ROMs, and other electronic sources.

■ U.S. Census Bureau. Website. Washington, D.C.: U.S. Census Bureau. <http://www.census.gov/main>

The main page for the census, with direct connections to all its other pages. Particularly useful for its collection of software tools for use with the data—these include calculators, table generators, and mapping software. The site also provides access to census databases and the census catalog.

State, County, and Local Data

■ Cities of the United States. 2d ed. Detroit: Gale, 1994. 4v.

Data for one to five cities per state. "State in Brief," then "City in Brief," then detailed descriptions of cities. General maps, photos. A cumulating index in each volume.

■ County and city data book, 1949– . Washington, D.C.: Govt. Print. Off., 1952– . Quinquennial. Also in several machine-readable forms from the government and private firms.

Covers all counties and most cities. Also has some summary stats for states, regions, urbanized areas, Metropolitan Statistical Areas (MSAs), and unincorporated places. Data cover all the subjects covered by the census and other data collected by the government.

■ County and city extra. Lanham, Md.: Bernan, 1992- . Annual.

Intended to update the *County and City Data Book,* covering places with a 1990 census population of at least 25,000. Easy to read, complete with colored maps, and based primarily on census data, with some other government sources and a few private sources as well. From 1993, places smaller than 25,000 are covered in a separate annual, *Places, Towns and Townships,* (Lanham, Md.: Bernan, 1993-).

■ MSA profile [year]. Washington, D.C.: Woods & Poole Economics, 1995. Also on CD-ROM. Annual.

Covers from the 1990 census to 2020, using Woods and Poole's own projections. Has been called by reviewers, "essential" and "very specialized." The disk is much easier to use to analyze data, but it lacks the introductory material, which, among other things, discusses the methodology of the projections. This is an unfortunate example of the dangers of relying only on electronic formats, which are not necessarily exact copies of the printed source.

■ State and metropolitan area data book. Washington, D.C.: U.S. Department of Commerce, Bureau of the Census, 1979- . Irregular. Also available for free on the Web.

Complements the *County and City Data Book* for census regions, states, metropolitan areas, and their constituent parts.

■ USA counties. Washington, D.C.: Govt. Print. Off., 1992- . Biennial. CD-ROM only.

Supplement to *Statistical Abstract,* giving all the data for counties in the *State and Metropolitan Area Data Book* (1986-) and *County and City Data Book* (1983-).

Foreign Government Statistics

■ Yearbook of international organizations. Brussels: Union of International Assn., 1948- . Annual since 1983. 4v. Also on CD-ROM.

Often said to be "the major source for international organizations." The first volume is the statistical volume.

CANADA

■ Canada year book [year]. Ottawa: Statistics Canada, 1868- . Annual.

Also issued in a French edition. Title varies, with current title since 1906. The standard Canadian statistical reference source covering economic, social, and political statistics. Detailed analytical index. Many tables with the text. Includes a directory of official sources and a bibliography of special materials in earlier editions.

■ Facts about Canada, its provinces and territories. Bronx, N.Y.: Wilson, 1995. 246p.

Brief introduction and many statistics from the 1991 census. Good bibliographies.

■ Historical statistics of Canada. 2d ed. Ottawa: Statistics Canada, 1983. 900p.

Very similar to *Historical Statistics of the United States* (*see* above, p. 408). Covers from 1867 to the 1970s, with notes and citations to sources. Detailed index.

LATIN AMERICA

■ Statistical abstract of Latin America. Los Angeles: Univ. of California at Los Angeles, Latin American Center, 1955- . Annual.

Covers the twenty nations traditionally considered as Latin America plus some data related to a broader definition of the area. Based both on data collected by the center and more than 200 other publications. Since 1970 irregular supplements on special topics have appeared.

■ United States–Mexico border statistics since 1900. Los Angeles: UCLA Latin American Center, 1990. 475p.
■ 1990 update. Los Angeles: UCLA Latin American Center, 1993. 137p.

Time series for all types of economic, political, demographic, and other statistics for the border regions. The update not only adds more recent material, but also includes data on the U.S. states that border Mexico, plus more textual analysis and a bibliography. The update's tables are keyed to the first title.

Subjects

Agriculture

■ Agricultural statistics, 1936– . Washington, D.C.: Govt. Print. Off., 1936– . Annual. Also on CD-ROM since 1994; some issues also on the Internet at <http://www.usda.gov/nass/pubs/agstats.htm>.

> Originally the statistical section of *Yearbook of Agriculture,* covering all aspects of agriculture and food (such as food prices, environmental costs, etc.). The *Yearbook* itself is no longer published, but the volumes from 1894 to 1936 are still useful for historical data.

■ Friedman, Catherine, ed. Commodity prices. 2d ed. Detroit: Gale, 1991. 630p.

> An extremely detailed index, arranged by more than 5,000 agricultural commodities (e.g., "Apples—Macintosh"), including unit measured, time coverage, etc., as well as citation to more than 150 U.S. and Canadian sources, mostly trade journals.

Averages

■ Gale book of averages. Detroit: Gale, 1994. 617p.

> More than 1,100 tables of all kinds of averages in all subjects, primarily contemporary. Numerical averages are listed by size under each subject, and sources are cited with each table. Indexed by subject.

Cost of Living

■ ACCRA cost of living index. Louisville, Ky.: American Chamber of Commerce Researchers Assn., 1968– . Quarterly.

> The most detailed and longest time series, emphasizing differences among urban areas.

For a convenient historical overview of both prices and income for many occupations, *The Value of a Dollar: Prices and Income in the United States, 1860–1989* (Detroit: Gale, 1994; 559p.) is handy. It draws on more than 500 sources, including such publications as Sears catalogs, for its data.

■ American cost of living survey. Arsen J. Darnay and Helen S. Fisher, eds. Detroit: Gale, 1994– . Biennial.

Covers 443 cities (at least one city or "Metropolitan Statistical Area" for each state), giving average prices of up to 600 items, if available for that city, starting with the overall cost of living. Entries give date and source, the cost and value in dollars, the quantity measured, and the time period covered. Most prices cover from 1990 to 1993 and are derived from about seventy sources, including the *ACCRA Cost of Living Index*, but not the federal government's Consumer Price Index (CPI).

■ CPI detailed report. Washington, D.C.: U.S. Bureau of Labor Statistics, 1974- . Monthly. Also on the Web.

Continues CPI (1913-1974). Contains monthly, quarterly, and annual time series based on a "typical" collection of goods and services, based on an index year (which changes over time). Gives breakdowns by region, urban areas, and overall average. The basic information is also contained in the *Monthly Labor Review.*

In recent years, there has been much debate over this index, which has become the basis for cost-of-living adjustments in labor contracts, pension plans, and social security payments. Depending on one's point of view, it has been said that the CPI overstates inflation by a full percentage point or even more and thus itself helps cause inflation. One of the issues is the "market basket" of goods and services—those items whose prices are used to create the index. Recent redefinitions are considered and explained in John S. Greenlees, *Overview of the 1998 Revision of the Consumer Price Index* (Washington, D.C.: U.S. Bureau of Labor Statistics, 1998; 83p.). In the meantime, several other organizations provide similar information:

■ The official guide to household spending: who spends how much on what. 4th ed. Ithaca, N.Y.: New Strategist, 1997. 803p.

A collection and guide to the data used to produce the CPI. More than 1,000 products and services cross-tabulated by age, income, and household size and type, with a detailed index. Includes projections to the year 2000.

■ PPI detailed report. Washington, D.C.: U.S. Department of Labor, 1996- . Monthly. Also on the Web.

Formerly *Producer Price Indexes* (1978-1996; title varies) and continues *Wholesale Prices and Price Indexes.* Unlike the more familiar *CPI Detailed Report,* this title provides data on the costs to produce goods and services and is sometimes said to be a more accurate barometer of future cost of living.

Crime

■ Sourcebook of criminal justice statistics. Washington, D.C.: U.S. Department of Justice, 1973– . Annual. Also online and on CD-ROM.

Data on prisons and the criminal justice system, opinion polls on crime and related subjects, and arrest and conviction statistics. Includes information in the following title, but updated and with time series instead of the more detailed annual information.

■ U.S. Department of Justice. Uniform crime reports for the United States and its possessions. Washington, D.C.: Govt. Print. Off., 1930– . Annual.

State, metropolitan, city, and, in recent years, university data on offenses, arrests, and police enforcement, based on reports from local policy agencies. Although often criticized as undercounting (or, in some cases, for overcounting) data, it is the definitive source.

Economics and Business

BIBLIOGRAPHIES AND INDEXES

■ Chapman, Florence. Investment statistics locator. Rev. ed. Phoenix, Ariz.: Oryx, 1995. 275p.

Index to data in twenty-two standard business serials, arranged by subject. More limited than *Wasserman* or *Andriot,* but helpful for the smaller library.

■ Daniells, Lorna M. Business information sources. 3d rev. ed. Berkeley: Univ. of California Pr., 1993. 725p.

A standard work but with a U.S. slant. Includes many statistical sources, but most are within the broader subject entries, rather than the statistic classification.

■ Directory of business and financial information services. 9th ed. New York: Special Libraries Assn., 1994. 471p.

Continues the SLA title *Directory of Business and Financial Services* (1963–1983). A standard directory to producers of statistical information with a subject index.

■ Freed, Melvyn N., and Virgil P. Diodato. Business information desk reference. New York: Macmillan, 1991. 513p.

A classified approach to reference in this area. In addition to the usual annotated bibliography, the authors provide lengthy sections for print and online sources by question-and-answer pattern: "Where should I go to find . . . ?" and "Try [this source]."

■ Ganly, John. Data sources for business and market analysis. 4th ed. Metuchen, N.J.: Scarecrow, 1994. 458p.

Lists print and online sources, often with brief descriptions. Has detailed coverage of the U.S. Bureau of the Census and other federal agencies. Also covers regional, local, and international sources. Index by subject, title, issuing body.

■ U.S. Bureau of the Census. Guide to foreign trade statistics. Washington, D.C.: Govt. Print. Off., 1967– . Irregular.

Imports, exports, shipping, and related information, with useful examples of the organization of the data.

DATA SOURCES

Several U.S. government publications are critical sources for data, including the economic census, which follows; but commercial publishers also provide excellent information.

■ U.S. Bureau of the Census. Economic censuses. Washington, D.C.: Census Bureau, 1954– . Also on CD-ROM and the Web since 1992. CD-ROM and Web only since 1997.

The economic censuses are required by law under Title 13 of the U.S. Code, Sections 131, 191, and 224, which require that they be taken at five-year intervals covering years ending in two and seven. These censuses constitute comprehensive and periodical canvasses of the nation's industrial and business activities. The first economic census of the United States was conducted as part of the 1810 decennial census, when inquiries on manufacturing were included with the census of population. Mineral data were first collected in 1840. The first censuses of construction and business were taken in 1929. An integrated economic census program was begun in 1954. In that year, the census covered retail and wholesale trades, selected service industries, manufacturers, and mineral industries. The basic procedures developed for these censuses have been used in all subsequent economic censuses, with appropriate revisions in specific details. As a harbinger of the future of all census data, the *1997 Economic Census* was the first to be provided in full only on CD-ROM and the Internet, with only summary reports provided in print.

■ Survey of current business. Lanham, Md.: Bernan, 1921- . Monthly, with annual cumulations. Also online and on CD-ROM in several formats.

Consists of general articles and surveys, with many statistical tables in a separate section. Emphasis is on U.S. business and industry but includes general information about the labor force, prices, and the like. Includes both specific numbers and various indexes, including price deflators. Offers coverage since 1929 for annual statistics and since 1946 for monthly and quarterly data. The printed version has a very detailed index.

■ Across the board. New York: Conference Board, 1976- . Monthly.

Continues *Conference Board Record* (1964-1976). The Conference Board, an economic and business research organization, supports its reports with statistics, graphics, and documentation.

■ Broadcasting and cable. Washington, D.C.: Broadcasting Pubs., 1963- . Weekly.

Former title *Broadcasting* (1931-1963). Data on radio and television broadcasting, including cable television; has had several title changes.

■ Business statistics, 1963-1991. Washington, D.C.: Govt. Print. Off., 1992. 343p.

Historical cumulation of about 2,100 series in the *Survey of Current Business,* plus monthly, quarterly, and annual data for about 260 of these series, with some other related statistics and methodological notes.

■ Business week. Hightstown, N.J.: McGraw-Hill, Sept. 7, 1929- . Weekly. Also on the Web.

A standard for current business information; many articles contain statistical tables and graphs.

■ CRB commodity year book. New York: Wiley, 1939– . Annual. CRB Year-book Statistical Update is available on disk only.

> Publisher varies; title varies slightly. Includes graphs, text, and tabular information on a selection of raw commodities and semifinished products, arranged alphabetically.

■ Current industrial reports. Washington, D.C.: U.S. Bureau of the Census [start date varies]. Monthly, quarterly, and annually. Also on the Web.

> Contains a number of series for different industries, generally including production, shipment, consumption, and inventories.

■ EconBase: time series and forecasts. Eddystone, Pa.: WEFA Group, 1990– . Online database only.

> Current and time series data from 1948 to date for business, economics, income, and related information, including demographics. Covers the United States, other countries, and international data. Each record for each table includes the entire time series (thus making this a more convenient source in many cases than the original, which does not repeat the whole series with each update). Source citation is abbreviated (e.g., title and date of beginning of series given but not specific months). Based on government, international, and commercial sources.

■ Economic indicators. Washington, D.C.: Govt. Print. Off., 1948– . Monthly. Also on the Web, free, since 1995.

> Data for the current month, quarter, and year from the Council of Economic Advisers, based on government and private sources.

■ Economic indicators handbook: time series, conversions documentation. Detroit: Gale, 1992– . Annual.

> All data updated through most current year available. Each chapter has formulas, definitions, and bibliographies for the indicator in question, as well as many tables. A majority of data are CPI by city, then by item. Recent editions have dropped 1967 and 1982 base years, replacing them with the base period 1982 to 1994. Includes a keyword index.

■ EDGAR. Washington, D.C.: U.S. Securities and Exhange Commission. <http://www.sec.gov/edgarhp.htm>

> By law, public companies are required to file quarterly and annual reports with the Securities and Exchange Commission (SEC). These are

available in several guises (including microform), but the SEC's website provides reports from the last several years and is more current than nearly any other source. Most of the business and investor services, and the major Web search services, provide access to this from their own sites. Although company annual reports (and websites) often provide much more information, the sets of reports here, the 10Q and the 10K, are in a standardized format, making comparisons easier. Of course, the enforced format and thus relative dullness of the reports also eliminates most of the public-relations hype, another positive factor for the information-seeking investor.

■ Editor and Publisher. Market guide. New York: Editor and Publisher, 1924– . Annual. Also on CD-ROM since 1994.

Data and rankings for "Metropolitan Statistical Areas" and for 250 top cities and 250 top counties. However, primarily useful for the survey data on U.S. and Canadian newspapers.

■ Federal reserve bulletin. Washington, D.C.: U.S. Board of Governors of the Federal Reserve System, 1915– . Monthly.

The best source of banking and monetary statistics, including commercial loans, consumer credit, production, and international finance.

■ Fortune. Chicago: Time, 1930– . Biweekly, with three issues in October. Also on the Web.

Carefully researched, with considerable use of colored graphics. Less number-intensive than some of the other business periodicals, but especially useful for lists, such as the "Fortune 500."

■ Industrial commodity statistics yearbook. New York: United Nations, 1974– . Annual.

Has had several title changes. Essentially is the only comprehensive source for international data on manufacturing.

■ International trade statistics yearbook. New York: United Nations, 1950– . Annual.

Formerly *Yearbook of International Trade Statistics.* The most comprehensive source of such data—but covering only trade across borders.

■ National trade data bank. Washington, D.C.: U.S. Department of Commerce, 1990– . Monthly. CD-ROM and on the Web only.

A general collection of international trade data, including most of the specific government sources listed in this section, as well as other data.

■ OECD main economic indicators. Historical statistics. Paris: OECD Pubs., 1960– . CD-ROM only. Annual.

Covers data from 1960, giving various economic indicators for the member countries of the Organisation for Economic Cooperation and Development.

■ Pierce, Phyllis S., ed. The Dow Jones averages, 1885–1995. Burr Ridge, Ill.: Irwin Professional, 1996. Unpaged.

Mostly charts for each year and month; probably the "most detailed listings to date," as one reviewer has put it.

■ Sales & Marketing Management. Survey of buying power and media markets. New York: Sales & Marketing Management, 1930– . Annual.

Population, effective buying power, and retail sales estimates for U.S. markets and annual projections for U.S. and Canadian markets.

■ Wall Street Journal. New York: Dow Jones, 1889– . Daily except Saturday, Sunday, and legal holidays.

The premier business journal for the United States. In addition to news and features, includes considerable statistical material.

■ World economic factbook. London: Euromonitor, 1993– . Annual.

Data for more than 200 nations for a three-year time series. Some unexplained standardization done to deal with unreliable data from some nations. Unlike some similar sources, provides ranking on all elements for all nations, not just the top. In addition to tables, includes a general country overview.

■ World tables. Baltimore, Md.: Johns Hopkins Univ. Pr. for the World Bank, 1991– . Annual. Also on tape, diskette, and on the Web.

Updated by semiannual *World Tables Update.* A standard source for economic and social time series data since 1972. Sources are based on World Bank, OECD, International Monetary Fund, and national publications. Includes twenty-two topical tables and data for 160 countries, with brief information for other nations.

RATIOS

A useful measure of a business or industry's success is to compare one set of data with another. The most familiar of these sorts of ratios is undoubtedly the price/earnings ratio, but there are many others. This information is clearly of interest to potential investors but is also often requested by job seekers and by economic researchers. Sheldon Gates's *101 Business Ratios* (Scottsdale, Ariz.: McLane, 1993; 288p.) is the fullest collection of such ratios generally available. Gates not only explains what the ratios are, but also tells how (including the mathematical formula) and why they are calculated and how to use and interpret each measure. Standard collections of the ratios may be found in a number of sources, notably the following:

■ Almanac of business and industrial financial ratios. Englewood Cliffs, N.J.: Prentice-Hall, 1971- . Annual. Also on CD-ROM, 1997- .

  Similar to Dun & Bradstreet's *Industry Norms and Key Business Ratios* and the Robert Morris Associates (RMA) *Annual Statement Studies* but includes graphs comparing across industries. Data are from the Internal Revenue Service; RMA uses data from commercial banks, and Dun & Bradstreet develops its own database.

■ Annual statement studies. Philadelphia: Robert Morris Associates, 1964- . Annual.

  Composite balance sheets, income data, commonly used financial ratios for 406 industries, including service as well as manufacturing, covering the last five years as well as the current year. Arranged by SIC number, then size. Unfortunately, the financial statements used to get data aren't really a good sample because only one SIC number is used per company, even if it has several product lines. Replaces *Statement Studies* (1923-1962).

■ Industry norms and key business ratios. Library ed. New York: Dun & Bradstreet Credit Services, 1982- . Annual. Also on the Web.

  Formerly *Selected Key Business Ratios*. In many ways, the standard for this sort of thing, covering more than 800 types of business in five segments. Supplies basic balance and income statements plus fourteen ratios for each firm, along with the full industry's quartile ratios.

LOOSE-LEAF SERVICES

Although most of the following are also available in electronic form, notably on the Web, many libraries retain them in their printed form. This involves a set of loose-leaf binders, permitting regular updates—to do this, individual pages are sent to replace superceded ones, thus the name.

■ Hoover's company capsules. Austin, Tex.: Hoover's, 1995- . Also on CD-ROM and the Web. Annual in print, quarterly on CD-ROM, and daily updates on the Web.

■ Hoover's company profiles. Austin, Tex.: Hoover's, 1995- . Also on CD-ROM and the Web. Annual in print, quarterly on CD-ROM, and daily updates on the Web.

■ Hoover's handbooks. Austin, Tex.: Hoover's, 1990- . Annual in print, quarterly on CD-ROM, and daily updates on the Web.

■ Hoover's online. Austin, Tex.: Hoover's. <http://www.hoovers.com>

A more recent player in this area than Moody's and Standard & Poor's, Hoover's produces a number of annuals that have already become very well respected. These include *American Business, Emerging Companies, Private Companies* (generally not well covered by other standard sources), and *World Business,* among others. Each of the separate publications includes several lists (top companies, most influential, ranked by size, etc.), plus company descriptions. The full set is available in the electronic forms—The longer entries are the "profiles," two printed pages that include basic description plus ten years of financial data. The shorter entries (capsules) give just the directory and basic descriptive information. In all, there are about 10,000 capsules and about 3,000 profiles in the system. The Web version also includes hypertext links from the companies to their Web pages, if any. The printed versions are all included in *Hoover's Handbooks Index [year],* which is obviously not needed for the electronic versions.

■ Moody's Investors Service. Moody's handbook of common stocks. New York: Moody's Investors Service, 1955- . Quarterly.

■ Moody's manuals. Charlotte, N.C.: Financial Communications, 1909- . Annual, with weekly updates. Also online and on the Web, and a full run on fiche (1909-).

The publisher has varied, and the title has varied, but it currently includes *Industrial, OTC Industrial, Transportation, Public Utility, Bank and Finance, Municipal and Government, OTC Unlisted,* and *International* manuals. Each manual is updated by the weekly *News*

Reports. In addition to data on all types of businesses and industries, the manuals include ratings of the quality of investments, using a scale from *Aaa* through *C.* Moody's also issues a series of *Investment Guides* and offers other related services. The full panoply of services may be obtained via the Web at <http://www.fisonline.com>.

■ Morningstar mutual funds. Chicago: Morningstar, 1984– . Biweekly. Also on CD-ROM and on the Web.

The basic publication of this service covering about 3,500 mutual funds electronically and about 1,000 in print. News plus index, followed by one-page profiles. Other services from this firm cover closed-end funds, Japan, variable annuities, and stocks. The website, as with the other source noted here, provides access to all of these, plus a news-and-investor-related site, and access to other company and fund information.

■ Standard & Poor's. Corporation records. New York: Standard & Poor's, 1914– . Semimonthly.

■ _____. Stock reports. New York: Standard & Poor's, 1971– . Monthly. Also on the Web.

The flagship publication, *Corporation Records,* provides regular reports on publicly held corporations on the New York and American stock exchanges, plus the larger of the other exchanges. A daily news section, plus a cumulated news section (changes in ownership, stock offerings, etc.), appears every two weeks, with a detailed index to the entire collection monthly. Full records include some company background, basic statistics on company size and product, and basic production data, balance sheets, etc., and, of course, the ratings of the value of the stocks.

Standard & Poor's also issues a number of other reports related to stocks and bonds, such as the *Stock Reports,* with the most up-to-date versions being those on the Web at <http://www.standardandpoors.com>.

■ Value Line investment survey. New York: Value Line, 1936– . Weekly.
■ Value Line mutual fund survey. New York: Value Line, 1993– . Weekly. Both are on the Web as part of the firm's investment services; the *Investment Survey* is also on disk or CD-ROM.

A very popular service, especially the first title, for many years. Includes detailed statistics on about 1,700 firms and on about 100 broad industry groups. *Value Line Investment Survey Expanded Edition* adds about as many small capitalization (small-cap) stocks. The mutual fund volume is set up on the same plan. Includes a weekly news summary and index to the whole; the main section consists of one-page reports that cover the past ten years and forecast ahead for three to five years. An especially handy feature is the inclusion of standard graphs for comparisons across companies within an industry. A third section gives advice for investors and a general analysis of the economy and the stock market.

As the variety and number of variant versions of such sources increase, more people will have to confront the question of whether all the formats are, in fact, delivering the same data. An example of the problem is discussed in Marydee Ojala's "The Many Moods of Moody's" (*Online* [July/Aug. 1998]: 46-48), which examines seven electronic variants (via Dialog, CD-ROM, and the Web) and the printed version. Her conclusion—none of the electronic versions duplicates the print, which not only has more data, but is often more accurate.

Education

▪ Chronicle of Higher Education. Almanac of higher education. Washington, D.C.: The Chronicle, 1988- . Annual.

Special insert to the *Chronicle of Higher Education.* All sorts of data, with an emphasis on such elements as costs and staff salaries. Many of the tables are at the institutional level.

▪ The condition of education. U.S. National Center for Education Statistics. Washington, D.C.: Govt. Print. Off., 1975- . Annual. Also online and on CD-ROM.

A regular report to Congress, using sixty indicators of the quality of U.S. education.

▪ Digest of education statistics, 1962- . Washington, D.C.: National Center for Education Statistics, 1962- . Annual. Also online and on CD-ROM.

Specific corporate author varies, and the title varies slightly. Data from government and private sources covering all aspects of American education from kindergarten through universities. Some time series go back to the 1870s. Coverage of libraries varies, with more data generally provided as the series matures.

- EDsearch: education statistics on disk. Washington, D.C.: National Center for Education Statistics, 1994– . Annual. CD-ROM only.

  Includes most (but not all) of the current editions of *Digest of Education Statistics* (Washington, D.C.: National Center for Education Statistics, 1962– ; annual); *The Condition of Education* (Washington, D.C.: National Center for Education Statistics, 1975– ; annual); *Projections of Educational Statistics* (Washington, D.C.: National Center for Education Statistics, 1964– ; frequency varies); *Historical Trends: State Education Facts, 1969-1989* (Washington, D.C.: National Center for Education Statistics, 1992; 198p.); *120 Years of American Education* (Thomas D. Snyder, ed. Washington, D.C.: National Center for Education Statistics, 1993; 107p.); *Education in States and Nations: Indicators Comparing U.S. States with the OECD Countries* (Washington, D.C.: National Center for Education Statistics, 1993– ; irregular); and *Youth Indicators* (Washington, D.C.: National Center for Education Statistics, 1988– ; irregular).

  The website, at <http://nces.ed.gov/>, includes a high proportion of all the statistics collected by the National Center for Education Statistics, in most cases beginning with the 1992 publications and also including a growing amount of raw data.

- Educational rankings annual. Lynn Hattendorf, comp. Detroit: Gale, 1991– . Annual.

  A complete compilation from all sorts of sources, including many scholarly journal studies. Unlike many sources, this is based on documented research and includes classic as well as current rankings. Not every table from every article is included, but some tables are repeated (covering more than one subject). Includes a detailed index to institution and person (e.g., each of the "most productive" faculty in a discipline). Each table gets a full citation and often an explanatory annotation. If you must have such rankings (which are a popular request), this is the only source you will need.

Ethnic Groups

In addition to the following titles, be sure to consider the *Statistical Handbooks* series and *Statistical Record Series* above, pages 408 to 409.

- African American almanac. 7th ed. Detroit: Gale, 1997. 3v. First five editions as *The Negro Almanac* (1967–).

Generally considered the standard on the subject, although the indexing has been criticized as incomplete. Thoroughly revised and expanded from earlier editions. Includes 800 maps and illustrations, lists of recipients of major awards, a bibliography, and many biographical entries, along with considerable statistics.

■ The Asian American almanac. Detroit: Gale, 1995. 834p.

ARBA 1996 called this "the single most important volume ever published on the subject. . . . the most substantial reference work in this area in many years." Contains data, in some cases from the 1830s, on all aspects of Asian Americans, with an emphasis on the Chinese but including all groups. As an almanac, includes considerable narrative text and illustrations as well as tables.

■ Black Americans: a statistical sourcebook. Palo Alto, Calif.: Information Pub., 1992– . Annual.

This supplements and to some degree updates *Statistical Record of Black America* (Detroit: Gale, 1990– ; biennial) with nearly all data from federal government sources. Nearly all tables include African Americans, whites, and all Americans, for comparison purposes; citations to the original; and a five- to ten-year time series.

■ Hispanic Americans: a statistical sourcebook. Palo Alto, Calif.: Information Pub., 1993– . Annual.

Based on government sources, primarily the census and especially the *Statistical Abstract*. However, because the group is not a clearly defined one, it is often difficult to find the data in the originals, which makes this source particularly useful. Full citations to the originals are provided for all tables.

■ Hispanic-American almanac. Nicolas Kanellos, ed. Detroit: Gale, 1993. 780p.

A bit misleading in title because this is a one-time publication, not an annual one. Twenty-five chapters cover all aspects of all parts of the Hispanic American community, including biographies, directory information, and history, as well as statistics. The data are also the basis for *Reference Library of Hispanic America* (Detroit: Gale, 1994; 3v.) and *The Hispanic Almanac* (Detroit: Invisible Ink, 1994; 644p.).

■ Historical statistics of black America. Jessie C. Smith and Carrell P. Horton, eds. Detroit: Gale, 1995. 2v.

A supplement and complement to *Statistical Record of Black America,* covering from the eighteenth century to 1975. Mostly from government sources, but also from *Negro Year Book* (Tuskegee, Ala.: Negro Year Book, 1912–38; 9v.) and *The Negro Handbook* (New York: Current Reference Pubs., 1942–49; 4v.). Nineteen chapters by topic. Indexed by subject and year, but the index has been criticized.

■ The Native North American almanac. Detroit: Gale, 1994. 341p.

Includes directory information also found in *Native Americans Information Directory,* but also has much information not in that title, including a biographical section on about 600 people—about one-third historical. Arranged in sixteen subject chapters.

■ Stuart, Paul. Nations within a nation: historical statistics of American Indians. Westport, Conn.: Greenwood, 1987. 251p.

A general collection from hundreds of different sources (but mostly twentieth century) on Native Americans. Arranged by eight major topics, with sources cited. Although good for the twentieth century, the lack of data, especially before about 1870, makes this source less helpful for earlier history.

Forecasts

■ Person, James E., and Sean R. Pollock. Statistical forecasts of the United States. Detroit: Gale, 1993–95. 2v.

In fourteen topic chapters with more than 800 tables as well as many charts and other graphics forecasting well into the twenty-first century. All entries cite sources in full and also the original if it is not the same as the source used. Depth of coverage varies with subject. Federal and state government publications, private books and articles, and non-government agencies are used. The index is by subject and also terminal year of forecast.

Government Activities, Including Elections

■ Almanac of American politics. Washington, D.C.: National Journal, 1972– . Biennial.

Combines biography with statistics on each politician, notably the current ratings by various political groups.

■ America at the polls: a handbook of American presidential election statistics. Storrs: Roper Center, Univ. of Connecticut, 1994– . Biennial.

Some data begin with Harding (1920), but most begin with 1932. Based on data collected by the center, provides summary tables of electoral votes and percentages, followed by detailed data by state. Generally, each volume is primarily a narrative with many graphs and tables interspersed.

■ America votes: a handbook of contemporary American election statistics. Washington, D.C.: Congressional Quarterly, 1956– . Biennial.

Election returns for president, Congress, and governor in considerable detail, to county and ward. Some data from 1920, but most from the 1960s. A highly respected source, even used by *Statistical Abstracts* for some data.

■ Book of the states, 1935– . Lexington, Ky.: Council of State Governments, 1935– . Biennial, with annual supplement. Also on CD-ROM.

Another standard tool, with statistical and directory information on all branches of state governments; many articles include bibliographies. Includes many types of data, but sometimes these are not current because of the slowness of state reporting. For a number of directory supplements, which keep the directory information up-to-date, *see* chapter 4, "Directories."

Cumulations of election data from 1920 to 1992 are available in *America at the Polls: A Handbook of American Presidential Election Statistics,* Richard M. Scammon and Alice M. McGillivray, eds. and comps. (Washington, D.C.: Congressional Quarterly, 1994; 2v.), which should not be confused with the Roper Center title.

■ Congressional Quarterly almanac. Washington, D.C.: Congressional Quarterly, 1939– . Annual.

A standard source, giving an overview of each session, membership lists, major presidential documents, etc. Includes data on major votes (who voted which way).

■ Congressional Quarterly's guide to U.S. elections. 3d ed. Washington, D.C.: Congressional Quarterly, 1994. 1543p.

Covers from 1789 to 1992, with election data through 1993, with data on presidential, congressional, and gubernatorial elections, plus narrative.

- Election results directory. Denver, Colo.: National Conference of State Legislatures, 1993- . Annual.

    Is probably the earliest source of election results. In addition to the data, updates *Congressional Staff Directory* (Mt. Vernon, Va.: Staff Directories, 1959- ; semiannual) and its Advance Locator, its update service.

- Municipal year book, 1934- . Washington, D.C.: International City Management Assn., 1934- . Annual.

    Statistics on and surveys of activities of city governments, including finance, public welfare, officials' salaries, etc. Also contains a directory of major city officials.

Health and Welfare

- Social security bulletin, v.1- , March 1938. Washington, D.C.: Social Security Administration, 1938- . Quarterly. Includes *Annual Statistical Supplement*, 1955- . Annual.

    Ongoing tables in each issue covering all aspects of social security, with some general data on the older population and analytical articles.

- World health statistics annual, 1962- . Geneva: World Health Organization, 1965- . Annual.

    Previously issued as *Annual Epidemiological and Vital Statistics*. Health, vital statistics, and medical data, by country and worldwide. Generally, data are for the year prior to the publication date. The basic source for such data across the globe. Supplemented by *World Health Statistics Quarterly* (1978-).

Libraries and Publishing

- Lynch, Mary Jo. Sources of library statistics, 1972-1982. Chicago: ALA, 1983. 48p.

    A brief listing but the most recent general source for summary data on all kinds of libraries, with numerous graphics.

- ACRL university library statistics. Chicago: ALA, 1980– . Biennial. Also on disk.

  Compiled by the Association of College and Research Libraries (ACRL), covers more than 100 U.S. and Canadian research and doctoral-granting universities not in the Association of Research Libraries.

- The Bowker annual library and book trade almanac. New Providence, N.J.: Bowker/Reed Reference, 1956– . Annual. Also on CD-ROM.

  A standard work, with narrative reports on major library conferences, special topics (e.g., copyright, library funding, employment), legislation funding and grants, library and information science education, research and statistics, reference information, directory of organizations, calendar of events, etc. Includes summary data on many aspects of publishing and libraries (including price indexes, average cost of books by subject, etc.). Much of the latter is based on and cumulates reports in *Publishers Weekly* and other Bowker periodicals.

- Eberhart, George M. The whole library handbook 2: current data, professional advice and curiosa about libraries and library services. Chicago: ALA, 1995. 521p.

  Complements but does not replace the 1991 first edition. Includes much information not in the *Bowker Annual.*

- Editor and Publisher international year book. New York: Editor and Publisher, 1959– . Annual. Also on CD-ROM.

  A complete listing of U.S. daily and weekly papers, schools of journalism, etc., as well as listing of Canadian and international dailies, syndicates, equipment, organizations, services (e.g., clip art), and personnel. Entries include basic directory information plus data varying with type of entry (e.g., news circulation statistics, newsprint consumption). Lack of a title index and a rather brief subject index make this hard to use in print, especially given the CD-ROM full-text search capability.

- Public libraries in the United States: [year]. Washington, D.C.: U.S. Department of Education, Office of Educational Research and Improvement, 1991– . Irregular.

  Based on data collected by the annual Public Libraries Survey conducted by the National Center for Education Statistics. Most data are at the state level.

■ Research library statistics, 1907–08 through 1987–88. Washington, D.C.: Assn. of Research Libraries, 1990. On disk only.

Includes the full run of the ARL statistics, plus R. E. Molyneaux, *The Gerould Statistics, 1907/08–1961/62* (Washington, D.C.: Assn. of Research Libraries, 1986; 268p.), which covers sixty libraries (but not consistently).

■ ARL statistics [year]. Washington, D.C.: Assn. of Research Libraries, 1961– . Annual. Also online and on CD-ROM.

Has been called "the bible" of data for major research libraries. Recent years have seen increased emphasis on service measures, as well as purely size data. Gives rank order plus data for the members of the ARL.

■ Wertsman, Vladimir F. The librarian's companion: a handbook of thousands of facts and figures on libraries/librarians, books/newspapers, publishers/ booksellers. 2d ed. Westport, Conn.: Greenwood, 1996. 225p.

A general summary of interesting facts about the subjects listed in the title, with lots of out-of-the-way statistics as well as material otherwise easily available. Not a first choice, but useful for the hard-to-find fact or statistics.

The ALA's Public Library Data Service and the Federal-State Cooperative System for Public Library Data, part of the National Center for Education Statistics (NCES), also collect and distribute national statistics on libraries. A detailed comparison of these two somewhat competing systems may be found in *Data Comparability and Public Policy: New Interest in Public Library Data. Papers Presented at Meetings of the American Statistical Association. Working Paper Series.* (Washington, D.C.: National Center for Education Statistics, 1994 [ERIC Document number ED 415 916]; 96p.).

Occupations

■ American salaries and wages survey. Detroit: Gale, 1988– . Biennial.

Relies heavily on federal and state government data, but each edition adds more numbers from trade associations and other private sources. Much of this information is hard to find in other sources.

■ Bulletin of labour statistics. Geneva: International Labour Office, 1965– . Quarterly.

Data are updated in a quarterly *Supplement* between regular issues. Articles, notes, and many statistical tables; update the *Yearbook of Labour Statistics.* Most data include time series for the last four years and for their quarters and months. In addition to the regular supplements, a special issue reports on the International Labour Office (ILO) "October Survey," giving wages and hours for about 160 occupations and retail prices for about 100 items. Data are based on national reports and thus are somewhat uneven and sometimes missing.

■ Employment and earnings. Washington, D.C.: U.S. Bureau of Labor Statistics, 1969– . Monthly.

Regular ongoing tables and special tables in each issue covering national and state data, plus 200 local areas.

■ Encyclopedia of careers and vocational guidance. 10th ed. Chicago: J. G. Ferguson, 1998. 4v. Also on CD-ROM.

Information on more than 2,000 jobs in 544 fields. Each printed volume has indexes to all four volumes. Searchable fields on the CD-ROM including job titles, industry profiles, school subjects, occupations (only twelve categories), interests (eighteen categories), level of education required, and earnings (five categories). Includes SIC and *Dictionary of Occupational Titles* codes.

■ Farr, J. Michael. The complete guide for occupational exploration: an easy-to-use guide to exploring over 12,000 job titles. Indianapolis, Ind.: JIST Works, 1993. 915p.

Expands the U.S. Department of Labor's *Guide for Occupational Exploration* (Washington, D.C.: U.S. Employment Service, 1979; 715p.) and Marilyn Maze and Donald Mayall's *Enhanced Guide for Occupational Exploration* (2d ed. Indianapolis, Ind.: JIST Works, 1995; 684p.) with additional information. Jobs in twelve major interest areas, sixty-six work groups, 348 subgroups, coded by *Dictionary of Occupation Titles* classification. Groups as well as jobs explained. Index by about 30,000 job titles.

■ Handbook of labor statistics. U.S. Department of Labor, 1926–89. Lanham, Md.: Bernan, 1997– . Annual.

Cumulates current and historical data for the series in *Monthly Labor Review, Employment and Earnings,* and other department publications. Much of the more recent data are also available on the U.S. Bureau of Labor Statistics' website: <http://stats.bls.gov>.

■ Monthly labor review. Washington, D.C.: Govt. Print. Off., 1915- . Monthly. Also on the Web.

Primarily ongoing statistical tables, with several analytical articles on employment and labor. Although the data are from the U.S. Department of Labor, many of the articles are from scholars with no such affiliation.

■ Occupational outlook handbook: employment information on major occupations for use in guidance. U.S. Bureau of Labor Statistics. Washington, D.C.: Govt. Print. Off., 1949- . Biennial. Also on CD-ROM.

Also has companion *Career Guide to Industries* (1992- , biennial) and *Occupational Projections and Training Data* (1971- , biennial). Also supplemented by *Occupational Outlook Quarterly* (1957- , quarterly). There are a total of six versions—three print, three CD-ROM, from both the government and private publishers. Describes 250 occupations in detail, covering about 87 percent of all U.S. jobs. Appendix with less data on about 80 more, or another 4 percent.

■ Statistical handbook of working America. Arsen Darnay and Helen S. Fisher, eds. 2d ed. Detroit: Gale, 1997. 934p.

A detailed collection of more than 900 tables based on data from government, academic, business, union, and other sources covering all levels from national to local and all sorts of topics (such as health, education, production, etc.) as well as wages, hours, and number of people employed.

■ Wright, John W. The American almanac of jobs and salaries. Newly rev. and updated 1997-98 ed. New York: Avon, 1996. 656p.

Like other sources in many ways but unique in its extensive data on salaries. An improvement on the *Occupational Outlook Handbook* in having citations to sources used.

■ Yearbook of labour statistics [year]. Annuaire des Statistiques du Travail. Anuario de Estadistica del Trabajo. Geneva: International Labour Office, 1936- . Annual.

National-level data on employment, earnings, and labor, based on each nation's own reporting. A set of methodology volumes called *Sources and Methods: Labour Statistics* is being issued to explain the methodology, history, and differences among the different national collections, as well as to provide various definitions as done by International Conference of Labour Statisticians. Updated by *Bulletin of Labour Statistics* (quarterly).

■ Yearbook of labour statistics: retrospective edition on population censuses, 1945–89. Washington, D.C.: International Labour Office, 1990. 1060p.

Covers 184 countries, based on ILO collections of data done since 1945. Each country gets four tables covering wages, labor supply, etc. Arranged by region with an index by country.

Population and Housing

CENSUS

The census, conducted every ten years since 1790, has increased its scope tremendously from its original charge to include considerable demographic and economic information. In the process, the increasing size of the questionnaire has engendered considerable controversy, both in terms of the perceived invasion of personal privacy and in accusations of undercounting specific groups (notably economic, racial, and ethnic minorities). The undercount controversy is well handled in Harvey M. Choldin's *Looking for the Last Percent: The Controversy over Census Undercounts* (New Brunswick, N.J.: Rutgers Univ. Pr., 1994; 264p.). Academe's response to such complaints and recommendations for changes may be found in *Modernizing the U.S. Census,* Barry Edmonston and Charles Schultze, eds. (Washington, D.C.: National Academy Pr., 1995; 460p.).

For a detailed discussion of all aspects of conducting a modern census, from early planning to publication and distribution of the results, *see 1990 Census of Population and Housing: History* (Washington, D.C.: Govt. Print. Off., 1993–95; 4v.).

■ The census and you. Washington, D.C.: U.S. Census Bureau, April 1988– . Monthly. Also on the Internet at <http://www.census.gov/prod/www/abs/cen-you.html>.

Formerly *Data User News* (1975-1988). A mix of how-to-use census publications, general news, and discussions of the most recent and next censuses.

■ Lavin, Michael R. Understanding the census: a guide for marketers, planners, grant writers and other data users. Kenmore, N.Y.: Epoch, 1996; distributed by Oryx. 545p.

  Details on how and why the census is conducted and specific questions are asked, with definitions of terms and concepts used, and descriptions of all census products, including the CD-ROM and online sources.

■ 1990 census of population and housing: guide. Washington, D.C.: Govt. Print. Off., 1992. 3v.

  Includes text, glossary, and an index to the summary tape files.

The publications of the U.S. Bureau of the Census itself are many and varied, with an increasing number available in electronic format, notably on the World Wide Web, and a growing number available *only* in such formats, not in print or microform. The basic citations for the primary publications, however, are

■ U.S. Bureau of the Census. Census of housing. Washington, D.C.: Govt. Print. Off., 1940- .

■ U.S. Bureau of the Census. Census of the population. Location varies: publisher varies, 1790- .

■ U.S. Bureau of the Census. Joint population and housing reports. Washington, D.C.: Govt. Print. Off., date varies.

BIBLIOGRAPHIES AND INDEXES

■ POPLINE. Bethesda, Md.: National Library of Medicine, 1970- . Monthly updates. Also known as Population Information Online. Online and on CD-ROM only.

  Citations to published and unpublished social science, biological, and medical literature (since 1827) on population and families, with abstracts. Includes vital statistics, demography, family planning, fertility, etc.

■ Population index. Princeton, N.J.: Office of Population Research, Princeton Univ. and the Population Assn. of America, 1935- . Quarterly. Also free, on the Web, at <http://popindex.princeton.edu/index.html>, from 1986 to date.

  Walford's calls this "a first-class example of an annotated bibliography in a special field." An annotated bibliography of all formats in the subject.

The backfile is indexed in *Population Index Bibliography, 1935-68* (Boston: Hall, 1971; 9v.) and *Population Index Bibliography, 1969-1981* (Boston: Hall, 1984; 4v.). The first is an author-and-subject index; the second adds a subject approach.

OTHER POPULATION DATA SOURCES

■ Demographic year book; Annuaire démographique. New York: United Nations. Statistical Office, 1949- . Annual.

Summaries of national data plus areas, with an emphasis on population data. Includes detailed technical notes with all tables. Each volume includes a cumulative list of special topics covered in earlier years and a cumulative index by subject. Special issues for 1978, *Historical Supplement,* and 1993, *Population Aging and the Situation of Elderly Persons,* were issued as volume 2. The 1948 (first) edition included time series from 1936 to 1947; the *Historical Supplement* covers from 1948 to 1978.

■ Demographics USA. New York: Market Statistics, 1993- . Annual. Also on CD-ROM.

Three editions: county, zip code, city. Detailed statistics, primarily in the form of cross-tabulated tables for more than 400 variables, including both numbers and ranks.

■ Population demographics. New York.: Market Statistics, 1990- . Online database only. Annual updates.

Based on the 1990 census, with estimates for the current year and five-year projections. Breakdowns for the entire United States by state, county, city, zip code, census division, Metropolitan Statistical Area (MSA), Consolidated Metropolitan Statistical Area (CMSA), and Designated Market Area (DMA) are possible. A useful set of data, but with the ready availability of the TIGER/Line files directly from the census, is becoming useful only for the projections. The attraction of online forms of such data is readily apparent in a case like this, because the same publisher produces a number of printed excerpts, unlikely to be held by the smaller library. The TIGER/Line database is a machine-readable file of geographic features that can be matched with machine-readable demographic (or other) data.

■ The sourcebook of zip code demographics: 1990 census edition. Arlington, Va.: CACI Marketing Systems, 1991- , annual; distributed by Gale. Also on disk and on CD-ROM.

Seventy demographic variables for each residential and nonresidential zip, information not presented in this form by the census itself, although much can be compiled one zip at a time using the TIGER/Line files. Updates a 1985 version. Includes information about zip code changes. CACI is a noted geodemographic information systems consulting firm, which also produces the very similarly arranged *Sourcebook of County Demographics* (12th ed., 1999; pagination varies).

■ The state of world population. New York: United Nations, 1988– . Annual.

A very brief handbook summarizing demographic data for the whole world, with some other data such as agricultural production, school enrollment, and more.

■ Vital statistics of the United States, 1937– . Washington, D.C.: Govt. Print. Off., 1939– . 3v. since 1960. Annual. Also on the Web.

Imprint and issuing agency vary. Updated by *National Vital Statistics Reports* (monthly). Volume 1 is *Natality,* volume 2 is *Mortality,* and volume 3 is *Marriage and Divorce.* The definitive source for this sort of information. Always national-level statistics, but in many cases, it also gives state-level data.

■ World population profile. Washington, D.C.: U.S. Bureau of the Census, 1986– . Biennial.

Summary information for nations, territories, regions, and similar units, with detailed notes on data sources and the techniques used for the projections, which tend to forecast about twenty years in the future and go back in many cases to the 1950s. Unlike the similar United Nations *World Population Prospects* (New York: United Nations, 1985– ; biennial), this provides data for much smaller units (population of at least 5,000 versus the UN volume's population of 200,000).

Public Opinion

■ American public opinion index. Boston: Opinion Research Service, 1981– . Annual. Also on CD-ROM as Polling the Nations, 1986 to date monthly updates.

Full text of questions and aggregate responses to more than 6,000 surveys from universities and corporations, as well as the usual polling organizations. Covers the United States and sixty other countries. The print product began as an index to a fiche set of the full text, and it tends to lack full citations to the originals; the CD-ROM remedies this defect and is otherwise much easier to use.

■ Index to international public opinion. Westport, Conn.: Greenwood, 1978– . Annual.

Complements *American Public Opinion Index,* with data from 127 reputable polling organizations in seventy-one nations. Includes a number of time series tables for the same question, plus a fifty-year retrospective. Classified arrangement by major topics and subtopics. Each entry gives sample size and source. Indexes by subject, location of poll, geographic area of poll.

■ Niemi, Richard G., John Mueller, and Tom W. Smith. Trends in public opinion. Westport, Conn.: Greenwood, 1989. 325p.

Based on the National Opinion Research Center's General Social Survey (GSS) (1972–) but supplemented to give time series back to about 1930. Its major value is the grouping of data on the same subject from different sources. Arranged by subject. Each table gives wording of question; percentage of responses in each category; GSS code, if available, for each year; plus a brief note on source, number of respondents, month/year of survey, and variants of the question over time. Indexed by GSS codes and subjects. A number of books and many research studies have used these data, which are generally available from the ICPSR (see above and below), but this is probably the handiest compilation.

■ Public opinion online. Storrs, Conn.: Roper Center for Public Opinion Research. Online only, with weekly updates.

Covers polls from 1936 to date, including information from Roper, Gallup, the National Opinion Research Center, Yankelovich Partners, and major television and newspaper polls, among others. Searchable by question, year, population, polling organization, and other elements. Includes the question, results (breakdowns as reported in the original survey), date of question, interview method, respondents, and population. Also includes citation to the original source. Unlike the ICPSR, which generally contains only the raw data, this source provides the data in a directly usable form.

■ Wood, Floris W. An American profile: opinions—behavior, 1972–1990. Detroit: Gale, 1995. 1065p.

Results from the General Social Survey of the National Opinion Research Center for 300 questions.

Religion

■ Eerdmans' handbook to the world's religions. 2d ed. Grand Rapids, Mich.: Eerdmans, 1994. 464p.

Much revision of entries from the 1982 edition, with many color illustrations and a new section on "Religion in Today's World." Still clearly concentrating on the West and Christianity, but with not too strong a bias against others.

Social Conditions

■ Social work almanac. 2d ed. Washington, D.C.: NASW Pr., 1995. 391p.

Not just social work, but general statistics on social problems and issues. Includes very useful discussion of the tables and features. Subject index also includes institutions and program names.

Weather

Current weather conditions and near-future predictions may be found in several online sources, of which the following are currently the most commonly used:

■ CNN.com.weather. <http://www.cnn.com/WEATHER>

From the television news service Cable News Network (CNN), providing much the same sort of data as the next source but with generally more emphasis on current and immediate future forecasts and less on general discussion of weather. As of this writing, also provides a direct link to the National Oceanic and Atmospheric Administration (NOAA) Weather Radio service, which provides warning of severe storms, tornadoes, and the like.

■ The weather channel. <http://www.weather.com>

Although the most detail is for North America, major cities in the rest of the world are also covered. Provides current data and several days' forecasts for cities, plus weather maps and nearly live graphic data on weather patterns. Produced by the television service, data are updated regularly. Includes general discussion of weather topics, such as the effect of tree pollen on health, and topical information (e.g., discussion of hurricanes in the spring and weather-related news).

Cumulations and historical data are also sometimes requested, in which case the following will be needed:

■ Climate Prediction Center. Monthly and seasonal weather outlook. Washington, D.C.: Climate Prediction Center, 1946- . Semimonthly.

Formerly *Average Monthly Weather Outlook.* A companion to the item below, this general analysis of weather patterns includes data for the past month and predictions for the next three months.

■ Climate Prediction Center. Daily weather maps: weekly series. Washington, D.C.: Climate Prediction Center, 1968- . Weekly. Also on the Web.

Four maps of the continental United States for each day, on one page showing the weather as of 7:00 A.M., EST; highest and lowest temperatures; and precipitation.

■ Climatological data [state]. Asheville, N.C.: National Climatic Data Center, 1897- . Monthly.

For greatest detail, one monthly volume per state listing data for each weather station, monthly precipitation for sixty years, and temperature and precipitation averages and variations from 1951 to date.

■ Weather America: the latest detailed climatological data for over 4,000 places, with rankings. Milpitas, Calif.: Toucan Valley, 1996. 1412p.

Thirteen data elements based on averages for the years 1965 to 1994, covering 4,158 places in all fifty states. Includes maps of the weather stations used.

For those with broader (in time or space) needs, a useful source is the World Climate Disc (Cambridge, England: Chadwyck-Healey, 1996; CD-ROM), which covers more than 7,300 sites worldwide, with much data from the mid-nineteenth century and some from even earlier.

Women

■ The world's women [year]: trends and statistics. 2d ed. New York: United Nations, 1995. 188p.

A combination collection of data and narrative on all aspects of women all over the world. The first edition (1991) was updated and expanded, but not completely replaced, by this one as an official publication of the Fourth World Conference on Women. *Choice* calls this source "extremely well organized."

Other Types of Statistical Sources

Emphasis has been given thus far to works that refer users to other sources or to general compendia of statistics. Others types of sources are also of value. Included here are representative examples of each type, together with their general characteristics. More will be found in the *Balay* and *Walford's* guides, especially statistical yearbooks of foreign countries and on special subjects.

Almanacs

Almanacs are frequently used as ready-reference sources of statistics because they make extensive use of government publications in their tables, giving citations to the source. The wide range of subjects covered and the adequate indexes to their arrangement recommend them for questions involving broad geographic areas, where the most recent statistics are not required. Emphasis is given to the country of publication, which makes it advisable for libraries to acquire almanacs published outside the United States. Several of these are included here, but first, a somewhat more limited version of the same idea:

- Chase's calendar of events [year]. Chicago: Contemporary Books, 1958- . Annual.

    Title varies. Arranged by date, giving events for each day with a short annotation. Tends to a U.S. and North American bias and a bit thin for religious events, but the standard. Includes a detailed index and a list of winners of major awards of all kinds for the past year.

GENERAL ALMANACS

True almanacs include the following sources:

- The annual register [year]: a record of world events. London: Keesing's, 1758- . Annual.

Title has varied over time. Retains a very strong British emphasis and an emphasis on Western-oriented and major nations only, but a classic and useful complement to the American almanacs.

■ Information please almanac, atlas and yearbook, 1947- . New York: Viking, 1947- . Annual. Also on the Web.

One of the standards, with many changes in arrangement and coverage over time. Though it has a U.S. bias, the sections on geography, space, awards, and current events are international. Many charts and graphs. Well indexed. Not ideal for current events of topical nature, but excellent for current and factual information about past events and geography. Its crossword-puzzle guide, guide to good English, and career-planning kit are notable features not in most other almanacs. The "People" section (with very brief entries) is good for celebrities but is not indexed in the general index.

■ Whitaker's almanack. London: The Stationery Office, 1869- . Annual.

The standard one-volume British source. Has been praised for its currency and index. Obviously has a British and Commonwealth bias and more detail on Europe than the U.S. productions.

■ World almanac and book of facts [year]. Mahwah, N.J.: World Almanac Books, 1868- . Annual. Also on CD-ROM and the Web as part of the Electric Library.

One of the basic library references. Includes some color photos. In addition to miscellaneous facts of all kinds, includes a review of important events of the past year and important Supreme Court decisions, making it more of a "yearbook" than most of those published with encyclopedias. Offers a list of Nobel Prize winners and a review of U.S. history with a time line. *American Reference Books Annual (ARBA)* in 1985 checked this and its major competitor, the *Information Please Almanac,* to find only about 70 percent overlap between the two. The CD-ROM permits searching by terms, Boolean logic, and phrases, with truncation allowed, as well as scrolling every word in text and subject categories.

SPECIALIZED ALMANACS

Some more-specialized titles of use follow:

■ The almanac of Canadian politics. 2d ed. Oxford and New York: Oxford Univ. Pr., 1996. 768p.

A primary statistical source, similar to the *Almanac of American Politics* (*see* above, p. 431). Each new edition covers different elections in great detail but does not replace earlier editions.

■ Nonprofit almanac. 5th ed. San Francisco, Calif.: Jossey-Bass, 1992– . Biennial.

Summary data on essentially all philanthropic, religious, advocacy, etc. groups and individuals in the United States but not individual organizations.

Statistical Yearbooks

More useful than almanacs in statistical reference work are statistical yearbooks because they concentrate on statistical data, often omitting the directory and miscellaneous information found in almanacs. They usually contain statistics covering a longer period of time, useful for comparative purposes by those seeking to establish trends in population, the economy, education, etc. These comparative tables are convenient because they make it unnecessary to consult so many individual annual volumes. This type of publication is covered well in both *Balay* and *Walford's,* and given below are only a few examples of frequently used annuals covering a wide range of subjects:

■ Statesman's year-book. New York: St. Martin's, 1864– . Annual.

Covers major international organizations, then countries and territories of the world. Statistics in entries under standard headings. Most entries have bibliographies, emphasizing statistical publications. Includes much historical data as well as current facts. A companion volume, with cumulated historical data, is *The Statesman's Year-book Historical Companion,* edited by John Paxton (London: Macmillan, 1988; 356p.).

■ UNESCO. Statistical yearbook. Paris: UNESCO; Lanham, Md.: Bernan, 1964– . Annual.

In French, English, and Spanish. Tables vary, but the general arrangement is similar to the United Nations (UN) *Statistical Yearbook,* cited in the next entry. This source covers educational, scientific, and cultural data for about 200 nations, based on annual surveys and generally giving the most recent ten years.

■ United Nations. Department of Economic and Social Affairs, Statistics Division. Statistical yearbook; annuaire statistique. New York: United Nations, 1949– . Annual. Also on CD-ROM since 1994.

All captions and text in French and English. Generally covers the most recent ten years, but remains about two years behind in publication data. Since the early 1990s, finally includes an index; since the early 1960s, also includes a world summary. Because of the increase in electronic data sources, the UN is gradually reducing the number of tables in this source, which remains a handy compilation of general socioeconomic, economic, scientific, technological, and industrial data. Heavy reliance on national governments for much of the information has led to criticism both for lack of accuracy and currency. Data are updated by *Monthly Bulletin of Statistics.* For data before 1949, *see Statistical Year-book of the League of Nations, 1926-1942/44* (Geneva: League of Nations, 1927-45; 14v.).

■ Great Britain. Office for National Statistics. Annual abstract of statistics. London: The Stationery Office, 1854- . Annual. Also published by Bernan.

Useful as an index to sources, as well as for wide coverage of all types of British statistics—economic, social, demographic, financial, etc.—generally for ten-year time series.

Atlases

Atlases are used primarily for economic and population statistics, and a number of such atlases have appeared in recent years. Only a few are listed here; for additional titles, see chapter 9, "Thematic Maps and Atlases," page 494.

■ Mattson, Mark T. Atlas of the 1990 census. New York: Macmillan, 1992. 168p.

Clear, concise maps (many in color) at state, regional, and national levels are supplemented by tables and charts. Includes regional county-locator maps. A useful graphic summary of the census.

■ Rand McNally commercial atlas and marketing guide. New York: Rand McNally, 1876- . Annual.

Based on the most recent census, plus updates based on estimates from the government and Rand McNally's own formulae. The metro areas are based on density of population rather than county lines, so are more accurate for much business work. As an atlas, covers small towns not in most atlases, with an index to more than 128,000 political units, such as villages, townships, towns, and cities.

■ TIGER/Line census files. Washington, D.C.: U.S. Bureau of the Census, 1991– . CD-ROMs, online, and Internet.

■ TIGER/Line 1992: the coast-to-coast digital map data base. Washington, D.C.: U.S. Bureau of the Census, 1993– . CD-ROMs, online, and Internet.

The TIGER (Topologically Integrated Geographic Encoding and Referencing system)/Line system provides the software to create maps based on the 1990 census. The data are coded to provide, in effect, overlays of the data; and a geographic information system must be used to actually create the maps. The data files are readily available, but probably the most convenient way to use TIGER is via the Internet on the Bureau of the Census's site. The CD-ROM versions may be more useful if extensive mapping is needed, because the free Internet site can have considerable traffic and thus be slow to load.

Historical Compendia and Dictionaries of Statistics

Historical compendia can be thought of as general compendia similar to the almanacs, with summary statistics covering wide areas (for the most part).

■ Dodd, Donald B. Historical statistics of the states of the United States: two centuries of the census, 1790–1990. Westport, Conn.: Greenwood, 1993. 478p.

Provides both a different and more convenient format than the U.S. Government Printing Office (GPO) title with a similar name, with an emphasis on state-level data. Appropriate notes and a number of subject-specialized tables are included.

■ Mitchell, B. R., comp. British historical statistics. Cambridge, England, and New York: Cambridge Univ. Pr., 1988. 886p.

Gives historical data from the twelfth century, and includes useful notes on collection methods and controversies involved in the subject.

The following series covers the more modern period:

■ Babuscio, Jack, and Richard M. Dunn. European political facts, 1648–1789. New York: Facts on File, 1984. 387p.

■ Cook, Chris, and John Paxton. European political facts, 1789–1848. New York: Facts on File, 1981. 195p.

- Cook, Chris, and John Paxton. European political facts, 1848–1918. New York: Facts on File, 1977. 342p.

- Cook, Chris, and John Paxton. European political facts, 1918–90. 3d ed. New York: Facts on File, 1992. 322p.

  Handy compilations, including (as much as possible) comparable data series over all volumes. Arranged by topic, then by nation. Each volume has a select annotated bibliography and an index.

- Mitchell, Brian R. International historical statistics, Europe, 1750–1988. 3d ed. Basingstoke, England: Macmillan; New York: Stockton Pr., 1992. 942p.

- _____. International historical statistics: Africa, Asia and Oceania, 1750–1993. 3d ed. London: Macmillan; New York: Grove's Dictionaries, 1998. 1113p.

- _____. International historical statistics: the Americas, 1750–1993. London: Macmillan; New York: Stockton Pr., 1998. 830p.

  Derived from official statistics for the most part, and lacking an index, these remain convenient compilations of statistics, mostly economic in nature. Each table includes useful notes and citations to sources. Because of the nature of the sources, most time series actually only go back to about the mid-1800s.

- Mulhall, Michael George. Dictionary of statistics. 4th rev. ed. London: Routledge, 1899. Reprint, Detroit: Gale, 1972. 853p.

  General statistics covering from Diocletian to 1890. Authorities for the data are not always cited, though a list of sources is included.

- Webb, Augustus Duncan. New dictionary of recent statistics of the world to the year 1911. London: Routledge, 1911. Reprint, Detroit: Gale, 1971. 682p.

  Supplements and updates Mulhall's volume, with a similar arrangement, covering from 1899 to 1909. Sources are cited with the data and in a separate bibliography, a major improvement over the former.

Handbooks

There are several standard handbooks, providing formulas and tables useful for interpreting statistics:

- Burington, R. S., and D. C. May. Handbook of probability and statistics with tables. 2d ed. New York: McGraw-Hill, 1970. 462p.

  Complements Burington's *Handbook of Mathematical Tables and Formulas* (5th ed. New York: McGraw-Hill, 1973; 500p.). Eighteen sections on elementary statistics and probability theory, then about 100 pages of tables. Index to tables and a subject index.

- CRC handbook of chemistry and physics. Boca Raton, Fla.: CRC Pr., 1922– . Annual.

  A classic source, needed in almost all libraries. Tables are revised with nearly every edition; recent editions have included more on the environment plus more verbal definitions as well as tables.

- CRC standard mathematical tables and formulae. 30th ed. Boca Raton, Fla.: CRC Pr., 1996. 812p.

  The standard for the professional but with major changes since the twenty-ninth edition, in 1991: many tables readily available on pocket calculators have been dropped or truncated; many chapters now include a short list of references; and Uniform Resource Locators (URLs) for websites are included. Given the changes, most libraries will probably want to retain at least the twenty-ninth edition.

- CRC standard probability and statistics tables and formulae. Cleveland, Ohio: CRC Pr., 1991. 503p.

  The current edition of another standard and a companion to the above but with a much higher proportion of actual tables as well as formulas and reasonably clear narratives explaining each table. Editions vary little.

- The Economist desk companion: how to measure, convert, calculate and define practically anything. New York: Henry Holt, 1994. 272p.

  Although the most common conversions (e.g., centigrade to Fahrenheit) may be found in the standard almanacs, this source gives many more measures, including local variations, and much more detail. There is a clear British slant, but relevant measurements are converted into both U.S. and British systems, as well as the ubiquitous metric.

- Fisher, R. A., and F. Yates. Statistical tables for biological, agricultural and medical research. 6th ed. Edinburgh, Scotland: Oliver & Boyd, 1963. 146p.

A standard source first published in 1938 but still with no index. The fifty tables, of course, change little, but this title is most useful for its introduction with examples.

■ New Cambridge statistical tables. D. V. Lindley and W. F. Scott, eds. 2d ed. Cambridge, England, and New York: Cambridge Univ. Pr., 1995. 96p. Also on the Internet.

Another standard, with more tables. The by-subscription Internet version makes this source an attractive choice, and the tables are, of course, accurate.

■ Platt, George. ISA guide to measurement conversions. Research Triangle Park, N.C.: Instrument Society of America, 1994. 172p.

Several thousand conversions listed in this definitive work. In two arrangements—by name and by classification. Gives the exact calculation and also a simpler way to convert within 5 percent accuracy.

■ Powell, F. C. Statistical tables for the social, biological and physical sciences. Cambridge, England: Cambridge Univ. Pr., 1982. 96p.

Extends the Fisher-Yates volume with line drawings and numerous tables.

Rankings

Librarians have seen an increasing call for rankings in recent years. Obviously, a number of the sources listed above either include indications of rank or can be used to calculate such ranks, but the following are particularly useful and generally reliable. One of the major questions to keep in mind whenever looking at a rank order is exactly what is being measured and how. For example, Lynn Hattendorf's *Educational Rankings Annual,* listed under "Education," on page 428, provides a discussion of the differences in rank that result when different measures are used (some being as obvious as the size of a library collection versus the size of its budget).

■ American suburbs rating guide and factbook. Milpitas, Calif.: Toucan Valley, 1993. 846p.

All suburbs with populations of 10,000 or more within the fifty largest metro areas. Based on the 1990 census and Uniform Crime Reports, with twenty-two rankings. Includes maps. Index by name covers 1,770 places.

■ CQ's state fact finder: rankings across America. Washington, D.C.: Congressional Quarterly, 1993– . Annual since 1996.

About 325 tables giving comparative statistics for states and the District of Columbia. Arranged by subject; includes a state profile section giving state ranks for all indicators. All sources identified with each table.

■ Gale country and world rankings reporter. 2d ed. Detroit: Gale, 1997. 1100p.

Gives about 3,200 tables in five broad categories based on more than 500 government and private sources (including newspaper articles, all with full citations), with full indexes by location and by keyword. The detailed introduction includes methods used for compiling the lists. Although coverage is the largest of any of the international sources, many tables have only a few countries.

■ Gale state rankings reporter. 2d ed. Detroit: Gale, 1996. 1580p.

Ranks more than 3,000 elements by all fifty states, primarily based on government statistics. Similar to *State Rankings,* published by Morgan Quitno (*see* below), which is an annual. Indexed by state and by keyword; all sources cited.

■ Heubusch, Kevin. The new rating guide to life in America's small cities. Amherst, N.Y.: Prometheus Books, 1997. 527p.

A companion to *Places Rated Almanac.* Gives ratings of more than 200 places of about fifteen square miles area and populations of 15,000 to 50,000.

■ Kurian, George T. Illustrated book of world rankings. 4th ed. Armonk, N.Y.: Sharpe Reference, 1997. 403p.

Compares 190 nations on about 300 key areas, with rankings as well as data. Each section includes discussion of the data and measurement methods, and there is a country summary at the end of the book.

■ Savageau, David. Places rated almanac. 5th ed. New York: Prentice-Hall, 1996. 485p.

Covers about 350 metro areas; each area gets entry description and ranking based on ten factors. Highly recommended by reviewers. Appendix lists cities and towns in each metro area. No index.

■ Showers, Victor. World facts and figures. 3d ed. New York: Wiley, 1989. 721p.

Ranks 218 countries and more than 2,600 cities on forty-five different elements, primarily in tables to allow for comparisons. Includes an index and bibliography.

■ State rankings. Lawrence, Kans.: Morgan Quitno, 1990- . Annual.

Covers the same territory as *Gale State Rankings Reporter,* above, but on an annual basis. Of course, each title includes some data the other lacks.

Summary

As the reader will note, this is a time of change, especially for numeric data sources, with the ease and sophistication of searching, combined with the ability to display in tabular or graphic form, causing an increasingly rapid migration to electronic sources. However, the basic principles of selection of any reference source remain—accuracy, completeness (within the source's stated limits), reliability and validity, and appropriateness, among others. Although ease of use is also a legitimate criterion, the user should remember that the primary purpose of a statistical data source is the provision of useful, meaningful, and accurate data—not merely ease of use, flashy graphics, or apparent timeliness.

9

Sources of
Geographical Information

$\mathbf{N}$either a purely natural nor a purely social science, geography has studied—from its development as an organized field of knowledge in classical Greece—human societies in their spatial and ecological environment. To be sure, geography is not alone in its concern for people and their environment:

> Many fields in the natural and social sciences study a particular category of phenomena, not excluding its distribution and variations over the earth. What geography, and geography alone, studies is the areal character of the earth in which man lives—the form, the content, and the function of each areal part, region, or place and the pattern of and interconnections between the areal parts. If the total diversity of places and their interrelations were simply the sum of areal variations and connections of physical, biological, and social phenomena, the subject could readily be divided into distinct fields: physical geography, biogeography, and human, or social, geography; or possibly two parts, the geography of nature and the geography of man. In reality, however, the phenomena of these several abstract categories are in many cases very closely interrelated in their areal variations and connections from place to place. Indeed, what the geographer observes as individual features—i.e., a soil, river water, a farm, a transport route—are element complexes in which factors of physical, animate, and social origin are so intricately interwoven as to require study within a single field. Places, or areas, large or small, may be studied either

specifically or generically. . . . Geography, like history, is ultimately concerned with attaining maximum comprehension of individual cases. An essential step in the description as well as the understanding of the individual areas is the determination of its generic characteristics. When we speak of places as "deserts," "canyons," "cities," "farms," or "culture areas," we limit the criteria in each case to a few closely interrelated features, overlooking aspects in which places of the same type may be radically different. Comparative study of the characteristics of places by kind may reveal indications of significant correspondence, leading to hypotheses of generic relationships [Richard Hartshorne, "Geography," in *International Encyclopedia of the Social Sciences,* v.6, p. 115-16].

Readers with an interest in additional overviews of the field of geography will be impressed with Chauncy D. Harris's chapter in William H. Webb's *Sources of Information in the Social Sciences* (3d ed. Chicago: ALA, 1986; p. 149-212) and the scholarly but readable overviews by Preston E. James and Geoffrey J. Martin, in *All Possible Worlds: A History of Geographical Ideas* (3d ed. New York: Wiley, 1993; 585p.), as well as that in Arild Holt-Jensen's *Geography, History and Concepts: A Student's Guide,* English adaptation and translation by Brian Fullerton (3d ed. London: Thousand Oaks, 1999; 228p.). Recent developments are well covered in James H. Bird's *The Changing World of Geography: A Critical Guide to Concepts and Methods* (2d ed. Oxford and New York: Oxford Univ. Pr., 1993; 307p.); a more cartographical emphasis is well developed in John Goss's *The Map-Maker's Art: A History of Cartography* (London: Studio Editions, 1993; 376p.).

Geographers, like members of other professions, do not want for organizations they may join. In the United States, the two principal geographical organizations are the Association of American Geographers (Washington, D.C.) and the American Geographical Society (New York); their publications are discussed later in this chapter. The International Geographical Union, founded in 1922, seeks to promote—through academies of science, research councils, or similar bodies, in more than eighty countries—international cooperation in geographical research and to organize international geographical congresses. With a very similar focus, the Pan American Institute of Geography and History (Mexico City) unites the countries of the Americas.

To serve the needs of geographers and others, many large academic and research libraries have extensive collections of maps and other geographical information. Their interests are seen in the activities of such organizations as the Geography and Map Division of the Special Libraries Association (SLA), the Western Association of Map Libraries (publishers of the Western Association of Map Libraries *Bulletin,* Sept. 1969-), and the Section of Geography and Map Libraries of the International Federation of Library Associations and Institutions (which publishes an Internet *Newsletter*). The great collections of the

Library of Congress and of the American Geographical Society (the latter held at the University of Wisconsin–Milwaukee Golda Meir Library) are evidence of the wealth of information being acquired and systematically organized.

Of interest to library school students and librarians is Lisa A. Recupero's "Map Users and Map Reference: Some Considerations for Map Librarians" (SLA Geography and Map Division *Bulletin,* no. 180 [June 1995]: 29–52), which provides an excellent overview of library aspects of map service. Regarding users, Recupero summarizes recent studies suggesting that most academic map users are undergraduates, primarily working on course assignments, and that most users (85 percent in one study) are generally happy with the service. A less reassuring piece of data is the very low percentage of library school students who use maps, especially because the evidence is fairly strong that the high percentage of user satisfaction is related to skillful assistance from library staff.

The various surveys are fairly consistent in which types of maps are most used—the U.S. Geological Survey (USGS) topographical map series. Unfortunately, it is not clear whether this is the result of this series' providing the most needed information or the result of librarian familiarity and the series' general availability—how many times would some other source have done as well or better but was not suggested by the librarian?

Other recent work discussing the important role of the librarian in both instruction and, if you will, "marketing" maps in the sense of bringing them to the attention of users as an important and desirable source includes Janet K. Rudd's "Map User Needs in Academic and Business Environments" (in *Maps in the Geoscience Community: Proceedings of the 19th Meeting of the Geoscience Information Society* [Alexandria, Va.: Geoscience Information Society, 1985]: 65–71). Mike Gluck and others' "Public Librarians' Views of the Public's Geospatial Information Needs" (*Library Quarterly* 66, no. 4 [1996]: 408–48) takes the librarian's point of view. The most recent detailed study of use is from Europe (where geographical knowledge seems at a higher standard than in the United States): Jan Smits, "Report on the Inquiry into Map-Use and User-Habits in Europe" (*LIBER Quarterly* 1, no. 3 [1991]: 283–310). All of these should be familiar to any reference librarian, especially because there is an unfortunate tendency (much as with government publications) to relegate geographical sources to some out-of-the-way place as a different type of source.

A different perspective is provided by Charles Seavey's "1991 ARL Cartographic Resources Survey" (Western Association of Map Libraries *Bulletin* 23 [July 1993]: 175–79). Seavey found substantial difficulties in getting data on the collections even of the large libraries in the Association of Research Libraries (ARL), but he has begun trying to collect consistent data over several years, both on map collections and such output measures as use, so that librarians can get a handle on what is really happening.

Glen Creason provides an easy, step-by-step program for overcoming what he calls "carto-phobia"—essentially, a description of map series of particular importance and heavy use from the public library perspective in "Wherever You Go, There You Are" (Western Association of Map Libraries *Bulletin* 25 [Nov. 1993]: 31-35).

Certainly, prospective librarians must be aware of map resources, and all libraries must keep their value and existence in mind.

School libraries and media centers are also faced with the problem of supplying materials needed in the teaching of geography. In this they are helped by such agencies as the National Council for Geographic Education, which is deeply concerned with the use of the newer media, as a cursory glance at its official publication, *Journal of Geography*, reveals.

It is not enough for the school library to have a good atlas (a volume of maps) and a few years of the *National Geographic* to augment the geographical information in school encyclopedias. Films, globes, videos, and an increasing number of computer databases and programs are needed; guides to these are noted later in this chapter. Jack Ferguson's "Using Road Maps in the Junior High School" (*Journal of Geography* 75 [Dec. 1976]: 570-74), although old, is still relevant; it exemplifies the usefulness of the *Journal of Geography*, which is equally valuable for teachers in colleges and universities as well as librarians.

But between the research worker and the elementary-school student is the general reader, whose demands and needs for geographical information will inevitably change as research activities and methods of teaching geography in schools and colleges change.

The biggest changes in geographic reference work (as in much of geographic information of all kinds) results from the development and increasing availability of "geographic information systems" (GISs).

Although many of the concepts as well as some of the tools of GIS date back to the early part of the twentieth century, GIS in the true sense developed in the 1960s as a result of the availability of modular programming languages. However, it was the ready availability of high-powered personal computers with good graphics that helped GIS mature. And, as one might expect with a new field, there is considerable, ongoing discussion about how to define GIS. One definition that seems to have had some stability is that of Dueker:

> A geographic information system is a special case of information systems where the database consists of observations on spatially distributed features, activities, or events, which are definable in space as points, lines, or areas. A geographic information system manipulates data about these points, lines and areas to retrieve data for ad hoc queries and analyses [K. J. Dueker, "Land Resource Information Systems: A Review of Fifteen Years' Experience," *Geo-Processing* 1, no. 2 (1979): 106].

In short, a GIS involves matching some kind of data with other data that provides information about some portion of the earth. Although oversimplified, one way of thinking of a GIS is the more traditional approach in many texts of providing a base map, on which one can place transparent overlays. For example, think of a map of a state showing county boundaries. One then obtains data by county, giving the number of registered voters, and colors in the numbers using several shades of green, putting this over the original map.

The attraction of GIS in this sort of application is that, assuming one has a sufficiently detailed map and sufficiently detailed data, one can create the overlay to show the numbers divided in five shades of color, or ten shades, or fifty. Or one could indicate the data as percentages rather than colors. Or, having created a map for the entire state, one could then enlarge the map to show just one county, and redo the overlay to show only the data by city blocks. Much of the attraction of a GIS to the layperson is the ability to manipulate the data and the map to create, on demand, new maps to answer a specific question.

Another very common GIS application is using the geographic information to create numeric data—for travelers, this means obtaining driving directions and specific mileage between two points, as in Mapquest or Maps on Us, two World Wide Web systems discussed below (pages 526 and 527).

However, although using GIS to produce and manipulate maps is common, many other applications exist in business, geography, social sciences, statistics, and the like. This may be clarified by a more detailed definition:

> The GIS . . . has the following subsystems:
>
> 1. A data input subsystem that collects and preprocesses spatial data from various sources. This subsystem is also largely responsible for the transformation of different types of spatial data. . . .
>
> 2. A data storage and retrieval subsystem that organizes the spatial data in a manner that allows retrieval, updating, and editing.
>
> 3. A data manipulation and analysis subsystem that performs takes on the data, aggregates and disaggregates, estimates parameters and constraints, and performs modeling functions.
>
> 4. A reporting subsystem that displays all or part of the database in tabular, graphic, or map form.
>
> [Michael N. DeMers, *Fundamentals of Geographic Information Systems* (New York: Wiley, 1997), p. 9].

In practice, libraries tend to use existing packages that already contain both the spatial and other data, plus the needed software for at least some manipulation. Some packages are available for local use, notably ArcView and MapInfo; others are available on the Web, either for a fee or for free.

In addition to knowing what systems are available for your library, the librarian should remember an important fact: GISs are fundamentally tools for dealing with geographic data and as such can easily be misunderstood or misused by those who lack understanding of geography. Thus, as with more traditional statistical packages, one can create meaningless displays or misunderstand the results of a display. But, unlike most use of numeric statistics, because the display is often in a colorful graphic form, one can easily forget that the choices of what to display and how to display it remain wide—maps (and other graphic information) are never complete representations of reality, but rather selected partial representations. In this regard, at least a brief reading of Monmonier's *How to Lie with Maps* is essential to doing reference work with these sources.

Finally, consider the pervasive role of governments in geography and cartography. The long and extensive involvement of the U.S. government affords a good example (although the considerable contributions of state and local governments must also be acknowledged).

No less a person than General George Washington was responsible for perhaps the first official mapping and map-collecting agency in the federal government. Apparently, because of Washington's complaints to the Continental Congress about the army's lack of accurate maps, Robert Erskine was appointed geographer and surveyor to the army in 1778 (Walter Thiele, *Official Map Publications* [Chicago: ALA, 1938], p. 104).

In the pre–Civil War years, the surveys conducted by the national government were chiefly exploratory in character—the most important of the early surveys was the expedition of Captains Meriwether Lewis and William Clark, who ascended the Missouri River to its source and then descended the Columbia River to the Pacific. The expeditions of Zebulon Pike in 1805 and 1807 were also significant, as were the 1820 expedition to Upper Michigan, Wisconsin, and Minnesota conducted by General Lewis Cass, then superintendent of the Bureau of Indian Affairs, and an expedition to one of the sources of the Mississippi in 1832, by Henry Rowe Schoolcraft, while traveling on behalf of the Bureau of Indian Affairs.

After 1835, the surveys and exploration under the auspices of the army were many. Of these, perhaps the most noteworthy were those of John C. Fremont of the Oregon and Upper California area and the survey of a railroad conducted under the War Department for a Mississippi to Pacific railroad. David Dale Owen conducted important surveys under the auspices of the General Land Office, covering the geology of what is now Illinois, Iowa, Wisconsin, and Minnesota.

Although no government survey of note was conducted during the Civil War, four major surveys of the West were conducted between 1867 and 1879. Known after the geologists in charge, two were conducted by the War Department and two by the Department of the Interior.

The King Survey (the Geological Exploration of the Fortieth Parallel), authorized by Congress in 1867, studied the belt of country along the fortieth parallel from longitude 120 to 105. The second, or Hayden, survey (under F. V. Hayden, and called Geological and Geographical Survey of the Territories) was also authorized in 1867 and eventually covered all the territories in the Far West, covering not only geology, but botany, topography, ethnology, philology, and other sciences as well. The third survey, the Powell survey, began in 1867 as an exploration of the Colorado River under the auspices of the Smithsonian Institution, under John Wesley Powell. Powell continued the survey into Utah and eventually the whole Rocky Mountain area, under the direction of the secretary of the Interior, again covering much more than merely geology.

The fourth, or Wheeler, survey, under the direction of Lt. George M. Wheeler of the War Department's Corps of Engineers extended over the western parts of the Dakotas, Nebraska, Kansas, and Texas, as well as the Rocky Mountain and Pacific Coast states. As with the others, in addition to its geographical and topographical emphasis, it covered "as far as practicable without greatly increasing the cost, all the information necessary before the settlement of the country."

In the early 1870s, there were thus four surveys in progress under specific congressional appropriations, each employing its own methodology and, in several places, duplicating coverage of the same areas. In addition, the Coast and Geodetic Survey (originally the Survey of the Coast, and renamed several times, to the National Ocean Survey in 1970) had also extended its work to the interior of the country.

As a result, Congress in 1878 called upon the National Academy of Sciences (NAS) for a less wasteful plan to carry on these activities. Congress acted upon the NAS's recommendations to create the USGS in 1879. The history of the USGS is well covered in Morris M. Thompson's *Maps for America: Cartographic Products of the U.S. Geological Survey and Others* (3d ed. Washington, D.C.: Govt. Print. Off., 1988; 265p.).

The above discussion of the federal government's cartographic/geographic activities to the landmark date of 1879 have relied heavily on Anne M. Boyd's *United States Government Publications* (3d rev. ed. by Rae E. Rips; New York: Wilson, 1952; 238–46); Brookings Institution, Washington, D.C., Institute for Government Research, *The U.S. Geological Survey: Its History, Activities and Organization* (New York: Appleton, 1918; Reprint, New York: AMS Pr., 1974; p. 1–13); Thiele (cited above); and Thompson (cited above). Information on recent activities of the government in this area may be found in the *U.S. Geological Survey Yearbook: Fiscal Year 1995* (Reston, Va.: USGS, 1995), also on the Web at <http://yearbook.usgs.gov>.

To meet the needs of various federal agencies to supply accurate and consistent place-names for the United States for use in maps, charts, and other federal publications, President Harrison created the U.S. Board on Geographical Names in 1890.

The twentieth century has witnessed dramatic increases in the nation's needs for and uses of geographical and cartographical materials. In many instances, existing federal agencies have assumed responsibility for appropriate materials; in other instances, new agencies have appeared, such as the Department of Transportation and the Tennessee Valley Authority.

Emphasis in this chapter is given to bibliographical sources, not only because of the development of library systems for resource sharing, which demands that librarians become and remain aware of what may be found outside their own collections, but also because of the ever-increasing amount of diversity of geographical sources.

Attention is also given to atlases, the most important source, and to a lesser degree to gazetteers and travel guides, particularly those most likely to be found in general collections and whose contents must be mastered for efficient reference service. Guidelines for reviewing atlases are in the appendix.

Because familiarity with the geographical information in general reference material will result in a wiser selection of geographical sources by avoiding those that merely duplicate the information in general sources, an overview of those types already discussed is in order. As in previous chapters, the types of information to be found in these sources will be briefly outlined.

1. Bibliographies, indexes, and abstracting services
   a. Trade bibliographies and national and union catalogs, useful for locating titles of atlases, handbooks, and travel guides for individual countries and cities, especially by use of the name of the place with the subdivision "Description and Travel"
   b. Bibliographic guides—to be discussed further below
   c. Indexes and abstracting services for periodicals. These are useful for locating information on cities, resorts, travel, and recreation and include collective indexes such as *Reader's Guide to Periodical Literature;* indexes to one periodical, such as the cumulated index to the *National Geographic Magazine;* and indexes to one type of source, such as *Bibliographic Index.* Often, sources with abstracts will indicate, either within the abstract or as a separate field, the presence of maps within nongeographic articles
2. Biographical sources. Useful for biographies of geographers and cartographers, as well as for information on place-names (many places, of course, are named after people)
3. Encyclopedias. As pointed out already, these are useful sources for geographical information. They contain descriptions of counties, cities, states, provinces, and the like; maps and plans of cities, states, and nations; and, often, atlases separate from the main body of the encyclo-

pedia. Less useful for small areas and for thematic maps than more specialized sources, but also useful for articles about maps and charts, photogrammetry, surveying, exploration, etc.

4. Dictionaries. Useful only for brief identification of larger places and for definitions of geographical terms. General dictionaries must be augmented with dictionaries of geographical and geological terms

5. Statistical sources. These are extremely useful, not only for data in tabular form, but increasingly for thematic maps such as those of the Bureau of the Census. In a growing number of cases, the machine-readable version of such sources includes software for the creation of maps showing the distribution of the data in geographical form

General Reference Works

Bibliographies

The bibliography of geography and cartography is wide and varied, as even a brief survey of its current state will reveal. Chauncy Harris's chapter in William H. Webb's *Sources of Information in the Social Sciences,* cited above, provides such a survey.

Bibliographic guides, catalogs of collections, bibliographies and indexes, abstracting services, special guides to government publications, and other sources are briefly described below.

To proceed from the general to the specific, the familiar guides to reference material offer a good beginning. *Walford's Guide to Reference Material* (6th ed. London: Library Assn., 1993; v.2), section 91, on geography, exploration, and travel, contains well-annotated lists of bibliographies, manuals, encyclopedias, dictionaries, and other formats, often with citations to reviews. A separate section on "Area Studies" reflects the great expansion of the literature in recent years and includes many geographical resources. Section CL, "Geography," and section D, "History and Area Studies," in *Guide to Reference Books,* edited by Robert Balay (11th ed. Chicago: ALA, 1996; 2020p.) are most useful in American libraries as sources of general works, gazetteers, dictionaries, handbooks, encyclopedias, and guidebooks.

Another general source, more restricted in the number of titles but recommended for its well-organized information, is the interestingly written chapter on geographical sources in William A. Katz's *Introduction to Reference Work,* volume 1, *Basic Information Sources,* 7th ed. (New York: McGraw-Hill, 1997; chapter 11) as is David A. Cobb's chapter, "Geographical Sources," in Richard E. Bopp and Linda C. Smith's *Reference and Information Services: An Introduction* (2d ed. Englewood, Colo.: Libraries Unlimited, 1995; 483p.).

Specific bibliographies and guides to the literature of geography and cartography include the following:

■ Dunbar, Gary S. The history of modern geography: an annotated bibliography of selected works. New York: Garland, 1985. 386p.

Definitive within its scope, which emphasizes the academic discipline in western Europe and North America. General/topical; various countries; biographical works. Indexed by author and by subject.

■ Encyclopedia of geographic information sources. 4th ed. Detroit: Gale, 1987. 2v.

One volume covers the Unites States; the other covers the rest of the world. Although very complete, especially for state and local resources, it is becoming dated, especially in its lack of reference to electronic sources.

■ Harris, Chauncy D. Bibliography of geography. Chicago: Dept. of Geography, Univ. of Chicago, 1976–84. 2 pts. (Research paper no. 179 for part 1; no. 206 for part 2).

By concentrating on the post-1945 period, this first-rate work is a true update to Wright and Platt's volume (*see* below). Entries are arranged primarily by format, with full bibliographic citations and careful annotations. Worthy of note is the core geographical reference collection in an appendix to part 1.

■ Harris, Chauncy D., and Jerome D. Fellman. International list of geographical serials. 3d ed. Chicago: Dept. of Geography, Univ. of Chicago, 1980. 165p. (Research paper no. 193).

Some 3,445 serials in 107 countries in fifty-five languages, including nonroman scripts. Index and cross-references. A selected list of more than 300 serials is given more detailed treatment in Harris's *Annotated World List of Selected Current Geographical Serials* (4th ed. Chicago: Dept. of Geography, Univ. of Chicago, 1980; 165p. [Research paper no. 194]).

■ The map catalog: every kind of map and chart on earth and even some above it. Joel Makower, ed. 3d ed., newly rev. New York: Vintage, 1992. 364p.

All kinds of maps, including historical, travel, water, and sky and images as maps. Includes information on accession, software, etc. Cross-references and comprehensive index. Appendixes include addresses for state and federal map agencies, map stores, and libraries. Excellent sections on choosing a map and general map skills. The first edition won a Reference and Adult Service Division (RASD) Outstanding Reference Source award in 1988.

■ Map Link catalog: travel maps and books for the entire world. Santa Barbara, Calif.: Map Link, 1990- . Annual.

Formerly *The World Map Directory,* from 1989 to 1993. Actually a sales catalog, with prices. Emphasizes tourist, city, and recreational maps; regional and country maps; topographical maps for most countries. Has been likened by reviewers to the traditional *Sears Catalog*—with uses as a reference tool far beyond its original purpose.

■ Wright, John Kirtland, and Elizabeth T. Platt. Aids to geographical research: bibliographies, periodicals, atlases, gazetteers, and other reference books. 2d comp. rev. ed. New York: for the American Geographical Society by Columbia Univ. Pr., 1947. Reprint, Westport, Conn.: Greenwood, 1971. 331p.

Still useful for the older material, especially for its comprehensive international coverage.

The following two "bibliographic" Internet sites, of the many available, are especially useful:

■ The AGS collection. Milwaukee, Wis.: American Geographical Society Collection, Golda Meir Library, University of Wisconsin–Milwaukee. 1996- . <http://leardo.lib.uwm.edu>

Information about the collection, one of the world's greatest, with links to other geographical and cartographical resources.

■ Odden's bookmarks: the fascinating world of maps and mapping. World Wide Web <http://oddens.geog.uu.nl/index.html>

The most complete maps and geography site on the Web, maintained by Roelof P. Oddens, at the University of Utrecht. Lists well over 6,500 sites classified by type of site, then by geographical region. As the name implies, does not rate or describe the sites, but merely provides hypertext links to them. Covers maps on the Web, departments of geography and cartography, library collections, commercial sites, sellers of maps and geography books, government agencies, etc. Includes a calendar of upcoming events (exhibits, conferences, and the like).

Indexes

Useful for more popular articles are the general indexes, such as *Readers' Guide;* and for those in more specialized journals, *Current Geographical Publications* (another American Geographical Society [AGS] publication) includes references to periodical articles.

■ American Geographical Society. Map Dept. Index to maps in books and periodicals. Boston: Hall, 1968. 10v. First supplement (1971, 603p.) second supplement (1976, 568p.); third supplement (1987, 668p.).

Although likely to be found only in larger libraries, this title should be known to all librarians. Its subject and geographical-political division entries include many hard-to-locate and little-known maps in the society's large holdings of books and periodicals from around the world (now at the Golda Meir Library of the University of Wisconsin–Milwaukee).

■ GEOBASE. Norwich, England: Elsevier/Geo Abstracts, 1980– . CD-ROM and online. Monthly updates (quarterly on CD-ROM).

Machine-readable version of *Geographical Abstracts* and its predecessors. About 60 percent of the entries cover physical and human geography.

■ Geographical abstracts. Norwich, England: Elsevier/Geo Abstracts, 1989– . Monthly.

In two parts, *Human Geography* and *Physical Geography.* Formerly *Geographical Abstracts* (1966-1971); then *Geo Abstracts* (1972-1985); then *Geographical Abstracts* (1986-1988) in several parts, which merged into these two. Retains topical arrangement. Regional index in each issue, cumulated annually, plus an annual author index. Also covers material in *International Development Abstracts; Geological Abstracts* series; *Mineralogical Abstracts;* and *Ecological Abstracts.*

■ National Geographic index, 1888-1988. Washington, D.C.: National Geographic Society, 1988. 1215p. National Geographic index, 1989-1993. Washington, D.C.: National Geographic Society, 1993. 117p.

Replaces and cumulates three earlier titles. Author/photographer, title, and subject indexes to the articles in this journal. Includes symbols to distinguish books, maps, TV programs. The index is continued in the annual index to the periodical itself, which is much more detailed than indexing in collective sources such as *Readers' Guide.*

■ Otness, Harold M. Index to nineteenth century city plans appearing in guidebooks: Baedeker, Murray, Joanne, Black, Appleton, Meyer plus selected other works to provide coverage of over 1,800 plans to nearly 600 communities, found in 164 guidebooks. Santa Cruz, Calif.: Western Association of Map Libraries, 1980. 84p.

■ Otness, Harold M. Index to early twentieth century city plans appearing in guidebooks: Baedeker, Muirhead-Blue guides, Murray, I.J.G.R., etc. plus selected other works to provide worldwide coverage of over 2,000 plans to over 1,200 communities, found in 74 guidebooks. Santa Cruz, Calif.: Western Association of Map Libraries, 1978. 91p.

Older guidebooks, especially, often have detailed plans that are otherwise very hard to find, because most atlases and tour guides emphasize the current state of the place in question. These are excellent and very handy guides for the historian and the historically minded traveler.

■ Walsh, Jim. Maps contained in the publications of The American bibliography, 1639–1819: an index and checklist. Metuchen, N.J.: Scarecrow, 1988. 367p.

Indexes the Evans and Shaw-Shoemaker bibliographies (see chapter 2). Arranged by item number, giving specific pages where maps can be found. Indexed by date of publication, place of publication, personal names (author, cartographer, etc.), title of both book and each map, and by geographic locations covered.

Literature Guides and Selection Aids

Guides to the literature of the field have increased in recent years. They include the following:

■ Brewer, J. Gordon. The literature of geography: a guide to its organization and use. 2d ed. London: Bingley, 1978. 264p.

A practical and useful guide, best, of course, for the older material, with emphasis on works in English.

■ Encyclopedias, atlases and dictionaries. Marion Sader and others. New Providence, N.J.: Bowker, 1995. 485p.

The most recent of the guides; titles selected with the assistance of several prominent educators and working reference librarians. Includes a section on atlases as well as a subsection on them in a chapter on electronic sources. Each section includes a "what to look for" guide, annotations for each entry, and a table summarizing features.

■ A geographical bibliography for American libraries. Chauncy D. Harris, ed. Washington, D.C.: Assn. of American Geographers, 1985. 437p.

Complements *Geographical Bibliography for American College Libraries* (rev. ed. Washington, D.C.: Assn. of American Geographers, 1970; 214p.), emphasizing publications from 1970 to 1984. This joint project of the Association of American Geographers (AAG) and National Geographic Society includes brief critical annotations for most titles and an index and is currently *the* source of recommended titles. Includes an "also recommended" list for school libraries. Annotated.

■ Information sources in cartography. R. B. Parry and C. R. Perkins, eds. London and New York: Bowker/K. G. Saur, 1990. 540p.

Aimed both at cartographers and map librarians, contains six parts, each with five to six bibliographic essays, primarily covering from 1960 to date. Indexes by subject and name. Good coverage of map publishers, with appendixes listing periodicals and societies.

■ Keyguide to information sources in cartography. New York: Facts on File, 1986. 253p.

The first section contains essays on maps and cartography and their literature. The remaining three sections include annotated bibliographies on the history of cartography and on contemporary cartography plus a directory of organizations. Index by author, title, subject, organizations, places (mainly countries). International coverage, but emphasis is on works in English and on the United Kingdom, United States, and Canada. Very well received when published; it is unfortunate that a new edition has yet to appear.

■ Kister, Kenneth F. Kister's atlas buying guide: general English language world atlases available in North America. Phoenix, Ariz.: Oryx, 1984. 236p.

Kister's usual excellent work, reviewing in detail more than 100 atlases. Unfortunately, now out-of-date in some respects, but it will remain an excellent example of detailed evaluative reviews even when completely superseded.

▪ Podell, Diana K. Thematic atlases for public, academic and high school libraries. Metuchen, N.J.: Scarecrow, 1994. 176p.

Evaluates 100 thematic atlases, giving a detailed description of topics and coverage and usually at least a brief table of contents. Emphasizes current material, with a slant toward those costing $100 or less, but with a few classics listed. Includes a list of published reviews for most entries and a glossary. Index by name/title, subject.

▪ Walsh, James P. General world atlases in print, 1972-73: a comparative analysis. 4th ed. New York: Bowker, 1973. 211p.

Although quite dated, the comparisons of about 140 atlases are still helpful as a guide to reviewing the atlas format; and in some cases, the information is still relevant to the current editions, as well as the older material.

Library Catalogs

The catalogs of major library collections in geography can be of considerable use, both for current information (especially with remote-access online catalogs) and for retrospective searching. The following are notable:

▪ American Geographical Society. Research catalogue. Boston: Hall, 1962. 15v. Map supplement (1962); supplement 1-2 (1972-78, 6v.).

Books, periodical articles, pamphlets, and government publications in one of the largest geographical libraries in the world, in a classified arrangement. Its update, noted below, has become the definitive current bibliography in the field. The supplements cumulate listings in *Current Geographical Publications,* volumes 25 to 39.

▪ American Geographical Society. Current geographical publications: additions to the Research catalog of the American Geographical Society. Milwaukee, Wis.: Golda Meir Library, University of Wisconsin–Milwaukee, 1938- . Monthly. Also on the Internet, 1996- .

Since 1964, contains a separate section on maps. Its classified arrangement is supplemented by annual indexes by subject, author, and region.

▪ Bibliographic guide to maps and atlases. New York: Hall/Simon & Schuster, 1979- . Irregular.

Supplements *Dictionary Catalog of the Map Division* of the New York Public Library (NYPL). Lists both NYPL Map Division and Library of Congress (LC) Geography and Map Division cataloging—maps, charts, atlases, globes, cartography, etc., including periodical analytics.

■ Library of Congress. Geography and Map Division. The bibliography of cartography. Boston: Hall, 1973. 5v. Supplements, 1980- .

Another G. K. Hall reproduction of a card catalog, with especially good coverage from 1895 to 1922. Probably the most complete bibliography of the subject within its time limits.

■ New York Public Library. Dictionary catalog of the map division. Boston: Hall, 1971. 10v.

In addition to maps and atlases, covers about 11,000 other titles on mapmaking, etc. Cards include analytics for periodicals and bibliographies. Updated by *Bibliographic Guide to Maps and Atlases,* above.

■ Library of Congress. Geography and Map Division. Panoramic maps of cities in the United States and Canada. Washington, D.C.: Library of Congress, 1984; distributed by Govt. Print. Off. 181p.

Offers 1,726 maps of cities in forty-seven states, the District of Columbia, and Canada. By state, then city. Indexed. Panoramic maps are, in effect, aerial maps from the days before aerial photography; and they often show nearly every building of every size.

■ A list of geographical atlases in the Library of Congress, with bibliographical notes. Washington, D.C.: Govt. Print. Off., 1909-92. 9v.

The catalog of one of the largest (if not *the* largest) atlas collections in the world, with generally full records.

The monthly *Journal of Geography,* the official organ of the National Council for Geographic Education, should be used regularly for information on all aspects of geographic media, as should the educational section of the USGS website, at <http://www.usgs.gov>.

Government Publications

All governments produce and distribute a wide variety of pertinent publications, some of which are extremely important in the field in geography. For example, during World War II, the U.S. government made and printed more maps than had been made throughout the previous history of the world.

Useful adjuncts to standard government indexes and catalogs, such as the *Monthly Catalog of United States Government Publications* and *Monthly Checklist of State Publications,* follow:

■ Maps and atlases. Washington, D.C.: Govt. Print. Off., 1994- . Annual. Subject Bibliography SB 102.

   An annotated bibliography of government publications about maps, mapping, and atlases.

■ Morehead, Joe, and M. Fetzer, eds. Introduction to United States government information sources. 6th ed. Englewood, Colo.: Libraries Unlimited, 1999. 491p.

   Similar to the previous editions but adds information on public access to electronic information and rearranges a number of other chapters. Indexes by name, title/series, subject. Has been called "probably the best general guide to U.S. government publishing available" by *Government Publications Review.* The chapter on mapping and geographic sources, like the others, is highly recommended.

■ Schmeckebier, Laurence Frederick, and Roy B. Eastin. Government publications and their use. 2d rev. ed. Washington, D.C.: Brookings, 1969. 502p.

   Chapter 16, "Maps" (p. 406–40) describes bibliographic sources, major atlases, various categories of maps, and the agencies responsible for their production. Although outdated in many respects, this remains important, especially for older material.

The 1992 National Geologic Mapping Act (PL 102-285) authorized a national mapping program to include the states as well as the USGS, again with the intent of creating a database rather than necessarily creating the maps themselves (Department of the Interior, *U.S. Geological Survey: Overview 1993* [Reston, Va.: USGS, 1993; 1v. Various pp.]).

As of 1993, the government began moving from traditional mapping to use of computerized cartography, with "partnerships" with both the public and private sector to produce data needed for GIS systems. Maps are becoming based on use of land data collected by satellite, with a conscious effort to reduce and eventually eliminate duplications in collection of data, notably the development of the geographic data for a new *National Atlas of the United States.* The USGS maintains the following files: National Digital Cartographic Data Base for digital map data and digital orthophotoquads; Geographic Names Information System; and Main Image File electronic catalog of about 10 million aerial photographs and satellite images.

Overall, the federal government's emphasis is changing from producing maps to producing the data so that maps can be produced for very specific needs. The USGS is also working with other agencies investigating natural phenomena and with the Federal Emergency Management Administration (FEMA) regarding the cause and prevention of natural disasters.

Maps and Atlases

The types of information conveyed by maps and atlases seem almost limitless. The following list merely illustrates their variety: bodies of water (oceans, rivers, lakes, etc.), mountains, deserts, highways, streets, railroads, airports, dams, canals, soils, forests, agriculture, minerals, political entities (boundaries between continents, nations, states, provinces, counties, capital cities, county seats, parks, school districts), fire insurance, weather, and climate.

Maps and atlases, so important a part of any good general reference collection, must be selected with care, especially as there are so many, with the number of electronic sources—too many of them with poor-quality maps—increasing almost daily.

Further information on sources of maps and atlases, representing a state-of-the-art summary just before the rapid acceptance of GIS, may be found in Donald A. Wise, "Cartographic Sources and Procurement Problems" (*Special Libraries* 68 [May/June 1977]: 198–205) and its eleven appendixes in the *Bulletin* of the Geography and Map Division of the Special Libraries Association, appearing in volumes 112 to 115, from 1978 to 1979.

FIRE INSURANCE MAPS

One type of very detailed map is the fire insurance survey, intended to provide risk-assessment data. The Sanborn Map Company provided such maps, with regular updates, beginning in the late nineteenth century and continuing well into the twentieth century. Unlike most city maps, these are detailed at the individual building level, including not only location, but building materials, use of the building, and the like. Chadwyck-Healey provides digital and microform copies of the maps held in the LC for the period from 1867 to 1970. Although the microform collections are quite expensive and, unlike the originals, filmed only in black and white, the maps are very popular, and many libraries will at least want the following as guides to the collection.

■ Library of Congress. Geography and Map Division. Fire insurance maps in the Library of Congress: plans of North American cities and towns produced by the Sanborn Map Company: a checklist. Washington, D.C.: Library of Congress, 1981; distributed by Govt. Print. Off. 773p.

Covers about 700,000 maps from 1867 to date and about 12,000 cities and towns in the United States, Canada, and Mexico. Arranged by state, county, and town. Indexed by county, city, and town.

Further information on this interesting series, often found second in popularity only to the USGS topographic maps, may be found in Diane Oswald's *Fire Insurance Maps: Their History and Applications* (College Station, Tex.: Lacewing Pr., 1997; 102p.).

Dissertations

■ Browning, Clyde E. Bibliography of dissertations in geography, 1901 to 1969: American and Canadian universities. Chapel Hill: Univ. of North Carolina Dept. of Geography, 1970. 96p.

■ _____. Bibliography of dissertations in geography, 1969 to 1982: American and Canadian universities. Chapel Hill: Univ. of North Carolina Dept. of Geography, 1970. 145p.

Based primarily on dissertation lists in *The Professional Geographer* (to 1979) and *The Guide to Programs in Geography in the United States and Canada* (1979–). Classified with author index.

Place-Names

■ Sealock, Richard Burl, and Pauline Augusta Seely. Bibliography of place-name literature: United States and Canada. 3d ed. Chicago: ALA, 1982. 435p.

Lists more than 4,800 items, including books, articles, and some manuscript collections. Arranged by states for the United States and provinces for Canada. Nearly all entries have brief annotations. Indexed by author and place-name. Much of the material is based on the periodical, *Names* (1953–), a quarterly publication of the American Name Society, whose recent issues update this exhaustive bibliography. *Names* has cumulative indexes covering volumes 1 to 15 and 16 to 30, easing the user's life.

Biographies

■ Geographers: biobibliographical studies. London: Mansell, 1977– . 19v. as of 1999 (in progress).

Intended to be definitive, has covered more than 200 individuals since the series began. Includes people who had been neglected. For each person, in addition to a biography, includes bibliography, list of sources, summary chronology of life, portrait.

Cartographic History and Map Librarianship

The history of maps is fascinating, and the study of them engages not only cartographers, but also amateur collectors, who search for them in secondhand dealers' shops. Brief accounts of maps and mapmakers are readily available in encyclopedias and provide good introductions to the subject, but for those seeking more information, the following books give one a fuller appreciation of the art.

■ The history of cartography. J. B. Harley and David Woodward, eds. Chicago: Univ. of Chicago Pr., 1987- . v.1- .

When the six volumes are complete, this will be the definitive work on the subject. This collection of essays covers the entire world (not just the West) and all of history to the present, with very good indexing.

A shorter work is Preston E. James and Geoffrey J. Martin's *All Possible Worlds: A History of Geographical Ideas* (3d ed. New York: Wiley, 1993; 608p.).

In the meantime, a number of titles have become classics, and will probably remain of interest even after *The History of Cartography* is completed.

■ Bricker, Charles. Landmarks of mapmaking: an illustrated survey of maps and mapmakers. Amsterdam: Elsevier, 1968. 276p.

Republished as *A History of Cartography.* A fine example of superb bookmaking, rich in reproductions of rare maps (with 200 maps), often from the best available copies. Deals only with European cartography from the fifteenth to the nineteenth centuries.

■ Brown, Lloyd A. The story of maps. Boston: Little, Brown, 1944. 397p.

Interesting, readable account of the mapmakers and how they made them, including the Egyptian astronomer, geographer, and mathematician Ptolemy, who faced the continuing problem of balanced coverage by making ten maps for Europe, four for Africa, and twelve for Asia.

■ Lister, Raymond. Antique maps and their cartographers. Hamden, Conn.: Archon Books, 1970. 128p.

Profusely illustrated with facsimiles of early maps (fifty-eight total); chapters with bibliographies cover up to the late nineteenth century.

■ Lister, Raymond. How to identify old maps and globes, with a list of cartographers, engravers, publishers, and printers concerned with printed maps and globes from c.1500 to c.1850. Hamden, Conn.: Archon Books, 1965. 256p.

Aimed at the collector and dealer, with many facsimiles, this is also a readable history of maps and charts, methods of early map production, and the like, covering flat maps and atlases plus globes and armillary spheres.

■ Lock, C. B. Muriel. Geography and cartography: a reference handbook. 3d ed., rev. and enl. London: Bingley, 1976. 720p.

As it says, a handbook, primarily a listing of materials. This edition, which tried to integrate the earlier material, including Lock's *Modern Maps and Atlases* (below), has, interestingly, received praise by geographers but mixed reaction from librarians. Altough somewhat dated, it is still an important source.

■ Lock, C. B. Muriel. Modern maps and atlases: an outline guide to twentieth century production. Hamden, Conn.: Archon Books, 1969. 619p.

Still considered important, especially for the discussion of cartographic methods and activities of government and private agencies.

■ Lynam, Edward. The mapmaker's art: essays on the history of maps. London: Batchworth Pr., 1953. 140p.

The author, once superintendent of maps for the British Museum, drew on that collection for this book, devoted to the history of English maps, with many facsimiles.

■ Skelton, Raleigh A. Maps: a historical survey of their study and collecting. Chicago: Univ. of Chicago Pr., 1972. 138p.

A well-written, informative overview of the study and collecting of maps by a leading authority.

■ Thrower, Norman J. W. Maps and man: an examination of cartography in relation to culture and civilization. Englewood Cliffs, N.J.: Prentice-Hall, 1972. 184p.

Particularly good for its attention to thematic mapping.

■ Woodward, David, ed. Five centuries of map printing. Chicago: Univ. of Chicago Pr., 1975. 177p.

> A scholarly examination of printing techniques, with superior reproductions. Given the changes in map production in recent years, this may well become the definitive discussion of traditional techniques.

Reproductions of old maps and atlases were made much more readily available to those who could afford them through the publishing program of Theatrum Orbis Terrarum, Ltd., in Amsterdam, which for several years reproduced a series of rare and important atlases in facsimile, beginning with Ptolemy's *Cosmographia* and Blaeu's *Light of Navigation.* The same company also issued *Acta Cartographica,* a series of unabridged reprints of monographs and studies dealing with the history of cartography, drawn from more than 150 of the foremost European and American historical journals from the first half of the eighteenth century, when interest in the history of cartography began to emerge. Although these publications are no longer in print, many map libraries are beginning to produce adequate computer-generated copies from their collections, often with at least a readable copy available on the Web for perusal.

But for every person interested in old maps, there are thousands who use modern maps and atlases, the products of cartographers who draw on what has been learned about the world from surveying, aerial photographs, and remote sensing. Thus, a thorough knowledge of atlases and their use is essential for librarians, who can learn their value only by examining their contents and noting their special features. A useful basic orientation may be found in the following:

■ Album of map projections. Washington, D.C.: Govt. Print. Off., 1989. Reprint 1994. 257p.

> Although thin on the details of the projections, which are well covered by Snyder (below), this inexpensive work provides an excellent set of examples of how the projections actually appear when used to make maps.

■ Canters, F., and H. Decleir. The world in perspective: a directory of world map projections. New York: Wiley, 1989. 181p.

> An illustrated overview of sixty-eight different map projections, with a section on general principles.

■ Larsgaard, Mary. Map librarianship: an introduction. 3d ed. Littleton, Colo.: Libraries Unlimited, 1998. 487p.

The first textbook aimed at American librarians (the first edition was in 1978), this has become the definitive work on the subject. Each edition to date has been much changed and enlarged from the previous.

■ Monmonier, Mark. How to lie with maps. 2d ed. Chicago: Univ. of Chicago Pr., 1996. 176p.

Explains the nature and method of necessary distortions of a round globe when drawing a flat map and how unnecessary ones can distort facts. Includes references to GIS systems, which can be used to manipulate "official data." Very entertaining as well as instructive.

■ Monmonier, Mark. Mapping it out: expository cartography for the humanities and social sciences. Chicago: Univ. of Chicago Pr., 1993. 301p.

Aimed at graduate students but accessible to any author who might benefit by using maps. Has the same purpose as literary-style manuals like Strunk and White's: how to use maps as a type of scholarly work— not just how to interpret maps. The chapter "Working with a Cartographic Illustrator" is particularly helpful for its intended audience.

■ Robinson, Arthur H. Elements of cartography. 6th ed. New York: Wiley, 1995. 674p.

A standard work for students in cartography since the first edition in 1953.

■ Snyder, John P. Flattening the earth: two thousand years of map projections. Chicago: Univ. of Chicago Pr., 1993. 365p.

Although useful to experts, this general history is aimed at the general reader, with the first four chapters providing an overview of the problem of creating an accurate two-dimensional map from a three-dimensional, roughly globular surface; the rest discuss in great detail the solutions to the problem in chronological order. A detailed glossary, bibliography, and index make this an important reference tool for those who might wish to learn more about the issues involved in any large-scale mapping project. Includes short biographies of each author of a projection, if available, and computerized reconstructions of most maps, to illustrate how they are done.

A number of journals in the field are worthy of perusal. For well-respected reviews of maps, atlases, and cartographical material, *see* the *Information Bulletin* of the WAML. Of course, all the titles also include articles of value, although some may be a bit technical. Most of these may be found in most academic libraries (and in geographical and cartographical collections): *Annals* of the AAG (often considered the major professional geographers' journal), *Cartography and Geographic Information Systems* (formerly *American Cartographer*), *Geographical Review, Journal of Geography,* and *Professional Geographer.*

And, although not directly connected with map librarianship, there is at least one useful title on the newest type of geographical representation—GIS: Micheal N. DeMers's *Fundamentals of Geographic Information Systems,* 2d ed. (New York: Wiley, 1999; 486p.). Unlike many similar books, this is accessible to the nongeographer and does not require much more than basic computer literacy to understand. This textbook should be at least familiar to (if not read by) all librarians who in any way deal with maps or their equivalent.

What to Look For

When looking for an atlas, be most aware of the maps themselves and not unduly impressed with photographs of countries and people or other extraneous material. Some American atlases have been criticized for including too much of the latter, using space that might better have been devoted to maps.

Note also balance of coverage, for most authorities agree that a fair allocation of space to maps on a worldwide basis is the most important criterion in judging a world atlas.

There is also general agreement that a good world atlas should consist of maps of all parts of the world, reproduced on a reasonably large scale, with a large number of place-names shown and with a good index. These should be accompanied by an adequate table of contents, instructions in the use of the atlas—including an explanation of symbols used, projections, and abbreviations—and sources used in its compilation. Careful reading of all these parts is as necessary for efficient use as reading the introductions of unabridged dictionaries, because, like the dictionary, the atlas conforms to set rules.

When looking at individual maps, note whether the copyright date is shown, for not all maps in an atlas are equally up-to-date. Note how relief is shown, whether by layer coloring to indicate different elevations above sea level, or by shading, or by hachures. Note the selection and application of the colors, bearing in mind that "maps should have harmony within themselves. An ugly map, with crude colors, careless line work, and disagreeable poorly arranged lettering may be intrinsically as accurate as a beautiful map, but it is less likely to inspire confidence" (John K. Wright, "Map Makers Are

Human," *Geographical Review* 32 [1942]: 542). In the past, few American atlases have been distinguished for their coloring, being excelled by the work of European cartographers. However, there has been much improvement in the past few decades, at least in printed maps and atlases. Some of the Web-based sites, on the other hand, seem to be regressing, at least as far as elegance of appearance is concerned.

Note the projections used, remembering that "a projection is a systematic compromise with accuracy of area or with true shape. The larger the area shown on the map, the greater is the distortion. The maximum difficulty is encountered in attempting to show the entire world on one flat map, and to meet this problem, mapmakers have, through the centuries, utilized a number of different projections. . . . A good reference atlas should use different projections, each best suited to the desired objective" (Walter W. Ristow, "World Reference Atlases," *Special Libraries* 38 [March 1974]: 71).

Note the scales used—they should be carefully chosen and as large as possible to show detail. Generally, it is recommended that all the maps of a given area, such as a continent, should use the same scale, so that the maps are comparable, and that there should be as few different scales used as possible. Remember that the conventional description of a scale is in a proportion of one unit on the map to a number of the same units in real life. Thus, 1:100,000 means a very *large* scale (one map inch represents 100,000 inches) and 1:10,000,000 is a *small* scale.

Note the treatment of place-names. Recent English-language atlases tend to follow the rulings of the U.S. Board on Geographical Names (BGN) or the Permanent Committee on Geographical Names in London (PCGN). These rulings are based on the local spelling of a name (on a standard transliteration of the local spelling). For places that have distinctive English names that differ from these, the English form is often given under the official form, and both forms will appear in the index. More and more, atlases reflect the UN Group of Experts on Geographical Names, a group of geographers, linguists, and historians, who, since 1960, have held conferences and made recommendations stressing the need for standardization of geographic names.

Publishers of good world atlases are concerned with all these aspects and, in this highly competitive field of publishing, continuously revise their works to meet the demand for well-balanced, handsome, accurate, and up-to-date atlases. Some have established reputations over the years, among them the distinguished John Bartholomew and Son in Edinburgh, responsible for the maps in the *Times Atlas of the World*. Also widely recognized is the Cartographic Department of the Oxford University Press, publishers of the *Oxford Atlas of the World* (*see* below, p. 487). In the United States, the most widely recognized publishers are Hammond, Rand McNally, and the National Geographic Society.

To cite but one instance of a foreign government agency that produced notable world atlases, consider the work of the (former) USSR Chief Directorate of Geodesy and Cartography, which issued the *Atlas Mira.*

Although there is considerable agreement among experts on which world atlases are superior, it is interesting to compare extended reviews, which vary greatly in particulars. For example, even the famous *Times Atlas of the World* was criticized by Roman Drazniowsky, then map curator of the American Geographical Society, for its spelling of foreign place-names and for its cartography, closing with, "The reviewer would like to add that some corrections of political division, changes in place-names, and the addition of some pipelines do not make this edition a superb atlas, as compared to the Mid-Century edition. It is hoped that this statement is not too harsh, but one sets and expects a high standard from the professional atlas makers and cartographers, and a high standard was achieved in the previous editions of the *Times Atlas,* particularly the superb Mid-Century edition" (SLA, Geography and Map Division *Bulletin* 73 [Sept. 1968]: 26–28). On the other hand, we find this same edition praised in *Booklist* (July 15, 1968) as "another landmark in cartography" and recommended by Daniel A. Gómez-Ibáñez ("World Atlases for General Reference," *Choice* 6 [July–Aug. 1969]: 628) as "by far the best English atlas, perhaps even the best atlas in the world."

All of which only serves to remind us that authorities do not always agree and that the art of atlas reviewing is not easily acquired, and seldom by the general reference librarian, who must often depend on critical evaluations by experts. It is always wise to be aware of the year in which a review was written, as atlases change (and so do world conditions, for that matter).

It is also wise to bear in mind the qualifications of the reviewer, for an atlas condemned by a cartographer or geographer for its lack of balance might be less severely criticized by a lay reviewer, who is pleased by that very lack of balance—if it favors his or her own point of view. And individual maps, praised for their uncluttered appearance by reviewers who are aware that users not proficient in map reading may find them easy to use, may be severely criticized by more sophisticated reviewers, demanding the maximum of detail, who label them flat and dull.

Librarians, knowing the kinds of people who use their atlases, will acquire the best and most recent atlases, whose maps may be heavily or lightly detailed, as well as those with emphasis on the country of origin or properly balanced coverage, depending on their users' needs and desires—a good idea in the development of any collection of any kind of material.

To demonstrate that reviewers do not always agree in their evaluation of individual world atlases, the titles below are accompanied by outlines of favorable and unfavorable comment.

General World Atlases

Most authorities agree that *The Times Atlas of the World* is the best world atlas published in recent times, essential in all libraries that can afford it. For this reason, it is described first:

■ The Times atlas of the world. 9th comprehensive ed. New York: Times Books, 1994. 514p.

> The largest (11½ by 18 inches) and most prestigious atlas currently sold. Contains mostly physical maps, mostly two-page spreads, with relatively few special features. Uses *eight* colors rather than the four in most atlases. Not unduly biased toward the United States or United Kingdom. Has larger maps and larger scales than any other general reference atlas—each type of map tends to have a standard set of scales, with some variation where needed. Several types of projection are used. Uses hypsometric tints to indicate elevation, unlike nearly all other general atlases. Very up-to-date, very legible. Endpaper maps with grid to indicate the location of a given map. Chinese names are in pinyin; the PCGN is used for the name authority (although local names are also usually present if space permits), and up to fifteen type fonts are used for labels. Scales in both ratio and bar graph give both miles and kilometers.

> *Pluses*

> > Lays flat; useful statistics with key to maps; regular and frequent revisions; large scales varying with map, mostly 1:250,000 and 1:500,000. Each map gives arrows to adjoining maps with page numbers; symbols are on a removable card as well as in the book. The gazetteer gives both grids and geographic coordinators and is the most complete gazetteer in an atlas available.

> *Minuses*

> > The atlas is large and heavy; no sources for statistics given; panhandles and similar features are often inset in larger maps and, thus, on a different scale than the rest of the area; the symbols card can get lost; there is very little information on how to use or interpret the maps. Given the emphasis on maps, there are relatively few special features found in most similar world atlases. The use of British name authority may sometimes be confusing to Americans.

■ The Britannica atlas. Chicago: Encyclopaedia Britannica, 1942– . Annual.

> This supersedes the *Encyclopaedia Britannica World Atlas* and *Encyclopaedia World Atlas International.* Reflecting the joint effort with

Rand McNally it is nearly identical to the Rand McNally *New International Atlas* (*see* below, p. 486). Thematic maps follow Goode's homolosine equal-area projection, also found in the *Rand McNally Goode's World Atlas* (*see* below, p. 488). Two sections contain general and thematic maps; the third section contains data, mostly in tabular form; and the fourth section is an index of about 170,000 place-names, giving latitude and longitude as well as page references and listing places both by English equivalent and local name (e.g., Vienna and Wein). The map has been praised by reviewers for its international coverage, overall balance, and annual updating. In fact, some reviewers see this atlas as equivalent to *The Times Atlas of the World*.

Pluses

More South American maps than most; excellent thematic maps; detailed city maps. Has a good glossary; current to year of publication. Very legible; clear political borders, especially versus *The Times Atlas of the World.* Summary index map. Maps have short glossaries for relevant terms, in the maps.

Minuses

Some thematic data are out-of-date; five languages lead to unclear legends. Index gives only latitude and longitude, not grid. And, obviously, it overlaps the *New International Atlas.*

■ CIA maps and atlases. Series. Washington, D.C.: Central Intelligence Agency, 1970– . Irregular.

Fairly inexpensive and a depository item, thus available in most government documents collections, these spiral-bound volumes are mostly maps with little text. The general pattern is regional maps followed by specific national maps. Appendixes include a glossary of historical regions; various charts and graphs giving national data for the area; text giving a general summary of the people, economy, government, and geography; and a bibliography. The various maps are consistently highly praised by reviewers.

Pluses

Lays flat; updated fairly often; inexpensive and readily available.

Minuses

Relatively little aesthetic appeal; lacks text and features many people expect to find in a world atlas; multiple volumes may lead to confusion.

- Cosmopolitan world atlas. Rev. ed. Chicago: Rand McNally, 1996. 304p.

Replaces the earlier *New Cosmopolitan World Atlas.* The United States and Canada get most detail (maps are from Rand McNally's *Atlas of the United States*). Has almost all political maps and essentially no physical maps. Scales vary from as small as 1:24,000,000 to as large as 1:3,000,000. Both vernacular and English names appear; 78,000 names are indexed. Tends to use text and photographs rather than maps to give information.

Pluses

Good U.S. and Canadian coverage, especially for a world atlas. Data as well as maps are updated regularly. Excellent essay on geography and map use called "The Real World," by Marvin Mikesell. Place-name index emphasizes country units and includes counties. Generally a user-friendly layout and design.

Minuses

Less comprehensive than competitors, with an incomplete index; not all symbols are explained in legend. Cluttered state and province maps; few thematic maps, even fewer physical maps. Each state and province gets a full page; thus, scales vary but level of detail the same. Therefore, smaller states look empty; larger look cluttered. Use of color and shading sometimes muddy and unclear.

- The great world atlas. Vera Benson, dir. of cartography. 4th ed. New York: American Map Corp., 1994. 367p.

A high-quality atlas of intermediate size (translated from a German atlas) that could be considered as an intermediate between the *Rand McNally Goode's World Atlas* and *The Times World Atlas.* The paper and printing are exceptionally good, thus giving what one reviewer called a "brilliant luminous quality." Coverage of the United States and South America is good, with the U.S. map scale slightly larger than that for Europe. Relatively few scales are used—the United States gets mostly 1:3,750,000; most others are 1:4,500,000. Unlike most of its competitors, here physical maps predominate, notably the seventeen natural-color satellite photos. This atlas prefers local spelling over English for place-names. The nearly 100,000 index entries generally cite only the largest scale map for a place.

Pluses

Best coverage of South America of any other general atlas; extremely good how-to-use features; good essays, statistics, and other features; excellent cartography and aesthetics.

Minuses

Projections are not given on maps. Color shades are too close to each other on relief; thus, it is hard to see differences. Doesn't give English equivalent for all terms on maps; labels and names are sometimes cut off at margin, and some information is lost in the gutters. The use of the same scale for sets of maps gives an unconventional grouping of nations.

■ Hammond atlas of the world. 2d ed. Maplewood, N.J.: Hammond, 1999. 312p. Also on CD-ROM, included with newer editions of the printed atlas, by itself, and as part of Microsoft Bookshelf.

Introduced in 1992 as the new top of the line for Hammond, based on a computer mapmaking system, it is the first such atlas, according to the publisher. Includes a new type of projection, "Optimal Conformal," for continents, to reduce distortion. Text includes an "Interpreting Maps" section with emphasis on computer systems plus many statistics but, overall, with less information and other special features than some competitors. The vast majority of maps are political or physical general maps, with a few thematic and purely physical maps (the latter are actually photos of three-dimensional models). Uses local names, translating the "hard" ones to English, plus giving the local in parentheses. Scales vary, with most at 1:3,000,000 and 1:6,000,000; U.S. maps are primarily 1:1,000,000. The place-name index lists about 115,000 items by page and grid number, to the largest scale map containing the place.

Pluses

About half the emphasis is on Europe and North America, but it has the best coverage of Africa of its competition and is good for South America and Australia. Uses abbreviations versus symbols for geographical features for clarity; excellent design; realistic relief; good colors and clarity; more comprehensive index than all but the largest atlases. The digital database permits rapid updates.

Minuses

Some maps are difficult to read; larger nations are often cut up into several maps. Statistical data are spotty and not all current—sources are not always given; symbols unstandard; nonstandard order of maps; some thematic maps are too small for easy reading. Coverage of the former Soviet Union and the Middle East is sparse. The opinions on the aesthetics of the maps vary—some reviewers are impressed with the clarity, but others feel this is achieved only at the expense of beauty.

The 1997 CD-ROM animations explain projections and permit looking at two national maps at the same time. Unlike Microsoft's Encarta product, the title is less confusing to use and requires less complex and expensive computers. The CD-ROM also includes almanac information, travel planning capabilities, and the ability to zoom in on maps for improved detail.

Hammond also produces a number of smaller atlases from the same database, notably *Centennial, New Century,* and *Citation,* which is aimed more at the school and home market. The latter includes maps plus all data and text on the same page.

■ National Geographic Society, Washington, D.C., Cartographic Division. National Geographic atlas of the world. 7th ed. Washington, D.C.: National Geographic Society, 1999. 280p.

This atlas's traditional strength is in political information and excellent graphics, but it also covers many names, with a comprehensive index of more than 150,000 items (including places not in most other general atlases). Although the Americas are at a larger scale than the rest of the world, one of its best features is color portraits of the world from satellite photos. Other than the emphasis on the Americas, it has a reasonable balance, but Third World nations tend to be shown in smaller scales compared with the rest of the world. Tends to more political information than competition and uses local place-names. Because page size is a bit larger than most and maps bleed to the edge, this has much larger maps than *Oxford Atlas of the World* or *Hammond Atlas of the World.*

Pluses

Includes a unique map of the universe and an indexed map of the moon. Striking organization and appearance; good feature articles and illustrations. Includes foldout maps, with a mix of satellite images and traditional maps. Generally good regional balance, although Africa is a bit thin; good statistics, fact boxes, etc. The index includes more than one map per entry and gives country and state and grid but not latitude and longitude.

Minuses

Biosphere map is hard to read; the large variety of scales can be confusing; sometimes borders between political units are unclear. Legends are not well explained. The city maps have small scales, and thus are not of much use. The physical volume is rather large and hard to handle.

■ New international atlas. 25th anniversary ed. Chicago: Rand McNally, 1996. 519p.

An attempt at a truly international atlas, complete with an introduction in five languages, country names in local language and English, and most other names only in local language. Five series of maps (239 in all) use a limited number of scales; uses the metric system only. Shaded areas versus tints are used to indicate relief. Includes a good glossary and an index of about 170,000 names (giving latitude and longitude). Has been recommended for "those who will get only one quality world atlas" and as a "basic reference source."

Pluses

The most international of the general world atlases. Very clear and easy-to-read maps, with good political and physical coverage; even many small towns are indicated. Detailed index with geographical coordinates allows use with multiple maps.

Minuses

Essentially the same as *The Britannica Atlas;* thus, it can be redundant in many libraries. Lack of English for most places can be confusing and will be off-putting to most American users. Three-dimensional shading can also be confusing; colors often drab. The detail on many maps leads to some cluttering.

■ The New York times atlas of the world. 3d rev. concise ed.; 3d U.S. ed. New York: Times Books, 1994. 67 + 245p.

Originally published in Great Britain as the *Times Atlas of the World, 6th Concise Edition,* in 1992; revised in 1994. Includes both a glossary and index. An up-to-date atlas using rather large basic scales for almost all maps, with a variety of projections. Has fairly balanced coverage, although North America and Europe are emphasized. As with the full *Times Atlas of the World,* lists all places shown on the maps, although only with the grid. One reviewer has commented on this edition: "In overall quality, however, it rivals any atlas on the market today at any price."

Pluses

Easy to handle because it is fairly thin. Europe and North America plus Australia and New Zealand get about half the coverage. Some statistics are given. The index gives grids, but not latitude and longitude. Maps are clear and easy to read, although not as good as the parent atlas.

Minuses

Idiosyncratic arrangement of maps. Has a much more Anglo-European slant than the Oxford or Hammond atlases. Sources are not given for statistics or text. The level of detail and cartographical style vary across maps. Some place-names cut across the gutter; typefaces vary with map, and thus may not match the legend. Use of hypsometric tints is off-putting, because colors may give a false impression of the environment.

■ Oxford atlas of the world. 4th ed. New York: Oxford Univ. Pr., 1996. 288p.

Published in Britain as *Philip's Atlas of the World;* the first edition sold out in four months. Has been called an "excellent reference source at a reasonable price." Clear, easy-to-read maps, with improving use of vivid colors and a few changes from edition to edition. Europe is covered by about one-third of the maps and North America by about one-eighth. Noteworthy are the diagrams of each area as well as the scale, and city maps detailed enough to be useful at 1:200,000. Uses color for relief; thus, color can't be used to indicate political borders as is more usual. Fewer place-names on maps than *Hammond Atlas of the World;* thus, fewer places can be found in the index. Thin border lines make it harder to see political borders. Gives the local name with English name in parentheses; still has some older names that have been superseded.

Pluses

Good margins; place-names not crowded; has locator maps; logical arrangement by geographic area; good index. Particularly good city maps, with their own gazetteer.

Minuses

Confusing use of symbols, which vary with different maps; smaller places are not shown in the index. Symbols are sparse compared with *The Times Atlas of the World* and other competitors; there is only one list of abbreviations versus the usual repeat on each map or page. Use of color for relief may be confusing and makes delineation of political boundaries difficult. Relatively small scales mean less detail than in some competitors' maps.

The same publisher also produces *Concise Atlas of the World* (4th ed. New York: Oxford Univ. Pr., 1999; 264p.) based on this. The maps are scaled down and text is reduced, but additional U.S. maps, including more cities, are added.

■ Peters atlas of the world. New York: Harper, 1990. 231p.

A wholly new atlas, using the new Peters projection: a cylindrical equal-area projection, intended to show continents in true proportion (but with distorted shapes). Contains 43 relief and 246 thematic maps. Relief is shown in a combination of shading, spot heights, and photography of models; color is used for vegetation, not relief. Some of the topics (e.g., sports, monogamy, direction of writing) are not readily found in other sources. Index includes both local and English form of place-name.

Pluses

Non-Eurocentric projections; inclusion of many thematic maps. Use of color for vegetation, though unconventional, approximates reality.

Minuses

Projection is confusing and does not reflect reality (notably, latitude lines increase spacing away from the equator, while all longitude lines remain the same—the opposite of reality). A very sparse gazetteer. This atlas has received generally poor reception from geographers.

■ Rand McNally Goode's world atlas. 19th ed. Chicago: Rand McNally, 1995. 371p.

A standard medium-sized atlas, originally *Goode's School Atlas* (1922–1950), but suitable for all ages. Updated about every four years with new maps and data as well as relevant changes and 34,000 index entries giving coordinates and pronunciations. In addition to general political and physical maps, it has many thematic maps. As with most U.S.-published atlases, is best on North America, followed by Europe, but does cover the entire world. Index includes pronunciation for most places. Various scales but consistent within given region. Including maps of major cities, many in a separate section, but others as inserts.

■ The world atlas in English. English ed. Moscow: 1967. 250p.

Translation of the *Atlas Mira* into English. When published, was the best balanced atlas in print, with excellent city plans, good coloring and relief, an extensive range of symbols, and comparatively large-scale maps for all nations. It was also praised for the separate index-gazetteer and for its unconventional framing, giving new insights on geographical relationships. On the other hand, several reviewers found evidence of an apparently deliberate misrepresentation of many locations, apparently because of concerns about national defense. And, of course, Russian conventions on non-Western place-names are different from those the average U.S. reader is used to, which makes it a bit difficult to use.

Finally, quite a different type of special-purpose atlas is of interest to librarians who work with the visually disabled:

■ Hammond large type world atlas. Boston: Hall, 1994. 144p.

First published in 1969 by Franklin Watts, this still holds the claim as the only atlas specifically designed for large-print readers. Uses wholly different cartography from the other Hammond atlases. Of the fifty-one three-color maps (9½ by 12¼), the emphasis is on the United States, with eight maps versus Europe with thirteen; North and Central America thirteen; and South America and Africa only five each. Maps drabber than usual; not as detailed as in regular atlases, but quite clear. Lists 3,100 entries in "Gazetteer Index" in front, giving grids. Minuses include no legends for maps and no abbreviation key; and it has some proofing errors.

School Atlases

There are many atlases aimed at schools, of which the following is a fair sample. The first title that should always be considered, however, has already been noted above: *Rand McNally Goode's World Atlas* began life as *Goode's School Atlas* and remains an excellent choice for both elementary and secondary schools.

■ The Dorling Kindersley world reference atlas. 2d American rev. ed. New York: Dorling Kindersley, 1998. 731p.

Begins with historical maps, then is arranged by nation rather than the usual regional arrangement. Lots of color, with a tendency to put information in tables, boxes, etc. rather than the more usual narrative. Has information normally not expected in an atlas. Clearly organized, graphic summaries of data, concise text, and up-to-date information, but the maps are too small and thus lack detail. Does not replace *Rand McNally Goode's* or similar atlases but a useful complement.

■ Encyclopedic world atlas. 4th ed. New York: Oxford Univ. Pr., 1997. 272p.

An excellent, rather traditional atlas aimed at middle and high schools. Includes encyclopedia-like essays for each nation, plus statistics, and thus in many ways complements the *Dorling Kindersley World Reference Atlas,* but for an older readership.

Electronic Atlases

■ Cartopedia: the ultimate world reference atlas. New York: Dorling Kindersley, 1995. CD-ROM only.

More of an encyclopedia than an atlas and generally aimed at elementary and middle schools. This title has received a number of awards for its good maps added to statistical data and its ease of use. Several types of access are available, and one can set up parallel comparative screens. The visuals include some animation.

■ PC Globe Maps 'n' Facts. Novato, Calif.: Broderbund, 1994. CD-ROM only.

For all ages, but generally marketed to schools by the same company that does the Carmen Sandiego series of geography and history games. Combines political and physical maps with almanac-type information. Can switch from map to text and back. Includes both old and newer versions of nations with recent boundary changes, such as Germany and Czechoslovakia. The maps are not particularly aesthetically pleasing and lack much detail, but the connection with the popular television and computer-game character Carmen Sandiego will probably attract students in a way that many other sources will not.

When talking about education and maps, one must mention the purely commercial Carmen Sandiego series, which generated a television series as well. The basic plot is a detective story, with the master spy Carmen Sandiego leading the user on a merry chase around the world. To win, one must follow geographical clues to her hideout. The software includes many graphics and, of course, maps as well as texts. Although aimed more at names, dates, and places than "real" geographic understanding, the series at least attempts to make some level of geographic learning fun. In addition to *Where in the World Is Carmen Sandiego?* and *Where in the USA Is Carmen Sandiego?* the publisher issues similar titles for arithmetic, history, and language.

Reproducible Maps

A relatively recent development is the production of atlases specifically designed for reproduction. Generally, these are in loose-leaf format, with fairly simple black-and-white maps, usually in an 8½-by-11-inch format suitable for making transparencies and photocopies. Purchase of one of these atlases includes appropriate permissions for copying. The following are good examples of the genre:

■ Geography on file. New York: Facts on File, 1995– . 1v. Annual updates.

> More than 250 maps, including graphics for geographical study as well as political maps. Updates with a new cumulative index available each year.

■ Maps on file. New York: Facts on File, 1997– . 2v. Annual updates.

> Offers 450 maps in a loose-leaf format, first produced in 1981, with strong black-and-white graphics, set up for copying onto standard letter-size paper. Index.

Similar specialized titles include *Outline Maps on File* (New York: Facts on File, 1997; 1v.), *Latin America on File* (New York: Facts on File, 1995; 1v.), *Africa on File* (New York: Facts on File, 1995; 1v.), *Middle East and North Africa on File* (New York: Facts on File, 1995; 1v.), *Historical Maps on File* (New York: Facts on File, 1984; 1v.), and *State Maps on File* (New York: Facts on File, 1993; 1v.). Although these have been criticized by some reviewers, they are quite popular with their intended audience, who need relatively undetailed maps, easily copied, for teaching and study purposes. An important point here is that purchase of any of these volumes includes a limited license to photocopy.

■ National Geographic picture atlas of our world. Mary B. Dickinson and others. Rev. ed. Washington, D.C.: National Geographic Society, 1993. 276p.

> Another standard, aimed at the middle- and junior-high-school student. Generally balanced geographical coverage, plus text on continents and nations, with many pictures and data. The introduction also includes information on cartography, map reading, and basic geological forces.

■ World Eagle's today series. Wellesley, Mass.: World Eagle, 1990– .

> Each one of the series consists of a loose-leaf set of pages with reproducible maps, with citations to the original map. Maps tend to be black-and-white reproductions of original maps, versus Facts on File's original line drawings.

■ Africa today: an atlas of reproducible pages. Rev. ed. Wellesley, Mass.: World Eagle, 1990. 172p.

■ Asia and Oceania today: a reproducible atlas. Rev. ed. Littleton, Mass.: World Eagle, 1995. 273p.

■ Europe today: a reproducible atlas. Rev. ed. Littleton, Mass.: World Eagle, 1996. 226p.

■ Latin America today: an atlas of reproducible pages. Rev. ed. Wellesley, Mass.: World Eagle, 1989. 153p.

■ Middle East today: a reproducible atlas. Rev. ed. Littleton, Mass.: World Eagle, 1997. 247p.

■ North America today: a reproducible atlas. Rev. ed. Littleton, Mass.: World Eagle, 1995. 193p.

■ The United States today: an atlas of reproducible pages. Wellesley, Mass.: World Eagle, 1990. 182p.

World Regional Atlases

Midway between the national atlas and the world atlas is the atlas covering a given region, often, but not always, a continent. A number of recent examples of the genre are included here:

■ Boustani, Rafic, and Philippe Fargues. Atlas of the Arab world: geopolitics and society. New York: Facts on File, 1992. 144p.

About 200 flat four-color maps and many color pictures, translated from the French. Index including maps and illustrations. A particularly useful feature is the "Data Bank," with summary statistics on each country (data are from the United Nations and French sources), providing hard-to-get facts and comparisons. Unfortunately, lacks political maps of the individual nations.

■ Brawer, Moshe. Atlas of Russia and the independent republics. New York: Macmillan/Simon & Schuster, 1994. 144p.

The first atlas to cover the area of the former USSR since the breakup. Arranged region by region. Unfortunately, has an out-of-date bibliography and typographical errors and uses only Russian names (e.g., not Ukrainian names for Ukraine maps). Includes chapters for each of the twelve Congressional Information Service (CIS) republics and the three Baltic states (each with a separate political, agricultural, and industrial map). Is very similar to Brawer's *Atlas of South America:* both have considerable text with maps—in the case of *Russia,* several shades of red.

■ Brawer, Moshe. Atlas of South America. New York: Simon & Schuster, 1991. 144p.

More than 100 two-color flat and relief maps plus many graphs and charts. Indexes of persons and places, glossary, and an annotated bibliography. Only black and green maps makes this ugly, but it offers lots of handy data. The most extensive section is the collection of country-by-country chapters providing uniform statistics plus graphs, etc., and up-to-date annotated bibliographies. Overall, this atlas has not received particularly good reviews, but it remains the only recent source for the area.

■ Diagram Group [London]. Atlas of Central America and the Caribbean. New York: Macmillan, 1985. 144p.

An atlas plus handbook with many color graphics, but its duotone green maps are not that easy to read.

National Maps and Atlases

Most countries have an established national cartographic agency, and their activities are well described in Lock's *Modern Maps and Atlases.* But not all areas are mapped at medium or large scale, nor is there the uniformity desired by certain international agencies, such as the United Nations Commission on National Atlases, which, starting in 1956, encouraged creation of national and regional atlases in individual countries and the unification and standardization of the contents of the principal maps.

National atlases are often fine examples of cartography, portraying the geographical, economic, and social aspects of the country and sometimes including historical maps as well. They require careful planning, and years of effort are spent in their compilation, as in the case of *The National Atlas of the United States.*

Other publications of the USGS are also of primary importance, and their topographic maps—familiarly known as the "quads" or "topos"; more formally, the Topographic series; and officially, the *7.5 Minute Topographic Quadrangle Series*—are widely used. Representing a quadrangular area bounded by lines of latitude and longitude, and taking their names from a town or prominent natural feature in the area represented, they are published on sheets about 22 by 27 inches. Each map covers an area 7½ minutes square (of the 60 minutes in one degree of latitude or longitude), at a scale of (usually) 1:24,000 (1 inch equals 2,000 inches, or 2,000 feet). As an example of their efficiency in data storage, it has been estimated that the average quadrangle contains more than 100 million bits of information. Even the smallest library should have at least the sheets of the area in which it is located, because these topographic maps show relief, drainage, and culture (towns, roads, railroads, and other man-made works, down to individual buildings). Separate index maps are published for each state, showing the extent to which the state is mapped (and giving all the quadrangles named).

Because these maps are so handy for hikers, travelers, and genealogists, as well as geographers and historians, the savvy librarian should also be aware of similar series for neighboring countries as well. To the north, *see Canada* (Ottawa: Department of Energy, Mines and Resources, 1923-); to the south, the series is Estados Unidos Mexicanos, *Carta Topografica* (Mexico: Instituto Nacional de Estadistica, Geografica e Informatica. Direccion General de Geografica, 1976-).

The USGS also publishes two series of base maps of states, showing counties, cities, towns, railroads, streams, public-land lines, highways, relief, and other features on a scale of either 1:500,000 (approximately eight miles to the inch) or 1:1,000,000 (approximately sixteen miles to the inch).

Other important government agencies are the Bureau of Land Management, for its wall map of the United States, showing national parks, forests and wildlife refuges, Native American reservations, and reclamation projects; the Soil Conservation Service of the Department of Agriculture, for its extensive series of county soil survey maps; and the National Ocean Survey, for its nautical charts. The U.S. Lake Survey publishes navigational charts of the Great Lakes and their connecting waters.

Although often neglected in small libraries, government publications (and not just maps) should not be overlooked as reliable and modestly priced sources that are especially valuable for small areas. In addition to the more exhaustive lists and indexes (some noted earlier), they are often listed in subject bibliographies available free from the Superintendent of Documents, including numbers 32: Oceanography, 102: Maps and Atlases, 160: Earth Sciences, 166: Foreign Country Studies, 183: Surveying and Mapping—to name just a few. Free pamphlets from individual agencies are also useful, such as those available from the USGS. The USGS operates the Earth Sciences Information Center, which collects, processes, and disseminates information concerning maps, aerial photography, geodetic positions, and elevations.

A full list of older atlases may be found in Clare E. Le Gear's *United States Atlases: A List of National, State, County, City, and Regional Atlases in the Library of Congress* (Washington, D.C.: Govt. Print. Off., 1950–53. Reprint, New York: Arno, 1971. 2v.

United States

Although they are discussed in more detail in chapter 8, "Sources of Statistics," one must mention the TIGER (Topologically Integrated Geographic Encoding and Referencing system)/Line files, produced by the Bureau of the

Census, in the context of national atlases. The database, created from the 1990 census, combines with software to create all sort of maps and can be merged with other databases to create a series of overlays on fairly detailed geographic and political maps. Although the graphics still leave something to be desired, the concept is interesting, and the ability to tailor a map to specific user requirements on demand is impressive.

■ The national atlas of the United States of America. Washington, D.C.: Govt. Print. Off., 1970. 417p.

An impressive work, consisting of 765 maps, often double-page spreads. Although this is being replaced by the new edition, this version continues to be of value.

■ National atlas of the United States of America. Washington, D.C. and other places: U.S. Geological Survey and "partners" [commercial firms], 1997- . Several formats, with CD-ROM and Internet emphasized.

A wholly new concept, with an emphasis on direct delivery to home computer users. At this writing, the following products are intended:

Spatial databases (zip code, latitude, longitude, addresses, congressional districts, etc.), with "metadata" (documentation); these are merely data, intended to be used with local mapping and information systems.

Maps: very few are planned by the government, but the USGS is trying to interest commercial publishers in some sort of printed atlas or map collection.

Desktop GIS: this will allow creation of maps and the addition of "overlays" via computer.

Multimedia products: such products include maps, overlays, sound, narration, etc.

Gradually, more and more overlays are appearing on the Web, with an increasing number being animated, for instance, to show growth over time (such as the spread of the zebra mussel). And, as of the early part of 2000, it appears that much of the basic material will be available for free download, and at least a few maps from the project are available at a nominal sum from the USGS.

Some specialized national atlases follow:

■ Atlas of historical county boundaries. New York: Simon & Schuster, Scribner, 1994- (in progress). 40v. projected.

Publisher varies. If the *National Atlas* is in effect a snapshot of counties, this is like a dynamic video even though printed. Gives every boundary change in detail, including county name changes, with very detailed maps (eight miles per inch). An index by places and counties, but to date, not to geographical features. When complete, this will supersede Long's five-volume *Historical Atlas and Chronology of County Boundaries, 1788–1980* (Boston: Hall, 1984; 5v.).

■ Lilley, William III, Laurence J. DeFranco, and Mark F. Bernstein. The almanac of state legislatures: changing patterns, 1990–1998: state data atlas. Washington, D.C.: Congressional Quarterly, 1998. 387p.

Covers more than 6,700 state legislative districts. For the first time, all congressional districts have been mapped in one volume. This is mostly an atlas of state political districts, with separate pages for larger cities (several on a page) per state and brief demographic data by district.

■ Street atlas USA. Freeport, Maine: DeLorme Mapping, 1995. CD-ROM only.

Contains maps of all fifty states. May be searched by city or town, zip, area code and exchange, street name, use of overview map, and by panning over a given map by use of an electronic compass rose. Printing and copying are easy to do. Includes more than 12 million street segments and more than 1.1 million geographic and other features.

Canada

■ National atlas of Canada. 4th ed. Toronto: Macmillan, 1974. 254p.

The standard atlas of the nation, this edition is the product of cooperation between the government and Macmillan. Physical and economic topics receive the most emphasis, although there are demographic and some historical maps as well.

■ Reader's Digest atlas of Canada. Montreal: Reader's Digest, 1995. 176p.

Has been praised by reviewers for its combination of a conventional atlas and its emphasis on both human and natural forces that affect the country's landscape. The first half includes forty thematic maps (all two-page) plus English text and many types of graphics to give a portrait of the nation. The second includes topographical and political maps (including thirty-five detailed city maps) and a 17,000-item gazetteer.

Thematic Maps and Atlases

Thematic maps are often simply defined as maps on a specific subject and are so described in glossaries of geographic terms in most world atlases. The same atlases also contain many thematic maps, as already shown. But recent years have seen great developments in this field, caused in part by the growing recognition of their efficiency for certain types of data storage. As Lock points out in the introduction to her extensive section on thematic maps and atlases:

> Much of the work being done in thematic mapping is still in its experimental stages; new combinations of coloring and symbols are being tried out in economic and population mapping. In the mapping of climate and oceanographic data, the work of numerous scientists is only now coming into maximum usage through international co-ordination. In the use and interpretation of all such maps also much remains to be learned and methods of reproduction are constantly under review [*Modern Maps and Atlases*, p. 404].

The use of thematic maps for problem analysis has greatly increased in recent years, and new technical developments have improved their production, such as greater precision of photographic and copying equipment and the continuing computerization of many aspects of cartography. Data gathered by remote sensing (the term applied to collecting data about objects or phenomena that are not in contact with the data-gathering device) have greatly increased, first, because of the wide use of aerial photography since World War II; second, with new types of advanced remote sensors, notably satellites; and finally, more elaborate and accurate systems for transmission, storage, and display of data. The recent development and wide availability of GIS have increased the capability of the ordinary user or library to create thematic maps as needed, in effect substantially increasing the number of thematic maps available.

All of these factors result in wider and more varied sources of thematic maps, which should be reflected in library collections. Here we can only consider several examples of thematic atlases of several kinds, some new and some with a longer history, which can be used to supplement the thematic maps in general atlases, among them the historical, economic, and several other special-purpose atlases to be found in most general reference collections.

As noted above, it is now increasingly possible to create customized thematic maps in many subjects, both through a mapping agency and by oneself, using online and CD-ROM systems. To date, the latter tend to lack much of the aesthetic appeal (and, sometimes at least, the extreme accuracy) of more traditional maps. However, the librarian must always keep in mind the potential for creating such maps, if needed.

General guides to reference materials, such as *Balay* and *Walford's,* contain many examples of thematic atlases, easily located through their indexes both under subject—Bible for example—and "Atlases." Subheadings in *Balay* under "Atlases" give a good idea of their variety, from agriculture to Civil War, from geology to Judaism, and from maritime to women.

Agricultural Atlases

■ 1992 census of agriculture. Volume 2. Subject Series. Part 1. Agricultural atlas of the United States. Washington, D.C.: Govt. Print. Off., 1995. 212p.

> Choropleth and dot-distribution maps based on the data found in volume 1 (actually part 1, with separate volumes for each state) and based on computer mapping technology. Most of the maps are less than one page in size, making detailed examination a bit difficult. Two different transparent overlays giving the outlines of each small area improve ease of use.

■ World atlas of agriculture: under the aegis of the International Association of Agricultural Economists. Novara, Italy: Instituto Geographic de Agostini, 1969–73. 4v.

> Based on *The Times Atlas of the World* maps, with considerable data added. Arranged by region, then nation, with most nations receiving a two-page spread (a few small countries are shown together on the same map). Includes brief citations to all maps and data sources used. Becoming a bit outdated (work began on this in 1961) but still monumental. (Some libraries have found all four volumes in one.)

Biblical and Archaeological Atlases

■ Hammond past worlds: the Times atlas of archaeology. Maplewood, N.J.: Hammond, 1988. 319p.

> Of several potential competitors, this generally has the best balance in terms of world coverage, with only about one-third devoted to Europe. Arranged chronologically, with two-page spreads including text, illustrations, and maps.

■ Macmillan Bible atlas. 3d ed. New York: Macmillan, 1993. 215p.

> The primary emphasis is on the maps: 3000 B.C. to A.D. 200, with about two-thirds of the maps related to the Old Testament and often includ-

ing adjacent areas. Gives a key to maps by books of the Bible; chronological tables listed under "East," "Palestine," "Egypt," and "West." Indexes all names on the maps, and notes the most important appearance of each name.

■ Oxford Bible atlas. Herbert G. May, ed. 3d ed. New York: Oxford Univ. Pr., 1984. 144p.

A standard work with considerable revisions in each new edition. Includes topographical as well as historical maps; each map has text relating to the Bible and the history of the period.

■ Pritchard, James B. Harper atlas of the Bible. San Francisco, Calif.: Harper, 1987. 254p.

More than just maps, this scholarly but accessible text provides a true chronology from prehistoric times through the Byzantine period by concentrating on the most important events versus a full chronology. Some maps are traditional; many use curved-earth forms. Indexes every place-name in the atlas (but no index to topical material); no grids or latitude or longitude (except for "standard Palestinian grid" found on endpapers). Includes much on background, customs, beliefs, and practices; the glossary summarizes biographies of most biblical personalities.

■ Rogerson, John. Atlas of the Bible. New York: Facts on File, 1985. Reprint, 1991. 237p.

Unlike many others, has a geographical rather than historical approach. Forty color maps, with many photos and site plans. The gazetteer indexes all locatable places mentioned in the Bible and lists all entries in the maps and illustrations. Map labels include Bible book, chapter, and verse in which the place is mentioned. Includes special features on food, writing, everyday life in biblical times and the area, etc.

Demographic Atlases

■ Mattson, Mark T. Atlas of the 1990 census. New York: Macmillan, 1992. 168p.

Provides clear maps for states and regions as well as the United States based on the census data provided for 100 percent of the population and comparing the 1990 and 1980 censuses. The maps are supplemented by many tables and charts. Additional features include regional county locator maps and a glossary of census terms. Because the Census Bureau has decided not to provide much in the way of print maps, this title is particularly useful, even for libraries with access to sophisticated GIS systems.

▪ Rand McNally zip code atlas and market planner. 2d ed. Skokie, Ill.: Rand McNally, 1990. 128p.

Basic maps with usual map features, including roads, lakes, towns, etc. Transparent overlays for five-digit zip code areas can be marked on and then cleaned. Arranged by state, with city inset maps.

▪ Thorndale, William, and William Dollarhide. Map guide to the U.S. federal censuses, 1790–1920. Baltimore, Md.: Genealogical Pub., 1987. Reprint, 1992. 420p.

Arranged by decennial census, giving county boundaries (modern in white and contemporary in black) and names as of each census, with an index by county. Also includes brief background of each census, a basic bibliography, and "Pitfalls in Mapping Boundaries."

Economic Atlases

Though thematic maps showing contemporary economic conditions will be found in general world atlases, and earlier conditions are included in historical atlases, the detailed and broader coverage in economic atlases makes them more useful to economists, businesspeople, geographers, and students interested in world economics. A few outstanding examples, some notable for their frequent revision, follow:

▪ The Economist atlas of the new Europe. New York: Henry Holt, 1992. 288p.

A well-respected atlas, although with much more text than maps. Combines basic economic maps with profiles of the countries and the region. More of a geographical representation of economic data than an atlas as such, with no physical/political maps at all. Maps are small scale but readable, with larger-scale insets when needed. Tables and charts provide much comparative data. This atlas is similar to *Oxford Economic Atlas of Europe* but provides more depth.

▪ Oxford economic atlas of the world. D. B. Jones, advisory ed. 4th ed. New York: Oxford Univ. Pr., 1972. 239p.

A number of regional atlases were also produced based on this. Maps giving world distribution patterns are accompanied by statistical tables and economic commentary. Maps include major trade flows, commodities, disease, medical care, education, employment, birth control, and similar topics, as well as purely economic topics.

■ Rand McNally commercial atlas and marketing guide. New York: Rand McNally, 1876- . Annual.

A standard source for more than 125 years. Data are updated annually, based on the most recent census, plus Rand McNally's own projection formulas. Here, metropolitan areas are based on population density rather than county lines, so the maps are more accurate for much business work. The index to more than 128,000 cities, towns, etc. includes hard-to-find smaller places not in most atlases. The maps include features not on most maps such as oil wells, bridges, tunnels, etc.

■ Rand McNally zip code atlas and market planner. 2d ed. Skokie, Ill.: Rand McNally, 1990. 128p.

By state with insets for metro areas. Base maps with usual map features, including roads, lakes, towns, etc. Transparent overlays for five-digit code areas can be marked on and then cleaned.

Educational Atlas

■ Fonseca, James W., and Alice C. Andrews. The atlas of American higher education. New York: New York Univ. Pr., 1993. 257p.

Statistics based on *Digest of Education Statistics, State Higher Education Profiles,* and others are the source of eighty-six maps. Each map includes citations to sources and detailed analysis of data, plus references to other maps.

Environmental Atlases

■ Couper, Alistair, ed. The Times atlas and encyclopaedia of the sea. 2d ed. New York: Harper, 1989. 272p.

Scientific, legal, economic, and environmental aspects of the water mass of the world in 105 two-page articles, 284 maps, more than 300 charts, and more than 140 pictures. Eleven appendixes of statistics. Well documented with attractive use of color. Index refers to the illustrations as well as the maps. Highly recommended, although not much different from its first edition, as *Times Atlas of the Oceans* (New York: Van Nostrand Reinhold, 1983; 272p.).

■ Earth book world atlas. Boulder, Colo.: Graphic Learning International, 1987. 327p.

A new kind of atlas, with about 200 full-color environmental maps (by the Swedish Esselte Map Service) that emphasize such things as vegetation rather than the traditional political or relief base. Includes a ninety-six-page "encyclopedia of the earth." Index to about 57,000 places.

■ Seager, Joni. The new state of the earth atlas: a concise survey of the environment through full-color international maps. 2d ed. New York: Simon & Schuster, 1995. 128p.

Thirty-seven large-format, double-page colored maps, with rather clever graphics, each on a different topic related to the earth's biosphere. The response to this particular work has varied with one's "environmental politics," for example, *Field & Stream* magazine felt it was antihunting. However, a large amount of data is made clear in a small space. This atlas is a good example of the points Monmonier makes (*see* above, p. 477) about the point of view possible in graphics.

■ WWF atlas of the environment. Rev. ed Geoffrey Lean and Don Hinrichsen, eds. Santa Barbara, Calif.: ABC-Clio, 1994. 192p.

A revised and updated version of *Atlas of the Environment* by Geoffrey Lean and others (London: Hutchinson; New York: Prentice-Hall, 1990; 192p.), with more recent statistics and some updated text, otherwise the same as the 1990 version. As one might expect from a World Wildlife Fund (WWF) product, the overall picture is rather depressing. Aesthetically, the color combinations are not good, projection and scale are not given, and there is no index. Even so, this atlas has received strong recommendations for the importance of its data.

Ethnic and Racial Groups

■ Allen, James P., and Eugene J. Turner. We the people: an atlas of America's ethnic diversity. New York: Macmillan, 1988. 315p.

Based on the 1980 census, 115 maps (mostly color) show population shifts and distribution of sixty-seven ethnic groups. Includes statistical tables, county-by-county ethnic census data, and a ten-page bibliography. Two indexes: "Index of Places" and "Index of Ethnic Populations." Unfortunately, there were some problems caused by census treatment of ethnicity. For example, all Jews are listed under People of Eastern

European Origin, and there is no distinction between Muslim and Christian Arabs.

■ Atlas of North American Indians. New York: Facts on File, 1985. 276p.

Covers the United States, Canada, and Mexico in about 100 maps and many black-and-white illustrations. Scholarly but readable text includes a chronology; description of the major tribes and their locations at present; and the location of federal reservations. Index is very comprehensive.

Historical Atlases

The importance of maps in teaching and studying history has long been recognized, and historical atlases have been published to provide a fuller coverage than that usually found in historical writing. Not all of them include the word *atlas* in their titles, though they usually do.

UNITED STATES

■ The American heritage pictorial atlas of United States history, by the editors of American heritage. New York: American Heritage, 1966. 424p.

Still of value for its color maps and for its "pictorial maps" of major battles of the Revolutionary and Civil Wars.

■ Atlas of early American history: the revolutionary era, 1760–1790. Lester J. Cappon, ed. in chief; Barbara Bartz Petchenik, cartographic ed.; John Hamilton Lang, assistant ed. Princeton, N.J.: for the Newberry Library and the Institute of Early American History and Culture by the Princeton Univ. Pr., 1976. 157p.

Nearly 300 superb maps and supporting text covering the period, divided into three time frames: pre–1776, the war, and the postwar years to 1790. Many maps have brief text in addition to the text pages following the map sections. Indexed.

■ Carnes, Mark C., and John Garraty. Mapping America's past: a historical atlas. New York: Henry Holt, 1996. 288p.

Not as large nor does it cover as many subjects as others here, but includes topics rarely covered by the competition, such as social and economic forces.

■ Ferrell, Robert H., and Richard Natkiel. Atlas of American history. Rev. and updated ed. [i.e., 4th ed.]. New York: Facts on File, 1995. 192p.

Covers from 1498 to 1992 in about 250 maps. Unlike most recent historical atlases, most of the maps are multicolored, and many of the photos are in color as well.

■ Gilbert, Martin. The Dent atlas of American history. 3d ed. London: J. M. Dent, 1993. 138p.

An update of Gilbert's *American History Atlas* (1985; 115p.). All black-and-white maps, with very little text. Although less flashy than some of the U.S.-produced atlases, this provides a different perspective, from a non-U.S. point of view.

■ Historical atlas of the United States. Rev. ed. Washington, D.C.: National Geographic Society, 1993. 289p.

Full-page and double-page maps, with smaller maps in borders, covering from 1400. Nearly 400 full-color maps, plus a plastic overlay of the United States in outline and a magnifying sheet. Also has many color photos and other graphics. As one would expect from the publishers, a high level of accuracy, an excellent index, and well-written text. The original edition was produced as a "gift to the nation" for the bicentennial, with a copy given to all U.S. high schools.

■ Jackson, Kenneth T. Atlas of American history. 2d rev. ed. New York: Scribner, 1984. 306p.

Continues the tradition of its first editor in chief, James Truslow Adams, who emphasized clear maps without the "clutter of distracting information." With 253 flat, black-and-white maps. Index to page and map number. Arranged by theme, in chronological order, with each map related in area and time to preceding and following ones. Clear, explicit, beautiful maps. The original was especially strong up to the Civil War; this edition adds more on the later period and includes a section on "Current Issues, 1978-1984."

■ Martis, Kenneth C. The historical atlas of political parties in the United States Congress, 1789-1989. New York: Macmillan, 1989. 518p.

The second volume of the Bicentennial Atlas project. No other title covers all Congresses. Multicolor maps for each Congress give party by district for the U.S. House of Representatives; smaller maps on the same page give U.S. Senate data. Facing pages list the senators and representatives. Includes an index, a 700-item bibliography, and a long introduction discussing the elections in general.

■ Martis, Kenneth C. The historical atlas of U.S. congressional districts, 1789–1983. New York: Free Pr., 1982. 302p.

Includes ninety-nine flat maps, nearly all black and white, with some color. Many maps include small, detailed inset maps for urban areas. Includes all congressional districts. Began as part of the Historical Records Survey of the Works Progress Administration (WPA) and the first volume of the Bicentennial Atlas project.

■ Martis, Kenneth C., and Gregory A. Elmes. The historical atlas of state power in Congress, 1790–1990. Washington, D.C.: Congressional Quarterly, 1993. 190p.

One of three similar award-winning atlases related to congressional history, this is based on the reapportionments in the U.S. House of Representatives done after every decennial census except 1920. Includes the maps, discussion of each change, and four case studies, along with reference to the laws, formulas, and other details of the process.

■ McPherson, James M. The atlas of the civil war. New York: Macmillan/ Simon & Schuster, 1994. 223p.

Compiled by McPherson and nine other historians. Narratives, participants' statements, 200 black-and-white and color illustrations, and 200 full-color maps done just for this atlas. Highly recommended by most reviewers, even though it does have a Northern point of view and a few minor errors.

■ The Naval Institute historical atlas of the U.S. Navy. Craig Symonds, ed. Annapolis, Md.: Naval Institute Pr., 1995. 241p.

Offers ten sections by time period, with ninety-four large full-color maps. Attached text gives brief accounts of all naval battles, with some information on political background as well. Complete index and well-constructed table of contents.

■ Paullin, Charles Oscar. Atlas of the historical geography of the United States. Washington, D.C.: Carnegie Institute of Washington and the American Geographical Society, 1932. 162p.

The first major historical atlas of the United States, notable for its 688 maps, some of them reproductions of earlier maps, with extremely broad coverage. Accompanied by excellent descriptive text.

■ Wexler, Alan. Atlas of westward expansion. New York: Facts on File, 1995. 240p.

Offers eight sections in roughly chronological order, emphasizing from 1754 to about 1900. A fairly dense text supplemented with maps, plus drawings, portraits, etc. Although this contains an extensive bibliography, the text lacks footnotes or endnotes. Index of names and topics.

WORLD

■ Atlas of maritime history. Antony Preston and Richard Natkiel. New York: Facts on File, 1986. 256p.

From the ancient Phoenicians to the 1980s in about 250 flat blue-and-gray maps, plus 200 black-and-white illustrations. Covers both battles and explorations, with a mostly British point of view. The index includes both the illustrations and the text. Also includes a glossary of obsolete and technical terms. Although many maps are original, others are from standard sources, such as Iain Parson's *Encyclopedia of Sea Warfare* (London and New York: Spring Books, 1975; 256p.).

■ Cambridge illustrated atlas of warfare: the Middle Ages, 768–1487; Renaissance to revolution, 1492–1792. New York: Cambridge Univ. Pr., 1996. 2v.

Text supported by excellent cartography. Includes a glossary of terms from many languages, including Latin, Mongolian, etc.; parallel chronological tables.

■ Gilbert, Martin. Recent history atlas: 1870 to the present day. Cartography by John R. Flower. New York: Macmillan, 1969. 121p.

Covers to 1960. Similar to his other works, notably the *Dent Atlas of American History,* with little text and black-and-white maps. Could be seen as an update of *Shepherd's Historical Atlas,* which stops with the late nineteenth century. A new edition was announced for 1999 but had not appeared by mid-2000.

■ The Harper atlas of world history. Rev. ed. New York: HarperCollins, 1992. 355p.

A revised and updated translation of the French *Histoire de l'Human-ité*. Considerable text, with mostly color maps, plus illustrations and many full-color photographs. Covers prehistory to the present, with considerable attention given to culture as well as politics and battles. Index is comprehensive, but doesn't highlight maps versus text. In some ways is more like a textbook with maps than an atlas.

■ Historical atlas of Canada. Toronto and Cheektowaga, N.Y.: Univ. of Toronto Pr., 1987–93. 3v.

Beautifully illustrated, and covers from the Ice Age to 1961. Flat color maps of Canada as a whole, then specific areas, including Greenland and the northern United States, etc. as relevant; many topical maps as well. Has been hailed as "magnificent, multidisciplinary achievement; exquisite; admirable." Text includes color illustrations, graphs, charts, and the like.

■ Muir's historical atlas, ancient, medieval and modern. London: G. Philip, 1976, 2v. in 1.

This is a reprint of the eleventh edition, in 1969. A classic, if somewhat traditional, atlas whose first edition was in 1911.

■ Rand McNally atlas of world history. Skokie, Ill.: Rand McNally, 1992. 192p.

The U.S. version of *Philip's Atlas of World History,* this is a slightly re-vised version of the 1982 edition—some maps are updated, as is the bibliography. The maps are detailed but still clear, and the text is well written. This work has been criticized as too garish and overly de-tailed, but it still receives purchase recommendations.

■ Shepherd, William Robert. Shepherd's historical atlas. 9th rev. ed. New York: Barnes & Noble, 1980. 226p.

Remains one of the best historical atlases in English, although few of the maps have been changed since the late 1960s. Includes a useful index of alternative place-names. Separate section with eight U.S. historical maps. Less flashy and thus often clearer than most of its competitors.

■ The Times atlas of world history. Geoffrey Barraclough, ed.; Geoffrey Parker, edition ed. 4th ed. Maplewood, N.J.: Hammond, 1993. 358p.

A truly new edition, wholly revised from the earlier, with nearly every article rewritten, new maps (now more than 600 maps) and text added, and most maps improved, notably with color improvements, better readability, and the use of American spelling. The focus is still "Western," but this is much less Eurocentric than its previous editions. This was the first historical atlas to rely on the latest mapping techniques and to include social history and cultural history. Includes an index to place-names, glossary with supplemental information about people and events, and a time line.

The abridged edition is Geoffrey Barraclough's *Times Concise Atlas of World History* (4th ed., rev. London: Times Books, 1995; 192p.). Also published as the *Hammond Concise Atlas of World History* (5th ed. Maplewood, N.J.: Hammond, 1998; 184p.). Almost 20 percent of the 320 maps are revised or new, thus making this a good compact historical atlas in its own right. Major revisions are primarily the result of new archaeological knowledge and the breakup of the USSR.

■ Van Der Heyden, A. A. M., and H. H. Scullard, eds. Atlas of the classical world. New York: Nelson, 1959. 221p.

For the layperson rather than professional scholars, but still a beautifully edited collection of colored maps and illustrations, including town plans.

Linguistic Atlas

■ Atlas of the world's languages. Christopher Moseley and R. E. Asher, general eds. London and New York: Routledge, 1994. 372p.

The only atlas of its kind, although with some flaws. This is the first attempt to show the distribution and changes in language distribution across the world. Includes excellent bibliographies and commentary but a flawed index. Although the title has received mixed reviews, this atlas has been quite successful.

Migration Atlas

■ Segal, Aaron. An atlas of international migration. New Providence, N.J.: Hans Zell/Reed Reference, 1993. 233p.

The first international atlas of its kind, with a stress on contemporary. Four sections of clear black-and-white maps cover voluntary and involuntary migrations, major diasporas, global migration characteristics.

Includes historical data, all sources given. Includes both an annotated and a separate unannotated bibliography, plus an excellent index.

Religious Atlas

■ Halvorson, Peter L., and William N. Newman. Atlas of religious change in America, 1952-1990. 3d ed. Atlanta, Ga.: Glenmary Research Center, 1994. 226p.

Based on four data sets, for 1952, 1971, 1980, and 1990. More complete than earlier versions of 1978 and 1981.

Space Atlas

■ Tirion, Wil, and Roger W. Sinnot. SkyAtlas 2000.0: twenty-six star charts, covering both hemispheres, and seven detailed charts of selected regions. 2d ed. Cambridge, England, and New York: Cambridge Univ. Pr., 1998. Various paging.

Currently the definitive atlas of the sky, with monthly maps showing the sky at different times of the year. A less detailed (and easier to use) version is Wil Tirion's *Cambridge Star Atlas* (2d ed. New York: Cambridge Univ. Pr., 1996; 90p.).

Women's Atlases

■ Seager, Joni. The state of women in the world atlas. New rev. 2d ed. London and New York: Penguin, 1997. 128p.

A clearly feminist perspective informs this atlas, whose first edition was in 1986. Offers forty chapters within ten broad themes; generally maps and short tables, with some text. Much of the data is not easily available elsewhere. Includes a brief subject index and a bibliography.

■ The women's atlas of the United States. Rev. ed. Timothy Fast and Cathy Carroll Fast. New York: Facts on File, 1995. 246p.

Replaces the 1986 edition, by Anne Gibson. In addition to the maps, tables summarize much of the same data. In another example of the changes in cartography, all the maps in this edition are produced by computer, while all in the first edition were drawn by hand. Has been particularly praised for its use of color, although some reviewers feel some of the captions are too flippant.

Gazetteers

A gazetteer is usually defined as a geographical dictionary or index. As already noted, many atlases have index-gazetteers or gazetteer-indexes; the items listed are generally more exhaustive. Ideally, a gazetteer should give the official standardized form of spelling of place-names, with cross-references to variant spellings; should give exact latitude and longitude, based on the latest information; and should give pronunciation. Emphasis should be on inclusiveness of entries rather than amount of historical and socioeconomic information for individual entries, because other sources, such as general encyclopedias, supply more information of this sort anyway.

For the most complete coverage, if not always the most information for each place, the following are becoming the standard:

World Gazetteers

■ GEOname digital gazetteer. San Diego, Calif.: GDE Systems, 1995- . CD-ROM. Also on the Web as GEOnet.

Based on the fifty-plus years of foreign geographic names collected by the U.S. Defense Mapping Agency, not including U.S. place-names. The multiple fonts on the disk provide the correct diacritics for most languages. In addition to the name, the system also provides the latitude and longitude as well as a brief description. Searching is fairly easy, as is exporting of data, in formats that can be pasted into electronic mapping products.

Covering fewer places, but probably sufficient for the smaller library most of the time is

■ Cambridge world gazetteer: a geographical dictionary. David Munro, ed. Cambridge, England, and New York: Cambridge Univ. Pr., 1990. 733p.

First published in 1988 as *Chambers World Gazetteer.* Has fewer but more detailed entries than *Merriam-Webster's Geographical Dictionary* (this includes pronunciations, for example), and includes a 100-plus-page atlas with maps by the Bartholomew firm.

■ Columbia gazetteer of the world. Saul Cohen, ed. New York: Columbia Univ. Pr., 1998. 3v.

A standard, formerly the *Columbia Lippincott Gazetteer.* Lists 165,000 places, including nations, towns, villages, monuments, natural features, theme parks, and even some fictional places. Includes pronunciation, latitude and longitude, distance from important places, official and variant place-names, and various data and historical information. Includes about 30,000 new entries compared with the last edition, plus generally more information for a given place.

■ Merriam-Webster's geographical dictionary. 3d ed. Springfield, Mass.: Merriam-Webster, 1997. 1361p.

Actually a pronouncing gazetteer rather than a dictionary of more than 47,000 places, current and historical, with about 15,000 cross-references for variants. Includes concise history for most entries. Available in Braille. Offers 252 detailed maps in black and white. Locates and identifies land features, human geography (e.g., states, cities, etc.), and major construction, such as dams, ruins, etc. More detail for the United States and Canada (but not Mexico) than for other nations. Pronunciation, current and former names and spellings, statistics and description, and historical information to about 1990. A new feature, in addition to more entries and more maps than the last edition (1972), is a brief glossary of geographic terms.

■ Times, London. Index-gazetteer of the world. Boston: Houghton, 1966. 966p.

Gives official spelling, cross-references from variants, and latitude and longitude for about 345,000 features, based on the Mid-Century edition of *The Times Atlas of the World* (plus the citations to that source for about 200,000 entries).

U.S. Gazetteers

■ Geographic names information system. Reston, Va.: USGS in cooperation with the U.S. Board on Geographical Names. CD-ROM and on the Web. <http://mapping.usgs.gov/www/gnis>

Official repository of U.S. geographic names. Includes official federal name and any other names, current or historical; latitude and longitude; reference to USGS 7.5-minute maps; state and county of location; elevation (where available); population of incorporated cities and towns; and links to permit generating a map. Searchable by feature, state or territory, feature type, elevation, county, population, size, range, map name.

■ National gazetteer of the United States of America. Washington, D.C.: Govt. Print. Off., 1983– . Also in fiche and on CD-ROM.

In effect, the printed version of the Geographic Names Information System (GNIS). When completed, there will be one detailed volume for each state. The first phase includes entering data for nearly all features on the USGS 7.5-minute maps, plus other federal mapping agencies, such as the Federal Aviation Administration (FAA), Federal Communications Commission (FCC), army, etc. A second phase involves collecting current and historical names from state and local materials. Finally, the state volume is published.

A commercial version, also in print and on CD-ROM, is *Omni Gazetteer of the United States of America* (Detroit: Omnigraphics, 1992; 11v.), with 1.5 million names from GNIS, National Register of Historic Places, Bureau of the Census, etc. Entry gives name, county, USGS map quadrangle, latitude and longitude, code for source of information. Some places also get elevation. Volume 10 is a complete index. Volume 11 has appendixes, including indexes to three scales of USGS maps, an index of feature types, lists of Native American reservations, airports, etc.

■ U.S. gazetteer. U.S. Bureau of the Census. Web. <http://www.census.gov/cgi-bin/gazetteer>

A detailed index of the United States, based on the 1990 census and the Census Bureau's TIGER/Line system. Covers only incorporated places. Searchable by town name, zip code, and state. Generates a map of the area, which can be enlarged or reduced (to cover more or less area). The system also permits a large number of overlays for additional information, such as counties, highways, Metropolitan Statistical Area (MSA)/Consolidated Metropolitan Statistical Area (CMSA) boundaries, census tracts, etc.

In summary, the smaller gazetteers may be used for pronunciation of place-names and for longitude and latitude of geographical features of the world. The larger ones are most useful for verification of the official spelling of a name and for locating obscure places whose names do not appear even in large world atlases. For most inquiries, however, the index to a good world atlas will supply the answers.

Place-Names

Related to gazetteers are more selective guides to place-names, usually giving the same information as in gazetteers, with the addition of the history and meaning of the name, often with anecdotes related to the name.

■ Canby, C. The encyclopedia of historic places. New York: Facts on File, 1984. 2v.

Towns, cities, deserts, fields, etc. of historic significance, including many places not usually in standard reference books. *Wilson Library Bulletin* called this the "librarians' first choice as a source of short histories."

■ Harder, Kelsie B., ed. Illustrated dictionary of place names, United States and Canada. New York: Van Nostrand Reinhold, 1976. 631p.

Often reprinted. About 15,000 names explained, giving origins and derivations. Includes bibliography and 200 illustrations. *See also* Stewart, below, for information not in this title.

■ Room, Adrian. Place-name changes, 1900–1991. 2d ed. Metuchen, N.J.: Scarecrow, 1993. 296p.

Given the changes in place-names in this century, this is helpful to any map user. Covers about 4,500 places, mostly Russian and Chinese. Includes earlier name cross-references; gives new name, old name, date of change, and type of place (e.g., town, hill). Extensive bibliography of place-name sources. Unfortunately, the title does not include all changes, especially since 1949, but it does include many of the most recent changes (e.g., in the Balkans).

■ Room, Adrian. Place-names of the world: origins and meanings of the names for over 5,000 natural features, countries, capitals, territories, cities, and historic sites. Jefferson, N.C.: McFarland, 1997. 441p.

Covers natural and man-made features, giving a short description, geographic location, brief etymology, and list of historical references.

■ Stewart, George R. American place-names: a concise and selective dictionary for the continental United States of America. New York: Oxford Univ. Pr., 1970. Reprint, 1985. 550p.

Some 12,000 entries in alphabetical order; good introduction on the general background and history of the name. Includes a bibliography. *See also,* Harder, above, for information not in this work.

Directories and Encyclopedias

Directories

■ Cobb, David A. Guide to U.S. map resources. 2d ed. Chicago: ALA Maps and Geography Round Table, 1990. 495p.

Directory and description of nearly 1,000 collections, with considerable detail in description and indexing. Has received mixed reviews, but is currently more recent and has more entries than *Map Collections.*

■ Directory of Canadian map collections. 6th ed. Ottawa: Assn. of Canadian Map Collections and Archives, 1992. 180p.

Detailed descriptions of 112 collections, in both English and French (depending on the working language of the library). Indexes by country, institution, and personal name.

■ Directory of geoscience libraries, United States and Canada. 4th ed. Alexandria, Va.: Geoscience Information Society, 1992. 135p.

All types of libraries, including government, corporate, and private, that have significant collections in geology, geophysics, and earth sciences. Of particular use is the (now outdated) appendix of Internet sites.

■ Guide to programs in geography in the United States and Canada. Washington, D.C.: Assn. of American Geographers, 1968– . Annual.

Formerly *Guide to Departments of Geography in the United States and Canada.* Descriptions of programs, a directory of geographers, general membership information for the AAG, and a list of theses and dissertations in geography completed in the past year.

■ Map collections in the United States and Canada. 4th ed. David K. Carrington and Richard W. Stephenson, eds. New York: Special Libraries Assn., 1985. 178p.

This edition covers 804 map collections in the United States and Canada and has a deserved reputation as the classic directory. Arranged by state, then city, it covers all special map collections as well as map reference departments of college and public libraries.

■ World directory of map collections. Lorraine Dubreuil, comp. 3d ed. Munchen, Germany, and New York: K. G. Saur, 1993. 310p. Produced by the Section of Geography and Map Libraries, International Federation of Library Associations and Institutions (IFLA).

Lists map collections in all national libraries and archives, the only map library in a nation, and collections that hold at least 1,000 maps or atlases, based on a mail survey. Includes standard directory information, plus narrative history or description of the collection and statistics of staff and holdings.

Encyclopedias

■ Background notes on the countries of the world. Washington, D.C.: U.S. Department of State, 1954– . Also on CD-ROM with other material as U.S. Foreign Affairs on CD-ROM and as Countries of the World and Their Leaders. Also on the Web.

A pamphlet series of four to sixteen pages, one pamphlet per nation. Each includes a small orientation map, and a full national map, both suitable for photocopying. Much of the information is not readily available in other general atlases or encyclopedias. The information is generally objective, with appropriate comments on official U.S. policy toward the nation. Each map is a different scale, with no indication as to which projection is used. About seventy-five of these are updated each year. Each pamphlet is dated. The series is available by subscription. A full list of the pamphlets can be found in Government Printing Office *Subject Bibliography SB-093, Background Notes* (Washington, D.C.: Govt. Print. Off., irregular).

■ Countries of the world and their leaders yearbook. Detroit: Gale, 1998– . Annual. Continues *Countries of the World and Their Leaders* [year]. Detroit: Gale, 1974– . 2v.

Primarily a compilation of *Background Notes,* with additional information on national leaders and the like from the U.S. Department of State. Also includes the addresses of U.S. embassies and consulates, the text of all Department of State advisories, and most of the Department of State's brochures of travel tips. Although the emphasis is on business travel, this is a useful compilation and general brief "encyclopedia" of the world.

■ eHRAF. Electronic human relations area files. New Haven, Conn.: Human Relations Area Files, 1996– . Online and on CD-ROM only.

Full text of material on sixty human societies from the printed and microform Human Relations Area Files (HRAF), arranged by subject in five volumes. Eventually intended to replace all other formats. Annual updates are planned to include about 50,000 or more pages of text on about fifteen cultural groups. The material includes both primary and secondary sources, plus summary and a bibliography.

■ Encyclopedia of world cultures: sponsored by the Human Relations Area Files at Yale University. New York: Macmillan, 1985–95. 10v.

Each of the first nine volumes covers a specific geographic area. Volume 10 consists of cumulated indexes, maps, and a bibliography. The

HRAF, the basis for this work, is the most comprehensive collection of materials on cultures as a whole ever compiled. Clearly, for the time being, this is a definitive work on the subject, although it is becoming superseded by the eHRAF title above.

■ Europa world year book. London and Detroit: Europa, 1926- . Annual.

A standard, formerly called the *Europa Year Book,* although it has undergone some additions and omissions in recent years. Includes data, plus information on government, religion, press, broadcasting, industry, etc. Seven regional volumes are based on this, with the same statistics but with longer narrative essays and bibliographies. Generally has been praised by reviewers for content and attacked for its hefty price.

The series, which is based on the above but with some more detail, includes these titles:

■ Africa South of the Sahara. London: Europa, 1971- . Annual.

■ Eastern Europe and the Commonwealth of Independent States. London: Europa, 1992- . Annual.

■ The Far East and Australasia. London and Detroit: Europa, 1969- . Annual.

■ South America, Central America and the Caribbean. London: Europa, 1990- . Annual.

■ The USA and Canada. London: Europa, 1989- . Annual.

Individual volumes have received very good reviews. Generally each follows the same format, heavy on text and tables, with hardly any maps or illustrations: mostly a nation-by-nation set with many statistics.

■ Geopedia. Chicago: Encyclopaedia Britannica, 1994. CD-ROM only.

A multimedia encyclopedia based on Britannica publications and aimed at upper-elementary through high school. More than 1,200 articles on major places and physical features, 3,000 visuals, a world atlas, statistical data, and fifty-five learning activities. "Chartmaker" software allows the reader to create graphs and charts.

■ Illustrated encyclopedia of world geography. New York: Oxford Univ. Pr., 1992. 11v.

Has what have been called "spectacular illustrations" (uncommon for Oxford publications), plus data, text, maps, charts, and graphs. Arranged by broad topic in each volume (e.g., world economy). Useful to the adult but generally understandable at the junior-high-school level.

■ Kurian, George Thomas. The encyclopedia of the third world. 4th ed. New York: Facts on File, 1991. 3v.

A standard reference set, first published in 1978. Generally reliable, current, and easy to use. Provides a wholly different point of view from most of the other similar sources, which tend to take the point of view of the country of publication. Of course, some commentators argue that the concept of "Third World" is no longer useful.

■ Kurian, George Thomas. World encyclopedia of cities. Santa Barbara, Calif.: ABC-Clio, 1993– . 6v.

Data on one to five cities per state or province (all with populations over 100,000). In addition to 200 fields of standardized numerical data, provides a map for each city. The first two volumes cover North America. More complete than most similar sources, but the emphasis on "equity" often means some cities are left out.

■ Lands and peoples. New York: Grolier, 1929/30– . 6v.

Another rather conservative "standard." Aimed at fifth grade and above. Each volume covers a given land mass, and is arranged by country. Many checklists of presidents, kings, etc. Information from each country follows a standard format and includes geography, history, culture, and economics, with sidebars for topics specific to a given country and lots of statistics. Updates are irregular. Three special volumes related to recent issues are *Crisis in the Middle East* (1992; 92p.); *Life after Communism* (1993; 108p.); and *The Changing Face of Europe* (1996; 130p.).

■ World factbook. Washington, D.C.: Central Intelligence Agency; Minneapolis, Minn.: Quanta Pr., 1981. Annual. Also on the Internet and on CD-ROM.

Very similar in content and arrangement to the *KGB World Factbook,* which Quanta also produces. Also available in print from the Government Printing Office (GPO), Brassey's, and Gale (as *Handbook of the Nations* [Detroit: Gale, 1981– ; annual]). Provides standardized up-to-date data at one to two pages per nation.

■ World geographical encyclopedia. New York: McGraw-Hill, 1995. 5v. Also on CD-ROM as GeoNavigator.

Based on the Italian *Enciclopedia Geografica Universale* (1994), in an excellent translation with 750 color photographs. Arranged by continent, each entry is in four sections: geopolitics, climate, administrative structure, and socioeconomic conditions. Indexes proper names but not subjects. Is a direct competitor with the *Worldmark Encyclopedia* but with more impressive production values.

▪ Worldmark encyclopedia of the nations. 9th ed. Detroit: Gale, 1998. 5v.

First edition produced in 1960. This is a well-known source, with fifty standard topics for more than 200 countries. Includes glossaries of special terms used in each nation and religious holidays; indexes to countries, territories, and international groups; and a special feature—the master index appears in each volume of the set. Ironically, although this is commonly found in libraries, critics are less impressed with this source than one would expect.

Dictionaries of Geographical Terms

Not to be confused with geographical dictionaries, such as those already described, these supplement unabridged dictionaries by giving fuller information on individual terms, with definitions restricted to geography (and related fields, in some cases). The following are useful:

▪ Clark, Audrey N., ed. Longman dictionary of geography. White Plains, N.Y.: Longman, 1985. 724p.

More than 10,500 main terms. Often cited as the best one-volume dictionary for this subject on the market and the first one-volume work to include both human and physical geography. Based on the fuller information in Stamp and Clark's *Glossary of Geographical Terms* and with an abridged version titled *New Penguin Dictionary of Geography* (London: Penguin, 1990; 359p.).

▪ Dictionary of human geography. R. J. Johnston and others, eds. 3d ed., rev. and updated. Oxford and Cambridge, Mass.: Blackwell, 1994. 724p.

Unlike the other sources listed in this section, includes much emphasis on the effects of social sciences and humanities on geographical thinking. Entries are arranged alphabetically, but there is also an index. Most entries have bibliographic references.

▪ The encyclopedic dictionary of physical geography. Andrew Goudie, ed. 2d ed. Oxford: Blackwell, 1994. 611p.

More than 2,000 entries—including long, signed articles as well as definitions—makes this live up to its title. With a strong British influence (U.S. variant terms are barely mentioned), this includes more biological and geomorphological terms than most U.S. works. Cross-references and an index.

▪ Huber, Thomas P., and others. Dictionary of concepts in physical geography. Westport, Conn.: Greenwood, 1988. 304p.

Concise definitions with considerable explanatory material, including origin of terms, background, changes in meaning, etc. in all fields of geography. Includes good bibliographies with each entry and a subject index.

▪ Larkin, Robert, and Gary Peters. Dictionary of concepts in human geography. Westport, Conn.: Greenwood, 1983. 286p.

More than 100 concepts in detail, with basic arrangements and treatment identical to the Huber dictionary, noted above.

▪ Small, Ronald J. A modern dictionary of geography. 2d ed. London and New York: E. Arnold, 1995. 265p.

This edition reflects changes in the discipline and discusses both human and physical aspects of the field. Includes 2,000 entries, many revised from the first edition, and more than 1,100 maps and illustrations. Aimed at advanced high school and undergraduate students, not specialists.

▪ Stamp, L. Dudley, and Audrey N. Clark, eds. A glossary of geographical terms. 3d ed. New York: Longman, 1979. 571p.

Comparative definitions, including many foreign terms, with many new entries in this edition. Generally gives rather brief definitions and concentrates on etymology, sources of terms, and changing meanings of terms in the field. Terms often include commentary on their use and meanings by experts. Includes bibliographic references.

Many other such dictionaries exist, with a preponderance of those having a British rather than North American focus. Although many terms (and meanings) do not change, the advances in cartography and changes in thinking (such as the now-general acceptance of the tectonic-plate theory) make use of older works a bit problematic.

Travel Guides

It has long been recognized that travel guides are a useful source of geographical and historical information, often augmenting gazetteers, with fuller descriptions of towns and historic sites and often more local maps and plans of cities than in atlases. They grow more popular every year.

Modern travel guides—intended to make it easier, more comfortable, and more pleasant to see the world—have multiplied so greatly, along with our mobility, that librarians may wish for the early nineteenth century, when the firm of Baedeker was the principal publisher of guides for most of the countries to which European and British travelers went. The excellence of its guides, the accuracy of detail, and the quality of its maps explain why they are still being updated and published today, and why *Baedeker* has so long been synonymous with *travel guide*.

There are many modern travel guides, both in series (such as the Rough Guides, the Let's Go, and other newer series, as well as older, more established series, like the Blue Guides and the Mobil Travel Guides) and individual titles. The next pages give a brief list of those likely to be found in a typical American library.

A growing amount of travel information is available online, especially on the World Wide Web. Although much of this is very useful, and at least some is produced by the same people and organizations as the more traditional sources, much is not. Naturally, the reader will be aware that descriptions published by groups such as the chambers of commerce will tend to list only favorable aspects of a place and that for-profit organizations such as hotel chains and consortia will usually list only their members. This logical phenomenon (that organizations will tend to put themselves in the most favorable light) is especially critical in the growing number of lists of recommended hotels and restaurants, which are convenient because rooms can be booked directly on the Web. However, remember that many other equivalent or better rooms may be available via other sources and that the quality of a website does not necessarily reflect the quality of the establishment. In addition, there is much else out there on the Web and in traditional sources that has no particular authority, other than the personal opinion of the writer—and nothing seems to be more conducive to personal opinion than travel.

Bibliographies

■ Anderson, Sarah. Anderson's travel companion: a guide to the best non-fiction and fiction for travelling. Brookfield, Vt.: Scolar Pr./Ashgate, 1995. 552p.

> A detailed and comprehensive guide to both modern and classical English travel writing, with many photographs. Includes standard guide-

books in a separate section; otherwise, geographical arrangement. Indexes by author, title, place, photographer.

■ Cox, Edward Godfrey. A reference guide to the literature of travel, including voyages, geographical descriptions, adventures, shipwrecks and expeditions. Seattle: Univ. of Washington Pr., 1935–49. 3v.

The standard for historical travel literature.

■ Hayes, Greg, and Joan Wright. Going places: the guide to travel guides. Boston: Harvard Common Pr., 1988. 772p.

A critical guide to nearly 200 English-language travel guides, including series. Appendixes list phrase books, travel stores and mail-order agents, travel book publishers, travel newsletters and magazines. Index by subject and by geographical location covered.

■ Heise, Jon O. The travel book: a guide to the travel guides. 2d ed. Metuchen, N.J.: Scarecrow, 1993. 397p.

A well-reviewed guide to the guides, by an author who has produced several similar guides over the years. Tends to be most complete for North America and Europe. Covers general series and all sorts of specialized titles (e.g., guides to ghost towns or shopping malls, travel guides for the disabled) with a subject index.

■ Simony, Maggy. The traveler's reading guide: ready-made reading lists for the armchair traveler. Rev. ed. New York: Facts on File, 1993. 510p.

Includes reading lists with comments, plus information on travel guides, travel bookstores, and a list of novels set in England.

Guidebook Series

Although there are many individual guides to cities, countries, and even specific locations, recent years have seen an increase in publisher's series. Some of the more helpful are listed here; others may be found in the bibliographies listed above.

■ American Automobile Association. Tour books. Heathrow, Fla.: AAA, 1928– . Annual.

Multiple volumes arranged by location, each covering several states. Gives tourist attractions and accommodations; admission fees and basic meal and room rates; basic information about temperature, local history, and the like; and small maps of major cities. Covers from Central America to Canada. Although much more comprehensive than the Mobil series, a mere listing no longer means much more than a minimal quality evaluation, contrary to the impression given by the rating system. The higher ratings, however, are still useful.

■ American guide series. Federal Writers' Project (later called Writers' Program), comps. [Various publishers], 1937- .

A classic, with separate volumes for each state and a few cities. Nearly all of the series are still in print, some updated. Covers history, geology, art, agriculture, industry, small towns, and villages, complete with recommended travel routes for the best highways as of the 1930s. Houghton Mifflin's New American Guide series has updated and corrected many titles, with better illustrations than the original. Remains an excellent example of both research and literary style, as well as covering material not in the standard guidebooks. Mark S. Selvaggio's *American Guide Series: Works by the Federal Writers' Project* (Pittsburgh, Pa.: Arthur Scharf, 1990; 176p.) indexes the whole series.

■ Baedeker handbook(s) for travelers. London: Allen & Unwin; New York: Macmillan, 1828- .

The oldest travel books of all, with an emphasis on popular sightseeing and shopping as well as history and culture. Includes *Baedeker/AA Country Guides* and *Baedeker/AA City Guides.* Most include a large foldout map as well as many smaller maps, plans, and diagrams. Similar to the *Blue Guide* volumes in many ways, although with more attention to lodging and meals.

■ Blue guide [place]. London: Ernest Benn [later A & C Black]; New York: Norton, 1918- .

A classic "standard" emphasizing cultural, historical, and architectural information; usually arranged geographically by "tours" (from point *A* to point *B*). Excellent detail maps and many plans of major buildings, such as castles and cathedrals. Several thousand titles in print cover nearly all nations and their major cities. The print is small (and that of detailed descriptions even smaller). Generally, however, other series are better for current information and essential for lodging and eating arrangements.

■ Eyewitness travel guides. New York: Dorling Kindersley, 1993- .

A newer series, with many color photos and three-dimensional aerial drawings of districts and historical buildings. To date, the emphasis is on cities rather than nations, regions, or even the countryside.

■ Fodor's comprehensive travel guides. New York: Prentice-Hall/Simon & Schuster, 1953- .

A highly successful series with more than 130 titles, at continental, regional, nation, and city levels. Well-written guide for the tourist, but tends to discuss only the more popular and obvious sights. The series has been criticized as stodgy and praised as suitable for the more mature traveler. Contains considerable, if sketchy, information on lodging, restaurants, and shopping. *Fodor's Budget Travel Guides* are based on these, with an emphasis on inexpensive places (but generally not hostels, campgrounds, and other nearly free places).

■ Frommer, Arthur. _____ [country, region, city] on _____ dollars a day. New York: Simon & Schuster. 1957- . Biennial.

Begun as *X on Five Dollars a Day,* this series remains one of the better budget-guide series. Discussions of the country's history, culture, and the like are rather brief, but these titles are excellent on transportation, food, and lodging. As with *Fodor's,* tends to emphasize the most popular and obvious tourist attractions.

■ ———. Let's go: the budget guide to _____. New York: St. Martin's, 1960- .

Subtitle varies. The premier budget guide for the truly impecunious, begun by the Harvard (University) Student Agencies in 1960. Tends to have better coverage of smaller cities and places off the tourist track than the other tourist guides (but no replacement for *Baedeker* or the *Blue Guide* volumes). Heavy reliance on student writers leads to outright errors at times and often an overemphasis on catchy writing rather than useful information (e.g., one military museum is described in full as "full of lots of bright shiny things").

■ Lonely planet travel survival kit series. Hawthorn, Australia: Lonely Planet, 1973- .

More than sixty guides to single countries or small groups of them. Unlike the other titles listed here, the emphasis is on the natural environment and areas definitely off-the-usual tourist routes. The *Lonely Planet Newsletter,* 1990- (quarterly), includes reviews of new books as well as updated travel information.

■ Michelin travel guide(s). Greenville, N.C.: Michelin Travel Pubs., 1900- .

Frequently revised. In two series. The Green guides are keyed to Michelin maps, as well as the self-contained maps in each guide, and have a deserved reputation as among the best sources for the sightseer. In addition to general maps, the guides include detailed directions and many floor plans of important buildings. The Red series is considered by many the premier guide to hotels and restaurants. Although many of both series are in English, others are only in French—for those who don't speak French, this is not a particular problem for the Red guides because of the clear rating systems.

■ Mobil travel guides. Chicago: Rand McNally, 1959- . 7v. Also on the Web and on CD-ROM as part of Rand McNally's TripMaker Deluxe.

Has been described as the Michelin for the United States. Definitely a guide to hotels, motels, and restaurants, with very sketchy information on sights, history, and the like (but always seems to mention theme parks, waterslides, and similar family oriented places). Includes ratings and cost information also, with standardized descriptions. Very reliable, but tends to ignore the chains.

■ Rough guide to [place]. Boston: Routledge & Paul/Methuen, 1982- . Many also on the Web.

One of the newer series, giving practical suggestions for travel. These have been praised for their sensitivity to life in the country and what tourists can expect. Tends to be aimed at the more adventurous than, say, *Fodor's,* and often lists out-of-the-way sights. Overall, approaches the ideal of the "traveler" over the "tourist." Although less comprehensive for historical sites than the *Baedeker* or *Blue Guide* volumes, the series provides more information on current life and culture.

Specialized Guides

■ Curtis, Nancy C. Black heritage sites: an African American odyssey and finder's guide. New York: New Pr., 1996. 677p.

Lists sites not usually covered or well covered in more general guides. Tends to emphasize the U.S. South, East, and Midwest, but is a bit weak for general sites that have some African American exhibits. Includes detailed descriptions and has more depth than its competitors, plus a very complete index.

■ Eagle Walking Turtle. Indian America: a traveler's companion. 3d ed. Santa Fe, N.Mex.: John Muir, 1993. 460p.

Lists reservations by state, including directory information, usually descriptions of public ceremonies and other events, history of covered groups, and some discussion of arts, etc. Indexed by subject.

■ Hecker, Helen. Travel for the disabled: a handbook of travel resources and 500 worthwhile access guides. Portland, Oreg.: Twin Peaks Pr., 1985. 185p.

Unfortunately, there is no truly current guide to facilities for the disabled, but this remains an excellent guide to resources that provide the guidance, including books, travel clubs and agencies, and specific guides to airports and cities. Includes a subject index.

■ Holidays and festivals index. Detroit: Omnigraphics, 1995. 800p.

An index to twenty-seven sources giving descriptions, locations, etc. for more than 3,000 events around the world. Indexed by date, name of person with whom associated, and religious, ethnic, and geographical associations. Includes saint's days, art festivals, fairs, and other functions.

■ Wasserman, Paul. Festivals sourcebook. 2d ed. Detroit: Gale, 1984. 721p.

Remains the most complete such list available. Similar in arrangement and entry to the *Encyclopedia of Associations,* classifies the events by type, then location. Gives a brief description and contact information; generally the latter is the most out-of-date information.

Other Travel Information

■ Hostelling international guides. Washington, D.C.: Hostelling International/ American Youth Hostels, 1977- . Also on the Web.

Often considered the lodging of choice for the youthful budget-conscious traveler, hostels in recent years have expanded their appeal to travelers of all ages and include an increasing number of facilities with semiprivate rooms and other amenities. The guide includes several volumes, with slightly variant titles; the one of most immediate relevance to most U.S. libraries is Hostelling North America [year]. Washington, D.C.: Hostelling International/American Youth Hostels, 2000- .

■ OAG business travel planner: North American edition. Oak Brook, Ill.: OAG Worldwide, 1990- .

Continues *Hotel and Motel Red Book* (1886–1986) and *OAG Travel Planner.* Arranged by city, a comprehensive listing of all lodgings. Larger cities are given more space, including airport maps, information on major events and climate, downtown street maps. Many listings include special services, general location, address, and basic size. The same publisher also produces European and Pacific Asia editions.

■ Official airline guide, 1943– . Oak Brook, Ill.: Official Airline Guides, 1943– . Monthly. Also in a number of electronic versions.

Title and publisher vary. In separate worldwide and North American editions. Includes all flight schedules and fares for airlines.

■ Rand McNally standard highway mileage guide. Skokie, Ill.: Rand McNally, 1997. 479p.

Covers 1,300 major and medium-sized cities in the United States and Canada, plus more than 130 pages of detailed highway maps, to permit calculation of mileages between the places in the tables. The user should remember that each city is listed only once as a main entry, so, for example, the distance between Yuma City, Arizona, and Los Angeles is only under the latter.

■ Woodall's campground directory. Highland Park, Ill.: Woodall, 1967– . 3v. Annual.

Covers the United States and Canada. Approximates the information the *Mobil Travel Guide* series provides for motels and hotels, but covers accommodations for tents, trailers, and recreational vehicles.

Road Atlases

■ Mapquest. New York: Mapquest.com. Internet: <http://www.mapquest.com>

Lacks the directory features of the next entry, but includes more types of travel information. At this writing, in addition to providing maps of both U.S. and foreign major cities and airports, Mapquest offers maps of any U.S. telephone area code and any U.K. postal code, as well as detailed maps for a given address (in the United States and some foreign countries). Users can also choose door-to-door or city-to-city route directions but cannot search by name, so if users lack the specific address, only the city-to-city directions are available. This site also includes travel information from the *Mobil Travel Guide* series, plus other local information. Again, beware of errors in the detailed itineraries.

■ Maps on Us. Westboro, Mass.: Switchboard.com. Internet: <http://www. mapsonus.com>

As with many similar sources, also provides a people and business or organization search feature (in effect, a combined white and yellow pages), but the interest here is its detailed coverage of the United States. The system permits searching by a known address (generating a surprisingly detailed map) or by keywords (e.g., for a business). The route planner is particularly interesting, because one may combine a known address (such as one's home) with a keyword search (including the condition "within X miles of city Y") and generate detailed directions as well as distances. An added fillip is the ability to include an intermediate destination. Directions include maps, with the ability to resize the scale to get larger or smaller sections of the entire route. However, as with competing products, the warning label should be heeded—often the directions are not the best route, and occasional errors will be found as well.

■ Rand McNally road atlas: United States, Canada, Mexico. Chicago: Rand McNally, 1924– . Annual.

A standard for many years, with insets for many cities and separate maps for some of the largest ones. Includes a brief mileage guide with each map and a complete index to all the maps.

■ TripMaker deluxe. Chicago: Rand McNally, 1999– . Annual. CD-ROM and on the Internet only.

Includes the information in the *Rand McNally Road Atlas* plus the *Mobil Travel Guide* series, other guidebook-type material (including preplanned "weekend adventures"), and support for personal digital assistants and global positioning software (of primary value to the individual rather than the library). Because most of the services of Maps on Us, Mapquest, and similar systems are free on the Web, this is aimed at value added, including portability.

This chapter has tried to give a brief overview of geography, a generally neglected field of study in the United States. It has briefly covered its methodology, organizations, and principal sources of information retrieval from basic types of sources. As with the other chapters, it must be augmented with more exhaustive guides.

Acronyms and Initialisms

Following are selected acronyms and initialisms used in *Fundamental Reference Sources.*

AAA	American Automobile Association
AAG	Association of American Geographers
ACCIS	Advisory Committee for the Coordination of Information Systems
ACCRA	American Chamber of Commerce Researchers Association
ACRL	Association of College and Research Libraries
AGS	American Geographical Society
ALA	American Library Association
ARBA	*American Reference Books Annual*
ARL	Association of Research Libraries
ASI	*American Statistics Index*
AV	Audiovisual
BGN	Board on Geographical Names
BIP	*Books in Print*
BLAISE	British Library Automated Information Service
BLS	Bureau of Labor Statistics
BMC	*British Museum Catalog*

BRD	*Book Review Digest*
BRI	*Book Review Index*
CAS	Chemical Abstracts Service
CBI	*Cumulative Book Index*
CD	Compact Disc
CD-I	Compact Disc—Interactive
CD-ISIS	Computerized Documentation—Integrated Set for Information Systems
CD-ROM	Compact Disc—Read Only Memory
CIA	Central Intelligence Agency
CIJE	*Current Index to Journals in Education*
CINAHL	*Cumulative Index to Nursing and Allied Health Literature*
CIP	Cataloging in Publication
CIS	*Congressional Information Service*
CMSA	Consolidated Metropolitan Statistical Area
COM	Computer Output Microform
CONSER	Conversion of Serials Project
CPI	Consumer Price Index
CQ	*Congressional Quarterly*
CRB	Commodity Research Bureau
CRC	Chemical Rubber Company
DAB	*Dictionary of American Biography*
DARE	*Dictionary of American Regional English*
DMA	Designated Market Area
DNB	*Dictionary of National Biography*
DOT	*Dictionary of Occupational Titles*
DSM	*Diagnostic and Statistical Manual of Mental Disorders*
DVD	Digital Versatile Disc
EAD	*Encyclopedias, Atlases and Dictionaries*
EB	*Encyclopaedia Britannica*
EB3	*Encyclopaedia Britannica, 15th edition*
eHRAF	Electronic Human Relations Area Files
EMTREE	Excerpta Medica Tree Structure (for subject headings)
ERIC/NTIS	Educational Resources Information Clearinghouse/National Technical Information Service
ESL	English as a Second Language
ESLC	*Elementary School Library Collection*
ESTC	*English Short Title Catalog*
ETS	Educational Testing Service
FEMA	Federal Emergency Management Administration
FTP	File Transfer Protocol
GIS	Geographic Information System
GNIS	Geographic Names Information System

GPO	Government Printing Office
GSS	General Social Survey
HRAF	Human Relations Area Files
HTML	Hypertext Markup Language
IAC	Information Access Company
IBZ	Internationale Bibliographie der Zeitschriftenliteratur
ICPSR	Interuniversity Consortium for Political and Social Research
IFLA	International Federation of Library Associations and Institutions
ILMP	*International Literary Market Place*
ILO	International Labour Organization
IPA	International Phonetic Alphabet
IRC	Internet Relay Chat
ISA	Instrument Society of America
ISBN	International Standard Book Number
ISI	Institute for Scientific Information
ISSN	International Standard Serial Number
KWIC	Keyword in Context
LC	Library of Congress
LCSH	Library of Congress Subject Headings
LISA	Library and Information Science Abstracts
LJ	*Library Journal*
LMP	*Literary Market Place*
MARC	Machine Readable Cataloging
MeSH	Medical Subject Headings
MLA	Modern Language Association
MOOs	Multiple User Dungeon—Object Oriented
MPAA	Motion Picture Association of America
MSA	Metropolitan Statistical Area
NAFTA	North American Free Trade Agreement
NAICS	North American Industry Classification System
NAS	National Academy of Sciences
NCES	National Center for Education Statistics
NGO	Non-governmental Organization
NICEM	National Information Center for Education Media
NIDS	*National Inventory of Documentary Sources*
NOAA	National Oceanic and Atmospheric Administration
NUC	*National Union Catalog*
NYPL	New York Public Library
OAS	Organization of American States
OCLC	Online Computer Library Center
OECD	Organisation for Economic Cooperation and Development
OED	*Oxford English Dictionary*

OEDII	*Oxford English Dictionary, 2d edition*
OLUC	OCLC Online Union Catalog
OPAC	Online Public Access Catalog
PAIS	Public Affairs Information Service
PCGN	Permanent Committee on Geographical Names
PDF	Portable Document Format
PRF	*[GPO Sales] Publications Reference File*
PTLA	*Publishers Trade List Annual*
RASD	Reference and Adult Services Division
RBB	*Reference Books Bulletin*
RIE	*Resources in Education*
RILM	Repertoire Internationale de la Litterature de Musique
RLG	Research Libraries Group
RLIN	Research Libraries Information Network
RMA	Robert Morris Associates
RUSA	Reference and User Services Association
S&P	Standard and Poor's Corporation
SALALM	Seminar on the Acquisition of Latin American Library Material
SCORPIO	Subject-Content-Oriented Retriever for Processing Information Online
SERVQUAL	Service Quality
SI	International System (of measurement)
SIC	Standard Industrial Classification
SIGLE	*System for Information on Grey Literature in Europe*
SLA	Special Libraries Association
SPDCD	Standard Periodical Directory on Compact Disc
STC	*Short-Title Catalog*
STN	Scientific and Technical Network
SuDocs	[U.S.] Superintendent of Documents
TIGER	Topologically Integrated Encoding and Referencing System
TQM	Total Quality Management
UAP	Universal Availability of Publications
UBC	Universal Bibliographic Control
UMI	University Microfilms International
UN	United Nations
UNBIS	United Nations Bibliographic Information System
UNESCO	United Nations Economic and Social Council
URL	Uniform Resource Locator
USGS	United States Geological Survey
WAML	Western Association of Map Libraries
WDEU	*Webster's Dictionary of English Usage*
WLB	*Wilson Library Bulletin*

WLN	Western Library Network
WOREP	Wisconsin-Ohio Reference Project
WPA	Works Progress Administration
WWF	World Wildlife Fund
WWW	World Wide Web

Guidelines for Particular Types of Reference Works

V. Criteria for Evaluating Specific Types of Materials

General English-Language Dictionaries

1. Authority, Scope, Purpose, and Objectives

Are the editors and contributors and their qualifications identified? Is their authority acceptable? Is the publishing house identified with quality works?

How many entries does the work include? What is the basis for inclusion?

Does the dictionary consist of word definitions only, or are additional (or integrated) listings for biographical, geographical, or other types of data included?

Does the dictionary fulfill its stated purpose? Is it appropriate for its intended audience?

Is the dictionary available in nonprint format (e.g., CD-ROM, online, etc.)? If so, are there significant differences between the various formats?

If the dictionary is electronic, is a site map provided? Is there a help page for using the dictionary that can be accessed at any time?

Reprinted from the *Reference Books Bulletin Editorial Board Manual,* revised (Chicago: ALA, 1999).

535

2. Vocabulary

What is the extent of the vocabulary? Is it, for example, limited to current usage? To what extent are special words and meanings covered (e.g., slang, dialect, obsolete and technical terms, and meanings)? Are there special designations (for example, obscene, colloquialism) for words of questionable propriety?

How is the vocabulary arranged? If in alphabetical sequence, is it letter by letter or word by word? If it is an electronic dictionary, does it provide searching options such as "exact spelling," "approximate spelling," or "floating searches" (searches that access words that contain the query word)?

3. Word Treatment

a) Spelling

What spelling guidelines are used?

Are variant spellings provided?

Is capitalization indicated?

Are British and American variants identified?

Are syllabication and hyphenation plainly illustrated and easily interpreted?

b) Parts of Speech

Are parts of speech clearly indicated?

Are past tenses of irregular verbs provided?

Are compound terms and phrase forms clearly presented?

c) Pronunciation

What system (e.g., diacritical marks, phonetic alphabet) is used to indicate pronunciation?

How is accentuation indicated?

Is the pronunciation key easy to use and readily accessible?

Are variations in pronunciation indicated?

Is there an audio pronunciation guide for electronic dictionaries?

d) Definitions

Are definitions accurate, clear, complete, and precise?

Are they geared to the level of the intended audience?

In what sequence are definitions given? Are they in historical sequence, with earliest meanings listed first, or are current meanings given first?

For electronic dictionaries, do the definitions provide links to related definitions in the dictionary? Are there hyperlinks within the definitions?

Are etymologies and word histories provided in sufficient detail, with changes in meanings and usage marked and dated?

If personal-name entries are included, do they include pronunciations and birth and death dates? Are there sufficient and current descriptive data? What proportion of the total number of entries do they represent?

If place-name entries are included, do they include pronunciation? Are there sufficient and current descriptive data? What proportion of the total number of entries do they represent?

What types of illustrations, videos, or audio clips are included in the definitions?

e) Usage

Is the dictionary prescriptive or descriptive? Does it establish rules regarding how words should be used or does it describe how words are being used?

Is informal and idiomatic usage indicated? Are obsolete and colloquial terms identified? Are these variances clearly marked?

Does the dictionary include sample sentences containing defined words? Are the sentences sufficiently descriptive and appropriate for the intended audience?

Are illustrative quotations provided? Do the selected quotations sufficiently describe the precise usage of the word? Are citations for source and date provided?

f) Synonyms and Antonyms

Are synonyms and antonyms included?

Are they listed under individual word entries or are they presented in a separate listing?

Do they represent sufficient variety? Are important variations in meaning noted?

4. Illustrations

What types of illustrations (e.g., line drawings, color photographs) are provided? How many? Are they of good quality?

Do the selection and placement of illustrations effectively complement the definitions?

5. Supplementary Material

What type of supplementary material is provided (e.g., abbreviations, statistical tables, maps, colleges and universities)? How is the information presented? Is it clear and easily accessible?

Is the supplementary information unique, or is it readily available in other sources? Is it accurate and up-do-date? Are sources cited?

Does the supplementary material contribute significantly to the achievement of the stated purpose of the resource?

6. Format

Is the publication a single volume or multivolume work? Is it physically easy to use?

Will the publication stand up to heavy use? Is the paper of adequate weight and quality? Is the binding substantial? Does the volume lie flat when opened?

Is the type clear and legible? Is page makeup conducive to easy reference? Are headings clear, simple, and easy to follow? Are margins adequate for rebinding?

Does the work feature an attractive layout, with balanced text and visuals?

General Encyclopedias

1. History of Publication

Is the encyclopedia a new work or is it a revision, abridgment, or alternate format (including CD-ROM and online) of a previous publication?

Is the work kept up-to-date by a policy of "continuous revision," by yearbooks, by links to online updates, or by other means? Do different formats of the same title have different revision policies?

2. Authority

Editors and Editorial Staff. Does the encyclopedia list the editors and editorial staff and their professional experience and qualifications?

Contributors. Are the contributors or consultants listed by name? Are the contributors qualified by experience or background? Are articles signed?

3. Scope and Treatment

Objectives and Purpose. What are the objectives, if stated, and are they accomplished? Does the work meet the needs of the intended audience/readership level?

Organization and Arrangement. How are articles arranged (e.g., alphabetically word by word or letter by letter, classified, thematic, via keyword retrieval)? What is the pagination (consecutive throughout the set, volume by volume, lettered for revised additions, e.g., 361a, 361b)? What is the cross-reference structure (e.g., embedded text references, end of article, *see* references; note if adequately hyperlinked for electronic products), and is it useful for identifying related information?

Indexing and/or Database Access. Is an index provided? What is the form of the indexing (dictionary, classified, "fact" index)? For electronic resources, note the access points: article-heading search, full-text keyword search, other searches (broad subject area, illustration, etc.), Boolean search capabilities, alphabetical browse. Does the index provide access to the entire contents of the work, including text, illustrations, multimedia elements, Internet links, etc.? Does the index analyze content? For example, does it cite topics that are not article headings? In electronic resources, do search mechanisms rank result sets so that more relevant materials are usually displayed at the top of the list? Overall, how accurate is the index?

4. Range and Quality of Contents

a) Text

Is article length appropriate to the subject?

Are articles factually correct?

Are sources cited where necessary to support facts?

Do articles give adequate treatment to opposing views in controversial areas?

Is there any indication of bias, be it political, racial, sexual, etc.?

Note new and revised articles and/or volumes.

b) Currency.
Taking into account the publication format, is the information up-to-date? Note editorial deadlines for print sets. Consider some of the following tests of currency:

List recent deaths of well-known persons and note whether articles (if present) note death date.

To what date do discussions of current events in countries generally extend?

Are new developments in fast-changing fields like medicine included?

Are tables of sports championships, literary awards, etc. up-to-date?

Are statistics up-to-date?

Look more for a pattern of statistics being five or ten years out-of-date throughout the work rather than being up to the prior year (which is often impossible, given the source material used).

For electronic encyclopedias, how often is the content updated? How often are Internet links validated and updated?

c) Style and Quality of Writing

Is the writing understandable and interesting in terms of the intended readership?

Are unfamiliar terms defined in articles on highly technical topics?

For electronic resources, are there hyperlinks to a dictionary for highly technical topics?

Are pronunciation guides provided?

Is a controlled vocabulary used if the work is for children?

d) **Bibliographies.** Consider whether they are consistently provided for major topics, where they are placed, whether standard data are provided, how up-to-date they are, and whether they cite "standard" works. Also, note whether bibliographies are limited to printed material, the English language, or books as opposed to periodical references.

e) **Study Guides.** Is a study guide included? If so, describe, noting whether it will help users.

f) **Illustrative Material.** Note what kind of illustrations are provided and how many there are. Consider their quality, placement, captions, cross-references to and from articles, and whether they are indexed. Note whether illustrations from previous editions have been substantially replaced or revised. For maps, note authority of producer, types (thematic, political, topographic, etc.), features (latitude/longitude shown, compass bearing, scale, keys). For electronic encyclopedias, note the kinds and quantities of multimedia elements (illustrations, animations, video clips, audio clips, etc.).

g) **Primary Source Documents.** Are primary source documents (e.g., full text of the *Contract with America, Paradise Lost,* or videos of speeches or events) included, and if so, how? Are there links to Internet resources, a CD-ROM, or site-resident text files, videos, or audiocassettes?

5. Physical Format (Print)

Binding: Durable? Attractive? Do volumes lie flat? Is spine lettering clear?

Paper: Consider quality and opacity.

Type: Attractive, easy to read?

Layout: Attractive? Sufficient margins? Running heads?

6. Physical Format (Electronic)

Consider page layout, fonts, navigation tools (running sidebars or footers with links, article outlines), length of text per page, ability to manipulate (copy, print) text and images, etc., in terms of how they add to or detract from use of the work and understanding of content.

Does the encyclopedia have basic search directions located near the point of query submissions?

Is there a help page that is accessible throughout the encyclopedia?

Are there various levels of searching complexity that would allow multiple patron proficiency levels to fully utilize the encyclopedia?

Are hyperlinked cross-references provided within the articles? These should be to sources within the encyclopedia, as well as sources on the Web.

Is there a hyperlinked dictionary so that patrons can look up the meaning of words within articles?

Is a site map of the encyclopedia available?

What types of interactive multimedia features are included (e.g., graphics, pictures, maps, diagrams, audio, etc.)? How do these enhance the text?

Are the screens easy to read (e.g., print size and color, graphics, no "cluttered" screens)?

Is there additional cost for any information accessed from the encyclopedia (e.g., other websites)?

Can searches be performed for sounds, maps, graphics, and other special features?

Are various searching structures allowed such as natural language, Boolean logic, keyword, and topic searching?

What special features are exclusive to the Web-based encyclopedia versus the disc version?

Are special plug-ins needed?

7. **Comparison with Alternate Formats, Previous Editions, and Similar Works**

If alternate formats are available (e.g., print, CD-ROM, Web), note how they differ in content and currency, as well as ease of use. If the work is revised, note major changes in scope, audience, structure, or features, if any. If appropriate, compare to other general encyclopedias that have similar scopes and audience.

Atlases

1. Authority

What is the reputation of the publisher? What is the copyright date? Does the copyright date refer to the date of the survey, compilation of the information, revision date, reprint date, edition, situation (current or old political situation, for example), statistical accuracy, publication date, or another date?

Is each map dated?

How are revisions done? Frequency? If the work is a previously reviewed edition, note *Reference Books Bulletin (RBB)* date and recommendation.

Are revisions complete or partial?

How accurate are the maps? For example, how current are political boundaries, name changes, and special maps?

How reliable are the sources of the data?

Who is identified in the statement of authorship (author, cartographer, editor, publisher, etc.)? What is their authority?

What is the accuracy and currency of supportive material, such as illustrations, bibliographies, and index?

2. Scope

What is the geographic area covered?

What type of atlas is it (road, state, or national parks/forests map, etc.)?

Is there balance in coverage?

How much detail is covered? For electronic maps, can the user get to a street map or just "city-to-city" maps?

Note if the atlas is a political, physical, or historical resource or a combination work. What types of maps are included (thematic, relief, political)?

How many maps are there?

What period of history does the atlas cover?

3. Treatment

Scale. Are the scales used appropriate for the amount of detail theoretically in the maps? Are scales represented by a numerical ratio, a graphic scale, or a verbal scale?

Projection. Are projections appropriate for the areas covered and type of maps?

Grid and Direction Devices. Are latitude and longitude indicated? How? Where?

Symbols and Legends. Are symbols readable? Easy to use?
- Are symbols distinct?
- Does each page contain a legend?
- Is the legend attractive and readable?
- Is the number of symbols used in the map appropriate?
- Who is the intended audience?

4. Arrangement

Is there an index to adjoining maps if the map is one of a series in the same format?

Does the table of contents list each map (and scale), as well as all tables, charts, and other supplementary materials?

Does the prefatory section (or the endpapers) provide a general key to the maps in the atlas?

What peripheral material is there?

Is the index just an index or is it a gazetteer?

Are the maps well cross-referenced?

Are the titles of the maps accurate and concise?

How does the index refer to location (e.g., latitude, longitude)?

For electronic atlases, is there a "getting started" tutorial? How easy is it to move from one map to another and within maps? For example, can the user "zoom" in and out or move to another area not currently on the screen?

5. Format and Appearance

How big are the maps? For electronic publications, are maps easy to read when the user has zoomed in as tight as the software allows?

How is color used? Are colors arranged in an attractive way? Are color changes and shadings distinct enough to be readily seen?

Are text designations clear? Are place-names and symbols clearly printed? Is the size of type appropriate for the areas designated? Is it difficult to read place-names and symbols through the color overlays? Are the maps as a whole clearly printed, with no blurring? For electronic publications, how do the maps print out? Will color maps print nicely on a black-and-white printer?

6. Special Features

Do the maps include mileage charts, enlarged or clickable inserts of certain areas, etc.?

If the atlas is electronic, does the software interface well with a Web browser?

What other special features are available? Is there text about different areas on the map? For electronic publications, can this text be accessed with a simple click? Do the maps show areas of interest such as museums and airports? Does the software for an electronic atlas indicate distances and other statistical information? Are there audio or video features?

Statistical Compilations

The term *statistical compilations* denotes works or parts of works that are devoted primarily to the presentation of numeric material in tabular or graphical format.

1. Structure

Does the work consist entirely of statistics or does it include text as well as tables, charts, etc.?

If text is included, are text and statistics well integrated?

What kind of introductory and end matter are included (e.g., introduction, interview guides or questionnaire forms, indexes, etc.)?

Does the electronic compilation have advanced searching options such as search forms, search customization, or topic search that would allow for efficient and exact searching of statistical data?

2. Authority

(In this section *authority* is used in reference to reliability of the methodology employed, as well as in its usual sense of author's authority.)

How were the statistics obtained? If the work compiles statistics from other sources, are those sources cited? If several sources have been used, is the source for each group of statistics clearly indicated? Where are the sources cited?

If the statistics represent the results of manipulations of data collected by the author, is the methodology clearly described? Have proper statistical and analytical techniques been used, insofar as these can be judged?

Are definitions, descriptions, or explanations of various categories of statistics and terms provided in the prefatory material or a glossary? (For example, if the work reports production statistics, are the units of measure defined? If it reports government revenues, are various kinds of taxes clearly indicated?)

Are there any peculiarities or exceptions noted in the various groups of statistics?

3. Time Period

Is the time period for which statistics are reported clearly indicated?

Does the work include historical data as well as current statistics?

How up-to-date are the statistics? Is coverage designed to be current?

If the work is a serial, does it generally cover the same categories of statistical information from issue to issue and for roughly the same time spans?

4. Coverage

What is the general topic covered by the work?

Is the work international, national, regional, or local in its coverage?

Is the work organized and are the data presented in a way that is appropriate for the topic(s) covered?

How detailed are the data?

Are the numerical data unique to this title or are the data available elsewhere?

5. Format

Are the statistics presented in tables, graphs, or by other means? Do the table titles accurately represent what is included? If the data are presented in a graph, is the baseline zero? If not, is the format appropriate for the data presented?

If other formats are used, are they appropriate, given the type of statistics, and are they clearly explained?

Does the work note whether or not the statistics are available in another medium (e.g., computer files)? If so, are the distributor and price noted?

Does the table of contents list all of the tables, graphs, etc.?

6. Special Features of Electronic Compilations

Does the electronic compilation allow for immediate conversion of statistical data into a spreadsheet format such as Lotus or Excel?

Can the searcher access the statistical data representing numerous years or is the compilation year-specific?

Does the electronic compilation allow the searcher to manipulate raw data in a customized statistical operation to achieve the desired end data?

Does the electronic compilation allow for regular updates to immediately be sent?

In what form can the data be viewed? Charts? Graphs? Tables? Can the searcher specify different formats?

Can maps be generated of statistical data where applicable?

Can several statistical sources be searched at the same time?

Are hyperlinks present in the accompanying explanation of data?

Can users access the statistical data through software (such as Adobe Acrobat) that will allow manageable and orderly hard-copy printing?

Does the compilation provide a tutorial or a help page that allows the searcher to successfully utilize the database?

Index

Full bibliographic citations are indicated by **boldface** page numbers.

547

Russian biographical archive, **221**
Russian dictionaries, 329
Russkii biograficheskii slovar', **242**

Sabin, Joseph, *Dictionary of books relating to America,* **54**
Sable, Martin H., *Research guide to the humanities, social sciences and technology,* **101**
Sader, Marion, and Amy Lewis, *Encyclopedias, atlases and dictionaries,* **263, 285, 467–68**
Salem, James M., *Guide to critical reviews,* **149**
Sales & Marketing Management, *Survey of buying power and media markets,* **424**
Sales product catalog, 66. *See GPO sales publications reference file*
Samples, Gordon, *Drama scholar's index to plays and filmscripts,* **151–52**
Savageau, David, *Places rated almanac,* **453**
Sawers, Robin. *See* Terrell, Peter
Saxton, Matthew L., 5
scales, map, 479
Scammon, Richard P., and Alice M. McGillivray, *America at the polls,* **432**
Scandinavian biographical archive, **221**
Schick, Frank L., and Renee Schick *Statistical handbook on aging Americans,* **408**
Statistical handbook on U.S. Hispanics, **409**
Schick, Renee. *See* Schick, Frank L.
Schlacter, Gale A., 195
Schlessinger, Bernard. *See* Karp, Rashelle S.
Schlessinger, June. *See* Karp, Rashelle S.
Schmeckebier, Laurence Frederick, and Roy B. Eastin, *Government publications and their use,* **471**
Schmid, Calvin F., *Statistical graphics,* **390**
Schmidt, Diane. *See* Davis, Elisabeth D.

Schmittroth, Linda
Statistical record of children, **409**
Statistical record of women worldwide, **410**
scholarships. *See* Grants
Scholze-Stubenrecht, W., and J. B. Sykes, *Oxford-Duden German dictionary,* 319, **325**
Schomberg Center guide to black literature . . . , **247–48**
school libraries. *See also* Children
atlases, 489–90
Elementary school library collection, **94–95**
Guide to reference books for school media centers, **16–17**
Middle and junior high school library catalog, **95, 285**
School library journal, **98**
Senior high school library catalog, **96, 285**
Thematic atlases for public, academic and high school libraries, **469**
School library journal, **98**
Schultze, Charles. *See* Edmonston, Barry
Schur, Norman W., *British English A to Zed,* **296**
Schwann CD review digest, **149**
science and technology. *See also* Biology; Chemistry
bibliographies, 92–93
biography, 258–60
CRC handbook of chemistry and physics, **451**
dictionaries, 315–17
directories, 207-8
Directory of published proceedings: series SEMT—science, engineering, medicine, technology, **158–59**
Directory of technical and scientific directories, **172**
in encyclopedias, 339
Index to scientific and technical proceedings, **159**
Index to scientific book contents, **145**